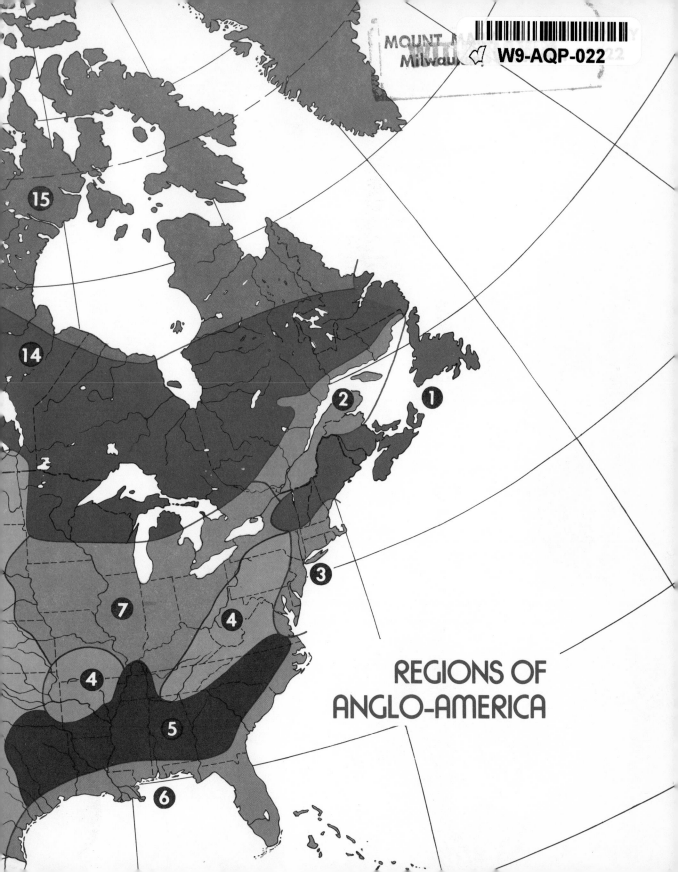

REGIONS OF ANGLO-AMERICA

REGIONAL GEOGRAPHY OF ANGLO-AMERICA

FIFTH EDITION

C. LANGDON WHITE

Professor Emeritus
Stanford University

EDWIN J. FOSCUE

Late of Southern Methodist University

TOM L. McKNIGHT

Professor of Geography
University of California,
Los Angeles

PRENTICE-HALL, INC., Englewood Cliffs, New Jersey 07632

regional geography of anglo-america

Library of Congress Cataloging in Publication Data

WHITE, CHARLES LANGDON (date)
  Regional geography of Anglo-America.

  Includes bibliographies and index.
1. United States—Description and travel—1960–
2. Canada—Description and travel—1951–
I. Foscue, Edwin J. (date) joint author.
II. McKnight, Tom Lee (date) joint author.
III. Title.
E169.02.W48   1979   973   78–23338
ISBN   0–13–770883–1

Printed in the United States of America

10 9 8 7 6 5 4 3 2 1

regional geography of anglo-america
FIFTH EDITION
C. Langdon White
Edwin J. Foscue
Tom L. McKnight

Cover photos (*clockwise from top left*) courtesy
of Alyeska Pipeline Company; Government of
Quebec, Tourist Branch; U.S. Army Corps of
Engineers, New Orleans District; USDA Soil
Conservation Service; New York State
Department of Commerce; Tom L. McKnight;
and Texas Forest Service.

Editorial/production supervision by
Lynda Heideman
Interior design by Judith Winthrop and
Lynda Heideman
Page layout by Judith Winthrop
Cover design by Judith Winthrop
Manufacturing buyer: Trudy Pisciotti

Frontispiece: The border between Canada and
the United States is often said to be invisible; this
infrared satellite image shows that such is not
the case. This is a Great Plains scene, with the
common meeting point of Montana, Alberta, and
Saskatchewan almost in the center of the photo.
Long, rectangular fields of grain appear in
differing patterns in both countries. The dark
tone of forest vegetation distinguishes the Sweet
Grass Hills (left center) and the Bear Paw
Mountains (lower right). The Milk River flows
southeasterly across the center of the scene,
and a portion of the Marias River is seen at lower
left (Landsat image).

Prentice-Hall International, Inc., *London*

Prentice-Hall of Australia Pty. Limited, *Sydney*

Prentice-Hall of Canada, Ltd., *Toronto*

Prentice-Hall of India Private Limited, *New Delhi*

Prentice-Hall of Japan, Inc., *Tokyo*

Prentice-Hall of Southeast Asia Pte. Ltd.,
Singapore

Whitehall Books Limited, *Wellington, New
Zealand*

CONTENTS

v

regional
geography

THE TUNDRA

20

546

PREFACE

Regional geography has recently passed through a period of relative disfavor. Its critics, encouraged by the quantitative revolution in many fields of learning, including geography, have found fault with its alleged lack of precision and methodological rigor. This is neither the time nor place to debate such charges, but it seems clear to the authors that regional geography meets a basic need in furthering an understanding of the earth's surface and that no surrogate has yet been devised to replace it.

The complexities of humanity's life on the earth are much too vast and intricate to be explained by multivariate analysis and related mathematical and model-building techniques. Such models may be useful, but any real understanding of people and the earth requires that words, phrases, photos, diagrams, graphs, and especially maps be used in meaningful combination. Conceptualization and delimitation of regions are critical exercises in geographic thinking, and the description and analysis of such regions continue as a central theme in the discipline of geography; some would call it the essence of the field.

It is a fundamental belief of the authors that a basic goal of geography is *landscape appreciation* in the broad sense of both words, that is, an understanding of everything that one can see, hear, and smell—both actually and vicariously—in humanity's zone of living on the earth. In this book, then, there is heavy emphasis on landscape description and interpretation, including its sequential development.

The flowering of civilization in Anglo-America is partly a reflection of the degree to which people have levied tribute against natural resources in particular and the environment in general. From the Atlantic to the Pacific and from the Arctic to the Gulf, people have been destroyers of nature, even as they have been builders of civilizations. Overcrowding of population and overconsumption of material goods have now become so pervasive that reassessment of goals and priorities—by institutions as well as by individuals—is widespread. Reaction to environmental despoliation is strongly developed, and ecological concerns are beginning to override economic considerations in many cases. In keeping with such reaction, environmental and ecologic issues are frequently discussed in this book.

Canada and the United States have a common heritage and have been moving toward similar goals. These factors, along with geographical contiguity and the binational influence of mass media, have produced both commonality of culture and mutual interdependence. Nevertheless, there are clear-cut distinctions between the two countries, and there is a particular concern among many Canadians to define a national character that is separate from both psychological and economic domination of the United States. These national interests and concerns, however, do not mask the fact that the geographical "grain" of Anglo-America often trends north-south rather than east-west; thus, several of the regions delimited in this book cross the international border to encompass parts of both countries.

A renewal of interest in regional geography is now becoming apparent, and nowhere is this more clearly shown than in the increase in publications dealing with aspects of the regional geography of the United States and Canada. There are more journals and more journal articles, and special publications of great significance have appeared. Perhaps most important, the output of state,

provincial, regional, and city atlases continues unabated. The chapter-end bibliographies of this book are overflowing with references to useful recent publications; it was more difficult than ever to choose among the plethora of available materials.

The major changes in this—the fifth—edition of the book include

1 updating of all, and rewriting of most, of the text

2 introduction in each regional chapter of a specialized vignette, in which a particular aspect of the region's geography is focused on in some depth

3 redrafting of many maps and addition of several new ones

4 expanded treatment of environmental issues

5 revision of several regional boundaries, particularly those of French Canada and the Appalachian and Ozark Region

6 updating and considerable expansion of the bibliographies at the end of each chapter

7 elimination of specific treatment of Greenland as a part of Anglo-America

acknowledgments

In writing this book, the authors have leaned heavily on many geographers and colleagues in associated disciplines. They have drawn especially on articles in the professional geographical journals and have relied significantly on data, both published and unpublished, from governmental sources.

A great many people have contributed thoughts, ideas, information, and critiques of value. Accordingly, the number to whom we are grateful is so large that only a general acknowledgment is possible. To two groups, however, our special thanks are due.

Several of our colleagues have commented critically upon specific chapters or issues of major importance in the organization and content of the book. These include

CHARLES S. AIKEN, *University of Tennessee*

GABRIEL P. BETZ, *California State College (Pennsylvania)*

J. BRIAN BIRD, *McGill University*

RICHARD G. BUCKSAR, *Bay de Noc Community College*

JOHN M. CROWLEY, *University of Montana*

RICHARD L. DAY, *University of Idaho*

GARY S. DUNBAR, *University of California, Los Angeles*

ALBERT G. FARLEY, *University of British Columbia*

J. FRASER HART, *University of Minnesota*

RALPH R. KRUEGER, *University of Waterloo*

ARLEIGH H. LAYCOCK, *University of Alberta*

RICHARD F. LOGAN, *University of California, Los Angeles*

STANLEY NORSWORTHY, *Fresno State University*

MERLE C. PRUNTY, JR., *University of Georgia*

OTIS W. TEMPLER, JR., *Texas Tech University*

NORMAN J. W. THROWER, *University of California, Los Angeles*

WILLIAM H. WALLACE, *University of New Hampshire*

WILLIAM C. WONDERS, *University of Alberta*

Some of the junior author's students, in seminars and independently, have contributed critical analyses of both substantive and methodological features of the book. Prominent among these contributors have been

GORDON AHLSCHWEDE

MARTIN CADWALLADER

JOHN COFFMAN

NANCY DANAHER

MICHAEL DONOHUE

ALAN FITZSIMMONS

G. THOMAS FOGGIN

RICHARD HAIMAN

FATIMAH HAMID-DON

JOHN KNODT

PETER MASON

JOEL MILLER

LINDA NEWBY

RICHARD NOSTRAND

NANCY ROCKOFF

DALE STEVENS

RICHARD STOWELL

OTIS TEMPLER, JR.

The maps and other line drawings of this volume demonstrate the notable cartographic talent of Patricia Caldwell.

Finally, to our very supportive wives, Mary and Marylee, the authors are particularly grateful for forbearance and encouragement.

C. Langdon White

Tom L. McKnight

REGIONAL GEOGRAPHY OF ANGLO-AMERICA

background

THE ANGLO-AMERICAN CONTINENT

1

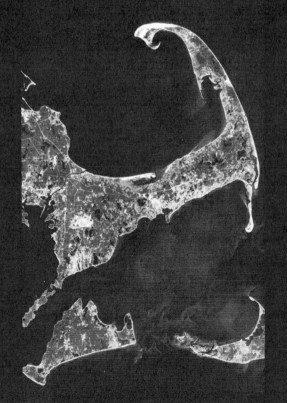

The Western Hemisphere is usually divided, for geographical purposes, into North America and South America. This is a satisfactory division from a physical standpoint, but on the basis of cultural, social, political, and economic contrasts it is much more meaningful to subdivide the continent into Anglo-America and Latin America.

Anglo-America is a generally recognized name that refers to the United States and Canada. The term is not definitively descriptive. It is a useful bit of general terminology that provides a brief form of reference to a major portion of the earth's surface; however, it also implies an important attribute of the population of the two countries. Their predominant origin is English, and most of the economic and political institutions of both countries have been derived from this heritage.

Nevertheless, within the United States and Canada there are numerous members of the population who are not descended from an Anglo (English) background. Some of these minority groups are sufficiently non-Anglicized and occur in sufficient concentrations to provide significant diversity in the human geography of the continent. Most notable in this regard is that part of eastern Canada that is predominantly occupied by people of French origin; this encompasses most of the settled portions of the province of Quebec, as well as adjacent sections of Ontario and much of New Brunswick.

Hawaii, with its prominent Asiatic and Polynesian elements, is another conspicuous exception to the cultural connotation of the term *Anglo*. Doubtless the reader can think of many other areas in the United States and Canada where non-Anglo ethnic groups are notable, such as a broad zone along the Mexican border from the Pacific Ocean to the Gulf of Mexico; the southeastern corner of Florida, where many Cuban refugees have settled in recent years; various Indian reservations in western United States and central Canada; concentrations of Eskimos and Aleuts in northern and western Alaska and northern Canada; areas of black population concentration in some rural parts of southeastern United States and many United States cities; and various concentrations of other non-Anglo peoples, primarily in urban ghettoes in both Canada and the United States.

continental parameters

Anglo-America, as defined above, encompasses an area of nearly 7.5 million square miles, which is larger than all but Asia and Africa of the seven recognized continents. It sprawls across 136 degrees of longitude, from 52° W.L. at Cape Spear in Newfoundland to 172° E.L. at Attu Island in the western extremity of the Aleutians. Its latitudinal extent is 64 degrees, from 83° N.L. at Ellesmere Island's Cape Columbia to 19° N.L. on the southern coast of the Big Island of Hawaii.

a view from space

The continent is roughly wedge-shaped, with its broadest expanse toward the north. The great bulk of Anglo-America is thus in the middle latitudes, with a considerable northern extension into the high latitudes and only Hawaii reaching into the Tropics.

If we can imagine a view of the entire Anglo-American continent from an orbiting space station on a clear day, there would be certain gross features that would appear prominently. Perhaps the most conspicuous configuration is the irregular continental outline; some extensive coastal reaches are relatively smooth, but by and large the margin of the continent is irregular and embayed, and there are numerous prominent offshore islands (fig. 1–1).[1]

The most notable indentation in the continental outline is Hudson Bay, which protrudes southward for some 800 miles from Canada's north coast. Despite its vastness, however, Hudson Bay is relatively insignificant in its influence on the geography of Anglo-America. Its surface is frozen for many months, and even the open water of summer supports only one sea route of importance and has minimal climatic effects on the surrounding lands.

Much more significant geographically are two extensive oceanic areas whose margins impinge less abruptly on the continent; both the Gulf of Mexico to the southeast

[1] The coastline of the high latitude portions of Anglo-America is much more uneven than that of other sections. For example, Alaska has more coastline mileage than the other 24 coastal states combined.

fig. 1–1   The irregular nature of the eastern coastline of Anglo-America is evident in southeastern Massachusetts and eastern Rhode Island. Cape Cod is composed of a complex of glacial moraines and sandy, current-built hooks, spits, and bars. From east to west the conspicuous islands are Nantucket, Martha's Vineyard, the Elizabeth Islands, and Block Island. Cape Cod is actually separated from the mainland by the smooth curve of the Cape Cod Canal, which extends from Cape Cod Bay to Buzzards Bay. Lighter tones distinguish the Boston urbanized area in the upper left of the photo and a portion of metropolitan Providence at the head of Narragansett Bay (Landsat image).

and the Gulf of Alaska to the west constitute gross irregularities in the continental configuration that are major climatic influences and also have great economic importance. Other coastal embayments that might be conspicuous from the viewpoint of a satellite include the Gulf of St. Lawrence, the Bay of Fundy, and Chesapeake Bay on the east coast; and Puget Sound, Cook Inlet, Bristol Bay, Norton Sound, and Kotzebue Sound on the west.

More than 70,000 islands are another feature that commands attention in the gross outline of the continent. Easily the most prominent island group is the Canadian Arctic Archipelago, an expansive series of large islands to the north of the Canadian mainland that constitutes more than 14 percent of the total area of Canada. The largest islands of the archipelago are Baffin and Ellesmere, and nine of the ten largest islands of Anglo-America are in the group.

Four other sizable islands are grouped around the Gulf of St. Lawrence. Prince Edward Island is a province of Canada, the island of Newfoundland is part of the province of the same name, Cape Breton Island is part of Nova Scotia, and Anticosti Island is part of Quebec.

With one major exception, the islands off the east coast of the United States are small and sparsely populated. The exception is Long Island, whose 1,400 square miles support a population in excess of 7 million. The other coastal islands of the Atlantic Ocean and Gulf of Mexico are nearly all long, narrow, low-lying sand ridges. There are a great many of them, but most are so close to shore and so narrow in width as to be indistinguishable from our theoretical high-altitude viewpoint.

The island pattern off the Pacific Coast is quite uneven. Only a few islands are found off the southern portion of the coast, and of these only the Channel Islands of Southern California encompass much acreage. The coast of British Columbia and southern Alaska, on the other hand, is extensively bordered by islands, and many of them are large. Most notable is Vancouver Island, which constitutes the extreme southwestern corner of Canada. Other major islands on this coast include the Queen Charlotte Islands of British Columbia, the Alexander Archipelago of southeastern Alaska, Kodiak Island of southern Alaska, and the far-flung Aleutian group.

the countries of anglo-america

In most of this book the material is presented by regions. As a prelude, it is well to look briefly at the nations as entities, noting a few general facts to serve as a context for regional analysis.

THE UNITED STATES OF AMERICA

The total area of the United States is 3,615,200 square miles, a figure exceeded by only three other countries—the Soviet Union, Canada, and China. The 1977 official population estimate was 216,294,000, which is also fourth-ranking among the nations of the world, after China, India, and the Soviet Union.

The United States is a federal republic with a division of power between federal and state governments. Both levels of government have a threefold administration: executive, legislative and judicial branches. There are 50 states, which vary greatly in size and population. The 48 "old" states, excluding Alaska and Hawaii, are collectively referred to as the *conterminous states.*

The states are subdivided into local governmental units called counties,[2] with the following exceptions: in Louisiana the units are called parishes; in Maryland, Missouri, Nevada, and Virginia there are cities that are independent of any county organization and thus constitute, along with counties, primary subdivisions of these states; and in Alaska the populated parts are subdivided into boroughs. Taken altogether, there is a total of about 3,100 counties and county equivalents in the United States.

The federal capital is the District of Columbia, which is territory on the northeast side of the Potomac River that was ceded to the nation by the state of Maryland (fig. 1–2). In addition to the 50 states and the District of Columbia, the United States governs a number of small islands in the Carib-

---

[2] Counties vary greatly in size and population. Delaware has the fewest, with 3, whereas Texas has the most, with 254.

fig. 1–2   The national Capitol of the United States. Pennsylvania Avenue extends beyond it, with Federal Court buildings in the upper right (courtesy Washington Convention and Visitors Association).

bean Sea, the most important of which is Puerto Rico, and in the Pacific Ocean. Further, the federal government administers the Panama Canal Zone, under a lease arrangement with Panama, and hundreds of tiny islands in Micronesia, as a trusteeship under United Nations' auspices. The political future of both the Canal Zone and the Micronesian trust territory is at present uncertain.

THE DOMINION OF CANADA

Canada is the world's second largest country, with an area of 3,851,800 square miles. It is not densely populated, however; its 1977 population total of 22,850,000 ranked only thirty-first among the nations.

The governmental organization of the nation is a constitutional monarchy that combines the federal form of the United States with the cabinet system of Great Britain. The cabinet system unites the executive and legislative branches of government; the prime minister and all, or nearly all, of the cabinet are members of the House of Commons. The reigning monarch of Great Brit-

ain is also the head of the Canadian state and is represented by a governor-general, whose duties are formal and rather perfunctory. The prime minister is the active head of the government. The members of the House of Commons are elected by the people of Canada. Members of the Senate, on the other hand, are appointed for life by the cabinet. The House of Commons is the dominant legislative body with many more powers than the Senate.

The Canadian confederation contains ten provinces and two territories. The easternmost provinces of Newfoundland, New Brunswick, Nova Scotia, and Prince Edward Island are often referred to as the Atlantic Provinces; the latter three are collectively called the Maritime Provinces. Alberta, Saskatchewan, and Manitoba, the three provinces of the western interior, are known as the Prairie Provinces. The other three provinces, Quebec, Ontario, and British Columbia, are not normally considered as members of groups. Most of northern Canada is encompassed within the Yukon Territory and the Northwest Territories. The various provinces and territories have differ-

fig. 1-3 The Canadian Parliament Buildings in Ottawa (courtesy Ontario Ministry of Industry and Tourism).

ent systems for administering local government; each is usually subdivided into counties or districts, which may be further fragmented into minor civil divisions.

The national capital of Ottawa does not occupy a special territory but is within the province of Ontario, adjacent to the border of Quebec (fig. 1-3).

selected general bibliography on canada and the united states

BENNETT, D. G., AND C. R. HAYES, *Selected Problems and Concepts in the Geography of the United States.* Dubuque, Iowa: Kendall/Hunt Publishing Company, 1974.

BROBST, DONALD A., AND WALDEN P. PRATT, eds., *United States Mineral Resources.* Washington, D.C.: United States Geological Survey, Professional Paper 820, 1973.

BROWN, RALPH H., *Historical Geography of the United States.* New York: Harcourt, Brace and Company, 1948.

BRUNN, STANLEY D., *Geography and Politics in America.* New York: Harper & Row, Publishers, Inc., 1974.

CAMU, P., "Introduction to Canada," *Canadian Geographical Journal,* 85 (August 1972), 40–51.

CHAPMAN, JOHN D., "Natural Resource Developments in Canada," *Canadian Geographer,* 20 (1976), 15–40.

CHAPMAN, JOHN D., AND JOHN C. SHERMAN, eds., *Oxford Regional Economic Atlas:*

United States and Canada. London: Oxford University Press, 1975.

CLARK, ANDREW H., "The Look of Canada," *Historical Geography Newsletter,* 6 (Spring 1976), 59–68.

DUNBAR, GARY S., "Illustrations of the American Earth: An Essay in Cultural Geography," *American Studies,* 12 (Autumn 1973), 3–15.

ECONOMIC RESEARCH SERVICE, U.S. DEPARTMENT OF AGRICULTURE, *The Look of Our Land: An Airphoto Atlas of the Rural United States.* Washington, D.C.: U.S. Government Printing Office.
1970. "The Far West"
1970. "North Central"
1971. "East and South"
1971. "The Mountains and Deserts"
1971. "The Plains and Prairies"

ESTALL, R., *A Modern Geography of the United States.* New York: Penguin Books, 1972.

FULFORD, ROBERT, "General Perspectives on Canadian Culture," *The American Review of Canadian Studies,* 3 (Spring 1973), 115–21.

GASTIL, RAYMOND D., *Cultural Regions of the United States.* Seattle: University of Washington Press, 1975.

GENTILCORE, R. LOUIS, ed., *Canada's Changing Geography.* Scarborough, Ont.: Prentice-Hall of Canada, Ltd., 1967.

————, *Geographical Approaches to Canadian Problems.* Scarborough, Ont.: Prentice-Hall of Canada, Ltd., 1971.

GERLACH, ARCH C., ed., *The National Atlas of the United States of America.* Washington, D.C.: United States Department of the Interior, Geological Survey, 1970.

GOUGH, B., *Canada.* Englewood Cliffs, N.J.: Prentice-Hall, Inc., 1975.

HAMELIN, LOUIS-EDMOND, *Canada: A Geographical Perspective.* Toronto: Wiley Publishers of Canada Limited, 1973.

HARRIES, KEITH D., *The Geography of Crime and Justice.* New York: McGraw-Hill Book Co., 1974.

HARRIS, R. COLE, AND JOHN WARKENTIN, *Canada Before Confederation: A Study in Historical Geography.* New York: Oxford University Press, 1974.

HART, JOHN FRASER, *The Look of the Land.* Englewood Cliffs, N.J.: Prentice-Hall, Inc., 1975.

HEADY, EARL, "The Agriculture of the United States," *Scientific American,* 235 (September 1976), 106–27.

IRVING, R. M., ed., *Readings in Canadian Geography.* Toronto: Holt, Rinehart & Winston of Canada, Ltd., 1972.

McNAUGHT, KENNETH, "The American Impact Upon Canada," *Canadian Geographical Journal,* 92 (January–February 1976), 4–13.

MARSCHNER, FRANCIS J., *Land Use and Its Patterns in the United States.* Washington, D.C.: U. S. Government Printing Office, 1959.

MORRILL, RICHARD L., AND ERNEST H. WOLDENBERG, *The Geography of Poverty.* New York: McGraw-Hill Book Co., 1971.

NICHOLSON, NORMAN L., "The Canadians and Their Country," *Canadian Geographical Journal,* 85 (August 1972), 52–79.

PATERSON, J. H., *North America (5th ed.).* New York: Oxford University Press, 1975.

PUTNAM, D. F., AND R. G. PUTNAM, *Canada: A Regional Analysis.* Toronto: J. M. Dent, 1970.

ROONEY, JOHN F., JR., *A Geography of American Sport.* Reading, Mass.: Addison-Wesley Publishing Co., 1974.

SAMPLE, C. JAMES, *Patterns of Regional Economic Change: A Quantitative Analysis of United States Regional Growth and Development.* Cambridge, Mass.: Ballinger Publishing Company, 1974.

SAUER, CARL O., *Sixteenth Century North America.* Berkeley: University of California Press, 1975.

SMITH, D. M., *The Geography of Social Well-Being in the United States.* New York: McGraw-Hill Book Co., 1973.

STARKEY, OTIS P., J. LEWIS ROBINSON, AND CRANE S. MILLER, *The Anglo-American Realm (2nd ed.).* New York: McGraw-Hill Book Co., 1975.

STATISTICS CANADA, *Canada.* Ottawa: Queen's Printer, annual.

————, *Canada Year Book.* Ottawa: Queen's Printer, annual.

STEWART, GEORGE R., *American Ways of Life.* Garden City, N. Y.: Doubleday & Co., Inc., 1954.

SURVEYS AND MAPPING BRANCH, *The National Atlas of Canada.* Ottawa: Surveys and Mapping Branch, Department of Energy, Mines and Resources, 1973.

UNITED STATES BUREAU OF THE CENSUS, *Statistical Abstract of the United States.* Washington, D.C.: U.S. Government Printing Office, annual.

WARKENTIN, JOHN, ed., *Canada: A Geographical Interpretation.* Toronto: Methuen Publications, 1968.

WATSON, J. WREFORD, *North America: Its Countries and Regions.* London: Longmans, Green and Co., Ltd., 1968.

ZELINSKY, WILBUR, *The Cultural Geography of the United States.* Englewood Cliffs, N.J.: Prentice-Hall, Inc., 1973.

THE PHYSICAL ENVIRONMENT OF ANGLO-AMERICA

2

We have seen that Anglo-America is largely a midlatitude continent, lying entirely north of the Tropic of Cancer, except for Hawaii, and mostly south of the Arctic Circle. It spreads broadly in these latitudes, fronting extensively on all three Northern Hemisphere oceans—Atlantic, Pacific, and Arctic. A wide variety of physical features is found, partly as a result of the great size of the continent; indeed, this diversity of environmental conditions is the keystone to an understanding of the physical geography of Anglo-America.

the pattern of landforms

The basic pattern of physiographic features in Anglo-America is a fourfold division roughly oriented north-south across the continent (fig. 2–1). In the west is a complex series of mountain ranges and lengthy valleys interspersed with numerous desert basins and plateaus toward the south; in the center is an extensive lowland area that widens toward the north; in the east is a broad cordillera of mountains and hills; and along part of the east coast is a coastal plain that swings westward to join the central lowland along the Gulf Coast.

In the conterminous states the western mountain complex consists of two major prongs. A number of steep-sided ranges more or less parallel the coast from Mexico to Canada; these vary in height from only a few hundred feet in parts of the Coast ranges of Oregon and Washington to more than 14,000 feet in the Sierra Nevada of California and the Cascades of Washington.

The Rocky Mountain cordillera consists of a series of southeast-northwest trending ranges that rise abruptly from the central plains and extend with only one significant interruption from north-central New Mexico to the Yukon Territory (fig. 2–2). Between the Rockies on the east and the Sierra Nevada–Cascade ranges on the west is an extensive area of dry lands where plateaus, mesas, desert basins, and short but rugged mountain ranges intermingle.

In western Canada the coastal mountains become more rugged and complex and are separated from the Canadian Rockies by mostly forest-covered, plateau-like uplands. To the northwest the highland orientation changes from south-north to east-west, with the broad lowland of the Yukon-Kuskokwim basins separating the wilderness of the Brooks Range to the north from the massive ranges of southern Alaska. These are the highest and most heavily glaciated mountains of the continent.

The central lowland should not be thought of as uninterrupted flatland. Much of the terrain is undulating or rolling, and there are many extensive areas of low hills,

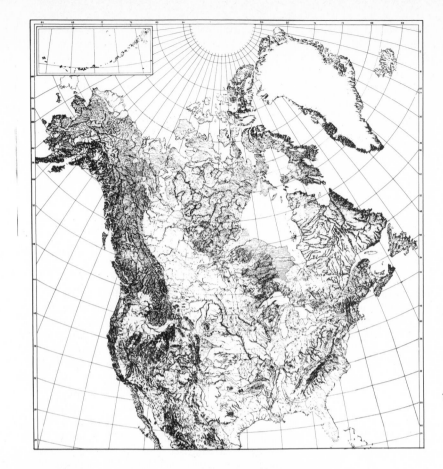

fig. 2–1 Physiographic diagram of Anglo-America (original map by A. K. Lobeck; reprinted by permission of Hammond, Inc.).

fig. 2–2 The mountains of western Anglo-America are generally high, steep, and rugged. In this central Colorado scene Hagerman Peak towers abruptly above Snowmass Lake (courtesy Colorado Department of Public Relations).

some of them quite steep-sided. By and large, however, most of the area between the Rockies on the west and the Appalachians on the east is a lowland of gentle relief. Its narrowest extent is toward the south, from which there is notable widening until the longitudinal extent in the north encompasses almost the entire width of the continent. The major exceptions to this pattern are in the rugged and glaciated eastern islands of the Canadian Arctic Archipelago: Baffin, Devon, Ellesmere, and Axel Heiberg.

The mountains of the east are not so high, rough, or obviously glaciated as are those of the west, and the eastern cordillera is only about half as long. Nevertheless, the Appalachian Mountain system extends almost without interruption from Alabama to the Gulf of St. Lawrence, and related ranges carry the trend through most of eastern Quebec and Labrador. The highest peaks are less than 8,000 feet, and most crests are less than half that height. The Appalachian system, however, is a broad one, and over much of its extent the slopes are steep and heavily wooded (fig. 2–3). An important outlier of the eastern highlands is found in the tristate area of Arkansas, Missouri, and Oklahoma, where the extensive hills of the Ozarks and Ouachitas are found.

fig. 2–3   The mountains of eastern Anglo-America tend to be lower, less rugged, and completely covered with forest. These are the Green Mountains in central Vermont (courtesy Vermont Development Department).

The east coastal lowland is a feature of lesser magnitude than the other three divisions previously discussed. It is a classic example of an embayed coastal plain, with many estuaries, bays, and lagoons. From its narrow beginning in southern New England it slowly widens southward, and then swings west in Georgia and Florida to link indistinguishably with the southern margin of the central lowland.

HYDROGRAPHY

Two prominent drainage systems, the Great Lakes–St. Lawrence and the Mississippi-Missouri, dominate the hydrography of Anglo-America (fig. 2–4). The five Great Lakes (Superior, Huron, Erie, Ontario, and Michigan, the first four shared by the United States and Canada) drain northeastward to the Atlantic via the relatively short St. Lawrence River. Many rivers flow into the Great Lakes, but they are all short. The drainage basin of the Great Lakes watershed is remarkably small; it is, for example, only one-seventh the size of the Mississippi-Missouri drainage area (fig. 2–5).

Most of the central part of the United States and a little of southern Canada is drained by the Mississippi River and its many tributaries. The Mississippi itself flows almost due south from central Minnesota to the Gulf of Mexico below New Orleans. Its principal left-bank tributary is the Ohio River. The Ohio River drains much of the northern Appalachians and the Midwest before being joined by the Tennessee River, which drains much of the southern Appalachians and adjacent areas. The far-reaching Missouri River, emanating from the northern Rockies of Montana and gathering tributaries all across the north-central part of the country, is the major right-bank tributary of the Mississippi.

Between the mouths of the St. Lawrence and Mississippi rivers the well-watered east coast of Anglo-America is drained by a host of rivers, most of which are of moderate length but carry much water. West of the Mississippi the rivers that flow into the Gulf

fig. 2–4   The principal hydrographic features of Anglo-America.
The drainage basins of the Mississippi and Great Lakes–St. Lawrence
systems are outlined in black.

are longer but do not have a large volume of flow.

In the western United States there is great variety in the rivers that reach the Pacific Ocean. The Colorado River is a lengthy desert stream that drains much of the arid Southwest and eventually debouches into the sea in Mexico. The complex Sacramento–San Joaquin system drains much of California. The Columbia, principal river of the Pacific Northwest, originates in Canada; traverses some 465 miles before crossing into the United States, where it is joined by its main tributary, the Snake; and finally flows

fig. 2-6 A satellite image of the lower end of the Great Lakes. Shown is the entirety of Lake Ontario and the eastern end of Lake Erie. The Niagara River flows northward to connect the latter with the former, and it is paralleled to the west by the Welland Canal. Leeward clouds are conspicuous around the eastern end of Lake Ontario (Skylab image).

for another 300 miles as the border between Oregon and Washington.

The Pacific drainages of Canada and Alaska encompass many short rivers and a few long ones, but heavy precipitation assures that the streams have a large volume of flow. The most notable rivers are the Fraser in southern British Columbia and the Yukon in the Yukon Territory and Alaska.

Most of the Arctic drainage of Anglo-America is accomplished by the Mackenzie system or by the myriad of streams that flow centripetally into Hudson Bay. The Mackenzie system is an unusually complex one; its major water sources are the Liard River and Great Slave Lake, the latter being fed by the extensive watersheds of the Hay, Peace, Athabaska, and Slave rivers.

It should also be mentioned that there are thousands of square miles in western Anglo-America that are not served by external drainage. Particularly in Nevada, Utah, and California, basins of internal drainage abound. Most of these basins contain either shallow or dry lakes in their center (of which Utah's Great Salt Lake is the most conspicuous) and are fed by streams that for the most part flow only intermittently.

In some parts of Anglo-America, lakes are a significant element in the landscape (fig. 2-6). As a result of more extensive glaciation, Canada has a much higher proportion of its surface area in lakes (as well as marshes and swamps) than does the United States. (There is some truth to Minnesota's claim to be the "land of 10,000 lakes," and Ontario's assertion to be the "land of 100,000 lakes" is equally valid.) Furthermore, many of Canada's lakes are large ones; Great Bear, Great Slave, and Winnipeg, for example, are larger than Lake Ontario, and Canada contains no less than eight lakes that are larger than any wholly United States lake except Lake Michigan.[1] In the United States there are relatively few natural lakes except in the glaciated sections, primarily New England, New York, and the upper Lakes states; in interior basins of the arid West; and in the flat limestone country of central and southern Florida.

In recent years there has been a great proliferation of artificial lakes (reservoirs) in Anglo-America, particularly in the southeastern, south-central, and southwestern states where natural lakes are rare. Most such reservoirs are formed by the simple damming of rivers, producing finger-like bodies of water that extend for long distances up former stream valleys, and are now prominent features on the large-scale maps of almost any area from Carolina to California.

GLACIATION

An understanding of the physical geography of Anglo-America requires that some attention be paid to the role of glaciation in creating the contemporary landscape, particularly in Canada. During the most recent Ice Age (Pleistocene time) that began 1 to 2 million years ago and may have ended less than 8,000 years ago, extensive continental ice sheets formed in northern and central Canada and made at least four major advances southward (fig. 2–7). At the height of Pleistocene glaciation, the ice sheets extended as far south as Long Island, the Ohio River, the Missouri River, and the middle Columbia River. At the same time, moun-

[1] There is a total of more than 250,000 square miles of fresh water lakes in Canada, which is an area almost as large as the state of Texas.

tain glaciers of considerable size developed throughout the ranges of the West; evidence of Pleistocene glaciation has been discovered as far south as central New Mexico and the San Bernardino Mountains of Southern California.

Glacial erosion and deposition have completely reshaped the terrain in all areas covered by Pleistocene ice. From the standpoint of geological time, the retreat of the ice is so recent that the critical factors of slope, drainage, and surficial material are more directly the result of the action of ice, and meltwater, than of any other landscape-shaping element. This is clearly shown by the deranged drainage patterns and the large amount of standing water (lakes, swamps, and marshes) now found in areas that were once covered by Pleistocene ice sheets.

Except in a few locations, ice is but a minor feature in the contemporary topography of Anglo-America. The only sizable ice sheets, although much smaller than those of Antarctica or Greenland, occur on the four large eastern islands of the Canadian Arctic Archipelago.

Mountain glaciers are also still found in Anglo-America, but they are slight remnants of their past extent. Small living glaciers, only a few acres in size, occur as far south as central Colorado in the Rockies and central California in the Sierra Nevada. Mountain glaciers appear with increasing frequency further north in the western cordilleras, but the only place in the conterminous states where their length is reckoned in miles is in the northern part of the Cascade Range.

Contemporary glaciation is much more extensive in western Canada, and mountain ice sheets occur in some parts of the Canadian Rockies and British Columbia's Coast Mountains (fig. 2–8). Mountain glaciation reaches its greatest extent in the ranges of southern Alaska and the southwestern corner of the Yukon Territory, where the length of many valley glaciers is measured in tens of miles and the areal extent of one piedmont glacier (the Malaspina) is greater than that of the state of Rhode Island.

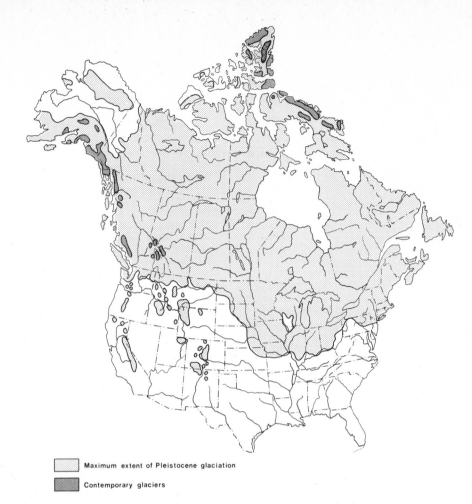

fig. 2-7 Glacial map of Anglo-America showing maximum ice extent during the Pleistocene Epoch as well as the extent of contemporary glaciation (after *National Atlas of the United States of America,* [Washington, D.C.: U.S. Department of the Interior, Geological Survey, 1970], p. 76).

Maximum extent of Pleistocene glaciation

Contemporary glaciers

fig. 2-8 Athabaska Glacier is one of the longest in the Canadian Rockies. The distance from the toe to the highest icefall, where the glacier issues from the Columbia Ice Field, is nearly ten miles (courtesy Information Canada, Photothèque).

MAJOR PHYSIOGRAPHIC REGIONS
OF ANGLO-AMERICA

Several geographers and geomorphologists
have subdivided the United States and
Canada into physiographic, or landform, regions based on various criteria but primarily
on the gross distribution of terrain features.
Figure 2–9 is a combination and modification of the work of a number of these
scholars.

The *Southeastern Coastal Plain* (1) is one of
the flattest portions of Anglo-America. Most
of the region slopes gently seaward, at the
rate of only a few feet or even a few inches
per mile, with the gentle slope continuing
under water for dozens of miles as a conti-

nental shelf. The uninterrupted flatness of
the landscape is relieved only sporadically
by low (10 to 50 feet) riverine bluffs alongside the broad river valleys or, particularly
west of the Mississippi River, by low linear
ridges (called cuestas) that parallel the
coast.

Most of the region has been submerged
in relatively recent geologic time, and its
surface layers consist of loosely consolidated
sands, gravels, marls, and clays. The coastal
margin is exceedingly irregular as a result of
recent submergence and embayment; it is
characterized by extensive drowned valleys
(estuaries) and many bays, swamps, lagoons,
and low-lying sand-bar islands. The portion
abutting the Appalachians encompasses the

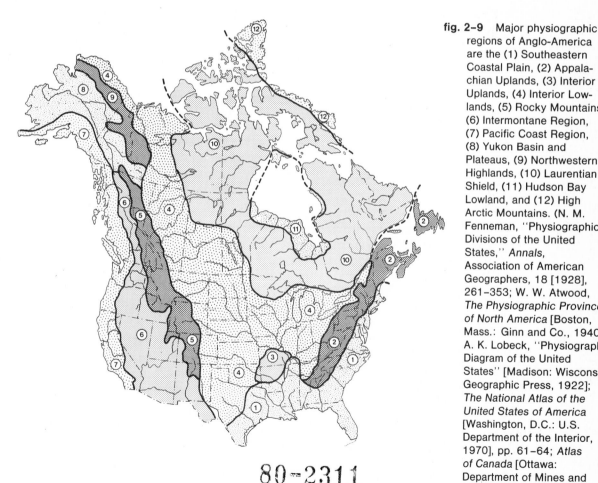

fig. 2–9 Major physiographic
regions of Anglo-America
are the (1) Southeastern
Coastal Plain, (2) Appala-
chian Uplands, (3) Interior
Uplands, (4) Interior Low-
lands, (5) Rocky Mountains,
(6) Intermontane Region,
(7) Pacific Coast Region,
(8) Yukon Basin and
Plateaus, (9) Northwestern
Highlands, (10) Laurentian
Shield, (11) Hudson Bay
Lowland, and (12) High
Arctic Mountains. (N. M.
Fenneman, "Physiographic
Divisions of the United
States," *Annals,*
Association of American
Geographers, 18 [1928],
261–353; W. W. Atwood,
*The Physiographic Provinces
of North America* [Boston,
Mass.: Ginn and Co., 1940];
A. K. Lobeck, "Physiographic
Diagram of the United
States" [Madison: Wisconsin
Geographic Press, 1922];
*The National Atlas of the
United States of America*
[Washington, D.C.: U.S.
Department of the Interior,
1970], pp. 61–64; *Atlas
of Canada* [Ottawa:
Department of Mines and
Technical Surveys, 1957],
plate 13.)

Piedmont where resistant crystalline bedrock has produced a more undulating surface.

The *Appalachian Uplands* (2) extend from Alabama to the Gulf of St. Lawrence, and the physiographic trend is continued in the island of Newfoundland. The region includes the "mountainous" part of eastern Anglo-America, although much of the terrain consists of low, forested hills. From Pennsylvania southward, most of the surface is underlain with sedimentary rocks. These sediments have been tightly folded in the eastern portion of the region to produce a remarkable sequence of parallel valleys and long, steep-sided ridges, although the easternmost ridge (the Blue Ridge) that contains the highest peaks in the eastern part of the continent is underlain with ancient crystalline rocks.

To the west of the ridge-and-valley section the sediments are more horizontal; here the so-called Allegheny and Cumberland Plateaus are thoroughly dissected by streams and give the appearance of an endless region of low hills. North of Pennsylvania the underlying rock is mostly crystalline (igneous or metamorphic), and there is great variety to the surface form, although hills and low mountains dominate the landscape. The most conspicuous ranges are the Adirondacks in New York, the Green Mountains in Vermont, the White Mountains in New Hampshire, the Notre Dame and Shickshock ranges in Quebec, and the Long Range in Newfoundland.

The *Interior Uplands* (3) bear considerable physiographic resemblance to the Appalachians, although both have less altitude and local relief. The Ozark section, mostly in southern Missouri and northern Arkansas, is a dissected plateau that consists of an amorphous pattern of low hills. Separated from the Ozarks by the transverse valley of the Arkansas River is the Ouachita section in western Arkansas and eastern Oklahoma. This is an area of east-west trending, linear ridges and valleys; it is markedly similar to the ridge-and-valley section of the Appalachians.

The *Interior Lowlands* (4) are a vast area of gentle relief that occupies much of the central portion of the continent. Some portions are remarkably flat, such as the High Plains of west Texas or the prairies of central Illinois; however, most of the region is characterized by undulating terrain or low, even hills. Relatively flat-lying sedimentary rocks underlie the surface in most places. The terrain was conspicuously modified by the action of Pleistocene ice sheets except in those portions south of the Missouri River. Numerous lakes, marshes, and ponds occur in the glaciated sections of the region, and many long rivers are found.

The *Rocky Mountains* (5), located just west of the flattish Great Plains portion of the Interior Lowlands, constitute a very abrupt physiographic change when approached from the east. They are characterized by high elevations—more than 50 peaks in Colorado reach above 14,000 feet—great local relief, rocky ruggedness, and spectacular scenery. Only in the Wyoming Basin area of southern and central Wyoming is there any significant section that is not dominated by mountainous terrain. There was great variety in the mountain-building processes that produced the Rockies. In the southern portions, extensive granitic intrusions have been thrust up many thousands of feet; whereas further north, sedimentary rocks have been drastically folded, and thrust and block faulting has taken place on a large scale. Throughout the region the recent action of mountain glaciers has deepened the valleys, steepened the slopes, and sharpened the peaks.

The *Intermontane Region* (6) encompasses a bewildering variety of terrain formed in many different ways. The southern and southwestern portions are basin-and-range country where numerous, discrete, short, rugged mountain ranges are interspersed with flat alluvial-filled valleys. In western Colorado and Utah, plateaus, mesas, cliffs, and buttes dominate the landscape, since weakly consolidated horizontal sedimentary rocks have been stripped and fretted by arid-land erosion processes (fig. 2–10). The

fig. 2-10 The spectacular starkness of the Intermontane West is demonstrated dramatically in Arizona's Grand Canyon, with the Colorado River visible in the inner gorge (courtesy Arizona Office of Tourism).

Columbia and Snake lava plateaus in Idaho, Oregon, and Washington have been deeply incised by major rivers and eroded into rolling hills in some areas. The various plateaus of the Canadian portion of the region (Fraser, Nechako, and Stikine) have been severely dissected and in many places appear as hills or mountains.

The *Pacific Coast Region* (7) is largely mountainous, with the trend of the ranges generally paralleling the coast. High and rugged mountains extend the entire length of the region, from the Sierra Nevada of California to the Alaska Range in the north (fig. 2–11). Several major valleys, particularly the Central Valley of California and the Willamette Valley of Oregon, are sandwiched between the massive interior ranges and the numerous smaller coastal ranges. The coastline itself is quite regular in the south, where the steep coastal ranges plunge abruptly into the sea; northward the coastline becomes exceedingly irregular, with lengthy bays and fiords interspersed with sinuous peninsulas and numerous islands.

The *Yukon Basin and Plateaus* (8) section occupies most of central Alaska and the southern part of the Yukon Territory, primarily within the drainage basins of the

fig. 2-11 The Cascade Range of the Pacific Northwest is surmounted by several prominent, cone-shaped volcanic peaks. This is Mount Hood in north-central Oregon (courtesy Oregon State Highway Travel Section).

Yukon and Kuskokwim rivers. Hill land predominates in the upstream areas, but much of central Alaska is a broad, flat-floored, poorly drained lowland. The lower courses of the two major rivers have built complex deltas.

The *Northwestern Highlands* (9) section includes the massive barren slopes of the Brooks Range in northern Alaska and a series of rugged mountains in northwestern Canada.

The *Laurentian Shield* (10) is an extensive, ancient, stable region floored with some of the world's oldest known crystalline rocks. With the exception of some relatively rugged hills in eastern Quebec and Labrador, this is a gently rolling landscape, typified by many outcrops of bare rock and an extraordinary amount of surface water in summer. There are hundreds of thousands of water bodies, ranging in size from gigantic to minute, connected by tens of thousands of rivers and streams.

The *Hudson Bay Lowland* (11) is a flat coastal plain that slopes imperceptibly northeastward toward the sea. It is underlain by recent sedimentary deposits that distinguish it from the surrounding, and underlying, Laurentian Shield.

High Arctic Mountains (12) occupy much of the four large eastern islands of the Canadian Arctic Archipelago. The region is typified by rugged and rocky slopes, large glaciers and ice sheets—several of which are larger than the province of Prince Edward Island—lack of vegetation and soil, and very deep permafrost.

the pattern of climate

Most of Anglo-America experiences climates in which seasonal changes are marked, as is characteristic of middle- and high-latitude portions of the world. Summer is generally hot and is the season of maximum precipitation; winter is cold and somewhat drier; and spring and fall are stimulating seasons of transition. There are many exceptions to these generalizations, particularly on the Pacific littoral where winter is the wet season and summer is quite dry.

CLIMATIC CONTROLS

Perhaps the most meaningful way to approach an understanding of the gross characteristics of Anglo-American climates is to consider the major climatic controls.

1 *Latitude* is the prime control. It has been stressed that Anglo-America is a mid-latitude continent with high latitude fringes; thus tropical characteristics of weather and climate are lacking except in Hawaii and the southern margin of the conterminous states.

2 The relationship of *land and water surfaces* is a major determinant of the continentality of a climate. Land heats and cools more rapidly and to a greater degree than water. Accordingly, coastal areas tend to have lessened temperature extremes and higher humidity and precipitation, whereas interior locations have greater temperature extremes and lessened opportunities for moisture. The relative nearness to oceans (Pacific, Atlantic, Gulf of Mexico, and to a lesser extent, Arctic) is reflected in temperature and moisture conditions.

3 *Air mass characteristics* influence the weather over broad areas and have long-term effects on climate. Anglo-America is a meeting ground of polar continental air, which is usually cold, dry, and stable, and tropical maritime air, usually warm, moist, and unstable; the former dominates in the winter and toward the north, and the latter exerts the most influence in summer and toward the south. In addition, there are relatively minor incursions of tropical continental air in the Southwest in summer and of polar maritime air in the Northeast and the Pacific Northwest.

4 The predominant *wind and pressure systems* of any continent have far-reaching effects on its climate. The systems are too complex for anything other than rough generalizations here. Basically, Anglo-America is under the influence of a westerly wind flow throughout the year, but with varying northerly and southerly flows in response to broader planetary circulation conditions. Further, easterly winds are characteristic in much of the Arctic and Subarctic; and southerly or southeasterly flow often dominates the Gulf and South Atlantic areas, particularly in summer.

5 Various kinds of *storms* are prominent in different parts of Anglo-America. From a climatic standpoint by far the most important are the extensive extratropical cyclones, which bring together tropical and polar air masses in broad low-pressure centers that move with the westerly wind flow and bring variable and unsettled weather to most parts of the continent many times each year (fig. 2–12). The more spectacular hurricanes, which affect southeastern coastal areas a few times each fall, and tornadoes, which are mostly restricted to the eastern two-thirds of the conterminous states, may have devastating local effects but climatically are of relatively minor importance.

6 The *topographic pattern* has great influence on wind flow. The western cordilleras of Anglo-America are generally oriented at right angles to the prevailing westerly flow, which strongly inhibits the movement of maritime characteristics inland. This "barrier" effect is not nearly so pronounced with the Appalachians, since easterly air flow from the Atlantic is uncommon. The lack of a significant topographic barrier along the Gulf Coast permits an inflow of warm moist air over the eastern United States with considerable frequency, especially in summer, and allows freezing conditions to reach the coastal areas and peninsular Florida sporadically in winter.

7 *Ocean currents* affect the temperature of the winds that blow over them and, hence, the climate of the adjacent coastal regions. Relatively warm waters are brought into the Gulf of Alaska by the Japan Current from the western Pacific, but the California Current, which flows southward along the coast from the Gulf of Alaska, is relatively cold. The warm Gulf Stream moves out of the Gulf of Mexico and northward along the Atlantic Coast until it pulls away from the shore between North Carolina and Nova Scotia. The cold Labrador Current flows southward from the vicinity of Davis Strait (between Greenland and Baffin Island) to displace the Gulf Stream seaward off New-

fig. 2–12 Floods occur sporadically and erratically but are especially likely in late spring and early summer, as here in Kansas City (Union Pacific Railroad photo).

foundland and sometimes even as far south as Virginia.

Other various climatic controls are influential to varying degrees in different places, but most of them, such as altitude and exposure, are of more local than regional importance.

CLIMATIC MODIFICATION

During the past few years people have devoted considerable attention to weather modification, primarily by cloud seeding to induce or inhibit precipitation. These attempts have been somewhat successful, but the overall climatic effect has been minimal. Of much greater importance have been the inadvertent effects of urbanization on climate. The increasing concentration of people, factories, and automobiles in cities influences climatic elements in many ways, not all of which are understood. Most conspicuous has been the acceleration of air pollution, which has not been proved to have far-reaching effects on regional climate but has clearly modified the immediate climate in many cities. The infamous smog of Los Angeles is the prime example of this phenomenon, but similar visibility and health deterioration can be detected on a smaller scale in and around most large Anglo-American cities.

MAJOR CLIMATIC REGIONS OF ANGLO-AMERICA

There are almost as many classifications of climate as there are climatologists. Although most classifications are fundamentally the same, their minor variations and specialized nomenclature may confuse the reader. No standard classification has been adopted for climates; the map used in this book shows one of the most widely accepted schemes (fig. 2–13).

The basic pattern that emerges is one of east-west trending climatic zones in the eastern and northern portions of the continent, with north-south trending zones in the west. Such a pattern reflects the fundamental significance of latitude, with topographic modification in the west. Generally similar patterns are evident in the succeeding maps of vegetation and soils.

In the southeastern quarter of the United States the climatic type is classified as *humid subtropical* (1). Summer is the most prominent season. Humid tropical air usually pervades most of the region, and high temperatures frequently combine with high humidity. Winter is short and relatively mild, although significant cold spells are experienced several times each year. Precipitation is spread throughout the year, with a tendency toward a maximum in summer, except in Florida where rains

fig. 2–13 Major climatic regions of Anglo-America are (1) humid subtropical; (2) humid continental with warm summers; (3) humid continental with cool summers; (4) steppe; (5) desert; (6) mediterranean, or dry summer subtropical; (7) marine west coast; (8) subarctic; (9) tundra; (10) icecap; and (11) undifferentiated highlands (after Glenn T. Trewartha, Arthur H. Robinson, and Edwin H. Hammond, *Elements of Geography*, 5th ed. [New York: McGraw-Hill Book Company, 1967]).

associated with hurricanes bring a fall maximum.

In east-central United States there is a large area of *humid continental with warm summer phase* (2) climate. This is a zone of interaction between warm tropical air masses from the south and cold polar air masses from the north, which results in frequent, stimulating weather changes throughout the year. Summers are warm to hot and are the time of precipitation maximums. Winters are cold, and there is considerable snowfall.

There is a broad east-west band of *humid continental with cool summer phase* (3) climate along the international border in eastern Anglo-America. It is distinguished from the previous climatic type by its shorter and milder summer and its longer and more rigorous winter (fig. 2–14).

The *steppe* (4) climate of the Great Plains and Intermontane areas is basically a semiarid climate with marked seasonal temperature extremes. Summers are hot, dry, and windy and punctuated by occasional abrupt thunderstorms; winters are cold, dry, and windy, with occasional blizzards. Intense and dramatic weather—hail, heat waves, tornadoes, windstorms, and the like—are typical of this region.

The *desert* (5) climate of the southwestern interior is characterized by clear skies, brilliant sunshine, and long periods without rain. Aridity is universal, except at higher elevations. Summer is long and scorchingly hot; winter is brief, mild, and delightful.

Central and coastal California is a region of *mediterranean* (6) climate, with its anomalous precipitation regime in which sequential winter frontal storms move in from the Pacific bringing alternating periods of rain and sunshine. Summer is virtually rainless, since stable high pressure conditions dominate the atmosphere. Coastal sections have mild temperatures throughout the year, whereas inland locations experience hot summers and cool winters.

The *marine west coast* (7) climate of the Pacific littoral is characterized by long, relatively mild, very wet winters and short, pleasant, relatively dry summers. The frequent movement over the region of maritime polar air from the Pacific and its

fig. 2–14 The beginning of spring thaw in eastern Canada. This is the Muskoka area of Ontario (courtesy Ontario Ministry of Industry and Tourism).

associated fronts account for the prominence of winter conditions. Exposed slopes at higher elevations receive some of the greatest precipitation totals (both rain and snow) in the world.

The climate of most of central Canada and Alaska is classified as *subarctic* (8). Winter is the dominant season and is long, dark, relatively dry, and bitterly cold. Summer occupies only a brief period, but the succession of long hours of daylight produces several weeks of warm to hot weather. Summer rainfall is scanty, but evaporation rates are low, so moisture effectiveness is high. Except in Quebec and Labrador, winter snowfall is also scanty, but there is little melting from October to May.

The *tundra* (9) climate of arctic Canada and Alaska is virtually a cold desert. There is little precipitation at any season; however, evaporation rates are also quite low. Winter is very long, although not so cold as in the subarctic areas. Summer is short and cool.

The *icecap* (10) climate of the High Arctic is rigorous in the extreme. Low temperatures and strong winds make these areas unendurable for humans and animals, except briefly.

The major mountain areas of Anglo-America are classified as having a *highland*

(11) climate. Generalizations concerning weather and climate in such areas can be made only with reference to particular elevations or particular exposures. On the average, temperature and pressure decrease with altitude; whereas precipitation and windiness increase. Thus vertical zonation is the key to understanding highland climates.

the pattern
of natural vegetation

Unlike landforms and climate, the natural vegetation of Anglo-America has undergone major changes brought about by humanity. The native flora has been so thoroughly removed, rearranged, and replaced that a discussion of natural vegetation in many areas is largely a theoretical or historical exercise. Still, from a broad standpoint it is possible to reconstruct the major vegetation zones and make some meaningful generalizations about them (fig. 2–15). The reader should keep in mind that in many parts of the continent, introduced plants—particularly crops, pasture grasses, weeds, and ornamentals—are much more conspicuous than native flora.

Anglo-America's natural vegetation associations can be divided into three broad classes: forests, grasslands, and shrublands.

FORESTS

The forests occur in six zones:

fig. 2–15 Major natural vegetation regions of Anglo-America are (1) broadleaf deciduous forest, (2) mixed broadleaf deciduous and needleleaf evergreen forest, (3) needleleaf evergreen forest, (4) grassland, (5) mixed grassland and mesquite, (6) broadleaf evergreen shrubland, (7) mediterranean shrubland, (8) tundra, and (9) little or no vegetation (after *The National Atlas of the United States of America*, pp. 90–92; and *Atlas of Canada*, plate 38).

1 the northern coniferous forests, or taiga
2 the eastern hardwood zone[2]
3 the eastern mixed forests
4 the southern pineries
5 the Rocky Mountain forests
6 the Pacific Coast forests

The taiga, composed mostly of coniferous trees growing under extremes of temperature in a region where the winters are very long, occurs widely across Canada and Alaska and dips into the north-central part of the conterminous states. For the most part the trees grow in relatively pure stands, with spruce, fir, hemlock, and larch dominating, although such nonconifers as aspen and willow also often cover extensive areas. The short growing season and relatively poor drainage of the region inhibit rapid growth, so that even old trees are not very tall.

Three belts of forested land extend southward from the taiga. One prong follows the Appalachian Mountains and adjacent lowlands, another the Rocky Mountains, and a third the ranges of the Pacific coastal states. The easternmost prong grades southward from the relatively pure softwood stands of the taiga through a zone of mixed broadleaf and needleleaf trees to an expansive region where hardwoods composed the original vegetation (fig. 2–16). South of the hardwood region is another area of mixed forest that gives way to extensive forests dominated by southern yellow pine in the Southeast.

fig. 2–16 Much of the northeastern United States was originally covered with a dense growth of mixed forest, as is still found on the slopes of Mount Katahdin in Maine (courtesy Maine Development Office).

[2] The terms *hardwoods* and *softwoods* are the most generally accepted popular names for the two classes of trees, the *Angiosperms* and the *Gymnosperms*. Most Angiosperms, such as oak, hickory, sugar maple, and black locust, are notably hard woods, and many Gymnosperms, such as pines and spruces, are rather soft woods. But there are a number of outstanding exceptions. Basswood, poplar, aspen, and cottonwood, all classified as hardwoods, are in reality among the softest of woods. Longleaf pine, on the other hand, is about as hard as the average hardwood, although it is classified as a softwood. The most accurate popular descriptions for the two groups are *trees with broad leaves* for the Angiosperms and *trees with needles or scale-like leaves* for the Gymnosperms (from Forest Products Laboratory, *Technical Note 187,* Madison, Wisconsin).

The Rocky Mountain prong is mostly mountain forest, with various species occupying altitudinal zones vertically arranged on the mountainsides. In the Southern Rockies trees grow only in the uplands, but in the Northern Rockies many of the lowlands between the ranges are also forested. Most of the trees are conifers, with spruce and fir occupying the wetter areas; pine and juniper grow in drier localities. Aspen, the first species to occupy an area after a fire, is one of the few deciduous trees and is quite widespread in some places.

The Pacific Coast prong also consists primarily of softwoods. Although the forested zone follows the mountain trend, most of the lowlands north of the Sacramento Valley (except the Willamette Valley) were also originally forested. This is a region of huge trees, generally the largest to be found on earth (fig. 2–17). Fir, spruce, and hemlock dominate in the north, whereas redwoods become conspicuous in northern

fig. 2–17 The evergreen forest association of the Pacific Northwest includes big tree species such as Douglas fir and western hemlock, as shown here in western Washington (courtesy Weyerhaeuser Company).

fig. 2–18 The bristlecone pines of desert mountain ranges in southern Nevada and adjacent parts of California are the world's oldest living things, some exceeding 4,000 years in age. This is Mount Wheeler in Nevada (courtesy Nevada Highway Department).

California. The drier slopes are almost invariably pine-covered (fig. 2–18).

GRASSLANDS

Grasslands are usually found in areas where the rainfall is insufficient to support trees, and most have never had any other kind of vegetation. Where grass is tall, it is often called *prairie;* where short, *steppe.* Toward the drier margin the short grass association grades into bunchgrass.

In Anglo-America the eastern portion of the Great Plains was originally clothed in prairie grasses, with a significant eastward extension in the so-called Prairie Triangle of Illinois. The western part of the Plains had a steppe association, and there were other significant areas of steppe in the Central Valley of California and in the northern part of the Intermontane Region.

The tundra of the far north is classified as a sort of pseudograssland. It is characterized by a low-growing mixture of sedges, grasses, mosses, and lichens, occurring in amazing variety of species.

SHRUBLANDS

Shrublands vary considerably in their characteristics but usually develop under an arid or semiarid climate. The typical plant association is a combination of bushes or stunted trees and sparse grasses. In southern and central Texas, the shrubby mesquite tree is the dominant plant. In the area from Wyoming to Nevada, sagebrush provides the most common ground cover. In the southwest, cacti and other succulents are characteristic (fig. 2–19). The chaparral-manzanita association of California is a dense, brushy vegetation that encompasses some broad reaches of grassland and some of open oak woodland.

the pattern of soil

The most complex feature of the environment is the soil. This is largely attributable to complicated chemical factors and reac-

fig. 2–19 Desert vegetation in southern Arizona. Spindly shrubs are characteristic, but the floristic landscape is often dominated by such conspicuous cacti as the organ pipe (left) and giant saguaro (right).

tions in soil development that are not only imperfectly understood, but also leave little or no mark on the landscape and so are difficult to ascertain without detailed microstudies. Also, minor differences in such related features as slope or drainage can be much more important than broader environmental parameters in determining significant soil characteristics; thus soil variations over short distances are often much more significant than broader regional variations.

The identification and distribution pattern of meaningful soil categories is consequently difficult to determine except on a very large scale. Most maps of soil categories are hopelessly complex for purposes of macrostudy. Moreover, the past few years have been a period of fundamental change in the way that soils are classified and categorized by pedologists and other scholars interested in soil distribution. Thus, an entirely new classification scheme has been adopted and many changes in nomenclature and terminology have been accepted.

With these caveats in mind, we can make only broad generalizations about the distribution of soil categories in Anglo-America. Figure 2–20 is based on the United States Comprehensive Soil Classification System that was developed slowly and laboriously during the 1950s and 1960s by the Soil Survey Staff of the U.S. Department of Agriculture.[3] The principal *orders* (the major categories in the hierarchical classification) are briefly described below:

Alfisols (A) are soils with mature profile development that occur in widely diverse climatic and vegetation environments. They have gray to brown surface horizons and a clay accumulation in subsurface horizons. They are most widespread in the Great Lakes area, the Midwest in general, and the northern part of the Prairie Provinces.

[3] Soil Survey Staff, *Soil Classification: A Comprehensive System—7th Approximation* (Washington, D.C.: U.S. Department of Agriculture, Soil Conservation Service, 1960); Soil Survey Staff, *Supplement to Soil Classification System—7th Approximation* (Washington, D.C.: U.S. Department of Agriculture, Soil Conservation Service, 1967); Soil Survey Staff, *Soil Taxonomy: A Basic System of Soil Classification for Making and Interpreting Soil Surveys* (Washington, D.C.: U.S. Department of Agriculture, Soil Conservation Service, 1976); Donald Steila, *The Geography of Soils* (Englewood Cliffs, N.J.: Prentice-Hall, Inc., 1976); J. S. Clayton et al., *Soils of Canada*, 2 vols. (Ottawa: Canada Department of Agriculture, 1977).

fig. 2–20 Major soils regions of Anglo-America: (A) Alfisols, (D) Aridisols, (E) Entisols, (H) Histosols, (I) Inceptisols, (M) Mollisols, (S) Spodosols, (U) Ultisols, (X) complex soil regions, and (Z) areas with little or no soils (after maps of Soil Geography Unit, Soil Conservation Service, U.S. Department of Agriculture).

Aridisols (D) are mineral soils that are low in organic matter and are dry in all horizons most of the time. They are associated primarily with arid climatic regimes and are most extensively found in the western interior of the United States, particularly in the Southwest.

Entisols (E) are mostly of immature development, with a low degree of horizonation. Characteristically they are either quite wet, quite dry, or quite rocky. They occur most widely in northern Quebec and Labrador but are also found in some of the High Arctic islands, in scattered localities in the West, and in southern Florida.

Histosols (H) represent the only order composed primarily of organic, rather than mineral, matter. They are often referred to with such terms as *bog, peat,* or *muck.* They can be found in any climate, providing water is available. In Anglo-America their most extensive occurrences are in subarctic Canada, particularly south of Hudson Bay and in the Great Bear Lake area.

Inceptisols (I) also occur in widely differing environments. They are moist soils with generally clear-cut horizonation. Leaching is prominent in their formation. They lack illuvial horizons and are primarily eluvial in character. They are wide-

30

spread in tundra areas of Canada and Alaska, where they are associated with permafrost, and are also notable in the Appalachians, the Lower Mississippi Valley, and the Pacific Northwest.

Mollisols (M) are mineral soils with a thick, dark surface layer that is rich in organic matter and bases. Their agricultural potential is generally high. They are mostly found in subhumid or semiarid areas and are the principal soils of the western Corn Belt and the Great Plains, as well as in interior portions of the Pacific Northwest.

Spodosols (S) have a conspicuous subsurface horizon of humus accumulation, often with iron and aluminum. They are usually moist or wet and heavily leached. They are often associated with the soil-forming process called podzolization and have limited agricultural potential. Their most extensive occurrence in Anglo-America is in southeastern Canada and New England, but they are also found in such divergent locations as northern Florida and the Great Slave Lake area.

Ultisols (U) are thoroughly weathered and extensively leached, and have therefore experienced considerable mineral alteration. Their principal locations are in the southeastern quarter of the United States.

Complex (X) soil associations are delineated on the map in many mountain areas and in much of California. Their variety is too complicated to allow generalization at this scale.

Areas with *little or no soil* (Z) are recognized in rugged mountain areas or where permanent icefields exist.

This soil classification differs from most previous ones in that it is generic (based systematically on observable soil characteristics) rather than genetic (based on soil-forming conditions and processes). The resultant distribution pattern is less easy to apprehend because soils with similar characteristics sometimes are found in widely differing environments; for example, Incep-

tisols dominate in both southern Louisiana and the Northwest Territories. Nevertheless, genesis is not completely ignored, as soil properties are directly related to soil development. Thus, the pattern of figure 2–20 reflects some environmental relationships. The zonation of soils in the eastern and northern parts of Anglo-America is generally in east-west bands, whereas that in the western part of the continent is banded north-south, thus emphasizing the roles of topography, climate, and vegetation in soil formation.

the pattern of wildlife

Unlike the environmental elements previously discussed, the faunal complement of Anglo-America is generally insignificant in the total geographic scene. The spread of civilization has been inimical to native wildlife, resulting in contracting habitats and decreasing numbers. A few species, such as opossum, coyote, armadillo, and raccoon, have withstood the onslaught of civilization and actually expanded their ranges in the last few centuries, but most forms of wildlife now occur in smaller numbers and with greatly reduced ranges.

People have also influenced wildlife patterns in Anglo-America in other ways. They have introduced new species, such as nutria, ring-necked pheasants, feral pigs, and feral horses, and have artificially rearranged the distribution of native species, for example, expanding the range of mountain goats by deliberate translocation.

In most parts of Anglo-America, wildlife is an inconsequential element in the landscape and does not attract much attention from students of geography. But in some areas, usually sparsely populated and with limited economic potential, wildlife assumes a more important role. Where such conditions pertain, the discussion takes place in the appropriate regional chapter of this book.

selected bibliography

ATWOOD, WALLACE W., *The Physiographic Provinces of North America*. Boston, Mass.: Ginn & Company, 1940.

BIRD, J. BRIAN, *The Natural Landscapes of Canada: A Study in Regional Earth Science*. Toronto: Wiley Publishers of Canada, Ltd., 1972.

BRYSON, REID A., AND F. KENNETH HARE, eds., *World Survey of Climatology: Vol. 2, Climates of North America*. New York: American Elsevier Publishing Company, 1974.

COURT, ARNOLD, AND RICHARD D. GERSHTON, "Fog Frequency in the United States," *Geographical Review*, 56 (1966), 543–50.

FALCONER, A., ET AL., *Physical Geography: The Canadian Context*. Toronto: McGraw-Hill Ryerson, Ltd., 1974.

FENNEMAN, NEVIN M., *Physiography of Eastern United States*. New York: McGraw-Hill Book Company, 1938.

————, *Physiography of Western United States*. New York: McGraw-Hill Book Company, 1931.

GERAGHTY, JAMES J., ET AL., *Water Atlas of the United States* (3rd ed.). Port Washington, N. Y.: Water Information Center, 1973.

GERSMEHL, PHILIP J., "Soil Taxonomy and Mapping," *Annals*, Association of American Geographers, 67 (1977), 419–28.

HARE, F. KENNETH, AND M. K. THOMAS, *Climate Canada*. Toronto: Wiley Canada, Ltd., 1974.

HUNT, CHARLES B., *Natural Regions of the United States and Canada*. San Francisco, Calif.: W. H. Freeman & Company, 1973.

IVES, J. D., "Glaciers," *Canadian Geographical Journal*, 74 (April 1967), 110–17.

KALNICKY, R. A., "Climatic Change since 1950," *Annals*, Association of American Geographers, 64 (1974), 100–112.

KUCHLER, A. W., *Potential Natural Vegetation of the Conterminous United States*. New York: American Geographical Society, Special Publications 36, 1964.

MacLENNAN, HUGH, *Rivers of Canada*. Toronto: Macmillan of Canada, 1974.

MARKHAM, CHARLES G., "Seasonality of Precipitation in the United States," *Annals*, Association of American Geographers, 60 (1970), 593–97.

McKNIGHT, TOM, *Feral Livestock in Anglo-America*. Berkeley: University of California Press, 1964.

NELSON, J. G., AND M. J. CHAMBERS, eds., *Vegetation, Soils, and Wildlife*. Toronto: Methuen Publications, 1969.

NELSON, J. G., M. J. CHAMBERS, AND R. E. CHAMBERS, eds., *Weather and Climate*. Toronto: Methuen Publications, 1970.

PIRKLE, E. C., AND W. H. YOHO, *Natural Regions of the United States* (2nd ed.). Dubuque, Iowa: Kendall/Hunt Publishing Company, 1977.

SEWELL, W. F. DERRICK, "Water Across the American Continent," *Geographical Magazine*, 46 (1974), 472–79.

SKAGGS, RICHARD H., "Severe Hail in the United States," *Proceedings*, Association of American Geographers, 6 (1974), 43–46.

STEILA, DONALD, *The Geography of Soils*. Englewood Cliffs, N. J.: Prentice-Hall, Inc., 1976.

STORRIE, M. C., AND C. I. JACKSON, "Canadian Environments," *Geographical Review*, 62 (1972), 309–32.

THOMAS, M. K., "Canada's Climates Are Changing More Rapidly," *Canadian Geographical Journal*, 88 (May 1974), 32–39.

THORNBURY, WILLIAM D., *Regional Geomorphology of the United States*. New York: John Wiley & Sons, Inc., 1965.

TULLER, S. E., "What Are 'Standard' Seasons in Canada?" *Canadian Geographical Journal*, 90 (February 1975), 36–43.

VISHER, S. S., *Climatic Atlas of the United States*. Cambridge, Mass.: Harvard University Press, 1954.

ZWINGER, A. H., AND B. E. WILLARD, *Land Above the Trees: A Guide to American Alpine Tundra*. New York: Harper & Row, Publishers, 1972.

THE
POPULATION
OF
ANGLO-
AMERICA

3

The areally vast and physically varied subcontinent of Anglo-America was sparsely populated until relatively recent times. Its aboriginal peoples were numerically few, geographically scattered, culturally diverse, and economically unsophisticated. The penetration and settlement of the continent by Europeans signaled an almost total change in its human geography; the aborigines were decimated and displaced, and in a few short decades virtually every vestige of their life style had been erased. The contemporary human geography of the United States and Canada, then, has been shaped almost completely by nonaboriginal people. Although the present population is mostly European in origin, it also contains other important elements. The saga of the blending of these elements is a chronicle of great complexity that is treated only briefly in this book.

nation building

Although the Norse had settled part of southern Greenland and sketchily explored a portion of the North Atlantic coastline (possibly as far south as Rhode Island and as far inland as Minnesota) a century or two earlier, effective European contact with Anglo-America began early in the sixteenth century shortly after Columbus's "discovery" of the New World. Across the North Atlantic came the Cabots, who discovered Newfoundland and the Gulf of St. Lawrence and claimed that territory for England. Later, Jacques Cartier, sailing under the flag of France, reached the Gaspé Peninsula.

About 1540, Cabeza de Vaca, after being shipwrecked on the Texas coast, wandered across the Southwest as far as Arizona, then turned southward down the west coast of Mexico. Coronado traveled through Arizona and New Mexico, Texas and Kansas, and then returned through the Southwest to Mexico. Having failed to discover the "fabulous" Seven Cities of Cibola, he considered the expedition a failure.

At about the same time, an expedition under Hernando de Soto advanced northwestward from Florida and crossed the Mississippi River to the south of the present city of Memphis. De Soto went as far west as the Ozarks, but on returning from that area he died and was buried in the Mississippi. In spite of the extensive explorations of the South and Southwest, Spain made no definite claims to the area because its explorers found no gold; thereafter its interests were concentrated largely in Mexico and South America.

It was not until the close of the sixteenth and the beginning of the seventeenth century that France and England made any further attempts to acquire colonies in North America. The French came to Canada, dominated the St. Lawrence Valley, then the Great Lakes area, and ultimately claimed all lands drained by the Mississippi River and its tributaries. The English, reaching Anglo-America later, settled only on the east coast and in the West Indies. Each country ignored the claims of the others, all the grants to the English colonies reading "thence westward to the Pacific." The Finns and Swedes settled in Delaware and were absorbed by the Dutch, who in turn were incorporated into the English colony.

By the early part of the eighteenth century the English were entrenched along the Atlantic coast from Nova Scotia almost to Florida. The French dominated the Great Lakes and the Mississippi Valley. Florida, Texas, New Mexico, and all lands westward to the Pacific were held by the Spanish.

The main base of Russian America was on Baranof Island at Sitka, Alaska. No one disputed the Russian possession of the region around the Aleutian Islands, but in southeastern Alaska there were conflicting claims. The Spanish had sent out an expedition from Mexico and claimed the coast as far north as 62° N. L. James Cook explored the Alaska coast and claimed much of it for Great Britain. American clipper ships had traded up the West Coast, discovering the mouth of the Columbia River and the lands of the Northwest. Spain and Russia withdrew from the quarrel about the southern part of the area, leaving it to the United States and England. Spain relinquished its claims to the United States in the Treaty of 1819, when Florida was purchased. In the early part of the nineteenth century, Russia ceased to make any further advances in the territory.

At the close of the French and Indian War, Canada became a part of the British Empire. Unlike the English colonies to the south, Canada remained loyal to Britain. The War of 1812 was largely a war between the United States and British Canada. At its close, the two countries agreed to abolish all fortifications along their common border and to maintain no navies on the Great Lakes. Since then, only customs houses mark the boundary between these two great nations on the longest unguarded international boundary in the world.

In the space of fifty years, 1803–53, the United States attained its initial continental size, acquiring much of the territory by purchase. Following the Revolutionary War and the creation of the United States as a new nation on the North American continent, the first land annexed was Louisiana in 1803. This territory had a complicated history. France had ceded Louisiana to Spain at the close of the French and Indian War to prevent it from falling into the hands of England. Spain, in accepting Louisiana, hoped to block the advance of the English colonists. Spain soon realized, however, that the advance of the new American republic could not be stopped and, hence, returned Louisiana to France so that France could act as a barrier between the young United States and Spanish Texas.

Spain was dismayed when France immediately sold the territory to the neighbor it dreaded most. American pioneers in the Ohio Valley had been demanding better treatment at New Orleans, their natural water outlet, and had begun to insist on the purchase of that port by the United States. Some trans-Alleghenian people even threatened secession because their economic interests were linked more closely with the port at the mouth of the Mississippi River than with any of the American ports on the Atlantic Seaboard.

President Jefferson, realizing the seriousness of the situation, opened negotiations with France for the purchase of New Orleans and ultimately secured the entire Louisiana Territory for $15 million. Although Congress had not authorized this purchase, Jefferson concluded the transaction because he recognized the importance of this tract of land to the growing United States. Immediately he sent out an expedition under Lewis and Clark to explore the new territory. They ascended the Missouri River to its headwaters, crossed the Rocky Mountains, and descended the Snake and Columbia rivers to the Pacific Coast. Organized expeditions were soon followed by trappers in the 1830s and 1840s. At this time the Great Plains were merely transit lands; no one was interested in occupying them or made any attempt to settle them.

Having lost most of its colonial possessions in the New World and realizing its inability to stop the territorial advance of the United States, Spain sold Florida to the new nation in 1821.

By 1820 settlers were rapidly moving westward. Meanwhile Mexico, having separated from Spain, controlled a broad area extending from Texas westward to the Pacific and as far north as the present northern boundary of California. Realizing that Texas should be immediately occupied, Mexico threw open the land to American settlers, giving them several times more land for homesteading than the United States later offered to its land-hungry population. Mexico soon saw the mistake of permitting Americans to homestead in Texas and tried to discourage further settlement by making it unpleasant for those already there, thus precipitating the Texas war for independence.

Texas was annexed by the United States after operating as an independent republic for nearly a decade. In the Mexican War that followed, the United States was victorious. Mexico then ceded to the United States all territory in dispute, established the Rio Grande as the southern boundary of Texas, and sold it the southwestern territories, including California. In 1853, the Gadsden Purchase was negotiated to extend the boundary of the United States south of the Gila River.

In Oregon, the claims of the United States and England conflicted. The former demanded the territory as far north as the southern boundary of Alaska, 54°40′, on the basis of exploration by fur traders and by Lewis and Clark. England claimed the entire region because its trappers had descended the Fraser and Columbia rivers. The United States dispached settlers over the Oregon Trail to clinch its claims. England also joined the race. The two countries compromised, however, on the 49th parallel,

which had already been agreed on as the boundary from Lake of the Woods to the Rocky Mountains. This boundary was projected across the mountains without regard to relief. The only exception in the use of that parallel was that all of Vancouver Island was recognized as Canadian territory.

As England extended its domain to the Pacific Ocean, need was felt for some type of home government. In 1867 the Dominion of Canada was organized. This included all of British North America north of the United States except Newfoundland. In 1949 Newfoundland became a province of the Dominion of Canada.

The purchase of Alaska from Russia in 1867 completed the acquisition of territory by the United States on the mainland of Anglo-America. The Hawaiian Islands were annexed by request in 1898 and achieved statehood in 1959, the same year in which Alaska's status was changed from territory to state.

melting pot or potpourri?

At the time of establishment of the first European settlements in Anglo-America, it is probable that the total population of the area now occupied by the United States and Canada did not much exceed 1 million. The population today is more than 240 times that figure.

It has often been stated that the United States and Canada are prime examples of a melting pot wherein people of diverse backgrounds are shaped in a common mold, thus becoming new citizens of new countries. There is some factual basis to this image, for tens of millions of immigrants have settled in the Anglo-American countries and, with the passage of time, many of their ethnic distinctions have been blurred into obscurity. But the melting-pot concept is only partially apt; in reality the population of the two countries consists of an imperfect amalgam of diverse groups. Some groups, and some individuals, assimilate more readily than others. Or, in Zelinsky's pithy prose, "The Melting Pot ... contains a lumpy stew; and ... the lumps will not cook away."[1]

By and large, the United States and Canada are Anglo-Saxon countries, and immigrants of British background are absorbed more neatly because of their basic similarity to and acceptability by the resident populace. Immigrants from other Northwest European areas also tend to be readily assimilable for the same general reasons, although the dichotomy of French Canada is an important exception to this generalization.

For people of Southern or Eastern European background, it is often more than one generation before the ethnic distinctiveness fades. Immigrants from Asian countries vary considerably in assimilability; distinctive physical features often belie adroitness in cultural absorption. The obvious pigmentation differences of nonwhites serve as an assimilation barrier that frequently calls forth cultural rejection on the part of whites; thus the aspirations of black people toward assimilation are often affected by their degree of acceptance in the white community.

the peopling
of anglo-america

The current population mix of the United States and Canada is continually being modified by the influx of immigrants and the egress of emigrants, as well as the rate of natural increase. It is a blend of varied origins, and its diverse patterns through the years continue in dynamic flux today. There were five major original source regions for the peopling of Anglo-America: indigenous, European, African, Asian, and Latin American.

[1] Wilbur Zelinsky, *The Cultural Geography of the United States* (Englewood Cliffs, N.J.: Prentice-Hall, Inc., 1973), p. 32.

NORTH AMERICAN ABORIGINES

The aboriginal population—mostly Indians but including a few thousand Eskimos and Aleuts—of Anglo-America at the time of European contact consisted of a great variety of tribes thinly scattered over the continent (Fig. 3–1). The largest concentrations were in the area presently called California, although there were some other notable groups in the Southwest, adjacent to the Gulf Coast, and along the Atlantic coastal plain.

The contrast with the relatively large population of *Indians* in Latin America is very marked and apparently has long been a feature of the Americas. There is nothing in North American archaeological evidence to suggest any developed Indian civilizations comparable with those of Mexico, parts of Central America, or the central Andes. The thin population density probably reflected a reliance on simple hunting and fishing or primitive agricultural economies.

It is generally accepted that the North American aborigines were relatively recent (within the last 30,000 years or so) arrivals from Asia, having entered the Western Hemisphere via Alaska and diffusing widely throughout the New World. There were many physical and cultural variations among the Indians; their diversity was at least as great as that of the Europeans, who later were to overwhelm them. Their only common physical attributes were black hair, brown eyes, and some shade of brown skin. There was much variety in both material and nonmaterial aspects of Indian culture, and hundreds of mutually unintelligible dialects (divided by scholars into six major linguistic groups) were spoken.

Eskimos and *Aleuts* are thought to be Asian immigrants of much more recent vintage, having crossed from Siberia as little as 1,000 to 3,000 years ago. The Eskimos spread all across the Arctic from the Bering Sea to Greenland, hunting and fishing for a living. The Aleuts, apparently branching off from the mainstream of Eskimo life, developed a distinctive culture of their own based

fig. 3–1 Generalized distribution of major tribal groupings in aboriginal Anglo-America.

on a fishing economy in the Aleutian Islands.

The initial relations between Europeans and Indians-Eskimos-Aleuts were not always unpleasant. Many tribes developed profitable trading patterns with the Europeans. Indeed, such tribes as the Iroquois in the East, the Crees south of Hudson Bay, the Comanches in the Great Plains, and the Apaches in the Southwest acquired metal weapons and horses and established short-lived empires at the expense of less fortunate neighboring tribes.

Within a few years or a few decades, however, the insatiable appetite of the land-hungry Europeans led to inevitable conflict. Although some of the tribes were fierce, brave, and warlike, the white settlers subdued them and relocated them in relatively short order. The aborigines were cruelly decimated by warfare, but introduced diseases were even more potent destroyers. For example, a smallpox epidemic wiped out more than 90 percent of the Mandans in the mid-1800s, at the same time that cholera was eliminating 50 percent of the Kiowas and Comanches.[2] An "Indian Territory" was established between Texas and Kansas, and nearly 100,000 Indians from east of the Mississippi were crowded onto the overutilized hunting grounds of the plains Indians.[3] Even this area was sporadically whittled down in size until it was finally thrown open to white settlement and became the state of Oklahoma.

Although there were occasional later outbursts by renegade Apaches in the Southwest, the last significant Indian conflict ended in the Wounded Knee massacre of 300 Sioux in 1881. By the turn of the century only a few tens of thousands of aborigines survived in all of Anglo-America.

During the twentieth century most Indians lived on reservations or entirely abandoned tribal life. Their numbers have been increasing at an accelerating rate in both Canada and the United States, constituting one of the fastest growth rates of any segment of the population, although the present aboriginal population is only about 0.5 percent of the total population of Anglo-America. There are now some 400,000 Indians living on about 280 reservations (including pueblos in New Mexico, colonies in Nevada, and rancherias in California) in the United States; the largest concentrations are in Arizona, New Mexico, and Oklahoma (fig. 3-2). Another 500,000 or so United States Indians are living outside reservations; most are in urban areas, and approxi-

mately one-third of the total is concentrated in Los Angeles.

About one-third of Canada's 300,000 Indians live on nearly 2,300 mostly small reserves. Another one-third of the Canadian Indians reside in cities, usually in unofficial ghettos; the remainder is scattered widely in rural areas and small towns. The province of Ontario contains by far the largest number of Indians.

In addition, there are about 35,000 Eskimos and Aleuts in Alaska and some 18,000 Eskimos in Canada.

THE PATTERN OF EUROPEAN IMMIGRATION

Anglo-America has been by far the principal destination of European immigrants. It is estimated that between 1600 and 1980 nearly 80 million people left Europe to settle elsewhere, and more than four-fifths of them went to the United States and Canada.[4] The pattern of immigration can be clarified if chronological periods are discussed. It is somewhat misleading to do so, however, for the social process of European immigration has varied little during the course of Anglo-American history.

[4] Extrapolated from data in Maldwyn Allen Jones, *American Immigration* (Chicago, Ill.: University of Chicago Press, 1969), p. 1.

[2] William T. Hagan, *American Indians* (Chicago, Ill.: University of Chicago Press, 1969), p. 94.
[3] The continual forced rearrangement of tribes caused great misery and frustration, which is indelibly echoed in the pointed question of the Sioux chief Spotted Tail: "Why does not the Great Father put his red children on wheels, so he can move them as he will?"

fig. 3–2 The Sandia Pueblo is one of several that is still in use in north-central New Mexico.

Before 1815 This is the period of primary European colonization of Anglo-America, when nearly all the migrants—with the important exception of early French settlers in Acadia (Nova Scotia) and Lower Canada (Quebec)—were of Anglo-Saxon ethnic stock and followers of reformed churches subsequent to the Reformation. They varied from High Church Anglican aristocracy to Puritan and Lutheran peasant dissenters. The majority were English, but there were important groups of Germans, Dutch, and folk from Ulster, Scotland, and Wales.

In total numbers they probably did not greatly exceed 1 million, but their descendants in all parts of the United States and Canada now form an important segment of the population. More significant than their actual numbers is the effect they had in establishing the foundations of the social and economic patterns of the continent for generations. Different regional frameworks were established in the Maritimes, Lower Canada, Upper Canada, New England, the Middle Colonies, and the Southern Colonies, many aspects of which are still evident today.

After the American Revolution, immigration from England declined drastically, and the most numerous of the newcomers, in most years, were Scotch-Irish. During the 1790s, European immigration to Anglo-America often exceeded 10,000 per year, but the flow slowed appreciably during the Napoleonic Wars and almost ceased during the War of 1812.

1815 to 1860s This period represented the first of the great waves of immigration to Anglo-America from Europe, a movement unprecedented in world history. Some 6 million immigrants were involved; the rate accelerated from about 200,000 in the 1820s to nearly 3 million in the decade of the 1850s. In comparison with the resident population at the time, this influx was enormous.

These were people drawn by the economic opportunities available in a virgin land, or driven from their homes by religious or political persecution or by revolution. Every country in Europe was represented, but the great majority were from the North Sea countries. More than half of the migrants in this period came from the British Isles, especially from Ireland. Germany was second only to Ireland as a source of immigrants; smaller numbers came from France, Switzerland, Norway, Sweden, and the Netherlands. Thus the immigrant mix of this period was less exclusively British, and there also was a larger proportion of Catholics (principally Irish and German) than previously.

1860s to 1890s The second great wave of European immigration occupied the three decades following the American Civil War. In composition and character it was much like the first wave, but it was nearly twice as great in magnitude. Most of the migrants were still from Northwestern Europe—Germany (250,000 German immigrants to the United States in 1882 constituted the largest number from any single country in any single year prior to the twentieth century) and the British Isles—and from Scandinavia, Switzerland, and Holland.

A significant feature of this period is that it was the only lengthy segment in Canadian history in which there was net outmigration. Some 800,000 Canadian-born people moved south of the international border during this era.[5] A postwar wave of prosperity in the northern states coincided with an economic depression in Canada and drew a great many people, particularly French-Canadians, to United States cities. In addition, farmlands in the Midwest were available for settlement, and this was a further inducement to Canadian immigration. In the later years of this period, the Canadian prairies were opened for settlement; but even the flood of Swedes, Ukrainians, Mennonites, Finns, Hungarians, and other Europeans to the Canadian West did not compensate for the southward flow.

[5] T. R. Weir, "Population Changes in Canada, 1867–1967," *The Canadian Geographer,* 11 (1967), 201.

1890s to World War I Numerically this was the most significant period, for in these two decades an average of nearly 1 million immigrants per year came from Europe to Anglo-America. Perhaps of equal significance was the change in origin of the flow. From a predominantly Northwest European source in the 1880s (87 percent in 1882, for example), the tide shifted to a predominantly Southern and Eastern European source after the turn of the century (81 percent in 1907).[6] Italy, Austria-Hungary (which included most of eastern Europe), and Russia were the homelands of the bulk of the immigrants,[7] but considerable numbers also came from such countries as Greece and Portugal. The change in Canadian immigration sources was almost as dramatic. The Canadian government had instituted a policy to induce and broaden the base of immigration in 1896, and during the succeeding decade immigrants to Canada from continental Europe were twice the number that came from the British Isles (fig. 3–3).

This was the period of the melting pot in Anglo-America, but the assimilation of vast numbers of people of different cultures and languages was a slow and difficult process. By the time of World War I, there was considerable agitation in the United States,

[6] Jones, *American Immigration,* p. 179.
[7] Peak-year immigration to the United States was 286,000 from Italy in 1907; 340,000 from Austria-Hungary in 1907; and 291,000 from Russia in 1913.

and some in Canada, to slow the pace of immigration.

World War I to 1960s Immigration to Anglo-America decreased markedly during World War I and then began a rapid climb in 1919. Concern mounted that "the greatest social experiment in human history" had become the "melting-pot mistake." Immigrants had contributed to material progress by opening new lands and providing a cheap labor pool for factories, mines, forestry, and construction, but it was becoming clear that the rate of influx was getting out of hand. There was further concern, particularly in the United States, about the "mix" of the immigrants, with increasing demand for restricting immigration from the Latin and Slavic portions of Europe and from Asia.

This led to the enactment of legislation in the United States in the early 1920s restricting the immigrant flow. Canada did not promulgate significant restrictions for another decade. The basis of the restrictions was the ethnic composition of the United States population prior to the war; thus the countries of Northwestern Europe were given relatively large annual quotas (65,000 for the United Kingdom and 25,000 for Germany, for example), whereas other countries received much smaller allotments (6,000 for Italy, 850 for Yugoslavia, 0 for Japan). Africa was ignored in the quota system.

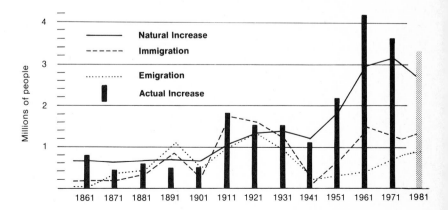

fig. 3–3 Canadian demographic trends. The major role of immigration in the early years of this century and in the period since World War II is notable. (T. R. Weir, "The People" in *Canada: A Geographical Interpretation,* ed. John Warkentin [Toronto: Methuen Publications, 1968], p. 141. Reprinted by permission.)

This resulted in a rapid decline in the total volume of immigration to the United States (down from 800,000 in 1921 to less than 150,000 by the end of the decade), whereas Canadian immigration maintained a relatively steady pace (between 100,000 and 150,000 per year during most of the 1920s). The depression of the 1930s and war in the early 1940s reduced immigration to insignificant totals for a decade and a half.

Although the quota system was still operating in the United States, after World War II there was a significant upturn in immigration to the United States and to Canada. The heaviest influx to both countries was from Great Britain, Italy, and Germany. Bulking large in the postwar migrant flow was the admittance of displaced persons and refugees (without regard to quotas in the United States) in considerable numbers, which significantly increased the influx from Eastern Europe until the Iron Curtain was closed.

Late 1960s to Present Drastically altered immigration laws in both countries (since 1965 in the United States and 1967 in Canada) have ushered in a new period in the immigration history of Anglo-America. In both cases immigration restrictions have been greatly liberalized and "universalized." In the United States system, immigration is on a first-come-first-served basis, up to a maximum of 20,000 per country in a single year and up to an annual quota of 170,000 for the entire Eastern Hemisphere. Canada's system is more complicated and flexible, making no reference to national origin; rather, it depends on a point system that puts a high premium on education and skills and varies annually with Canada's anticipated migrant needs.

These revised immigration policies have resulted in major changes in the flow of migrants to both Canada and the United States. In the first place, the total net gain from immigration has increased significantly in the former (averaging between 150,000 and 200,000 per year) and remarkably in the latter (between 300,000 and 400,-000 annually). When combined with the declining rate of natural increase in both countries, the contribution to population growth from net immigration is now about 25 percent in the United States and nearly 50 percent in Canada.

Another notable result has been a marked decrease in the European component of total immigration. Whereas 80 percent of the immigrants to Canada in the early 1960s were from Europe, they are now less than 40 percent of the total; there has been a somewhat smaller proportional decrease in the United States. Although Britain is still the single leading source of immigrants to Canada, the great bulk of European immigrants to Anglo-America now emanates from Mediterranean countries, particularly Portugal, Italy, Greece, and Yugoslavia.

INVOLUNTARY IMMIGRATION: THE AFRICAN SOURCE

Soon after the first white settlers occupied the land of coastal Virginia there arose the problem of labor for clearing the forests, cultivating the soil, and harvesting the crops. Since land was free, few settlers would consider working for others when they could have their own land, and the local Indians could not be enslaved. At first, indentured workers—Englishmen who temporarily sold their services for the price of ship passage to the New World—met the labor requirements. But they did not prove satisfactory because they were not numerous enough and because it was difficult to keep them as workers once they reached the frontier.

To help solve the labor problem, Negro slaves were imported from West Africa, initially via already established slaving areas in the West Indies. The first African slaves in the English colonies were landed at Jamestown in 1619. By the 1630s, slaves were being brought in each year. They were not very popular at first, and by the end of the century there were less than 10,000 in the tobacco colonies. But at about that time the British government began to restrict the sending of convicts (another source of labor) to America, and cotton became an important crop as a result of Eli Whitney's cotton gin. Thus, slaveholding began in earnest, and direct slave trade with the Guinea Coast of West Africa developed.

On the eve of the American Revolution there were about half a million Negroes (mostly slaves) in British North America, and nine-tenths of them were in the Southern Colonies. Despite their servile status, they exerted a significant influence upon many aspects of Southern life, from language to social customs. By 1808, when further importation of slaves was prohibited, nearly 20,000 were being brought into the United States every year.

Slavery was abolished at the time of the Civil War in the 1860s, and very few African immigrants have entered Anglo-America since that time. The descendants of those involuntary immigrants of the seventeenth to nineteenth centuries numbered nearly 9 million by 1900, however, and more than 24 million in the late 1970s.

Throughout most of these centuries the black population has been concentrated in the southeastern part of the United States. In this century, however, there has been a major movement northward and westward. As recently as 1950 blacks lived in approximately equal numbers in three situations: one-third in the rural South, one-third in the urban South, and one-third in cities of the North and West coasts. But the continued rural-to-urban movement has significantly decreased the proportion of nonurban blacks. Most are now city dwellers, with the largest concentrations in New York, Chicago, Detroit, Philadelphia, Washington, Los Angeles, and Baltimore.

Only a small number of blacks reside in Canada, largely in Toronto, Montreal, Halifax, and Windsor. Recent immigration from several black Caribbean nations—particularly Jamaica, but also Trinidad, Haiti, and Guyana—has made a large proportional increase, however.

THE IRREGULAR SEQUENCE OF ASIAN IMMIGRATION

Until very recently the immigration of people from Asia to Anglo-America has been quite limited in number and extremely sporadic in occurrence. Occasionally Asian workers have been imported or have come of their own volition in large numbers, but throughout most of history their entry has either been severely curtailed or totally prohibited.

The earliest Asian immigration was also the largest; some 300,000 Chinese came to California between 1850 and 1882, when the passage of the Chinese Exclusion Act halted the flow. During this same period several thousand Chinese entered British Columbia; originally they came from California, and later directly from China. The great majority of these immigrants were males, and after working in railway construction or gold mining for a while, many of them returned to China. Most remained on this continent, however, settling in "Chinatowns" in San Francisco, Los Angeles, Seattle, Vancouver, New York, and Chicago.

The first Japanese immigrants came to Hawaii as contract laborers to work on sugar cane plantations in the 1880s. After Hawaii became a territory of the United States in 1898, the Japanese were free to come directly to the mainland, and several tens of thousands did so during the early years of this century. A few thousand Japanese also immigrated to British Columbia.

The quota system stopped Japanese immigration to the United States after World War I, and Canada effectively stopped Chinese immigration by legislation in 1923.[8]

[8] Some 4,300 Chinese had immigrated to Canada in 1919, a larger total than from any other countries except the United Kingdom and the United States. The Chinese Immigration Act of 1923 resulted in such restriction that an average of only one Chinese immigrant per year entered Canada during the next two decades. See W. H. Agnew, "The Canadian Mosaic," in *Canada One Hundred: 1867–1967,* ed. Dominion Bureau of Statistics (Ottawa: Queen's Printer, 1967), p. 89.

The new immigration policies of the 1960s have once again opened the doors to Asian settlers, and in the United States this has resulted in a veritable flood of Asian immigrants. In the first few years under the new laws, more Chinese (from Taiwan and Hong Kong) and Filipino immigrants have entered the United States than citizens of any other Eastern Hemisphere countries; and there has also been a great upsurge of immigrants from India and Korea (fig. 3–4). Overall, Asians constituted nearly one-third of total immigrants to the United States in the 1970s, in comparison with only one-fifteenth in the mid-1960s. The Asian proportion is smaller in Canada, but there have been notable increases in immigrants from Hong Kong, India, and the Philippines in particular. The great majority of all Asian immigrants has settled on the West Coast, particularly in California. Most are urban dwellers, joining the swelling Chinese, Japa-

nese, and Filipino minorities of Los Angeles, San Francisco, Seattle, and Vancouver, with some spillover into Arizona and Alberta and conspicuous nodes in New York, Chicago, and Toronto.

It should be noted that Hawaii has long had a significant Asian population. The majority of the contemporary populace of that state is of Asian extraction, particularly Japanese and Chinese but with large numbers of Filipinos and Koreans.

LATIN-AMERICAN IMMIGRANTS

Throughout the twentieth century there has been a fluctuating pattern of immigration to Anglo-America, primarily the United States, from Latin America. With the exception of the recent massive influx from Cuba, this has been primarily a move toward economic betterment and has often been on a short-term rather than permanent basis.

Latin Americans were totally exempted (as were Canadians) from the quota provisions of United States immigration laws in the 1920s, which meant that they essentially enjoyed unrestricted immigration most of the time. Under current immigration regulations, there is a total Western Hemisphere quota of 120,000, with a maximum of 20,000 from any single country.

By far the largest, most continuous, and most conspicuous flow has been from Mexico. Legal immigration from Mexico began about the turn of the century, and several million immigrants, both legal and illegal, have entered since that time. Most Mexican immigrants have settled in the Southwestern border states, Texas to California, plus Colorado, although there is a significant concentration in Chicago.

Immigration from the West Indies is also of long-standing duration. Puerto Rico has been the principal source but is not considered to be a foreign country. In most recent years Jamaica has furnished more immigrants to the United States than any other country except the Philippines, Italy, Greece, and Hong Kong–Taiwan. More than half a million Cubans migrated to the

fig. 3–4 Principal components of recent Asian immigration to the United States.

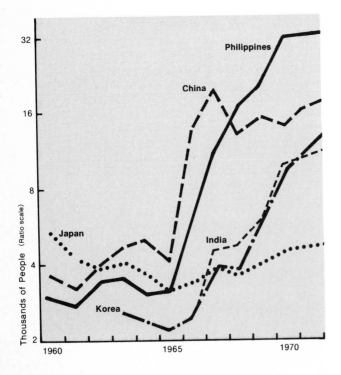

United States in the decade following 1965, about half of them on the twice-daily "Freedom Flights" that operated between Havana and Miami from 1965 until 1974.

the contemporary population of anglo-america

The 240 million Anglo-Americans represent about 6 percent of total world population. They occupy a land area of some 8.3 million square miles, or 14.5 percent of the land area of the planet. This population is very unequally divided between the two countries, with about ten people in the United States for every one person in Canada. The 10 to 1 ratio has been maintained throughout the past century and indicates that the rate of population growth in the two countries has been approximately equal for several generations.

DISTRIBUTION

The principal population concentrations are in the northeastern quarter of the United States (fig. 3–5) and adjacent parts of Ontario and Quebec. The most notable clusters are in the Megalopolis Region of the Atlantic seaboard, around the shores of Lake Erie, and around the southern end of Lake Michigan (fig. 3–6). In the southeastern quarter of

fig. 3–5   Distribution of population in the United States, according to the 1970 census.

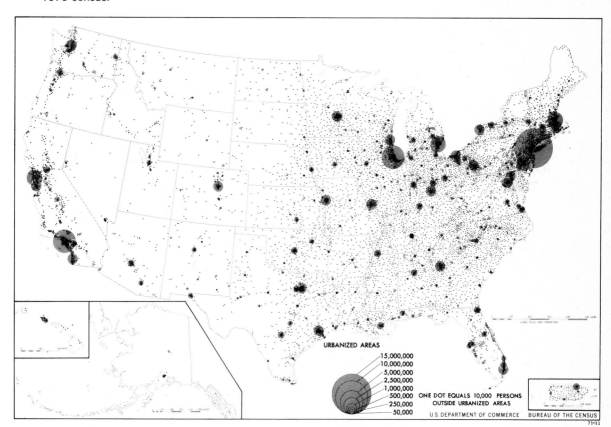

URBANIZED AREAS

15,000,000
10,000,000
5,000,000
2,500,000
1,000,000
500,000
250,000
50,000

ONE DOT EQUALS 10,000 PERSONS OUTSIDE URBANIZED AREAS

U.S. DEPARTMENT OF COMMERCE   BUREAU OF THE CENSUS

71-11

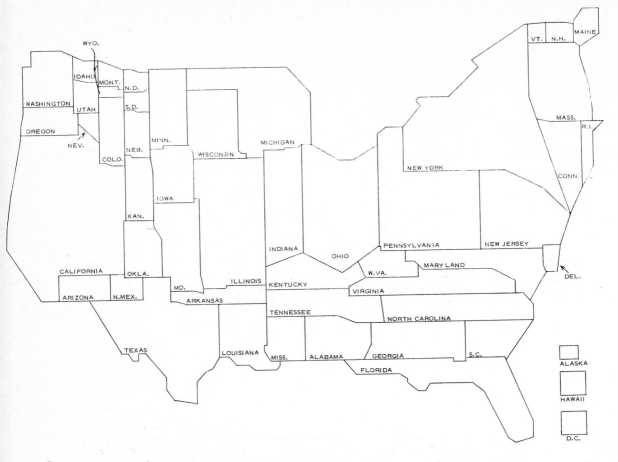

fig. 3-6 The states shown with their areas proportionate to the size of their population. (Map by Division of Research and Statistics, Ohio Bureau of Employment Services, based upon Census of Population, April 1970, Bureau of the Census, U.S. Department of Commerce.)

the United States and in parts of southern Ontario there is a moderate population density, fairly evenly distributed except for agglomeration around urban nodes. In the Atlantic Provinces there is an irregular pattern of moderate density alternating with patches of little population. In the central plains and prairies there is a generally decreasing density from east to west, with obvious concentrations along the major river valleys and at the eastern edge of the Rocky Mountains. The intermontane West is sparsely populated, with a few minor concentrations around cities.

On the Pacific Coast there is moderate to heavy population density in the valleys, with conspicuous agglomerations around the six principal urban areas. The vast expanses of central and northern Canada and most of Alaska are practically unpopulated; indeed, 90 percent of Canada's population is within 200 miles of the international border (fig. 3-7).

As it has for some years, the greatest *absolute* population growth continues to be in the states of California, Texas, and Florida and in the provinces of Ontario and British Columbia. The fastest *rates* of increase are in

The group defined by the U.S. Census Bureau as of Spanish origin is another Caucasian minority that is sufficiently prominent in terms of population concentration and distinctive cultural attributes that it merits particular attention. The number of people involved is unknown, for the Census Bureau readily admits that they have been underenumerated in official counts. As of the late 1970s, a conservative population estimate would be between 11 and 12 million citizens and legal aliens of Spanish origin, with perhaps half again that many who lead a surreptitious existence as illegal aliens. Of this total, about two-thirds of the legal residents and most of the illegal ones are of Mexican origin (Chicanos). About nine of every ten Chicanos live in the five southwestern states of California, Arizona, New Mexico, Colorado, and Texas.[9] The second largest component of the Hispanic minority consists of emigrants from Puerto Rico, of whom there are some 2 million in Anglo-America. Puerto Ricans mostly inhabit the metropolises of the Northeast, with the greatest concentration by far in New York City (fig. 3–9). There are more than 700,000

[9] Richard L. Nostrand, "The Hispanic-American Borderland: Delimitation of an American Culture Region," *Annals*, Association of American Geographers, 60 (December 1970), 638.

fig. 3–9 Ethnic neighborhoods are notable in many Anglo-American cities. This is the well-known sidewalk market along 125th Street in New York City's Spanish Harlem, where the bulk of the population is of Puerto Rican origin.

people of Cuban extraction in the United States, largely consisting of recent self-exiles from the Castro regime in Cuba. Despite massive efforts at resettlement, more than half reside in southern Florida. Cubans are a majority of the population of Miami, which is now legally a bilingual city.

Although most Hispanic-Americans are fluent in English, the majority consider Spanish to be their mother tongue. Most are at least nominally Roman Catholic, and they tend to be disadvantaged socially, economically, and politically, although they have recently developed considerable political leverage in south Texas, New Mexico, southern Arizona, and southern Florida.

Blacks are only a tiny fraction of the Canadian population, but they make up more than 11 percent of the populace of the United States. As in the past, blacks are more numerous in the Southern states than elsewhere; more than half of the nation's blacks live in the South. Moreover, the proportion is now increasing. After many decades of massive out-migration to the North and West, during the middle and late 1970s a reverse trend developed. More blacks are now moving to the South from the West, and particularly from the North, than are leaving the South.

The black population has become highly urbanized. The long continuing rural-to-urban flow has slowed but is still a clear trend. Washington, Newark, Atlanta, and Baltimore now have a black majority population within their political limits, and in New Orleans, Detroit, Birmingham, Richmond, St. Louis, Memphis, and Cleveland the black proportion is above 40 percent. In absolute terms, New York City contains far more blacks than any other city: 1.9 million, or 23 percent of the total population. In most instances the black population is concentrated in central areas and is a very minor element in the suburbs. More than 25 percent of the total population of *all* central cities in the United States is black, whereas less than 5 percent of the suburban population is black.

Other "nonwhites" are prominent in the contemporary population only in the major

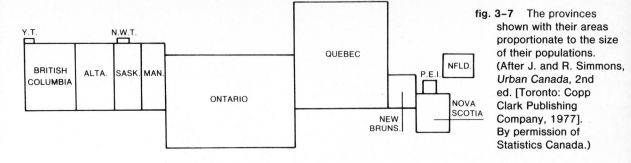

fig. 3–7 The provinces shown with their areas proportionate to the size of their populations. (After J. and R. Simmons, *Urban Canada*, 2nd ed. [Toronto: Copp Clark Publishing Company, 1977]. By permission of Statistics Canada.)

the southwestern states, especially Arizona and Nevada; Florida and Alaska; and the western provinces of Alberta and British Columbia.

ETHNIC COMPONENTS

Most of the people in both countries are of Anglo-Saxon background, but there are a number of significant minorities. The most prominent non-Anglo minority in Canada is the French, who live mostly in Quebec and in adjacent portions of New Brunswick and Ontario. French-Canadians have constituted about 30 percent of the national population total ever since Confederation, and in

recognition of this fact, Canada has long been officially a bicultural nation (fig. 3–8). This situation is discussed in greater detail in chapter seven.

Although people of German, Italian, Dutch, Scandinavian, Polish, Russian, and other European nationalities are significant components of the population in both countries, they are for the most part relatively inconspicuous as minorities. They are sometimes prominently associated with particular areas—as Scandinavians in Minnesota and Wisconsin or Ukrainians in the Canadian prairies—but a detailed consideration of their distribution is beyond the scope of this general treatment.

fig. 3–8 Ethnic origin of the Canadian population. The rapid recent increase of the non-British, non-French component is striking. (T. R. Weir, "The People," in *Canada: A Geographical Interpretation*, ed. John Warkentin [Toronto: Methuen Publications, 1968], p. 138. Reprinted by permission.)

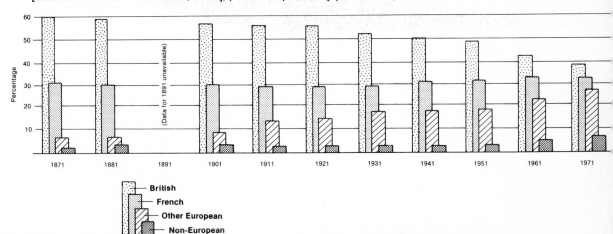

West Coast cities and a few Western farming areas and in ghetto situations in the largest Eastern cities. The total population of Asian origin in Anglo-America is estimated to be about 2.5 million, with Japanese, Chinese, and Filipinos dominating in roughly equivalent total numbers. Hawaii has long been the major North American domicile of people of Asian extraction, but the great flood of immigrants in the late 1960s and 1970s has given California the principal concentrations of all significant Asian minorities except Japanese, who are still slightly more numerous in Hawaii.

DEMOGRAPHIC CHARACTERISTICS

After World War II there was a population explosion in both Canada and the United States. Initiated by a postwar baby boom, the birth rate remained relatively high for many years. Population growth was also augmented by a high rate of immigration. Beginning about 1960, however, there was a downturn in the birth rate in both countries, which was sharpened in 1965. This continuing slow rate of natural increase has been partly compensated for by an increase in net immigration in both countries, so that there is still substantial net growth—averaging about 2 million people annually for Anglo-America in recent years. Nevertheless, this short-run slowdown in the rate of population increase is being watched with interest. Will it become a long-run phenomenon?

The average age of the population is now about 29 and has been slowly increasing in recent years. The overall age pyramid, however, is relatively symmetrical, except for a significant constriction in the 35 to 45 age group.

There is a slowly decreasing proportion of males in the population of both countries. In Canada there are about 101 males per 100 females, whereas in the United States women outnumber men at a ratio of 100 to 95. The higher proportion of males in Canada is a reflection of the more "frontier" nature of life in parts of that country and the higher rate of immigration, which often involves males rather than families.

RELATED CULTURAL CHARACTERISTICS

The cultural geography of Anglo-America is diverse, complex, and imperfectly understood. No attempt will be made to explore it in systematic fashion here, although the accompanying map of culture areas (fig. 3–10) is offered as a summary.

It is, however, appropriate to discuss a few details about certain nonmaterial culture elements that are closely associated with population: language, religion, and politics.

In terms of language, the United States is one of the least complex large areas in the world. Well over 90 percent of the population is fluent in English, and no sectional dialect is different enough to cause any problems in intelligibility. In the areas near the Mexican border, a large proportion of the people utilizes Spanish as either a primary or secondary tongue. In southern Louisiana, French is important, normally in a creolized form, but only in remote rural areas is English not dominant.

On some of the larger Indian reservations, particularly in Arizona, Indian languages are in everyday usage. In the larger metropolitan areas there are various ethnic enclaves where some non-English language dominates. This is most conspicuous in Spanish Harlem and other parts of New York City where Puerto Ricans have settled, in different big-city Chinatowns, in areas of Italian and Polish settlements, and in the recent Cuban settlements of Florida.[10]

The linguistic pattern in Canada is much more heterogeneous; English and French are dominant, although many people prefer another language. Census statistics show that English is the mother tongue

[10] A 1975 Census Bureau study quantified the linguistic simplicity of the United States by calculating that the usual language spoken by 96 percent of the population over four years of age was English. The usual language for 2 percent of the population was Spanish. Other leading languages were Italian, 0.2 percent; Chinese, 0.15 percent; French, 0.15 percent; and German, 0.07 percent.

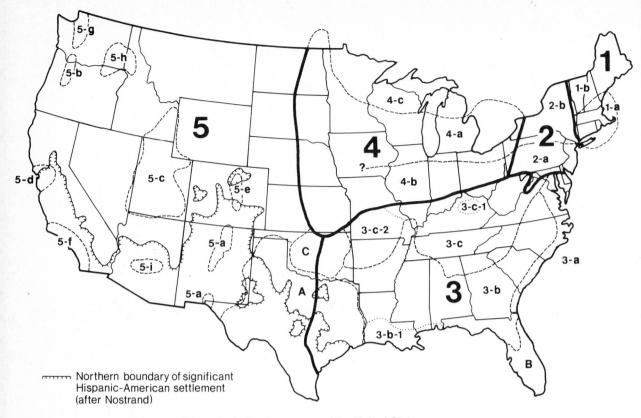

fig. 3–10 Zelinsky's view of the principal culture areas of the United States.

1 New England
  1–a Nuclear New England
  1–b Northern New England
2 The Midland
  2–a Pennsylvanian Region
  2–b New York Region, or New England Extended
3 The South
  3–a Early British Colonial South
  3–b Lowland, or Deep South
    3–b–1. French Louisiana
  3–c Upland South
    3–c–1 The Bluegrass
    3–c–2 The Ozarks
4 The Middle West
  4–a Upper Middle West
  4–b Lower Middle West
  4–c Cutover Area

5 The West
  5–a Upper Rio Grande Valley
  5–b Williamette Valley
  5–c Mormon Region
  5–d Central California
  5–e Colorado Piedmont
  5–f Southern California
  5–g Puget Sound
  5–h Inland Empire
  5–i Central Arizona
Regions of uncertain status or affiliation are
  A Texas,
  B Peninsular Florida
  C Oklahoma

(After Wilbur Zelinsky, *The Cultural Geography of the United States,* © 1973, pp. 118–19. Reprinted by permission of Prentice-Hall, Inc.)

for 60 percent of the Canadian population but is the principal language for 68 percent. French is the mother tongue for 25 percent of the population, whereas more than 14 percent of the population has a mother tongue that is other than English or French. Canada is officially a bilingual country, and the cultural dualism thus posed is a major stumbling block in any attempt at recognizing a national identity.

Canadian novelist Mordecai Richler oversimplified the situation but reached to the heart of the matter when he noted that there is no such thing as a Canadian national character; rather "there are the French, sheltered by a language and traditions all their own, and there are English-speaking Canadians who are essentially Americans and whose cultural capital, like it or not, is New York."[11]

Religious affiliation is more varied. In the United States approximately 67 percent of the population professes some branch of Protestantism, with Baptists and Methodists as the largest denominations. The southeastern states, the Midwest, and much of the West are dominantly Protestant. Roman Catholics constitute about 25 percent of the total population, with particular concentrations in the Southwest, southern Louisiana, parts of New England, and many of the larger cities of the Northeast. Only about 3 percent of the population is Jewish, and it is distinctly concentrated in the large cities; half the nation's Jews live in New York City, with other major concentrations in Los Angeles, Philadelphia, Chicago, and Boston.

Some 46 percent of the Canadian people profess Roman Catholicism; Catholic strongholds are in Quebec and the Atlantic Provinces. Most of the remainder of the population is Protestant, of which the two dominant denominations are United Church of Canada and Anglican.

Political affiliations have changed markedly in the past two decades in both countries. Two parties, Democratic and Republican, dominate the political scene in the United States at federal, state, and local levels. Democratic strongholds have traditionally been in the southeastern states, in the big cities of the Northeast, and among certain minority groups, particularly blacks and Jews. Republican strength has been concentrated in the Midwest, in the interior states of the West, and in rural New England. Significant regional trends in the last few years have been the resurgence of Republicans in the Southeast and of Democrats in New England and parts of the Midwest.

There is intense provincialism in Canadian politics, and dominant parties at the provincial level are often much less important nationally. The two principal national parties are Liberal and Progressive Conservative, but it is often the case (as throughout the 1960s and much of the 1970s) that neither is able to gain a majority in the House of Commons, resulting in either a precarious minority government or a shaky coalition. Three other parties are particularly notable at the provincial level: (1) the New Democratic Party is a socialist party that has become third-ranking at the national level and is provincially strong in the eastern Prairies, Ontario, and British Columbia; (2) the Social Credit Party was in power in Alberta for the better part of four decades until its 1971 defeat, was long dominant in British Columbia until 1972, and more recently has made a significant impact in Quebec; and (3) the Parti Québécois, the political embodiment of the French Canadian separatist movement, finally came to power in Quebec in 1976, virtually assuring an impending national political crisis.

trends and questions

The population of Anglo-America will undoubtedly continue to grow, but the predicted rate of growth is a matter for considerable debate. Projections based simply on the changing age structure of the population would indicate an upsurge in the rate of increase, for the number of young adults in the population is growing rapidly and these are the prime childbearing years. But fertility has been declining at a record rate, presumably as a result of changing attitudes by young adults, and this is a huge imponderable for prognostication. Some authorities have gone so far as to predict the possibility of achieving zero population growth within this century, which is considered by many as a most worthy goal. It is logical to expect a continued high rate of net immigration to both countries; but natural increase is the principal source of population growth, and

[11] Quoted in "Canada: Down Under Up There," *The Bulletin,* 89 (22 April 1967), 25.

it is difficult to predict natural increase rates.

The regional pattern of population growth, or nongrowth, is easier to foresee. The westward movement of people in Canada and in the United States has been pronounced for years and gives every evidence of continuing, although perhaps differing in detail. British Columbia gained more interprovincial migrants during the decade of the 1960s than the other nine provinces combined, although this pattern slackened considerably during the early 1970s. It is expected that Canadian population expansion will be concentrated in the relatively faster growing economic regions, notably Ontario, British Columbia, and the western Prairies, with probable net outflows from the Atlantic Provinces, Quebec, and the eastern Prairies. California is still the principal goal of interstate migration in the United States, but the rate of flow has declined. Growth in the so-called Sunbelt states (the southern tier from Florida to California and Hawaii)

has been notable and relatively continuous in recent years, reflecting the desire of an affluent and footloose population to settle in warmer areas. Related but less pronounced movements to scenic, high amenity, Western states, such as Colorado, Utah, Nevada, Oregon, and Alaska, are also conspicuous (fig. 3–11).

The most notable trend in population movement in recent decades has been the flow to cities (fig. 3–12). There is, however, strong evidence that this tendency has been significantly slowed, if not reversed, in the late 1970s. For some time it has been clear that suburbs were expanding while central city areas often stagnated or declined. Recently, however, net migration flow has been increasingly directed away from metropolitan areas to their hinterlands.[12] Various hy-

[12] Between 1970 and 1976, for example, the population of United States metropolitan areas increased by 4 percent, while the nonmetropolitan population increase was 8 percent.

fig. 3–11 Gainers and losers in domestic net migration, United States, 1970–76 (based on U.S. Bureau of Census estimates).

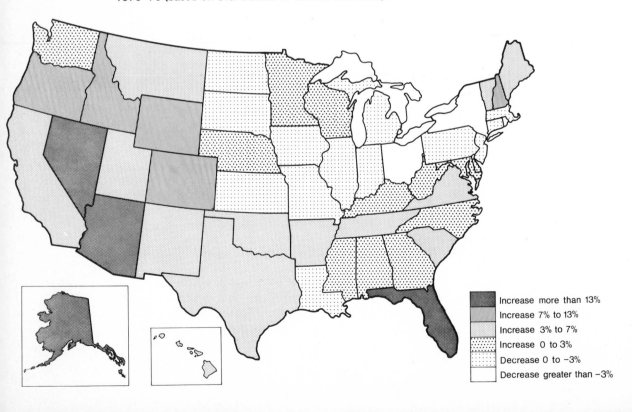

Increase more than 13%
Increase 7% to 13%
Increase 3% to 7%
Increase 0 to 3%
Decrease 0 to −3%
Decrease greater than −3%

fig. 3–12 Most Anglo-Americans are urbanites. This is Fifth Avenue in New York City (courtesy New York State Department of Commerce).

potheses have been advanced to explain this phenomenon.[13] In part it is reflective of predictable economic stimuli, such as changes in traditional location factors, an increasingly service-oriented economy, and metropolitan spread effects. There are, however, apparently other, less obvious factors that are at least as influential, including personal preferences for rural or small town living, a wider horizon for retirees, and the increasing attractiveness of amenity-rich locations.

Whatever the causes, the results signal a remarkable change in Anglo-American migration habits. Areas previously noted as sources of population flight, such as southern Appalachia, the Arkansas Ozarks, and north-country Michigan, are increasingly being sought as destinations for settlement. It is highly unlikely that this trend presages an end to the dominance of urbanism on this continent, but it does show that even the most clear-cut geographical patterns may be subject to radical change.

[13] Richard F. Lamb, "Intra-Regional Growth in Non-Metropolitan America: Change in the Pattern of Change" (unpublished manuscript, 1977).

selected bibliography

ALLEN, JAMES P., "Recent Immigration from the Philippines and Filipino Communities in the United States," *Geographical Review,* 67 (1977), 195–208.

BALLAS, DONALD J., "Geography and the American Indian," *Journal of Geography,* 65 (1966), 156–68.

BEALE, CALVIN L., *The Revival of Population Growth in Nonmetropolitan America.* Washington, D.C.: U. S. Department of Agriculture, Economic Research Service Report 605, 1975.

BIKALES, GERDA, "Immigration Policy: The New Environmental Battlefield," *National Parks and Conservation Magazine,* 51 (December 1977), 13–16.

BROWNING, C. E., "The Shifting Winds of Population Change in the United States," *Geographical Review,* 66 (1976), 94–95.

DAVIS, GEORGE A., AND O. FRED DONALDSON, *Blacks in the United States: A Geographic Perspective.* Boston, Mass.: Houghton Mifflin Company, 1975.

DENEVAN, WILLIAM M., *The Native Population of*

the Americas in 1492. Madison: University of Wisconsin Press, 1976.

DRIVER, HAROLD E., *Indians of North America.* Chicago, Ill.: University of Chicago Press, 1961.

GREBLER, LEO, ET AL., *The Mexican-American People: The Nation's Second Largest Minority.* Glencoe, Ill.: The Free Press, 1970.

GREELEY, A. M., *Ethnicity in the United States.* New York: John Wiley & Sons, 1974.

HAGAN, WILLIAM T., *American Indians.* Chicago, Ill.: University of Chicago Press, 1961.

HANSEN, MARCUS LEE, *The Immigrant in American History.* New York: Harper & Row, Publishers, 1964.

HARRIES, KEITH D., "The Geography of American Crime," *Journal of Geography,* 70 (1971), 204–13.

HAWKINS, FREDA, *Canada and Immigration.* Montreal: McGill-Queen's University Press, 1972.

HAWTHORNE, H. B., ed., *A Survey of Contemporary Indians of Canada.* Ottawa: Indian Affairs Branch, 1966.

JOHNSON, D. W., ET AL., *Churches and Church Membership in the United States.* Washington, D.C.: Glenmary Research Center, 1974.

JONES, MALDWYN ALLEN, *American Immigration.* Chicago, Ill.: University of Chicago Press, 1960.

KOSINSKI, LESZEK A., "How Population Movement Reshapes the Nation," *Canadian Geographical Journal,* 92 (May–June 1976), 34–39.

KUBAT, DANIEL, AND DAVID THORNTON, *A Statistical Profile of Canadian Society.* Toronto: McGraw-Hill Ryerson, 1974.

LEWIS, G. M., "The Distribution of the Negro in the Coterminous United States," *Geography Magazine,* 54 (1969), 410–18.

LEWIS, PIERCE F., "Common Houses, Cultural Spoor," *Landscape,* 19 (January 1975), 1–22.

MARSDEN, L. R., "Is Canada Becoming Overpopulated?" *Canadian Geographical Journal,* 89 (November 1974), 40–47.

NEILS, E. M., *Reservation to City: Indian Migration and Federal Relocation.* Chicago, Ill.: University of Chicago Press, 1971.

PALMER, H., ed., *Immigration and the Rise of Multiculturalism.* Toronto: Copp Clark Publishing Company, 1975.

PIERSON, GEORGE WILSON, *The Moving American.* New York: Random House, 1973.

ROSEMAN, CURTIS C., *Changing Migration Patterns within the United States.* Washington, D.C.: Association of American Geographers, Resource Paper 77–2, 1977.

SAUER, CARL O., "European Backgrounds," *Historical Geography Newsletter,* 6 (Spring 1976), 35–58.

SCHNELL, GEORGE A., AND MARK S. MONMONIER, "U.S. Population Change 1960–1970: Simplification, Meaning, and Mapping," *Journal of Geography,* 75 (1976), 280–91.

SHORTRIDGE, JAMES R., "Patterns of Religion in the United States," *Geographical Review,* 66 (1976), 420–34.

SUTTON, IMRE, *Indian Land Tenure: Bibliographical Essays and a Guide to the Literature.* New York: Clearwater Publishing Co., 1975.

TAEUBER, I. B., AND C. TAEUBER, *People of the United States in the Twentieth Century.* Washington, D.C.: Government Printing Office, 1971.

WINKS, ROBIN W., *The Blacks in Canada.* New Haven, Conn.: Yale University Press, 1971.

ZELINSKY, WILBUR, "Changes in the Geographic Patterns of Rural Population in the United States 1790–1960," *Geographical Review,* 52 (1962), 492–524.

———, "Selfward Bound? Personal Preference Patterns and the Changing Map of American Society," *Economic Geography,* 50 (1974), 144–79.

THE ANGLO-AMERICAN CITY

4

The prominence of an urban way of life for most of the population has emerged as the single most important geographical fact in contemporary Anglo-America. More than three-fourths of the people of the United States and Canada are urbanites, and the proportion increases every year. Furthermore, as the urban population burgeons, the concentration of people in very large cities increases even faster. By the late 1970s there were 38 metropolitan areas in Anglo-America with populations exceeding 1 million, and another 137 with populations in excess of 200,000 (fig. 4-1).

Despite the dominance of cities in the life style of Anglo-Americans, this book does not emphasize urbanism in its regional treatment. There are several reasons for this, but the most important is that most Anglo-American cities are quite similar in their urban aspects. They have developed, at approximately the same time and in roughly the same fashion, in countries that are characterized by a relatively high standard of living and in which people, ideas, and money are shifted easily from one region to another (mobility of population, pervasiveness of mass media, and fluidity of capital).

There are some exceptions to this generalization. Some cities have a character of their own; nobody would be likely to accuse

New Orleans, Quebec City, or San Francisco of being undistinctive. Nevertheless, for the vast majority of Anglo-American cities within the general size-category there is a sameness in appearance, morphology, and function that is almost bewildering to a visitor from another continent where cities have grown up more individualistically over a much longer period of development (fig. 4-2).

Even though the two nations of Anglo-America have been politically separate for the better part of two centuries, cities on both sides of the international border tend to be remarkably alike. In both countries it is the urban areas that absorb practically all the continuing high rate of population and economic growth; in both countries the automobile has assumed a dominant role in shaping city form and patterning urban life; and in both countries the similarity in the standard of living and in personal motivation and aspiration is reflected in urban function and morphology. Canadian cities are spread in a long east-west band that has a very narrow north-south breadth, and each tends to be more like American cities of similar longitude than like Canadian cities significantly farther east or west; thus Calgary is more like Denver than like Toronto, Winnipeg more resembles Minneapolis than

fig. 4–1 The 50 largest metropolitan areas in Anglo-America (based on 1975 estimates of United States Bureau of the Census and 1976 Census of Canada).

it does Vancouver, and Toronto is more reminiscent of Cleveland than of Montreal.

There are, however, also some differences between cities on opposite sides of the border. These differences reflect variation in the recent economic history, ethnic population mix, and urban institutional patterns of the two countries, among other things. Where pertinent, such differences are pointed out in the chapters.

This chapter considers Anglo-American cities in general, commenting on the major characteristics of their urban geography. In each of the regional chapters that follow there is a section devoted to the leading cities of the region or to atypical aspects of urbanism in the region or to a particular urban theme that is pertinent to the region.

fig. 4–2 The epitome of modern urbanization. The central business district of Houston is dominated by new skyscrapers, fringed with extensive parking lots, and ringed by freeways (courtesy Houston Chamber of Commerce

the location
of anglo-american cities

Cities develop as a result of functions that they can perform. Some functions result directly from the ingenuity of the citizenry, but most are a response to the needs of the local area and the surrounding hinterland (the region that supplies goods to the city and to which the city furnishes services and other goods).

Geographers often make a distinction between the *situation* and *site* of a city. Situation refers to the general position in relation to the surrounding region, whereas site involves physical characteristics of the specific location.

Situation is normally much more important to the continuing prosperity of a city. If a city is well situated with regard to its hinterland, its development is much more likely to continue. Chicago, for example, possesses an almost unparalleled situation: it is located at the southern end of a huge lake that forces east-west transportation lines to be compressed into its vicinity, and at a meeting of significant land and water transport routes; it also overlooks what is perhaps the world's finest large farming region. These factors assured that Chicago would become a great city regardless of the "vile" characteristics of the available site, which

was prone "to flooding and unable to furnish drainage for storm waters that tend to collect in areas so subject to sharp thunderstorm activity."[1]

Similarly it can be argued that much of New York City's importance stems from its early and continuing advantage of situation. Philadelphia, Boston, Halifax, and Montreal all originated at about the same time as New York and all shared New York's location at the western end of the world's most important oceanic trade route, but only New York City possessed an easy-access functional connection (the Hudson-Mohawk lowland) to the vast midwestern hinterland. This simplistic explanation does not alone account for New York City's primacy, but it is clearly a major factor.[2]

Among the many aspects of situation that help to explain why some cities grow and others do not, original location on a navigable waterway seems particularly applicable (fig. 4–3). Most important Anglo-

[1] James E. Vance, Jr., "The American City: Workshop for a National Culture," in *Contemporary Metropolitan America, Vol. 1, Cities of the Nation's Historic Metropolitan Core,* ed. John S. Adams (Cambridge, Mass.: Ballinger Publishing Company, 1976), p. 15.

[2] See R. G. Albion, "New York Port and Its Disappointed Rivals," *Journal of Economic and Business History,* 3 (August 1931), 602–29.

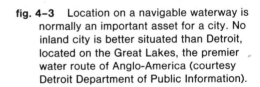

fig. 4–3 Location on a navigable waterway is normally an important asset for a city. No inland city is better situated than Detroit, located on the Great Lakes, the premier water route of Anglo-America (courtesy Detroit Department of Public Information).

American cities are located on the edge of an ocean, a canal, or a navigable river or lake. Of the 50 largest cities in Anglo-America, only 14 are not situated on navigable waters, and all but 2 of the 14 are relative newcomers to the big-city list.

To be sure, site factors are also significant in the founding and growth of cities. Slope, drainage, power resources, river crossings, coastal shapes, and other physical characteristics help to determine city location, and such factors are normally more significant in the early stages of city development than later.

The momentum of an early start is another important advantage for city development. This concept of initial advantage implies that an existing location generates significant inertia to inhibit a shift to another location that may appear more advantageous at a later date and that such concentration tends to be self-perpetuating.[3] Growth is likely to beget growth, and the economy of a city can almost literally support itself after reaching a certain size—barring unforeseen economic catastrophe—by nonbasic activities, that is, circulating money within the city rather than bringing in money from outside. It is likely that at least two dozen Anglo-American cities have reached this self-sustaining plateau, with a diverse economic base and self-generating growth impetus. "It means that they will share in all the future growth of the national economy, and presumably play a larger and larger part within the nation. They are more able to control their own fortunes, maintain their images, and use their political power."[4]

[3] See Allan Pred, "Industrialization, Initial Advantage, and American Metropolitan Growth," *Geographical Review*, 55 (April 1965), 158–85. This concept has been propounded in various forms by many economic geographers and economists, perhaps most conspicuously in Gunnar Myrdal's "principle of circular and cumulative causation," stated in *Rich Lands and Poor* (New York: Harper, 1957).

[4] James and Robert Simmons, *Urban Canada* (Toronto: Copp Clark Publishing Co., 1969), p. 60.

historical development of anglo-american cities

PRIOR TO 1800

In early colonial days small towns sprang up along the Atlantic Seaboard, mostly in what are now New England and the Middle Atlantic States in the United States, and in the Maritime Provinces and Lower St. Lawrence Valley in Canada. This was natural because these areas were nearest England and France, particularly the former, whence came immigrants, capital goods, and many consumer goods. Accordingly, merchandising establishments were more advantageously located in port cities from which goods could be more readily distributed to interior settlements. Here, too, were the favored locations for assembling raw materials for export and for performing what little processing was necessary for shipment abroad. There were a number of small ports, but Baltimore, Boston, Philadelphia, New York, and Montreal soon began to exert dominance (although for several decades Quebec City grew almost as rapidly as Montreal).

Urban growth was less impressive in the Colonial South, where life centered around the plantation rather than the town. The local isolation and economic self-sufficiency of the plantation were inimical to the development of towns. Thus nearly all Southern settlements were located on navigable streams, and each planter owned a wharf accessible to the small shipping of that day. Both Charleston and Savannah were founded early and developed various urban functions, but after a short time neither rivaled the North Atlantic cities in urban development.

At the time of the first census of the United States, in 1790, there was not a city in Anglo-America with as many as 50,000 inhabitants, and only Baltimore, Boston, Charleston, New York, Philadelphia, and Montreal exceeded 10,000. No city yet showed any indication of urban dominance; each Atlantic port served a small hinterland

and was primarily oriented toward the sea and Europe.

1800–1870

Penetration of the interior and the use of inland waterways (Ohio River, lower Great Lakes, Erie Canal) began to produce a few inland urban centers: Richmond, Lancaster, Pittsburgh, and Albany; and a bit later, St. Louis, Cincinnati, Louisville, Buffalo, and Rochester. But the Atlantic ports retained their regional primacy, and the Louisiana Purchase added another primary port, New Orleans.

Montreal had grown to dominate a large share of the trade of the interior of the continent and challenged New York, Philadelphia, and New Orleans. The partitioning of British North America into Upper Canada (Ontario) and Lower Canada (Quebec) and the choice of York (later to be named Toronto) as capital of Upper Canada added a significant dimension to the urban scene in the north. For Toronto, the "law of initial advantage operated fully, and by 1830 all rivals to regional control had been subdued."[5]

Still, rural dominance was clear-cut until the 1840s when railways began to develop, the factory system became established, and the industrial function of cities began to grow. The mechanization of spinning and weaving had set the pace in the previous two decades, but other types of manufacturing were oriented mostly toward household and workshop, often in rural locations, until the 1840s.

The large port cities grew especially in size with the building of canals, roads, and railways to the interior. A series of regional rail networks developed, with the larger networks converging at important inland waterway connections.[6] Each important coastal port began to organize its own railway and push it inland. Of the major American ports, Boston alone was forced to content itself with connecting lines; its Boston and Albany Railway never got beyond the Hudson River. There was little railway development at this time in Maritime Canada. The Grand Trunk Railway, built after 1850 from Chicago through Toronto and Montreal, reached the Atlantic in the United States at Portland, Maine. Hence, Canada's Atlantic port cities grew very slowly.

The midcentury period was a transition time for city development. Before then, industrialization was quite subordinate, except in the five great Atlantic port cities that dominated trade relationships between the Anglo-American agricultural economy and Europe. The mercantile syndrome continued to pervade most other cities for some years, but industrial development and urban growth began to be much more closely linked. Labor supply was enhanced by the attraction of farm youths to cities and by accelerating immigration; after 1840 foreign immigrants began to concentrate on the edge of the expanding central business district in many urban areas, presaging the large-scale development of ethnic ghettos in decades to come.[7]

New York City rose to undisputed continental primacy at this time, partly because the opening of the Erie Canal cemented its western trade advantages but also because it was able to control much of the external trade of the South. "Indeed, it was largely because the merchants of New York and their itinerant factors controlled the cotton trade that urbanization in the South was extremely slow."[8] Thus Charleston and New Orleans were unable to wrest control of the cotton trade from New York. From roughly equal size with Philadelphia and Boston at

[5] Donald P. Kerr, "Metropolitan Dominance in Canada," in *Canada, A Geographical Interpretation*, ed. John Warkentin (Toronto: Methuen Publications, 1968), p. 540.

[6] John R. Borchert, "American Metropolitan Evolution," *Geographical Review*, 57 (July 1967), 315.

[7] David Ward, "The Emergence of Central Immigrant Ghettoes in American Cities: 1840–1920," *Annals*, Association of American Geographers, 58 (June 1968), 343.

[8] David Ward, *Cities and Immigrants: A Geography of Change in Nineteenth Century America* (New York: Oxford University Press, 1971), p. 29.

the turn of the century, New York's population exceeded half a million by 1850; this population was more than twice that of any other city on the continent.

Inland regions of urbanization were limited mostly to the Ohio Valley (Cincinnati, Pittsburgh, Louisville) and upstate New York (Albany, Troy, Rochester, Buffalo), although Toronto had almost kept pace with Montreal's *rate* of growth with nearly a 50 percent increase during the decade of the 1850s.

The growth rate of Canadian cities sharply declined during the 1860s, apparently owing to large-scale emigration to the United States. In the Midwest, urban populations were booming. Water transport helped Cincinnati and St. Louis to grow rapidly, but by 1870 they were being challenged by the swiftly growing Great Lakes cities of Detroit, Milwaukee, Cleveland, and especially Chicago. There was also continued fast growth in New England and the Middle Atlantic states, especially near New York. Brooklyn was the third largest city in the nation, and Newark and Jersey City were both sizable. In the South, only New Orleans had continued major growth and numbered nearly 200,000 people, whereas the only Western city that had developed to more than 25,000 was San Francisco, with a population of 150,000.

Thus the development of a more-than-regional transportation system, combining regional rail networks with inland waterways, revolutionized urban development in this period. Industrial growth had been an important stimulant in the larger cities, but major industrial development came later.

1870–1920

This was an era of maturing for Anglo-American cities, the previous period being a formative one. The national transportation systems were completed. National accessibility was extended to the South, the Southwest, and the Far West. The remaining agricultural lands of the West, from Texas to British Columbia, were opened. A variety of major mineral deposits was developed.

But the principal stimulus to urban growth was industrial development. The economy of the two countries changed from a commercial-mercantilistic base to an industrial-capitalistic one.[9]

The coastal cities became increasingly important, but much of the growth was concentrated in the industrial belt of northeastern United States and southern Ontario and Quebec. The geographical division of labor, a basis for present-day regionalism, was beginning to be apparent by the end of the Civil War period. There followed a quarter century of accelerated westward movement, rapid population increase, heavy immigration, and burgeoning urban growth. Cities found their functions multiplying, but the growth of manufacturing was usually at the core.

The big cities became bigger, but there were also developments among smaller centers. Toronto, only half the size of Montreal at the beginning of the period, began to capture trade territory to the north and west and, by the turn of the century, had approached parity in size; the growth rates of the two cities have been quite similar ever since. Winnipeg began to grow in the Prairies, and Los Angeles experienced the early stages of its spectacular population increase. There were boom times in Florida urban areas, in Appalachian coal towns, and in cities of the Carolina Piedmont.

1920 TO PRESENT

By 1920 half of the population of Anglo-America was urban, and the proportion continued to increase. There has been substantial and continued growth in the older urban areas of the United States and Canada, but the most flamboyant developments have been in new cities far removed from the traditional urban centers. The most spectacular growth has been on the West Coast, from San Diego to Vancouver, and similar trends have taken form in Florida, in

[9] Pred, "American Metropolitan Growth," p. 161.

Texas, in the desert Southwest, and on the inland side of the Rockies (Colorado and Alberta).

By the beginning of the 1960s approximately 25 percent of the world's population lived in cities of 20,000 or more inhabitants; the comparable figure for Anglo-America was 55 percent, the highest proportion of any populous part of the globe.[10] Thus the concentration of urban population on this continent is not only of recent vintage and sizable magnitude but also has occurred at a remarkably rapid rate.

Since World War II our cities have developed many new characteristics and trends. Urban sprawl, freeways, central city decay, urban renewal, air pollution, suburban high-rise, planned industrial districts, and many other developments typify contemporary urbanism in Anglo-America. We examine some of these features in succeeding chapters of this book.

urban morphology: changing patterns

Viewed from the air, a typical Anglo-American city appears as a sprawling mass of structures of varying size, shape, and construction, crisscrossed by a checkerboard street pattern that here and there assumes irregularities. The general impression is one of stereotyped monotony. The pattern of form and structure is so repetitive that one can anticipate a characteristic location of specialized districts and of associations of activities within them.[11] The stylized arrangement and predictable interrelations make it possible to formulate broad generalizations about Anglo-American urban anatomy that are particularly valid if confined to cities of similar size, function, and regional setting.

[10] Derived from data in Leroy O. Stone, *Urban Development in Canada* (Ottawa: Dominion Bureau of Statistics, 1967), p. 16.
[11] Howard J. Nelson, "The Form and Structure of Cities: Urban Growth Patterns," *Journal of Geography*, 68 (April 1969), 199.

THE PATTERN OF LAND USE

When considered in detail, the pattern of land use varies with every city. There are, however, such basic similarities that general patterns can be described and, to some extent, explained. The resulting generalizations are broadly valid for most cities whether they are older and slower-growing cities with rigid zoning restrictions, such as Buffalo, or newer, burgeoning cities with only limited land-use zoning regulations, such as Tucson.

Theoretical Models of Urban Structure Many urbanologists have pointed out commonalities of pattern in the structure of American cities, and several simplified models have been designed to give graphic portrayal to theories of urban structure. The three most widely followed are outlined briefly here.

Burgess's *concentric zone* theory recognizes five zones of variable width and dynamic boundaries, situated concentrically about a central point (fig. 4–4).[12] The zones are

[12] Ernest W. Burgess, "Growth of the City," in *The City*, ed. Robert E. Park, Ernest W. Burgess, and Roderick D. McKenzie (Chicago, Ill.: University of Chicago Press, 1925), pp. 47–62.

fig. 4–4 The Burgess concentric zone theory of urban structure.

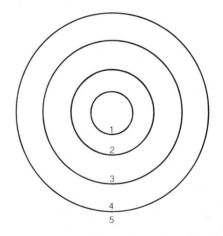

1 central business district, including retail and wholesale sections

2 transition zone of business, light manufacturing, and deteriorating residences

3 working class residential zone

4 middle-class residential zone with business subcenters

5 commuting zone, primarily residential

The *sector* theory was developed by several theorists but was most prominently advanced by Hoyt (fig. 4–5). It contends that rent is the principal guide to urban residential structure; that rent areas conform to a pattern of pie-shaped sectors radiating outward from the city center, these sectors tending to retain their basic rental character with the passage of time and the outward growth of the city; and that the historical shift of high-rent areas is the major influence on city expansion.

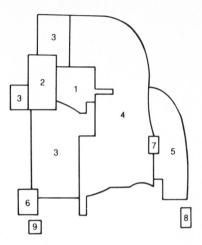

fig. 4–6   The multiple nuclei theory of urban structure.

fig. 4–5   The Hoyt sector theory of urban structure, based on a generalized diagram of Des Moines. The darker the pattern the higher the residential rental (based on Homer Hoyt, *The Structure and Growth of Residential Neighborhoods in American Cities* [Washington, D.C.: Federal Housing Administration, 1939].

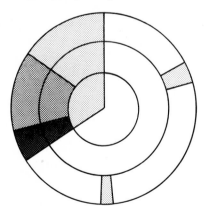

The *multiple nuclei* theory of Harris and Ullman combines elements of the two previous concepts and adds other features to produce a schematic representation that is both more complex and more flexible than the

others (fig. 4–6).[13] This theory contends that a city's land-use pattern is built around more than one discrete nucleus, these nuclei attracting urban forms and functions in differing patterns that can be further generalized:

1 central business district
2 wholesale/light manufacturing
3 low-class residential
4 medium-class residential
5 high-class residential
6 heavy manufacturing
7 outlying business district
8 residential suburb
9 industrial suburb

All three theories have many followers and many detractors. They have also been frequently modified by their original authors as well as by other theorists. In general, each theory has a certain validity, and they might best be thought of as cumulative and elaborative explanations of the internal pattern of cities. In any case, such models can only summarize certain dimensions in the

[13] C. D. Harris and E. L. Ullman, "The Nature of Cities," *Annals*, American Academy of Political and Social Science, 242 (November 1945), 7–17.

spatial variation of residential land use.[14] Many variables are involved, and it may well be that land cost or rent is not the most important. James Vance, for example, argues that "the fundamental processes at work in American cities are those of congregation and segregation," in which the former represents deliberate clustering in social groupings and is by far more significant for almost all elements in urban society except blacks, even pertaining to blacks where they have "normal income mobility."[15]

It is the total pervasiveness of the automobile, however, that particularly causes the blurring of the classical models of city structure.[16] Now that the urbanite is so fully committed to the automobile as a means of travel, intraurban distances mean much less than they did in the past. Tentacles of urbanization, related to major transport routes, extend irregularly outward from the city center and establish new kinds of patterns that are often associated with temporal rather than spatial dimensions.

The impact of the automobile on city form is somewhat less conspicuous in Can-

ada than it is in the United States, although it is a difference in degree rather than in kind. The surge of automobile ownership and low density urbanization came later to Canada; thus urban sprawl and decentralization are less prominent north of the international border.[17] The same processes are at work in both countries, however, and the same generalizations are broadly applicable.

Commercial Land Use   Most cities are primarily commercial centers. Their attraction as a place for people to live is largely predicated on the concentration of commercial or business activities. For Anglo-American cities as a group, more than half of all jobs are in commercial fields: wholesale trade, retail trade, finance, insurance, real estate, and various kinds of services. Although the proportion of a city's land area that is devoted to these activities is very small—generally less than 4 percent of the total—the structures in which the activities take place are often conspicuous and involve the tallest and most obtrusive buildings in the urban area.

The *central business district* (CBD) is the commercial heart of the city. It normally occupies an area near, but slightly removed from, the original town site (fig. 4–7). It usually has a geographically central position in relation to the urban area as a whole; in some cases, however, it may be situated well off center, particularly where prominent physical features, such as coastline, mountain front, or river, are involved. The CBD is normally characterized by the greatest intensity of urban activity: highest daytime population density, most crowded sidewalks, most used surface streets, focus of mass transit routes, principal concentration of taxis, and greatest concentration of high-rise buildings. It also contains the most valuable land in the city and is the principal location of office space, large department stores, restaurants, theaters, hotels, government offices, financial institutions, corporation headquarters, and auto parking facilities.

[14] L. S. Bourne et al., eds., *The Form of Cities in Central Canada* (Toronto: University of Toronto Press, 1973), p. 47.
[15] Vance, "The American City: Workshop for a National Culture," p. 44.
[16] Harold M. Mayer, "Spatial Change Inside the American City," in *Problems and Trends in American Geography,* ed. Saul B. Cohen (New York: Basic Books, Inc., 1967), p. 54.

fig. 4–7   The conspicuous central business district of Denver.

[17] Simmons, *Urban Canada,* p. 14.

In part as a response to the almost over-whelming economic challenge of sparkling new outlying shopping centers, downtown merchants have begun to develop extensive, climate-controlled shopping malls within the CBD. Such malls are usually located on two or three underground levels beneath large buildings or street-level plazas and have direct connections both to major buildings on the surface and to subsurface mass or rapid transit facilities, if any exist. They provide an almost fully self-contained environment for urbanites that is a long overdue and eminently logical adjustment to winter in northern cities. Montreal's pioneering example in Place Ville Marie has stimulated similar developments in many other cities, even in such mild winter locations as Los Angeles.

With or without underground malls, however, the CBD is the core of downtown, and its function is preeminently commercial. Certain other aspects of urban life are also prominent in or near the CBD: manufacturing is often represented by printing-publishing plants and a concentration of loft-type garment factories; theaters, hotels, night clubs, and bars highlight the recreational function; and a surprising number of people is likely to reside near, if not actually within, the area.

Marginal to the CBD is the so-called *transition zone.* This is a discontinuous area of irregular shape and unpredictable size that has an almost continually changing land-use pattern.[18] Its commercial prominence is often more oriented to wholesaling than to retailing, and industrial activities, in the broad sense, are usually notable (fig. 4-8). Still, much of the land in a typical transition zone is occupied by residences; this is a characteristic location for slum and ghetto development. In general, the transition zone is seedy and dilapidated, although

fig. 4-8   The transition zone adjacent to the Minneapolis CBD (courtesy Greater Minneapolis Chamber of Commerce).

some sections may be uncharacteristically bright and even prosperous owing to public or private urban renewal and slum clearance projects. Grandiose high-rise office buildings or apartment houses sometimes tower above the general obsolescence.

Another significant proportion of a city's commercial land-use is found along *string streets,* which are usually major thoroughfares of considerable length and are lined on both sides by varied businesses. The development may be patchy and discontinuous, but in larger cities the extent of string street commercial zones may be measured in consecutive miles. Characteristically the businesses along a string street are small and diverse; however, there may be concentrations of specific types of enterprises, the best known of which is "automobile row" where new and used car lots are clustered. A recent and growing trend is the construction of high-rise office buildings along string streets, away from the CBD.

The most remarkable change in commercial land use in Anglo-American cities since World War II is the emergence of planned *suburban shopping centers.* Continually increasing amounts of a city's retail and service business are being carried out in these outlying centers, which are geared to the automobile era, with much more aceage de-

[18] There is considerable literature on the transition zone. One of the more definitive statements of the concept is found in Donald W. Griffin and Richard E. Preston, "A Restatement of the 'Transition Zone' Concept," *Annals,* Association of American Geographers, 56 (June 1966), 339-50.

fig. 4–9 The compact sprawl of a planned suburban shopping center, the Southdale center in Edina, Minnesota (courtesy Greater Minneapolis Chamber of Commerce).

voted to parking spaces than to shopping areas (fig. 4–9). In the early years (1940s and early 1950s) such shopping centers emerged gradually; more recently, however, the planned shopping plaza has emerged full-grown at birth (fig. 4–10).

[It is] a complete shopping centre planned and erected all at once to serve a specific area and a specific number of customers. Now plazas are established at the farthest edges of the city long before an area is completely built up. They dominate the retailing in those parts of the city built in the last fifteen years, yet they pose some difficult problems for orderly urban growth because of their inflexibility. . . . All aspects of such a plaza—the physical plant, the number, size and layout of stores, the parking spaces, as well as the type of re-

fig. 4–10 Major new shopping centers often focus on indoor malls that are intensively landscaped, tastefully decorated, and climate-controlled, whether in warm climates or cold. Shown here are the Winter Park Mall (courtesy Florida Division of Tourism) and the IDS Crystal Court (courtesy Greater Minneapolis Chamber of Commerce).

tail activities—are geared to a specific size of centre, and thus to a specific location.[19]

The larger new shopping centers are often enclosed under a single massive roof that towers high enough to encompass three or four levels of walkway- and escalator-connected shops of varying sizes that are clustered around one or more spacious atria containing fountains, waterfalls, resting areas, and other attractions for the weary shopper.

Residential Land Use By far the most extensive usage of land in Anglo-American cities is for residences, which occupy 30 to 40 percent of an average city's area.[20] Single family dwellings (normally separate but sometimes attached to one another as row houses) are not always numerically in the majority, but they occupy more than three-fourths of the area devoted to housing.

Within the CBD, residences are scarce, although some housing units are often found on the upper floors of buildings. The greatest residential density in any city normally occurs in and near the transition zone, where grand old homes of the past (frequently converted to rooming houses) are mixed with vast expanses of low-quality residences and occasional redevelopment pockets of high-rise apartments. This is typically the tenement section that constitutes the bulk of the city's slums and ghettos. The inhabitants of such areas are normally blue-collar workers with relatively low incomes, and a large proportion is likely to consist of ethnic minorities and, particularly, black Americans.

The *black ghetto*[21] has, almost within the space of a single generation, become one of the two most rapidly expanding spatial configurations in large cities of the United States (the suburb is the other). Ghettos have been a prominent part of the Anglo-American metropolitan scene for many decades,[22] but the rapid expansion, consolidation, and conspicuous social isolation of the black ghetto in recent years has produced what amounts to a new urban subculture. In most cities of the United States and in the few Canadian cities where blacks reside in any numbers, there is very strong de facto segregation between areas of white and black households; this holds true in central cities as well as in suburbs, in the North or the South, and in large cities or small.[23] But it is in central-city locations that blacks find easiest access to housing, and it is here that ghetto formation is pronounced and growing.

These ethnic enclaves usually occupy the least desirable parts of the city and strongly tend to be blighted zones, except in newer cities where there is a prevalence of relatively new single-family residences located in the path of ghetto expansion (as in Denver, Phoenix, and some California cities).[24] Black ghettos tend to be poverty areas, although there is often a concentration of blacks with an income above poverty level. The ghetto is normally but not always a forced development; nevertheless, it performs the important function of providing a sense of community to its residents, who are often at a critical stage in their lives. Ghettos obviously offer more disadvantages than advantages, but with continued white abandonment of the central city as a place of residence, territorial dominance has clearly been relinquished to ghetto residents.

Other types of ghettos are also found in and around the transition zone of Anglo-American cities, but rarely are they as large or as conspicuous as the black ghettos. Probably most notable are the Hispanic ghettos,

[19] Simmons, *Urban Canada*, p. 121.
[20] Jerome D. Fellmann, "Land Use and Density Patterns of the Metropolitan Area," *Journal of Geography,* 68 (May 1969), 265.
[21] Harold M. Rose, "The Origin and Pattern of Development of Urban Black Social Areas," *Journal of Geography,* 68 (September 1969), 328.

[22] For a succinct account of ghetto formation, see Mayer, "Spatial Change Inside the American City,", pp. 58–59.
[23] Karl E. Taeuber and Alma F. Taeuber, *Negroes in Cities* (Chicago, Ill.: Aldine Publishing Company, 1965), p. 2.
[24] Rose, "Urban Black Social Areas," p. 331.

fig. 4–11 High-rise apartment buildings in the Century City area of Los Angeles.

which include Chicano ghettos in many cities of the Southwest, Puerto Rican ghettos in New York and in other cities of the Northeast, and Cuban ghettos in several cities of southern Florida.

With the general outward shift of population distribution in cities, there tends to be a similarly centrifugal displacement of residential zones based on economic factors. The vast expanse of middle-class housing, normally situated beyond the transition

fig. 4–12 Some suburban housing areas appear to sprawl endlessly, as here in Fort Lauderdale, Florida.

zone, has an inner boundary that moves outward with pressures from the central city. This usually creates a "gray" area that serves as buffer between middle- and lower-class housing, attracts an upwardly mobile segment of the central city population, and is often a determinant of the direction of ghetto expansion.

There is also a general centrifugal gradation in population density throughout the residential areas from the transition zone to the outer suburbs. Multifamily housing is more common near the city center, and lowest population densities are in the outer areas where relative remoteness reduces the price of land and subdivision ordinances require greater spacing between houses. There are, however, numerous variations from this pattern (fig. 4–11). The unremitting monotony of detached single-family dwellings has been significantly leavened by garden apartment complexes, mobile home developments, cluster housing, and contemporary townhouse variations of the old row house form. Such variety produces not only higher population densities but also diversity of residents. The old stereotypes of "suburban sameness" are less valid today than they were a couple of decades ago, when an entire school of social criticism was nurtured on attacking the aesthetics of suburbs.[25]

In the suburban fringe there are initially independently planned street systems in separate communities or subdivisions, often with curvilinear pattern and considerable sprawl (fig. 4–12). These discrete areas are subsequently joined, and the open spaces among them are filled in with further urban (usually residential) development, producing irregular but not necessarily displeasing patterns of urban sprawl. The disparate densities between close-in and more remote residential areas tend to lessen with time as the settlement pattern ages and intensifies.

The *suburb* has a special place in the contemporary folk history of Anglo-America; it is The Place that connotes status, security,

[25] Dennis J. Dingemans, "The Urbanization of Suburbia: The Renaissance of the Row House," *Landscape*, 20 (October 1975), 31.

comfort, and convenience—the calm of country living with the amenities of the city within easy reach. The surge to the suburbs is nothing new; since at least the 1920s there has been a well-established tradition for the maturing generation, providing it had the income and the means of internal transportation, to move to the edge of the city and establish yet another peripheral band of housing.[26] The post–World War II expansion of the suburbs, however, is on a heretofore undreamed of scale. The nearly 100 million Anglo-American suburbanities of the late 1970s amount to more than 40 percent of the total population (fig. 4–13).

Suburbanites are generally but by no means universally well off financially and are somewhat insulated from the decay and social trauma of the central city (fig. 4–14). To move to the suburbs is not to escape the problems of the city because congestion, soaring taxes, crime, drugs, and pollution tend to follow, although generally to a lesser extent.

Although historically considered as bedroom zones for a population that commuted to the central cities to work, suburbs have increasingly become more complex in structure and function as their size and extent have burgeoned. Jobs have followed people to the suburbs, and numerous nodes of high density commercial and industrial development—high-rise office buildings, sprawling industrial parks, and immense shopping centers—scattered throughout suburbia are now typical. The usual movement of people, moreover, is from one suburb to another, rather than commuting to the CBD, and a certain amount of reverse commuting has become established as central city blue collar workers increasingly must go to the suburbs to find work.

Industrial Land Use Although land devoted to industrial usage occupies only an average of 6 to 7 percent of the city's area,[27]

[26] James E. Vance, Jr., "Cities in the Shaping of the American Nation," *Journal of Geography*, 75 (January 1976), 50.
[27] Fellman, "Land Use and Density Patterns of the Metropolitan Area," p. 265.

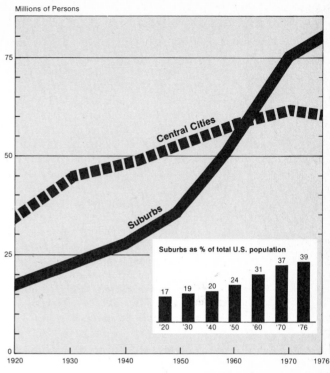

fig. 4–13 The suburbanization of United States population continues to increase (based on U.S. Bureau of the Census tabulations and estimates).

fig. 4–14 Variety and attractiveness in the suburbs is sometimes carefully planned, but it is often a reflection of the affluence of the homeowners. This scene is in Edmonton, Alberta.

in most cities the significance of factories as employment centers is so great that industrial activity is critical to the local economy. Industrial areas may be widely scattered, but generalizations can be made about their location pattern. Most cities have one or more long-established and well-defined factory areas near the CBD, often containing several large firms as well as many smaller ones. These districts were usually established during the era of railway dominance and are characterized by the presence of rail lines and flat land.

If there is a functional waterfront (ocean, canal, or navigable river or lake) in the city, another old industrial area is likely to be located there. Heavy industry may be congregated in such an area, typically primary metals plants, oil refineries, and chemical plants. Often these areas were originally swampy or marshy and have been reclaimed by drainage, landfilling, or both.

Planned industrial districts are the product of more recent years. They are variously located, but usually the site was chosen with care so that ample space is available and access to a major transport route is assured. Many planned industrial districts have been sited along railway lines, but more recently the critical site factor has been a prominent road or highway, since motor trucks are used more often than railways in transporting goods to and from factories. Perimeter or belt-line highways are particularly attractive to the builders of planned industrial parks.

There are many other kinds of locations in which factories may be found in Anglo-American cities. The principal industrial areas, however, tend to fall into one of the previously discussed categories.

Transportation Land Use A surprisingly large amount of land in most cities is devoted to transportation of one sort or another, including the storage of vehicles (fig. 4–15). This is the second greatest consumer of city space, exceeded only by residential land use. Most of the acreage in this category is occupied by streets, highways, and off-street parking spaces for automobiles. Relatively small proportions of the city area are required by other modes of transport, although airports can be very expansive and new container ship terminals require extensive dockside storage space.

Other Types of Land Use Many other kinds of activities are carried on in a city, but their locational patterns are less predictable. Parks and other kinds of green spaces are found in all cities and in some cases occupy a large share of the total city area. Institutions of various kinds tend to be widespread but scattered—for example, schools, cemeteries, museums. Government office complexes are relatively insignificant in most cities but may be particularly prominent in a national (Washington and Ottawa) or state (as Albany or Sacramento) capital or in a city that is a significant regional headquarters for federal activity (as Denver or San Francisco). Vacant land is another category that occupies varying amounts of space; even the most crowded cities have a certain amount of land that is at present not being utilized for any purpose.

fig. 4–15 Complex freeway interchanges are commonplace in and around Anglo-American cities. This is a part of the Miami system, with Miami Beach in the background (courtesy Florida Division of Tourism).

THE PATTERN OF TRANSPORTATION

There are two different but overlapping facets to transportation in cities: internal movement within the city and external movement to or from the city. For either facet, the dominant fact of life is the pervasiveness of the automobile. Of all the money spent in the United States for freight transportation, 75 percent is for motor trucking, and more than 90 percent of the total outlay for passenger movement goes to automobiles and buses.[28] Although facilitating the movement of goods and people, the massive increase in rubber-tired transport threatens to overwhelm the system of streets and highways. The wastes of congestion become progressively worse despite every effort to facilitate traffic flow. In the New York area, for example, 33 percent of the trucks do not move at all on a given day, and 20 percent of the remainder move empty.

Internal Transport Movement within Anglo-American cities depends primarily on the traffic flow of streets and highways.[29] A large and increasing share of total city area must be devoted to routeways and storage lots for cars and trucks. Some 60 percent of the central square mile of Indianapolis consists of streets and parking lots; similarly more than 33 percent of the Loop area of Chicago is devoted to motor vehicles. Most Anglo-American CBDs are heavily congested throughout the business hours of the day; yet the number of people entering them has not increased over the past two or three decades.

Essentially every Anglo-American city has a rectangular grid as the basic pattern for its street network—at least in the older portions of the urban area. The pattern has nearly always been modified by subsequent departures from the original layout, and in

fig. 4–16 Kansas City was the first Anglo–American metropolis to have its CBD encircled by a close-in ring of freeways. The final link in the loop was completed in 1972. This view across the CBD looks toward the southeast (courtesy Chamber of Commerce of Greater Kansas City).

many cases there is a series of separate grids, adjusted to topography or to surveying changes, that are joined in variable fashions. The grid scheme, with its right-angled intersections, dominates the layout of Anglo-American CBDs. The streets were usually established in the preautomobile era and are normally too narrow to facilitate traffic flow; thus, they engender massive downtown congestion and tax the ingenuity of traffic specialists to devise techniques to unclog the streets.

Away from the city center there is usually a greater diversity in the street pattern, particularly in newer subdivisions. Even so, it is rare for regularity to be maintained over a very large area, since varied sequences of development and annexation lead to heterogeneity in planning.

Superimposed on the pattern of surface streets in all large Anglo-American cities as well as in many small ones is a network (or the beginning of a network) of freeways or expressways (fig. 4–16). These are high-speed, multilaned, controlled-access traffic-ways that are laid in direct lines across the

[28] Gilbert Burck, "Transportation's Troubled Abundance," *Fortune*, 84 (July 1971), 60–61.

[29] Important elements of this discussion are extracted from Harold M. Mayer, "Cities: Transportation and Internal Circulation," *Journal of Geography*, 68 (October 1969), 390–408.

fig. 4-17 A typical freeway scar, in this case across north Dallas.

metropolis from one complicated interchange to another, making functional connection with the surface street system at sporadic intervals by means of access ramps (fig. 4–17).

Modern freeways carry a large share of travel in most cities, permitting rapid movement (except at rush hours) at about one-third the accident risk of surface streets. Characteristically the freeway network of a city radiates outward from the CBD. Even though functional connection to a freeway is restricted, its route is often an axis along

fig. 4-18 Freeways attract industry, and vice versa. Most large suburban factories are deliberately located adjacent to freeways, if at all possible. This is the Texas Instruments plant north of Dallas (courtesy Texas Instruments Inc.).

which urban development takes place at higher densities than in the intervening wedges, with the most intensive development likely to occur near access ramps and freeway interchanges.

Almost every large city has one or more belt-line routes, often but not always a freeway, that roughly circles the city at a radius of several miles from the CBD. Probably the most famous example of this phenomenon is Boston's Circumferential Highway (Route 128), but the pattern is now common, from Miami's Palmetto Parkway to Seattle's Renton Freeway. Such perimeter thoroughfares often attract a considerable amount of secondary and tertiary industry; for example, Boston's Route 128 has some 600 plants employing 60,000 people along its right-of-way. This very attractiveness inhibits the proper functioning of the beltway concept (fig. 4–18). These routes are intended to move traffic around urban centers, but they frequently become so overloaded with local traffic that they generate a need for new circumferential routes still farther out to carry the through traffic.

As congestion threatens to choke the cities of the continent, it is often suggested that the only hope for urban survival is *mass transit* with emphasis on *rapid transit*. But unfortunately the panacea effect seems to be overestimated. Mass-transit patronage in the United States has absolutely declined more than one-third over the last four decades, in a period when the urban population was more than doubling. Patronage of rapid transit, on the other hand, has declined only slightly over the same period, although urban governments either subsidize or own (and operate at a loss) all systems that are in operation. Rapid transit is now functioning in Montreal, Toronto, Boston, New York, Philadelphia, Washington, Cleveland, Chicago, and San Francisco (fig. 4–19), and is under construction in Atlanta. Anglo-American urbanites, however, seem to be wedded to their automobiles, and their interest in transit facilities is limited. Also, the relatively low population density in most areas means low volumes of traffic, which

fig. 4-19 The most celebrated, and problem-plagued, new rapid transit system in Anglo-America is BART, which serves the San Francisco–Oakland metropolis. It first went into service in 1972 (San Francisco Visitor Bureau photo).

militate against the feasibility of substantial investments in rapid transit facilities.

There is no way to avoid the fact that rapid transit systems are relatively idle most of the time and are in demand only at rush hours. Furthermore, who is served by rapid transit systems? New lines in Chicago and Toronto were found to draw 90 percent of their passengers from bus lines and only 10 percent from automobiles.[30] Most systems accommodate commuters rather than the poor, the aged, and the handicapped, who, some would argue, need public transit most of all. The basic inadequacy of rapid transit to solve automobile-related problems has been trenchantly summarized by Vance, in his comment on the situation in San Francisco:

Here in the Bay Area we have begun what is a terribly limited rapid-transit system whose main use will be in the commuting of office workers from middle-income East Bay and the Sunset district of San Francisco to work in downtown San Francisco. Such a scant and specialized system has already cost almost a billion and a half dollars, money that cannot be used for housing or schools or parks or improving the life of the poor and the nonwhite.[31]

[30] Burck, "Transportation's Troubled Abundance," p. 139.
[31] James E. Vance, Jr., "Man and Super-City: Complex Structures of the Bay Area in the 'Seventies'," in *California: 1970, Problems and Prospects*, ed. David W. Lantis (Chico, Calif.: Association of American Geographers, 1970), p. 39.

If not mass transit, and not rapid transit, then what will prevent the Anglo-American city from grinding to a halt some day under the sheer bulk of its street and freeway traffic?

External Transport The movement of people and goods into and out of cities is accomplished in a great variety of ways, although auto and truck transportation is dominant. Cities are hubs in the cross-country highway networks of the United States and Canada, with routes converging to join the internal street system of the hubs. Despite the construction of bypasses and beltways, there is much mixing of a city's internal and external roadway traffic, with each contributing to congestion for the other. Even the building of the unprecedented ($70 billion in construction over a 21-year period) Interstate Highway System in the United States has done little to improve traffic within cities; it has immensely facilitated cross-country travel but clearly failed to alleviate urban congestion, which was one of its principal objectives.

Railways were generally very important in the founding and growth of Anglo-American cities, but in most cases they are relatively less significant today. Nevertheless, railroad facilities are still quite conspicuous in most cities. Rail lines converge on cities in the same fashion and sometimes in the same pattern as highways. For large cities, there are also railway belt-lines to facilitate the shifting of rail cars from one line to another. Major passenger and freight terminals are usually located in the transition zone near the CBD, but in some cases the latter have been shifted to more distant sites. Most cities have a single passenger terminal ("Union Station"), but busier railway centers may have two, and Chicago, the world's leading rail hub, has four. An important specialized feature of railway transport is the classification yard where freight trains are assembled and disassembled; yards of this kind are now usually located on the very outskirts of the urban area.

The very rapid recent expansion of air travel in Anglo-America has meant that most cities are now engaged in the construction of new, or the expansion of old, airports. There is little in the way of a predictable pattern, except that an airport is usually located several miles (in some cases, several tens of miles) from the CBD, where an extensive area of flat and relatively cheap land is available (fig. 4–20). Normally a major freeway or other thoroughfare is designed to give the airport a direct connection with the CBD. The long-predicted development of intracity helicopter travel in the larger metropolitan areas is as yet relatively insignificant.

Water transportation may be important to the economy of many ocean, river, and Great Lakes ports, but the amount of space utilized for port facilities is usually small in comparison with the total area of the city. Piers, docks, and warehouses are normally the most conspicuous permanent features along a port's waterfront, although the recent rapid change to containerization of cargo has led to enormous aggregations of container vans in open spaces adjacent to the docks.

Pipeline transportation is highly specialized and relatively inconspicuous in most cities. Internal networks distribute water and gas and collect sewerage, but these are ubiquitous and largely underground features. External pipeline systems are normally associated with liquid or gaseous fuels, bringing petroleum or gas into the city for either refining or distribution to consumers. In any case, most pipelines are buried, and the prominent landscape features associated with this activity are huge storage tanks at the terminals.

VERTICAL STRUCTURE

The building of skyscrapers and other high-rise buildings is not peculiar to Anglo-America, but the concept achieved its first real prominence in New York City, and the vertical dimension of the Anglo-American skyline has continued to be significant in any consideration of city form (fig. 4–21). In the past, the vertical structure of cities was predictable. Within the CBD there would be an irregular concentration of tall buildings, with a rapid decrease in height centrifugally in all directions to the very low profile that characterized the vast majority of the urbanized area. The only significant exception to that generalized scheme was New York, with its prominent dual concentration of skyscrapers: the major one in Midtown

fig. 4–20 Modern urban airports are both expansive and busy. This is the Miami International Airport (courtesy Miami-Metro Department of Publicity and Tourism).

fig. 4-21 Although there has been some decentralization of high-rise construction in Anglo-American cities, most tall buildings are still concentrated in CBDs, as in Edmonton.

Manhattan; and the secondary, but still very impressive, one in Lower Manhattan.

In recent years the pattern of high-rise building has become more diffuse. The CBD still has the conspicuous skyline, but tall buildings are being built ever more widely throughout the urban area. Secondary aggregations of high-rise structures are often associated with major suburban shopping centers, planned industrial districts, and even airports. Tall buildings are also being built increasingly along principal string-street thoroughfares, usually in a very sporadic pattern. Los Angeles's famous Wilshire Boulevard, for example, is now marked along its entire 15-mile length from the CBD to the Pacific Ocean by an irregular string of high-rise office buildings and apartments.

In Anglo-America the greatest concentrations of tall buildings have always been in the older, more crowded cities of the Northeast; the newer, less intensively developed cities of the West tended to sprawl outward rather than upward. But since World War II this pattern has been changing; prominent skylines now sprout from such plainsland cities as Dallas, Denver, and Winnipeg, and the trend extends to almost all the large cities of the continent.

New York City still contains the greatest concentration of skyscrapers in the world; two-thirds of the world's tallest buildings and more than half of the nation's buildings over 500 feet in height are located on Manhattan Island. Chicago is the only other Anglo-American city with a skyline that includes a number of very tall buildings, but its total is only about 20 percent as large as New York's. The construction of skyscrapers continues apace, and the present roster of cities with tallest buildings (Boston, Chicago, Dallas, Houston, New York, Pittsburgh, San Francisco, and Toronto) will undoubtedly change from year to year.

The skyscraper is a visible symbol of high land values, and of congestion. Although the skyscraper permits many more people to live and work in a restricted area, it also adds to traffic confusion. The streets of most cities were designed for smaller populations, lower buildings, and more limited movement; hence they cannot carry the present traffic load without friction and delays. Traffic slows to a snail's pace in the very places where speed and promptness are most desired. The diffusion of high-rise building away from the CBD is a partial response to this problem.

Most Anglo-American cities are visually similar, a generalization that is a logical outgrowth of the morphological similarity that has been chronicled on preceding pages. Within the CBD, tall buildings dominate the scene. Elsewhere in the urban area, even in the transition zone, the most conspicuous visual element consists of trees, generally rising above low-level residential and commercial rooftops. The visual dominance of trees is interrupted wherever there are extensive special-use areas, such as airports or planned industrial districts, but in general their pervasiveness can be seen in cities throughout Anglo-America.

Building ordinances and zoning restrictions, which tend to be much the same from city to city, are another reason for the visual similarity of cities in the United States and in Canada. Many examples could be cited, but perhaps the most prominent is the requirement that residences be set back from the street; thus in most parts of most cities front yards are required, even though their functional role is a thing of the past.

A more detailed look at cities shows their many differences in appearance. Every city has a certain visual uniqueness on the basis of street pattern, architecture, air pollution, degree of dirtiness, and a host of other elements. But often such distinctiveness is a function of site (slope land versus flat land or coastal versus inland, for example), regional location (as the widespread adoption of "Spanish" architecture in the Southwest), or relative age.

The federal program of *urban renewal* in the United States, along with its other consequences, has had a marked effect on the appearance of many cities. There is no similar national program in Canada, although provincial and municipal authorities have inaugurated various urban renewal efforts on a much smaller scale. The idea behind urban renewal is simple enough: communities acquire large parcels of slum property (using the power of eminent domain where necessary) and sell or lease them for massive public or private redevelopment, using mostly federal funds for capital requirements. The program was initiated under the auspices of the Federal Housing Act of 1949, although its legal origin dated from state-enabling legislation as early as 1944. Subsequent amendments broadened the action beyond slum clearance to provide for the conservation and rehabilitation of areas that do not require demolition.

An overriding consideration in urban renewal philosophy was the acceptance of the need for federal aid to revitalize the economic base and taxable resources of cities. Several thousand urban renewal projects have been carried out under the program, with erratic results. The principal objections are that more low-income housing is removed than is replaced and that the costs are much greater than the benefits. In any event, the replacement of slums by modern high-rise buildings and greenspaces has changed the face of many American cities, from Boston's West End to Los Angeles's Bunker Hill. The greatest emphasis on urban renewal has been in the Northeast, particularly in the cities of Pennsylvania.

urban functions:
growing diversity

As well as being a morphological form that occupies space, a city is a functional entity that performs services for both its population and the population of its hinterland. In doing so, it may also provide services for people in more distant regions or even in foreign lands. Every Anglo-American city is multifunctional in nature, being involved in several different kinds of economic activities (fig. 4–22).[32]

[32] Urban function is treated extensively in geographical literature. One important summation of the topic is found in Howard J. Nelson, "A Service Classification of American Cities," *Economic Geography,* 31 (July 1955), 189–210.

urban population:
variety in abundance

Whatever else a city is, it is primarily a group of people who have chosen to live in an urban environment because of the economic opportunities, the amenities that are close at hand, or inertia. Whatever the reasons, the population of Anglo-America is becoming increasingly urbanized (fig. 4–23). The pell-mell rate of urbanization that characterized the 1950s and 1960s slowed down in the 1970s, in part because of a trend toward nonmetropolitan living but in part simply because the vast majority of the populace already lived in cities.

We have already noted that the population of central cities in metropolitan areas, particularly the largest metropolitan areas, has stagnated or declined in recent years, with all or most growth being confined to the expanding suburbs. Indeed, it was during the 1950s that many large cities had their last great growth, having actually lost population within their political limits since that time.[33] One notable result is that contemporary urbanites have more living space than they did a decade or two ago: the population per square mile in Anglo-American urbanized areas has decreased by more than 50 percent in the last half century.

There are many aspects to the population structure of cities. Three of the most important are age, sex, and ethnicity.

AGE STRUCTURE
OF THE URBAN POPULATION

For most Anglo-American cities there is a general sameness to the age structure. The age pyramid for the city is likely to resemble the age pyramid for the nation: a broad symmetry except for constriction in the zone of younger middle-age.

An important exception to the generally uniform age structure involves cities in which there is a preponderance of older

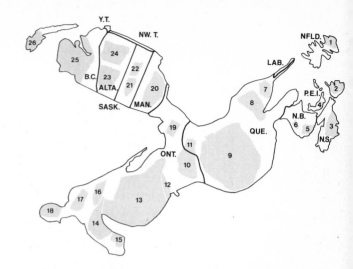

fig. 4–23 Isodemographic map of Canada. The areas of the provinces and major cities are shown proportional to their population. The remarkable urbanization of the population is striking. The cities are as follows: (1) St. John's, (2) Sydney, (3) Halifax, (4) Charlottetown, (5) Saint John, (6) Fredericton, (7) Chicoutimi-Jonquiere, (8) Quebec City, (9) Montreal, (10) Ottawa, (11) Hull, (12) Oshawa, (13) Toronto, (14) Hamilton, (15) St. Catharines, (16) Kitchener-Waterloo, (17) London, (18) Windsor, (19) Sudbury, (20) Winnipeg, (21) Regina, (22) Saskatoon, (23) Calgary, (24) Edmonton, (25) Vancouver, and (26) Victoria (based on Statistics Canada, *Perspective Canada II: A Compendium of Social Statistics, 1977* [Ottawa: Minister of Supply and Services, 1977], p. 194).

people. This is usually the result either of deliberate settlement by older people or of a residual concentration of the elderly in places from which younger people have moved. Some parts of Anglo-America, basically areas with warm sunny climates, are attractive to older people for retirement purposes. St. Petersburg is probably the most famous of the retirement cities, although other urban areas in Florida and various cities in the Southwest, particularly Tucson and Phoenix, also show this phenomenon. The trend is less marked in Canada, for there are few areas that could be classed as warm and sunny for much of the year; however, Victoria is somewhat representative of this kind of development. On the other hand there are areas where there

[33] Ronald Boyce, "Urban Growth and Urban Decline in the United States," *Geographical Review,* 63 (April 1973), 272.

has been a significant out-migration of young adults, resulting in a population structure weighted toward older people. This shows up only in smaller cities, most conspicuously in Appalachia (especially West Virginia), the central plains (Iowa and the Dakotas), and the Atlantic Provinces.

At the other extreme are cities with an unusually high proportion of younger people in their population. Certain minority groups, such as Indians, have particularly high birth rates, and where there are small cities containing a significant component of such a minority the age pyramid may be quite extended for the younger years. In still other cities there may be a greater-than-average proportion of young adults in the population; this is likely to be associated with new cities with recently expanded specific employment opportunities, such as mining towns, cities with military installations, and cities prominent in the space program.

SEX RATIO
OF THE URBAN POPULATION

The male-female ratio of the Anglo-American urban population tends to be quite uniform. The sex ratio in most cities is well balanced, with a slight excess of females. Any variation from this norm tends to be regional in nature. Marked female dominance in population numbers is essentially nonexistent. Marked male dominance is not unusual in frontier towns; there are many small cities in Alaska, the Canadian "north country," and the intermontane West where men significantly outnumber women. There is also an excess of males in the cities of the Hawaiian Islands, presumably as a result of immigration (mostly from the Orient and various Pacific island areas) of men who do not have or do not bring families.

ETHNIC PATTERN
OF THE URBAN POPULATION

Anglo-American cities have a remarkably varied array of ethnic mixes. The variety generally follows a regional pattern, but in some cities there are significant variations

from the regional trend. It should be noted that it does not require a very large number of people of a particular ethnic group to put a significant imprint on a city or on that city's image.

The situation in Canadian cities is quite different from that in United States cities. Every Canadian city of any size is at least 40 percent British or 40 percent French in terms of the lineage of the population. This bicultural bifurcation identifies the two main groups in any ethnic classification of Canadian urban areas.[34] Figure 4–24 illustrates the magnitude of this bifurcation. The average Canadian urbanite is an Anglo-Saxon Protestant, normally of British descent but sometimes of German or Dutch extraction. In the province of Quebec, on the other hand, urban-dwellers are overwhelmingly French; only in Montreal is the population less than 80 percent French.

There is a varied although largely European ethnic mix among the non-British, non-French minority in Canadian cities; however, there is no large, underprivileged, vocal ethnic group around which racial antagonisms cluster. Canadian urban minority groups tend to be upwardly mobile in both social and economic status. Ethnic ghettos occur in Canadian cities, but they are not—except for some French-Canadian areas in predominantly Anglo-Canadian cities—particularly conspicuous in most cases. The most clustered and easily identified small ethnic minorities are probably the Chinese (largely in Vancouver and Toronto), Hungarians, Greeks, Portuguese, and West Indians.

In cities south of the international border, black Americans are often a prominent minority that is all the more conspicuous because of the racially segregated housing pattern that usually prevails and the generally low economic level of the group as a whole. We have already noted that blacks are predominantly ghettoized throughout the nation. The central city ghettos continue a rapid outward expansion, but only a small

[34] Simmons, *Urban Canada*, p. 41

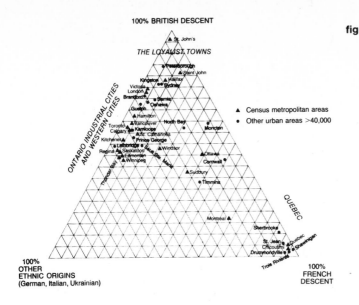

fig. 4–24 The ethnic pattern of Canadian cities (1971). This chart indicates the proportion of the city's population composed of each of three different ethnic origins. The closer a city is to a point of the triangle, the more homogeneous is its origin. Note the extreme homogeneity of most Quebec cities, and the spectrum of British and other origins in the remainder of the country. (From J. and R. Simmons, *Urban Canada*, 2nd ed. [Toronto: Copp Clark Publishing Company, 1974], p. 40. By permission of Statistics Canada.)

proportion of the black population moves to the suburbs. Although the rate of such movement has been increasing, the proportion of black suburbanites has remained fixed at about 5 percent since 1950.[35] Random examples from the 1970 census show that Lakewood, Ohio, a suburb of Cleveland, had 21 blacks in a population of 71,-000; Anaheim, California, near Los Angeles, had 170 blacks in a population of 167,000; blacks constituted 47 percent of the population of the city of Baltimore, but only 7 percent in the suburbs of Baltimore. Blacks are particularly concentrated in the large cities; one-third of all black Americans resides in eighteen cities, and one-fourth is concentrated in only six metropolitan areas.

Hispanic-Americans are another prominent urban minority, although their numbers are fewer and their distribution is less widespread than that of blacks. In cities of the Southwest, from California's Central Valley to the piedmont of north-central Colorado to the east Texas metropolises of Dallas and Houston, Chicanos are frequently found in large numbers. There are other

concentrations of this minority in Chicago (largely of Mexican origin), the major cities of Megalopolis (primarily Puerto Ricans), and various urban areas in Florida (mostly Cubans). Although less ghettoized than the urban blacks, Chicanos are often clustered in distribution, and their generally low economic status is likely to be reflected in slum housing.

urban ills: massive maladjustments

The big city everywhere is the object of criticism. Critics insist that all cities are ailing and are not good places in which to live. They point to smog, crowding, strain on family life, snarled traffic, segregation of minorities, drugs, juvenile delinquency, riots, impersonality, and a host of other urban evils. The long-continued growth of our cities begets massive growing pains. The worst problem is urban sprawl. As the urbanized area expands in all directions, the provision of necessities, such as water, sewerage, paved streets, utilities, refuse collection, police and fire protection, schools, and parks, becomes a continuing headache, particularly when more than one municipal

[35] Harold M. Rose, "Migration and the Changing Status of Black Americans," *Geographical Review,* 61 (April 1971), 298.

governing body is involved. Also, as the flight to the suburbs continues, it is generally accompanied by a degeneration of much of the core of the city; the results are intensified slums, loss of merchandising revenue, and a decline in the tax base.

As the metropolitan area expands, local transportation becomes more complicated. As many more cars drive many more miles on only a few more streets, relatively speaking, traffic congestion becomes intense, the journey to work lengthens, and parking facilities become inadequate. The big city must maintain constant vigilance to keep from choking.

The maintenance of enough good domestic water also challenges the exploding metropolis. In subhumid regions, cities must sometimes reach out dozens or hundreds of miles to pipe in adequate water; even such humid-land cities as New York and Boston have to extend lines farther and farther to tap satisfactory watersheds.

Where humans congregate, the delicate problem of pollution is accelerated. Rare indeed is the stream in any urban area that is not heavily infiltrated by inadequately treated liquid waste from home and factory. The shocking condition of American waterways has caused some civic groups to wage stringent cleanup campaigns, with emphasis on adequate sewerage treatment. The result has been heartening improvements in such infamous rivers as the Ohio and Philadelphia's Schuylkill—improvements that show this problem can be solved in other areas. More recently the menace of atmospheric pollution has arisen. The highly (and justifiably) publicized smog of Los Angeles is the most striking instance, but "smust" in Phoenix, "smaze" in Denver, and smoke in Montreal are further examples of an undiminishing phenomenon in most large cities. Industrial vapors and burning refuse contribute, but automobile exhaust fumes are generally believed to be the major cause. The air pollution problem will undoubtedly get worse before it gets better.

Wherever people live close together, social friction escalates, and the city is the seat of continually burgeoning social problems. Crime statistics increase, with the annual rate climbing above one crime for every 30 urbanites and one violent crime for every 250 urbanites. Similar trends can be seen for juvenile deliquency, drug abuse, and alcoholism.

Coping with the ills of the city and planning to avoid unending escalation of these problems are immensely complicated by the fragmentation of administrative responsibility that is so widespread in the United States, although less so in Canada. Broad planning is inhibited and effective implementation of general solutions is prevented by the multiplicity of municipalities, townships, counties, school districts, and other special districts (everything from cemetery districts to mosquito abatement units). There are more than 81,000 units of government in the United States, most of them empowered to levy taxes. The average 1-million-population metropolitan area in the United States encompasses nearly 300 separate governmental jurisdictions. A few attempts at formation of a metropolitan government for large cities and their suburbs have been mooted, but as yet nothing very effective has resulted.

The situation is less chaotic in Canada, primarily because the provincial governments have considerable power to regulate municipal institutions. Canadian cities are not surrounded by as many small independent municipalities as their counterparts in the United States, and urban problems can be approached on a broader front. The most far-reaching attempt at metropolitan government was established in Ontario in 1953, when Metro Toronto was created. It has been quite successful in providing integrated services to the metropolitan area for which high capital expenditures were necessary; other aspects of its operation have been less satisfactory. Metro Toronto is at least an innovative guidepost for the future; subsequent experiments along the same line, as in Winnipeg Unicity, will be watched with interest by urban administrators throughout Anglo-America.

urban delights:
the proof of the pudding

If cities are such bad places, why do so many people live there? Anglo-Americans still flock to urban areas, and cities continue to increase in size. It is clear that the number of urban critics is significantly less than the number of people who choose to live in urban areas. Disadvantages may be legion, but the attractions are also multitudinous. Most notable, probably, is the ready availability of material and nonmaterial satisfactions. A vast quantity of goods and services can be purchased, a variety of entertainment may be sampled, and a plethora of mass media provides almost unlimited information and mental stimulation. For many urbanites, however, it appears that the opportunity for social interaction may be even more important than economic advantage or amenity attraction: in cities one can expect to find like-minded people with whom to interact (in a process that Vance called "congregation"). For most people, this combination of positive attributes apparently far outweighs the detrimental aspects of urban life.

urban dichotomy:
central cities versus suburbs

For several decades Anglo-American urban areas were dichotomized into a dualistic division between the cores and the suburbs. It is only in the last few years, however, that the suburban peripheries have experienced such spectacular growth, not only in residential population but also in many other functions that were traditionally restricted to the central areas. As a result, Anglo-American metropolitan areas "have undergone a remarkably swift spatial reorganization from tightly focused single-cores to decentralized multinodal" systems.[36] At first there was

[36] Peter O. Muller, "Toward a Geography of the Suburbs," *Proceedings,* Association of American Geographers, 6 (1974), 36.

merely a cautious outward drift of store clusters in the wake of new residential subdivisions, but the almost instantaneous success of these retailing pioneers encouraged bolder innovations, which were epitomized by the development of immense regional shopping complexes that attracted other kinds of employers to their vicinity. The transportational convenience of suburban freeway and beltway locations has encouraged successive waves of retailing, wholesaling, manufacturing, and service-oriented activities to abandon the CBD and shift to the suburbs.

Central cities thus provide a continually decreasing variety and magnitude of functions. "The leading residual activity is office functions, a set of interdependent activities requiring face-to-face contact and the external economies of the CBD's specialized services."[37] Increasingly, however, office activities are also moving to the suburbs. This is not to say that the CBDs are dying. To the contrary, a resurgence of downtown construction activity in recent years has greatly proliferated the availability of white-collar jobs in the central cities (fig. 4–25). Between 1960 and 1972 gross office

[37] Ibid., p. 38.

fig. 4–25 Enclosed, elevated skyways represent one imaginative approach to augmenting the comfort and convenience of workers and shoppers in CBDs. Such skyways, which enable passage from one building to another without having to deal with inclement weather or automobile traffic, have been constructed in several cities; this one is in Minneapolis (courtesy Greater Minneapolis Chamber of Commerce).

floor space increased by 74 percent in Manhattan; similar proportional growth was experienced in the CBDs of Atlanta, Boston, Cleveland, and Dallas; and in Houston, Minneapolis–St. Paul, and San Francisco the increment was more than 100 percent.[38] A significant proportion of this downtown investment is seen as "defensive," a civic responsibility to the wider urban community to maintain the economic viability of the core. "These new investments represent what could well be the last major defense of the central city against the persistent and ever-growing challenge of the suburbs."[39]

The crux of the dichotomy revolves around money and jobs. A very large share of suburban growth is beyond the political limits of the central cities, which severely undercuts their tax base and payrolls. Thus there are relatively prosperous suburban communities and destitute central cities. Suburbanites largely ignore the central cities, and the inner city blue-collar workers are often unable to find replacement jobs downtown and must face either unemployment or the prospect of long-distance reverse commuting to outlying industrial concentrations. The heightened unemployment problem is only one aspect of the increasing social upheavals resulting from inner city economic stagnation, or what George Sternlieb called the "defunctioning" of the central city.[40]

Suburbs, on the other hand,

have achieved critical mass, a scale of population and buying power which permits them to sustain amenities of a type and at a level which once only the central city was capable of sustaining. The shopping center which had at best a single department store branch now has

three and soon will have four. The suburban music calendar is evolving from a marginal summer collection of odds and ends to a year-round independent activity. Small suburban hospitals have grown to thousand-bed monsters which can supply all the services and specialists available in the biggest central-city hospitals.[41]

It is clear that our cities will never again be the same (fig. 4–26). The domination of the suburbs will continue to grow, but so will their diversification. An understanding of the varied geography of the suburbs is critical to any comprehension of the future geography of Anglo-America.

urban tomorrow:
the outreach of city life

What will the city of tomorrow be like? Many radical designs have been produced and grandiose predictions made, but only one thing is clear: the urban place of the future will be a combination of elaborate planning and unstructured eventuality.

The surest bet for the short-run is the continuance of urban sprawl. The areal expansion of individual cities will result in the increasing coalescence of adjacent metropolitan areas and the creation of more supercities around the western end of Lake Ontario, around the margin of Lake Erie, around the southern end of Lake Michigan, and along the coast of Southern California. The metropolis expands, and so do the suburbs and ghettos.

Innovations in the use of urban space will surely proliferate, although surrealistic cities of the future may still be a few decades away. Many cities have experimented with pedestrian malls and walkways, and this is likely to continue. The advantages of separating pedestrian and vehicular traffic are clear, and in intensive-use areas such separation is worth almost any cost. Increasingly there will also be construction of buildings above transportation routes. The concept of air rights above railway tracks, highways,

[38] Gerald Manners, "The Office in Metropolis: An Opportunity for Shaping Metropolitan America," *Economic Geography,* 50 (April 1974), 93.

[39] Ibid. p. 95.

[40] George Sternlieb, "The City as Sandbox," in *Suburbanization Dynamics and the Future of the City,* ed. James W. Hughes (New Brunswick, N.J.: Center for Urban Policy Research, Rutgers University, 1974), p. 225.

[41] Ibid.

fig. 4-26 The dichotomy of urban Anglo-America
is symbolized by the massive edifices
of Midtown Manhattan (occupying most of the photo)
and the distant sprawl of conspicuous buildings
on the New Jersey side of the Hudson River
(courtesy New York State Department of Commerce).

and transport terminals is now well accepted and will be resorted to more and more.[42]

If the morphology of Anglo-American urban areas is changing, so is the life style of its citizens. "A new kind of large-scale urban society is emerging that is increasingly independent of the city."[43] The distinction between urban and rural is blurred. Cities can no longer be understood as configurations of population density, for the functional linkages among their far-flung parts and the interactions with nonmetropolitan peripheries

are so complex that urban influence extends well beyond the traditional boundaries of metropolitan areas. Urban researchers have increasingly turned their attention to wider reaches. Concepts such as *urban field* and *daily urban system* have been developed to incorporate these vaster functional zones that include not only the central cities and the suburbs but also the extensive, urban-related commuting fields in the nearby hinterlands.[44] In such conceptualizations, well over 90 percent of all Anglo-Americans are urbanites, for better or for worse.

[42] Prominent examples of the use of air rights include one of New York's largest office buildings, the Pan-American Building, over a railway station; Chicago's Merchandise Mart, the world's most spacious office building, over railway lines; and part of the grounds of the United Nations complex over a major Manhattan parkway.

[43] Melvin M. Webber, "The Post-City Age," in *Suburbanization Dynamics and the Future of the City,* ed. Hughes, p. 246.

[44] The term *urban field* was introduced in John Friedmann and John Miller, "The Urban Field," *Journal of the American Institute of Planners,* 31 (November 1965), 310–21; the term *daily urban system* was coined by C. A. Doxiadis, but the concept has been most thoroughly developed in Anglo-America by Brian Berry (see, for example, *Growth Centers in the American Urban System,* 2 vols. [Cambridge, Mass.: Ballinger Publishing Co., 1973]).

selected bibliography

ABLER, RONALD, JOHN S. ADAMS, AND KI-SUK LEE, *A Comparative Atlas of America's Great Cities: Twenty Metropolitan Regions.* Minneapolis: University of Minnesota Press, 1976.

ADAMS, JOHN S., ed., *Urban Policy-Making and Metropolitan Dynamics: A Comparative Geographical Analysis.* Cambridge, Mass.: Ballinger Publishing Company, 1976.

ADAMS, RUSSELL B., "Metropolitan Area and Central City Population, 1960–1970–1980," *Annales de Geographie,* 81 (1972), 171–205.

BERRY, BRIAN J. L., *Growth Centers in the American Urban System,* 2 vols. Cambridge, Mass.: Ballinger Publishing Company, 1973.

BERRY, BRIAN J. L., AND QUENTIN GILLARD, *The Changing Shape of Metropolitan America: Commuting Patterns, Urban Fields, and Decentralization Processes.* Cambridge, Mass.: Ballinger Publishing Company, 1977.

BORCHERT, JOHN R., "America's Changing Metropolitan Regions," *Annals,* Association of American Geographers, 62 (1972), 352–73.

BOURNE, L. S., "Some Myths of Canadian Urban Growth: Reflections on the 1976 Census and Beyond," *Programme and Abstracts,* Canadian Association of Geographers, University of Regina (1977), pp. 40–43.

BOURNE, L. S., AND R. D. MACKINNON, eds., *Urban Systems Development in Central Canada: Selected Papers.* Toronto: University of Toronto, Department of Geography Research Publication 9, 1972.

BOURNE, L. S., R. D. MACKINNON, AND J. W. SIMMONS, eds., *The Form of Cities in Central Canada: Selected Papers.* Toronto: University of Toronto, Department of Geography Research Publication 11, 1973.

BOYCE, RONALD, "Urban Growth and Urban Decline in the United States," *Geographical Review,* 63 (1973), 272–73.

BRECKENFELD, G., "Downtown Has Fled to the Suburbs," *Fortune,* 86 (October 1972), 80.

CONZEN, MICHAEL P., "The Maturing Urban System in the United States, 1840–1910," *Annals,* Association of American Geographers, 67 (1977), 88–108.

DINGEMANS, DENNIS J., "The Urbanization of Suburbia: The Renaissance of the Row House," *Landscape,* 20 (October 1975), 20–31.

FARLEY, REYNOLDS, "The Changing Distribution of Negroes within Metropolitan Areas: The Emergence of Black Suburbs," *American Journal of Sociology,* 75 (1969–70), 512–29.

FELLMANN, JEROME D., "Land Use and Density Patterns of the Metropolitan Area," *Journal of Geography,* 68 (1969), 262–66.

FORD, LARRY R., "The Urban Skyline as a City Classification System," *Journal of Geography,* 75 (1976), 154–64.

GIBSON, LAY J., AND RICHARD W. REEVES, "The Roles of Hinterland Composition, Externalities, and Variable Spacing as Determinants of Economic Structure in Small Towns," *Professional Geographer,* 26 (1974), 152–58.

GLANTZ, F. G., AND N. J. DELANEY, "Changes in Nonwhite Residential Patterns in Large Metropolitan Areas, 1960 and 1970," *New England Economic Review,* Federal Reserve Bank of Boston (March–April 1973), pp. 2–13.

GRIFFIN, DONALD W., AND RICHARD E. PRESTON, "A Restatement of the 'Transition Zone' Concept," *Annals,* Association of American Geographers, 56 (1966), 339–50.

HARRIS, CHAUNCY D., "A Functional Classification of Cities in the United States," *Geographical Review,* 33 (1943), 89–99.

HARTSHORN, TRUMAN A., "Inner City Residential Structure and Decline," *Annals,* Association of American Geographers, 61 (1971), 72–96.

HUGHES, JAMES W., *Suburbanization Dynamics and the Future of the City.* New Brunswick, N.J.: Rutgers University, Center for Urban Policy Research, 1974.

JACKSON, JOHN N., *The Canadian City: Space, Form, Quality.* Toronto: McGraw-Hill Ryerson, 1973.

KASAHARA, Y., "A Profile of Canada's Metropolitan Centres," *Queen's Quarterly,* 10 (1963), 303–13.

LEY, DAVID, *The Black Inner City as Frontier Outpost.* Washington, D.C.: Association of American Geographers, 1974.

LITHWICK, N. H., *Urban Canada: Problems and Prospects.* Ottawa: Central Mortgage and Housing, 1970.

LITHWICK, N. H., AND G. PAQUET, *Urban Studies: A Canadian Perspective.* Toronto: Methuen Publications, 1968.

Louis, Arthur M., "The Worst American City," *Harper's Magazine*, 250 (January 1975), 67–71.

Manners, Gerald, "The Office in Metropolis: An Opportunity for Shaping Metropolitan America," *Economic Geography*, 50 (1974), 93–110.

Marshall, John U., "City Size, Economic Diversity, and Functional Type: The Canadian Case," *Economic Geography*, 51 (1975), 37–49.

Maxwell, J. W., "The Functional Structure of Canadian Cities: A Classification of Cities," *Geographical Bulletin*, 7 (1965), 79–104.

Mayer, Harold M., "Cities: Transportation and Internal Circulation," *Journal of Geography*, 68 (1969), 390–408.

Morrill, Richard L., "The Persistence of the Black Ghetto as Spatial Separation," *Southeastern Geographer*, 11 (1971), 149–56.

Mulhern, John J., ed., *The Future of American Cities*. Philadelphia, Pa.: Federal Reserve Bank of Philadelphia, 1976.

Muller, Peter O., *The Outer City: Geographical Consequences of the Urbanization of the Suburbs*. Washington, D.C.: Association of American Geographers, Resource Papers for College Geography 75-2, 1976.

———, "Suburbia, Geography, and the Prospect of a Nation without Important Cities," *Geographical Survey*, 7 (1978), 13–19.

———, "Toward a Geography of the Suburbs," *Proceedings*, Association of American Geographers, 6 (1974), 36–39.

Murphy, Raymond E., *The American City: An Urban Geography* (2nd ed.). New York: McGraw-Hill Book Co., 1974.

Nader, George A., *Cities of Canada, Volume One: Theoretical, Historical and Planning Perspectives*. Toronto: MacMillan of Canada, 1975.

Nelson, Howard J., "The Form and Structure of Cities: Urban Growth Patterns," *Journal of Geography*, 68 (1969), 198–207.

———, "A Service Classification of American Cities," *Economic Geography*, 31 (1955), 189–210.

———, "Town Founding and the American Frontier," *Yearbook*, Association of Pacific Coast Geographers, 36 (1974), 7–24.

Phillips, Phillip D., "The Changing Standard Metropolitan Statistical Area," *Journal of Geography*, 75 (1976), 165–73.

Rose, Harold M., "The Development of an Urban Subsystem: The Case of the Negro Ghetto," *Annals*, Association of American Geographers, 60 (1970), 1–17.

———, ed., *Geography of the Ghetto: Problems, Perception, and Alternatives*. Dekalb, Ill.: Northern Illinois University Press, 1972.

Schwartz, Barry, ed., *The Changing Face of the Suburbs*. Chicago, Ill.: University of Chicago Press, 1976.

Simmons, James, and Robert Simmons, *Urban Canada* (2nd ed.). Toronto: Copp Clark Publishing Company, 1976.

Sternlieb, George, and James W. Hughes, eds., *Post-Industrial America: Metropolitan Decline and Inter-Regional Job Shifts*. New Brunswick, N.J.: Rutgers University, Center for Urban Policy Research, 1975.

Stone, Leroy O., *Urban Development in Canada*. Ottawa: Dominion Bureau of Statistics, 1967.

Ullman, Edward, Michael Dacey, and H. Brodsky, *The Economic Base of American Cities*. Seattle: University of Washington Press, 1969.

Vance, James E., Jr., "The American City: Workshop for a National Culture," in *Contemporary Metropolitan America, Vol. I, Cities of the Nation's Historic Metropolitan Core*, ed. John S. Adams, pp. 1–49. Cambridge, Mass.: Ballinger Publishing Company, 1976.

———, "Cities in the Shaping of the American Nation," *Journal of Geography*, 75 (1976), 41–52.

Ward, David, *Cities and Immigrants: A Geography of Change in Nineteenth Century America*. New York: Oxford University Press, 1971.

———, "The Emergence of Central Immigrant Ghettoes in American Cities: 1840–1920," *Annals*, Association of American Geographers, 58 (1968), 343–59.

Yeates, Maurice, and Barry Garner, *The North American City* (2nd ed.) New York: Harper & Row, Publishers, 1976.

regional geography

THE REGIONS OF ANGLO-AMERICA

5

It is convenient, and in many ways useful, to refer to Canada and the United States as discrete units that are sufficiently similar to support generalizations that apply to both nations. But in actual practice, such unitary consideration is likely to be misleading or inaccurate. Generalizations about either nation usually force a vast number of unlike areas into the same category. It is more meaningful to think of these countries as composed of a large number of parts that are more or less dissimilar. Geographers call these parts *regions*. Although the concept of regions leaves something to be desired, it continues "to be one of the most logical and satisfactory ways of organizing geographical information."[1]

It is well known that people vary, in speech, customs, habits, mores, and other ways, from region to region; however, there is no simple explanation for such variations (fig. 5–1). In some cases it may be attribut-

[1] Peter Haggett, *Locational Analysis in Human Geography* (London: Edward Arnold, Ltd., 1967), p. 241.

fig. 5–1   This historic note from the Great Plains is a restored sod house, mainstay of early settlers, in western Nebraska. A contemporary Great Plains scene is a cattle feedlot in northeastern Colorado (Union Pacific Railroad photos).

able to aspects of the environment, whereby an element or complex of the physical realm exerts a pervasive influence on the population. Such effects appear to be most significant in areas where human activity is hindered by environmental extremes, such as deserts, mountains, or swamplands. In other cases, the regional variation of people is more closely related to culture than to nature. Whereas land is relatively changeless, man is the active agent; movements of people, changing stages of occupance, or different assessments of the resource base may occasion significant variations in the geography of regions.

The United States and Canada are nations composed of many political units, but they are also large portions of the earth's surface and comprise many varying regions. Each region differs from the others in one or more significant aspects of environment, culture, or economy; indeed, the magnitude of regional differences is often vast and complex. This book treats Anglo-America by regions, with broad sweeps of the brush; it is hoped that such treatment will bring readers a fuller appreciation of regionalism, a vital concept to those who seek a better understanding of the world.

Even in such affluent and economically integrated nations as Canada and the United States, regional considerations have long been recognized in business and government. Federal Reserve banking districts were formalized as early as 1913, and there are now more than 50 United States government bureaus in the executive branch alone that are organized with regional divisions. Businesses have likewise created regional offices, mail-order houses, and magazines to cope with the varied problems and opportunities that are faced in operations covering such extensive areas as the United States and Canada. By working with large units, regional geography can make a more meaningful contribution to understanding national life. The often unsatisfactory artificiality of political boundaries becomes particularly apparent when attention is focused on regions.

Geography, which links the data of the social sciences with those of the natural sciences, is the logical discipline for dealing with regions. It sees in the region not only the physical, biological, social, political, and economic factors, but it also synthesizes them. In short, it considers the region in its totality—not merely the elements that are there, but also the processes and relationships that have operated, are operating, and presumably will operate in the future. As J. Russell Smith once said, "The geographer is like the builder of a house who takes brick, stone, sand, cement, nails, wire, lath, boards, shingles, and glass—the products of many industries—and builds them into a symmetrical structure which is not any one of the many things that have entered into it, but is instead a house for the occupancy of man."[2]

the geographical region

Geographers generally recognize two kinds of regions: *uniform* regions and *nodal* regions. The former possess significant aspects of homogeneity throughout their extent, whereas the latter are very diverse internally and are homogeneous only with respect to their internal structure or organization. A nodal region always includes a focus, or foci, and a surrounding area tied to the focus by lines of circulation. A city and its hinterland illustrate, in crude fashion, the concept of a nodal region.

The authors feel that at macroscale the geography of Anglo-America can best be understood by reference to uniform regions; accordingly the ensuing discussion and the regional breakdown are related solely to the concept of uniform regions.

Every uniform region has a core area of individuality in which the regional characteristics are most clearly exemplified. The core possesses two distinct qualities that may be blurred in the periphery:

[2] J. Russell Smith, *School Geography and the Regional Idea* (Philadelphia, Pa.: John C. Winston Co., 1934), p. 2.

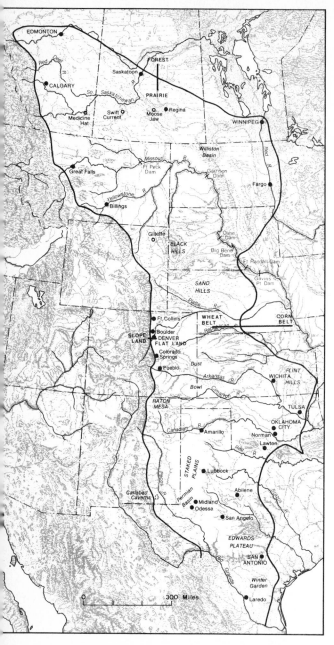

fig. 5–2 The Great Plains Region, showing the boundary transects discussed in this chapter.

1 It differs noticeably from neighboring core areas.

2 It exists as a recognizable and coherent segment of space defined by the criteria whereby it is selected.

Beyond the core lies a marginal area. Regional boundaries are usually not lines but rather transitional zones that partake of the character of adjoining regions or cores. The width may vary from a few feet to many miles; thus the field geographer making a reconnaissance survey seldom knows when he or she leaves one region and enters another. At some point, of course, he or she passes from one to the other, but the human eye usually cannot perceive it at the moment of change. The distinguishing features of one region melt gradually into those of the neighboring region, except perhaps along a mountain front or along the shore of a large body of water.

the problem of regional boundaries

Consider, for example, the problem of delimiting the boundaries of one of the most universally recognized and precisely bounded regions of Anglo-America, the Great Plains. The eastern boundary is the least exact; in this book it is considered to be an irregular north-south zone extending from Texas to Manitoba. Several criteria are employed in positioning the boundary line shown in figure 5–2, but most significant is the change from a predominantly Corn Belt type agriculture on the east to a predominantly Wheat Belt type agriculture on the west. To locate this boundary at any particular point is an exercise in frustration. Southeasternmost Nebraska is clearly Corn Belt, and southwesternmost Nebraska is clearly Wheat Belt, but where is the boundary?

In an east-west transect of this area, one slowly passes from a corn-dominated crop pattern to a wheat-and-grain sorghum-dominated crop pattern before reaching the midpoint of the transect. But then corn appears significantly again, and there is an erratic alternation of the two crop combinations for many tens of miles until the wheat-and-grain sorghum pattern clearly prevails in southwesternmost Nebraska; thus, the eastern boundary of the Great Plains—as exemplified by this single transect—that is portrayed as a black line in figure 5–2 is actually a broad transition zone that approaches 300 miles in width in some places.

The northern boundary of the Great Plains Region is somewhat easier to delimit but is still far from precise. Once again several criteria are used, but the most prominent criterion is the change from grass-and-grain in the south to forest in the north. In theory it is reasonable to expect an abrupt and conspicuous demarcation between such different vegetation associations, but in actuality the change is again transitional. A south-north transect through central Saskatchewan would find a significant interfingering of grass-and-grain with forest, the whole pattern being complicated by enclaves of forest well to the south and patches of grassland scattered deep in the forest. Again, the map shows a precise line as boundary, and again, the boundary (as generalized from this transect) is erratically transitional, embracing a zone that is in some places almost 100 miles in breadth.

The western boundary of the Great Plains Region is much more clear-cut, but even this is imprecise. The principal criterion for pinpointing the boundary is the change from flat land on the east to sloping land on the west; this change is particularly pronounced where the Great Plains meet the front ranges of the Rocky Mountains. An east-west transect in northern Colorado finds essentially flat land around Denver becoming virtually all slopeland west of Golden, only 25 miles away. But the intervening area fits well in neither region, since the pervasive flatness of the plains is interrupted by the gentle slopes of the Colorado Piedmont, the somewhat steeper slopes of scattered foothills, and the varied terrain of mesas and hogbacks before it is replaced by the more precipitous slopes of the mountain ranges. Thus even one of the most abrupt

regional boundaries that can be marked has a transition zone several miles in width.

the problem of regional statistics

Although many geographers agree that regional geography is a fundamental part of their subject—that it is even the heart of the discipline—students of regional geography usually face an enormous handicap for precision study because of the unavailability of quantitative data. Statistics produced by the various data-collecting agencies (government and otherwise) normally are applicable only to political units (states, provinces, counties, townships, and other civil divisions) and therefore are difficult to apply to the more functional and less precise geographical regions. As a partial response to this problem, more refined statistical units, such as urbanized areas, standard metropolitan statistical areas, state economic areas, industrial areas, and labor market areas, have been designated in recent years; statistics applicable to such areas are often more meaningful for the regional geographer to use. The difficulty of fitting statistics to regions still persists, but improvements continue to be made.

determination of regions

Dividing a continent into regions is a matter of "scientific generalizing." It serves the dual purpose of facilitating the assimilation of large masses of geographic information by students and organizing data into potentially more meaningful patterns for researchers. One recognizes a region by noting the intimate association existing between the people of an area and their occupance and livelihood pattern within that area. Similarity of interest and activity sometimes indicates a similarity of environment.

Geographers deal with both natural and cultural landscapes. Everyone who has traveled, even if only slightly, has noted that the natural landscape changes from one part of the country to another. When two unlike areas are adjacent, the geographer may separate them on a map by a line and thereby recognize them as separate natural regions. Similarly he or she may study the cultural or artificial landscape and delineate it into separate cultural regions.

Whenever people come into any area they promptly modify its natural landscape, "not in a haphazard way but according to the culture system which [they bring with them]. . . . Culture is the agent, the natural area is the medium, the cultural landscape the result."[3] They cut down the forest, plow under the native grass, raise domesticated animals, erect houses and buildings, build fences, construct roads and railroads, put up telephone and telegraph lines, dig canals, build bridges, and tunnel under mountains. All this constitutes the cultural landscape of a region.

Geography consists of more than the mere distribution of humanity and things in the landscape. The distribution of races, climates, or landforms by themselves is never geography. Rather it is ethnology, climatology, and geomorphology. Such distributions become geographically significant only as they function in the mutual relationship of people to natural environment, for these relations are themselves recorded in the landscape (fig. 5–3).

[3] Isaiah Bowman, *Geography in Relation to the Social Sciences* (New York: Charles Scribner's Sons, 1934), p. 150.

changing regions

In several of the disciplines closely related to geography the regional systems are fixed by nature; climatic, pedologic, physiographic, and vegetation regions are all based on relatively static natural boundaries. But geographical regions are not fixed; instead of having hard-and-fast boundary lines, they have ever-changing ones. When people push wheat culture farther north in Canada or farther west in Kansas, or when they grow cotton farther north and west in Texas or Oklahoma, they are responsible for changes in geographical regions because raising wheat or cotton may be of such significance in the regional totality that a shifting of cultivation limits requires a similar shifting of regional boundaries.

Thus an inherent characteristic of a geographical region is that it is dynamic. It changes with time as people learn to assess and utilize their natural environment in different ways, with changing economic, political, or social conditions or with the advance of technology (fig. 5–4). It may contract, expand, fragment, or drastically change its character through the years.

Regional analysis can be carried out at different levels of generalization, and conclusions derived at one scale may be invalid at another.[4] It has been pointed out by various geographers that a change in scale often requires a restatement of problem, and "there is no basis for presuming that asso-

[4] See Haggett's discussion of this point in *Locational Analysis in Human Geography,* p. 263.

fig. 5–3 Human adjustment to environmental restrictions is illustrated by this Indian corn in the arid environment of Monument Valley. The individual hills are widely spaced in each direction, and the seeds are planted deeply in order to come in contact with moist soil.

fig. 5–4 Leisure time activities play an increasingly important role in the lives of Anglo-Americans and in the geography of Anglo-America. Pictured here is the most-visited entertainment feature on the continent, Walt Disney World in central Florida (courtesy Florida Division of Tourism).

ciations existing at one scale will also exist at another."[5] One implication of this situation is that a hierarchy of regions can be designed. The creation of such a hierarchy is a useful exercise of geographical scholarship. It is beyond the intent of this book to do so; nevertheless the understanding of some regions appears to be enhanced by the designation of subregions, and subregions are delimited in some chapters.

the goal
of regional geography

Anglo-America is a fabric of regions; it is the functioning of these interrelated areas that gives a balance between regional and national life through specialization on one hand and integration on the other. Regional study is helpful in social science research

[5] H. H. McCarty, J. C. Hook, and D. S. Knos, *The Measurement of Association in Industrial Geography* (Ames: State University of Iowa, Department of Geography, 1956), p. 16.

and in governmental regional planning because it provides the most useful framework within which to organize the use of resources. Regional inventories can determine what resources are available, and regional plans can provide for their wisest use.

Every region offers its people a certain range of possibilities; however, the actual use made of these possibilities depends heavily on the economic, social, and cultural heritage of the people. In other words, such additional factors as ideals, psychology, and inherited intellectual habits—all derived from the inhabitants of a region—function along with the natural environment.

In the following chapters, mutual relationship (cultural, psychological, and economic) between the people of the region and the conditions of the natural environment is discussed, and the current conditions of life in the different parts of the continent are dealt with broadly. The reader has ample opportunity to judge the proposition that the division of Anglo-America into geographical regions provides the most meaningful way to understand the whole.

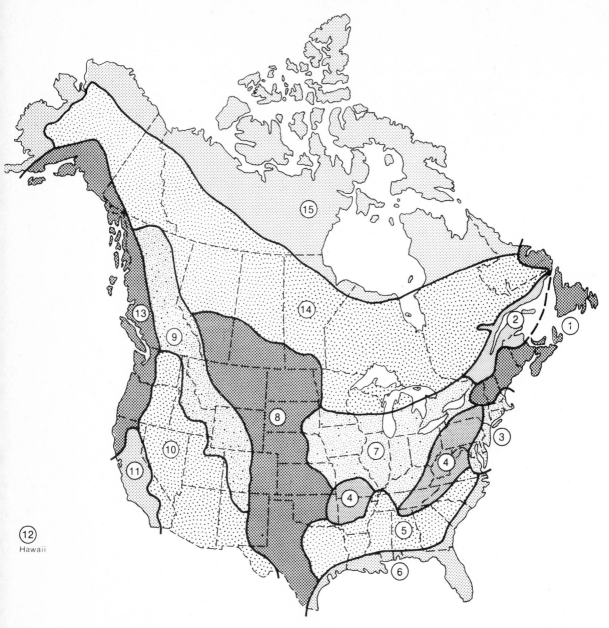

fig. 5–5 Geographic
regions of
Anglo-America.

12
Hawaii

regions of anglo-america

In this book, Anglo-America is divided into 15 regions. The criteria chosen for making the regional divisions are both multiple and varied. In some cases physical considerations have been dominant, and in others cultural factors have been more important. But in all instances the broad regions defined reflect as accurately as possible the basic features of homogeneity inherent in the various parts of Anglo-America at the present time. In general the principal criteria used in determining regional boundaries are the socioeconomic conditions currently characteristic, which often have been decisively influenced by the physical environment and historical development. The regions, as numbered in figure 5–5, are as follows:

1 Northeastern Anglo-America
2 French Canada
3 Megalopolis
4 the Appalachians and the Ozarks
5 the Inland South
6 the Southeastern Coast
7 the Anglo-American Heartland
8 the Great Plains
9 the Rocky Mountains
10 the Intermontane Basins and Plateaus
11 the California Region
12 the Hawaiian Islands
13 the North Pacific Coast
14 the Boreal Forest
15 the Tundra

selected bibliography

BERRY, BRIAN J. L., "Approaches to Regional Analysis: A Synthesis," *Annals,* Association of American Geographers, 54 (1964), 2–11.

FISHER, C. A., "Whither Regional Geography," *Geography,* 55 (1970), 373–89.

GASTIL, RAYMOND D., *Cultural Regions of the United States.* Seattle: University of Washington Press, 1975.

GUELKE, LEONARD, "Regional Geography," *Professional Geographer,* 29 (1977), 1–7.

JAMES, PRESTON, "Toward a Further Understanding of the Regional Concept," *Annals,* Association of American Geographers, 42 (1952), 195–222.

JENSEN, MERRILL, ed., *Regionalism in America.* Madison: University of Wisconsin Press, 1965.

KOHN, CLYDE F., "Regions and Regionalizing," *Journal of Geography,* 69 (1970), 134–40.

KRUEGER, RALPH R., ed., *Regional Patterns: Disparities and Development.* Waterloo, Ont.: Canadian Association of Geographers/Canada Studies Foundation, 1975.

McDONALD, JAMES R., *A Geography of Regions.* Dubuque, Iowa: William C. Brown Company, Publishers, 1972.

MINSHULL, ROGER, *Regional Geography: Theory and Practice.* London: Hutchinson Libraries, 1967.

NICHOLSON, N. L., AND Z. W. SAMETZ, "Regions of Canada and the Regional Concept," in *Regional and Resource Planning in Canada,* ed. Ralph R. Krueger et al., pp. 6–23. Toronto: Holt, Rinehart and Winston of Canada, Ltd., 1963.

RAY, D. MICHAEL, *Dimensions of Canadian Regionalism.* Ottawa: Department of Energy, Mines and Resources, Policy Research and Coordination Branch, 1971.

SCHWARTZ, M. A., *Politics and Territory: The Sociology of Regional Persistence in Canada.* Montreal: McGill-Queens University Press, 1974.

TURNOCK, D., "The Region in Modern Geography," *Geography,* 52 (1967), 374–83.

WADE, MASON, ed., *Regionalism in the Canadian Community.* Toronto: University of Toronto Press, 1969.

6

NORTHEASTERN ANGLO-AMERICA

Northeastern Anglo-America is a predominantly rural region that contrasts sharply with the highly urbanized region to its south. It is a region in which the forest and the sea have been pervasive influences on the life style of its inhabitants. There is a sense of history and tradition, reflecting the relatively limited resources of the land and the relative richness of the adjacent ocean.

Included within the region are the less populated, rougher parts of northern New England and New York State, all of the Maritime Provinces except that portion of New Brunswick that is predominantly French-Canadian in population and culture, and the island of Newfoundland with a portion of the adjacent Labrador coast that is oriented toward "Newfoundland-type" commercial fishing (fig. 6–1). Interior Labrador is not included because of its sparse population and similarity to the Boreal Forest Region. Northern New Brunswick and adjacent Quebec are excluded because of the significant cultural differences in French Canada.

The most difficult decision to be made in delimiting Northeastern Anglo-America as a region is the separation of northern and southern New England. Throughout most of its history the people of New England have manifested a regional consciousness in greater degree, perhaps, than in any other part of Anglo-America. Their traditions, institutions, and ways of living and thinking have exhibited considerable uniformity; however, in recent years there has been a sharply increasing divergence between the way of life of the urbanites in southern New England and the people of the small towns and rural areas that characterize northern New England.[1] Furthermore, the economic and psychological orientation of much of southern New England is increasingly dominated by New York. It seems clear to the authors that urbanized southern New England is more logically a portion of the megalopolitan region to the south than it is of the rurally oriented region to the north. Accordingly, the southern boundary of Northeastern Anglo-America is considered to lie just north of the urbanized areas of Portland in Maine, the Merrimack Valley in New Hampshire, the small cities of western Massachusetts, and the Mohawk Valley of New York State.

[1] This New England dualism has been noted by several scholars in recent years. See, for example, Saul B. Cohen, "New England's Boundaries: How Realistic Are They?" *The New Englander* (August 1964), p. 8; and George K. Lewis, "Population Change in Northern New England," *Annals,* Association of American Geographers, 62 (1972), 308.

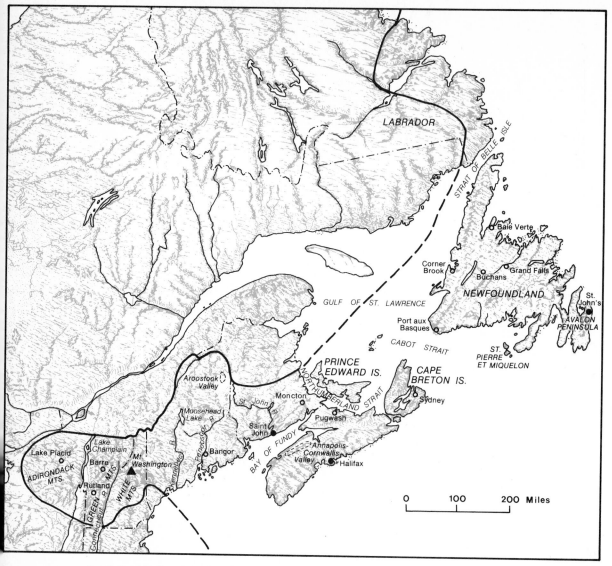

fig. 6–1 Northeastern Anglo-America (base map copyright A. K. Lobeck; reprinted by permission of Hammond, Inc.).

a region of scenic charm and economic disadvantage

Northeastern Anglo-America is a region that abounds in scenic delights: the verdant slopes of the Adirondacks, the rounded sky-line of the Green Mountains, quaint covered bridges and village greens, sparkling blue lakes, Maine's incredibly rockbound coast, the tide-carved pedestal rocks of the Bay of Fundy, the classical symmetry of Prince Edward Island's farm landscape, the ordered orchards of the Annapolis-Cornwallis Valley, the splendid harbors of Halifax and St.

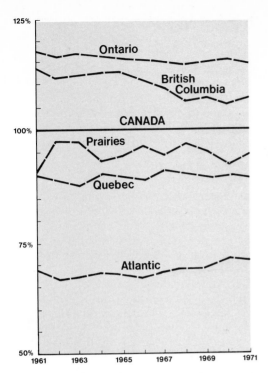

fig. 6-2 Regional personal income per capita as percentage of Canadian average. The significantly and persistently low position of the Atlantic Provinces is conspicuous. (After Ralph R. Krueger, "Regional Disparities and Regional Development in Canada," in *Regional Patterns: Disparities and Development*, ed. Ralph R. Krueger et al. [n.p.: Canadian Association of Geographers/Canada Studies Foundation, 1975] p. 6).

replacement takes many decades. Fishing was the mainstay of the economy for a great many years and has continued in declining importance, but the sea's contribution to the regional economy has been erratic and unstable. The rushing streams of the region were early sources of hydraulic and later hydroelectric power; but their productive capacity is limited, and Northeastern Anglo-America is a power-deficient region today.

The foreland location of the region gives it a closest-to-Europe position that provided early economic advantage; indeed, the port of St. John's has been referred to as being located halfway across the Atlantic. The foreland, however, can be easily bypassed in contemporary times. The more westerly location of the commercial-industrial heartland of the continent has drawn most trade either into the Boston–New York–Philadelphia axis or up the St. Lawrence River. The foreland position regained some of its former importance in war time, and there is an annual regeneration of activity for the Maritime ports when the St. Lawrence is closed by ice; but the long run commercial and strategic value of the foreland location is in marked decline.

This region has experienced slow economic growth, even in periods of national affluence. Its resources are too small and too scattered to tempt external investors. The region has been described as one of "effort" rather than of "increment."[2] Even government infusion of capital tends to be easily dispersed without bringing about much growth.

The population of the region is scattered, and there are only a few nodes of urban-industrial concentration. Essentially this is a region of emigration. The rates of population increase for the portions of four states and four provinces included in the region have consistently been among the

John's, the Old World charm of Newfoundland outports. Yet this region of delightful views has suffered longer and more continually from economic handicaps than any other on the continent (fig. 6-2).

Much of the problem is environmental. Soils are generally poor, the growing season is short and cool, the winter is long and bleak, mineral resources are scarce, and second-growth timber grows slowly. Timber, fish, and running water have been the chief physical advantages, but all three have handicaps. The readily accessible forests have long since been cut, and second-growth

[2] David Erskine, "The Atlantic Region," in *Canada: A Geographical Interpretation*, ed. John Warkentin (Toronto: Methuen Publications, 1968), p. 233.

lowest recorded on the continent. There has been a continual trend of Maritimers moving to Ontario, and northern New Englanders moving south.[3] And there has been no large influx of immigrants to compensate. Northern New England has absorbed a steady stream of French-Canadians into its forest industries, but mostly the region has not shared in the continent's high rate of net immigration or of net population growth. St. John's and Saint John have consistently been at the bottom of the list of population increment among Canada's metropolitan areas, with Halifax not far above.

Northern New England is economically depressed, and the four Atlantic Provinces have a long record as Canada's economic problem region. The extremes are all there, including lower income per person, lower goods output per capita, lower average investment of new capital, and higher unemployment. The Atlantic Provinces overall average nearly 30 percent below the per capita income for all Canada, a disparity that has persisted for decades.[4]

Many study committees have been established in both countries to prescribe remedies for the ills of Northeastern Anglo-America. Various assaults on economic deprivation have been mounted, and many palliatives have been tried. Some local benefits have been derived from these efforts, but the region as a whole continues to suffer; it remains a scenically attractive area, but many of its residents are economically disadvantaged.

---

[3] It has been noted that the Atlantic Provinces have furnished more migrants to Ontario than has any other area except Great Britain.

[4] A 1971 study showed that 37 percent of the population of the Atlantic Provinces had incomes below "the poverty line"; the next lowest showing was by the Prairie Provinces, with 27 percent; the all-Canada average was 23 percent. See Ralph R. Krueger, "Regional Disparities and Regional Development in Canada," in *Regional Patterns: Disparities and Development*, ed. Ralph R. Krueger et al. (n.p.: Canada Studies Foundation/Canadian Association of Geographers, 1975), p. 10.

the physical setting

Northeastern Anglo-America is a region of slopeland, forest, and coast; of bare rock, cold waters, and leaden skies; and of thin soils, swift streams, and implacable tides. It is a land where beavers still build dams, moose feed on lake bottoms, and Atlantic salmon come upstream to spawn.

SURFACE FEATURES

The coastal area consists primarily of low rounded hills and valleys. Most of the region is traversed by fast-flowing streams, and much of it is dotted with small lakes. The coastal area has been slightly submerged; accordingly, ocean waters have invaded the lower valleys, creating bays or estuaries. Often branch bays extend up the side valleys. The coast is characterized by innumerable good, if small, harbors. Superficially the coasts of Maine and Nova Scotia appear to be fiorded, but they are probably drowned normal river valleys that have been slightly modified by ice action. The restricted and indented nature of much of the coastline has given rise to some of the greatest tidal fluctuations to be found anywhere (fig. 6–3). Many rugged and rocky headlands extend to the water's edge, especially in Maine and Newfoundland. Beaches are relatively small and scarce.

All mountains of the upland area are geologically old and have been worn down by erosion. The Green Mountains of Vermont have rounded summits, the result of the great ice sheets that covered ridges and valleys alike. The highest peaks are less than 4,500 feet above sea level. The White Mountains are higher and bolder and were not completely overridden by the ice, as is shown by the occurrence of several cirques (locally called "ravines"); their highest points are in the Presidential Range, where Mount Washington reaches an elevation of nearly 6,300 feet. Northeastward the mountains become less conspicuous, although their summits remain at an approximate elevation of 5,000 feet.

fig. 6-3   The phenomenal tidal
fluctuations of the Bay of
Fundy serve as significant
erosive agents on softer
rocks. The 20-foot-high
evergreen trees growing on
this tide-carved pedestal
rock along the New
Brunswick coast give an
indication of scale.

The mountains of eastern Canada are lower and more rounded, having been subdued through long periods of erosion. Their general elevation is slightly more than 2,000 feet above sea level. The Adirondacks, geologically an extension of the Laurentian Uplands, are also considered a part of this region because of the similarity of the activities of the inhabitants. Although an older upland mass, the Adirondacks underwent changes at the time of the Appalachian mountain-building movement that caused a doming of the upper surface; furthermore, they were eroded profoundly during glacial times. Although not so high as the White Mountains, the Adirondacks cover more area.

The entire upland is composed largely of igneous and metamorphic rocks—granites, schists, gneisses, marbles, and slates—so valuable that this has become the leading source of building stones on the continent.

The stream courses of the upland area were altered by glaciation. Many water bodies, such as Lake Placid, Lake Winnipesaukee,[5] and Moosehead Lake, characterize the region (fig. 6-4). They have been of inestimable value in the development of the tourist industry.

The Aroostook Valley, occupying the upper part of the St. John River drainage, is the result of stream erosion in softer rocks. The Lake Champlain Lowland and the Connecticut Valley were severely eroded by tongues of ice that moved southward between the Green Mountains and the Adirondacks, and between the Green Mountains and the White Mountains. Many of the valleys and lowlands are underlain by sedimentary rocks.

Newfoundland consists of a combination of moorland and forest, with an abun-

fig. 6-4   There are thousands of lakes in the
region. This is Lake Willoughby in northern
Vermont (courtesy State of Vermont).

[5] There are on record 132 different ways of spelling this name. *Sixth Report of the United States Geographic Board* (Washington, D.C.: Government Printing Office, 1933), p. 822.

dance of rocks, ponds, and shrubby barrens. It has been described as

a queer dishevelled region where the Almighty appears to have assembled all the materials essential to a large-scale act of creation and to have quit with the job barely begun. Ponds are dropped indiscriminately in valleys and on hilltops, rocks strewn everywhere with purposeless prodigality.[6]

Much of the island is a rolling plateau 500 to 1,000 feet above sea level, with elevations above 3,000 feet in the Long Ranges. The coastline is severely indented; the juxtaposition of bay and peninsula is the most conspicuous feature of the littoral landscape. The coast of southern Labrador is the rugged, elevated, fiorded edge of the Laurentian Shield and is strewn with small offshore islands.

CLIMATE

Because of the maritime influence, the coastal areas, particularly in Maine and Nova Scotia, generally have a milder and more equable climate than might be expected in these latitudes. Nova Scotia's mean January temperature is about the same as that of central New York, despite being two to five degrees of latitude farther north. Winters, although long and cold, are not severe for the latitude. Temperatures may fall below zero, however, and snow covers the ground throughout most of the winter. Spring surrenders reluctantly to summer because of the presence of ice in the Gulf of St. Lawrence and because of the cold Labrador Current. Summers are cool, temperatures of 90° being extremely rare. The growing season varies from 100 to 160 days in Nova Scotia.

The precipitation of 40 to 55 inches is well distributed throughout the year. Southeast winds from the warm Gulf Stream blowing across the cold waters between the Gulf of Maine and Newfoundland create the summer fogs that characterize the coasts of New England, New Brunswick, and Nova Scotia. Newfoundland itself is famous for its foggy coasts.

The upland area lies within the humid continental climatic regime, with the Atlantic Ocean exerting little influence. The growing season is short, averaging less than 120 days. Summers are cool and winters extremely cold, temperatures dropping at times to 30° below zero. The abundant precipitation is evenly distributed throughout the year, but in winter most of it falls as snow. This seeming handicap has been turned to economic advantage by the commercial development of winter sports.

In Newfoundland and south coastal Labrador the climate is largely the result of a clash between continental and oceanic influences, with the former dominating. The winters are much colder than those in British Columbia or Britain in the same latitude. Altitude plays its role, as evidenced by the replacement of forest by tundra at elevations exceeding 1,000 or 1,200 feet.

No point in Newfoundland is more than 70 miles from salt water, but the ocean's relative coldness and the prevailing westerly winds, which bring continental influences, do not permit much amelioration of the temperatures. In the Gulf of St. Lawrence all harbors freeze over in the winter, the Strait of Belle Isle being completely blocked by ice. The bays on the Labrador coast and large areas of the adjacent sea freeze solid by October or November. Summers everywhere are cool because the Labrador Current, laden with ice floes and icebergs, moves southward along the east and south coasts.

Except for the south coast of Newfoundland, the entire island gets more than 100 inches of snow in winter. Ice storms, more common here than elsewhere in Anglo-America, occur when a south wind sets in. Rain freezes as it comes in contact with the colder ground. Fog is prevalent on the coasts and on the Grand Banks, but no more so than on the southern coasts of Nova Scotia.

---

[6] Edward McCourt, *The Road Across Canada* (Toronto: Macmillan of Canada, 1965), p. 16. By permission.

NATURAL VEGETATION

The great majority of the land included within this region was once covered with trees; however, it is difficult to get an accurate word-picture of the forest in its primitive state (fig. 6-5). The principal treeless localities were small areas of dunes, marshes, meadows, bogs, and exposed mountain summits, except in Newfoundland and coastal Labrador, where temperature, wind, and moisture conditions of the more extensive reaches of low scrubby barrens and modified tundra were inhibitory to tree growth.

The New England section was originally covered with a relatively dense forest of mixed deciduous and coniferous species. Even today more than 80 percent of the land is forested by a mixture of northern hardwoods, with white pine, spruce, and fir. Originally white pine was the outstanding tree; attaining a height of 240 feet and a diameter of 6 feet at the butt, it dwarfed even the tall spruce. It was sometimes called the "masting pine" because the larger trees were marked with the Royal Arrow and reserved for masts for the Royal Navy. Maine is still referred to as the "Pine Tree State." Most of the existing forest is second-growth; the original timber was cut for lumber and fuel or cleared for agriculture many decades ago. Only in the more remote parts of the uplands, primarily in Maine, are there still virgin stands of trees.

In the Maritime Provinces a mixed forest cover is also still widespread. Although it has been thoroughly removed from Prince Edward Island, most of the land is still forested in Nova Scotia, and forest clearing was even less common in southern New Brunswick. Some large areas of relatively pure hardwood or softwood species may be found, but mixed growth is much more common. Spruce, hemlock, fir, pine, maple, and birch are the typical trees.

The forests of Newfoundland are much more predominantly coniferous, with balsam fir, white and black spruce, larch, and some pines widespread. Birch and some

fig. 6-5 Most of Notheastern Anglo-America was originally forested, and much of it still is. This is the Adirondack Mountains (courtesy New York State Department of Commerce).

maples are associated. Nowhere are the trees large; as a result there is not much lumbering carried on, although pulping is important. The coast of Labrador is almost completely lacking in forest; but the sheltered stream basins support some tree growth, particularly in the Churchill River Valley.

SOILS

Due to differences in parent rock, slope, drainage, and previous extent of glaciation, the soils of Northeastern Anglo-America are varied; nevertheless, the dominant soils throughout the region are Spodosols. The only other soil order represented importantly in the region is Alfisol. These are soils that have developed under cool, moist conditions and are thus leached and acidic in nature. Usually there is a layer of organic accumulation near the surface, and more characteristically, considerable accumulation of compounds of iron and aluminum. A layer of clay accumulation is often found in the Alfisols of the valleys.

Agricultural productivity of these soils is undistinguished. Those that are derived from shales, especially in New Brunswick and northern Nova Scotia, are heavy and poorly drained. The sedimentary floored lowlands give rise to soils that are more fertile for farming; the shales of Vermont and the sandstones of the Annapolis Valley and Prince Edward Island yield more productive agricultural soils than are found elsewhere. Rockiness, poor drainage, and peat formation are major and widespread handicaps to crop and pasture development. Alluvial soils, occurring on narrow valley floodplains, are extremely important to agriculture even though their total acreage is small.

FAUNA

There is nothing out of the ordinary about the wildlife in most of the region; it is a "north woods" environment that contains a predictable faunal complement. One anomalous situation does prevail in Newfoundland. This large island was singularly lacking in a number of the common mainland terrestrial species. There were, for example, almost no rodents, especially the smaller varieties. Three very characteristic denizens of the north woods, porcupine, mink, and moose, were also missing. To remedy these deficiencies, introductions of exotic animals have been accomplished at various times during the past century. The most spectacular success resulted from the introduction of six moose about the turn of the century; the moose is now more numerous and widespread than the native caribou and has yielded more than 100,000 legal kills to hunters. Chipmunks and mink were also successfully introduced, and shrews were brought to Newfoundland to control a larch-destroying sawfly.

settlement
and early development

Northeastern Anglo-America was not settled by immigrants from a single country. The earliest settlers in New England were British, those in the Maritime Provinces were French, and both British and French originally settled in Newfoundland.

THE NEW ENGLAND SEGMENT

The first important settlement in what is now New England was founded at Plymouth in 1620. All the early colonies, including those before and immediately after the landing of the Pilgrims, were planted on the seaboard. The coast was, then, the first American frontier. Its settlements were bounded by untamed hills on the west and by the stormy Atlantic on the east. Beckoned by the soil and the sea, its shore-dwelling pioneers obeyed both, and their adjustments to the two environments laid the foundations for the land life and sea life of the nation.

As population became more dense in maritime New England and Canada, the more venturesome settlers trekked farther into the wilderness. So long as the French controlled the St. Lawrence Lowlands, the Indians of the upland remained entrenched in this so-called neutral ground, thus restricting white settlements to the seaboard. In the Adirondacks, hostile Iroquois kept the English confined to the Hudson and Mohawk valleys until the close of the Revolutionary War. Feeling that at last the power of the Indian had been broken after the conquest of Canada by the British, pioneers from the older parts of New England penetrated the upland. By the 1760s most of the lower valleys in New Hampshire and Vermont were occupied. The clearing of the forest for farms led to an early development of logging and lumbering, which could be carried on in winter when farm work was not feasible. The logs, dragged on the snow to frozen streams, were floated to mills in the spring when the ice melted; thus a supplemental source of income was provided for the pioneers, which continued to be important until the latter part of the nineteenth century.

MARITIME CANADA

The first permanent settlement in North America north of Florida was at Port Royal on the Bay of Fundy in 1605. Here the French found salt marshes that needed no clearing. This environment was attractive to people from the mouth of the Loire, whose forebears for generations had reclaimed and diked somewhat similar land. These French called their new home *Acadie* (Acadia). The Acadians converted the river marshes into productive farmland that characterized the cultivated area almost exclusively for a century.

The French population grew rapidly after the Treaty of Utrecht in 1713. Louisburg was fortified to guard the mouth of the St. Lawrence and the fishing fleet. The Acadians remained until the outbreak of hostilities between the British and French preceding the Seven Years' War in the 1750s. Then more than 6,000 of them were rounded up and banished; they were scattered from Massachusetts to South Carolina. Some fled into the forests of what are now New Brunswick, Prince Edward Island, and Quebec; some made their way to Quebec City, the Ohio Valley, and even to Louisiana; and others joined the French in St. Pierre, Miquelon, and the West Indies. Many starved. The reason most commonly given for their expulsion was fear on the part of England that such a heavy concentration of French in this part of the continent was a menace to English safety.

This dispersal continued for eight years, ending in 1763; then individuals and groups began to trickle back. Though denied their old properties, they found abodes here and there, mostly on the gulf coast of New Brunswick, the western part of Prince Edward Island, and at scattered localities in Nova Scotia. Frenchmen never returned to Newfoundland in any meaningful numbers.

The first significant arrival of British settlers in the Atlantic Provinces was in 1610 in Newfoundland. Despite a hard and lonely life, oriented almost exclusively toward export of salted codfish, increasing numbers of English and Irish settlers occupied the numerous bays of southeastern Newfoundland through the seventeenth century. By 1750 British settlers and New Englanders were beginning to come in large numbers to Nova Scotia and New Brunswick. Shortly afterward 2,000 Germans founded Lunenburg. Large migrations of Scottish people, principally from the Highlands, came after 1800, dominating the population of Nova Scotia and, to a lesser extent, Prince Edward Island.

the present inhabitants

There is a remarkable homogeneity to the contemporary population of Northeastern Anglo-America. The vast majority of the people are of white Anglo-Saxon ancestry. English is the only language of importance, except along the northern margin of the region and in scattered pockets of French settlement; the religious affiliation over large areas is dominantly Protestant except in locales of French or Irish Catholic settlement; and most of the people who live in the region were born in the region, often the offspring of several generations in the region.

The taciturn, traditionally conservative Yankee stereotype is still dominant in northern New England. Yankees descended from antecedents who during a "period of poverty and struggle . . . beat down the forest, won the fields, sailed the seas, and went forth to populate Western commonwealths."[7] Similar British stock, often referred to as Loyalists, originally peopled much of the Atlantic Provinces of Canada and remains dominant today.

The population of the Atlantic Provinces is somewhat less uniform than that of northern New England because large blocks of immigrants settled in groups and have generally tended to occupy the same areas for generations. The origins are usually English, Scottish, or Irish. For example, in eastern Newfoundland in general and the Avalon Peninsula in particular the population is about 95 percent Irish Catholic, except for the city of St. John's. Similarly most of Cape Breton Island is a stronghold of Highland Scots, and people of Scottish ancestry predominate throughout northeastern Nova Scotia, eastern New Brunswick, and Prince Edward Island.

[7] J. Russell Smith and M. Ogden Phillips, *North America* (New York: Harcourt, Brace & Co., 1940), p. 113.

The French component of the population, so important in the early days of Acadian settlement, is today largely marginal. A large proportion of the New Brunswick population is of French origin, but their dominance is in the northern part of the province, which is considered to lie outside this region. With increasing distance from Quebec, the French element in the New Brunswick population rapidly decreases. Along the northern margin of New England, from Maine's Aroostook Valley to the northeastern New York counties of Clinton and Franklin, there is a significant number of French-Canadians who have migrated across the international border to work in forests and mills.[8] Otherwise, clusters of French-Canadians are found at several places in Nova Scotia and

Prince Edward Island. Wherever the French occur in Northeastern Anglo-America, the traditional manifestations of their culture, typified by the French language and the Roman Catholic religion, are prevalent.

As a general rule, the cities of Northeastern Anglo-America have a more variegated populace than the small towns and rural areas. The larger the urban place, the more cosmopolitan its population is likely to be; thus all the cities of the region have various minority ethnic groups, although their numbers are few (fig. 6–6).

The people of this region are mostly long-time residents. Emigration takes place to Megalopolis, to Toronto, and to the Prairie Provinces, but there is little immigration to balance it. This can be illustrated by comparing the birthplaces of the people of Atlantic cities with those of other Canadian cities.[9] Of the nineteen metropolitan areas in Canada, the three Atlantic cities of St. John's, Saint John, and Halifax rank second, third, and fourth, respectively (exceeded only by Quebec City), in proportion of their population born in Canada; and second, fifth, and sixth, respectively, in proportion of their population born in the same province.

Most of the character of any region is asserted by the attitudes, traditions, and values of its people and by the imprint of these intangibles on the regional landscape. Northeastern Anglo-America is singularly rich in this regard. The relative homogeneity and stability of the populace over a long period of time has produced a regional image that is part fact and part fiction, but that could be produced only as a consequence of people of the same background living in comparative isolation and eking out an existence in a harsh environment.

The elements of this image are difficult to define and the cause-and-effect relationships are obscure, but some of its manifesta-

---

[8] Bilingual (English and French) road signs are found in northern Vermont.

fig. 6–6 Principal ethnic components of cities in the Atlantic Provinces. Relative homogeneity is typical. (After C. N. Forward, "Cities: Function, Form and Future," in *The Atlantic Provinces*, ed. Alan Macpherson [Toronto: University of Toronto Press, 1972], p. 146. Reprinted by permission.)

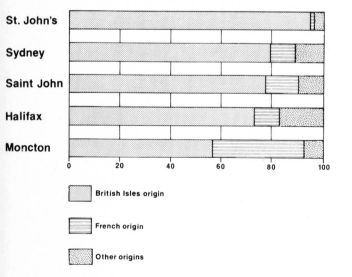

[9] Adapted from James and Robert Simmons, *Urban Canada* (Toronto: Copp Clark Publishing Company, 1969), p. 43.

tions are conspicuous. As Edward McCourt has observed about "Newfies," the people of this region "have evolved their own mores, created their own culture, made and sung their own songs, and added to the language according to their need."[10]

One aspect of the cultural character of the region relates to the form and charm of the small units of settlement, the hamlet and village. The name of the village is likely to sound as pleasant as it appears. Thus travelers in central New Hampshire can stop at the hamlet of Sandwich; if unsatisfied there, they can drive on to the next village, Center Sandwich; or the next, North Sandwich. Vivid place names persist throughout the region. Consider a selection from Newfoundland: Harbour Grace, Heart's Delight, Witless Bay, Doting Cove, Bay Bulls, Maiden Arm, Uncle Dickies Burr, Come By Chance, and Hug My Dug Island.

The village form has a certain uniformity: the fishing hamlet clustered on a tiny beach about the head of a bay and the farming town rectangularly arrayed around the village green. Actually village greens are present in almost every town in northern New England but very uncommon in Canada's Atlantic Provinces. White, tall-spired churches with their adjacent cemeteries are, however, the dominant edifices in villages throughout the region.

The rural landscape also has characteristic regional forms. The covered bridge, for example, is a famous feature in northern New England and is often carefully cultivated as a tourist attraction. Covered bridges are common throughout the Maritimes and are more prevalent in New Brunswick than in any part of New England. House-and-barn arrangements are also interesting. The attached house and barn is notable in New Hampshire and Maine. In Vermont, on the other hand, the house and barn are often located adjacent to the road but on opposite sides, presumably to take advantage of the snow-clearing efforts of the road crews.

[10] McCourt, *The Road Across Canada*, p. 30.

the decline of agriculture

Although Newfoundlanders were fishermen from the start, farming was the first occupation of the colonists in the Maritime Provinces and northern New England. It was on a small scale and usually on infertile soil; moreover, the short, often overly wet summers and the long, cold winters retarded the development of a thriving agriculture.

NEW ENGLAND

Despite environmental difficulties and a scarcity of accessible markets, agricultural settlement had spread widely over northern New England by the beginning of the nineteenth century. Farms were small and not very prosperous, but an agrarian way of life was clearly established.

The opening of the Erie Canal across New York State in 1825 ushered in major changes in the land use and settlement patterns of rural New England. The accessibility of much better farmland in the Midwest attracted some New Englanders, but more significant was the sudden competition from lower-cost producers of crops and livestock in these new areas.

The peak in rural population and agricultural development in northern New England occurred in about the 1820s, and a large-scale exodus of population began soon afterward, continuing for decades (fig. 6–7). In New Hampshire, for example, most towns (the name given to minor civil divisions in New England) lost population in every census for a century.[11] Cultivated fields were downgraded to hayfields, then to rough pasture, and ultimately reverted to woodland. Today there is abundant evidence of farm abandonment in the form of ramshackle stone walls that used to bound the fields but now merely border plots of tangled and forested wilderness. Also, the large

[11] William H. Wallace, "A Hard Land for a Tough People: A Historical Geography of New Hampshire," *New Hampshire Profiles* (April 1975), p. 26.

1920 POPULATION
LESS THAN 1860

1920 POPULATION MORE THAN
1860 BUT MAXIMUM BEFORE 1920

1920 POPULATION
MORE THAN 1860

40 MILES

fig. 6–7 Population change in New Hampshire from 1860 to 1920. The long-term population decline was experienced in all parts of the state, a typical situation in northern New England. (After William H. Wallace, "A Hard Land for a Tough People: A Historical Geography of New Hampshire," *New Hampshire Profiles* [April 1975] p. 28.)

shade trees that were planted along many country lanes are now almost indistinguishable from the naturally regenerated forest.

Overall, then, farming in northern New England has been on a declining trend for well over a century. New Hampshire exemplified the pattern: by the middle of the nineteenth century about 40 percent of the state's area had been cleared, mostly for farming; one hundred years later cleared farmland was only 7 percent of the total area.

THE MARITIME PROVINCES

Agriculture began in the Maritimes in the seventeenth century when, by diking, the Acadians reclaimed the tidal marshes along the Bay of Fundy. Before their expulsion in 1755, some 10,000 Acadians were comfortably supported in Nova Scotia. It is estimated that they had put 100,000 acres of land into pasture, orchard, and garden.

Because much of Nova Scotia and New Brunswick is characterized by low rounded mountain ranges, lakes, swamps, and forests, arable land has always been restricted. Most of New Brunswick is still in forest. Nova Scotia, although more favored, is not well endowed for agriculture; scarcely one-third of its area is occupied as farmland. Its productive areas are confined primarily to the western coastal belt, the Atlantic Coast being an upland of crystalline rocks. The first successful farming colony was in the meadows around Port Royal (now Annapolis). Subsequent settlement was along the more extensive marshlands around Minas Basin and Cobequid Bay and at the head of Chignecto Bay.

present-day agriculture

Today agriculture throughout Northeastern Anglo-America continues on a small scale.

NEW ENGLAND

Dairying is the principal farm activity in northern New England, and with excellent transportation facilities, the emphasis is on whole-milk production. In addition to hay, corn is widely grown as a feed crop for the dairy herds. It is mostly cut green for silage. The better soils of Vermont are reflected in corn production statistics; Maine and New Hampshire combined yield only half as much silage corn as Vermont.

The most dynamic aspect of northern New England agriculture in recent years has been the poultry industry. Although there is some emphasis on egg production, the principal focus is the raising of broilers (young, tender-meated chickens weighing about three pounds). Income from poultry exceeds that from dairying in both New Hampshire and Maine, and there is a particular concentration of the industry in Waldo County of the latter state. Gigantic, multistory chicken "hotels" dominate the farm scene in this area; the industry is mostly an indoor operation throughout the year (fig. 6-8). The Maine operations are relatively costly in comparison with their competitors in the southern states, but quality control is much closer owing to highly integrated production procedures, with the result that Maine birds command premium prices on the New York market.

Aside from corn, field crops are relatively minor on the farm scene except in a few specialty areas. Vegetables are grown near the southern margin of the region, for sale in megalopolitan cities, and potatoes are fairly widespread, especially in the upper Connecticut Valley. For the most part, agriculture in northern New England means hay, dairying, and chickens.

THE ATLANTIC PROVINCES

In Nova Scotia the cultivated land lies mostly in the northwestern lowland, the granitic interior and the Atlantic Coast tending to discourage settlement; 75 percent of the land is still in forest. The diked lands of Old Acadia, made famous by Longfellow in *Evangeline,* are still fertile, easily cultivated, and productive. Farm crops are primarily those that mature in a short growing season: forage crops, potatoes, vegetables, and fruits.

In New Brunswick the area in farms is about equal to that in Nova Scotia, but the area in field crops is nearly twice as great. That the province is not outstanding agriculturally seems proved by the fact that forest still covers nine-tenths of the land. An exception is the Saint John River Valley, which is farmed almost as intensively as the Connecticut Valley, although the crop possibilities are more limited (fig. 6-9). The upper part of the valley is a major potato-growing area. Pasture is less important here than in Nova Scotia. Dairying is favored in southern New Brunswick by heavy summer precipitation and proximity to urban markets. Farming in New Brunswick is characterized by small and fragmented areas of

fig. 6-8　A typical, enormous broiler "hotel," near Waterville, Maine.

fig. 6-9　The principal agricultural area of New Brunswick is the St. John Valley, where much of the forest has been cleared (courtesy Tourism New Brunswick).

fertile soil, a large proportion of part-time farmers, and a 70-year history of farm abandonment.

Prince Edward Island, with about two-thirds of its inhabitants engaged in farming, sustains a relatively prosperous agriculture (fig. 6-10). About two-thirds of the total area of the province is in farms, a much

113

fig. 6–10 Many of the "ordinary" farms of Prince Edward Island have the appearance of country estates, with their large and immaculate buildings.

higher ratio than in any other political unit in Anglo-America. Overall, the countryside is a delight to the eye, with alternation of field and woodlot, unbelievably green cultivated land, neat farmsteads, and a frequent view of water. The principal commercial crop is potatoes. The island enjoys an international reputation for certified seed potatoes.

The rigorous physical environment of Newfoundland militates against significant agricultural development; however, it has been pointed out that institutions and land policy of the past may be equally important in explaining why only 1/5000 of the area of the island is in improved farmland.[12] In any event, subsistence farming is now less important than at any time in Newfoundland's history, and the number of farms on the island continues to decline. But both the number and acreage in commercial farms is slowly rising, and some farms in the vicinity of St. John's are actually turning a profit.

[12] Peter Crabb, "Some Aspects of Agriculture in Newfoundland," in *Newfoundland: Introductory Essays and Excursion Guides* (St. John's: Department of Geography, Memorial University of Newfoundland, 1969), p. 21.

agricultural specialization

AROOSTOOK COUNTY AND POTATOES

Northeastern Maine produces nearly one-tenth of the total potato crop of the United States. The area lies in a narrow belt from one to three townships wide along the northeastern border of the state. It has a short growing season and easily cultivated silty loam glacial soil. Large-scale enterprises and highly mechanized production methods have built up a sizable industry in this remote corner of the United States. Emphasis is on the growing of seed potatoes for sale in other parts of the country.

THE ANNAPOLIS-CORNWALLIS VALLEY AND APPLES

A large proportion of Canada's leading fruit crop, the apple, is produced in the Annapolis-Cornwallis Valley, the only area of outstanding commercial agriculture in Nova Scotia. This fairly level valley, 70 miles long and 2 to 8 miles wide, is sheltered from northwest winds and fogs by North Mountain, which lies along the Bay of Fundy. The valley trends in a general west-east direction from Annapolis to Wolfville, with the bulk of the orchards concentrated in the eastern end.

Despite its favorable production factors,[13] the growers of the valley have faced an abnormal number of marketing problems, owing in part to an individualized approach to selling (neither cooperative nor centralized marketing has attracted a majority of the growers). After the wartime loss of their

[13] The valley has long enjoyed a lower per-tree cost of production than any other major orchard area in Anglo-America, according to Ralph R. Krueger, "The Geography of the Orchard Industry in Canada," in *Readings in Canadian Geography*, rev. ed., ed. Robert M. Irving (Toronto: Holt, Rinehart and Winston of Canada, Limited, 1972), p. 223.

critical British market, the growers underwent a lengthy period of restructuring their operations, primarily by decreasing the number of trees and changing the varieties of apples grown. The number of apple trees today is only about one-tenth as large as it was in the peak years early in the century, but production is nearly one-fourth of Canada's total. More than two-thirds of the output is converted into processed apple products, rather than being sold fresh.

forest industries

Northeastern Anglo-America, the continent's pioneer logging region, possessed an almost incomparable forest of tall straight conifers and valuable hardwoods. Perhaps nine-tenths of the region was forest-covered. For 200 years or more after the landing of the Pilgrims in 1620, the settlers uninterruptedly continued the removal of trees.

The heyday of forest industries in New England is long since past. There is still considerable woodland, but much of the good timber is inaccessible and much of the accessible timber is of poor quality. Even so, a moderate quantity of sawtimber is cut each year, although no state in the region ranks among the 20 leaders in annual lumber production. Pulpwood production is more significant; in most years only a half dozen states yield more than Maine.

Most of the forest land in Maine is owned by large corporations. In the northern two-thirds of the state, some 75 percent of the land is in only 20 ownerships. Timber cutting for pulp and paper manufacture is the predominant activity; lumbering is still important but is declining. The operations of the logging companies have enhanced forest recreation by permitting increased accessibility over logging roads, improved wildlife habitats by opening up the dense forest stands, and provided artificial lakes. But the damming of Maine's few remaining wild rivers is a source of great controversy among conservationists, and debates over the value of wildland development policies promise to be long-continuing.

Logging and lumbering have also been important in the Canadian portion of Northeastern Anglo-America, especially in New Brunswick where all other economic activities have been secondary. Trading in lumber in the Maritimes began as early as 1650. Mariners returning to Europe took cargoes of masts, spars, and ship timber.

New Brunswick produces nearly half of all lumber and pulpwood in the Atlantic Provinces (fig. 6–11). Moreover, its sawmills and pulp mills are mostly larger than the ones in the other provinces. Nova Scotia's forest land, unlike that of New Brunswick and Newfoundland, is largely in private ownership; there is a roughly even balance between output of lumber and pulpwood, with processing mostly in small mills. In Newfoundland most of the productive forest land is owned or leased by three large pulp and paper companies; commercial output is heavily oriented toward pulpwood, although there is also a great deal of subsistence logging for firewood. The limited forest land of Prince Edward Island is mostly in small, individually owned woodlots. For the Atlantic Provinces as a whole, the cutting of pulpwood is nearly twice as great as timber harvesting for all other purposes combined.

fig. 6–11 Clearcutting is now a widely used logging technique in Northeastern Anglo-America. This area is near Fredericton, New Brunswick.

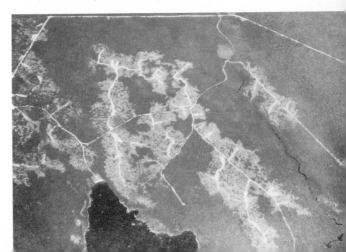

fishing

Fish was the first export from the New World. From Newfoundland to Cape Cod lie offshore banks that are one of the richest fishing grounds in the world. These banks were frequented by Scandinavian, Portuguese, Dutch, English, and French fishermen before the period of colonization in America. As early as 1504, Breton and Norman fishermen were catching cod in the western North Atlantic; and by 1577 France had 150 vessels, Spain 100, Portugal 50, and England 15, fishing for cod on the banks.[14]

Banks are shallows in the ocean at or near the outer margin of the continental shelf. Occasionally they reach the surface, although ordinarily they lie 100 to 200 feet below it. Banks are invaluable for fishing: their very shallowness makes fishing convenient, and their waters are rich in fish because the sun's rays penetrate to an adequate depth for the abundant growth of plankton, which is the primary unit of the food chain.

The early fisheries concentrated largely on cod, which was salted, pickled, and especially, dried for export to European, largely Mediterranean, and tropical markets. Maximum production of dried salted cod was reached in the 1880s, but changing fishing conditions and market requirements caused a gradual decline that has continued to the present. Around the turn of the century lobster replaced cod as the principal source of income to New England and Maritime fishermen, although the trade in fresh and processed fish has continued to flourish with irregularity.

During the present century freezing replaced drying, salting, and pickling as the major technique of preserving fish en route to market. Two important technological improvements have reshaped the industry during this period. The first, developed in the 1920s, was the technique of filleting and the quick-freezing of the fillets. Then in the 1950s came the change to fish sticks, made by cutting small rectangular pieces from fillets and cooking them in batter prior to freezing.

COASTAL FISHING

Usually coastal fishing is done within a few miles of shore in small motorboats carrying two or three people. The catch is brought into port each day; however, some "draggers" (inshore trawlers) from 30 to 50 tons in size may stay away from port as long as 48 hours. The fish caught are primarily cod, haddock, mackerel, and herring. Herring and squid are used for bait. The bulk of the catch, after gutting and washing, is kept fresh in ice-packed chambers.

DEEP-SEA FISHING

For banks or deep-sea fishing, large vessels are used in the deeper waters over the extensive reaches of the banks where bottom fish such as cod, cusk, flounder, and haddock are sought. Most of the vessels are trawlers that are designed for the wholesale taking of demersal (bottom-feeding) fish by scooping them into a long, funnel-shaped net-bag. Also important are midwater trawlers, which drag their trawls at predetermined depths above the ocean floor to catch free-swimming fish; seiners; purse-seiners; offshore long-liners; and scallop draggers.

In the last decade the stern trawler has been introduced and has rapidly become the most popular and efficient of the fishing vessels. It drags a conventional otter or midwater trawl, but the trawl is handled over the stern of the boat rather than over the side, which permits the fishermen to continue operating in heavy weather and allows for the handling of the catch below decks rather than topside.

LOBSTER FISHING

From Newfoundland to Massachusetts, millions of lobsters are caught each year. Although the catch has been reduced by

---

[14] R. H. Fiedler, "Fisheries of North America," *Geographical Review*, 30 (April 1940), 201.

overfishing in the past, it has held its own in recent years. Lobsters are usually taken in baited traps (called lobster pots) as they crawl about in shallow water looking for food, but more recently deep-sea trawlers have been taking large quantities of lobsters further out on the continental shelf.

Lobsters provide the principal source of income for commercial fishermen in Maine and all three Maritime Provinces but are less important in Newfoundland. Nova Scotia fishermen take more than half of all Canadian lobsters, and fishermen from Maine catch over 50 percent of the total in the United States. Most of the catch is marketed alive or freshly boiled, or the frozen tail is sold.

FISHING IN NEWFOUNDLAND AND COASTAL LABRADOR

Newfoundland from its earliest days was a staple product colony, the staple being codfish. For three centuries the bulk of the populace was fishermen. They sold their catch to local merchants, who passed it on to exporters in St. John's, who depended on distant and unstable markets. The consequence was a precarious economy with continuing poverty for most of the fishermen and an uncertain opulence for the St. John's exporters.[15] Catching cod in inshore waters remained the unchallenged base for Newfoundland's limited economy until the close of the nineteenth century.

In this century Newfoundland's seaward outlook has weakened, and the contribution of fishing to the provincial income has declined steadily; it is now substantially below that from mining and forestry. But there are still more than 12,000 inshore fishermen in Newfoundland, mostly living in small villages (called outports) at the heads of innumerable bays scattered around the island. Most of their fishing is done within the bays or slightly beyond them; they set

cod traps in the bay mouths, use a variety of nets, and use hook-and-line further out. Before being marketed in Europe, most of the cod used to be cleaned and then dried on racks (called flakes) in the uncertain Newfoundland sun. Nowadays a small percentage of the catch is still handled in this fashion, but the great bulk is filleted, frozen, and sold in the United States.

The Labrador coastal fishery is similar; relatively small-scale fishing for cod is done in bays or near-coastal waters. The permanent residents of this coast are called *liveyeres* (presumably a corruption of those who "live here"), but they are outnumbered by summer fishermen who come up from Newfoundland either as "stationers" (who live ashore in temporary camps) or as "floaters" (who live aboard their schooners).

While the inshore fishing industry of Newfoundland and coastal Labrador has been retrenching, the capital-intensive offshore fishery has been expanding. This operation involves larger boats fishing out on the banks or along the Greenland coast and is oriented toward fish other than cod, especially herring. Competition from European fishermen in the same waters is strong.

THE VALUE OF THE FISHERIES

Despite continuous exploitation for more than four centuries, the western North Atlantic fisheries continue to provide a large and important supply of food—more than 2 billion pounds a year. Two-fifths of the total annual Canadian catch and about one-tenth of the total United States catch are from this area (fig. 6–12). In total value of landings among Canadian provinces, Nova Scotia, Newfoundland, New Brunswick, and Prince Edward Island rank second, third, fourth, and fifth, respectively (British Columbia is first.)

In Nova Scotia, Prince Edward Island, and Newfoundland, the catching and processing of fish contribute about 14 percent of the value added in all "commodity-producing industries" (essentially all primary and

---

[15] A. R. M. Lower, " 'British North America' in the 1860's," *Canada: One Hundred, 1867–1967* (Ottawa: Dominion Bureau of Statistics, 1967), p. 7.

fig. 6-12 Small fishing villages, such as Peggy's Cove, Nova Scotia, dot the coastline of the region (courtesy Canadian Pacific Railway).

the possibility of diversifying the catch increases the technological challenge.

Mounting concern for the conservation of fish stocks has brought about the formation of an International Commission for the Northwest Atlantic Fisheries, with membership from the 16 nations that do most of the banks fishing. Probably the most useful action of the commission has been in instituting minimum mesh sizes in otter trawls to permit the escape of smaller fish. But as with most such maritime resource-control organizations, the effectiveness of the commission is limited by the extent of cooperation among the individual fishermen.

secondary production).[16] In no other province does it exceed 5 percent of the total. To Canada, the world's fourth leading exporter of fish products (exceeded only by Japan, Norway, and Denmark), the northwestern Atlantic fisheries continue to be very significant. They are less important to the United States; Massachusetts (with fishermen operating mostly in this area) ranks fifth among the states in total catch, and Maine ranks eighth.

The fishery of Northeastern Anglo-America continues to be a troubled industry. The growing scarcity of fish increases operating costs.[17] The continuing need for modernization requires much capital investment at a time when profits are not high. Well-established European fishermen provide effective competition. Pollution is affecting many of the inshore fishing areas, having decimated the clam fishery along the coast of Maine. As shown in recent expansion of Cape Breton swordfishing and dragging for deep-sea scallops off Nova Scotia,

[16] Fisheries and Marine Service, Environment Canada, *Annual Statistical Review of Canadian Fisheries*, vol. 9 (Ottawa: Environment Canada, 1976), p. 26.
[17] Fish landings in the region have declined every year but one since 1968.

mining

There is a long history of mining in the region, particularly in relation to coal in Nova Scotia and iron ore in Newfoundland; however, productivity has been irregular and prosperity has been limited. Still, mining is an important contributor to regional income, especially in Newfoundland.

Coal has been mined in Nova Scotia for more than a century, mostly on the north shore of Cape Breton Island. Production has declined for the last three decades, however, and it was anticipated that all mining would cease early in the 1980s. The energy crisis of the mid-1970s suddenly provided an impetus to turn the situation around, and a sizable expansion of activity is now under way.

Another traditional mining activity of the region is the production of *iron ore* on the flanks of the Adirondack Mountains in northern New York state. Output has been erratic for more than 100 years, but large reserves of magnetite are still present, and in most years New York is the fourth-ranking state in iron ore production.

There are a half dozen notable mining localities on the island of Newfoundland. Most significant is Buchans, in the western interior, where sulfide ores holding copper, lead, zinc, silver, and gold are extracted. At Baie Verte on the north coast are large mines yielding asbestos and copper.

Most of Canada's gypsum is produced in Nova Scotia. There is considerable output of rock salt in the northwestern corner of that province, at Pugwash.

The *quarrying* of building stone has for many decades been the only significant "mining" activity in northern New England. The hard rock complex underlying most of this subregion has long been an important supplier of granite, marble, and slate, particularly from several locations in Vermont. Demand for these high-quality stones has decreased in recent years, however, and the prominence of quarrying has declined.

recreation

Tourist-oriented recreation has been a mainstay of northern New England's economy since World War II. The relatively cool summers are attractive to most tourists, and the snowy winters are popular with skiers (fig. 6–13). Moreover, the area is immediately adjacent to the huge population of Megalopolis, and there are well-developed expressways and toll roads to enable urbanites to reach secluded rural retreats and wildlands in a relatively short time.

Within the last decade there has been a great upsurge in interest in owning second homes in northern New England. Rural land values, which had remained remarkably depressed considering their nearness to large population clusters, have now skyrocketed. Condominium clusters and other kinds of resort living have mushroomed on mountainsides and lakeshores.

Tourism is less significant and more seasonal in the Atlantic Provinces. The great majority of visitors during the relatively short summer tourist season comes from nearby localities in the Maritimes or from neighboring Quebec. There are six national parks in the Canadian section of this region, but the visitors seem to be particularly attracted to the beach resorts of Prince Edward Island. The two ferry systems connecting the island to the continent are drastically overcrowded during the summer;

fig. 6–13 The ski slopes are shorter and gentler in the East than in the West, but the reliability of snowfall attracts great hordes of winter sports enthusiasts from nearby locations as well as from more distant cities. This is Stratton Mountain in Vermont (courtesy State of Vermont).

consequently there is much interest in the idea of constructing a bridge-and-tunnel connection from Prince Edward Island to the mainland.

urbanism and urban activities

We have seen that Northeastern Anglo-America is largely a region of rural charm, rural activities, and economic impoverishment. The people of the region, as with almost all regions in Anglo-America, are now mostly urbanites, however, and the endeavors that provide most of the jobs and contribute most to the economy of the region are urban-oriented endeavors. The primary activities of farming, mining, and fishing are quite important and are conspicuous in the landscape; but the secondary and tertiary activities of manufacturing, trade, services, construction, and governmental functions actually dominate the economy, and their locus is mostly in urban areas.

There are no large cities in the region. There are, however, many long-established urban places, and it is in these that economic growth is concentrated and population growth is taking place. As of the late

1970s, approximately one-half of the inhabitants of Northeastern Anglo-America were urban.

Much of this pattern of urban growth and rural stagnation is also common to other regions of Anglo-America. Both economic opportunities and the material amenities of life tend to be prevalent in cities; consequently, immigrants from other regions or other continents usually settle in the cities. And as rural opportunities diminish, particularly in agriculture and fishing,

there is a rural-to-urban population drift—especially among younger people—which is long-established and well-recognized. There is a specialized regional component to this "normal" pattern in Newfoundland, where a deliberate government resettlement scheme is significantly restructuring the pattern of small urban communities (see vignette below).

The industrial functions normally associated with cities are limited and specialized in Northeastern Anglo-America. Among the

newfoundland outport resettlement

fig. 6-a A representative Newfoundland outport, The Battery.

fig. 6-b Distribution of outports in Newfoundland, ca. 1947.

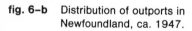

Ever since the beginning of European settlement in Newfoundland, most of the residents have been inshore fishermen living in hundreds of tiny outports scattered around the highly embayed coast of the island (fig. 6-a). Although there had been a general drift of people to larger urban places for some years, at the time Newfoundland became a province of Canada in 1949 more than half the population of the island still resided in outports, of which there were some 1,200 (fig. 6-b). The typical outport was a small but sprawling (unless the site was too steep) settlement at the head of a mainland bay or in a sheltered cove of an offshore island in which a few dozen to a few hundred people lived. Most homes had seaside locations, so that each family could have space for both a wharf and a garden.

The traditional outport economy was a more-or-less balanced combination of subsistence and commercial production.[a] The former included produce from the garden, products from the few livestock on hand, and miscellaneous items gleaned by cutting in the forest or by hunting and fishing. In most outports the only commercial product was fish, and this was dominated by cod. The cod was dried and sold to the local fish-buyer or merchant, the transaction often being on a credit basis with little or no cash changing hands.

[a] Cato Wadel, *Marginal Adaptations and Modernization in Newfoundland*, Newfoundland Social and Economic Studies, no. 7 (St. John's: Institute of Social and Economic Research, Memorial University of Newfoundland, 1969), p. 9.

cities of this region, Halifax alone is large enough to encompass a relatively full range of manufacturing activities, but it is by no means a major industrial center. Notable specialized industrial centers include Sydney–North Sydney (fig. 6–14) in Nova Scotia (iron and steel) and Bangor in Maine (lumber and pulp).

Many of the more prominent manufacturing facilities of Northeastern Anglo-America are located in small towns or even in rural localities several miles from any town. This is particularly true of wood-processing plants, both those producing sawn lumber and those whose output is pulp and/or paper. Some of the major mills are located in medium-sized "cities," such as Corner Brook, Newfoundland; but more often the mill site is associated with much smaller urban places, such as Berlin, New Hampshire, or Millinocket, Maine. Fish-processing facilities, too, are often found in small coastal settlements rather than in the larger cities.

The small size, great dispersal, and frequent lack of landward accessibility meant that most outports were greatly lacking in social services and normal amenities. Such basic requisites as schools, doctors, and roads were either absent or scarce. Thus, the majority of the population was characterized by a low level of income, education, and social well-being.

Both the provincial and federal governments became convinced that the only likely amelioration of this situation would have to come about through population resettlement, that is, phasing out an "obsolete" distribution pattern by shifting people from the many tiny outports to larger, more centralized communities. Although a number of outports were voluntarily abandoned in the early 1950s, it was in 1954 that the Newfoundland government formalized its "Centralization Program," in which each family would be paid $600 if the whole community moved within two years.[b] In the ensuing decade nearly 200 small communities were abandoned, with some 8,000 people resettling elsewhere.

In 1965 the federal government joined the provincial government in offering a "Household Resettlement Program" that would provide each migrating householder with $1,000 plus $200 for each member of the family, as well as the actual cost of moving. Moreover, only 80 percent of the community had to agree to move to become eligible for financial assistance, but the move was supposed to be only to designated growth centers.[c] Under this legislation, an average of about two dozen outports has been abandoned annually, with resettlement of about 3,000 persons per year (fig. 6-c).

[c] J. Lewis Robinson, "Changing Settlement Patterns in Newfoundland," *Geographical Review*, 65 (April 1975), 268. (*Continued*)

fig 6–c Outport closure is a continuing process. This map shows the communities in Newfoundland that were resettled in the earlier years of the program. (Based on data in Cato Wadel, *Marginal Adaptations and Modernization in Newfoundland* [St. John's: Memorial University of Newfoundland, Institute of Social and Economic Research, 1969], p. 4.)

[b] C. Grant Head, "Settlement Migration in Central Bonavista Bay, Newfoundland," in *Canada's Changing Geography*, ed. R. Louis Gentilcore (Scarborough, Ont.: Prentice-Hall of Canada, Ltd., 1967), p. 109.

50 Miles

• Communities Resettled Up To September 1967

fig. 6-14 One of Canada's major steel mills is located at North Sydney, Nova Scotia (courtesy Nova Scotia Communications and Information Centre).

The major urban centers of Northeastern Anglo-America are ports, and most of the larger ones have experienced a remarkable increase in traffic in the last decade or so. *Halifax* is clearly the most important port in the region, as well as being by far the largest city (fig. 6–15). It normally accommodates more overseas shipping than any other Canadian Atlantic coast city below Montreal. Winter is its most active season, of course, as Canada's St. Lawrence and Great Lakes ports are closed by ice for several months. Halifax is not really a primate city for the region, but its magnificent harbor and reasonably diversified economic base assure its relative prosperity.

fig. 6–d Case studies of outport resettlement. On the left is shown the agglomeration of people from several outports to the reception center of Englee; on the right is shown the dispersal of people from the evacuated outport of Williamsport. (After Alan Macpherson, "People in Transition: The Broken Mosaic," in *The Atlantic Provinces*, ed. Alan Macpherson [Toronto: University of Toronto Press, 1972], p. 71. By permission.)

In most cases the resettled families have not moved great distances, but the movement has always been to larger centers and is resulting in a continually decreasing pattern of dispersion (fig. 6-d). Most movers take all their belongings with them, often including houses, shops, and sheds, which they either shift intact or dismantle and rebuild.

If present resettlement rates continue, it is estimated that about 17 percent of all Newfoundlanders, amounting to some 40 percent of the rural population, will eventually move.[d] This is clearly a major redistribution of the population and will certainly bring more people within reach of basic social services. Its success in terms of reducing poverty, however, is much more problematical. Newfoundland already has a high rate of urban unemployment to go along with its traditionally low average income, and it is unreasonable to anticipate that the urban-industrial sector of the provincial economy can absorb the continuing influx of resettled outporters.

[d] Alan G. Macpherson, "People in Transition: The Broken Mosaic," in *The Atlantic Provinces*, ed. Alan G. Macpherson (Toronto: University of Toronto Press, 1972), p. 70.

Englee
Reception center

Williamsport
Evacuated community

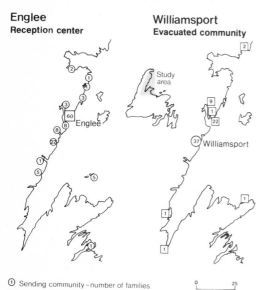

ⓘ Sending community – number of families

☐ Reception center – number of families

0 25
Miles

fig. 6–15 The principal commercial port of the Atlantic Provinces is Halifax, with its combination of enclosed finger piers and modern container-handling facilities (courtesy Nova Scotia Communications and Information Centre).

St. John's also has a splendid protected harbor, although its mouth ("the Narrows") is occasionally choked with ice. Its extreme foreland location provides little opportunity for service to anything more than a provincial hinterland, and even this port-of-entry and distribution function is being challenged by smaller Newfoundland ports.[18] But the harbor facilities have recently been modernized, and St. John's is magnificently situated to serve as a base for the offshore fishery fleets in the northwest Atlantic and as the only effective storm port in a region of stormy seas.[19]

Saint John is a port about the same size as St. John's, but its situation is quite different. It serves as one Atlantic terminus (Halifax and Portland are the others) of Canada's transcontinental railway system and thus has a busy season of general cargo activity in winter; however, its somewhat more remote location than Halifax from the Atlantic side

and its less suitable harbor give it a secondary rank among Atlantic ports.

Other cities of moderate size in Northeastern Anglo-America are listed in table 6–1. Each regional chapter includes a table that gives the population for the metropolitan area and the political city, as tabulated in the 1976 census of Canada and estimated for 1976 by the United States Bureau of the

[18] Charles N. Forward, "Recent Changes in the Form and Function of the Port of St. John's, Newfoundland," *Canadian Geographer*, 11 (1967), 101.

[19] When storms, particularly hurricanes, come to the banks area or other parts of the western North Atlantic, less durable craft, particularly fishing vessels, often make for a protected port. St. John's is conspicuously the most suitable anchorage in the area and may become crowded with ships seeking refuge.

table 6–1 Largest Urban Places of Northeastern Anglo-America

name	population of principal city	population of metropolitan area
Bangor, Maine	32,262	
Burlington, Vt.	37,133	
Charlottetown, P.E.I.	16,508	
Corner Brook, Nfld.	24,798	
Dartmouth, N.S.*	64,452	
Fredericton, N.B.	44,572	
Halifax, N.S.	113,036	261,366
Moncton, N.B.	53,418	
Saint John, N.B.	82,976	109,700
St. John's, Nfld.	84,994	140,883
Sydney, N.S.	30,087	

* A suburb of a larger city.

Census. The cities in each table are arranged in alphabetical order; only the more important ones, based on population and lying within the region under consideration, are included.

On the regional maps at the beginning of each chapter, the following urban places are shown:

1 Those with a 1976 population exceeding 250,000 are indicated by a large dot, and their names are shown in all capital letters (as BOSTON).

2 Those with a population between 50,-000 and 250,000 are shown by a large dot, and their names are in capital and lower case letters (as Halifax).

3 Those with a population of less than 50,000 that are mentioned prominently in the text are indicated by an open circle, and their names are in capital and lower case letters (as Bangor). To assure legibility, cities and towns that are distinctly suburbs of larger urban places are not shown.

the outlook

In spite of a long history and a distinguished heritage, Northeastern Anglo-America has not been a favored region from an economic standpoint. Its natural resources are limited, and its position in the northeast and southeast corners of the two countries involved has cut it off from the mainstream of activity just enough to inhibit its commercial vitality. In few other significant parts of Anglo-America are there so many part-time workers—part-time farmers, part-time fishermen, part-time loggers. The rest of their time is spent in another wage-earning capacity, in doing odd jobs, or in subsisting on welfare payments (the latter is often a significant portion of total income). There is no reason to expect a change in this broad pattern.

The region has a disproportionately large number of people engaged in marginal activities in the fields of farming, fishing, and logging, even though in recent decades there has been a steady decline in employment in all three. There is a dearth of arable land that must circumscribe agricultural growth. Product specialization (especially in orchards, beef, tobacco, and poultry) and, in some cases, intensification should have a salutary effect in some areas.

There is likely to be a trend toward larger-scale enterprises in farming, forestry, and fishing. The future of fishing is clearly in mechanized offshore operations rather than small-scale inshore activity. Although such an emphasis will help to stabilize the industry, it will actually decrease employment and thus does not address the core problem of local dependence on inshore fisheries. The Canadian government estimates that nearly three-fourths of all communities in the Atlantic Provinces are involved in commercial fishing, and more than 20 percent of these rely exclusively on fish catching and processing for their economic support. In 1975 the government instituted yet another fisheries strengthening program in the Atlantic Provinces, infusing capital for both inshore and offshore fishermen and for processors. Recent international conservation agreements and the decision of both Canadian and United States governments to control foreign fishing within 200 miles of the coastline should aid domestic fishermen in both the short- and long-run. Market prices for fish have been strong in recent years, but the serious long-term decline in landings, apparently due primarily to overexploitation (particularly by foreign fishing interests), is a nagging worry. Moreover, the future of displaced fishermen is a continuing problem, especially in Newfoundland where the greatest displacements will occur in association with the abandonment of outports.

Mining will probably continue to flourish unevenly in Newfoundland, but the bright spot on the economic horizon is in the long-declining Nova Scotia coal fields. Rather than facing abandonment, the coal-mining industry is expanding, in response primarily to the need to develop energy alternatives to petroleum but also in line with the interest of Ontario steel makers in using more Canadian coking coal.

The entire region is heavily dependent on imported oil for electricity generation. Intensive exploration on the continental shelf, especially off Nova Scotia, has thus far been unproductive, but the possibility of a significant petroleum discovery is still there. Meanwhile, construction and expansion of hydroelectric and coal-fired thermal electric generating plants are being emphasized.

The problem of provincial budgets continues to be a major cause of concern. Nearly half of the total Maritime provincial revenues emanate from Ottawa, in part as pump-priming measures that have not been very effective. One prominent and radical suggestion that has been made is for a full political union of the Maritime Provinces; this would presumably have the dual benefit of reducing the wasteful costs of three governmental infrastructures and of blending three relatively small and interdependent economies into a unit that could be more effectively planned for development programs. Actual implementation of such a political amalgamation is highly unlikely; nevertheless, it is an interesting possibility.

Northern New England has undergone repeated economic readjustments. Pulp and paper production should continue to be important, and hydroelectric developments will probably continue; however, both these activities are coming under increasingly severe scrutiny by advocates of wildland preservation. Agricultural specialization should continue but not on a large scale. Poultry raising, dairying's only rival to agricultural dominance, is expected to increase. Farm abandonment is already a seemingly permanent feature of the agricultural scene.

Urban activities throughout the region, especially manufacturing, can be expected to grow steadily—if slowly. The rate of expansion will remain well below the average growth rate for both nations, and most industrial growth will be in production of items for the local or regional market. But despite the prospect of increased urbanization, Northeastern Anglo-America is never likely to be famous for its urban-industrial advantages. Rather, rural amenities are emphasized as the regional attraction. It has been said that "Vermont is the only place within a day's drive of New York that is fit to live in."[20] Or, stated differently, David Erskine has noted that the region's "compensation must be in a life that is freer, or lived in more attractive surroundings, or with closer family ties."[21] As recently as a decade ago much of the rural land in northern New England could have been purchased as cheaply as it was selling for a century earlier. Such conditions are now gone, presumably forever. The tourist, the second-home owner, the developer, and the speculator have landed in force. Short- and long-term visitors arrive in ever greater numbers during the summer, and winter recreation also continues to expand. The wider dissemination of such activities over the region of Northeastern Anglo-America augurs well for a more balanced economic gain.

[20] Joe McCarthy and the Editors of Time-Life Books, *New England* (New York: Time Incorporated, 1967), p. 163.
[21] Erskine, "The Atlantic Region," p. 280.

selected bibliography

ALLEN, J. P., "Migration Fields of French Canadian Immigrants to Southern Maine," *Geographical Review*, 62 (1972), 366–83.

BELLIVEAU, J. E., "The Acadian French and Their Language," *Canadian Geographical Journal*, 95 (October–November 1977), 46–55.

BLACK, W. A., "The Great Northumberland Ice Barrier," *Canadian Geographical Journal*, 87 (October 1973), 30–39.

BOGUCKI, DONALD J., AND MALCOLM FAIRWEATHER, "Hypsometry and Relief Characteristics of the Adirondack Province," *Ecumene*, 9 (April 1977), 17–21.

BRACK, DAVID M., "The Ocean Coasts of Canada,'' *Canadian Geographical Journal,* 87 (October 1973), 4–15.

CLARK, ANDREW H., *Acadia: The Geography of Early Nova Scotia.* Madison: University of Wisconsin Press, 1968.

————, *Three Centuries and an Island.* Toronto: University of Toronto Press, 1954.

CLARK, R. H., ''Energy from Fundy Tides,'' *Canadian Geographical Journal,* 85 (November 1972), 150–63.

COLLIE, M., *New Brunswick.* Toronto: MacMillan of Canada, 1974.

DUNBAR, M. J., ''Resource Management for the Gulf of St. Lawrence?'' *Canadian Geographical Journal,* 87 (August 1973), 4–13.

FORWARD, CHARLES N., ''Parallelism of Halifax and Victoria,'' *Canadian Geographical Journal,* 90 (March 1975), 34–43.

GILLESPIE, G. J., ''The Atlantic Salmon,'' *Canadian Geographical Journal,* 76 (June 1968), 186–99.

HALLIDAY, H. A., ''The Lonely Magdalen Islands,'' *Canadian Geographical Journal,* 86 (January 1973), 2–13.

HARRINGTON, MICHAEL F., ''St. John's, Newfoundland,'' *Canadian Geographical Journal,* 81 (September 1970), 84–95.

KRUEGER, RALPH R., ''Changes in the Political Geography of New Brunswick,'' *Canadian Geographer,* 19 (1975), 121–34.

LEBLANC, ROBERT G., ''The Acadian Migrations,'' *Canadian Geographical Journal,* 81 (July 1970), 10–19.

LEVY, THOMAS A., ''The International Economic Interests and Activities of the Atlantic Provinces,'' *American Review of Canadian Studies,* 5 (Spring 1975), 98–113.

LEWIS, GEORGE, ''Population Change in Northern New England,'' *Annals,* Association of American Geographers, 62 (1972), 307–22.

MCLAREN, I. A., ''Sable Island: Our Heritage and Responsibility,'' *Canadian Geographical Journal,* 85 (September 1972), 108–14.

MACPHERSON, ALAN G., ed., *The Atlantic Provinces.* Toronto: University of Toronto Press, 1972.

MANNION, JOHN J., *Irish Settlements in Eastern Canada: A Study of Cultural Transfer and Adaptation.* Toronto: University of Toronto Press, 1974.

MEEKS, HAROLD A., *The Geographic Regions of Vermont: A Study in Maps.* Hanover, N.H.: Dartmouth University, Geography Publications at Dartmouth 10, 1975.

MOFFATT, THOMAS F., ''Beauty in Crisis at Passamaquoddy Bay,'' *Canadian Geographical Journal,* 94 (February–March 1977), 8–17.

REES, RONALD, ''Changing Saint John: The Old and the New,'' *Canadian Geographical Journal,* 90 (May 1975), 12–17.

ROBINSON, J. LEWIS, ''Changing Settlement Patterns in Newfoundland,'' *Geographical Review,* 65 (1975), 267–68.

VICERO, RALPH D., ''French-Canadian Settlement in Vermont Prior to the Civil War,'' *Professional Geographer,* 23 (1971), 290–94.

WALLACE, WILLIAM H., ''A Hard Land for a Tough People: A Historical Geography of New Hampshire,'' *New Hampshire Profiles* (April 1975), 21–32.

WELSTED, JOHN, ''Post-Glacial Emergence of the Fundy Coast: An Analysis of the Evidence,'' *Canadian Geographer,* 20 (1976), 367–83.

WOOD, KENNETH SCOTT, AND J. PALMER, *Natural Resources of Northeastern Nova Scotia.* Halifax: Dalhousie University, Institute of Public Affairs, 1970.

FRENCH
CANADA

7

Of all the major regions of Anglo-America, French Canada is the most culturally distinctive. For more than three and a half centuries it has been occupied by people whose primary cultural attributes are different from the settlers of the other regions of the continent. It has been a Franco-culture island in an Anglo-culture sea, and this unique cultural expression has been maintained without significant external reinforcement. In the last two centuries there has been very little immigration, or even much tangible support, from France; yet the settled southern portions of Quebec continue to be dominated by a solidly French culture, and the areal extent of this influence has continued a slow expansion into adjacent parts of New Brunswick and Ontario, and even into New England.

The predominant expression of French-Canadian culture is, of course, the use of the French language. More than 80 percent of the people of the province of Quebec consider French as their mother tongue, and if the cosmopolitan city of Montreal is excluded from the statistics, more than 90 percent of the people are Francophones (linguistically French), with many of the remainder (the Angolophones) being bilingual. Indeed, in most of the St. Lawrence Valley and estuary downstream from Montreal the proportion of French-speakers exceeds 98 percent of the total population. Hand-in-hand with the French language in the region goes the Roman Catholic religion. Catholicism in Canada is not restricted to Francophones, but more than 85 percent of the inhabitants of Quebec profess to be followers of the Roman Catholic faith. It is in the French-Canadian region, then, that the Catholic Church has its firm Canadian base, largely accounting for the fact that some 45 percent of the Canadian population professes to be Roman Catholic.

These two important social attributes—language and religion—are not the only nonmaterial elements of the distinctive French-Canadian culture, but they are clearly the most conspicuous. Other intangible culture traits, such as cohesiveness of family life or dietary preferences, are less easily identified and quantified but may be equally significant in some areas.

Although recognizing the importance of nonmaterial culture elements, a geographer is continually seeking to identify and interpret expressions of culture in the landscape. In French Canada this search is amply rewarded. Physical manifestations of the dominant culture can be recognized in farmscapes and townscapes, fences and signs, field patterns and architectural styles, general appearance, place names, and many other facets of the landscape.

Consider, for example, the matter of place names in French Canada. The great majority of all places—towns, rivers, streets, mountains—is named for saints. Any map of the region shows this dominance: St. Laurent, St. Maurice, Ste. Anne de Bellevue, Ste. Foy, St. Hyacinthe, St. Jérôme, St. Félix-de-Valois. The principal areas where such names are not dominant are those where a later spread of French settlement was superimposed on an already established Anglo framework, as in the Eastern Townships of Quebec or parts of New Brunswick.

The prominence of the church in the French-Canadian way of life is manifested in the landscape by many features other than place names. Roman Catholic religious institutions are numerous and conspicuous. Churches, seminaries, monasteries, convents, shrines, retreat houses, cemeteries, and other edifices are prominent throughout the settled parts of the region. They are usually large in size, in comparison with other structures in the area, and often solid and massive in style. Their prominence is somewhat subdued in cities, where secular buildings may also be large and massive. But in smaller towns and villages, church-related structures usually dominate the scene; indeed, most towns in the region cluster about a large, stone Roman Catholic church.

The rural landscape, too, has its characteristic features. Most notable is the pattern of land ownership and field alignment. Most farms are shaped as long and narrow rectangles, and the fields within the farm repeat the pattern on a smaller scale. The background to this unique pattern is discussed subsequently.

Centrally located within the fields are often long heaps of stones that have been gathered by the farmer after years of winter frost-heave and accumulated in piles. Surrounding the field is likely to be a cedar pole fence, although wire fences have been increasingly adopted in recent years, particularly in the upstream portions of the region. The farmstead, too, often has predictable characteristics. The buildings are likely to

fig. 7–1   One of the many manifestations of French-Canadian culture is in architectural styles. The wraparound veranda with its decorative wooden trappings and the conspicuous dormers are typical of many homes in the region. This scene is near Levis, Quebec.

be constructed of unpainted wood, somewhat unkempt, gray, and bleak in appearance. Certain architectural styles are common: the farmhouse often has a lengthy veranda or porch, a certain amount of "gingerbread" on the exterior, and several high dormers (fig. 7–1); the barn is likely to be of the inclined-ramp variety with livestock housed on the lower floor and a wooden ramp leading to the second story where machinery, tools, and feed are kept.

a culturally oriented region

The designation of French Canada as a major region of Anglo-America is primarily in recognition of its cultural uniqueness and the significance of this cultural imprint on its geography. There are other factors, environmental and economic, that contribute to regional unity, but it is the manifestations of French-Canadian culture that are the principal shapers of the total geography of this region.

No other Anglo-American region, as delineated in this book, is recognized principally on the basis of its cultural components.

129

Some other sections of the continent have important elements of non-Anglo culture, but in every case the designation of a culturally oriented region is felt to be unwarranted either because the culture does not sufficiently permeate the geography of the region or because the area and population involved are too small to justify separation as a region.

A case might be put, for example, that the southwestern borderlands of the United States—those parts of Texas, New Mexico, Arizona, and California that are close to Mexico—contain hundreds of thousands of people of Mexican extraction who have an Hispanic culture that is analogous in many ways to the French-Canadian culture region in eastern Canada.[1] Although recognizing the validity of this assertion, the authors feel that the form and function of life in the borderlands are clearly dominated by an Anglo pattern that is insufficiently different to justify regional recognition. Similar reasoning holds true for the Hawaiian Islands, with their significant Oriental and Polynesian culture complexes, although Hawaii is delineated as a separate region for other reasons.

True cultural distinction is also shown in certain parts of Anglo-America where the bulk of the population is aboriginal in origin. For example, the Navaho-Hopi-Ute Indian complex of the Four Corners country has recognizable cultural uniqueness. Also, in large stretches of subarctic and arctic Canada and Alaska varying degrees of distinctive Indian, Eskimo, and Aleut culture predominate. But in each instance regional recognition does not seem warranted on a largely cultural basis because of the small size of the population involved or its highly fragmented settlement pattern over broad areas where environmental considerations seem more important as regional delineators.

[1] See, for example, Richard L. Nostrand, "The Hispanic-American Borderland: Delimitation of an American Culture Region," *Annals,* Association of American Geographers, 60 (1970), 638–61.

french canada as a region and as a concept

The region of French Canada, as delineated here, does not include all the province of Quebec and is not limited by the borders of Quebec (fig. 7–2). It is considered to encompass that portion of eastern Canada that is dominated by French-Canadian culture, except where significant areas of non-French-Canadian culture or nonsettlement intervene. Thus, the region includes most of the southern settled parts of Quebec: from the lower Ottawa River Valley in the west; down the St. Lawrence Valley to include the Gaspé Peninsula, Anticosti Island, and the north shore of the Gulf of St. Lawrence in the east; as well as the relatively densely settled portion of the Shield that encompasses the Lake St. John lowland and the Saguenay River Valley. It is also considered to include the French-dominated portions of the province of New Brunswick (largely the area north of 47° N.L.) and limited areas in the extreme eastern part of Ontario. With a few minor exceptions in northeasternmost New York State, northernmost Vermont, and the Aroostook Valley of Maine, the area of French-Canadian dominance ends abruptly at the international boundary; so the United States border can be considered as the southern margin of the region.

As thus delimited, the region of French Canada includes 90 percent of the population of Quebec, about 33 percent of the population of New Brunswick, and a small percentage of the population of Ontario. This amounts to some 27 percent of the population of Canada, or 6.5 million people as of the late 1970s.

It is important to note that there are a few hundred thousand French Canadians who live outside the region of French Canada described above. They are found throughout the settled parts of Canada, although usually in small numbers. The principal concentrations of French Canadians who live outside the French Canada Region are in the Abitibi-Timiskaming area of

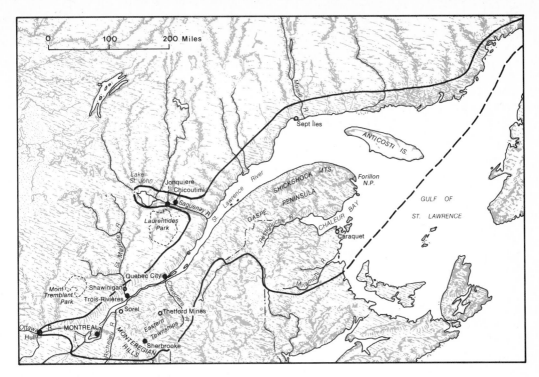

fig. 7–2 The French Canada Region (base map
copyright A. K. Lobeck; reprinted by
permission of Hammond, Inc.).

west-central Quebec, in the iron mining
towns of the Labrador-Quebec border country, in scattered mining communities of
east-central Ontario, in southeastern Manitoba (especially the Winnipeg suburb of St.
Boniface), and in various parts of the Maritime Provinces mentioned in the previous
chapter.

The French Canadians living in these
other parts of Canada maintain most of the
same cultural attributes as those who live
within the French Canada Region, except
that the French language becomes decreas-
ingly important with increasing distance
from Quebec.[2]

²Ludger Beauregard, "Le Canada Francais
par la Carte," *Revue de Géographie de Montréal*, 22
(1968), 35.

the region and its parts

The location of the region is a great paradox; it is isolated from surrounding regions
by natural barriers and yet has served
throughout history as the principal thoroughfare connecting Canada with the Old
World. To the north of French Canada is
the rocky forested fastness of the Laurentian
Shield, largely unpopulated. To the south
the Appalachian highlands of Northeastern
Anglo-America serve as a very effective barrier, with the single important exception of
the Champlain lowland, to connection with
the populous parts of the United States. To
the east is the vastness of the Atlantic
Ocean, ice-locked for part of the year. Only
to the west is there a relatively easy route to
connect "Lower Canada" (as Quebec was
formerly called) to "Upper Canada," and

even here the zone of settlement is a narrow one, pinched between the southward extension of the Shield and the Adirondack Mountains.

Despite the difficulties imposed by white-water rapids on the rivers, an estuary and gulf with seasonal ice problems, and rocky impediments to land transport, the St. Lawrence corridor has been the major routeway providing the Canadian heartland with access to Europe and the rest of the world. The development of the St. Lawrence Seaway system over the past several decades has reinforced the importance of the corridor.

There are various parts, even to a region as small as French Canada, and the parts demonstrate differing characteristics. The St. Lawrence Valley is the central part and core of the region; it is a broad lowland in the southwest that narrows progressively downstream until the estuary of the river occupies almost all the flat land below the Ile d'Orléans. Southeast of the valley and extending to the international border lie the gently rolling and hilly lands of the Eastern Townships where early English settlers have been largely replaced by more recent French arrivals. South of the Gulf of St. Lawrence is the rocky, tree-covered peninsula of Gaspé, occupied by marginal farmers and hardy fishermen. The portion of the region in New Brunswick encompasses a peripheral circle of fishing, farming, and forestry around an interior that is almost totally unpopulated. The pattern of life in each of these sections has much in common, but there are important differences, the most striking being between the upstream and downstream portions of the region.

the environment

In many ways the environment of French Canada is similar to that of Northeastern Anglo-America: rocky uplands, extensive forests, bleak winters, rushing streams, and limited mineral resources. There are also important differences; the most significant is the amount of flat land and relatively pro-

ductive soil that have made possible a widespread agricultural base to the region's economy.

TOPOGRAPHY

The St. Lawrence corridor consists of a long stretch of flat, valley-bottom land that varies greatly in width. It is broadest in the Montreal plain and on the right bank of the river between Montreal and Quebec City. Former beach terraces and strand lines, indicating relatively recent emergence of the lowland from beneath the sea, are commonplace. The surface materials of the lowland are mostly sands and other recent deposits of marine, fluvial, or glacial origin, which cover the bedrock foundation quite deeply in places. The major irregularities in the plain are the Monteregian Hills, scattered remnants of old volcanic stocks that rise several hundred feet above their surroundings; most famous is the westernmost, Mount Royal, in the heart of the city of Montreal.

On the left-bank side of the St. Lawrence River the flat land soon gives way to the sloping edge of the Laurentian Shield, which rises rockily and in many places abruptly in steep hills or complex escarpments. The only significant extensions of the lowland on this northwest side of the St. Lawrence are where major tributaries—such as the Ottawa, the St. Maurice, and the Saguenay—have breached the Laurentian escarpment.

Southeast of the St. Lawrence there is much flat land that extends well into the Eastern Townships. But slopelands are more characteristic, with stretches of rolling hills becoming higher and more complicated mountain ranges near the United States border. The mountains become higher toward the northeast, forming a sort of rolling plateau that in places is deeply dissected by rivers. Elevations of more than 4,000 feet are reached in the rocky fastness of the Shickshock Mountains of the Gaspé Peninsula. Northern New Brunswick is a mixture of rolling lowland and rocky hill, with major valleys carved by the Restigouche, Nipisguit, and Miramichi rivers.

CLIMATE

Winter is the memorable season in French Canada, both because of its coldness and its length. Qualitative descriptions may vary,[3] but there is no dispute that there is a long period of low temperature in the region. Even the areas of mildest climate have a winter period of five and a half or six months, with early frosts beginning in October and streams not running freely in the new year until April.[4] January temperatures average below 20°F. throughout the region, with Montreal recording a mean of 14° and Quebec City, 10°. Snowfall is heavy (100 inches annually is not unusual, even at sea-level localities), and weather changes are frequent, although warm periods are brief (fig. 7–3). Storm tracks converge in the region in winter, and migratory cyclones and anticyclones pass with frequency.

But winter's icy grip is not an unmixed blessing. The deep snow cover enables easier movement for both men and logs in the forest and facilitates the accumulation of logs on frozen waterways for floating downstream in the spring thaw. The "dead" navigation season on the St. Lawrence, occasioned by the winter freeze-up, has sometimes lasted from December to April. More recently the energetic use of icebreakers has permitted the port of Montreal to function for all but a few days of the year; Quebec City's port is closed only occasionally since high tides keep the ice broken and shifting in the estuary.

Summer weather is quite varied in the region. The upstream portion of the St. Lawrence Valley experiences much warmth and humidity and has a growing season of approximately five months. Higher elevations and the more easterly coastal areas (Gaspé, both sides of the estuary, and Anticosti Island) have mild to cool summers,

fig. 7–3   Winter is a prominent fact of life in French Canada. Here the frozen St. Charles River in Quebec City serves as a temporary walkway and skating rink (courtesy Government of Quebec, Tourist Branch).

with a frost-free period of less than 100 days. Summer is a time of generally abundant rainfall, which is a distinct agricultural advantage to the warmer upstream areas. Annual precipitation totals about 40 inches at both Montreal and Quebec City.

SOILS

Soils are quite variable, but most are heavily leached, acidic, deficient in nutrients, and poorly drained. Those that have developed on glacial deposits are very stony, and sands and clays are prominent where marine deposits are the parent material.

Spodosols dominate in the upland areas and in the downstream parts of the region. These are poor soils for agriculture; they are totally leached in the upper horizons, quite acidic, and ash-gray in color. Alfisols are the chief soils of the upstream areas, especially on the terraces, and although somewhat leached and acidic in nature, they respond well to fertilizer and are important agricultural soils. Small areas of alluvial soils in the valley bottoms are the most productive for farming in the region.

[3] For example, three different textbook descriptions use the following adjectives: "cold but not bitter," "harsh," and "severe."

[4] Pierre Biays, "Southern Quebec," in *Canada, a Geographical Interpretation,* ed. John Warkentin (Toronto: Methuen Publications, 1968), p. 291.

Originally almost the entire region was forested, except for poorly drained, marshy areas in the lowlands and some of the higher, rocky upland slopes. Softwoods were dominant, with magnificent stands of white pine and fir, particularly in the downstream areas and in northern New Brunswick. The upstream sections and much of the Eastern Townships were covered with a mixed forest in which maple, elm, beech, and birch were prominent. Most of the uplands are still forested, although logging has removed all the accessible timber at least once. The lowlands have long since been cleared for farming; yet extensive woodlots have been maintained in the agricultural areas throughout the region.

settling the region

At the time of European contact, most of the St. Lawrence Valley and associated lowlands were occupied by Iroquoian tribes. Several relatively small Algonkian tribes inhabited the southern edge of the Laurentian Shield, but none was significant in the settlement history of the region except for the Ottawas along the Ottawa River. In Gaspé and northern New Brunswick were the equally unobtrusive Micmacs and Malecites, who fished along the coast in summer and hunted in the forest in winter.

The Huron tribe, of Iroquoian stock, occupied a territory in southern Ontario and was probably the most active trading tribe in eastern Canada and the northeastern United States.[3] Furs were the basis for their trading relationship with the French, with whom the Hurons acquired a trade monopoly from the earliest days of settlement. The tribes of the Iroquois League (Mohawk, Seneca, and others) that occupied lands east and south of the Hurons were active traders with the Dutch in New York. By 1640 the Iroquois had run out of beaver to trade and

took to active conflict with the Hurons, hijacking fur canoes and trying to preempt trading rights with the French and Algonkians. In 1649–50 a series of Iroquois attacks, combined with appalling winter starvation, virtually eliminated the Huron people and wiped out their tribal identity.

During the subsequent decade the Iroquois annihilated or adopted most of the other small tribes in this region, except for the Ottawas. The Iroquois signed a treaty with the French at Montreal in 1688 and for some decades continued to serve as a buffer between the settlements in Quebec and those in the American colonies to the southeast.

European settlement in the region dates from 1608, with the founding of Quebec City by Champlain.[6] "New France" was to be an agricultural colony, but throughout the early decades it was fur trading that attracted the most interest and enthusiasm and pulled French explorers ever deeper into the interior of the continent. Agricultural settlement moved slowly up the St. Lawrence and some of its major tributaries; Trois-Rivières was founded as a trading center in 1634, and the first settlers disembarked on Montreal Island in 1642.

The initial settlement and land-ownership pattern in rural Quebec was quite different from that in most of the rest of the continent. Today its imprint on the landscape is both unique and notable (see vignette on next page).

In 1763 France gave up its claim to New France, and the 65,000 *canadiens* came under British rule. A land survey was soon carried out, and rectangular townships were laid out between the seigneuries of the St. Lawrence and the international border (the Eastern Townships), with the area being thrown open to Anglo-Saxon colonists. Other townships were surveyed sporadically around the margin of the seigneurial territory until it was completely surrounded by

---

[5] Harold E. Driver, *Indians of North America* (Chicago: University of Chicago Press, 1961), p. 235.

[6] The city's proper name is simply Quebec. But in order to spare confusion, in this book Quebec refers to the province and Quebec City refers to the city.

lands earmarked for British settlement. Many of the early settlers were "Loyalists" immigrating from the new American republic to the south; English, Scottish, and Irish immigrants also came. Farms were typically square or rectangular, and the pattern was totally unlike the long-lot system, although farmsteads sometimes appeared to be aligned because they were built along access roads.

a long-lot landscape

The most striking feature of the landscape in rural French Canada is the almost limitless array of long, narrow rectangles that subdivides the agricultural land. With the notable exception of the Eastern Townships, property lines and field boundaries replicate the pattern with faithful precision, disdainful of topographic variation, throughout most of the region. Moreover, the farmsteads are almost invariably positioned at the same ends of adjacent rectangles, so that neighboring farmhouses exist in close proximity to one another with remarkable linearity of location. This distinctive contemporary landscape morphology is a heritage of the earliest days of French settlement in Lower Canada and has survived with tenacious persistence and little change for three centuries.

The first element in the pattern was the establishment of a seigneurial system. In the seventeenth century the kings of France awarded land grants (called *seigneuries*) with feudal privileges to individual entrepreneurs (*seigneurs*). The seigneurs, in turn, were expected to subgrant parcels of land to peasant farmers (*habitants*). The seigneuries varied greatly in size, but each fronted on a river and extended inland for a mile or two in some cases and up to almost 100 miles in others.

The typical land grant (called a *roture*) within a seigneury was a long, narrow rectangle, fronting for 150 to 200 yards along the river and extending inland for a mile or more.[a] This gave each farm direct access to the river, which was the only transportation route in the early years. When all the riverside rotures had been granted, a road would be built along their inland margin, paralleling the river, and a second rank (or *rang*) of rotures would be developed. In some cases there were up to a dozen rangs successively arrayed back from the river, separated from one another by parallel concession roads that ran without break for dozens, or occasionally even hundreds, of miles (fig. 7-a).

(Continued)

fig. 7-a A hypothetical model of rang settlement patterns in Quebec. (From *Canada Before Confederation: A Study in Historical Geography* by R. Cole Harris and John Warkentin, p. 74. Copyright © 1974 by Oxford University Press, Inc. Reprinted by permission.)

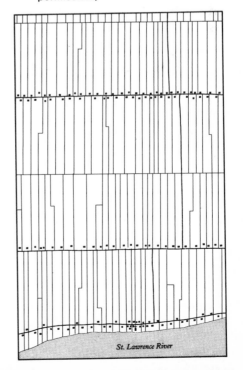

[a] R. Cole Harris, "Some Remarks on the Seigneurial Geography of Early Canada," in *Canada's Changing Geography*, ed. R. Louis Gentilcore (Scarborough, Ont.: Prentice-Hall of Canada, 1967), p. 31.

St. Lawrence River

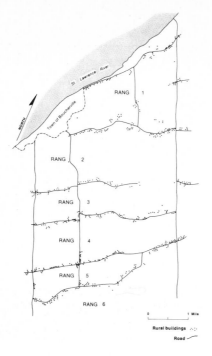

For the better part of a century after France's retirement from Canada, the French populace remained within the seigneurial domain; as the population expanded rapidly, it filled in the as yet unsettled parts of the seigneuries. But by the middle of the nineteenth century the French Canadians were more than half a million strong and were overflowing into the Anglo-Saxon townships. In some cases they took over British holdings, usually resulting in only minor landscape changes. But many of the French-Canadian settlements in the Eastern Townships during this period were on empty

fig. 7–4 An example of the rang-long lot pattern of rural settlement in a portion of the St. Lawrence Valley. The land ownership pattern of such an area can be visualized as long, narrow properties running at right angles to the roads (map data from Army Survey Establishment 1:50,000 series, Beloeil 31H/11W sheet, 1965).

fig. 7–b Distribution of rotures in the Seigneurie of St.-Sulpice. The river-oriented pattern is striking. (From *Canada Before Confederation*, by Harris and Warkentin, p. 39. Copyright © 1974 by Oxford University Press, Inc. Reprinted by permission.)

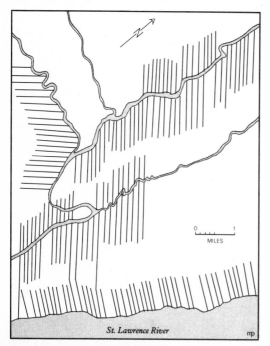

The habitants invariably built their farmsteads at the end of their rotures adjacent to the river or road; thus there grew up an almost continuous string of individual settlements along the transportation routes.[b] The most common settlement pattern was the *rang double,* in which houses were built on either side of the concession road, thus serving rotures that extended off in opposite directions from the road. By the early 1800s many seigneuries contained six or seven rangs double along roads roughly parallel to the river and linked by occasional crossroads with no settlement along them.[c] The custom of equal inheritance rights resulted in increasing fractionization of the rotures along the lines of

[b] Deffontaines noted that at the end of the French rule a traveler could have seen almost every house in Canada by making a canoe trip along the St. Lawrence and Richelieu rivers. P. Deffontaines, "Le Rang: Type de Peuplement Rural du Canada Francais," *Proceedings,* 17th International Congress of the International Geographical Union (1952), p. 723.

[c] R. Cole Harris and John Warkentin, *Canada Before Confederation* (New York: Oxford University Press, 1974), p. 73.

lands among the Anglo-Saxon settlers and were nearly always organized on the rang-long lot pattern (fig. 7–4); even when far removed from a navigable river, the rangs were arranged systematically along roads (fig. 7–5).

In the two decades prior to Canadian confederation (1867), the French population of the Eastern Townships increased by 120 percent, while the British population of the same area was only increasing by 6 percent. The total numbers of the two groups were approximately equal by the date of confederation, but the continuing rapid increase of the French population soon greatly exceeded that of the British. On the other side of the St. Lawrence, on the edge of the Laurentians, the French-Canadian settlement also rapidly expanded, filling in the interstices among the predominantly Irish

settlers in those townships and in townships in northeastern Ontario. Soon there was a French-Canadian majority on the edge of the Shield, and a "spillover" of farmers and

fig. 7–5 Contemporary rural settlement and field patterns southeast of Montreal.

the original subdivision, with each succeeding fraction becoming narrower so that each farmer still had access to river or road (fig. 7-b). The original "long lot" farms were designed to be about ten times as long as they were wide, but repeated linear subdivision sometimes created units that were virtually too narrow to farm economically.[d]

The French population grew slowly at the outset, reaching about 3,000 by 1660, but the seigneurial domain continued to expand along the St. Lawrence, reaching downstream to the Gaspé Peninsula and upstream to the border of Upper Canada; it also extended up a number of tributaries, particularly the Chaudière, the Richelieu, and the Ottawa (fig. 7-c).[e]

[d] Peter Brooke Clibbon, "Evolution and Present Pattern of the Ecumene of Southern Quebec," in *Quebec*, ed. Fernand Grenier (Toronto: University of Toronto Press, 1972), p. 17.
    [e] This long lot arrangement of properties and fields was developed in other areas of French settlement on the continent, notably in sections of the Maritimes, in Manitoba, in Louisiana, and along the Detroit River, but nowhere did it reach anything like the magnitude or the permanence of its extent in Quebec.

fig. 7-c Population distribution in early Quebec. The people settled almost exclusively in riverside locations. (From *Canada Before Confederation*, by Harris and Warkentin, p. 35. Copyright © 1974 by Oxford University Press, Inc. Reprinted by permission.)

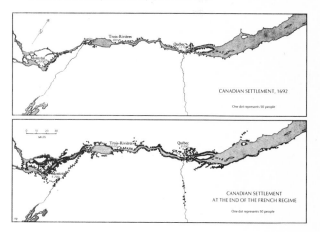

loggers occupied the Saguenay Valley and Lake St. John lowland in considerable numbers.

At the time of confederation, the population of the French Canada Region was overwhelmingly rural; it is estimated that more than 80 percent of the population at that time derived its livelihood from agriculture.[7] Montreal and Quebec City were the only urban centers of note, with populations of about 100,000 and 60,000, respectively. By the time of confederation, the occupance of French Canada was virtually complete.

Few new areas of rural settlement have been established since then except in the area northwest of Montreal and north of Ottawa—particularly in Terrebonne and Labelle counties—which reached its maximum extent in the 1930s and 1940s. In some other sections the rural population density has increased in this century, but in most it has actually declined because of farm abandonment. The major change in population distribution has been the growth of cities. French Canada today, like the rest of the country, is overwhelmingly urban.

the contemporary population

Urbanism is the most significant characteristic of the contemporary population of French Canada. The image of the region has always been one of hard-working, conservative farmers surrounded by large and cohesive families. But the proportion of urbanism in Quebec is now almost exactly the same as for Ontario or for Canada as a whole. The development of such an urban society has understandably meant a more radical change for French Canada than for other portions of the continent. The psychology and value system of a peasant society is rapidly being replaced by the dynamic and liberalized outlook of an urban-industrial milieu. Submissive traditionalism is giving way to restive concern.

[7] Biays, "Southern Quebec," p. 289.

The degree of urbanism is not the same throughout the region. Montreal has been the growth pole and leader of modern Quebec. The population of the city has increased more than tenfold in the last century. There are other examples of spectacular urban increment in the region, but of a lesser degree of magnitude. Urbanization has had a much less dramatic impact in the northern part of the Eastern Townships, along the right bank of the St. Lawrence below Sorel, in the Gaspé Peninsula, and in the interior of northern New Brunswick.

Urban growth has not meant absolute rural decline. Even though the proportion of the population that is nonurban has dramatically decreased, the total rural population in French Canada today—roughly 950,000—is approximately the same as it was one hundred years ago. It is the rural "surplus" that has moved away: to Montreal especially, but also to smaller cities in the region, to both urban and rural areas in northern New England, and to mining towns and agricultural communities on the Shield in both Quebec and Ontario.

The principal component of population growth in the region in the past was natural increase, but this, too, is changing. Average family size in Quebec was greater than in any other province, but the figure has declined over the past two or three decades until now it is just equal to the Canadian average. Immigrants come to this region at a lesser rate than to most of the rest of the nation. Most in-migration to French Canada in recent years has involved non-British, non-French Europeans, and most have settled in metropolitan Montreal.

One other important point about the contemporary population is that the "Frenchness" of French Canada has continued to intensify. Only a few small areas in the region do not have a French-Canadian majority, and in many places French-Canadians constitute more than 95 percent of the population. In the Eastern Townships, for example, Anglo-Canadians continue to sell their farms to French-Canadians and move to urban areas either within or without the region. (This has resulted in many curious combinations of English and French place names, such as Rue Notre Dame de Boundary Line or St. Calixte de Somerset.) The trend, however, has been toward an increase in French population and influence in cities.

Virtually every city in the region records a higher proportion of French-Canadians with each succeeding population census. In the case of Quebec City there was a 70 percent French majority a century ago; today 97 percent of its citizens are Francophones, and of necessity, almost all the remaining fraction are bilingual. Only in Montreal is the pattern different; approximately 67 percent of all Montrealers have been French-Canadians since the turn of the century; the non-French proportion is maintained largely by immigration from continental Europe, rather than by growth of the Anglo-Canadian populace.

the bilingual road to separatism

The cultural diversity of Montreal provides a dynamic focus for what is certainly the most significant social and political problem facing Canada today: the accommodation of a large and vibrant French-Canadian minority within a predominantly Anglo-Canadian nation. As a leading Anglo-American geographer has pointed out, the most important political fact in Canada is that a third of its citizens do not speak the majority language as a mother tongue, if at all.[8] The special position of the French-Canadian minority has been legally recognized since the establishment of the Canadian nation; the British North America Act of 1867, which established the federation, included various irreducible obligations to the province of Quebec. Quebec was guaranteed its civil law, its religious liberty, jurisdiction over its educational system, and the equality of its

language in both the Parliament and the federal courts of the nation, as well as in the Legislature and courts of the province. It is unlikely, however, that the framers of this remarkably tolerant legislation anticipated the cultural tenacity of the French Canadians. In every decennial census since 1867, the population of French origin has remained at approximately 30 percent of the Canadian total "despite immigration, emigration, differential birth rates, and the addition of six new provinces to the original four. From the standpoint of numbers ...the balance between the two cultures has been stable for the past century."[9]

Other aspects of the cultural dichotomy have been less stable, however. Much lip-service was given to the principle of Canada as a bilingual and bicultural nation. In the real world of government and business, however, Canada functioned as an English-oriented country with Quebec as a French-oriented enclave. French-Canadian objections to the status quo have been increasingly strident since World War II, the summary complaints being that English is the language of business so that Francophones must use English in order to advance and that the Franco community is being assimilated by the Anglo community.

Quebec's *revolution tranquille* (quiet revolution) of the 1960s brought French- and English-speaking Canadians into direct large-scale competition for jobs and power in modern business and government. This effort was slow in attracting national attention, but the abrupt actions of a fanatic extremist group (the FLQ, or Front de Libération du Québec) shocked the nation with bombing, kidnapping, and murder. Strong government and private efforts were then instituted to assuage the situation. The "special relationship" of Quebec to the confederation was heartily affirmed, bilingualization of the federal civil service was accelerated, and the prime minister (a

[8] Andrew H. Clark, "Geographical Diversity and the Personality of Canada," in *Readings in Canadian Geography*, 2nd ed., ed. R. M. Irving (Toronto: Holt, Rinehart & Winston of Canada, Ltd., 1972), p. 7.

[9] Kenneth D. McRae, "The Structure of Canadian History," in *The Founding of New Societies*, ed. Louis Hartz (New York: Harcourt, Brace & World, 1964), p. 220.

In the past, forest exploitation was restricted almost exclusively to winter. Trees were cut and hauled by various means to the rivers, where they were dumped on the ice. At the time of the spring thaw vast flotillas of rough logs came churning down to the mill sites, where they were caught and processed. This seasonality made part-time logging an important source of income for many residents of the region, especially small farmers whose winter labors were few. But in the last two decades forest exploitation has become virtually a year-round operation, and the opportunities for part-time employment are quite limited.

The rivers still serve as log thoroughfares, with bumpers and booms to guide the logs to the proper catchment areas in quiet water (fig. 7–8). A large proportion of the cut nowadays is, however, transported by truck or train; thus, the gathering of logs can go on in every month. Still, the important milling sites are along the streams, especially in the St. Maurice and Saguenay valleys and where major tributaries—such as the Ottawa and the St. Maurice—join the St. Lawrence; indeed, every river junction on the left bank of the St. Lawrence has a sawmill, pulp mill, or both nearby. Other types of wood-processing plants, such as those making doors, plywood, and pressed wood products, tend to be located in the major industrial centers.

fig. 7–8 Many of the region's rivers are still heavily used for transportation and storage of logs. This is the St. Maurice River upstream from Trois-Rivières.

FISHING

In the total view, fishing makes a trivial contribution to the regional economy. The principal species caught by French-Canadian fishermen are cod, redfish, and herring. Less than 10 percent of the total value of Canadian Atlantic fisheries is landed at ports in French Canada, and less than 1 percent of the regional work force is employed in catching and processing fish. Nevertheless, around the Gaspé Peninsula and in northern New Brunswick fishing is a significant enterprise, and in many places fishing villages and fishermen's houses literally line the bay shores. The village of Caraquet, New Brunswick, for example, is said to be the longest town in Canada. It consists of an almost-continuous line of homes along the south shore of Chaleur Bay, some 20 miles long and less than one block wide.

MINING

Mining is another primary activity with significance only in a limited part of the region. The world's largest commercial deposits of asbestos, with an annual output amounting to more than one-fourth of the world total, are located in the "Serpentine Belt," which extends in an arc northeastward from the Vermont border through the Eastern Townships. More than 6,000 workers are employed by ten mining companies in various mines between the valleys of the St. Francis and Chaudière rivers. Three sizable towns, Thetford Mines, Asbestos, and Black Lake, are supported by the industry; the two larger ones are sited over ore bodies, and the encroachment of open-pit mines has brought about great conflicts with urban land use.

urban-industrial french canada

As in most of Anglo-America, the true dynamism of this region's geography is found in its urban-industrial development. The rapid and significant growth of urbanism, based on solid industrial development, has made the French Canadian as much an urbanite as the New Englander or the Southern Californian.

Industrial output in the region, mostly concentrated in metropolitan Montreal, amounts to about 25 percent of the Canadian total. More than half of the Canadian production of tobacco products, cotton textiles, leather footwear, aircraft, and ships comes from French Canada. The single most important industry in the region is pulp and paper, with more than 50 large plants producing about 40 percent of Canada's total output.

The urban system of French Canada includes many small cities, a few medium-sized ones, and two dominant metropolises (see table 7–1 for a listing of the region's largest urban places). The medium-sized centers include the Trois Rivières–Cap-de-la-Madeleine conurbation of nearly 100,000 people at the confluence of the St. Maurice and St. Lawrence rivers; the notable industrial (especially aluminum refining and forest products) and commercial complex of Chicoutimi-Arvida-Jonquiere in the upper Saguenay Valley; Sherbrooke, the subregional center of the Eastern Townships; the prominent industrial city of Shawinigan in the St. Maurice Valley; and Hull, essentially an industrial suburb of Ottawa but located on the Quebec side of the Ottawa River.

But it is the bipolar axis of Montreal and Quebec City that dominates the region. Quebec City is the hearth of French-Canadian culture and serves as the political, religious, and symbolic center of French Canada. Montreal is French Canada's contribution to the world, a vibrant and exciting commercial, industrial, and financial node that shares with Toronto the primacy of all Canada.

MONTREAL

The city of Montreal spreads over most of the island of the same name that is located adjacent to the first major rapids on the St. Lawrence River. The city also overflows onto the nearby Île Jésus and eastward

table 7–1   Largest Urban Places of French Canada

name	population of principal city	population of metropolitan area
Cap-de-la-Madeleine, Que.	31,788	
Charlesbourg, Que.*	62,366	
Chicoutimi, Que.	56,702	
Drummondville, Que.	28,894	
Granby, Que.	36,674	
Hull, Que.	58,160	
Jonquiere, Que.	60,373	127,181
Lachine, Que.*	40,948	
LaSalle, Que.*	75,361	
Laval, Que.*	241,297	
Langueuil, Que.*	119,994	
Montreal, Que.	1,060,033	2,758,780
Montreal-Nord, Que.*	94,980	
Pointe-aux-Trembles, Que.*	37,463	
Quebec, Que.	173,959	534,193
Rimouski, Que.	27,550	
Sherbrooke, Que.	75,137	
St-Hubert, Que.*	48,385	
St-Hyacinthe, Que.	36,832	
St-Jean, Que.	34,048	
St-Laurent, Que.*	62,826	
St-Leonard, Que.*	78,619	
Ste-Foy, Que.*	70,356	
Trois-Rivières, Que.	51,772	
Verdun, Que.*	74,520	

* A suburb of a larger city.

across the river into Chambly County. Its site is dominated by the hill of Mount Royal, which rises directly behind the central business district (fig. 7–9).

Cartier discovered an Indian fort and settlement (Hochelaga) on Montreal Island. Soon a French town was founded there, for the location was superb. "Standing on an island, splitting the St. Lawrence at the confluence of the Ottawa, it commands the historic riverways of Canada. It is also north of the Champlain gap, and the way to New York."[12] Montreal was a fur and lumber

[12] J. Wreford Watson, *North America: Its Countries and Regions* (London: Longmans, Green and Co., 1968), p. 350.

143

fig. 7–9 Looking southeastward across the central business district of Montreal, from Mount Royal toward the St. Lawrence River.

trading center for the French, but its principal business and industrial growth was brought about by the British. It has long been the largest city in Canada, as well as being by far the nation's leading port. It shares commercial, industrial, and financial primacy with Toronto.

With its sprawling suburbs, numerous industrial districts, massive skyscrapers, and heavy traffic, Montreal has much the look of any Anglo-American metropolis. But it is about two-thirds Francophone and is called the second largest French-speaking city in the world. The remainder of its population mix is quite varied, and the life of the city is cosmopolitan. Old World charm is shown in the streets and squares of the older sections; the excitement of modern architecture dominates Place Ville Marie and its downtown surroundings; the attractive and efficient Metro subway system gives a fresh dimension to internal transport; the new Mirabel airport is one of the largest and most modern in the world; and the lingering and dramatic effects of the 1967 World's Fair and the 1976 Olympics are still strong.

This is not to say that Montreal is without problems; they exist in profusion, including the massive debt incurred in constructing the Olympic facilities. But imaginative approaches have been applied to attacking many of them. One of the most successful has been the rejuvenation of downtown, accomplished in part by a covered-city development in which about 65 acres have thus far been linked in sheltered promenades, walkways, shopping malls, and Metro stations to provide a year-round environment of comfort, safety, and convenience.

QUEBEC CITY

Quebec City is much smaller than Montreal, and its importance to Canada is therefore much less, although its significance to French Canada can hardly be overstated. Its famous site crowns 300-foot cliffs that rise abruptly from river level just upstream from the Île d'Orléans, where the St. Lawrence River opens out into its estuary. The historic fort of the Citadel still stands above the cliff ramparts, connected by Canada's most famous boardwalk with a castle-like hotel, the Château Frontenac, whose imposing turrets command a breathtaking view downriver (fig. 7–10).

The old walled portion of the city (called Upper Town) with its narrow, cobbled streets adjoins the Citadel. Below the cliffs lies Lower Town, also with a large older section of narrow streets and European

fig. 7-10 The spired turrets of Chateau Frontenac (on the right) and the sprawling stone walls of the Citadel (on the left) dominate the cliffs of Quebec City. Modern office towers rise in the distance, beyond the walled premises of Upper Town (courtesy Government of Quebec, Tourist Branch).

charm. More modern residential and commercial areas sprawl to the north and west. Industrial districts are mostly close to the harbor, which is increasing its shipping by virtue of expanded container facilities and efforts to keep the port open all winter. Although the importance of manufacturing in the economy is growing, Quebec City's major functions are administrative, commercial, and ecclesiastical. Tourism is another important activity in this city, which is probably the most picturesque of the continent.

recreation

The unique cultural attributes of French Canada make it a most attractive goal for tourists from non-French parts of the continent, and the large population centers of southern Ontario and northeastern United States are near enough to make accessibility no problem. The landscape, the architecture, the institutions, and the cuisine are the principal attractions; tourist interest centers on things to see rather than things to do, except perhaps in Montreal.

There are a number of areas to attract the nature-lover and outdoor enthusiast in and near the region. The provincial parks of Mont Tremblant and Laurentides, on the nearby Shield margin, draw many visitors, especially from Montreal and Quebec City; many of them come for winter sports. New national parks have been established at Forillon in the Gaspé and La Maurice north of Trois Rivières.

Beaches are few and inadequate in the region. But along the St. Lawrence estuary there is a surprising amount of tourist development, often consisting of small cottages situated above mud flats, and summer visitors from nearby inland areas are accommodated in large numbers. Still, the principal attractions for tourists in the region are cultural. Essentially all visitors go to Montreal, and most also visit Quebec City; if there is time left over, they may sample some of the areas of rural charm.

the outlook

French Canada has long been a region of economic disadvantage. Although not as serious as in the Atlantic Provinces, there has been a persistently high rate of unemployment as well as an even greater amount of seasonal unemployment. These factors are most notable in the eastern part of the region—the shores of the estuary, the Gaspé

Peninsula, and northern New Brunswick. In the last few years the regional economic disparity has decreased somewhat, although much of the improvement has been focused in the Montreal area. This trend is likely to continue, although slowly and irregularly.

Agriculture can be expected to contract on the one hand and intensify on the other. Farm abandonment and farm consolidation will probably continue for some years in the less favored agricultural areas. The more productive farmlands of the Montreal plain and the Eastern Townships are not likely to experience such a trend; rather, more intensive output of specialty crops and livestock products is anticipated, particularly in response to the growing Montreal market.

Quebec's manufacturing expansion since World War II has been dramatic and is likely to continue. The region, overall, has been changed from agrarian to industrial in three decades, and the general advantages of market, labor, power, and transportation are still there. Most of the industrial prosperity and growth will continue to occur in the already established centers, especially Montreal, but also Quebec City, Trois Rivières, Hull, and Shawinigan.

The effect of the St. Lawrence Seaway Project has been broadly detrimental to the commercial sector of the region's economy, but the impact has not been as unfavorable as was anticipated in many quarters. Larger ships can now bypass Montreal and cruise directly into the Great Lakes, with the result that Ontario's port business has been expanding more rapidly than Quebec's; nevertheless, traffic continues to increase in the ports of French Canada. In addition to the important ports of Montreal and Quebec City, the iron-ore shipping port of Sept Iles (on the north shore of the estuary) continues to be one of Canada's busiest ports in terms of volume handled.

In recent years, the tertiary sector of the economy—trade, finance, services—has been growing rapidly and accounting for much of the improvement in average per capita income in the region. Such growth should continue, although it will be focused principally in Montreal; indeed, Montreal will continue as the dominant growth center in almost all phases of the regional economy. It is a world-class metropolis, with influence beyond regional, national, and continental boundaries.

The primacy of Montreal is such that the provincial economy has been summed up as "Montreal and the Quebec desert." Certainly the upstream part of French Canada participates much more fully in the advantages of urbanization and industrialization than does the rest of the region. This economic disequilibrium will undoubtedly persist and perhaps become even more unbalanced as time passes.

The French Canada Region faces three general economic problems in the near future:

1 Labor unrest is a continuing threat to economic stability. French Canada probably has a higher rate of work stoppages than any other region on the continent.

2 The government debt burden, exacerbated by the Olympics, is so high that it acts as a drag on investment.

3 Most significant, however, is uncertainty over the political situation. It is reported that nearly 100 Canadian companies or subsidiaries of United States companies moved their corporate headquarters out of Quebec within four months of the accession of the Parti Québécois to power in 1976. The now-required Frenchification of businesses in the province is clearly a deterrent to most Anglo-based companies.

selected bibliography

BALDWIN, BARBARA, "Forillon—The Anatomy of a National Park," *Canadian Geographical Journal*, 82 (1971), 148–57.

BARRETT, F. A., "The Relative Decline of the French Language in Canada," *Geography*, 60 (1975), 125–29.

BEAUREGARD, LUDGER, "Le Canada Français par la Carte," *Revue de Géographie de Montréal,* 22 (1968), 35–44, maps.

———, "Le Québec et Ses Problémes de Population," *Canadian Geographer,* 18 (1974), 3–15.

BELZILE, MARCEL, "The Canada Land Inventory in Quebec," *Virginia Geographer,* 7 (Fall–Winter 1972), 13–14.

BROUILLETTE, NORMAND, "L'industrie Manufacturière du Québec: Development et Tendances Récentes," *Canadian Geographer,* 18 (1974), 26–38.

CERMAKIAN, JEAN, "The Geographic Basis for the Viability of an Independent State of Quebec," *Canadian Geographer,* 18 (1974), 288–94.

ECCLES, W. J., "New France and the French Impact on North America," *American Review of Canadian Studies,* 3 (1973), 173–82.

FALAISE, NOEL, "Les Iles de la Madeleine," *Canadian Geographical Journal,* 69 (1964), 116–25.

GREENING, W. E., "Sherbrooke: The Queen of the Eastern Townships," *Canadian Geographical Journal,* 69 (1964), 12–19.

GRENIER, FERNAND, ed., *Quebec.* Toronto: University of Toronto Press, 1972.

HALLIDAY, HUGH A., "Pushing the Road to Havre-St.-Pierre: And What Then?" *Canadian Geographical Journal,* 87 (December 1973), 28–35.

HAMELIN, LOUIS-EDMOND, "French Soul in a British Form," *The Geographical Magazine,* 44 (1972), 744–52.

HARRIS, RICHARD C., *The Seigneurial System in Early Canada.* Madison: University of Wisconsin Press, 1966.

JOY, RICHARD J., "Languages in Conflict: Canada, 1976," *American Review of Canadian Studies,* 6 (Autumn 1976), 7–21.

MAROIS, CLAUDE, *Employment Atlas, City and Island of Montreal.* Montreal: Les Presses de l'Universite du Québec, 1972.

ROSS, W. GILLIES, "Encroachment of the Jeffrey Mine on the Town of Asbestos, Quebec," *Geographical Review,* 57 (1967), 522–37.

SQUIRE, W. A., "New Brunswick's Hills and Mountains," *Canadian Geographical Journal,* 77 (1968), 52–57.

STEED, GUY P. F., "Centrality and Locational Change: Printing, Publishing, and Clothing in Montreal and Toronto," *Economic Geography,* 52 (1976), 193–205.

VELTMAN, C. J., "Ethnic Assimilation in Quebec: A Statistical Analysis," *American Review of Canadian Studies,* 5 (Autumn 1975), 104–29.

8

MEGALOPOLIS

The Megalopolis Region is one of the smallest major regions in Anglo-America, encompassing only about 50,000 square miles, or less than 1 percent of the continent. Its population of some 42 million people, however, is the second largest population of any region, amounting to 18 percent of the Anglo-American total.

It is a coastal region, and although not now primarily oriented toward the sea, it serves as the major western terminus of the world's busiest oceanic route that extends across the North Atlantic to Western Europe. Its role as eastern terminus of transcontinental land transportation routes and as two-way terminal (international to the east and transcontinental to the west) for airline routes is equally significant.

The region was a major early destination of European settlers. Thus, most of its cities have a long history in comparison with others on the continent, and the region is rich in historical tradition. Yet it is pulsing with change.

It is the premier region of economic and social superlatives to be found in Anglo-America. It represents the greatest accumulation of wealth and the greatest concentration of poverty, it has the greatest variety of urban amenities and the greatest number of urban problems, it has the highest population densities and the most varied population mix, and it is clearly the leading business and governmental center of the nation. Its economic and social maladjustments are legion, and yet its attempts at alleviating them are imaginative and far-reaching.

Most of all, however, it is an urban region. Its geography is a geography of cities and supercities. It is one of the most highly urbanized parts of the world, and its life style is geared to the dynamic bustle of urban processes, problems, and opportunities.

extent of the region

Megalopolis, the world's greatest conurbation, has developed along a northeast-southwest axis approximately paralleling the Middle Atlantic and southern New England coast of the United States (fig. 8–1). Its core is the almost completely urbanized area extending from metropolitan New York across New Jersey to metropolitan Philadelphia. It extends northeastward from New York City through a number of smaller cities to metropolitan Boston, and southwestward from Philadelphia to Baltimore and Washington.

For a number of years this metropolitan complex from Boston to Washington has been recognized as a major urban region. The concept of a unified Atlantic seaboard metropolitan region was notably publicized

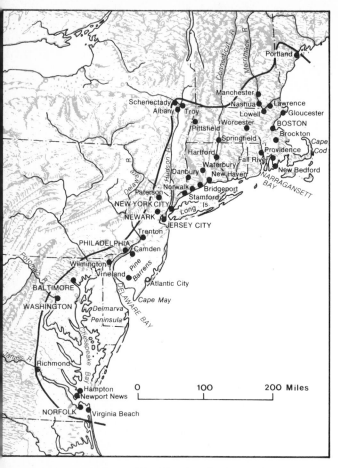

fig. 8–1 The Megalopolis Region (base map copyright A. K. Lobeck; reprinted by permission of Hammond, Inc.).

by Jean Gottmann's epic study of 1961, in which he adopted the ancient Greek name *Megalopolis* to apply to the region.[1] Since the time of Gottmann's work, continued urban expansion at either end has made it logical to extend the area under consideration northward in New York and New England and southward in Virginia.

[1] Jean Gottmann, *Megalopolis, The Urbanized Northeastern Seaboard of the United States* (New York: Twentieth Century Fund, 1961).

The Atlantic coastline marks the eastern margin of the region, which means that fairly extensive rural areas—particularly in southeastern Massachusetts, southern New Jersey, the Delmarva Peninsula, and eastern Virginia—are included within the confines of Megalopolis. These lands, however, are used primarily for urban-serving agriculture or recreation and can thus logically be accepted as part of the region.

The western boundary of Megalopolis is considered to be where urban population densities and land-use patterns fade and are replaced by rural densities and patterns to the west of the principal urban nodes of the region. This zone is fairly easy to demarcate in the south, where the Hampton Roads cities, Richmond, Washington, and Baltimore are involved. West and northwest of Philadelphia the distinction is less clear, as is the case north of New York City and north of Boston. In the first-mentioned district, the megalopolitan boundary is drawn to exclude most of southeastern Pennsylvania beyond the immediate metropolitan area of Philadelphia, with the reasoning that the Pennsylvania Dutch farming counties of Lancaster and York and the small industrial cities of Reading and Allentown-Bethlehem are relatively independent of Megalopolis and more logically associated with the Appalachian Region to the west. North of New York City the boundary is drawn to include that portion of the Hudson Valley as far as the Albany-Schenectady-Troy metropolitan area. North of Boston the extent of Megalopolis is considered to include the urbanized lower portion of the Merrimack Valley as far as Concord and the urbanized coastal zone as far as Portland and Lewiston.

As thus delimited, the Megalopolis Region encompasses a number of significant urban nodes and complexes, most of which have important interconnections while remaining relatively discrete urban units.

1 In southern New Hampshire and northern Massachusetts are the old but still highly industrialized mill towns of the Merrimack Valley.

150

2 Metropolitan Boston, with its many suburbs and related towns, spreads over much of eastern Massachusetts.

3 Metropolitan Providence includes most of Rhode Island and small cities of related economic structure in adjacent Massachusetts.

4 The Lower Connecticut Valley area includes a number of closely spaced, medium-sized cities, especially Springfield, Hartford–New Britain, Waterbury, and New Haven.

5 The urbanized node of Albany-Schenectady-Troy.

6 The New York City metropolitan area sprawls over parts of three states and encompasses such adjacent major cities as Newark, Jersey City, Paterson, Elizabeth, and Stamford.

7 Metropolitan Philadelphia includes an extensive area along the lower Delaware River Valley, including Trenton and Camden in New Jersey and Wilmington in Delaware.

8 Metropolitan Baltimore.

9 Metropolitan Washington, which spreads widely into Maryland and Virginia.

10 Metropolitan Richmond.

11 The Hampton Roads urban complex includes the urbanized areas on either side of the mouth of the James River estuary.

character of the region

Nowhere else in Anglo-America is there such a concentration of the physical works of humanity to dominate the land and the horizon for square mile after square mile; yet there is a surprisingly rural aspect to much of the region. Despite the prominence of tall skyscrapers, controlled-access highways, massive bridges, extensive airports, and noisy factories, the green quietness of the countryside is also widespread.

There are many places in Rhode Island, a tiny state but one with the second greatest population density, where a person can stand on a viewpoint and look in all directions and see no evidence of people or their works; there is nothing but trees and clouds and sky. In an extensive area in southern New Jersey, that most urbanized of states, birds nest, streams run pure, and forests are virgin. The deer population of the region is now greater than it was a decade or even a century ago.[2] In many areas there is actually more woodland than there was ten or twenty years ago because of farm abandonment. For Megalopolis as a whole, it is estimated that only about 20 percent of the land is in urban use.[3]

From the viewpoint of an orbiting satellite, it would probably be the interdigitation of urban and rural land uses that would be the most prominent aspect of the geographical scene. But by no stretch of the imagination is the region entirely urbanized; neither does it form any sort of a single urban unit. Rather there are major nodes of urbanization that are growing toward one another, usually along the radial spokes of principal highways, with much rural land between the spokes. In some cases, particularly around New York, Philadelphia, and Boston, nodes have coalesced; but in most parts of the region the nodes remain discrete, and a great deal of nonurban land is interlocked.

Another important facet of the regional character is its dependence on interchange with other regions and countries. Although the full range of urban functions occurs in multiplicity in Megalopolis, the region generates a monstrous demand for primary goods (foodstuffs and industrial raw materials), most of which it cannot produce. There

[2] For example, in the five states that are entirely within the Megalopolis Region—Connecticut, Delaware, Massachusetts, New Jersey, and Rhode Island—the estimated deer population in 1970 was 106,000, in comparison with a 1940 estimate of approximately 63,000. (Personal communications from Fish and Game agencies of the respective states, October 1971.)

[3] Irving Cutler, "Megalopolis: Intermetropolitan Coalescence," *Journal of Geography,* 68 (November 1969), 463.

is an almost equally significant need for the movement of regional products to extraregional markets; thus major transportation terminals, which are numerous, are loci of much activity and of extensive storage and processing facilities.

Most significant of all, in assessing the geographic character of Megalopolis, is probably the intensity of living that prevails there. This is shown in its crudest form by the high population density, both as a general average for the whole region and more specifically for the urbanized nodes. The av-erage population density for the region is 850 persons per square mile. In the most urbanized state, New Jersey, average density is 936 per square mile. In some of the cities population density reaches remarkable levels, the highest being on Manhattan Island with a night-time density of more than 80,000 and a daytime density of almost 200,-000 per square mile.

There are many other elements to "intensity of living." Where people live close together, there is also a clustering of structures, activities, and movements. Such agglomeration is advantageous in providing concentrated opportunities for variable want-satisfaction within a limited space. Yet it also engenders the handicaps associated with crowding: waste of space and time, frustration and psychological trauma, pollution and health problems, stifled transportation, and so on.

fig. 8-2   The urban complexes of Megalopolis:
(1) the Merrimack Valley, (2) Metropolitan Boston,
(3) the Narragansett Basin, (4) the Lower Connecticut Valley,
(5) Albany-Schenectady-Troy, (6) Metropolitan New York City,
(7) Metropolitan Philadelphia, (8) Metropolitan Baltimore,
(9) Metropolitan Washington, (10) Metropolitan Richmond,
and (11) Hampton Roads.

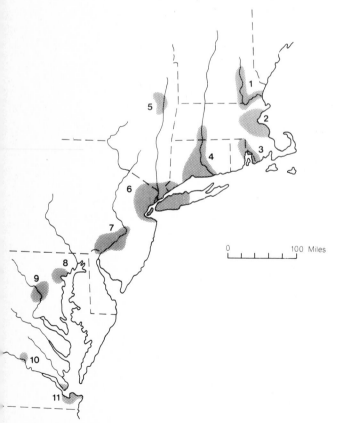

the urban scene

The urban complex of Megalopolis is almost overwhelming in its magnitude and diversity. Within the region there are nearly 1,000 places that are classed as urban by the Census Bureau, more than 4,000 separate governmental units, and a population of about 42 million of which nearly 90 percent is urban (see table 8-1 for a listing of the region's largest urban places). For convenience of discussion, the region is subdivided into eleven urban groupings, to be considered successively from north to south (fig. 8-2).

THE MERRIMACK VALLEY

With a total population of half a million, the Merrimack Valley of New Hampshire and Massachusetts includes five small cities: Manchester, Nashua, Lowell, Lawrence, and Haverhill. These former mill towns, highly industrialized and specialized toward textiles and shoes, have mirrored the economic pattern and problems of southern New England for many decades (fig. 8-3). As New England's advantages for making these products declined, areas that could not

table 8–1   Largest Urban Places of the Megalopolis Region

name	population of principal city	population of metropolitan area	name	population of principal city	population of metropolitan area
Albany, N.Y.	110,311	799,000	New Bedford, Mass.	100,133	463,800
Alexandria, Va.*	105,220		New Britain, Conn.	78,556	
Arlington, Mass.*	49,815		New Brunswick, N.J.	47,420	589,600
Arlington, Va.*	152,000		New Haven, Conn.	126,845	
Atlantic City, N.J.	43,969	189,800	Newport News, Va.	138,760	351,800
Baltimore, Md.	851,698	2,136,900	New Rochelle, N.Y.*	71,841	
Bayonne, N.J.*	73,574		Newton, Mass.*	88,559	
Bloomfield, N.J.*	52,162		New York, N.Y.	7,567,800	9,635,200
Boston, Mass.	636,725	3,914,600	Norfolk, Va.	286,694	772,600
Bridgeport, Conn.	142,960	793,900	Norwalk, Conn.	76,688	
Bristol, Conn.	58,560		Norwich, Conn.	41,060	240,600
Brockton, Mass.	95,878		Passaic, N.J.	49,900	
Cambridge, Mass.*	102,420		Paterson, N.J.	139,098	452,700
Camden, N.J.	89,214		Pawtucket, R.I.	72,024	
Chesapeake, Va.*	104,459		Petersburg, Va.	45,245	124,200
Chester, Pa.*	48,529		Philadelphia, Pa.	1,815,808	4,797,300
Chicopee, Mass.*	57,771		Pittsfield, Mass.	54,893	149,000
Clifton, N.J.	79,467		Portland, Maine	59,857	229,100
Cranston, R.I.*	74,381		Portsmouth, Va.	108,674	
Danbury, Conn.	54,512		Poughkeepsie, N.Y.	31,608	234,800
East Hartford, Conn.*	54,132		Providence, R.I.	167,724	851,100
East Orange, N.J.*	73,420		Quincy, Mass.*	91,494	
East Providence, R.I.*	49,636		Richmond, Va.	232,652	581,500
Elizabeth, N.J.	104,405		Rockville, Md.*	44,299	
Fairfield, Conn.*	58,084		Schenectady, N.Y.	74,995	
Fall River, Mass.	100,430		Somerville, Mass.*	80,798	
Framingham, Mass.	65,540		Stamford, Conn.	105,151	
Greenwich, Conn.*	59,566		Springfield, Mass.	170,790	597,400
Hampton, Va.	125,013	351,800	Suffolk, Va.	49,210	
Hartford, Conn.	138,152	1,059,800	Taunton, Mass.*	41,935	
Holyoke, Mass.	46,435		Trenton, N.J.	101,365	320,500
Irvington, N.J.*	58,196		Troy, N.Y.	60,312	
Jersey City, N.J.	243,756	582,800	Union City, N.J.*	52,648	
Lawrence, Mass.	67,390		Vineland, N.J.	53,637	132,900
Lewiston, Maine	41,045	94,600	Virginia Beach, Va.	213,954	
Long Branch, N.J.	31,007	486,700	Waltham, Mass.*	56,251	
Lowell, Mass.	91,493		Warwick, R.I.	85,875	
Lynn, Mass.*	79,327		Washington, D.C.	722,700	3,015,300
Malden, Mass.*	55,778		Waterbury, Conn.	107,065	
Manchester, N.H.	83,417	243,800	West Hartford, Conn.*	66,605	
Medford, Mass.	60,769		West Haven, Conn.*	53,002	
Meriden, Conn.	57,697		Weymouth, Mass.*	56,815	
Milford, Conn.	49,704		White Plains, N.Y.*	48,327	
Mount Vernon, N.Y.*	67,687		Wilmington, Del.	79,152	517,300
Nashua, N.H.	61,002		Woonsocket, R.I.	46,888	181,800
Nassau-Suffolk, N.Y.		2,622,000	Worcester, Mass.	171,566	648,100
Newark, N.J.	339,568	1,995,900	Yonkers, N.Y.	191,509	

* A suburb of a larger city.

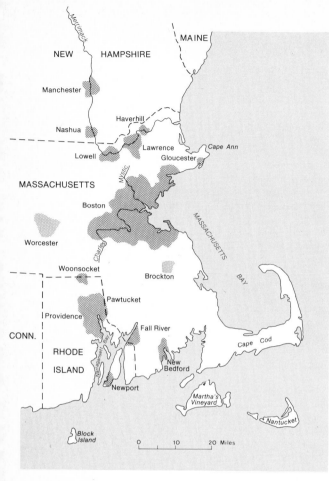

fig. 8–3 The metropolitan areas of southeastern New England.

find satisfactory replacements were subjected to increasing unemployment and economic distress.

Since the prosperous years of the 1920s the textile industry, which employed well over half of all industrial workers in the valley, has declined to a fraction of its former magnitude (fig. 8–4). The manufacture of leather goods, primarily shoes, has decreased much less precipitously and is still the leading type of manufacturing in the valley. Electrical machinery production has been the principal growth industry, and there has been increasing diversification. The valley is a low wage area with generally depressed incomes, but during the 1970s there was rapid economic and population growth, particularly in the New Hampshire portion.

METROPOLITAN BOSTON

The dominant city of New England is located at the western end of Massachusetts Bay, a broad-mouthed indentation that is generally well protected by the extended arms of Cape Ann and Cape Cod. The site of the original city was a narrow-necked peninsula of low glacial hills and poorly drained swamps. The Charles and Mystic rivers flow into the bay, and much of the older part of the city now occupies land that had to be drained before construction could take place.

Shortly after the founding of Boston in 1630, other towns, such as Cambridge and Quincy, were established on better drained land nearby. Boston with its numerous protected wharves was, however, the dominant

fig. 8–4 An old textile mill, still operating at Ipswich, Massachusetts.

settlement from the outset. By the end of the colonial period it was exceeded in size nationally only by Philadelphia and New York, and it maintained this third-ranking position for more than a century. Further, by the middle of the nineteenth century there were more towns exceeding 5,000 population in eastern Massachusetts (largely within Boston's orbit) than in any other cluster in Anglo-America.

Boston's central business district was extended after further drainage projects were completed but has remained mostly concentrated near the original nucleus. Urban sprawl has widely expanded the city to the north, west, and south of the original area, and many of the ancillary settlements have been absorbed into the metropolis.

Although early significant as an industrial center, the economy of Boston has become increasingly oriented toward tertiary and quaternary activities—trade, services, and government employment—which provide more than 70 percent of the jobs in the metropolitan area. This is a somewhat higher proportion than in most large Anglo-American cities and can be accounted for primarily by Boston's dominant commercial relationship to most of New England (except Connecticut) and to the concentration of government offices and educational institutions in Boston. The port of Boston is a busy one, but the lack of an extensive hinterland has resulted in a relative decline in its importance; it is a major importing port, but in total trade it is outranked by four other ports in the Megalopolis Region alone.

The industrial component of Boston's economy is a prominent one and, as with most cities, tells much about the distinctiveness of the city's function. Total employment and output in manufacturing have been approximately static over the past two decades, which means that there has been a relative decline in the importance of manufacturing to the city's economy; manufacturing is down from about one-third of total metropolitan employment in the early 1950s to one-fourth in the early 1970s. Although textiles and leather goods have been the traditional mainstays of manufacturing in New

England, the former has not been important in Boston for several decades, and the latter has been on an erratic but declining trend for several years, even in the historic shoe-making suburbs of Brockton and Beverley. The leading manufacturing industry in Boston since World War II has been the production of electrical machinery, particularly electronics equipment, which employs about one-sixth of the city's industrial workers. The principal growth industry in the last few years, however, has been nonelectrical machinery. Despite the relative decline of manufacturing in Boston, its size is so great that it still ranks as the eighth largest industrial center in Anglo-America.

As one of the oldest major cities on the continent and one that was quite prominent in colonial times, Boston maintains an air of historic charm in many of its older sections. Narrow twisting streets, colonial architecture, and tiny parks are widespread. But modernity is increasingly evident even in the central city, as evidenced by skyscrapers, freeways, an airport on reclaimed land in the bay, and even a multilevel parking garage under the famed Boston Common. Boston also has one of the first beltways completed around a major American city; the Circumferential Highway (Route 128), at a radius of about 12 miles from the city center, has become a major attraction for light industry and suburban office buildings (it is sometimes referred to as the "electronics parkway"). The pattern is now being repeated on Interstate 495, an outer beltway some 25 miles from the central business district, with many planned industrial parks at intersections of the freeway and express arterials from downtown.

Boston has long been known as an elitist city and cultural center with many attractions for living; yet, numerous problems exist. Lack of money to meet governmental expenses is at the root of many of them. In Boston, 20 percent of the residents of the city are on the welfare rolls. Most of the city budget (70 percent) comes from property taxes, and yet almost half of all municipal property is untaxed, such as the home of state government, hundreds of churches, and many educational institutions. In the past, the city population has been dominated by Europeans, particularly the Irish and a large Italian minority.[4] In recent years there has been a rapid influx of less readily assimilable people, particularly blacks and Puerto Ricans, resulting in ethnic hostility that had been dormant for decades. Black and Puerto Rican residential areas are more highly segregated than in perhaps any other major Anglo-American city, and the areas of lowest per capita income coincide precisely with these districts.[5]

Even so, metropolitan Boston continues to grow and the average family income is one of the highest of any large city. Imaginative attempts are underway to assuage two urban problems for which Boston has long been famous: reorganization and extension of mass transit facilities to prevent traffic strangulation of an auto-oriented city that is plagued by an infamous maze of narrow twisting streets, and a major start toward metropolitan government. Boston remains the primate city of northern and eastern New England and continues as the northern bastion of Megalopolis.

NARRAGANSETT BASIN

New England's second largest city and second-ranking industrial center is Providence, situated where the Blackstone River flows into the head of Narragansett Bay. The Providence area, with its industrial satellites of Pawtucket and Woonsocket to the north and Fall River and New Bedford to the southeast, represents in microcosm the industrial history of southeastern New England, demonstrating graphically the economic displacement that occurs in a heavily industrialized area when its leading industry falters.

[4] The largest population component of "foreign stock" (first, second, and third generation) in metropolitan Boston is Canadian, however.
[5] Michael P. Conzen and George K. Lewis, *Boston: A Geographical Portrait* (Cambridge, Mass.: Ballinger Publishing Co., 1976), p. 38.

From colonial days southern New England was the center of the American cotton textile industry. Initial advantages included (1) excellent water power facilities; (2) a seaboard location for importing cotton; (3) damp air, which was essential to prevent twisting and snarling during spinning and to reduce fiber breakage in weaving; (4) skilled labor; (5) clean, soft water; and (6) location in a major market area. Since the 1920s most of the cotton textile industry has relocated in other areas, particularly in the southern Appalachian Piedmont where labor, taxes, power, and raw materials were all less expensive. The greatest concentrations of cotton textile factories in New England were in the Narragansett Basin and the Merrimack Valley; their attrition has been a damaging blow to the local economy. The last cotton-weaving mill in Rhode Island ceased operation in 1968, and both cotton spinning and weaving are almost gone from adjacent parts of Massachusetts.

The woolen textile industry of New England prospered longer. In the early days there was local wool in addition to waterpower, skilled labor, and an appreciable nearby market. Further, Boston has always been the major wool-importing port of the nation. Rapid decline engulfed New England's woolen textile industry in the late 1940s, and the downward trend has continued at a slower pace. The Narragansett Basin has been particularly hard hit. Fall River, once the single leading producer of cotton textiles in the country, now has fewer than 3,000 textile workers, and nearly all are in the woolen industry. The textile industry once employed more than half of all manufactural workers in Providence; it now provides jobs for barely one-seventh of the total.

The very high rate of industrialization in the Narragansett Basin emphasizes the magnitude of the problem. In the late 1940s Providence was the most highly industrialized large city in the nation, with more than 55 percent of its work force employed in factories. Fall River, New Bedford, and Pawtucket were even more dependent on manufacturing, with nearly 65 percent of their work force employed in factories. Comparable figures in the late 1970s are 40 percent for Providence and about 50 percent for the three smaller centers.

It should be noted that even with a declining rate of industrial employment, the Narragansett Basin cities are still heavily dependent on manufacturing. Providence, with its preeminent rank as a producer of jewelry and silverware, is still among the twenty leading industrial employment centers in Anglo-America.

CONNECTICUT VALLEY

The broad lowland drained by the lower Connecticut River contains a number of prosperous,[6] medium-sized cities, with a total population of about 2.5 million (fig. 8–5). The Springfield-Chicopee-Holyoke complex in Massachusetts and Hartford in Connecticut are located on the river; the other cities of New Britain–Bristol, Waterbury-Naugatuck, Meriden, New Haven, and Bridgeport are a bit further west.

This is a long-standing industrial district of importance. The factories specialize in diversified light products requiring considerable mechanical skill: machinery, tools, hardware, firearms, brass, plastics, electrical goods, electronics equipment, precision instruments, watches, and clocks. These are mostly products of high value and small bulk, which require little raw material and can easily stand transport charges to distant markets.

This southwestern part of New England has adjusted much better than southeastern New England to changes in the economy. The flight of textiles has not resulted in nearly so many abandoned factories; rather, other types of manufacturing were attracted to utilize the cadre of trained workers and the available buildings. The growth in electrical machinery production has been steady, partly because of the research and product-development facilities of the dis-

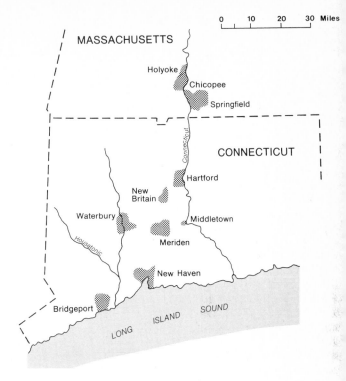

fig. 8–5 Metropolitan areas of the lower Connecticut Valley.

trict. Aircraft engine manufacture is significant in Connecticut, even though airframe assembly is accomplished in other parts of the country. Various kinds of machinery and hardware and other light metal goods are produced in quantity in several cities.

Although there is heavy dependence on manufacturing (more than 40 percent of the Connecticut labor force is employed in factories, a higher proportion than in any other state), the economy of the subregion is broadly diversified and includes a notable concentration of the nation's insurance industry in Hartford. The commercial orientation of the valley is largely westward toward New York, which apparently is an important catalyst.

This is a district with no major cores. The nineteenth century industrial cities have persisted but have not dominated. Rather, many nodes of specialized activities

---

[6] Connecticut normally ranks first among the states in per capita income.

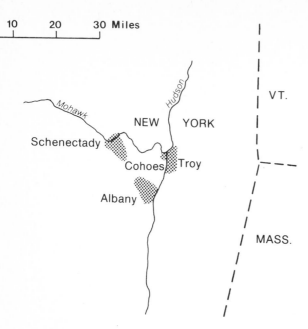

fig. 8–6　The Albany-Schenectady-Troy metropolitan area.

have emerged.[7] The result is a noncentric population pattern, with much daily movement among a wide range of foci.

[7] David R. Meyer, *From Farm to Factory to Urban Pastoralism: Urban Change in Central Connecticut* (Cambridge, Mass.: Ballinger Publishing Co., 1976), p. 32.

fig. 8–7　The heart of Megalopolis is the expansive urban complex of New York–northeastern New Jersey (Landsat image).

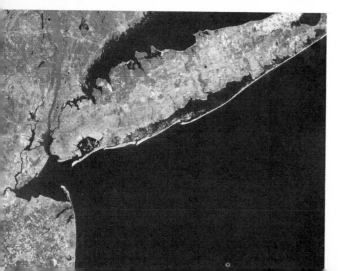

ALBANY-SCHENECTADY-TROY METROPOLITAN AREA

Situated at the commercially strategic confluence of the Mohawk and Hudson Rivers, the old Dutch settlement of Albany has become a metropolitan area of 800,000 people clustered about multiple nuclei in parts of four counties (fig. 8–6). As the upstream end of the Hudson River axis and the eastern end of the low-level Mohawk corridor to the Great Lakes, the Albany area had major crossroads significance from its earliest days. By late in the 1600s Albany was the leading fur-trading center for the English colonies, and a century later it was declared the state capital. The completion of the Erie Canal in 1825 was a major stimulus to economic prosperity and population growth. Despite many changes in transportation orientation, the urban node still functions as a transshipment point between river or ocean traffic on one hand and canal or overland traffic on the other.

The area has been an important industrial center for many decades. It had initial raw material advantages (sand, limestone, and nearby iron ore) that provided an early start for manufacturing, and the industrial component of the economy remained strong through the years. Troy has been noted as a center for making men's shirts; Albany was a wood-manufacturing center; and Schenectady was most famous for General Electric and the American Locomotive Company.

More recently, the area's industrial importance has declined, with a commensurate expansion in trade, services, and especially, government employment.

METROPOLITAN NEW YORK

The metropolitan area of New York City, which occupies two dozen counties in parts of three states, is the core of Megalopolis (fig. 8–7). It is the principal city of the United States and, in many ways, is the most important if not dominant city in the world. The massing of people and activities around the mouth of the Hudson estuary represents Megalopolis at its most intensive.

The economic primacy of New York cannot be satisfactorily explained in any simple fashion. It is the result of a continuum of complex interactions that are worldwide in scope and spread over several centuries in time. In elementary terms, it can be viewed as the result of an economic struggle among several competing ports to dominate the juncture of two major trade routes: the North Atlantic shipping lanes to Europe and the continental connections to the Anglo-American interior. New York's location did not initially appear to be more advantageous than that of its major competitors, notably Baltimore, Boston, Halifax, Montreal, and especially, Philadelphia. The others, however, suffered from various handicaps. Baltimore, Philadelphia, and Montreal all had to be reached by tortuous navigation up narrow estuaries, and Montreal was iced in for several months each winter. Both Boston and Halifax had less extensive harbors than New York, and Boston, particularly, was plagued by shallow water in its harbor.

The major advantage for New York was access to the interior. The availability of an easy water-level route to the Midwest via the Hudson River and the Mohawk Valley gave New York a preeminence over its nineteenth-century competitors that was never relinquished. In 1800 New York handled less than 10 percent of United States foreign trade, but by 1830, after the opening of the Erie Canal, New York's share was nearly 40 percent.[8]

New York has a magnificent site for waterborne traffic. It is located at the mouth of the navigable Hudson River on a well-protected harbor that is continually scoured by the river, which keeps the channel deep. The channel leading to the Atlantic is direct and broad. The tidal range is so small that ships may come and go at almost any time. The harbor is well protected from storms and is never blocked by ice. The principal

[8] Robert McNee, "New York," in *Geography of New York State*, ed. John H. Thompson (Syracuse, N.Y.: Syracuse University Press, 1966), p. 428.

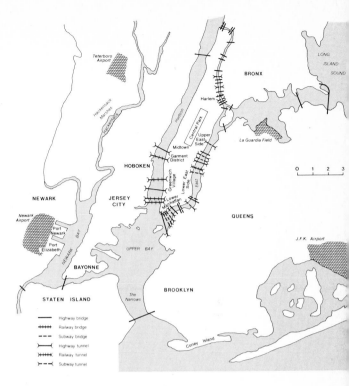

fig. 8-8   Manhattan Island and its connections with other parts of the metropolitan area.

handicaps involve rapid and tricky currents and the occasional presence of dense fog.

A look at any large-scale map shows the exceeding fragmentation of the city's site (fig. 8-8). This fragmentation was a boon to waterborne commerce but constitutes a major problem to internal communication. Manhattan Island is a narrow finger of land (13.5 miles long by 2.3 miles wide at its broadest point) situated between the broad Hudson River on the west, the narrow Harlem River on the north, and the East River (really a tidal estuary connecting New York Harbor and Long Island Sound) on the east (fig. 8-9). Long Island extends eastward for 100 miles between Long Island Sound on the north and the Atlantic Ocean on the south. Staten Island, nearly three times the size of Manhattan, huddles close to the New Jersey shore to the southwest of New York Harbor. Rivers, estuaries, and marshes add to the fragmentation along the Jersey shore.

fig. 8-9 The island of Manhattan extends
southward from the distant Bronx mainland,
sandwiched between the Hudson River on
the left and the East River on the right.
The twin towers of the World Trade Center
dominate the Lower Manhattan scene at
the southern tip of the island (courtesy
Port Authority of New York and New
Jersey).

Function Owing to the immense size
of its population and its location at a focus
of land, water, and air transport routes, New
York City has become preeminent in most
fields of urban activity in the United States.
By almost any measure—retail sales, wholesale sales, foreign commerce handled—of
commercial activity, New York is the unchallenged national leader. Its port activities
have declined relatively (but not absolutely)
from the peak year of 1870, when nearly 60
percent of all United States foreign trade
passed through New York, to a contemporary level of between 35 and 40 percent.
This is five times greater than that of the second-ranking port (see vignette below).

Although commerce has contributed
more to the city's primacy than has industry, New York is—almost incidentally—the
nation's and the world's largest manufacturing center. Within the metropolitan area is
nearly 10 percent of the country's factory
output, which, for example, exceeds the
combined total for the six New England
states. Despite its magnitude, the industrial
structure is not highly diversified. One type
of manufacturing, the making of garments,
predominates. About one-fourth of all the
apparel manufactured in the United States
is produced in New York factories. Only five
other Anglo-American cities have more employees in all manufacturing combined than
are employed in New York in this single industry. Most of the garment factories are
concentrated in an area of 200 acres in central Manhattan, where they occupy the
upper floors of moderate-height buildings

the changing geography of the port of new york

One of the most striking changes in the geography of New York in recent years has been the
shift of port activities from one area of the harbor to another, particularly for general cargo
movements. The Hudson River waterfront has
almost faded away, particularly on the Manhattan side; the Brooklyn waterfront has declined
but survived; and the dynamic area of contem-

porary port activity is in the heretofore remote
reaches of Newark Bay.

Throughout the nineteenth century most of
the area's general cargo oceangoing traffic was
accommodated along the Manhattan shorelines, particularly by finger piers that were constructed out into the relatively deep water of the
Hudson and East rivers. Early in the present

and are so inconspicuous as to pass unnoticed by the casual visitor.

The second-ranking manufacturing industry is printing and publishing; about one-sixth of total national output is in the metropolitan area. There is a pronounced trend for production (printing) to be shifted to suburban locations, whereas the publishing activities remain concentrated in Manhattan. A great variety of other types of manufacturing is found in New York, but none is nearly so significant as the two discussed; and there is a virtual absence of some types of heavy industry, particularly primary metal production.

New York City continues as the leading financial center of the world. The great money market is focused in the Wall Street district of Lower Manhattan, where a proliferation of financial specialists can provide external economies to businesses at all scales of operation. As a result of the great concentration of financial institutions, the velocity of demand deposits (relative frequency of use of a deposited dollar) is greater than elsewhere in the nation. Furthermore, the two securities exchanges (stock markets) in this district handle nearly nine-tenths of the organized stock and bond transactions of the country.

As a headquarters and managerial center, New York is also unsurpassed. It houses far more corporate headquarters than any other city, despite recent decentralization tendencies that have seen literally thousands of offices, and tens of thousands of white-collar jobs, shifted to the suburbs and be-

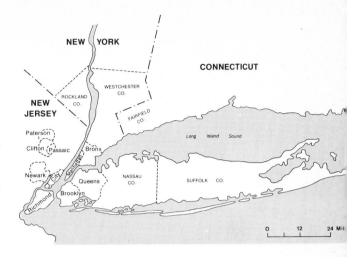

fig. 8–10 Metropolitan New York.

yond. Still, the wide variety of business services and skills available in New York provides a spectrum of expertise that is not remotely approached by any other city.

New York's entertainment, cultural, and tourist functions are outstanding. The city is national leader in theaters, museums, libraries, art galleries, mass media headquarters, higher education institutions, hotel rooms, and most other significant urban amenities.

Morphology The political city of New York is composed of five boroughs: Manhattan, Bronx, Queens, Kings (Brooklyn), and Richmond. The metropolitan area, however, sprawls widely on the mainland and on Long Island (fig. 8–10).

---

century, however, the New Jersey side of the harbor (primarily at Hoboken, Jersey City, and Bayonne) became increasingly active, and the Brooklyn waterfront was upgraded, becoming dominant in the post–World War I years.

By the time of World War II most general cargo traffic was handled on the New York side of the harbor. Brooklyn was the principal center

of activity, followed by the Hudson River waterfront of Manhattan. Bulk cargo facilities, then as now, were concentrated along the Jersey City waterfront and in upper Newark Bay. The principal passenger terminals, mostly catering to transatlantic liners, were on the Hudson side of Manhattan directly opposite Midtown.

The states of New York and New Jersey

(Continued)

fig. 8–11 The blocky skyscrapers of Midtown Manhattan, with Central Park beyond (to the north). The George Washington Bridge and the palisades of the Hudson River show at upper left.

Manhattan Island is the nerve center of the city. The island is composed of an ancient, stable rock mass that is rigid enough to support the tall buildings for which the city is famous. In the middle of Manhattan is Central Park, one of the largest and best-known greenspaces in the world. Just to the south is the Midtown district, which contains the world's greatest collection of skyscrapers (fig. 8–11). Slightly southwest of this area and across Times Square is the "garment district," an area of moderate-sized buildings, clogged streets, and jam-packed sidewalks. Further south is the old "Bohemian" district of Greenwich Village, now becoming fashionable again, and the more recent, art-oriented neighborhood of

had been involved for decades in acrimonious quarrels, litigation, and competition involving all manner of harbor-related use. They finally agreed, under prodding by the federal Interstate Commerce Commission, to establish a bistate authority to plan, construct, and administer most commerce facilities within the Port District, which was considered to be the area within a radius of approximately 25 miles of the Statue of Liberty. The original administrative body was created in 1921 and is known today as the Port Authority of New York and New Jersey.

There were many technological developments in maritime shipping during the 1950s and 1960s, but by far the most revolutionary was the introduction and widespread adoption of containerized shipping, in which an increasing proportion of all general cargo is sealed in standardized boxes (usually 40 x 8 x 8 feet or 20 x 8 x 8 feet) before shipment. This greatly simplifies loading into and unloading from vessels, largely eliminates pilferage and breakage, and significantly reduces handling time and cost. It also requires major changes in dockside facilities: immense specialized machinery is needed to shift the containers from shore to ship and vice versa, most cargo sheds become redundant, extensive dockside storage areas are required (the accepted ratio is now about 50 acres of supporting space for each con-

tainer ship berth), and ready access for trucks is necessary.

The advent of containerization hastened the demise of the cramped and outmoded finger piers that studded the waterfronts of Manhattan and Brooklyn and the Hudson River shorelines of New Jersey. In the last few years expansive new cargo facilities have been constructed, most notably on filled land along the western side of Newark Bay, and to a lesser degree on the north side of Staten Island and on the Brooklyn waterfront. The Newark Bay facilities are oustanding (fig. 8-a). Thirty-six deepwater (35 feet) berths are available along two channels: Port Elizabeth is completely containerized, and Port Newark is partly containerized but with extensive facilities for handling conventional general cargo. In addition there is a scrap steel terminal, a pelletized lumber port, an automated (pipeline) wine terminal, a cold storage meat terminal, and expansive facilities for handling imported automobiles.

By the late 1970s more than half of the area's oceangoing general cargo traffic was passing through Port Elizabeth and Port Newark. The Brooklyn waterfront has declined but is still a large handler of general cargo, and other container facilities are planned there. The Jersey City–Hoboken waterfront handles only a fraction of its former traffic. Almost all of the Manhattan cargo facilities are now rotting in

Soho. At the southern end of the island is Lower Manhattan, dominated by the Wall Street financial district and another cluster of skyscrapers (fig. 8–12). The southeastern section is called the Lower East Side, an area with a lengthy history of crowded tenements, low incomes, and ghettoized ethnic groups (Chinatown, Little Italy, the Bowery, the East Village, and so on).[9] To the east of Central Park is the Upper East Side, an area

[9] A record 335,000 people per square mile was documented in this area in 1890. See George W. Carey, "East Side of Manhattan," in *Guidebook for Field Excursions,* ed. John E. Brush and George W. Carey (Washington, D.C.: Association of American Geographers, 1976), p. 52.

fig. 8–12   Looking south on Manhattan Island. This view, taken from the Empire State Building in Midtown, shows the skyscraper complex of the financial district, dominated by the twin towers of the World Trade Center.

disuse, and a part of the waterfront is being filled and redeveloped for office and apartment buildings.

All passenger traffic has been concentrated in the new three-pier passenger terminal on the Hudson River side of Manhattan at about 50th Street. The number of passengers has declined almost every year since the early 1960s; transatlantic passenger business has faded badly, and cruise ships have not taken up all of the slack.

fig. 8-a   The new cargo-handling facilities of Newark Bay are very expansive and mostly adapted to containerization. This view looks northward (courtesy Port Authority of New York and New Jersey).

known for its affluence. Northeast of Central Park is the expanding Puerto Rican ghetto of Spanish Harlem, and north of the park is the long-established black Harlem district.

Manhattan is a veritable hodgepodge of functional areas. It includes the greatest concentration of manufacturing facilities (the garment district), commercial buildings (Midtown), and financial institutions (Lower Manhattan) on the continent; yet its residential function is a major one. Detached, single-family dwellings are unknown, and the 1.4 million inhabitants of the island live in multistoried apartments.[10] Commuters swell this population total considerably during daylight hours; it is estimated that there are more than 2 million jobs between Central Park and The Battery (southern tip of the island) and that 1.5 million of those are filled by commuters.[11]

The *Bronx* is the only borough of the city that is on the continental mainland. It is a moderately hilly district that is primarily residential in function. Close settlement in apartments characterizes the southern portion, but further north there is a sparser density and some single-family homes. The population of the Bronx is approximately equal to that of Manhattan.

The borough of *Queens* occupies more than 120 square miles at the western end of Long Island, extending from Long Island Sound across the island to Jamaica Bay. It is primarily a residential borough but also has large commercial and industrial districts. Individual homes are more commonplace than in the other boroughs, but multiple residences are in the majority. Kennedy International and La Guardia, two of the four principal metropolitan airports, are located in Queens. The borough's population is about 2 million.

There are more people in *Kings* (*Brooklyn*)—about 2.4 million—than in any other

borough. (Indeed, if Brooklyn were a separate city, it would be the fifth largest in Anglo-America.) It occupies the southwestern tip of Long Island and is closely connected to lower Manhattan by bridges and tunnels. The business center of Brooklyn is near the eastern end of the Brooklyn Bridge and would be an imposing central business district if it were not under the shadow of Manhattan skyscrapers. Brooklyn contains considerable industrial land, but for the most part it is a residential area, largely developed for multifamily apartments.

The borough of *Richmond* occupies Staten Island, which until the early 1960s had no direct connection with the rest of the city except by ferry. As a result, much of Staten Island is still suburban or semirural. The completion of the Verrazano Narrows Bridge (the world's longest suspension bridge) to Brooklyn has changed all that, and the population of Richmond has now passed 300,000 and is growing steadily.

The urban spillover into *outer Long Island* has reached beyond Queens and spread throughout most of Nassau County (population, 1.4 million) and deep into Suffolk County (1.3 million). The eastern end of Long Island is still rural, but urban sprawl reaches ever farther eastward along the main transport routes.

North and east of the Bronx, the metropolitan area extends into *mainland New York.* Westchester County, with its numerous elite residential areas, has a population of nearly 1 million. Rockland County (300,000) and Fairfield County (in Connecticut) are on the fringes of growth.

On the *Jersey side* of the Hudson, the urban agglomeration extends north, south, and west so that essentially all of northeastern New Jersey is encompassed. Urbanization is not complete in the area, but it is both expanding and intensifying. The Jersey City peninsula has a population of some 600,000; the Newark area, which occupies three counties, has nearly 2 million; and the Paterson-Clifton-Passaic area claims nearly 1.4 million. Of great significance to the entire metropolitan area are the reclaimed marshlands along the western shore of the

---

[10] For New York City, 75 percent of the residences are rental units. For Manhattan itself, the proportion is well above 90 percent.

[11] Seymour Freedgood and Editors of Time-Life Books, *The Gateway States* (New York: Time Incorporated, 1967), p. 105.

Hudson estuary and New York Harbor, which are utilized for heavy and nuisance industries (such as oil refineries and chemical plants) and as railway marshaling yards.

Population As in other metropolises, the flight to the suburbs, particularly of middle-class whites, has been a prominent feature of the area's demography for some years. In this case, however, there are several central cores that are losing people and jobs to the outlying districts. The most notable effects are in Manhattan, Newark, and Jersey City, where a decline in employment opportunities and burgeoning welfare rolls have produced unprecedented financial crises. For the metropolis as a whole, the rate of population growth during the 1970s has been very slow.

New York has always had an extraordinarily diverse population mix. For example, at the turn of the century it was estimated that 80 percent of the population of Manhattan consisted of foreign-born people or their first-generation children.[12] There are still many languages to be overheard in walking the streets of the city, but in recent years the most notable minorities have been blacks and Puerto Ricans, whose influx since World War II has been very rapid. The 2 million blacks and Puerto Ricans in New York are mostly crowded in ghettos, particularly in Harlem and Bedford-Stuyvesant (central Brooklyn).

Viewed in historical perspective, the presence of these ghettoized minorities does not present radically different problems to a city whose history has been replete with ghettoized minorities, although racial antagonisms and prejudices complicate the situation. Nevertheless, it is true that the blacks and Puerto Ricans are mostly poor and needful of many social services but contribute very little tax revenue. Even New York City's welfare-swollen budget (larger than that of any state) is extremely inadequate to clear the slums and educate the

slum dwellers. This vicious circle is no different in other large cities, but in New York its very magnitude is of mind-boggling proportions.

On the other hand, metropolitan New York contains a populace that is, in Gottmann's words, "extremely distinguished." Here, on the average, is a population that is the wealthiest, best educated, best housed, and best serviced of any metropolis of comparable size in the world.

METROPOLITAN PHILADELPHIA

Metropolitan Philadelphia, the fourth largest urban complex in Anglo-America, is not so densely populated or so sprawling as New York. Its principal axis lies parallel to the lower course of the Delaware River, extending from Wilmington, Delaware, in the southwest to Trenton, New Jersey, in the northeast, a distance of some 50 miles (fig. 8–13). Its southeast-northwest dimension is less than half as great, reaching from Camden, New Jersey, up the Schuylkill Valley to Norristown, Pennsylvania.

William Penn selected and planned the initial settlement in 1682 on well-drained

fig. 8–13 Metropolitan Philadelphia.

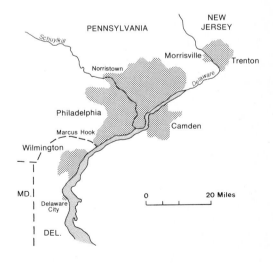

---

[12] Oscar Handlin, *The Newcomers* (Cambridge: Harvard University Press, 1959), p. 89.

land a short distance north of the marshy confluence of the Schuylkill and Delaware rivers. Penn's rectangular street pattern with wide lanes and numerous parks was well designed for a relatively small city. As Philadelphia grew, however, it absorbed other settlements so that the street layout is heterogeneous and irregular away from the present central business district. Hills, marshes, and valleys further complicated the pattern in outlying areas. Converging highways and railways have produced a radial design for the major thoroughfares.

Much has been written about Philadelphia's misfortune in not having an easy access route to the interior of the continent. It is true that the ridge-and-valley section of the Appalachians, lying athwart the direction of westward penetration, inhibited Philadelphia's competitive position vis-à-vis New York. Nevertheless, Philadelphia was the largest city in Anglo-America for most of the eighteenth century, and the Pennsylvania Railroad, completed in the mid-1800s, gave Philadelphia a much more direct (if more costly) route to the Midwest than New York's Hudson-Mohawk corridor provided. For many years the "Pennsy" was one of America's busiest and most prosperous railways.

The harbor activities of the lower Delaware are administered by a tristate authority that coordinates the lengthy port facilities and maintains a dredged channel as far upstream as Morrisville. Both banks of the river are lined with piers and wharves downstream from Philadelphia for several miles, continuing on the right bank below Wilmington to New Castle and Delaware City. Oil refineries, chemical plants, shipyards, and other heavy industrial facilities are also numerous in riverside sites. Most of the port business consists of imported raw materials, particularly petroleum (from both overseas and coastwise traffic) and iron ore (largely from Venezuela and Canada). In comparison with New York, the Delaware River port complex is very minor as an exporter.

Metropolitan Philadelphia is the fifth ranking manufacturing center of the continent. Its industrial structure is extremely well balanced, in contrast to the other urban centers of Megalopolis; indeed, it is considered to be the most diversified in the United States. Philadelphia has large apparel and publishing industries, but unlike New York City, they do not dominate the manufactural scene. Also important are the electrical and nonelectrical machinery industries, which together provide jobs for almost one-fourth of the area's factory workers. Total manufacturing employment has been declining for several years, but a steady increase in nonmanufacturing jobs has mostly compensated for the decline.

That portion of the riverfront between Philadelphia and Wilmington contains a notable assortment of chemical plants, especially those associated with the Du Pont Company. These factories produce a variety of items ranging from refrigerants to explosives and paints and are highly mechanized. Relatively few production workers are required, with the result that more than three-quarters of the employees are in administrative and research capacities. E. I. du Pont de Nemours & Company is the world's largest producer of chemicals and maintains its corporate headquarters as well as many of its production facilities in and around Wilmington. The high rate of remuneration for its 26,000 local employees has helped to give Delaware the second highest per capita income in the nation.

Further upstream on the Delaware, around Marcus Hook, is a significant concentration of petroleum refineries. These are market-oriented plants that receive their crude oil via inexpensive sea transportation.

At Morrisville, a cross-river suburb of Trenton, is one of the newer and larger steel mills of Anglo-America. The Fairless Works spreads over 2,000 acres and employs 6,000 workers. Coal is railed in from western Pennsylvania and West Virginia, and ore is brought by sea from Venezuela.[13]

---

[13] The deep-draft ore vessels are unable to negotiate the river all the way to the Fairless plant. They must be partially unloaded at Philadelphia, which adds significantly to transport costs.

The urban opportunities and problems of Anglo-America in general and Megalopolis in particular are exemplified in Philadelphia. The central business district has been revitalized by some of the most efficient urban renewal on the continent. Modern bridges have replaced ferries across the Delaware; acres of decaying buildings, just north of Independence Hall, have been removed in favor of a graceful mall; and the modern complex of Penn Center buildings now stands where the "Chinese Wall" muddle of elevated railway tracks once congested downtown traffic flow.

Some of the continent's most lavish and opulent suburbs are found to the west and south of Philadelphia; yet just beyond the revitalized central business district stand 80,-000 units of substandard housing that are mostly occupied by blacks, who constitute more than one-third of the city's population. Philadelphia has become a deeply rifted city, a battleground of different interest groups.[14] It is, with the exception of New York, probably the most socially and ethnically heterogenous city in the country.[15]

METROPOLITAN BALTIMORE

Baltimore is a seaport on Chesapeake Bay but is located in what is almost the remotest corner of the bay (nearly 200 miles from its mouth) where the estuary of the Patapsco River provides a useful deepwater harbor (fig. 8–14). It was founded relatively late (1729) at a Fall Line power site, and its exports of agricultural produce (largely flour and tobacco) soon assured its preeminence over Annapolis, an administrative center already eight decades old. By the end of the eighteenth century it was the fourth-ranking

fig. 8–14 Metropolitan Baltimore and Washington.

port in the nation; ever since it has maintained a high position among American ports, based in part on a productive hinterland, in part on excellent railway connections to the interior, and in part on prosperous local manufacturing. Even its distance from the open sea has been reduced by the construction of the Chesapeake and Delaware Canal across the narrow neck of the Delmarva Peninsula, and its relatively inland location, in comparison with other North Atlantic ports, gives it a comparative freight-rate advantage to the Midwest.

Although its exports (particularly grain and coal) are not inconsiderable, Baltimore is primarily an importer of bulk materials from both foreign and Gulf Coast sources; many of these materials are processed locally. Copper, sugar, and petroleum refin-

---

[14] Peter O. Muller, Kenneth C. Meyer, and Roman A. Cybriwsky, *Metropolitan Philadelphia: A Study of Conflicts and Social Cleavages* (Cambridge, Mass.: Ballinger Publishing Co., 1976), p. 11.

[15] For example, in 1978 Philadelphia had an Italian mayor, an Irish police commissioner, a Jewish city council president, and a majority party leader who was a Polish Protestant.

fig. 8-15 The heavy industry complex at Sparrows Point, Maryland, includes an enormous steel mill and (at left) a large shipyard (courtesy Bethlehem Steel Corporation).

ing, as well as fertilizer manufacture, are significant port-related industries, but most prominent in this regard is the Sparrows Point steel complex (fig. 8-15).

This Bethlehem Steel Corporation mill is the largest single steel-producing facility in Anglo-America, with a capacity of nearly 11 million tons. Although all the production materials come from some distance—limestone from Pennsylvania, coal from West Virginia, ore from Venezuela—the material assembly costs are probably lower than anywhere else in the nation. The ready availability of finished steel has attracted various metal-using industries, especially shipbuilding, and also machinery and machine tools production.

Apart from a dominance of primary metals production (steel and copper), Baltimore's industrial structure is moderately well diversified. The most prominent industry during the 1940s and 1950s, aircraft and missile production, has declined in recent years, as has shipbuilding. Baltimore is now much more notably a commercial than an industrial city.

The city—which has been called "the most southerly northern city and the most northerly southern city"—sprawls widely in all directions but is not restricted by adjacent urban centers and has considerable room for expansion. Although relatively near the larger Washington conurbation to the southwest, Baltimore's quite different economic orientation has minimized the disadvantages of the shadow effect, except in the matter of air-transport development.

METROPOLITAN WASHINGTON

It is only 35 miles from Baltimore to Washington; yet the rural area in between is still far from being completely suburbanized, and the two cities are remarkably unlike. Originally laid out in the 1790s, Washington was designed as a governmental center that was relatively centrally located to the population distribution of that time. The original District of Columbia was a square of land ceded approximately equally from Maryland and Virginia. The latter state was allowed to reannex its portion in 1846, so that the present 69 square miles of the District is all on the Maryland side of the Potomac River.

Much of the original site was low-lying and swampy, but extensive drainage and an elaborate municipal plan produced a city of orderly pattern and impressive appearance. The original street pattern combined the regular form of a rectangular grid with a diagonal network of avenues and traffic circles. Massive complexes of government buildings are mixed with attractive parks between the Potomac River and the central business district, with the landscaped mall that connects Capitol–White House–Washington Monument as the hub of activity. Both government offices and commercial districts are scattered over the metropolis, although square mile after square mile of residences—ranging from stately old mansions to modern high-rise apartments to monotonous row houses—dominate the surroundings. In the last four decades runaway growth has overwhelmed orderliness, and the metropolitan area sprawls well beyond the District's boundaries into the two adjoining states.

Overcrowding and congestion have become a trademark of the Washington scene. The Capitol Beltway around the city is helpful, but routes in and out become traffic quagmires during rush hours, and inadequate bridging of the Potomac aggravates the problem. Washington is largely a white-collar city, and most employment opportunities are downtown, not in the suburbs. Accordingly the daily commutation flow, on a per capita basis, is higher than anywhere else in Megalopolis. Attempts to alleviate this situation have been made by locating some government complexes in the suburbs and by opening the continent's newest rapid transit system, the Washington Metro.

An increasing proportion of the population resides in suburbs outside the District proper. The total population of the District decreased by 9 percent between 1970 and 1977, although all of the suburban counties were growing rapidly. By the late 1970s, the city of Washington was more than 75 percent black, and the public school enrollment was more than 90 percent black. Unlike most large cities, however, there is an increasing flow of blacks to the suburbs, particularly southeastward into Prince Georges County.

The economic function of Washington is unlike that of any other major Anglo-American metropolis. In four important respects the employment structure is unusual:

1 Most obvious is the remarkably high percentage of federal government workers, amounting to about 45 percent of the District's work force. This is much higher than for any other major city on the continent.

2 The proportion of females in the work force is abnormally high, reflecting the large number of clerical jobs in government offices.

3 The proportion of blacks in the work force is also higher than in other large cities; the lack of hiring discrimination in federal employment accounts for much of the black population influx.

4 Only 4 percent of the jobs in metropolitan Washington are in manufacturing, which is by far the lowest proportion in the nation, and half of that 4 percent is employed in printing and publishing, indicating the great flood of government publications.

Two other facets of the city's economy should be mentioned. Its financial community has been expanding, largely as a result of increasing federal controls and regulations; in no other part of Megalopolis outside New York has the *relative* growth of financial services been as marked. Also, Washington continues to be a major tourist attraction; its many government offices, monuments, and museums are high on the list of sights to see for American and foreign visitors alike.

METROPOLITAN RICHMOND

The rapidly growing capital of Virginia is a Fall Line city on the James River, some 75 miles south of Washington (fig. 8–16). Its inclusion in the Megalopolis Region cannot be justified by contiguous urban land use, although the strip between Richmond and Washington is rapidly being suburbanized from both ends. Rather it is the city's business orientation to the north and east and its efficient transport connections with Washington and Norfolk that suggest a logical extension of Megalopolis as far southwest as Richmond.

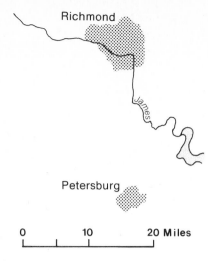

fig. 8–16 Metropolitan Richmond.

cals, which together provide nearly half of total manufactural jobs.

HAMPTON ROADS

Just inland from the mouth of Chesapeake Bay is the commodious harbor of Hampton Roads, situated where the north-flowing Elizabeth River enters the mouth of the James River estuary and slightly upstream of the latter's confluence with Chesapeake Bay (fig. 8–17). The resultant natural harbor is one of the finest in the Western Hemisphere, and around it has developed one of the largest maritime, military, and shipbuilding complexes in the world. Clustered about the mouth of the Elizabeth River are the cities of Norfolk (Virginia's largest), Chesapeake, and Portsmouth, and on the tip of the peninsula across the mouth of the James River are Newport News and Hampton.

Military and port-related activities dominate the economy of this group of cities, sometimes nicknamed "Tidewater." There are more than a dozen military bases in or adjacent to the urbanized areas, and their payrolls constitute a large share of the total metropolitan income. The strategic location in the middle of the nation's Atlantic coast and splendid harbor make Hampton Roads a logical center for protective naval and air facilities.

The export of coal is the most prominent shipping activity of the Hampton Roads ports. The coal-handling facilities at Norfork and Newport News are among the largest and most automated in the world and make Hampton Roads the leading coal-exporting port of the nation. Other exports include grain and general cargo; imports are modest and varied. Channel deepening, primarily to accommodate supercolliers, and new piers have contributed to a considerable increase in traffic in the last decade.

Manufacturing, with one exception, is not of major importance in the Hampton Roads cities. The exception is shipbuilding, which employs more than half of the indus-

The city was founded in early colonial days and became a bastion of Southern culture and Confederate politics. It has experienced rapid growth as a commercial and, to a lesser extent, financial center in recent decades. Its moderate level of industrial development (25 percent of the labor force is employed in factories) is highly specialized toward production of cigarettes and chemi-

fig. 8–17 Hampton Roads.

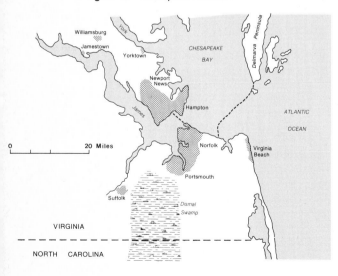

trial workers in the area and is dominated by the massive shipyards at Newport News.

There are nearby recreational attractions on three sides of Hampton Roads, which generate much tourist as well as local business. A few miles northwest of Newport News are three outstanding historic restorations: Williamsburg, Yorktown, and Jamestown. East of Norfolk are the tidewater beach areas, focusing on Virginia Beach. To the northeast are the waters of Chesapeake Bay, with their fishing and boating interest, and the bridge-tunnel route that crosses the bay mouth to the relatively unspoiled southern reaches of the Delmarva Peninsula.

the rural scene

Despite the predominance of an urban life style, population, and economy, most of the land in Megalopolis is actually rural. It is estimated that some 80 percent of the total land area of the region supports nonurban land uses. This rural land is important for many things. It supplies a great volume of foodstuffs to the cities of the region, although the majority of the food for Megalopolis is actually produced elsewhere; its rivers, streams, springs, and lakes provide much of the region's water supply, although many of the urban watersheds extend far beyond the confines of Megalopolis. Perhaps most important of all, the rural lands provide breathing space and recreational areas for the 42 million megalopolitans. The significance of green spaces becomes greater with the construction of each new high-rise apartment block, with each passing day of expanding urban sprawl.

THE COAST AND THE COASTAL PLAIN

The most pervasive aspect of the regional environment is the sea and its interface with the land. The long axis of Megalopolis parallels the Atlantic, and there are many hundreds of miles of coastline along the irregular shore. People turn to the ocean and

its edge for much of their commerce and recreation and for some of their food. No part of Megalopolis is more than 100 miles from the coast.

The most striking characteristic of the coast is its irregularity. Few parts of the Anglo-American coastline, and certainly no section with such a sizable population, have such an uneven, embayed, island-studded outline. Different parts of the present shoreline have varied origins, and their diversity of form is striking.

The principal embayments each have different shapes and different patterns of river flow into them. From north to south they include Cape Cod Bay, protected from the stormy North Atlantic by the hooked peninsula of Cape Cod; Narragansett Bay, Rhode Island's island-dotted waterway; Long Island Sound, sandwiched between the Connecticut coast and the north shore of Long Island; Lower New York Bay, the broad entryway to the Hudson lowland, between New Jersey and Long Island; Delaware Bay, the extensive estuary of the Delaware River; and Chesapeake Bay, the continent's most complex and second largest estuary.

There are three prominent peninsulas along this stretch of coast. Cape Cod is a long, low-lying sandy hook that is world famous as a summer recreational area. Cape May is a peninsula at the southern tip of New Jersey that shelters Delaware Bay from the open ocean. The Delmarva Peninsula, largest on the east coast north of Florida, encompasses parts of the three states for which it is named.

The numerous offshore islands, with one outstanding exception, are crowded summer vacationlands that are largely depopulated in winter. Most famous are the islands off the southeastern coast of Massachusetts: Nantucket, Martha's Vineyard, the Elizabeth Islands, and Block Island. Many of the sand bar islands off the Long Island, New Jersey, and Delmarva coasts are also popular holiday spots. Long Island itself, of course, is much larger and more complex in its function.

The coastal plain is underlain by relatively unconsolidated sediments, most of which are of geologically recent vintage (Tertiary and Quaternary), although the inner margin of the plain has some older (Cretaceous) deposits. Beneath the sediments is a base complex of ancient igneous and metamorphic rocks, which reaches the surface in a very complicated pattern in southern New England, the New York City area, and northern New Jersey.

After a long period of gentle uplift of the continental shelf in Tertiary time, in which a series of broad open valleys was developed, there was a significant drowning of the coastal plain, presumably as a combined result of the weight of the Pleistocene ice load and the postglacial rise in sea level attributable to glacial meltwater.[16] Glaciation modified the northern part of the coastal plain, primarily by the laying down of extensive glacial and glaciofluvial deposits; indeed, the size of Long Island, Cape Cod, Martha's Vineyard, and Nantucket Island was significantly increased by the deposit of terminal moraines. The most recently developed terrain features of the region are ephemeral beaches, coastal dunes, and sand bars, with their associated shallow lagoons.

The resulting topographic pattern throughout the Megalopolis Region is one of exceedingly flat land sloping gently toward the sea. Along the inner (western) margin of the region there is a rise toward rolling land or occasional steep-sided hills, but in the plain itself there are only minor prominences that appear above the uniform level; these are mostly in the north and are mostly related to accumulations of glacial deposition. Hard rock bluffs (the "Palisades") lining the lower course of the Hudson River are exceptions to this generalization.

The continental shelf offshore of the Megalopolis Region is one of the best-known shelf areas in the world. It is in reality a submerged extension of the coastal plain, and its surface is a continuation of the smooth and remarkably uniform terrain characteristic of the coastal plain. The shelf is quite broad off the coast of Massachusetts but narrows southward to a width of only about 50 miles off southern Virginia. There are a number of prominent submarine canyons cut into the outer edge of the continental shelf in this area, most of which do not seem to be simply drowned extensions of the surface river system.

WATERS OF LAND AND SEA

The megalopolitan coast is a well-watered region: its coastal plain is crossed by a large number of important rivers flowing southward or southeastward to the Atlantic. These rivers originate in the interior uplands of the Appalachian system and move swiftly off the crystalline rocks of the Piedmont onto the softer sedimentaries of the coastal plain. The lithologic change from hard rock to softer rock is usually marked by a steeper gradient, producing a rapids or small waterfall, and a line drawn on a map to connect these sites is often referred to as the *Fall Line*.[17]

Most of the rivers of the region carry a large volume of water throughout the year. Heaviest annual discharges are from the Susquehanna and the Potomac, but the

---

[16] William D. Thornbury, *Regional Geomorphology of the United States* (New York: John Wiley & Sons, Inc., 1965), p. 36.

[17] Several cities of varying sizes have riverside sites along the Fall Line between New Jersey and Georgia. Some scholars believe that there is a causative relationship involved, for the rapids often served as both an early source of power generation and as head of navigation on the coastal plain rivers, thus providing economic incentive for town sites. This contention has been challenged in recent years, particularly by Roy Merrens, who has marshaled an impressive array of evidence to refute the notion that any functional relationships between river rapids and town sites along the Fall Line do, in fact, exist. See H. Roy Merrens, "Historical Geography and Early American History," *William and Mary Quarterly*, 3rd series, 22 (October 1965), 529–348.

Merrimack, Connecticut, Hudson, and James all have average flows exceeding 5,000 cubic feet per second. None of the rivers flows swiftly, however, and there is a fairly high tidal range in their lower courses. Several are deep enough to be navigable, but only the Hudson, the Delaware, and the James are significantly used in this regard. Almost all the rivers of the region receive sewerage from the cities and industrial waste from the factories along their courses, and as a result the rivers and the estuaries into which many of them flow are heavily polluted.

Despite the large number of rivers on the coastal plain, its very flatness ensures that much of the lowland is not naturally well drained. There is a general absence of lakes, but much marsh and swamp was originally found in the region, although most of it has been artificially drained over the years to allow for urban or industrial construction. The two most famous areas of ill-drained land that remain are the Hackensack Meadows, the last major remnant of once extensive marshland on the New Jersey side of the lower Hudson River, and the Dismal Swamp, a vast area at the southern tip of the region just south of the Hampton Roads cities.

The ocean waters are relatively warm most of the time, partly because of the northeastward-flowing Gulf Stream some miles offshore. Colder waters, related to the southward-flowing Labrador Current, sometimes wend their way along the coast inshore of the Gulf Stream. The shallow waters of the coastal estuaries and lagoons have been famous for their abundant aquatic life, especially shellfish. Most notable by far is Chesapeake Bay, which is said to be the most biologically productive body of water in the world on a per-acre basis. In recent years the habitats have seriously deteriorated and the biota has significantly decreased, particularly owing to pollution and overfishing.

The varied interlocking of land and sea in Megalopolis—river, estuary, bay, peninsula, lagoon, strait, island—provided a number of useful sites for cities and forts in the early years of settlement. Many of the resulting settlements have grown to great size, and the interfingering now proves to be a mixed blessing. What was advantageous for waterborne commerce is now deleterious for urban traffic movements. This factor contributes significantly to the congestion of Megalopolis.

CLIMATE

The climate is classified as humid midlatitude and semimarine. The coast has a leeward location on the continent, relative to the general west-to-east movement of weather systems, which mutes the maritime influence. Still, the effect of the adjacent ocean is to ameliorate both summer and winter temperatures, to lengthen the growing season, to assure that the region's harbors remain ice-free (with rare exceptions), and to increase the moisture content of the atmosphere.

Precipitation is the most consistently prominent feature of the climate. Most of the region receives between 40 and 50 inches of moisture annually, with a few localities getting up to 55 inches. It is generally well distributed throughout the year, with a slight maximum in summer.

Storms of various kinds are not uncommon, and most bring considerable precipitation. Thundershowers are prevalent during the warmer months, and late summer occasionally brings a "northeaster," a rainstorm with high wind that may last for several days. Every few years in late summer or fall the region may be visited by an errant tropical hurricane that has worked its way north from the Caribbean; heavy rain and roaring winds may whip up the sea sufficiently to cause considerable coastal damage and occasional loss of life. Winter snowstorms in the northern part of the region are often abrupt, and the deep snow is occasionally paralyzing.

"WILD" VEGETATION

Most of what is now the Megalopolis Region was originally covered with a mixture of woodland and forest in which deciduous species predominated but coniferous trees sometimes occurred in significant concentrations, especially on areas of sandy soil. Much of the forest and woodland was cleared for farming and other purposes by the middle of the nineteenth century. Since that time, there has been a resurgence of trees, largely occasioned by farm abandonment. About "half of the whole area of Megalopolis is [now] green,"[18] mostly in forest and woodland but some in scrubby brush. The proportion of land in trees and brush has been increasing steadily for several decades—Connecticut, for example, was one-third wooded in 1850 but is two-thirds wooded today—and the trend seems likely to continue for some time to come.

The present vegetation associations of woods and brush are difficult to classify as natural vegetation; there has been too much human interference, both deliberate and accidental, in most areas. Many exotic species, especially shade trees and weeds, have been added to the floristic inventory. Still, there are vast sectors where woods and forest predominate, and in a few localities the natural vegetation has not been changed or altered by humanity.

Of particular interest is the so-called pine barrens area of New Jersey. Located in the most densely populated state and just southeast of the most densely traveled traffic corridor in the world, this 650,000 acres of pitch pine and oak has a population density of only about 15 people per square mile.[19] It has remained virtually intact for several hundred years, apparently because of lack of agricultural potential. It also has an extensive aquifer of pure, soft water. Many real-estate schemes have threatened the barrens, but so far only the edges have been nibbled away.

SOILS

The soils of Megalopolis vary widely in characteristics. Still, three principal kinds may be noted: sand or sandy loams in the better-drained parts of the coastal plain, hydromorphic soils in the numerous areas of marsh and swamp, and varied residual soils in scattered localities.

Spodosols, with their subsurface accumulations of iron, aluminum, and organic matter, dominate in southern New England. Thin, light-colored Inceptisols are typical of the New York–northern New Jersey area. Clayey or sandy Ultisols predominate in the southern part of the region.

Although agriculture is well entrenched, it is not primarily because of the soils; indeed, few of the soils are inherently very fertile for crop growing, and high agricultural productivity is usually associated with heavy use of fertilizer. In many farming areas the natural soil is simply a medium through which to feed the crops. Even the relatively productive soils of the Connecticut Valley and parts of New Jersey are heavily fertilized wherever cash crops are grown.

SPECIALIZED AGRICULTURE

Throughout recent decades there has been a continuing attrition of farmland in the Megalopolis Region. Urban sprawl has pushed many farms out of production, and woodland spread has replaced cultivated land where marginal farms have been abandoned for agriculture. The long-run trend has been for general farming to decline and specialty farming to increase, and for total farm acreage to decrease while total value of output continues to rise. In other words, with the pressures from expanding urban land use on one side and increasing costs of farming on the other, the megalopolitan farmer has tended to abandon the poorer land and the

[18] Gottmann, *Megalopolis,* p. 234.
[19] John A. McPhee, *The Pine Barrens* (New York: Farrar, Straus & Giroux, Inc., 1968), p. 38.

less valuable products and concentrate on high-value output. The remaining farms tend to be efficient and specialized, emphasizing the production of perishables either for local consumption or immediate canning or freezing. Despite the relatively small acreage in farmland, between 5 and 10 percent of the total value of agricultural products sold in this country is produced in Megalopolis.

Although the region has a generally favorable climate for agriculture and soils that are only moderately fertile but responsive to fertilizer, it is not the physical advantages that undergird farming in Megalopolis; indeed, "there is practically nothing in this area which could not be grown as well or better in other parts of the United States."[20] The great advantage is market, and most agricultural production is market-oriented. Megalopolitan agriculture is not significant for its total quantity of output; rather "because it has the best market in the country, the most customers with the highest incomes."[21]

Market Gardening The typical farm of contemporary Megalopolis is engaged in the raising of fresh vegetables and fruits in a market-gardening type of operation. The sandy loams of southern New Jersey are particularly favored for vegetable production and have given New Jersey its reputation as "the Garden State." A great many kinds of vegetables are raised in the area, but nearly one-third of the harvested value is in tomatoes. More than half the New Jersey vegetable output is sold fresh, but a large share is contract production for the freezing and canning industries.

South of Chesapeake Bay the pattern is somewhat different. Increasing distance from large urban markets diminishes the

[20] Lewis M. Alexander, *The Northeastern United States*, 2nd ed. (New York: D. Van Nostrand Company, 1976), p. 72.
[21] Edward Higbee, "Megalopolitan Agriculture," in *Megalopolis*, Gottmann, p. 259.

emphasis on market gardening, although truckloads of vegetables from southeastern Virginia make nightly runs as far as New York City. Corn remains a dominant crop, and such specialties as tobacco, peanuts, and cotton are often of greater value than vegetables.

Specialty Horticulture Horticulture flourishes in close proximity to the big cities. Megalopolis leads the nation in the output of horticultural specialties: cut flowers, trees and shrubs for landscaping, bulbs, flower seeds, and other greenhouse specialties. A large, affluent, nearby market is the most important attraction for horticulture; labor is another requisite. Horticulture normally occupies the most valuable real estate of any agricultural land; thus there is a continuing sequential change of land use as subdivision displaces horticulture, and horticulture moves a bit further out to displace something else.

Dairying Dairying is widespread in Megalopolis but tends to be concentrated on the western margin of the region where urban pressures are less and land prices are lower. There is also notable development of dairying in parts of southern New Jersey near Philadelphia and in the northern portion of the Delmarva Peninsula. Much of the milk for Megalopolis is, however, brought in from milksheds to the north and west of the region. Similarly most of the dairy farms within the region depend on feed grains that are shipped in from elsewhere.

Poultry Raising Another farm enterprise that is well adapted to small amounts of relatively expensive land near large markets is the raising of poultry, particularly chickens for broiling and frying. Contemporary poultry husbandry is large-scale and specialized. Most of the feed is brought in from outside the region, constituting the major item of expense; thus, no crop acreage is required. The Delmarva Peninsula is the

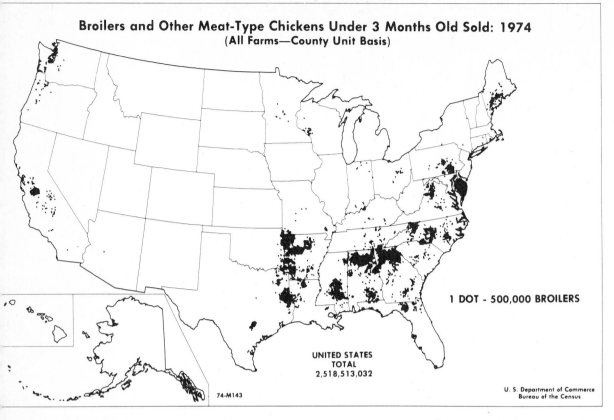

Broilers and Other Meat-Type Chickens Under 3 Months Old Sold: 1974
(All Farms—County Unit Basis)

1 DOT - 500,000 BROILERS

UNITED STATES
TOTAL
2,518,513,032

74-M143

U. S. Department of Commerce
Bureau of the Census

fig. 8–18 Distribution of commercial chicken-raising in the United States. Broilers account for most of the sales. The Delmarva Peninsula stands out prominently.

fig. 8–19 A successful fishing trip for menhaden. The hold of the boat is full, and they are piled more than a foot deep on the deck. The port is Gloucester, Massachusetts.

principal area of chicken-raising, mostly broilers (fig. 8–18). Eastern Connecticut also has many broiler farms. An interesting poultry specialty on Long Island (mostly in Suffolk County) is the raising of ducks.

COMMERCIAL FISHING

Although the commercial fishing industry of Megalopolis has a long history of successful operation, its significance, both absolutely and relatively, continues to decline through the years. Mostly the fishing fleets operate relatively close to home, in near North Atlantic waters, although some of the boats—particularly those from New England ports—regularly visit the "banks" area. Shellfish (primarily oysters, clams, scallops, and crabs), menhaden, and flounder are the principal catch (fig. 8–19).

Menhaden, a fish little known to the general public, is taken in far greater volume by United States commercial fishermen than is any other product of the sea. In most years it amounts to nearly 40 percent by weight of the total United States catch, which is about five times as much as shrimp, the second variety; but it is a low-value fish, rarely providing more than 5 percent of the total value of the United States catch. About one-third of the menhaden caught in the United States comes from the waters off the Atlantic coastal plain. In part because of its extreme oiliness, menhaden is not generally considered as a food fish. It is used primarily as a source of oil and meal for the making of stock and pet feed and commercial fertilizers.

The mid-Atlantic coast has a long history as the leading oyster fishery of the continent, but this reputation is in serious jeopardy owing to declining yields. The many bays, estuaries, and tidal flats of the region, with their relatively warm and shallow water, are an ideal location for oyster propagation. Chesapeake Bay is by far the leading source of oysters, and strict conservation laws have been enacted in both Maryland and Virginia to sustain long-run production. Some parts of the bay are closed to fishing; sailboats are mandatory in areas where dredging is permitted; and old-fashioned and relatively inefficient hand tongs are required in other areas.

In total the commercial fishery of the Megalopolis Region yields about one-fourth of the United States catch, whether measured by weight or value. Virginia is the fourth-ranking state in volume of catch, largely because of menhaden landings. Massachusetts is the fifth-ranking state in value of catch and sixth in volume; New Jersey ranks seventh in volume of catch. The leading fishing ports of Megalopolis are Gloucester and New Bedford in Massachusetts and Cape May in New Jersey.

recreation and tourism

The tourist and recreational attractions of Megalopolis are numerous and varied, as might be expected in such a populous region. Local people spend much of their holiday or vacation time within the region, and in addition, a great many visitors are attracted from other regions and overseas. Tourist interest is mostly focused on three general categories of attractions: cities and their points of interest, coastal areas, and historical sites.

Without doubt it is the urban attractions of Megalopolis that are most attractive to resident and visitor alike. New York City is the number one tourist goal on the continent, and Washington is not far behind. In these, as in the other large cities of Megalopolis, there is a host of things to see and do, although famous buildings, such as the Empire State Building, United Nations, National Capitol, and the White House, seem to rank first in popularity.

The long seacoast and numerous islands of Megalopolis are very important summer playgrounds, but their recreational significance in winter is limited (fig. 8–20). There are scores of beach resorts; the more famous

fig. 8–20   A coastal scene near Newport, Rhode Island (courtesy Rhode Island Development Council).

fig. 8–21 Cape Cod has one of the busiest beaches of Megalopolis (courtesy Massachusetts Department of Commerce and Development).

are Cape Cod (fig. 8–21), Nantucket Island, Martha's Vineyard, Asbury Park, Atlantic City, Ocean City, and Virginia Beach.

The almost-continuous beaches of southern New Jersey attract the greatest flood of patronage; some 30 million people (including repeats) are estimated to visit this area each summer.[22] The resort towns, from Point Pleasant in the north to Cape May in the south, are built right along the beach, usually separated from the sand by only a boardwalk. Real estate prices continue to soar, and construction of motels, condominiums, town houses, and other types of housing units flourish, catering to the immense nearby markets of Philadelphia, New Jersey, and New York. The oldest and most famous of the Jersey resorts, Atlantic City, has been passing through a declining phase, however, its economy faltering, its appearance dilapidated and run-down, and its population diminishing by one-fourth in the period between 1960 and 1975. But in 1976 the citizens of New Jersey voted to legalize casino

gambling in Atlantic City, and the economic future of the city now seems assured. The first casino was in operation by the end of 1977, and others were under construction. Projections of future jobs, payrolls, and visitors are astronomical. This may be a mixed blessing to the ordinary citizens of the area, but it is likely that the glory days of yesteryear will be surpassed by the flamboyant future of "Las Vegas East."

The historical attractions of Megalopolis may occupy the visitor for a shorter period of time than does city or shore, but the great number of historic sites and the frequently intriguing nature of their presented interpretation make many of them hard to pass up. Most of the states of the region have capitalized on "selling" history to tourists; but Virginia, with hundreds of permanent historical markers along its highways, Pennsylvania, and Massachusetts have done the most thorough jobs. Battlefield sites of the Revolutionary and Civil wars are particularly notable. An interesting and popular trend is the integrated restoration of early settlements on a large-scale basis—for example, the Pilgrim village of Plymouth, Massachusetts; the restored seaport of Mystic, Connecticut; and the colonial town of Williamsburg, Virginia.

---

[22] Evan B. Alderfer, "Sun, Surf, and Sand: Times and Tides on the Jersey Shore," *Business Review*, Federal Reserve Bank of Philadelphia (November 1973), p. 15.

the role of the region

The significance of Megalopolis is much greater than its area or even its population would indicate. It is not enough to say that within the region are 20 percent of the people, 23 percent of the industrial production, and 29 percent of the wholesale sales of the nation. It must be reiterated that Megalopolis is also the financial heart of the country—six of the ten largest banks in the nation are in New York City—a particularly significant fact in any country with a capitalistic economy. Of even greater importance, Megalopolis is the brain and nerve center of the nation. In this region is made a large share of the decisions that shape the economy and government of the United States and thus significantly influence economic and political decisions and events over most of the world.

It is impossible to quantify the magnitude of the decision-making role of Megalopolis, but some indication of this factor can be seen by tabulating the locations of the headquarters of the major business corporations of the nation. According to the annual *Fortune* magazine survey for 1977, 33 percent of the 500 largest industrial corporations in the nation were headquartered in Megalopolis. The region was also headquarters for 33 percent of the 50 largest utilities, 42 percent of the 50 largest life insurance companies and the 50 largest retailing firms, and 28 percent of the 50 largest commercial banks and the 50 largest transportation companies. Add to this the Megalopolitan location of both the seat of government of the United States and the United Nations, as well as a host of state, city, and local government centers, and it becomes clear that much of the economy and politics of the nation is guided from Megalopolis—for better or for worse.

Another way in which the importance of Megalopolis transcends its size is in its manner of coping with urban problems. This is an urban region with an unmatched intensity of living. Its urban problems, too, are unmatched in their complexity and magnitude. Equally abundant within the region are workers, brainpower, skills, and technology with which to face the problems. Gottmann called Megalopolis the "cradle of the future," implying its role, both actual and potential, in meeting the challenge of an urbanized world.

There is yet another way in which Megalopolis has a role to play. What can it show the world in the matter of despoliation or protection of the environment? As cities grow and green spaces shrink, how does humanity's relationship to nature change, and how does this affect the qualify of life for people and all other living things? Must air pollution forever worsen, since there are increasing numbers of machines and people to expel pollutants into the atmosphere? Will New York harbor eventually be so choked with garbage scows that there will be no room for ocean liners? Must Chesapeake Bay become as sterile as Newark Bay, where in some reaches even coliform (intestinal) bacteria cannot survive?[23] The citizenry, abruptly and increasingly conscious of ecological relationships, watches with interest and apprehension.

[23] George W. Carey, *A Vignette of the New York–New Jersey Metropolitan Region* (Cambridge, Mass.: Ballinger Publishing Co., 1976), p. 207.

selected bibliography

ALEXANDER, LEWIS M., *The Northeastern United States* (2nd ed.). New York: D. Van Nostrand Company, 1976.

ALFORD, JOHN J., "The Chesapeake Oyster Fishery," *Annals*, Association of American Geographers, 65 (1975), 229–39.

BERGMAN, EDWARD F., AND THOMAS W. POHL, *A Geography of the New York Metropolitan Region*. Dubuque, Iowa: Kendall/Hunt Publishing Company, 1975.

BOSWELL, T. D., "Residential Patterns of Puerto Ricans in New York City," *Geographical Review*, 66 (1976), 92–94.

BOYLE, ROBERT H., AND MARK KRAM, "A Gift of Place," *Sports Illustrated*, 43 (21 July 1975), 56–64.

BRODSKY, H., "Land Development and the Expanding City," *Annals*, Association of American Geographers, 63 (1973), 159–66.

BROWNING, CLYDE, ed., *Population and Urbanized Area Growth in Megalopolis, 1950–1970*. Chapel Hill: University of North Carolina, Geography Department, Studies in Geography Series 7, 1974.

CAREY, GEORGE W., *A Vignette of the New York–New Jersey Metropolitan Region*. Cambridge, Mass.: Ballinger Publishing Company, 1976.

CONZEN, MICHAEL P., AND GEORGE K. LEWIS, *Boston: A Geographical Portrait*. Cambridge, Mass.: Ballinger Publishing Company, 1976.

DANSEREAU, PIERRE, ed., *Challenge for Survival: Land, Air, and Water for Man in Megalopolis*. New York: Columbia University Press, 1970.

The Delaware River Basin: An Environmental Assessment of Three Centuries of Change. Washington, D.C.: Government Printing Office, 1976.

ESTALL, R. C., *New England: A Study in Industrial Adjustment*. New York: Frederick A. Praeger, 1966.

FRIEDLAND, WILLIAM H., AND DOROTHY NELKIN, *Migrant Agricultural Workers in America's Northeast*. New York: Holt, Rinehart & Winston, 1971.

GOTTMANN, JEAN, *Megalopolis: The Urbanized Northeastern Seaboard of the United States*. New York: The Twentieth Century Fund, 1961.

———, *Virginia in Our Century*. Charlottesville: University of Virginia Press, 1969.

KANTROWITZ, N., *Ethnic and Racial Segregation in the New York Metropolis: Residential Patterns Among White Ethnic Groups, Blacks and Puerto Ricans*. New York: Praeger Publications, 1973.

LIPPSON, ALICE JANE, *The Chesapeake Bay in Maryland: An Atlas of Natural Resources*. Baltimore, Md.: Johns Hopkins University Press, 1973.

LOWENTHAL, DAVID, "New York's New Hispanic Immigrants," *Geographical Review*, 66 (1976), 90–92.

McMANIS, DOUGLAS R., *Colonial New England: A Historical Geography*. New York: Oxford University Press, 1975.

McPHEE, JOHN A., *The Pine Barrens*. New York: Farrar, Straus & Giroux, Inc., 1968.

MEYER, DAVID R., *From Farm to Factory to Urban Pastoralism: Urban Change in Central Connecticut*. Cambridge, Mass.: Ballinger Publishing Company, 1976.

MULLER, PETER O., KENNETH C. MEYER, AND ROMAN A. CYBRIWSKY, *Metropolitan Philadelphia: A Study of Conflict and Social Cleavages*. Cambridge, Mass.: Ballinger Publishing Company, 1976.

OLSON, SHERRY, *Baltimore*. Cambridge, Mass.: Ballinger Publishing Company, 1976.

ROBICHAUD, BERYL, AND MURRAY F. BUELL, *Vegetation of New Jersey: A Study of Landscape Diversity*. New Brunswick, N.J.: Rutgers University Press, 1973.

THOMAS, JEAN-CLAUDE MARCEAU, "Washington," in *Contemporary Metropolitan America, Vol. 4, Twentieth Century Cities*, ed. John S. Adams, pp. 297–344. Cambridge, Mass.: Ballinger Publishing Company, 1976.

THOMPSON, DEREK, ed., *Atlas of Maryland*. College Park, Md.: University of Maryland, Department of Geography, 1977.

THOMPSON, JOHN H., ed., *Geography of New York State* (2nd ed.). Syracuse, N.Y.: Syracuse University Press, 1977.

TILDEN, PAUL M., "Planning in the Pine Barrens," *National Parks and Conservation Magazine*, 45 (1971), 22–26.

VERNON, RAYMOND, *Metropolis: 1985*. Garden City, N.Y.: Doubleday & Co., Inc., 1961.

WACKER, PETER O., *Land and People: A Cultural Geography of Pre-industrial New Jersey: Origins and Settlement Patterns*. New Brunswick, N.J.: Rutgers University Press, 1975.

WALLACE, WILLIAM H., "The Future of the Freight Train in New England," *Proceedings*, Association of American Geographers, 2 (1970), 145–49.

THE
APPALACHIANS
AND
THE
OZARKS

9

The Appalachian Highlands and the Ozark-Ouachita Uplands are two disconnected segments of a single region, separated by the broad expanse of the Mississippi Valley. The Appalachians extend from central New York State, south of the Mohawk Valley, to central Alabama, where they terminate on the Gulf Coastal Plain (fig. 9–1).

fig. 9–1   The Appalachian and Ozark Region (base map copyright A. K. Lobeck; reprinted by permission of Hammond, Inc.).

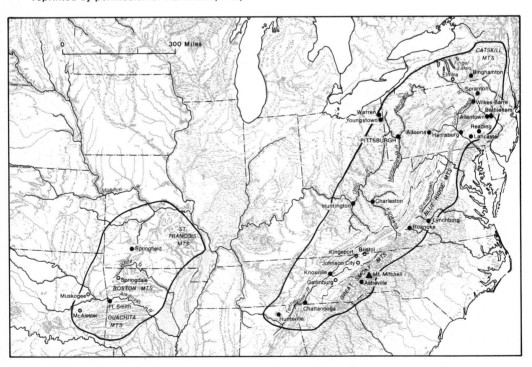

The general trend of the mountains and their intervening valleys is northeast-southwest.

Geographically the eastern boundary of this subregion follows the contact between the southern Piedmont and the Blue Ridge–Great Smoky Mountains. Northward from central Virginia, other factors seem to be more significant in locating the boundary. The northeastern margin of the subregion is deemed to lie along the western edge of Megalopolis, where rural land use replaces urban land use; thus, the northern part of the Appalachian Piedmont is included within the Appalachian subregion. The western boundary of the subregion is generally along the western edge of the Appalachian "Plateaus."

Although the two parts of this region are separated by extensive lands that do not belong within the regional boundaries, it seems desirable to consider them as forming one region because of their remarkable similarity both in physical appearance and in human responses.

This is a diversified region topographically, climatically, and economically; nevertheless, a thread of internal unity holds the several parts together, making them one major geographical region. The most densely settled areas, those with more than 100 persons per square mile, are the valleys; the sparsely settled areas, with less than 10 inhabitants per square mile, are those of broken relief. Considerable discrimination is shown in the selection of places for settlement, especially regarding the suitability of land for crops.

the regional character

As with any large region, generalizations about predominant characteristics are fraught with exceptions. There are many differences in the various parts of the region. Some authorities would say that the northern Appalachians (roughly from the Kanawha River northward) are quite distinct from the southern Appalachians; others would note that the main differences are between coal-mining areas and noncoal-mining areas; and still others would point up differences between the Appalachians and the Ozarks. Throughout the region there are also pronounced variations in life style among the citizens: between the black factory worker in Chattanooga and the white subsistence farmer on Hickory Ridge, between the family-centered Pennsylvania Dutchman of Lancaster County and the externally oriented resort operator on Lake of the Ozarks.

It has been tempting to paint the region as a hill people haven, replete with colorful speech, a charming folk culture, and hidden moonshine stills. This exaggerated image belongs to another era, if indeed it ever pertained. Hill people and mountain folk certainly exist today in various parts of the region, but with few exceptions their isolation and distinctiveness are gone forever. As Thomas Ford has pointed out about the southern Appalachians:

The sprawling growth of . . . metropolitan areas and the abandoned cabins up narrow hollow roads provide impressive evidence of major population shifts. Brush cover and second-growth timber reclaiming mountain slopes once cultivated to the very ridges, and unfamiliar silhouettes of industrial smokestacks . . . bear equally eloquent testimony of a transforming economy. Hard-surface highways along mountain streams which themselves a scant generation ago served as roadbeds, and television antennas clustered on mountain tops are functional symbols of the intrusion of contemporary mass culture into even the most isolated areas.[1]

There are elements that contribute to geographical generalizations about the region. Most of the land is in slope, and the slopes are often steep. As a result, life is focused in the valleys; settlements, transportation routes, and industrial developments compete with river or stream for the limited

[1] Thomas R. Ford, "The Passing of Provincialism," in *The Southern Appalachian Region: A Survey,* ed. Thomas R. Ford (Lexington: University of Kentucky Press, 1962), p. 9.

amount of flat land on the valley floor. Another pervasive aspect of the region is forest; almost all of the area was originally forest covered, and the great majority of it is still clothed with virgin or second-growth trees.

Another significant facet of regional character is recent population trends. During the middle decades of the twentieth century—the 1940s and 1950s—there was an actual population decline in most parts of the region, a situation that pertained to no other populous portion of Anglo-America. Appalachian birth rates, long among the highest on the continent, declined rapidly. More significant, however, was the impact of out-migration, predominantly teenagers and young adults, that characterized most of the region until the mid-1960s. Beginning in the late 1960s, however, more people moved into the region than left. This pattern accelerated in the 1970s, and the traditionally declining areas of Southern Appalachia and the Ozarks-Ouachitas are now experiencing a population resurgence that is not restricted only to urban areas but also includes a great many rural counties.

The population growth is indicative of greater economic opportunities in the region, but it does not necessarily indicate a reversal of the long-standing economic plight of the people of Appalachia and Ozarkia. The 1930 Census of Agriculture showed that the Appalachians encompassed the highest proportion of low-income farms in the country. Later the significant decline in coal-mining employment added another dimension to economic difficulty, as farming and coal-mining had long been the principal occupations of the people of Appalachia; thus this region came to be recognized as the number one long-run problem area (in a geographical sense) in the nation's economy. Any discussion of the region's geography must consider the low incomes and restricted economic opportunities of a large proportion of the population.

the environment

Although the Appalachian and Ozark portions of the region are separated from one another by several hundred miles, their geologic and geomorphic affinities are so marked that there is general agreement that Appalachian lithology and structure continue westward beneath coastal-plain sediments to reappear at the surface in the Ozark-Ouachita subregion.[2] The result is notable similarity in rock types, structure, and landform patterns, which give the Appalachian and Ozark Region topographic distinctiveness that provides a convenient rationale for delineating physical subregions. The prominent subregions are (1) the Northern Piedmont; (2) the Blue Ridge–Great Smoky Mountains; (3) the Ridge and Valley section; (4) the Appalachian Plateaus, often further subdivided into the Allegheny Plateau in the north and the Cumberland Plateau in the south; (5) the Ouachita Mountains and Valleys; and (6) the Ozark Plateaus (fig. 9–2).

fig. 9–2 Topographic subdivisions of the Appalachian and Ozark Region: (1) the Northern Piedmont, (2) the Blue Ridge–Great Smoky Mountains, (3) the Ridge and Valley section, (4) the Appalachian Plateaus, (5) the Ouachita Mountains and Valleys, and (6) the Ozark Plateaus.

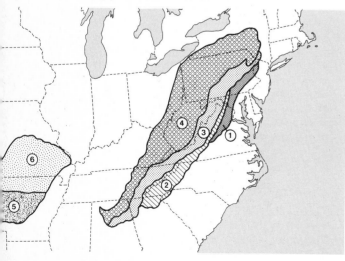

[2] William D. Thornbury, *Regional Geomorphology of the United States* (New York: John Wiley & Sons, Inc., 1965), p. 262.

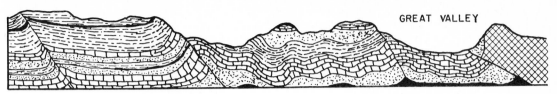

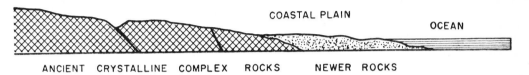

fig. 9-3 Generalized geologic cross-section of the Appalachian subregion.

THE NORTHERN PIEDMONT

The Northern Piedmont occupies an area extending from central Virginia across central Maryland and southeastern Pennsylvania into northern New Jersey. Its gently undulating surface reaches to only a few hundred feet above sea level in its highest parts. The underlying metamorphic and plutonic rocks are crystalline and ancient (fig. 9-3).

Along the inner (western) margin of the Northern Piedmont is a lengthy lowland tract that has developed on sedimentary rocks of mostly Triassic Age. This so-called Triassic Lowland encompasses some of the finest agricultural land on the continent, in part attributable to the soils that have developed there.

THE BLUE RIDGE–
GREAT SMOKY MOUNTAINS

The Blue Ridge consists largely of crystalline rocks of igneous and metamorphic origin: granites, gneisses, schists, diorites, and slates. Extending from Pennsylvania to Georgia, in altitude the Blue Ridge exceeds

all other mountains in the East. North of Roanoke it consists of a narrow ridge cut by numerous gaps; south of Roanoke it spreads out to form a tangled mass of mountains and valleys more than 100 miles wide. The mountains are steep, rocky, and forest-covered. The highest peak is Mount Mitchell in North Carolina (6,684 feet), in the range known as the Great Smoky Mountains.

Because of heavy rainfall, the Blue Ridge was covered with magnificent forests, originally consisting of hardwood trees, especially oak, chestnut, and hickory. The greater part of the original forest was logged years ago, part of it being converted into charcoal for iron furnaces in the nineteenth century. Much of the area has been cut repeatedly, and a great deal has been burned; however, most of the subregion is still cloaked with extensive forest.

THE RIDGE AND VALLEY

This subregion consists of a complex folded area of parallel ridges and valleys and is well-developed in Pennsylvania and southwestern Virginia (fig. 9-4).

fig. 9–4 Ridge and valley country in the western part of the state of Virginia.

The Great Valley This nature-chiseled groove that trends northeast-southwest from the Hudson Valley of New York to central Alabama is one of the world's longest mountain valleys. Its flattish floor is divided into separate sections by minor cross ridges that serve as watershed separations for the several streams that drain the valley. Different names are applied to various segments of the Great Valley. Near the Delaware it is called the Lehigh Valley; north of the Susquehanna, the Lebanon Valley; south of the Susquehanna, the Cumberland Valley; in northern Virginia, the Shenandoah; in Virginia as a whole, the Valley of Virginia; and in Tennessee, the Valley of East Tennessee.

The Great Valley has long been the north-south highway in the Appalachian region as well as one of the most productive agricultural areas in the East. It has never been of outstanding industrial importance, although several of its cities (particularly in Pennsylvania and Tennessee) have important manufacturing establishments.

The eastern and western confines of the Great Valley are definite: the knobby wooded crest of the Blue Ridge towers above the valley floor on the east, and the wild, rugged, though less imposing, Appalachian ridges bound it on the west.

The Ridge and Valley Section West of the Great Valley is a broad series of roughly parallel ridges and valleys that has developed along parallel folds in Paleozoic sediments. Topographical development results primarily from differential erosion, with the configuration based on differences in the resistance of the bedrock. The ridge-makers are mostly sandstones.

The ridges are not the same everywhere: some are low and narrow, others high and fairly broad. Most of the valleys are narrow, flattish, and cleared for agriculture. From the air, the forested ridges show up as dark parallel bands, and the cleared valleys as light ones.

This area gets less rainfall than other parts of the Appalachians—about 40 inches. This difference is ascribed to the sheltering effect of the Blue Ridge on the one side and the Allegheny-Cumberland Escarpment on the other. The seasonal distribution is quite even, although autumn is somewhat more dry than spring. About half the precipitation falls during the growing season, the average length of which varies from 176 days in the north to more than 200 days in the south.

The natural vegetation of the valley lands consisted primarily of oak and hickory, with sycamore, elm, and willow near the streams. On the ridges it was similar to that found on the Blue Ridge Mountains to the east. Some of this magnificent forest was destroyed by the pioneers who settled in the area, but the ridges are still tree-covered even though much of the cover is second and third growth. There were also areas of grassland in the broader river valleys—the result of burning by the Indians.

THE APPALACHIAN PLATEAUS

The western division of the Appalachian Highlands is a broad belt of land known as the Appalachian Plateaus. Along its eastern edge it has a bold high escarpment, the Allegheny Front, that is so steep that roads and railroads ascend it with difficulty. Most of the layers of rocks that form the plateaus lie flat, one on the other. This subregion extends from the Catskill Mountains to north-central Alabama, and from the Allegheny Front to the Interior Lowland. The term *plateau* is applicable in a structural sense, but the present topography is mostly hill country, with only accordant summits as reminders of any previous plateau surface. The area can be subdivided into the Allegheny Plateau (glaciated and nonglaciated sections) and the Cumberland Plateau.

The Glaciated Allegheny Plateau Rounded topography puts its stamp on most of this area, which on the north is bounded by the Mohawk Valley and the Ontario Plain. The nearly flat-lying sandstones and shales are much dissected by streams that have cut down and back into the plateau. In the northern part—the Finger Lakes country—six slender lakes, trending north-south, occupy the valleys of preglacial streams that were modified by ice erosion and blocked by ice deposition. Here is an area of rolling terrain. In northeastern Ohio and adjacent northwestern Pennsylvania, the plateau was modified by the ice, and the relief is gentle, with broad divides. Northeastern Pennsylvania consists of a hilly upland with numerous streams, lakes, and swamps.

The Unglaciated Allegheny Plateau Topographically this plateau is more rugged than its glaciated neighbor to the north. Most of the area might properly be regarded as hill country, for the plateau has been maturely dissected. In the Kanawha Valley, the streams lie 1,000 to 1,500 feet below the plateau surface. Some of the valleys are so narrow and canyonlike as to be uninhabited; some have inadequate room even for a railroad or highway.

The Cumberland Plateau This "plateau" is mostly rugged hill country that is so maturely dissected that practically none of its former plateau characteristics remains except locally, as in parts of Tennessee. No sharp boundary separates it from the Allegheny Plateau to the north; thus the Cumberland Plateau is regarded here as beginning in southern Kentucky (the upper reaches of the Kentucky River) and extending to the Gulf Coastal Plain. It includes parts of southeastern Kentucky, eastern Tennessee, and northern Alabama.

THE OZARK-OUACHITA UPLANDS

The Ozark-Ouachita subregion is composed of three major divisions:

1 The Ozark section, consisting mainly of eroded plateaus such as the Salem and Springfield plateaus and two hilly areas, the St. Francois Mountains in Missouri and the Boston Mountains in Arkansas (fig. 9–5).

fig. 9–5   The heavily forested Ozark Mountains in northern Arkansas (courtesy Arkansas Department of Parks and Tourism).

2 The broad structural trough of the Arkansas River Valley.

3 The Ouachita Mountains, whose strongly folded and faulted structures result in ridge and valley parallelism similar to the Ridge and Valley section of the Appalachians. The Ouachita Mountains reach their highest elevation—about 2,800 feet above sea level—near the Arkansas-Oklahoma border.

settlement
of the appalachian highlands

It was a century and a half after the founding of Atlantic seaboard colonies before settlement began to push into the hill country of the Appalachians, although the Northern Piedmont was settled 50 years earlier. Welsh Quakers and Scotch-Irish Presbyterians were in the vanguard that funneled through William Penn's Philadelphia and spread out in southeastern Pennsylvania. It was German Protestants, however, who were the bulk of the settlers, attracted by both economic opportunity and the promise of religious freedom. By 1750 half of the population of the Pennsylvania colony consisted of immigrant Germans.[3]

From the Pennsylvania Piedmont through the Triassic Lowland was the only easy route to the Great Valley of the Appalachians. Into this valley in the early part of the eighteenth century came pioneer settlers from Pennsylvania; later they were joined by a trickle, and then a flood, of people moving more directly west from tidewater Virginia and Maryland. A road was finally cut through the western mountains via the Cumberland Gap, providing access to the interior. This "Wilderness Road" furnished the only connection to the infant settlements in Kentucky for several decades, later being supplemented by the old national road west from Baltimore.

In the latter part of the eighteenth century and the early part of the nineteenth, the coves and valleys of the Appalachians began to be occupied. "Many of the early settlers were hardy Ulster Scots, descendants of Scots who had been settled in the ancient Irish province of Ulster more than a century before they had moved to the New World."[4] People of English and German stock were also numerous, and there was a minority of French Huguenot and Highland Scots as well. The Great Valley, with its prime agricultural land, was fairly densely occupied before the settlers began to push into the mountains in large numbers. By the 1830s, following the eviction of Cherokees from their homes in northern Georgia, that area was occupied by whites, and the settlement of the Appalachians was more or less complete.[5]

Why did people choose to settle in these mountains at all, when much "better" land lay to the west? One view is that this was "the place where the axle broke" and that the discouraged pioneer was too shiftless to fix it and move on. Others hold that this was a place where a dream was realized, where free-spirited people could live as they wanted in a place of their liking.[6] It seems clear that many, if not most, of the early settlers were of lower economic levels and were nonconformist sectarians in religious belief. Settlement in mountainous isolation reinforced their tendencies toward clannishness, religious fundamentalism, and suspicion of, or hostility to, centralized authority. In any event, after the initial decades of settlement, there were few in-migrants who joined them, and time seemed to pass most of the subregion by. Such isolation reinforced the perpetuation of a folk culture based on the traditions of previous generations.

[3] Ezra Bowen and Editors of Time-Life Books, *The Middle Atlantic States* (New York: Time-Life Books, 1968), p. 35.

[4] John Fraser Hart, *The South* (Princeton, N.J.: D. Van Nostrand Company, 1976), p. 52.

[5] John C. Belcher, "Population Growth and Characteristics," in *The Southern Appalachian Region: A Survey,* Ford, p. 38.

[6] Wilma Dydeman, James Stokely, and Editors of Time-Life Books, *The Border States* (New York: Time-Life Books, 1968), p. 36.

For many years most of the Appalachians south of Pennsylvania was a sort of land-locked island, isolated from the rest of the country. Most rivers were too swift to be used for transportation, and the rugged terrain inhibited railroad and highway construction. Even today most of the railways are branch lines built solely to exploit the coal and timber resources.

When the attractions of urban living became known to the hill people, particularly during World War II, an out-migration began that has continued. The availability of industrial employment and urban amenities has drawn tens of thousands of inhabitants from the Appalachians eastward to Washington, southward to Atlanta and Bi .ningham, and especially westward and northward to Nashville, Louisville, Cincinnati, Pittsburgh, Cleveland, Detroit, and Chicago. There they often settle in relatively close-knit neighborhood communities, maintaining a strong flavor of hill country living in the midst of the city until time eventually wears away the traditions.

The Great Valley has not significantly shared in the egress; rather its attractions of cities, industry, and better farming areas have brought about population increase. Population in the Blue Ridge has remained virtually static for the past three decades; it is the Cumberland and Allegheny plateaus that have been the major losers.

The present population of the Appalachians is preponderantly native-born and white. Blacks constitute a significant minority in the Pittsburgh area, in some of the other Pennsylvania and Ohio industrial towns, and in parts of the Piedmont; elsewhere they live mostly in Chattanooga and Charleston.

settlement of the ozark-ouachita uplands

The earliest white settlements in the Ozark-Ouachita Uplands were those of the French along the northeastern border in Missouri. They were only feeble attempts and were based on the presence of minerals, especially lead and salt. Since silver, the one metal they wanted, was lacking, the French did not explore systematically or try to develop the subregion. The first recorded land grant was made in 1723. The French, who never penetrated far into the Upland, were reduced to a minority group by English-speaking colonists toward the close of the eighteenth century. After the purchase of this territory in 1803 by the United States, settlement proceeded rapidly.

The Upland was occupied before settlements were made in the lowland prairies to the northwest, west, and southwest. The area immediately to the west was set aside by the United States government between 1820 and 1837 as the Indian Territory and for many years was not opened to white settlement. After the initial occupance of the Missouri, Mississippi, and Arkansas river valleys, succeeding pioneers entered the rougher and more remote sections of the Upland and remained there. The hilly, forested habitat, which provided so amply for the needs of the pioneers, later retarded their development by isolating them from the progress of the prairies.

World War I was an important factor in the breakdown of isolation in this subregion. The draft and the appeal for volunteers caused many ridge dwellers to leave the hills to join the armed forces. High wages in the cities during the war also enticed many from their mountain fastnesses. After the war, those who returned brought back new ideas. But the Depression following 1929 had a regressive effect, for many who went to the cities lost their jobs and returned to the Upland, and a large part of the plateau population went on relief when various relief agencies were developed under the New Deal.

World War II repeated the effect of the first war. Selective Service and high wages, particularly in munitions and aircraft factories in St. Louis, Kansas City, Tulsa, Dallas, and Fort Worth, attracted many of the younger persons away from the hills.

Modern highways have opened most of the subregion to much greater interaction with the surrounding lowlands. In the last few years the long-term trend of out-migration has been reversed. Increasing numbers of people are settling in the Ozarks and Ouachitas, not only in the urban areas but also throughout the rural counties. The attraction is in part the availability of jobs in a more diversified industrial scene, but in large measure it is based on tourism and retirement, reflecting the recreational, climatic, and scenic amenities of the subregion.

agriculture

Most of the early settlers of the Appalachian and Ozark Region depended largely on crop growing and livestock raising for their livelihood, and farming continues as a prominent land use throughout most of the region today. In general, however, agriculture has not been a very prosperous occupation. Niggardly environmental provisions of flat land and fertile soils have combined with lack of accessible markets to circumscribe the agricultural opportunities.

Historically, farms have been small, and cropped acreage per farm is limited. Even in recent decades of increasing average farm size elsewhere, many parts of Appalachia have experienced an opposite trend. Farm mechanization also lags behind the rest of the country. Generally, farm income and living standards continue to be the lowest in the nation.

A common generalization is that the characteristic Appalachian land use pattern is one of forested slopes and cleared valley bottoms. Such a pattern clearly prevails in many of the more productive areas, such as the ridge-and-valley portion of Pennsylvania. For most of the region, however, this generalization is invalid; the countryside appears disorganized and patternless, with a hodgepodge of land use on both slopeland and bottomland. As J. Fraser Hart has pointed out:

As you travel through the core of Appalachia . . . you quite literally do not know what to expect when you turn the next corner or go over the crest of the next hill. . . . Field, forest, and pasture are scattered across flat land and hillside alike, with no apparent logic, and the slope of the land seems to have scant power to predict how man will use it. Steep slopes are cultivated but level land is wooded. The tiny tobacco patches stick to the more or less level land, but rows of scraggly cornstalks march up some treacherously steep hillsides, often just across the fence from stands of equally scraggly trees. On the far side of the woods, as like as not, and on the selfsame slope, a herd of scrawny cattle mopes through a gulley-scored "pasture" choked with unpalatable grasses, unclipped weeds, blackberry briers, sumac bushes, and sprouts of sassafras, persimmon, thornapple, and locust.[7]

The seemingly random and nondescript character of land use can be explained in part by the small size of many holdings and the relatively high rate of farm abandonment that has prevailed for some time.[8] More fundamental, however, is the more-or-less inadvertent cycle of land rotation that is traditional in much of the region: land is cleared and cultivated as cropland for some years and then allowed to lapse into a state of less intensive use (pasture) or disuse (woodland) for a period. This is usually a lengthy cycle, the farmer clearing, or abandoning, a particular piece of land only once in a working lifetime (perhaps without realizing that he is reclearing a parcel that had previously been cleared by his father or grandfather).[9] The long-range nature of such a cycle makes it difficult to delineate and comprehend.

Crops and livestock are varied over this extensive region. It is primarily a general farming area, and most farms yield a variety of products, generally in small quantities. Corn is the most common row crop, although it is usually not grown for commercial purposes. Hay growing is widespread and occupies the greatest acreage of cropland. Tobacco is the typical cash crop, although average acreages are quite small.

[7] John Fraser Hart, "Land Rotation in Appalachia," *Geographical Review,* 67 (April 1977), 148.

[8] Decline in farm acreage has been endemic in eastern United States for many years, but nowhere has the abandonment been so great as in Appalachia.

[9] Hart, "Land Rotation in Appalachia,", p. 154.

Livestock is very significant and often provides the greater part of farm income (fig. 9–6). Beef cattle, dairy cattle, and poultry are widely raised; hogs and sheep are important locally.

Products specialization is notable in some areas. The Finger Lakes district of New York, for example, is famous for grapes, fruits, and a variety of vegetables. Apple-growing is an important specialty in parts of the Great Valley and associated ridges from southern Pennsylvania down into central Virginia. Cotton is a major crop in the Arkansas Valley. The most widespread specialty farms, however, are engaged in dairying, particularly in the northern part of the region (New York and northern Pennsylvania) and in the Springfield Plateau of the Ozark section.

NORTHERN PIEDMONT

In marked contrast to the general regional picture, agriculture in the Northern Piedmont, especially in southeastern Pennsylvania, is notably successful and prosperous. Dairy products, grains, tobacco, and apples are the major sources of farm income. There are also local specialty crops such as mushrooms. The raising and fattening of beef cattle are increasing throughout the area.

One of the most productive, interesting, and attractive farming sections in Anglo-America is the Pennsylvania Dutch country of southeastern Pennsylvania, which centers on Lancaster County but also includes most of Berks County to the east and York County to the west (fig. 9–7). The original settlers were mostly *Deutsch,* or German, in nationality, and the term was corrupted to *Dutch.* Other settlers hailed from Switzerland, Austria, France, and Holland, but whatever their origin, the majority shared a common bond of piety and had come to America largely to escape religious persecution. Their descendants have clung remarkably to tradition as well as to land. Unlike farmers in many areas, generations pass through the same homesteads; sons follow fathers on the same soil.

fig. 9–6 Beef cattle (in the foreground) and chicken (houses in the middleground) are livestock specialties in the Shenandoah Valley of Virginia.

The industrious, devout, old-fashioned farm population of the area can be divided into two groups:

1 The *plain Dutch* are mostly pious Amish, Mennonites, Quakers, and Brethren (Dunkards) who are dedicated to a tradi-

fig. 9–7 The Pennsylvania Dutch country of southeastern Pennsylvania.

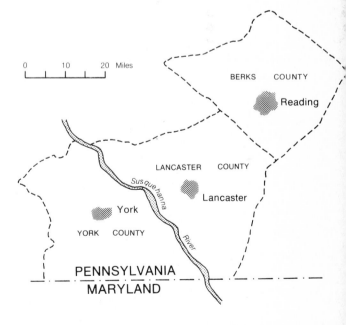

fig. 9–8 A modern scene in Lancaster County. Plain Dutch people still travel by horse-and-buggy, and one-room schoolhouses are still in use (courtesy Pennsylvania Dutch Tourist Bureau).

tional way of life that preserves the peaceful, family-centered, home-oriented style of living for which the Pennsylvania Dutch are justly famous (fig. 9–8). For the most part they wear homespun clothing, insist on their own approach to close-knit education, travel in buggies, and eschew such modern conveniences as electricity, telephones, and farm machinery. Most Amish married men wear full beards but not mustaches.

2 A significant segment of the farm population has drifted away from the strict life style of the plain Dutch; they are re-

fig. 9–9 Barns decorated with hex symbols, near Reading, Pennsylvania.

ferred to as the *gay Dutch.* Although they retain many aspects of the traditional values, their pattern of living is more outgoing, and they have embraced many aspects of modernity, such as automobiles, electricity, modern dress, and farm machinery. A notable feature of gay Dutch farmsteads is the painting of hex symbols on their barns; these are circular designs whose primary purpose is decoration of the otherwise unrelieved whiteness or redness of their immaculate farmsteads (fig. 9–9).

Few farming areas in Anglo-America have been as richly endowed by nature and as well handled by people as the Pennsylvania Dutch country. The gently rolling terrain, abundant summer rainfall, relatively long growing season, and fertile, limestone-derived soils provide a spendid environment for agriculture. The Pennsylvania Dutch farmers are legendary for their skill and industriousness, although at least one authority has challenged the widespread belief that the eighteenth century *Deutsch* were better farmers than those from the British Isles.[10] In any event, the farm landscape provides ample evidence that this is an area of rich and productive agriculture. The fields are well tended, the abundant livestock is well fed, scientific techniques are widely used (with some ingenious devices to compensate for the lack of machinery on plain Dutch farms), and most farmsteads are virtual showplaces (fig. 9–10).

Although most of the local farmers do not personally use tobacco, it is the principal cash crop of the area. The Pennsylvania Dutch country produces more than half of the nation's cigar fillers. Wheat is also an important source of farm income, although much of it is fed to livestock in the area. Corn and hay are widely grown for stock feed, and potatoes for sale. Almost every farm raises cattle, pigs, and poultry; how-

[10] James T. Lemon, "The Agricultural Practices of National Groups in Eighteenth-Century Southeastern Pennsylvania," *Geographical Review,* 56 (October 1966), 467–96.

fig. 9–10 A typical prosperous Lancaster County farm includes fields of tobacco and corn, as well as a large and immaculate farmstead.

ever, commercial dairying is less significant here than in sorrounding areas.

forest industries

Practically all of this upland region was originally forested and, at one time or another, supported logging or lumbering activities. Well over half of the area is now tree-covered, although much is second growth. Relatively valuable hardwoods are a majority of the total stand, sometimes in relatively pure situations but often intermingled with softwoods.

A large proportion of total forested acreage is within the boundaries of national forests. In some districts, however, extensive tracts are owned by major forest products companies, and there are a great many small private holdings, particularly in Pennsylvania and Virginia.

In recent years there has been a modest resurgence of forest industries in the Appalachians. With increasing farmland abandonment, it is obvious that woodland acreage is expanding. The replacement process has been described as follows:

A hard-scrabble, hillside farm is finally abandoned. The first summer, weeds quickly take over. The next summer some grass gets a foothold under the weeds, and blackberry seedlings make their appearance. After several more years, clusters of trees push up above the brambles. The trees may be gray birch from wind-borne seeds, and Eastern red cedar trees from seeds dropped by birds that had dined on red cedar berries. Ultimately

maples and oaks crowd the birches and red cedars for sunlight. By and by the oaks and maples predominate.[11]

Forestry is generally minor in the total economy of the region, but practically every county has at least a little of it, and its local significance may be great even though it is usually characterized by low wages and temporary employment. Logging and lumber camps are essentially a thing of the past, having been initially replaced by small portable mills. More recently there has been a decline in these small "peckerwood" mills and a tendency toward larger-scale operations at a relatively few permanent mill sites.

In most areas lumber is the principal product, but there has been a continuing increase in pulping operations. No part of the region is a major lumber producer, but taken as a whole, some 40 percent of the nation's hardwood lumber comes from the Appalachians and Ozarks.[12]

mineral industries of the appalachians

Various ores and other economic minerals are produced in the Appalachians, but coal is much more important than all the rest

[11] Evan B. Alderfer, "A Jogtrot Through Penn's Woods," *Business Review*, Federal Reserve Bank of Philadelphia (February 1969), p. 11.

[12] Only a miniscule proportion of United States softwood lumber is produced in the region.

combined. No other activity has made such an imprint on the subregion and is so intimately associated with the "problem" of Appalachia.

BITUMINOUS COAL

A large proportion of the Appalachian subregion is underlain by seams of bituminous coal, which occur in remarkable abundance. This area has been the world's most prolific source of good quality coal and still yields about two-thirds of the nation's total output. Now that United States oil production is not only increasingly expensive but also declining in output, that natural gas reserves are dwindling, and that the future of large-scale nuclear power is unclear, the Appalachian coal fields have assumed an overwhelming significance in the total energy picture (see vignette below).

ANTHRACITE COAL

In the northern end of the Ridge and Valley country in northeastern Pennsylvania lies the once important anthracite coal field of Anglo-America. The anthracite region,

the resurgence of king coal

fig. 9-a Idealized cross-sections of anthracite and bituminous coal beds. Mining is difficult and costly in the highly folded seams (above) of the Pennsylvania anthracite district, while it is much simpler and more economical in the horizontal bituminous beds (below) of the Appalachian Plateau.

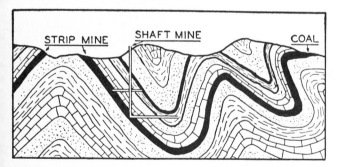

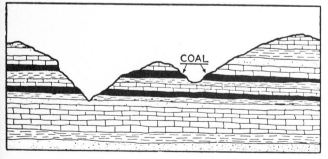

Coal mining has long been the dominant industry of the Appalachian and Ozark Region. Every state in the region except New York and North Carolina is a producer of bituminous coal. The history of the industry is one of ups and downs, but the energy crisis of the early 1970s demonstrated conclusively that the United States must rely heavily on its domestic resources, and its reserves of coal are far larger than its supplies of all other practical energy sources combined. Consequently, coal production has been on a continually upward trend for several years, providing increasing employment opportunities. These developments are particularly significant for Appalachia, which furnishes more than two-thirds of the bituminous coal mined in the United States (fig. 9-a).

Coal mining had been declining from the end of World War II until the early 1960s, losing its two biggest markets, railway steam engines and domestic heating, and experiencing a national employment decrease from 400,000 to 150,000. Increasing use of coal in electric power generation halted the decline in the early 1960s, but there was only a slow growth in output and almost no increase in employment until the accelerated demand of the early 1970s. By 1975 domestic bituminous coal production had surpassed the previous record-year output (1947), and a new peak has been reached every year since. Moreover, by the late 1970s

characterized by narrow valleys, is clogged by large mine buildings, enormous piles of waste, and many railroads. Though only 480 square miles in extent, this area produces all of the anthracite of the United States.

As a result of folding and faulting, as well as of the presence of much earthy material, anthracite is neither so easily nor so cheaply mined as the bituminous coal of western Pennsylvania; accordingly more labor is required in mining and separating the coal from slate. Both strip and underground mining are carried on, but the former is more important.

Because of its smokelessness and high heat-producing efficiency, anthracite was long in demand for domestic heating. The industry peaked in 1917, however, and has been generally declining ever since, unable to compete with natural gas and other "clean" sources of heat. Contemporary production is at an all-time low, although some 3,500 people are employed and reserves are far from exhausted.

Despite what amounts to a national monopoly of this resource, the anthracite district has experienced a long history of economic distress. It has suffered from five

employment in coal mines had grown to more than 225,000, despite heavy reliance on mechanization (fig. 9-b).

There are nearly 6,000 coal mines in the Appalachian and Ozark Region, employing about 170,000 miners. Many of the mines are small operations ("dogholes") with only a few workers, but the majority of the output comes from large mines owned by only a dozen or so companies, most of which are subsidiaries of giant corporations.

About 60 percent of the coal is extracted from strip mines, in which gigantic power shovels, the largest machines ever to move on land, exploit seams that are close to the surface. Mechanization is virtually complete in the larger underground shaft mines as well. "Continuous mining" machines have whirling teeth that tear the coal from the seam at a rate of ten tons per minute, and "longwall" machines have a spinning planer that shaves coal from an exposed surface; in both cases the loosened coal is automatically gathered onto a conveyor belt for removal to the surface. Wherever possible (only involving about 7 percent of total output) extremely efficient horizontal power augers denude a coal seam without the expense of either removing the overburden or sinking a shaft.

Mechanization has meant a dramatic increase in productivity per miner but a significant decrease in the number of miners needed.
(Continued)

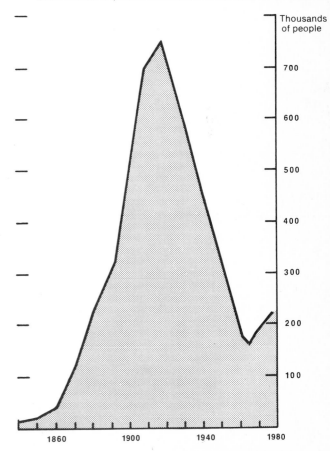

fig. 9-b Historical fluctuations in coal mining employment in the United States. The half-century downtrend has now been reversed (based on Bureau of the Census statistics).

decades of chronic unemployment, and attempts to attract industry to utilize the available labor have not been particularly successful. Several large manufacturing facilities have been established. They mostly produce apparel and textiles and thus usually employ women workers at low wages, which does not alleviate the problem significantly.

PETROLEUM

Petroleum has long been important in Pennsylvania, Kentucky, and New York. The nation's first oil well was put down near Titusville in northwestern Pennsylvania in 1859, and that state led all others in the production of crude oil until 1895. Pennsylvania reached its peak output about 1891, when it produced 31,424,000 barrels of petroleum. Although still productive, the area is outstanding more for the high quality of the lubricants derived from the oil than for the quantity of production. Today less than 2 percent of the country's petroleum is produced in the Appalachians and Ozarks, and only one of the sixty leading oil fields (the Bradford-Allegheny field in Pennsylvania and New York) lies in the region.

CEMENT

Widespread limestone deposits encouraged industrial development in the Appalachians, especially the manufacture of cement. Pennsylvania's Lehigh Valley produced more than one-half of the nation's supply half a century ago. Today it produces only a fraction of that proportion, although its actual output has increased considerably. The reason for its relative decrease in production is that the cement industry is now decentralized, for the market is nationwide and the product is one of relatively low value and great weight. Freight rates accordingly set a definite limit on the area a given source can serve. But with many good sources of argillaceous limestone or of ordinary limestone and silica, the principal raw materials needed in cement making, the Appalachian subregion is relatively significant as a producer of cement. Other notable production, in addition to that of the Lehigh Valley, occurs in the Kanawha Valley of West Virginia and at various places along the Ohio River.

COPPER AND ZINC

Numerous small deposits of metallic ores yielding copper, zinc, and small quantities of other metals are worked along the western flanks of the Great Smoky Mountains in Tennessee. That state is the leading zinc producer of the nation, with nine mines in the area just east of Knoxville. In the extreme southeastern corner of Tennessee are five underground copper mines, the only significant source of copper in the eastern United States.

The working miners receive substantial wages and generally have full-time jobs; thus they are better off than in the past. But unemployment is a continuing reality in the coal areas, despite the recent upturn in both output and employment. The unemployment has resulted partly from stringent federal mine safety regulations that have been imposed since 1969; the larger companies have been able to accommodate the new rules, but several hundred smaller mines have been forced to close.

In the last few years coal production has been increasing most rapidly in the southern Appalachians, in part because of the higher proportion of more desirable coals with low sulfur content. West Virginia continues as the leading Appalachian coal-producing state, and five of the six leading coal mining states are in the region (Kentucky, Pennsylvania, Virginia, and Ohio are the others).[a]

For the last decade or so a major problem for the coal industry has been environmental

[a] Kentucky is actually the single leading coal-producing state in the nation, but about one-third of its output is from the western part of the state, which is not in the Appalachian and Ozark Region.

mineral industries
of the ozark-ouachita uplands

For an upland area, the Ozark-Ouachita subregion is poor in minerals—with two exceptions. In southeastern Missouri is one of the oldest mining areas of the United States, having produced almost continuously since 1725. This is the principal source of lead ore in the nation, with much of the output from recently developed or expanded mines. In the Tri-State District where the Missouri, Kansas, and Oklahoma borders meet is another underground mining district that has been prominent during the past half century. A leading zinc producer in the past, the Tri-State District now yields mostly lead. Combined output from mines in these two districts makes Missouri by far the leading lead-producing state, normally with more than 80 percent of national output.

river basin "development"

In the twentieth century, the "taming," or "harnessing," of a river has become one of the favorite tools for local or regional economic development. All across the United States, from the Penobscot to the Sacramento, rushing rivers have been turned into quiet reservoirs by the straightening of channels, the construction of levees, and particularly, the building of dams. In most cases such development waves the banner of multiple use, emphasizing the resulting advantages of flood control, decreased erosion, improved navigation, expanded hydroelectricity potential, increased water availability, and broadened recreational opportunities. Opponents of river development schemes point out that the economic logic of such projects is nearly always suspect, at best, and that often ecological disconformities are caused.

The controversy between proponents and opponents of river development is long-continuing. In the meantime most of the rivers of the nation have experienced some sort of development, and plans are on the drawing boards for the rest. In the Appalachian and Ozark Region lie major portions of two of the most integrated and best-known of all river-basin development schemes: the Tennessee Valley Authority and the Arkansas River Waterway.

THE TENNESSEE VALLEY AUTHORITY

To date, the TVA is perhaps the greatest experiment in regional socioeconomic planning and development carried out by the federal government. It was created in the 1930s to aid in controlling, conserving, and utilizing the water resources of the area. It deals with such diverse matters as flood control, power development and distribution,

despoliation. The abrupt rise of ecological awareness in the nation has brought about strong protests, and varied regulations, concerning the effects of coal mining on land, water, and air. Strip mining is particularly deplored because of the desolated landscape it produces. All of the principal coal-mining states have enacted stringent laws requiring the reclamation and revegetation of stripped land, and at least two counties have banned stripping altogether.

Whatever the difficulties, the industry is booming, and United States coal reserves are prodigious. With current technology and at contemporary levels of production, there is still more than three centuries worth of coal in the ground. Moreover, in the future coal should become increasingly substitutable for other energy sources, being convertible—although presently only at inordinate cost—into gasoline, synthetic natural gas, and feedstocks for various chemical industries.

Coal has been a mixed blessing for Appalachia in the past. The industry's long-term prognosis, however, looks relatively stable and prosperous. This should result in increasing prosperity for the region, with much better environmental safeguards as a bonus.

navigation, fertilizer manufacturing, agriculture, afforestation, soil erosion, land planning, housing, and manufacturing. Dams were constructed along the Tennessee River and some of its headwater tributaries, backing up the river in a series of contiguous reservoirs throughout almost its entire length.

The area of the Tennessee Valley Authority encompasses the watershed of the Tennessee River and its tributaries—more than 40,000 square miles in parts of seven states (fig. 9-11). This area was selected because it was the most poverty-stricken major river basin in the country. Except that it is a drainage basin, it is not a unified region because land utilization, agriculture, manufacturing, transportation, and the dis-

tribution of power all cut across the drainage boundary.

There are no longer any free-flowing stretches of the river, except in its upper headwaters; it has been dammed into a series of quiet lakes for its 650-mile length from Knoxville to its confluence with the Ohio River near Paducah. In addition to the nine mainstream dams, there are more than two dozen others on tributaries. Hydroelectricity is generated at each of the dams, but the majority of TVA's power output now emanates from a dozen thermal electric plants (mostly coal-fired) that it controls. This comprehensive electric system was a great boon to the valley, but it is also the most controversial feature of the TVA's operation. Private power companies contend

fig. 9-11 The TVA (courtesy Tennessee Valley Authority).

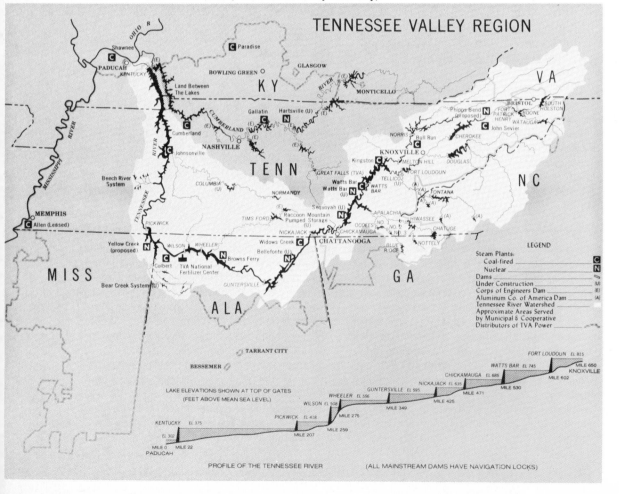

that their very existence is threatened by the cheaper TVA power, part of the cost of which is federally subsidized. Further, many of the complaints about destructive strip mining in the region are aimed at the TVA, which is the single largest purchaser of coal.

A major initial purpose of the TVA was to control flooding in the valley, which was a sporadic, major hazard. This goal has largely been achieved, but some critics point out that flood damage has been prevented by permanently flooding much of the best valley land.

Other benefits attributable to the TVA include attraction of industry to the region, alleviation of much accelerated soil erosion, provision of new water recreational areas, and maintenance of a permanent 9-foot navigation channel. There is no question of the good works that have resulted, but there is considerable difference of opinion about the costs in relation to the benefits. Critics claim that the money could have been used more effectively in other ways.

The controversy will doubtless continue; nevertheless, many lessons may be learned from the experiment. The TVA functions at a level between centralized federal government and fragmented local authorities, and yet on an interstate basis. It is blessed by some and cursed by others but is often referred to—particularly by foreigners—as a comprehensive and relatively successful example of functional regional planning. On the other hand, many residents of the region consider the TVA to be little more than a large electric power utility.

THE ARKANSAS RIVER NAVIGATION SYSTEM

On a somewhat smaller scale, but not at a significantly lower cost, is the Arkansas River Navigation System, dedicated in 1971 after nearly two decades of construction. Its purpose was to produce a 440-mile navigable channel (9 feet in depth) up the Arkansas River from its confluence with the Mississippi, via Pine Bluff, Little Rock, Fort Smith, and Muskogee, to the head of navigation near Tulsa. Eighteen dams have "stabilized" the river, thus adding flood control and hydroelectricity production to the project's benefits (fig. 9–12).

fig. 9–12   Major components of the Arkansas River Navigation System.

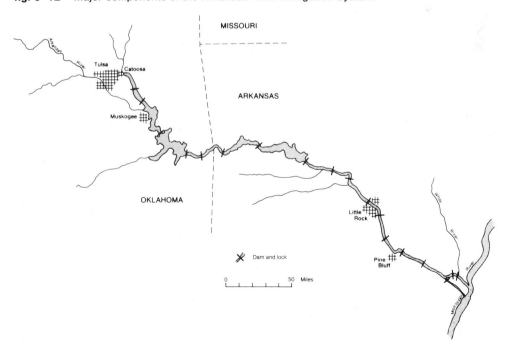

There is no doubt that the local areas are benefited by cheaper transportation, power generation, and industrial attraction; however, the expense of the undertaking—which was approximately equal to the amount spent on construction of the Great Lakes–St. Lawrence Seaway—makes it one of the most costly public works projects in the history of the nation. Critics who con-

tend that "it would be cheaper to pave it" are speaking only partly in jest.

cities and industries

The Appalachian and Ozark Region is not highly urbanized. Urbanization is a much more recent phenomenon here than in most of the rest of the nation, and in many extensive areas rural dwellers are in the majority (see table 9–1 for the region's largest urban places).

Pittsburgh is the only major metropolis in the entire region. Including associated industrial satellites in the valleys of the lower Monongahela and Allegheny rivers and the upper valley of the Ohio and the nearby complexes of *Youngstown* and *Wheeling,* the Pittsburgh district is one of the great metal-manufacturing areas of the world. Its long-time economic focus has been on the production of primary iron and steel and on further processing in fabricated metals and machinery industries.

In addition to this notable urban agglomeration, there are four general areas in which loose clusters of medium-sized cities occur:

1 In northeastern Pennsylvania and adjacent parts of southern New York State are several cities whose economy has significantly depended on coal mining or specialized manufacturing for several generations. The decline of the anthracite coal industry and various industrial problems have caused considerable economic hardship in this area in the past three decades.

The *Allentown-Bethlehem-Easton* urban complex on the lower Lehigh River is highly industrialized—with about half of its work force employed in factories—particularly emphasizing steel, fabricated metals, and apparel production. In the upper valley of the Susquehanna River are the congested anthracite towns of *Scranton* and *Wilkes-Barre,* where coal decline has caused particular hardship and apparel manufacture now dominates the industrial scene. *Binghamton* and *Elmira* are separate urban nodes in

table 9–1 Largest Urban Places
of the Appalachian and Ozark Region

name	population of principal city	population of metropolitan area
Allentown, Pa.	106,624	621,500
Altoona, Pa.	59,692	133,400
Asheville, N.C.	59,591	167,900
Bethlehem, Pa.	73,827	
Binghamton, N.Y.	60,666	303,200
Charleston, W.Va.	67,348	257,300
Chattanooga, Tenn.	161,978	393,000
Elmira, N.Y.	37,320	100,100
Fayetteville, Ark.	33,405	149,100
Fort Smith, Ark.	64,734	201,400
Harrisburg, Pa.	58,274	425,300
Hot Springs, Ark.	38,207	
Huntington, W.Va.	68,811	289,600
Huntsville, Ala.	136,419	286,200
Johnson City, Tenn.	39,325	399,000
Johnstown, Pa.	40,044	265,000
Joplin, Mo.	40,139	
Knoxville, Tenn.	183,383	436,100
Lancaster, Pa.	56,669	341,300
Lynchburg, Va.	63,006	142,300
Parkersburg, W.Va.	38,882	
Pittsburgh, Pa.	458,651	2,315,900
Reading, Pa.	81,592	305,100
Roanoke, Va.	100,585	215,100
Scranton, Pa.	95,884	639,900
Springfield, Mo.	131,557	187,300
Steubenville, Ohio	28,280	165,800
Warren, Ohio	60,486	
Wheeling, W.Va.	44,369	
Wilkes-Barre, Pa.	57,040	
Williamsport, Pa.	35,915	114,900
York, Pa.	48,587	347,400
Youngstown, Ohio	132,203	548,500

southern New York that have fairly well-balanced economies and have absorbed considerable in-migration from the Pennsylvania anthracite area.

2 Several other old, medium-sized cities are scattered over the Piedmont of southeastern Pennsylvania. *Reading, Lancaster,* and *York* are commercial centers for the Piedmont in general and the Pennsylvania Dutch country in particular; however, their principal function is industrial. About 50 percent of the labor force in each city is employed in factories. Their industrial structures are well diversified, with an emphasis on metalworking and machinery production. *Harrisburg* is larger than the other three cities and much less dependent on manufacturing. It is an important railway center, and as the state capital, its governmental employment is sizable.

3 The middle valley of the Ohio River and the adjacent valley of the lower Kanawha have experienced an industrial boom in the last two or three decades. The lure of "firm" power has been particularly important as an industrial attraction; large nearby coal supplies are much more reliable than hydroelectricity with its seasonal vagaries. Inexpensive river transportation and a nearby surplus of suitable labor are other recognizable assets for industry. This is primarily a heavy industry center, with metallurgical and chemical factories particularly notable.

The principal urban nodes are the tricities of *Huntington* (West Virginia)-*Ashland* (Kentucky)-*Ironton* (Ohio) on the Ohio River, and *Charleston* on the Kanawha (fig. 9-13). But many of the most spectacular industrial developments in this area have taken place away from the older centers, often in the splendid isolation of a completely rural riverside setting some distance from any urban area.

4 In the valleys of eastern Tennessee there has been considerable urban and industrial growth, much of it associated with TVA power development. The principal nodes are *Chattanooga, Knoxville, Johnson City, Kingsport,* and *Bristol.*

fig. 9-13 Large factories, especially those producing chemical products, crowd the valley of the Kanawha River around Charleston, West Virginia (courtesy Charleston Chamber of Commerce).

resorts and recreation

The highlands of the northeastern Appalachians are not particularly spectacular or unusually scenic; they consist of pleasant, forested hills, with many rushing streams and a number of lakes. They also contain, particularly in the Catskill and Pocono mountains, one of the densest concentrations of hotels, inns, summer camps, and resorts to be found on the continent. The great advantage is that these are literally next door to Megalopolis and provide a relatively cool summer green space for urban millions to visit.

fig. 9–14 The Pennsylvania Turnpike is the longest, and one of the earliest and most successful, of the modern toll roads. Its construction was complicated by the large number of ridges and mountains that extended perpendicularly across the generally east-west route of the turnpike. Many of these topographic barriers had to be tunneled through, as shown here (courtesy Pennsylvania Turnpike Commission).

The principal tourist attractions of the Pennsylvania Piedmont and the Shenandoah Valley are historical. This was an area of almost continual conflict during the Civil War; in few other areas are historical episodes presented so clearly and accurately to the visitor, most notably at Gettysburg. The Pennsylvania Dutch culture is another major attraction of the area. Tourists are disliked by the plain Dutch, but they and their dollars are welcomed by most other residents of the area (fig. 9–14).

Further south, the national parks attract large numbers of tourists. Shenandoah National Park, with its beautifully timbered slopes and valleys, is well known for picturesque Skyline Drive. Great Smoky Mountains National Park is a broad area of lofty (by Eastern standards) mountains clothed with dense forests of pine, spruce, fir, and hardwoods. In most years it receives more visitors than any other national park on the continent.

In the southern part of the Appalachians, recreational interest centers around water sports on the area's many reservoirs, most of which are products of the TVA.

The recreational possibilities of the Ozark-Ouachita Uplands were recognized by Congress as early as 1832,[13] but the resort industry as it exists today is a recent development. Although Hot Springs and other centers became important locally in the 1890s, the present development had to wait until better railroads and highways were built into the mountains of the area and until the urban centers in surrounding regions attained sufficient size to support a large nearby resort industry. Both of these goals have now been achieved, and today the Ozark-Ouachita Uplands occupy the unique position of being the only hilly or mountainous area within a few hours' drive of such populous urban centers as Kansas City, St. Louis, Memphis, Little Rock, Dallas, Fort Worth, Oklahoma City, and Tulsa. The most remote of these lies less than 300 miles from the center of the subregion.

The climate is only reasonably favorable for resorts, and this tends to offset the advantages of location and mountain scenery. Winter temperatures are cold. There is considerable snow on the higher slopes but not enough for winter sports. The spells of hot, humid weather in the summer are far from desirable in a resort area.

As in other parts of the Southeast and Gulf Southwest, some of the most successful recreational areas have developed around the large, branching reservoirs that have been constructed in various river valleys. Water sports, in the form of boating, fishing, swimming, and skiing, are now very much a part of holiday living for hundreds of thousands of families in an area where natural

---

[13] An area around Hot Springs was set aside as a federal preserve some four decades before Yellowstone, normally considered to be the first of the national parks, was established.

lakes are almost nonexistent. Most important as a recreational center is Lake of the Ozarks in Missouri but also notable are Lake O' the Cherokees in Oklahoma, Lake Ouachita in Arkansas, and Bull Shoals Reservoir on the Arkansas-Missouri border.

the "appalachia problem"

The Appalachian and Ozark Region has long been a poor one. Yet it is only in the last few years that the widespread prevalence of poverty in the Appalachians has been brought to national attention. In the late 1950s and early 1960s the mass media of the nation frequently focused on the "Appalachia problem," featuring the bleak towns, impoverished agriculture, problem-plagued coal mines, underdeveloped economies, wasted lives, and despoiled landscape of the subregion.

The federal government initiated large-scale action with the enactment of the Area Redevelopment Act of 1961. This legislation set up loan funds for commercial and industrial development and for the provision of public facilities, as well as for establishing occupational training programs for workers with obsolescent skills. Much more comprehensive legislation was enacted in 1965 with the Appalachian Regional Development Act. The act established the Appalachian Regional Commission, under whose aegis nearly $1 billion has been appropriated in an attempt to revitalize the Appalachian economy. Local initiative was emphasized in planning, implementing, and administering projects, although Congress dictated that the major thrust of the overall program would be in highway development. Other major expenditures so far have been in health demonstration projects, vocational education, mine reclamation, and land stabilization.[14]

It is as yet premature to assess the effect of the federal program, although it is clear

that the short-run results have been less far-reaching than was hoped. The subregion as a whole was better off in the 1970s than it was in the 1960s. Employment has increased, and unemployment has declined. The economic base has been broadened, with more jobs available in construction and services. But the implementation of the program has attracted strong critics. The ratio of publicity handouts to solid results is said to be inordinately high. Highway development, the very basis of the program, has been brought under fire with the notation that Appalachia has more rural highway mileage in proportion to population and area than the national average.[15]

One clear result has been a change in the economic psychology of the people. The tradition of rugged individualism in Appalachia has been severely eroded. The people now "expect and receive more outside relief and subsidy from government, churches, and private agencies in proportion to their own contributions, than any area of comparable size in the nation."[16] An important exception to this generalization applies to Appalachian farmers. Their small farms cannot afford a cutback in crop acreage; thus, they generally cannot comply with acreage-reduction requirements for federal agricultural subsidies.

the outlook

The plight of the Appalachian and Ozark Region has been celebrated in song and story. It has been recognized as a major negative economic anomaly, an extensive region of poverty in the heart of the richest nation on earth. Its way of life has been called a "culture of despair." The reasons underlying such a situation are complex and imper-

[14] Shirly A. Goetz, "Appalachia: Back from the Brink?" *Business Review,* Federal Reserve Bank of Philadelphia (November 1969), p. 12.

[15] John Munro, "Planning the Appalachian Development Highway System: Some Critical Questions," *Land Economics,* 45 (May 1969), 160.

[16] Rupert B. Vance, "The Region: A New Survey," in *The Southern Appalachian Region: A Survey,* Ford, p. 7.

fectly understood but certainly include a litany of environmental difficulties and a variety of questionable economic approaches and negative human attitudes.

Into a region of small, hill-country farmers came three waves of economic development, each largely financed by "outside" entrepreneurs, each largely sending the profits outside the region, and each despoiling the environment to a notable (sometimes disastrous) degree.[17] The story of logging and mining, the first two waves, is well known. Some local people made money from sale of land or resources, and many jobs were provided; however, many of the sales were at relatively low prices and most of the jobs were low-paying, part-time, or both. Recreation and tourism, the third wave, is more recent but is nearly as massive and sudden as the other two. Developers, usually corporate and often from outside the region, have purchased large acreages of high-amenity (scenic or waterside) land on which to build massive recreational and housing projects. Lack of integrated planning and zoning allows development that often does not conform to the landscape.

Federal and state governments have attempted to alleviate the situation with massive infusions of capital and ambitious development programs. Such efforts, most notably represented by the TVA, the Arkansas River Waterway, and the Appalachian Regional Commission, have provided many advantages to the region but usually at a cost-benefit ratio of depressing proportions.

Until recently the popular solution has been graphically shown by migration statistics; most parts of the region have experienced a massive and continuous out-migration and population decline for several decades. Beginning in the late 1960s, however, and continuing through the 1970s, new demographic trends have appeared. In many sections, particularly in southwestern Appalachia (Kentucky, Tennessee, and Alabama) and the Ozarks of Arkansas and Missouri, there has been an upsurge of population growth. This growth is based partly on expanded employment opportunities in manufacturing (new factories) and recreation (mostly reservoir-related services) that have stemmed the prevailing out-migration of working-age people, and partly on an influx of older people who have opted for retirement in the pleasant rural surroundings offered by the hill country.

Some parts of the region have functioned for a considerable period as pockets of prosperity, for example, the Poconos, the Pennsylvania Dutch country, and much of the Great Valley. Economic stimulation has been provided by long-term government installations at such places as Oak Ridge, Tennessee, and Huntsville, Alabama. And many of the larger cities, such as Pittsburgh, Chattanooga, Knoxville, and Springfield, have continued to experience "normal" urban growth patterns based on their diversified economies.

The renewed importance of coal in the national energy scene provides for long-term stability for this industry and augurs well for the economy of most of the coal-mining counties.

It seems likely that the Appalachians and Ozarks have partly broken free of the traditional syndrome of regional poverty and depression. Agricultural specialization, especially in beef cattle and poultry, will result in more efficient and profitable output in many farming areas. Industrial and recreational developments will continue to make contributions to economic diversification. Population statistics will be watched with interest to see if the recent short-term growth in rural areas develops into a long-term trend.

Many parts of the region, however, have not gotten away from the patterns of the past. There will still be many areas of poor farms, eroded soil, and marginal mines with underpaid workers interspersed among the districts of improving conditions.

---

[17] See Edgar Bingham, "Appalachia: Underdeveloped, Overdeveloped, or Wrongly Developed," *The Virginia Geographer,* 7 (Winter 1972), 9–12.

selected bibliography

BINGHAM, E., "Appalachia: Underdeveloped, Overdeveloped, or Wrongly Developed?" *Virginia Geographer*, 7 (Fall–Winter 1972), 9–12.

CLEMENTS, DONALD W., "Recent Trends in the Geography of Coal," *Annals*, Association of American Geographers, 67 (1977), 109–25.

FORD, THOMAS R., ed., *The Southern Appalachian Region: A Survey*. Lexington: University of Kentucky Press, 1962.

GERLACH, RUSSELL L., *Immigrants in the Ozarks: A Study in Ethnic Geography*. Columbia: University of Missouri Press, 1976.

GERSMEHL, PHIL, "Factors Involved in the Persistence of Southern Appalachian Treeless Balds: An Experimental Study," *Proceedings*, Association of American Geographers, 3 (1971), 56–61.

GIBSON, ARRELL MORGAN, *Wilderness Bonanza: The Tri-State District of Missouri, Kansas, and Oklahoma*. Norman: University of Oklahoma Press, 1972.

GRAFF, THOMAS O., "Arkansas Population Change: 1940–1970," *Ecumene*, 9 (April 1977), 22–28.

GROSSMAN, DAVID A., AND MELVIN R. LEVIN, "The Appalachian Region: A National Problem Area," *Land Economics*, 37 (1961), 133–41.

HART, JOHN FRASER, "Land Rotation in Appalachia," *Geographical Review*, 67 (1977), 148–66.

KARAN, P. P., AND COTTON MATHER, eds., *Atlas of Kentucky*. Lexington: University of Kentucky Press, 1977.

LANDING, JAMES E., "The Amish, the Automobile, and Social Interaction," *Journal of Geography*, 71 (1972), 52–57.

LEMON, JAMES T., *The Best Poor Man's Country; A Geographical Study of Southeastern Pennsylvania*. Baltimore, Md.: Johns Hopkins Press, 1972.

LINEBACK, NEAL G., "Low-Wage Industrialization and Town Size in Rural Appalachia," *Southeastern Geographer*, 12 (1972), 1–13.

MILLER, E. JOAN WILSON, "Ozark Superstitions as Geographic Documentation," *Professional Geographer*, 24 (1972), 223–26.

————, "The Ozark Culture Region as Revealed by Traditional Materials," *Annals*, Association of American Geographers, 58 (1968), 51–77.

MILLER, E. WILLARD, *Socioeconomic Patterns of Pennsylvania: An Atlas*. Harrisburg: Pennsylvania Department of Commerce, 1975.

MITCHELL, ROBERT D., "The Shenandoah Valley Frontier," *Annals*, Association of American Geographers, 62 (1972), 461–86.

NELSON, J. G., "Some Effects of Glaciation on the Susquehanna River Valley," *Annals*, Association of American Geographers, 55 (1965), 404–48.

RAFFERTY, MILTON D., RUSSEL L. GERLACH, AND DENNIS J. HREBEC, *Atlas of Missouri*. Springfield, Mo.: Aux-Arc Research Associates, 1970.

RIZZA, PAUL F., JAMES C. HUGHES, AND ALLEN R. SMITH, *Pennsylvania Atlas: A Thematic Atlas of the Keystone State*. Berlin, Conn.: Atlas Publishing Inc., 1975.

STRAHLER, A. H., "Forests of the Fairfax Line," *Annals*, Association of American Geographers, 62 (1972), 664–84.

VERNON, PHILIP H., AND OSWALD SCHMIDT, "Metropolitan Pittsburgh: Old Trends and New Directions," in *Contemporary Metropolitan America, Vol. 3, Nineteenth Century Inland Centers and Ports*, ed. John S. Adams, pp. 1–59. Cambridge, Mass.: Ballinger Publishing Company, 1976.

WOODRUFF, JAMES, "Debris Avalanches as an Erosional Agent in the Appalachian Mountains," *Journal of Geography*, 70 (1971), 399–406.

ZELINSKY, WILBUR, "The Pennsylvania Town: An Overdue Geographical Account," *Geographical Review*, 67 (1977), 127–47.

ZELINSKY, WILBUR, ET AL., *Population Change and Redistribution in Non-Metropolitan Pennsylvania, 1940–1970*. University Park: Pennsylvania State University, Population Issues Research Office, 1975.

IO

THE
INLAND
SOUTH

The southeastern interior of the United States has been one of the most distinctive regions of the continent for many decades. Although its boundaries have never been easily delimited, it has retained certain cultural (that is, economic, demographic, and social) characteristics that have tended to set it apart as an easily recognizable region. This region has been designated by a number of names, the most popular being "Cotton Belt" and "Old South." Both these names are now anachronistic and misleading, but the region to which they refer is nevertheless conspicuous on the contemporary scene.

The Inland South Region encompasses most, but not all, of the "cultural South." Its boundaries are largely determined on the basis of land use and topography. As delineated in figure 10-1, the region occupies

fig. 10–1 The Inland South Region (base map copyright A. K. Lobeck; reprinted by permission of Hammond, Inc.).

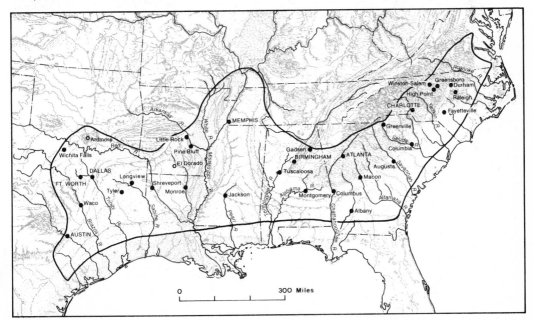

most of the broad coastal plain southward of the Appalachians and the Ozark-Ouachita Uplands.

The northern boundary, then, is primarily marked by the southern margin of the two upland areas. Between and on either side of the uplands—in the Mississippi River lowland, in Virginia, and in Oklahoma-Texas—the extent of the Inland South is determined by variation in crop patterns. In each of these three areas there is a transition from a Southern pattern featuring cotton to some other pattern: a Wheat Belt pattern in Oklahoma-Texas, a Corn Belt pattern in the Mississippi Valley, and a less distinctive general farming pattern in Virginia.

The southern and eastern boundaries of the Inland South are in a transition zone that roughly parallels the Gulf and South Atlantic coasts, some 75 to 100 miles inland. Dense forest, poor drainage, and spotty agriculture predominate coastward; more open woodland, better drainage, and less discontinuous agriculture are found interiorward. The littoral zone of the southeastern states is prominently oriented toward the sea; its port activities, industrial development, and seaside recreation set it apart from the Inland South.

The western boundary of the region is less clear-cut than the others. Differences in land use seem to be the most important criteria. In south central Texas the change from flat land to the short but steep slopes of the "hill country" is accompanied by a change from crop-farming to pastoralism. North of the "hill country," however, there is only an indefinite transition from relatively small general farms eastward to somewhat larger specialty farms (grain sorghums, wheat, irrigated cotton, and cattle) westward.

the physical environment

There is widespread uniformity of physical attributes in the Inland South, several of which provide conspicuous elements of unity for the region. The land surface is quite flat in most places, the drainage pattern is broadly centrifugal and functionally simple, summer and winter climatic characteristics are grossly uniform, and red and yellow soils of only moderate fertility predominate. It is, however, the prevalence of forest and woodland over almost all of the region that is the most noticeable feature of the regional landscape.

THE FACE OF THE LAND

The Inland South is primarily a coastal plain region; the flat or gently undulating land surface is only occasionally interrupted by small hills or long, low ridges. The underlying rocks consist of relatively thick beds of unconsolidated sediments of Tertiary or Cretaceous Age. These beds have a monoclinal dip that is gently seaward, so that progressively older rocks are exposed with increasing distance from the coast.

Along the interior margin of the region in the east is an extensive section of older crystalline rocks that form the Southern Appalachian Piedmont. The topography here is somewhat more irregular than in the coastal plain, although slopes are not steep and the landscape is best described as gently rolling. Between the rocks of the Piedmont and those of the coastal plain is a continuation of the Fall Line. The Southern Piedmont extends in an open arc from central Virginia to northeastern Alabama.

That portion of the Inland South Region that is north of the Gulf of Mexico exemplifies a pattern of landform development known as a belted coastal plain. The sedimentary beds outcrop in successive belts that are arranged roughly parallel to the coast. Some of these strata are less susceptible to erosion than others and, thus, stand slightly above the general level of the land as long, narrow, resistant ridges called cuestas (fig. 10–2). The overall pattern is a series of broad lowlands developed on weaker limestones and shales, which are bounded on the seaward side by the low but abrupt scarps that mark the inward edge of the resistant sandstone cuestas (fig. 10–3). In some cases the cuestas extend for hundreds of miles. They are more numerous in the west Gulf Coastal Plain of Texas and Louisiana but are slightly bolder and more conspicuous in the east Gulf Coastal Plain of Mississippi and Alabama.

Between the two belted zones of the coastal plain is the broad north-south alluvial plain of the Mississippi Valley. This alluvial lowland varies in width from 25 to 125 miles and is bounded on the eastern and western sides by prominent bluffs that rise as much as 200 feet above the lowland. Although a few residual upland ridges interrupt the valley floor, most of the lowland is extraordinarily flat and has a southward slope averaging only about 8 inches per mile. With such a gentle gradient, the Mississippi River and its lower tributaries meander broadly and produce many oxbow lakes and winding scars.

The general drainage pattern of the region consists of a number of long, relatively straight rivers that flow sluggishly toward the ocean from interior upland areas (Appalachians, Ozarks, Ouachitas, and high plains of West Texas). The normally dendritic pattern of their tributaries is interrupted in several places by the cuestas, resulting in right-angle bends and trellising. Very few natural lakes, other than small oxbows, are found along the rivers, but

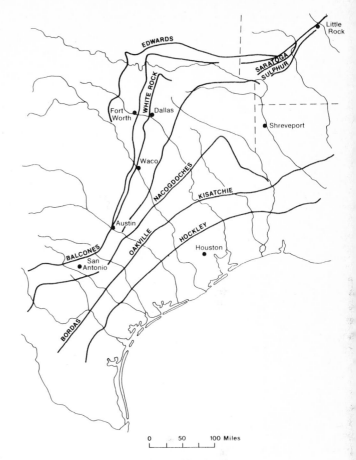

fig. 10–2 Principal cuestas making up the belted coastal plain of the western Gulf area. (From N. M. Fenneman, *Physiography of Eastern United States* [New York: McGraw-Hill Book Company, 1938]. Reprinted by permission.)

fig. 10–3 Generalized geologic cross-section of the western Gulf Coastal Plain, extending northwest-southeast across Texas. (From Fenneman, *Physiography of Eastern United States*. Reprinted by permission.)

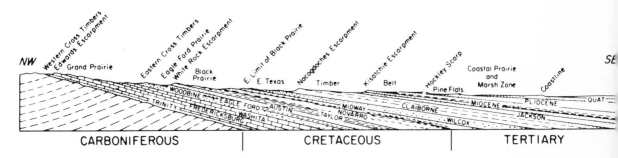

swamps and bayous, indicative of poor drainage, are widespread.

CLIMATE

The climate of the Inland South is sometimes described as humid subtropical, but such terminology is belied by occasional severe winter cold spells. Nevertheless, summer is clearly the dominant season in this region. It is a long period of generally high humidity that is hot by day and warm by night. Summer is also the time of maximum precipitation, with most rainfall coming in brief convective downpours.

Winter is a relatively short season, but it is punctuated by sporadic sweeps of continental polar air across the region, which push the normally mild temperatures well below the freezing point. In no part of the region is snow unknown, and most sections can anticipate one or more snowfalls each winter, although the length of time of snow cover is usually measured in hours rather than days. Winter is only slightly less moist than summer, and most winter precipitation falls in protracted drizzles rather than in brief showers. Total annual rainfall in the region varies from about 55 inches in the east to about 20 inches on the western margin.

Spring and fall are relatively long transition seasons, marked by pleasant temperatures. The former is a notably windy time of the year and, in the western part of the region, is often characterized by major dust storms carried on westerly winds.

SOILS

The most widespread soils of the Inland South are Ultisols. These are mostly red or yellowish-gray in color, indicating a considerable degree of leaching and the subsequent concentration of insoluble iron and aluminum as well as accumulation of a clay horizon. With careful management, these can be agriculturally productive soils; unfortunately, however, careful management has often been lacking, and some of the nation's

worst examples of accelerated soil erosion can be found in the region.

In the Black Belt of Alabama-Mississippi and the Black Waxy Prairie of central Texas are extensive areas of soils derived from underlying limestone and marl. Classed as Mollisols, these are among the most naturally fertile soils anywhere; but they, too, have been subjected to severe erosion, and in many localities, the black topsoil has been stripped away and reveals the lighter-colored subsoil.

The rich alluvial soils of the Mississippi Valley are also dark in color, rich in organic matter, and highly productive. They are mostly classed as Inceptisols and Alfisols.

NATURAL VEGETATION

The Inland South was originally a timbered region characterized by southern yellow pines on most of the interfluves and southern hardwoods (gums, oaks, cypress) in the stream valleys, with a proportion roughly half pine and half hardwood. There are eleven species in the group called southern yellow pines, of which seven are prominent in the Inland South. The most widespread pine species in the region are loblolly, shortleaf, and longleaf.[1] The principal concentrations of hardwoods are in the Mississippi River lowland and scattered widely over the northern portion of the state of Mississippi. In the natural state, three parts of the region apparently were relatively treeless. The Black Belt and Black Waxy Prairie were probably covered with prairie grasses,[2] and the extreme western part of the

[1] Elbert L. Little, Jr., and William B. Critchfield, *Subdivisions of the Genus Pinus (Pines)* U.S. Department of Agriculture Miscellaneous Publication no. 1144 (Washington, D.C.: Government Printing Office, 1969).

[2] As is the case with many seemingly "natural" grasslands, there is considerable debate as to whether the prairie association of the Black Belt was indeed natural or had been induced by repeated burning by Indians. See, for example, Erhard Rostlund, "The Myth of a Natural Prairie Belt in Alabama: An Interpretation of Historical Records," *Annals,* Association of American Geographers, 47 (December 1957), 392–411.

region had a mixed cover of grassland, low open woodland, and scrubby brush.

Although not part of the natural vegetation, there is an introduced species that has become so prominent in the vegetational landscape of the Inland South that it deserves special mention. The kudzu plant (*Peuraria lobata*) is a leguminous, climbing vine that was imported from the Orient for the dual purpose of holding the soil against erosion and providing livestock forage. It has flourished remarkably in its adopted environment in the southeastern states and is now considered a pest species in many localities because of its propensity to climb on and inundate anything (trees, telephone poles, barns, and even houses) that is not protected from it (fig. 10–4). Throughout the Inland South, from Virginia to Texas, the kudzu covers an inordinate amount of surface.

fig. 10–4   A kudzu landscape in central Mississippi. The vines have overgrown all trees and bushes on the left of the road.

peopling and people of the inland south

The aboriginal inhabitants of the Inland South consisted of several strong and well-organized Indian tribes and a number of minor ones. Most important were the "Five Civilized Tribes"—Cherokee, Choctaw, Chickasaw, Creek, and Seminole—that originally occupied most of the area between the Mississippi River and the Atlantic coast. West of the Mississippi, the Caddo, Osage, and Apache were important; later the Comanche moved down from the northern plains and dominated the western frontier of the region for several decades.

During the early years of European contact, conflict with the Indians was relatively limited, mostly because profitable trading relationships had been established between tribesmen and coastal merchants and because pressure for European settlement in the region was slow in building up. Once the Europeans began to move inland significantly, however, the days of the Indian were numbered, regardless of the treaties that were frequently promulgated and just as frequently dishonored by the colonial and federal governments.

Indian wars became commonplace in the early 1800s, and before long most of the recalcitrant tribes had either been wiped out or shifted to new homes west of the Mississippi. An acerbic contemporary critic described the process in which "the most grasping nation on the globe" would take the Indians "by the hand in brotherly fashion and lead them away to die far from the land of their fathers . . . with wonderful ease, quietly, legally, and philanthropically. . . . It is impossible to destroy men with more respect for the laws of humanity."[3]

European settlement in the eastern part of the Inland South was little more than a tiny trickle until the eighteenth century, and the occupance of most of the region dates from the early nineteenth century. Five generalized tides of settlement can be discerned:

1 From the early colonial coastal settlements of Virginia and Maryland, freemen moved west and southwest, joined by settlers coming directly from Europe but funneled through the Chesapeake Bay ports; this stream was augmented by a flow up the

[3] Alexis de Tocqueville, *Democracy in America*, trans. George Lawrence (New York: Harper & Row, 1966), p. 312.

211

Shenandoah Valley into eastern Tennessee and beyond.

2 From the South Atlantic coastal ports, particularly Charleston and Savannah, more European settlers were channeled into the interior.

3 A third route of settler flow was southward from the Midwest and the Upper South (Kentucky and Tennessee) and, in part, down the Mississippi Valley.

4 A fourth stream moved northward through the Gulf Coast ports of New Orleans and Mobile.

5 There was also an early movement of settlers of Spanish ancestry northeastward from Mexico into central and eastern Texas; this flow was circumscribed first by contact with the French in Louisiana and later by the persistent movement of Anglos into Texas from the east and northeast.

Except for those coming from Mexico, nearly all the settlers of the region were Northwest European in origin. It is probable that most of the initial settlers were American-born, but many came directly from Europe, and certainly the great majority were of recent European ancestry. British people (English, Welsh, Scots, and Scotch-Irish) were the most numerous, but Germans, French, Swiss, and Irish were also significant.

COTTON AS A SETTLEMENT CATALYST

By the 1790s most of the Carolina portion of the Inland South and part of eastern Georgia had been settled, and there were other small settled districts in the lower Mississippi Valley and in central Texas. In 1793 young Eli Whitney, visiting on a Georgia plantation near Savannah, developed a vastly improved cotton gin. It was the first practical machine for separating "green seed" cotton lint from seed.[4] With remark-

[4] For amplification of this point, see C. S. Aiken, "An Examination of the Role of the Eli Whitney Cotton Gin in the Origin of the United States Cotton Regions," *Proceedings*, Association of American Geographers, 3 (1971), 5–9.

able suddenness cotton was adopted as the commercial crop of settlement, for it could be produced on small farm or large plantation, providing cheap labor was available. Thus, cotton production boomed, settlement spread, and slave importation expanded.

By 1820, eastern and central Georgia were fully occupied, the good lands of central and western Alabama were settled, much of the Mississippi Valley was being farmed, and settlements in eastern Texas were expanding. Within another three decades nearly all of the Inland South was under settlement except for much of the alluvial Mississippi valley. Plantations, with large slaveholdings, were widespread. There were also many small farmers engaged in limited commercial enterprises with only a few slaves.

Yeoman farmers, who operated without labor assistance, were commonplace, especially in areas of less productive soil or steeper slope. A few freed slaves were farming in Virginia and North Carolina. The total slave population amounted to more than 3 million in 1850, in comparison with a white population of twice that number.

THE CONTEMPORARY POPULATION

The present population of the Inland South is more homogeneous than that of most regions. It has two principal components: some 20 million whites, who are mainly of Anglo-Saxon ancestry and Protestant religious affiliation, and 8 million blacks, who are also mostly Protestant. The largest denominational affiliations in the region are Baptist and Methodist, although various evangelical Protestant groups are strongly entrenched and are experiencing a rapid growth in membership.

In comparison with the total population of the region, adherents of Roman Catholicism are relatively few in number, except among the large Hispano minorities of several Texas cities. Jews constitute an extremely small proportion of the population but have a disproportionately large impact because of their prominence in economic and civic affairs.

In terms of population mobility in the region, there are three recognizable trends in partial opposition to one another:

1 A large share of the people who live in the Inland South were born there. For example, more than 80 percent of the population of Mississippi, Alabama, Georgia, and South Carolina are still living in the state of their birth, in contrast to the national average of less than 70 percent.

2 The urban areas, particularly the larger ones, are significant foci of in-migration from outside the region as well as from rural areas within the region.

3 The long-run high rate of net out-migration of blacks from the Inland South apparently has now been reversed (see vignette below).

reversal of black migration patterns

For the better part of a century there has been a migratory flow of blacks from the Inland South to other parts of the country. For the first few decades the movement was entirely northward, essentially to the larger cities of the Northeast and Midwest. Beginning in the 1920s and accelerating in the 1940s, there was an added flow to the urban areas of the West. This pattern was well established and clear-cut until about 1970, when significant changes began to appear. These changes have become increasingly pronounced through the decade of the 1970s and now seem to be more than temporary aberrations.

For the first time in history more blacks are moving into the region than out, and the tendency appears to be accelerating. Although precise data are unavailable, Census Bureau samples and estimates indicate that there is now a net inflow of blacks to the Inland South, primarily from Northeastern cities. From 1965 to 1970 there was a net outflow of blacks from the region at a ratio of about 2.3 to 1 (a proportion that had been about the same for many years), but during 1970–75 there was a net inflow of blacks at a ratio of about 1.1 to 1.[a]

A summary of the interregional flow patterns shows that the Northeast is the principal area of change, closely followed by the Midwest. In 1965–70 there was a 2 to 1 net outflow of blacks from the Inland South to the Northeast; in 1970–75 this had reversed to a 2 to 1 inflow (fig. 10-a). A 1965–70 net outflow of In-

(Continued)

fig. 10-a Black migration to and from the South in recent half decades (for data source, see footnote a).

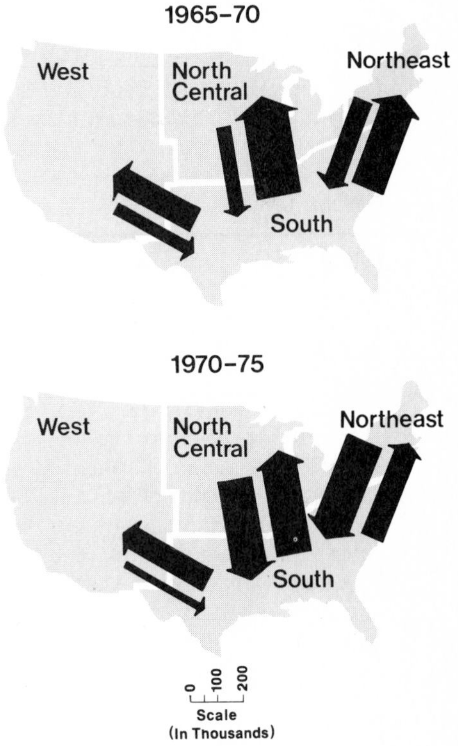

1965–70

1970–75

Scale
(In Thousands)

[a] Based on unpublished Census Bureau data and Patricia Faulkinberry, "New Faces in the South," *Monthly Review,* Federal Reserve Bank of Atlanta, 62 (February 1977), 15–23.

the changing image
of the inland south

Perhaps in no other part of Anglo-America is the sense of regional identity so pervasive as it is in the Inland South. The Southern way of life is recognized by Southerner and non-Southerner alike as being regionally distinctive, partially in tangible ways and partially as a state of mind. For many people this regional identity arouses strong emotions, ranging from reverence to abhorrence. To some, the Southern way of life is "genteel"; to others, "decadent." The strongly entrenched and nondiversified economic base of the Southern past is part of the image, but more a part of contemporary consciousness are feelings about social conditions, particularly as regards the black minority of the population.

The origin of the Southern way of life is complex and beyond the scope of this presentation. Briefly, a generation or two ago there was a regional character to the Inland South that was simple of generalization, even if imperfect of image: the region was economically depressed and socially divided. Agriculture—the traditional basis of the Southern economy—was straitjacketed by corn for subsistence and by cotton and tobacco for cash. The unholy duo of tenancy and soil erosion had a stranglehold on rural life. Industry was present, but it was undi-

land South blacks to the Midwest at a 3 to 1 ratio shifted in 1970–75 to an approximately even interchange (a 1 to 1 ratio). For the West, on the other hand, the long-established pattern of outflow had not reversed; in fact, a 1965–70 net migration of blacks from the Inland South at a 3 to 1 ratio increased to a 4 to 1 ratio during 1970–75. The principal sources of the incoming black migrants are New York, Philadelphia, Cleveland, Detroit, Chicago, and St. Louis.

Within the Inland South the primary areas of settlement for incoming blacks are in the eastern part of the region, particularly Atlanta, but also Charlotte and other Carolina Piedmont cities and Richmond. In-migration of blacks is somewhat less pronounced in the western part of the region, although Dallas and Fort Worth are growth centers. Black inflow is least conspicuous in the central area (Mississippi-Tennessee-Arkansas-Louisiana), except for Memphis and Little Rock.

Sampling indicates that the principal component of the inflow consists of native Southern blacks who had once moved away and are now returning to their natal areas. The migratory pattern appeared to be from the rural South to the urban North; there now appears to be a return to the urban South. Increasingly, however, there is also a southward flow of Northern-born blacks.

The reasons behind this startling change in migration patterns are complex. For some it is an attempt to escape the urban problems of life in big Northern cities, and for others it is a response to family ties or family responsibility. Many retired persons return to the South to stretch out their pensions in a region of generally lower cost of living. But the principal impetus seems to be simply a matter of economic opportunity. Unemployment is generally less severe in the Inland South than in many Northern regions, and increasing numbers and varieties of jobs are available.

Despite the striking nature of this migration reversal, it should be viewed in the general context of population mobility. The Inland South has been attracting white migrants for several decades. Total net migration to the region during 1970–75 showed a 3 to 1 net inflow from the Northeast, a 2 to 1 net inflow from the Midwest, and a slight net inflow from the West. Nearly 90 percent of all migrants into or out of the Inland South are non-blacks, and the net impact of migration on the racial composition of the region is to make it whiter rather than blacker. Thus the net inflow of blacks to the region is remarkable not for the numbers involved but for the drastically changed direction of flow.

versified and paid low wages. Per capita income was well below the national average, and poverty was relatively widespread. Average educational attainment was low, and illiteracy was a problem. Practically speaking, only one political party was extant. Class distinctions were strong, and the Negro was universally accorded—by white and black alike—the bottom rung of the social and economic ladder. There was more to the image—veneration of womanhood, religious piety, economic pluck, and patriotic valor; only inadequacies have been emphasized. The point is that the Inland South displayed certain significant disadvantages and faced certain significant handicaps.

What of its regional character today? Certainly many of the "old" elements of regional distinctiveness still prevail. Regional speech characteristics, for example, show no significant change; the Southern drawl is as distinctive today as it has ever been, despite population diversification and the influence of mass media. Dietary preferences have been modified, particularly in the large cities, but there is still a pronounced regional "flavor" to both choice of food and method of cooking; corn bread, hominy grits, hush puppies, pot likker, black-eyed peas, turnip greens, and other delicacies are distinctly Southern. Protestant religious fundamentalism continues to be strong despite weakening trends in the cities, and the term "Bible Belt" is still quite apt. And "Southern hospitality" is more than a cliché; there is a regional claim to personal warmth and friendliness that is readily discernible.

Race relations in the Inland South, as in most of the nation, are far from tranquil. The servile Negro of yesterday has become the proud black of today who demands equality and seeks redress. Racist feelings of the white majority have considerably softened, and overt discrimination has been eliminated or notably reduced. Public as well as most private facilities have been desegregated, and blacks are accorded the rights and responsibilities of full citizenship in most places and activities. Black legisla-

tors have been elected in Georgia, black mayors in Mississippi, and black sheriffs in Alabama. Perhaps more important, state and local administrations in such key states as North Carolina and such major cities as Atlanta, Birmingham, and Dallas have become more congizant of and more responsive to the needs of their black citizens. Still, there are many race-related difficulties and potential difficulties. Militants, both white and black, are stridently active, and the pathway toward tranquil equality is haunted by mistrust and misunderstanding.

The economy of the Inland South has undergone expansion, diversification, and substantial strengthening. Industrial growth has been notable and widespread. In every state of the region, value added by manufacturing far exceeds the value of agricultural production. As recently as 1947 Atlanta was the only city in the region that ranked among the 50 leading industrial centers of the nation, whereas by 1977 the region had Dallas, Atlanta, Greensboro–Winston-Salem, Charlotte, Greenville-Spartanburg, and Fort Worth among the top 40 industrial cities. The tertiary and quaternary components of the economy have also expanded and diversified, with greatly increased employment opportunities in trade, services, finance, construction, transportation, and government.[5]

It may be, however, that the changing character of the South is best exemplified by the agricultural scene. The cotton-and-corn, plantation-oriented duoculture (never merely a cotton monoculture) that characterized primary production in the region for several generations has given way to a diversification of significant proportions. This diversification is most conspicuously demonstrated by the dethroning of "King Cotton."

[5] For further elaboration of the changed character of the South, see Merle C. Prunty, "Two American Souths: The Past and the Future," *Southeastern Geographer,* 17 (May 1977), 1–24.

the rise and decline
of cotton
in the inland south

When the American Southeast was first settled by Europeans, the colonists felt that whites could do little sustained physical labor in its tropical summers. Accordingly Charleston and Savannah became great slave-importing cities. The first crops raised with the help of slave labor were rice, indigo, sugar cane, tobacco, and some cotton. In 1786, long-fibered Sea Island cotton was introduced and successfully grown along the coastal lowlands.

In 1793 Whitney's invention of the cotton gin revolutionized the cotton industry. Until then cotton had been one of the more expensive vegetable fibers because its separation from the seed was so difficult that large-scale operation was impossible. The textile industry in northwestern Europe began to demand increasing quantities of raw cotton. Southern planters—of the Carolinas and Georgia—having had little success with crops previously grown, then saw new opportunities in cotton. More acreage and more slaves were needed, and the plantation system began to expand rapidly in this region.

WESTWARD MOVEMENT
OF COTTON

Westward expansion of cotton growing was temporarily blocked by Indian tribes in western Georgia, Alabama, and eastern Mississippi. At the beginning of the nineteenth century the white settlements that composed the "cotton" South were confined to a relatively narrow strip along the Atlantic Coast and to the Southern Piedmont. Acquisition of Louisiana and the opening of the bottom lands along the Mississippi and its tributaries made large areas available for the establishment of the plantation system. The intervening areas were also thrown open to settlement. It was at this time that the Black Belt of Alabama and Mississippi became the heart of the Old South.

With the separation of Texas from Mexico, the establishment of the Republic, and its annexation to the United States in 1845, cotton migration continued westward until it reached the treeless prairies of central Texas, where it halted because of the pioneer's distrust of grasslands, the heavy soil that was difficult to till with the iron plow then in use, and the lack of protection from nomadic, warlike Indians. It was thus during the first half of the nineteenth century that cotton became "king" in the area between the Atlantic Ocean and the Texas prairies.

THE CIVIL WAR
AND ITS EFFECTS

By the time of the Civil War, many Southern planters realized that slavery was no longer economical. Had some practical method been suggested at that time to compensate the owners, in part, for their heavy investments in slaves, secession might have been averted; however, the strong agitation of the abolitionists of the North encouraged these planters to hold their slaves even at a financial loss. At that time most planters had many more slaves than were needed as laborers or as domestic servants.

In 1860 the United States shipped more than 4 million bales of cotton to Europe, as against 779,000 supplied by the rest of the world. By 1864, federal blockade of all Southern ports and decreased production owing to the war reduced exports to 241,000 bales (most of these smuggled out). Foreign regions supplied 2,300,000. So began foreign competition in the production of cotton. Immediately on the resumption of normal trade after the Civil War, however, the South again became the greatest cotton-producing area in the world.

Two other factors must be considered as consequences of the war: the freeing of slaves and the abandonment of many plantations in the southeast that, along with increasing population pressure, resulted in a second westward movement. Southern planters, as soon as they became reconciled to the fact that they no longer owned slaves, set about rebuilding their farm economy. If the planters' land had not become worn out by continuous cotton cultivation, they subdivided the plantation into small plots to be tilled by former slaves who had refused to leave when freed. This led to share-cropping, a Southern heritage that only recently disappeared. It was a natural outgrowth of the former plantation-slavery system, and throughout much of the Old South it was the only solution. Negro farmers had no experience in planning for themselves, neither did they have land nor the financial backing necessary for independent farming.

Many old plantations were so completely ruined and the planters' families so broken up that they could only move westward to make a new start. Some planters settled in unoccupied lands of east Texas; some moved to the Black Prairie, and with the help of ex-slaves again planted cotton; and still others went farther west where they engaged in the cattle business on the High Plains.

THE BOLL WEEVIL
AND ITS EFFECTS

Another westward shift in cotton production took place in the early twentieth century with the invasion of the boll weevil. Since the weevil thrives best under the more humid conditions of the eastern Cotton Belt, many areas were abandoned in favor of the dry lands to the west and northwest. The boll weevil, a native of the plateau of Mexico and Central America, first appeared in the United States in 1892 near Brownsville, Texas. By 1894 it had spread through southern Texas. By extending its range annually from 40 to 160 miles, it reached virtually every part of the Cotton Belt by 1921.

When the boll weevil first appeared it damaged as much as 50 percent of the crop, creating panic among cotton planters. Later this loss was reduced considerably by the use of insecticides and by burning or plowing under, in autumn, cotton stalks that otherwise would be used by the weevils as hibernation shelters.

The pink boll worm, also a native of Mexico, first appeared in Texas in 1920. Although its effect on the cotton industry was not so severe as that of the boll weevil, it has brought about the division of infested areas into districts with varying regulations for its control. Cotton seed is treated as it is ginned, and both the fiber and seed are shipped under regulations.

THE PEAK OF THE CROP

During the Civil War, Southern cotton growers were cut off from foreign markets. This situation greatly stimulated foreign production; nevertheless, as previously pointed out, the South resumed its lead after the war. There was an almost uninterrupted expansion of cotton acreage from post–Civil War days until the peak planting year of 1926. Accompanying this expansion were continuing increases in the supporting infrastructure: corn acreages for feeding mules, the major power source; cotton gins; small farm supply businesses; and the farm labor force.

By the late 1920s the United States accounted for 51 percent of world cotton acreage and 58 percent of total world production. United States cotton exports reached an all-time high of 11.3 million bales in 1926.

THE DECLINE
OF THE SOUTH'S SUPREMACY
IN COTTON PRODUCTION

The onset of the economic depression of the 1930s, along with the cumulative effect of soil erosion, insect pests, and plant diseases, caused a downturn in acreage and production at that time. Market prices were low, and in 1933 government controls limiting acreage planted and controlling prices were established. One important development in this period was the program of the Soil Conservation Service to institute better agricultural practices through incentive payments that subsidized farmers when they adopted recommended practices. The great demand for cotton, together with competition from foreign areas, forced farmers to improve

fig. 10-5 Harvested cotton being dumped from cotton-picker into hopper in which it will be transported to a gin. The scene is in northern Louisiana (courtesy USDA Soil Conservation Service).

methods of production (fig. 10-5). But these measures were not enough to maintain United States dominance, and today the South is only one among several leaders in cotton production. Furthermore, most of the principal cotton-producing areas are now on irrigated lands to the west of the old Cotton Belt. Output has declined in most parts of the old "Cotton Belt," and cotton is now virtually absent in two areas that were originally major producers—the "Sea Island" coastal country of Georgia and South Carolina, and the Southern Piedmont of Georgia and the Carolinas.[6]

UNCLE SAM AS FARMER

Low cotton prices in the early 1930s contributed materially to the passage of the Agricultural Adjustment Act of 1933, which brought the federal government into the

[6] See Merle C. Prunty and Charles S. Aiken, "The Demise of the Piedmont Cotton Region," *Annals,* Association of American Geographers, 62 (1972), 283–306.

business of partially managing the farm economy of the nation. Since then government's participation in agriculture in general, and cotton farming in particular, has become increasingly deep and complicated.

The government's role in cotton is very complex but essentially involves acreage controls on one hand and price supports on the other. Acreage restraints and diversion programs have been instrumental in reducing cotton acreage, although farm income has been more or less maintained by price support loans and direct payments to farmers. The program changes on a year-to-year basis, with the result that allotment-and-support manipulations have been a major cause of the remarkable fluctuations in cotton production in recent years.

As recently as 1965, national output amounted to 15 million bales, but as a result of government incentives to reduce production, cotton plantings were sharply reduced thereafter. Production was halved by 1967, which was the second-smallest output since 1896 and the fewest harvested acres since 1871. The program was then changed again, and an irregular upturn in production resulted. During the 1970s national production fluctuated between 8 and 13 million bales, but output was at its lowest persistent level since the first decade of this century. Plantings generally increase in response to a rise in worldwide cotton prices, but any change in Washington's cotton policy triggers a much more abrupt response, either upward or downward.

QUANTITY PRODUCTION

Of the five leading cotton-producing states, only Mississippi, Arkansas, and part of Texas are located in the Inland South (fig. 10–6). Texas, the leading cotton-growing state for many decades, has experienced significant internal production shifts but remains the principal producer by far. Although its average yield per acre is the lowest of any major state, in most years it accounts for nearly one-third of the national harvest. Mississippi is the third-ranking cotton producer (after California), yielding about 10 percent of the nation's output. Arizona ranks fourth, followed by the southeastern states of Arkansas, Louisiana, Alabama, Tennessee, and Georgia.

fig. 10–6 Distribution of cotton production in the United States. Although the middle Mississippi Valley is still outstanding, many of the other major producing areas are beyond the margins of the classical Cotton Belt.

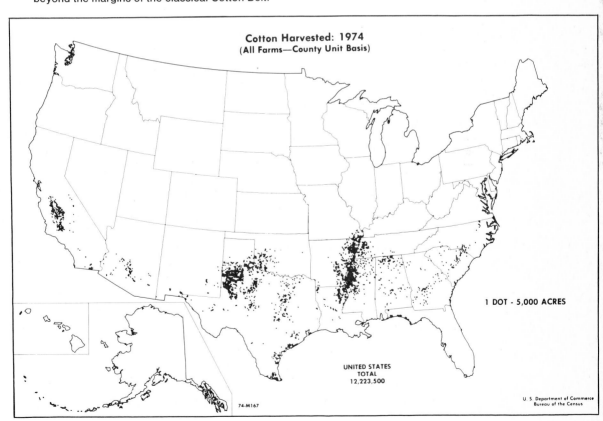

farming in the inland south: productive diversity

For several decades social scientists have made much of the "changing South," listing tendencies and prognosticating trends in economic and social matters that will make a "New South" out of the "Old South." Many of the predicted changes have long since materialized, and in no field have they been more striking than in agriculture.

Crop rotation, improved soil management and fertilization, supplemental irrigation, variation in field crops, and increased mechanization are all part of the scheme, but the most pronounced aspect is the shift toward mixed farming, with pastures for cattle as the dominant feature of the landscape. Cropped acreage, especially of cotton, has decreased, and many eroded fields have been restored to useful production by the planting of forage and pasture.

With the decline of cotton as undisputed king, many attendant evils have also diminished. Soil erosion and fertility loss have been decreased. The established and practical but often corrosive pattern of absentee ownership and farm tenancy has been broken—presumably forever (fig. 10–7).[7] The general dietary level in the region has been raised, and the feast-or-famine economy that was utterly dependent on world cotton prices is gone.

[7] Farm tenancy, under many circumstances, is no longer considered to be a bad thing. It allows a farmer to put his capital to work without having it tied up in land. See the relevant discussion in John Fraser Hart, *The Look of the Land* (Englewood Cliffs, N.J.: Prentice-Hall, Inc., 1975), 77–79.

fig. 10–7 Tenant farming is now much less notable in the Inland South than it used to be. The principal concentrations are in the middle portion of the Mississippi Valley and in the Carolina coastal plain.

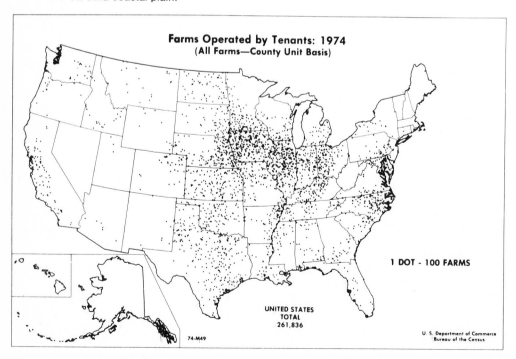

Farms Operated by Tenants: 1974
(All Farms—County Unit Basis)

1 DOT - 100 FARMS

UNITED STATES
TOTAL
261,836

U. S. Department of Commerce
Bureau of the Census

74-M49

The plantation, however, is not gone; it is merely concealed with modified characteristics, a disguised appearance, and perhaps, a pseudonym such as "ranch," "neoplantation," "fragmented neoplantation," or "industrialized crop farm."[8] Merle Prunty has pointed out that the plantation has experienced a significant renaissance, as shown by an increase in the number of

[8] Charles S. Aiken, "The Fragmented Neoplantation: A New Type of Farm Operation in the Southeast," *Southeastern Geographer,* 11 (April 1971), 43–51; Howard F. Gregor, "The Large Industrialized American Crop Farm," *Geographical Review,* 60 (April 1970), 151–75; Merle Prunty, Jr., "Deltapine: Field Laboratory for the Neoplantation Occupance Type," *Northwestern University Studies in Geography,* 6 (1962), 151–72.

farms that have much land, large fields, mechanization, and centralization of administrative and cultivating power.[9]

If Southern agriculture has diversified and cotton acreage has declined, what has replaced cotton and what are the elements of diversification? In terms of gross acreage, the answer is pasture and woodland. A great deal of former crop land, especially cotton land, has been returned to a grass or tree cover and is now used mainly for grazing cattle and, to a lesser extent, as a source of pulpwood (fig. 10–8). (It should be noted that an opposite trend is taking place in the

[9] Merle Prunty, Jr., "The Renaissance of the Southern Plantation," *Geographical Review,* 45 (October 1955), 459–91.

fig. 10–8 Decrease in cropland acreage, 1944–64. In most parts of the Inland South, except for the middle Mississippi Valley, there has been a notable decrease in cropland acreage, with the crops being replaced by pasture and forest.

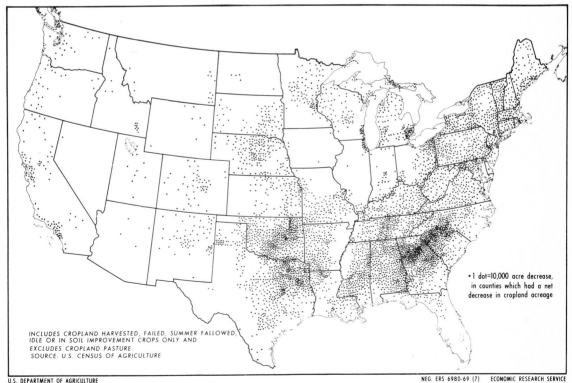

• 1 dot=10,000 acre decrease, in counties which had a net decrease in cropland acreage

INCLUDES CROPLAND HARVESTED, FAILED, SUMMER FALLOWED, IDLE OR IN SOIL IMPROVEMENT CROPS ONLY AND EXCLUDES CROPLAND PASTURE.
SOURCE: U.S. CENSUS OF AGRICULTURE

U.S. DEPARTMENT OF AGRICULTURE

NEG. ERS 6980-69 (7)   ECONOMIC RESEARCH SERVICE

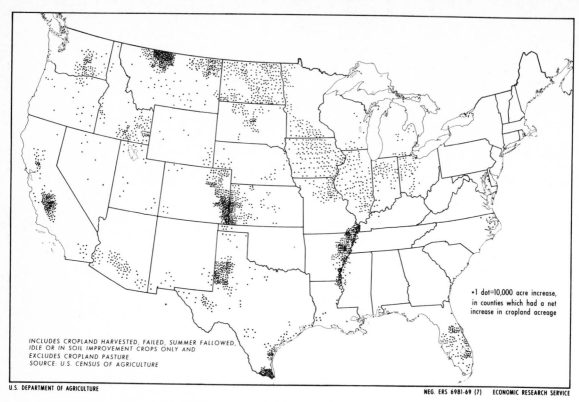

Within the map:

•1 dot=10,000 acre increase, in counties which had a net increase in cropland acreage

INCLUDES CROPLAND HARVESTED, FAILED, SUMMER FALLOWED, IDLE OR IN SOIL IMPROVEMENT CROPS ONLY AND EXCLUDES CROPLAND PASTURE
SOURCE: U.S. CENSUS OF AGRICULTURE

U.S. DEPARTMENT OF AGRICULTURE

NEG. ERS 6981-69 (7)   ECONOMIC RESEARCH SERVICE

fig. 10–9   Increase in cropland acreage, 1944–64. Since World War II there has been a significant increase in cropland acreage in the middle Mississippi Valley of the Inland South Region, as well as in several parts of the Great Plains.

Mississippi River lowland, from southern Missouri to northern Louisiana, where crop acreage expanded by nearly 40 percent between 1950 and 1970 mostly as a result of the clearing of forests [fig. 10–9].) The major component of agricultural diversification has been a shifting emphasis from crops to livestock, particularly beef and dairy cattle and, locally very important, poultry. The most notable cropping diversification has been the expanding cultivation of soybeans; in parts of the Mississippi Valley they are the dominant crop, and in the eastern part of the Inland South Region the acreage devoted to cotton, corn, and soybeans is approximately equal.

CORN

The principal system of farming in the region was long based on two crops, cotton and corn, and virtually every farmer grew both. Since 1938, however, total corn acreage has been decreasing. This decrease has been greatest in the western areas where corn has been largely replaced by grain sorghums and small grains. During the same period, the yield per acre has materially increased, and further increase on an even more reduced acreage seems to be the trend for the future. With corn, as with cotton and some other crops, definite rotation systems are not common. Fields that are well adapted may be planted more or less continuously to it, and high yields are obtained even over long periods if adequate fertilization and other good management practices are followed.

SOYBEANS

The soybean became significant in the Mississippi Valley during the early 1930s when its introduction was encouraged by the Soil Conservation Service as a legume soil-building crop. Yields per acre were low, and the soybean was not in any way considered a rival to cotton. Cotton farmers, attracted by the adaptability of soybeans to mechanized farming and by their value as a cash crop, began to increase acreage when faced with a shortage of labor during World War II. Continued research to improve the quality and productivity of the bean and to extend its utilization has resulted in such an increase in cultivation that the middle Mississippi Valley is now the second largest soybean-producing area in the United States (after the Corn Belt) and probably the most intensive in the world.[10] In more than 50 counties of the area soybeans occupy more than 60 percent of all harvested acreage, and the five states that share the valley (Missouri, Arkansas, Mississippi, Louisiana, and Tennessee) all rank among the ten leaders in national soybean output.

BEEF CATTLE

Since the early 1950s livestock has yielded more income than cotton, or any other crop, to farmers of the Inland South, with beef cattle in the forefront (fig. 10–10). In association with cattle raising, the acreage of grass and legume meadows for pasturage has been greatly increased; however, a considerable amount of grazing is carried on in

[10] L. Arnold Siniard, "Dominance of Soybean Cropping in the Lower Mississippi River Valley," *Southeastern Geographer*, 15 (May 1975), 27.

the fairly open forest that characterizes more than half of the region. It is estimated that five-sixths of the forested area is grazed.[11] The most widespread beef breed is the Hereford, but Angus, Brahma, and Santa Gertrudis are also popular.

Many of the cattle enterprises of the Inland South are operated more or less as an avocation by urban business executives who derive satisfaction and a tax shelter from a ranch of their own. The quality of their livestock is often high, and their willingness to experiment and innovate makes them a powerful force for upgrading the entire industry, even though their ranch may be more for outdoor recreation than for livestock operation.

POULTRY

In the past, poultry raising—particularly chickens—has been of importance for home consumption and local market only; today there are certain areas in the South where

[11] F. J. Marschner, *Land Use and Its Patterns in the United States,* Agriculture Handbook No. 153, U.S. Department of Agriculture (Washington, D.C.: Government Printing Office, 1959), p. 85.

fig. 10–10 Pastures and cattle are a dominant part of the farm scene in the Inland South today. These dairy cattle are grazing on fescue and clover in southern Alabama (courtesy USDA Soil Conservation Service).

fig. 10–11   A typical complex
of commercial broiler
houses, in the Piney
Woods of eastern Texas.

the raising of poultry for commercial consumption dominates farm activities. There is some emphasis on producing eggs, frying chickens, and turkeys, but the principal product is broilers, and these constitute more than two-thirds of all poultry consumed in the United States.

Much of this industry is handled under a contractual agreement whereby a feed merchant or meatpacker provides chicks, feed, vitamins, medicines, scientific counsel, and a market, and the farmer supplies only housing and labor (fig. 10–11). The contractee is benefited by needing little capital and having an assured market; the contractor, by having an assured supply of dependable quality; and the consuming public, by lower poultry prices. Skyrocketing poultry consumption has resulted, but an insecure national market, labor disputes at packing plants, and cutthroat competition have combined to inhibit stability in the industry. Nevertheless, five of the seven leading chicken-producing areas in the nation are in the Inland South: northern Georgia, northern Alabama, central Mississippi, eastern Texas, and central North Carolina.

Commercial egg production has also increased enormously in the region over the past decade, which is in contrast to the national trend whereby nearly two-thirds of the states have recorded absolute decreases in egg output. The Inland South now ranks second only to Megalopolis in the number of eggs sold annually.

TOBACCO

An outstanding specialty crop in the northeastern portion of the region is tobacco. More than half of the nation's output comes from eastern and central North Carolina, and adjacent parts of southern Virginia and northern South Carolina (fig. 10–12). Tobacco was introduced here in the early days of settlement by in-migrants from the tobacco section of eastern Maryland, but it did not become a popular crop until the time of the Civil War. Since then it has been the most important cash crop in the area and has attracted to the North Carolina Piedmont the greatest concentration of cigarette factories to be found anywhere in the world.

Of the seven classes of tobacco cultivated in the United States, this area concentrates almost totally on one that is synonymously called "flue-cured," "Virginia," and "bright." Most of the tobacco is grown on small to medium-sized farms, which are

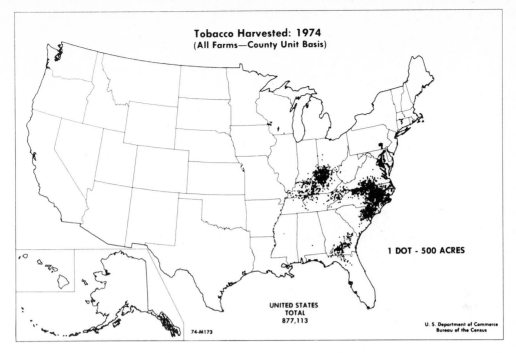

Tobacco Harvested: 1974
(All Farms—County Unit Basis)

1 DOT - 500 ACRES

UNITED STATES
TOTAL
877,113

74-M173

U. S. Department of Commerce
Bureau of the Census

fig. 10–12   The leading area of tobacco
growing in the United States is on the
Piedmont and Inner Coastal Plain of the
Carolinas and Virginia.

distinguished by the presence of small square barns in which the leaves are cured by flue-piped heat from a brick furnace outside the barn. Tobacco harvesting extends over a period of four to eight weeks during which the pickers comb the field about once a week, selecting ripe leaves from the bottom of the stalks. Although mechanization is being introduced into tobacco growing, a great deal of labor is still required on most farms, and therefore the tobacco district has the densest rural farm population in the country.[12] Many of the workers are blacks, and this is one of the very few parts of the rural South where out-migration of rural blacks has not been significant.

[12] John Fraser Hart, *The South,* 2nd ed. (New York: Van Nostrand Reinhold Co., 1976), p. 47.

OTHER CROPS

Other crops are grown significantly in the region. One-fourth of the national production of *rice* comes from eastern Arkansas and adjacent parts of Mississippi. One-half of the national output of *peanuts* is in southwestern Georgia and southeastern Alabama, and most of the rest is from northeastern North Carolina and southeastern Virginia and from scattered localities in central Texas and Oklahoma (fig. 10–13). More than half of national production of *sweet potatoes* and *watermelons* is widely scattered over the region. South Carolina and Georgia rank second and third among states producing *peaches.* Three-fourths of national output of *pecans* is from this region, especially from Georgia. *Truck crops* are also important.

225

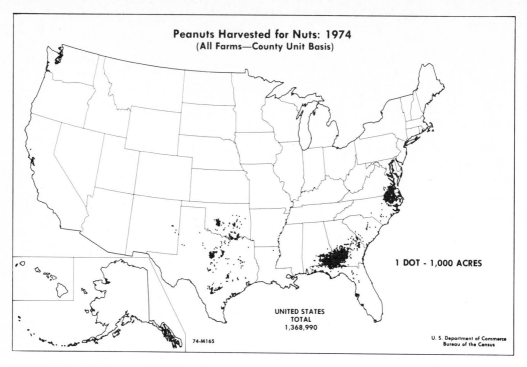

Peanuts Harvested for Nuts: 1974
(All Farms—County Unit Basis)

1 DOT - 1,000 ACRES

UNITED STATES
TOTAL
1,368,990

74-M165

U. S. Department of Commerce
Bureau of the Census

fig. 10–13 Peanuts are grown widely in the Inland
South Region, with the heaviest concentration
in southern Georgia and Alabama.

forest products

The Inland South Region lies in the southern part of the eastern forest, which once
was one of the greatest stretches of timber in
the world. Originally almost every portion
of the region was forested. Demand for cotton land coupled with reckless burning reduced the supply of standing timber long
before lumbering began on a commercial
basis. The early days of forest exploitation
were characterized, as in most parts of the
nation, by a thoughtless and wasteful "cut
out and get out" approach. But the long
growing season and heavy rainfall of the region make for rapid tree growth, and forest
industries have become well established in
every state. A forest planted with pine seedlings can be thinned for pulpwood after
only 12 to 15 years, and a mature crop of
sawtimber can be harvested within four
decades.

Roughly half of the present forest acreage is in small farm woodlots, which taken
as a whole are characterized by poor timber
management. Most of the remainder is
owned by large corporations (fig. 10–14).
Forest fires, most of which are caused by
people and many of which are deliberately
set, are more numerous here than elsewhere
in the country and are one of the most dis-
couraging aspects of timber management.

SOFTWOOD LUMBERING

The cutting of southern yellow pines for
lumber was the first forest industry to be
widespread in the region. Small operations,
feeding small sawmills, have been characteristic. Prior to the 1960s, there had been a
long-term decline in regional lumber output. The trend, however, was reversed in
that decade, and production has been stead-

fig. 10–14 Clearcutting has come to the Inland South, as shown by this "tree farm" in eastern Texas (courtesy Texas Forest Service).

ily increasing, owing partly to tree farming and partly to increased scale of operations and the establishment of larger sawmills. The region yields about one-fourth of the nation's softwood lumber and the same proportion of the nation's plywood.

HARDWOOD INDUSTRIES

Hardwood logging is much more localized. The greatest concentration is in the Mississippi River lowland, where cutting is a seasonal operation because of the boggy conditions brought about by winter rains. Hardwood output is also notable in the Carolina Piedmont, where it is carried on year-round. Southern hardwoods—oak, hickory, cypress, gums—are in great demand for furniture, veneers, and shingles, and are used increasingly in pulp and paper making.

PULP AND PAPER INDUSTRY

This branch of forest industries has become the leading source of income in the region, having grown very rapidly in the last few

decades. The region yields nearly half of the total pulpwood cut, with Georgia as the national leader. Throughout the Inland South, a conspicuous feature of the landscape is a clearing along a railway or highway that serves as a depot (called a *woodyard*) for stacking pulpwood cut in nearby areas (fig. 10–15). From the woodyard the pulpwood is shifted, usually by rail, to a pulp mill. Many of the mills—especially the larger ones—are located outside the Inland South in the

fig. 10–15 A typical pulp log woodyard in central Georgia.

fig. 10–16 An integrated wood products plant in southeastern Arkansas. Included in this complex are a sawmill, chemical plant, and paper mill (courtesy Georgia-Pacific Corporation, Crossett Division).

Southeastern Coast Region, often at a seaport (fig. 10–16).

minerals and mining

Geographic regional boundaries, which seldom are determined by mineral distribution, frequently cut across mineralized areas. Thus many minerals of the South, such as iron ore, phosphate, sulfur, salt, and coal, lie largely if not entirely outside the boundary of the Inland South Region and are therefore not considered in this chapter. In fact, the only ones of major importance in this region are those hydrocarbons—petroleum and natural gas—found largely in the trans-Mississippi portion. In addition, some bauxite, lignite, iron ore, and salt are mined. Apart from hydrocarbons, however, the region is poor in economic mineral resources.

PETROLEUM

The first commercial production in the Inland South began in the 1890s with the discovery of oil in a well being drilled for water near Corsicana, Texas. Texas production climbed from 50 barrels in 1895 to nearly 66,000 in 1897. In the following year it reached 546,000 barrels, and the great oil industry of the region was under way. Although numerous small fields were brought in during the next decade, no important development took place within the Inland South until 1911, when the Electra Field, near Wichita Falls, Texas, was discovered. Many large fields were then developed in rapid succession—including other famous producers such as Ranger, Burkburnett, Mexia, and Powell in Texas; numerous fields in southern Oklahoma; Smackover and El Dorado in Arkansas; and some important ones in Louisiana.

The major oil boom, however, dates from 1930 when the East Texas field, the most prolific in Anglo-American history, was brought in. At maximum extent the field was 42 miles wide and 9 miles long. Within an area of about 300 square miles were more than 27,000 producing wells. This field has yielded more than 5 percent of all oil ever produced in the United States, nearly three times as much as any other field.

The five western states of the Inland South are all among the national leaders in petroleum production: Texas, first; Louisiana, second; Oklahoma, fourth; Mississippi, ninth; and Arkansas, fifteenth (see also table 10–1). Other than the East Texas Field, there are three principal areas of production: north-central Texas and south-central Oklahoma, centering on Wichita Falls and Ardmore; the northwestern corner of Louisiana and the southwestern corner of Arkansas, with adjacent portions of northeastern Texas, centering on Shreveport and El Dorado; and northeastern Louisiana and adjacent portions of Mississippi.

The domestic petroleum industry faced major economic problems throughout the 1960s, but the energy crisis of the 1970s provided a strong upward impetus. Higher oil prices spurred a significant increase in production and a spectacular boom in exploration. Production soon began to decline again, however, and it is probable that no major new fields will be discovered. There are also increasingly efficient efforts to recover additional oil from existing fields. In some cases secondary recovery (injecting gas or water into oil formations to maintain field pressures that allow more oil to be pumped) has significantly extended the life and total output of a field, and sophisticated tertiary recovery techniques (treating oil horizons with chemicals or heat to loosen the crude and push it to producing wells) offer promise for further gains.

NATURAL GAS

Production and consumption of natural gas have increased dramatically in Anglo-

table 10–1 Production of Leading United States Oil Fields

rank	field	state	production since discovery (thousand barrels)	rank based on production in 1974
1	East Texas	Tex.	4,241,715	3
2	Wilmington	Calif.	1,681,810	4
3	Panhandle	Tex.	1,283,585	41
4	Midway-Sunset	Calif.	1,192,592	8
5	Sho-Vel-Tum	Okla.	1,002,456	9
6	Huntington Beach	Calif.	923,820	23
7	Long Beach	Calif.	884,872	–
8	Ventura	Calif.	793,393	46
9	Oklahoma City	Okla.	756,241	–
10	Wasson	Tex.	703,095	1

Data Source: Bureau of Mines, Department of the Interior, Minerals Yearbook, 1974, vol. 1 (Washington, D.C.: Government Printing Office, 1975), p. 984.

America over the last three decades. Proved reserves are now at critically low levels, however, and production trends continue downward despite accelerated exploration. Texas and Louisiana are by far the leading producers of natural gas, although most of their production is outside the Inland South Region. In recent years, natural gas production from these two states has amounted to about three-fourths of total national output.

BAUXITE

Although seven-eighths of the bauxite ores used in the United States are imported (largely from the Caribbean area), domestic production is also important. All domestic supplies now being worked lie within the boundaries of the Inland South Region. About 85 percent of the output comes from several mines, both underground and strip, in Saline County of central Arkansas. Three counties in Alabama and Georgia supply the remainder.

urban-industrial dynamism

An important part of the new look of the Old South is furnished by the dynamic urban and industrial growth of the region (see table 10–2 for the region's largest urban places). From an area of sparse and specialized manufacturing in small cities, it has developed into a region of notable industrial diversity and strength in booming metropolises. For example, Dallas, Atlanta, and Fort Worth, the three largest urbanized areas in the region, increased in population by more than 35 percent and in value of industrial output by more than 100 percent during the decade of the 1960s.

PRIMACY OF THE GATEWAY CITIES

At the top of the urban hierarchy of the Inland South are two dominant metropolises that epitomize the concept of the gateway city. *Atlanta* (fig. 10–17) in the east and *Dallas* in the west serve as regional capitals in terms of commerce, finance, transportation, and other economic aspects. These two cities are the principal funnels and nerve centers through which extraregional goods, services, ideas, and people are channeled into the Inland South, and to a lesser extent, they accommodate the reverse flow of regional output to the nation. This gateway function

---

table 10–2   Largest Urban Places of the Inland South Region

name	population of principal city	population of metropolitan area	name	population of principal city	population of metropolitan area
Albany, Ga.	73,373	100,300	Greenville, S.C.	58,518	526,300
Alexandria, La.	49,481	135,800	High Point, N.C.	61,330	
Anniston, Ala.	30,622	106,400	Irving, Tex.*	103,703	
Arlington, Tex.	110,543		Jackson, Miss.	166,512	288,400
Athens, Ga.	49,457		Jackson, Tenn.	43,357	
Atlanta, Ga.	436,057	1,806,100	Killeen, Tex.	49,307	210,500
Augusta, Ga.	54,019	276,400	Little Rock, Ark.	141,143	367,300
Austin, Tex.	301,147	394,800	Longview, Tex.	52,034	125,300
Birmingham, Ala.	276,273	793,000	Macon, Ga.	121,157	235,900
Bossier City, La.*	46,565		Memphis, Tenn.	661,319	873,300
Bryan, Tex.	37,160	72,300	Meridian, Miss.	46,256	
Burlington, N.C.	37,586	99,400	Mesquite, Tex.*	61,933	
Charlotte, N.C.	281,417	594,500	Monroe, La.	61,016	125,600
Columbia, S.C.	111,616	370,700	Montgomery, Ala.	153,343	249,600
Columbus, Ga.	160,200	222,900	N. Little Rock, Ark.*	61,768	
Dallas, Tex.	812,797	2,552,800	Pine Bluff, Ark.	54,631	83,700
Danville, Va.	45,563		Raleigh, N.C.	134,231	473,200
Durham, N.C.	101,224		Richardson, Tex.*	59,190	
Fayetteville, N.C.	65,915	232,900	Sherman, Tex.	26,049	79,000
Florence, Ala.	34,402	123,600	Shreveport, La.	185,711	345,000
Fort Worth, Tex.	358,364		Spartanburg, S.C.	46,929	
Gadsden, Ala.	50,357	95,400	Texarkana, Tex.	21,249	45,000
Garland, Tex.*	111,322		Tuscaloosa, Ala.	69,425	123,900
Gastonia, N.C.	49,343		Tyler, Tex.	61,434	107,400
Grand Prairie, Tex.*	56,842		Waco, Tex.	97,607	156,700
Greensboro, N.C.	155,848	765,000	Wichita Falls, Tex.	95,008	130,700
Greenville, Miss.	42,449		Winston-Salem, N.C.	141,018	

* A suburb of a larger city.

fig. 10–17 Atlanta is the booming gateway city of the Southeast.

is best shown by the magnitude of wholesale sales, the concentration of financial institutions—especially banks and insurance companies—the large number of national and regional corporate headquarters, and the daily passenger flow through the respective airports.

Although approximately the same in size and function, the two cities have quite different origins and histories. Their spectacular industrial growth since 1940 overshadows the fact that neither is among the top 25 manufacturing cities of the nation. In both cities the bulwark of industrial expansion has been in the related fields of aircraft-missiles-electronics, although both have significant apparel and food-processing industries. Their functions, however, are much more significantly commercial than industrial, and the impressive skyline of Dallas and the progressive atmosphere of Atlanta suggest the improving economic and cultural image of the region.

SECONDARY REGIONAL CENTERS

One step lower in the regional hierarchy are the medium-sized cities of Memphis, Fort Worth, and Birmingham, each of which is also growing rapidly. *Memphis* is the traditional river city of the middle Mississippi basin, dominating the area between the spheres of New Orleans and St. Louis.

Fort Worth, although near enough to have a twin-city relationship with Dallas, is remarkably different from its neighbor.

Whereas Dallas's eastward orientation has been specialized toward commerce, finance, and oil, Fort Worth is clearly oriented to the west, with emphasis on cattle, railways, and industry.

The story of *Birmingham* is unusual; it has long been the only heavy-industry center in the South. Local deposits of iron ore and coal made it the least expensive place in the nation to manufacture steel. Distance from major markets inhibited its growth and the nearby ore deposits have been depleted, but Birmingham has developed a variety of manufactures and is also an important commercial center.

THE CAROLINA URBAN-INDUSTRIAL COMPLEX

Although lacking a major metropolis, there is a zone of notable urban and industrial development centered on the Piedmont of North Carolina (fig. 10–18). This zone extends northward into southern Virginia, southwestward across South Carolina into northern Georgia, and eastward onto the North Carolina coastal plain. The heart of the district is the North Carolina Piedmont, with its medium-sized cities of *Charlotte, Winston-Salem,* and *Greensboro.* This is a highly industrialized district; many of the factories are located in smaller towns, such as Reidsville and Shelby, and in nonurban areas, especially in Gaston and Cabarrus counties. New industries have tended to locate in rural areas or in small towns rather

231

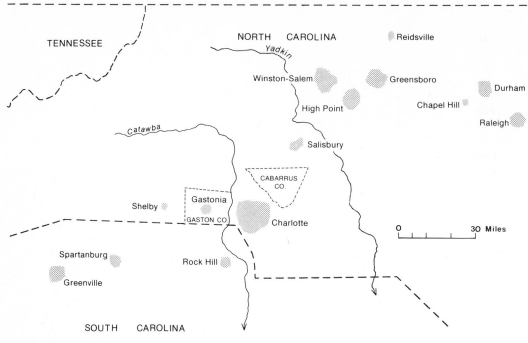

fig. 10–18   The urban-industrial complex of the Carolinas.

than in the cities, partly because of a tight labor market.[13] Manufacturing is not diversified in the district, being mainly tobacco, textiles, chemicals, and furniture. The area contains the greatest concentrations of cigarette, cotton-textile, and furniture factories to be found in the nation.

The importance of manufacturing to the local economy is shown by the fact that only Connecticut and New Hampshire, among the 50 states, have as great a proportion of their labor force employed in factories as South and North Carolina. This Piedmont industrial district contains approximately 50 percent as many manufactural facilities and employees as the six New England States—about 4 percent of the national total. Other facets of urbanism are also notable in the district. For example, in the area between *Raleigh, Durham,* and *Chapel Hill* is the "Research Triangle," probably the most successful corporate research center in the nation. It is related to the three major universities of the area but oriented toward industrial and environmental research.

[13] Richard E. Lonsdale and Clyde E. Browning, "Rural-Urban Locational Preferences of Southern Manufacturers," *Annals,* Association of American Geographers, 61 (June 1971), 255–68; Ray M. Northam, "Recent Industrialization in the Appalachian Piedmont: The Case of Northeastern Georgia," *Northwestern University Studies in Geography,* 6 (1962), 93–112.

the outlook

The Inland South is a region with a distinctive cultural heritage, but the only really unifying physical phenomena are climate and forest. It is a region that has traditionally produced a few staple commercial crops but where an agricultural revolution has taken place. It is a region that has been traditionally rural and agrarian but is rapidly becoming urban and industrial.

Cattle raising will continue to replace cotton farming as the chief agricultural activity in many areas. Since improved permanent pasture is the key to a livestock system in such a climate, there will be a continual expansion of grass and legume meadows—in some cases at the expense of good timberland. Cattle feeding will also become more important.

Dairying will slowly increase, as will the acreage devoted to peanuts and soybeans. The raising of specialty products, such as poultry, tree crops, and vegetables, will probably intensify. Supplemental irrigation will become commonplace to carry crops vigorously through short dry spells and to increase overall yields. Contract-farming agreements will become more numerous. The permanent farm population will continue to decline, but migratory workers will probably increase in numbers. Only in the Mississippi River lowland is there likely to be any significant increase in cropland acreage.

The continued decrease of rural population, both white and black, will likely be a blessing rather than a curse to the region. The displaced marginal agriculturalists will probably find more satisfactory urban employment—both within and without the Inland South; and either machinery or migrant workers will take up the labor slack on the fewer but larger remaining farms.

Production from timberlands will become increasingly important for both lumber and pulp. The trend toward clearcutting will probably spread throughout most of the larger pine holdings, although its efficiency as a management technique will at least be partly counterbalanced by environmental and aesthetic objections. This issue promises to become one of sharp controversy in the region.

The economic outlook in nonagricultural fields is generally promising, although less so in some areas than in others. The attraction of the Inland South to manufacturing industries is solidly based on inexpensive labor, expanding markets, certain types of raw materials in abundance, low power and fuel costs, and miscellaneous financial considerations, such as reduced taxes or direct subsidies by local governments. Although manufacturing in the Inland South is unlikely to rival that in the Southeastern Coast Region in growth, it will undoubtedly play an increasingly important role.

Urban growth and associated commercial expansion seem assured. Some of the nation's fastest-growing medium-sized cities are in this region, and the two gateway metropolises continue as leaders of expansion. At the other end of the urban spectrum, however, many smaller towns seem destined to wither.

The population mix will probably become more diverse with continued influx of people from other regions. Black migration trends will be watched with special interest to see if net in-migration becomes the norm. The concentration of blacks in the larger cities, particularly the inner-city districts of Atlanta, Birmingham, and Memphis, will provide increased political power to black voters.

All things considered, the passage of time will continue to blur the image of the Inland South as a distinctive region, even as the region's economic and social role in the nation becomes more significant.

selected bibliography

ADKINS, HOWARD G., "The Imported Fire Ant in the Southern United States," *Annals*, Association of American Geographers, 60 (1970), 578–92.

AIKEN, CHARLES S., "The Fragmented Neoplantation: A New Type of Farm Operation in the Southeast," *Southeastern Geographer*, 11 (1971), 43–51.

ARBINGAST, STANLEY, ET AL., *Atlas of Texas* (3rd ed.). Austin: University of Texas Press, 1973.

BEDERMAN, SANFORD H., "Recent Changes in Agrarian Land Use in Georgia," *Southeastern Geographer*, 10 (November 1970), 72–82.

BEDFORD, JOHN L., "Rainfall Regimes and the Surface Energy Balance in the Southeastern United States," *Southeastern Geographer*, 16 (November 1976), 98–112.

BOUNDS, JOHN H., "The Alabama-Coushatta Indians of Texas," *Journal of Geography*, 70 (1971), 175–82.

CLAY, JAMES W., AND DOUGLAS M. ORR, JR., eds., *Metrolina Atlas*. Chapel Hill: University of North Carolina Press, 1972.

CLAY, JAMES W., DOUGLAS M. ORR, JR., AND ALFRED W. STUART, eds., *North Carolina Atlas: Portrait of a Changing Southern State*. Chapel Hill: University of North Carolina Press, 1976.

CONWAY, DENNIS, ET AL., "The Dallas-Fort Worth Region," in *Contemporary Metropolitan America, Vol. 4, Twentieth Century Cities,* ed. John S. Adams, pp. 1–37. Cambridge, Mass.: Ballinger Publishing Company, 1976.

CROSS, R. D., ET AL., *Atlas of Mississippi*. Jackson: University of Mississippi Press, 1974.

DAVIS, SID, AND TRUMAN HARTSHORN, "The Changing Pattern of Activity Location in the Atlanta Metropolitan Area," *Atlanta Economic Review*, 13 (July–August 1973), 4–13.

FOSCUE, EDWIN J., "East Texas: A Timbered Empire," *Journal of the Graduate Research Center,* Southern Methodist University, 28 (1960), 1–60.

FUSSELL, MICHARD, *A Demographic Atlas of Birmingham*. Tuscaloosa: University of Alabama Press, 1975.

HANSEN, N. M., *Location Preferences, Migration and Regional Growth: A Study of the South and Southwest United States*. New York: Praeger Publications, 1973.

HART, JOHN FRASER, "The Demise of King Cotton," *Annals,* Association of American Geographers, 67 (1977), 307–22.

HARTSHORN, TRUMAN A., ET AL., "Metropolis in Georgia: Atlanta's Rise as a Major Transaction Center," in *Contemporary Metropolitan America, Vol. 4, Twentieth Century Cities,* ed. John S. Adams, pp. 151–225. Cambridge, Mass.: Ballinger Publishing Company, 1976.

HAYES, CHARLES R., AND NORMAN W. SCHUL, "Why Do Manufacturers Locate in the Southern Piedmont?" *Land Economics*, 44 (1968), 117–21.

HAYNES, KINGSLEY E., AND G. KELL, "The Changing Role of the CBD, Dallas, Texas," *Ecumene*, 7 (February 1975), 42–45.

JORDAN, TERRY G., "Antecedents of the Long-Lot in Texas," *Annals,* Association of American Geographers, 64 (1974), 70–86.

———, "Early Northeast Texas and the Evolution of Western Ranching," *Annals,* Association of American Geographers, 67 (1977), 66–87.

———, *German Seed in Texas Soil: Immigrant Farmers in Nineteenth Century Texas*. Austin: University of Texas Press, 1967.

LAMB, ROBERT BYRON, *The Mule in Southern Agriculture*. Berkeley: University of California Press, 1963.

LINEBACK, NEAL G., ed., *Atlas of Alabama*. Tuscaloosa: University of Alabama Press, 1973.

———, ed., "Manufacturing in the South" *Southeastern Geographer*, 14 (November 1974), entire issue.

LONSDALE, RICHARD E., AND CLYDE E. BROWNING, "Rural-Urban Locational Preferences of Southern Manufacturers," *Annals,* Association of American Geographers, 61 (1971), 225–68.

LORD, J. DENNIS, "The Growth and Localization of the United States Broiler Chicken Industry," *Southeastern Geographer*, 11 (1971), 29–42.

———, "School Busing and White Abandonment of Public Schools," *Southeastern Geographer*, 15 (November 1975), 81–92.

LOWRY, MARK, "The Mississippi Chinese," *Geographical Review*, 63 (1973), 560–61.

MANOGARAN, CHELVADURAI, "Climatic Limitations for Tree Growth Potential in Southern Forests," *Southeastern Geographer*, 13 (November 1973), 71–81.

MEINIG, DONALD W., *Imperial Texas: An Interpretive Essay in Cultural Geography*. Austin: University of Texas Press, 1969.

MELAMID, ALEXANDER, "The Texas-Louisiana Boundary Dispute," *Geographical Review*, 65 (1975), 268–70.

MURRAY, MALCOLM A., ed., *Atlas of Atlanta: The 1970's*. Tuscaloosa: University of Alabama Press, 1974.

PANNELL, CLIFTON W., "Recent Metropolitan Growth in the Southern United States,"

Southeastern Geographer, 14 (May 1974), 7–16.

PRUNTY, MERLE C., "Some Contemporary Myths and Challenges in Southern Rural Land Utilization," *Southeastern Geographer,* 10 (1970), 1–12.

————, "Two American Souths: The Past and the Future," *Southeastern Geographer,* 17 (May 1977), 1–24.

PRUNTY, MERLE C., AND CHARLES S. AIKEN, "The Demise of the Piedmont Cotton Region," *Annals,* Association of American Geographers, 62 (1972), 283–306.

SCHRIVER, WILLIAM R., "The Industrialization of the Southeast Since 1950," *American Journal of Economics and Sociology,* 30 (1971), 47–69.

SINIARD, L. ARNOLD, "Dominance of Soybean Cropping in the Lower Mississippi River Valley," *Southeastern Geographer,* 15 (May 1975), 17–32.

THOMAS, BILL, "Congaree: Last of the Bottomland Forests," *The Living Wilderness,* 40 (July–September 1976), 16–21.

TRIMBLE, STANLEY W., *Man-Induced Soil Erosion on the Southern Piedmont, 1700–1970.* Ankeny, Iowa: Soil Conservation Society of America, 1974.

WHEELER, JAMES O., "Studies of Manufacturing Location in the Southern United States," *Geographical Review,* 65 (1975), 270–72.

WINBERRY, JOHN J., AND DAVID M. JONES, "Rise and Decline of the 'Miracle Vine': Kudzu in the Southern Landscape," *Southeastern Geographer,* 13 (November 1973), 61–70.

11

THE
SOUTHEASTERN
COAST

The Southeastern Coast Region is attenuated along the "subtropical" shores of the eastern United States. It is long and narrow in shape (fig. 11–1), dynamic in recent development, and a curious mixture of the primitive and modern. It is a region that contains some of the most undisturbed natural areas as well as some of the most

fig. 11–1   The Southeastern Coast Region (base map copyright A. K. Lobeck; reprinted by permission of Hammond, Inc.).

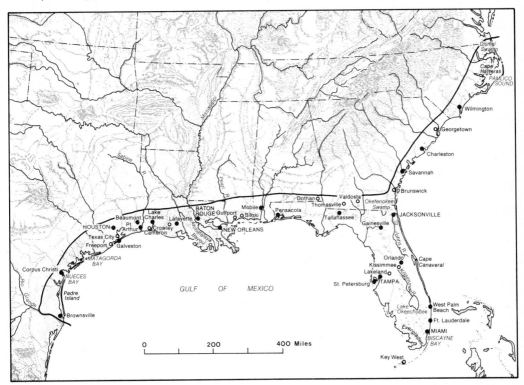

thoroughly built-up areas to be found anywhere on the continent. Burgeoning cities and expanding factories nestle side-by-side with quiet backwaters where fin and feather and fur dominate life, a juxtaposition restricted to places where a low-lying coastal environment permits an infinite variety of land-and-water relationships. Sophisticated urbanites live close to backwoods trappers, and some of the nation's most scientific and mechanized agriculture is carried on only a stone's throw from areas of hardscrabble subsistence farms.

The region extends from the Dismal Swamp of southeasternmost Virginia along the littoral zone of the Atlantic Ocean and Gulf of Mexico to the international border at the Rio Grande; thus it abuts the Inland South Region along most of its interior margin, brushing the Great Plains Region in southern Texas and touching the Megalopolis Region in southern Virginia.

The inland margin of the Southeastern Coast Region is not clearly defined. Physically it is marked by a transition zone that separates the poorly drained coastal lands from the better-drained country interiorward. Culturally it can be considered to be inland of the seacoast cities and their immediate city-serving farmlands. As thus defined, this region encompasses a relatively narrow coastal strip of Virginia, the Carolinas, Georgia, Alabama, Mississippi, and Texas; it also includes about half of Louisiana and all of Florida.

the physical setting

RELIEF OF THE LAND

Although almost uniformly characterized by flatness and impeded drainage, the regional topography is remarkably varied in detail and primarily reflects variations in geomorphic history. Except in much of Florida, where Tertiary formations predominate, almost the entire region is underlain by relatively unconsolidated Quaternary sediments of marine origin. These beds extend seaward to constitute also the continental shelf. The shelf offshore of this region is quite broad—generally more than 75 miles in width—everywhere except off the southeastern corner of Florida and near the delta of the Mississippi River. Along almost all of the coast the ocean is very shallow for a considerable distance offshore; in many localities a swimmer must wade out tens or even hundreds of yards to find water deep enough to swim in.

Low-lying, sandy islands occur off the coast of most of the region except parts of Louisiana and the Gulf side of peninsular Florida. The almost continuous chains of islands off the North Carolina and Texas coasts represent barrier sandbars at an extreme stage of lengthwise development; they are long, narrow, and low, and they encompass lagoons and sounds that are in the process of being filled in as the coastline progrades outward. Other offshore islands (along the Georgia and Mississippi coasts, for example) are more varied in origin, ranging from erosional remnants to old beach ridges, with gradations in between. The Florida Keys are totally different in formation. The eastern keys are mostly uplifted coral reefs, whereas the western keys represent limestone shoals upraised from an earlier sea bottom.

With the important exceptions of peninsular Florida and southeastern Louisiana, the topography of the mainland is generally uniform throughout the region. The land is exceedingly flat, sloping gently toward the sea. A great many rivers meander across this lowland. The lower reaches of most of the streams have been drowned by coastal subsidence; thus, the coastline is studded with estuaries and bays in addition to the lagoons and sounds previously mentioned. Inadequate drainage is, therefore, common, and there are extensive stretches of swampland as well as some large marshes. The two largest and most famous of these poorly drained lands are Okefenokee Swamp in Georgia-Florida (fig. 11–2) and Dismal Swamp on the Virginia–North Carolina border.

The topography of peninsular Florida is distinctive from that of the rest of the region. The peninsula is a recently emerged mass of carbonate rocks, largely limestone, characterized by karst features in the north and immense areas of inadequate drainage in the south. The caves and sinks of typical karst regions are modified in Florida by the uniformly high water table; most of the caverns are water-filled and most of the sinks have become small lakes. There are so many sinkhole lakes in central Florida that this area is referred to as the "lakes district."

Associated with the karst is the most extensive artesian system in Anglo-America. Some components of the system are deep and discharge on the sea bottom many miles offshore. Shallower components often discharge as artesian springs. Florida has the greatest concentration of these in the country, and many of them serve as the source of short rivers. Silver Springs is the largest known of the artesian outflows, with an average daily discharge of nearly half a billion gallons of water.[1]

The exceedingly flat terrain of southern Florida has a natural drainage system that is both complex and delicate. Lake Okeechobee, with a surface area of about 750 square miles and a maximum depth of less than 20 feet, is fed in part by overflow from the Kissimmee Lakes to the north. Lake Okeechobee, in turn, overflows broadly southward with a 50-mile-wide channel that maintains the natural water supply of the Everglades and Big Cypress Swamp. Human interference with this drainage system has caused major problems, as we shall see subsequently.

The area around the mouth of the Mississippi, the continent's mightiest river, is generally flat and ill-drained, and its detailed pattern of landforms is notably complex. Essentially all southeastern Louisiana within the Southeastern Coast Region is a part of the Mississippi River deltaic plain. During the past twenty centuries the lower course of the river has shifted several times, producing at least four different subdeltas that are the principal elements of the pres-

fig. 11-2 Moss-draped cypress and pines tower over Okefenokee Swamp on the Georgia-Florida boundary (courtesy Georgia Department of Industry and Trade).

ent complicated "bird's foot" delta of the river. The main flow of the river during the past 400 years or so has been along its present course extending southeast from New Orleans. This portion of the delta has been built out into the Gulf at a rate of more than 6 miles per century in that period (fig. 11-3).

The Atchafalaya distributary is the principal secondary channel of the river. If unhindered by people, it is estimated that in only a few years the main flow of the Mississippi would shift to the shorter and slightly steeper channel of the Atchafalaya.[2] The terrain of the Mississippi deltaic plain consists of many bayous and swamps, with

[1] William D. Thornbury, *Regional Geomorphology of the United States* (New York: John Wiley & Sons, Inc., 1965), p. 47.

[2] H. N. Fisk, *Geological Investigation of the Atchafalaya Basin and the Problem of Mississippi River Diversion* (Vicksburg: Mississippi River Commission, 1952).

fig. 11–3 The lower end of the Mississippi Delta, where the separation of river, land, and sea is virtually indistinct (courtesy U.S. Army Corps of Engineers, New Orleans District).

marshes occupying all the immediate coastal zone. In addition to the natural bayous, the coastal marshlands are criss-crossed by a maze of artificial waterways, mostly shallow, narrow ditches (called *trainasse*) that were crudely excavated by local people to provide small boat access. Many of these simple canals are now established elements of the drainage systems. The only slightly elevated land is along natural levees, which parallel the natural drainage channels, and on low sandy ridges (*cheniers*) that roughly parallel the coast of southwestern Louisiana.

CLIMATE

This region is typical of the warmer, more humid phase of the humid subtropical climate. It is characterized by a heavy rainfall and a long growing season (from 240 days in the north to the almost frostless areas of southern Florida). The total annual precipitation decreases from more than 60 inches in southern Florida and along the east Gulf Coast to less than 30 inches in the southwest. Over most of the region the rainfall is evenly distributed throughout the year, but the maximum comes during the summer and early autumn, which are thunderstorm and hurricane seasons. The torrential rains (most stations in this region have experienced more than 10 inches of rain in a 24-hour period) coupled with high-velocity winds have caused considerable damage to crops and wrought great destruction to many coastal communities at some time or other.

From the psychological standpoint, mild, sunny winters largely offset the hurricane menace and thus enable this region to capitalize on climate in its agriculture and resort business. But severe, killing frosts affect part of the region almost every year.

SOILS

The region has a considerable variety of soil types but most are characterized by an excess of moisture, quartz particles, or clay. Most widespread are hydromorphic (poorly drained) varieties, but sandy soils are also common. From a taxonomic standpoint, the soils of the Southeastern Coast Region are the most complex of the continent. All of the soil orders except Aridisols are extensively represented, often in a complicated patchwork pattern.

NATURAL VEGETATION

Because of heavier rainfall, the eastern part of the region is largely covered with forests, mainly yellow pines and oaks on the better-drained, sandy lands, with cypress and other hardwoods dominating the swamps and other poorly drained areas. Hardwoods were probably more widespread long ago, before the Indians began burning the woodlands in winter to aid their hunting. Periodic burning favored the pines and oaks, since they are more resistant to fire than other trees and shrubs. Until fairly recently burning was commonplace in the region, generally done on a casual and indiscriminate basis in order to "improve" grazing for scrub cattle. A common feature of the region is the so-called Spanish moss, which festoons live oaks and cypress but is much less abundant on pines except in swampy areas.

Some extensive grasslands, usually marshy, are found along the coast. Dotted irregularly through these marshlands are bits of elevated ground, usually called *islands* or, in Louisiana, *cheniers*, which are generally covered with big trees laden with moss. From southwestern Louisiana westward, most of the natural vegetative cover is coastal prairie grassland; this is partially replaced by scrubby brush country south of Corpus Christi.

Most of Florida south of Lake Okeechobee is part of the Everglades (literally "sea of grass") where tall saw grass dominates the landscape. Patches of woodland, slightly elevated above the surrounding Everglades marsh, are called *hammocks* (fig. 11-4); these are the favorite haunts of Florida's most vicious wildlife, mosquitos. The littoral zone of the coastal Everglades has Anglo-America's only extensive growth of tangled mangroves.

WILDLIFE

The Southeastern Coast Region contains the only part of the conterminous states that is a major wintering ground for migratory

fig. 11-4   A hammock in the Everglades. The tall sawgrass is interrupted by a slightly elevated patch of ground on which many species of trees are crowded together.

birds, particularly waterfowl. From Florida to Texas, the coastal marshes and swamps provide a last stronghold for the wintering (for example, whooping cranes) or breeding (various egrets and spoonbills) of numerous rare and endangered birds, as well as seasonal or permanent homes for many other avian species.

The region's poorly drained wild areas also provide an important habitat for a number of native quadruped species. Mustelids, such as mink, otter, and skunk, are prominent, but muskrats and raccoons are the most numerous of the region's fur-bearers. Here, too, is the last stronghold for the cougar in the eastern United States.

The American alligator, Anglo-America's only large reptile, is found exclusively in the Southeastern Coast Region. Heavily persecuted in the past, it responded to stringent protection in the 1960s, and by the late 1970s the alligator was once more abundant in Louisiana and Florida and was increasing in suitable areas from the Big Thicket of Texas to the Dismal Swamp of Virginia.

The vast expanses of marshes and other types of wilderness and the relatively mild winters in this region make the Southeastern

241

Coast an attractive habitat for a host of exotic animals that have been introduced either deliberately or inadvertently. It is in Florida, where the natural ecosystems have been most disturbed and where the winter weather is most permissive, that the greatest variety of alien species has become established. Siamese walking catfish, Mexican armadillos, African cattle egrets, Indian rhesus monkeys, South American giant toads, and Australian parakeets represent only a sampling of the international Noah's ark that Florida is becoming.

The exotic species that has become most conspicuous in the regional biota, however, is the South American nutria (*Myocastor coypu*). It was deliberately brought to Louisiana in the 1930s as a dual-purpose introduction: to provide another source of furs for trappers of the area and to help in controlling the rapid expansion of water hyacinth (another exotic from South America) in the state's bayous and lakes. The nutria is larger than the muskrat and its fur is richer, more akin to beaver fur; hence nutria pelts are considerably more valuable than muskrat. The first nutria brought to the United States were kept on fur farms, and today there are several hundred operating nutria farms in Louisiana. In the 1940s, however, nutria were released or escaped from farms and are now very numerous in Louisiana and adjacent parts of Texas and Mississippi. The animal has now become well established, is a major quarry for trappers, and has found many things that it prefers to eat other than water hyacinths.

primary industries

In a region that is close to nature a variety of primary economic activities is likely to be carried on, provided basic resources are present. The Southeastern Coast is such a region, and primary production significantly contributes to both the regional economy and the regional image.

TRAPPING

Although swamps and marshes are widespread in the region, Louisiana is the only major source of wild fur; it is the leading producer among the 50 states, with an annual take twice as great as any other state. Over 1 million muskrats are trapped every year in Louisiana. Mink, otter, skunk, and other mustelids are also trapped in Louisiana, but the second most important species is nutria.

Trapping is a full-time occupation for only a relatively few people in the Southeastern Coast Region. For the most part it is a sideline of fishermen, shrimpers, and farmers, particularly in the Louisiana bayou country and less commonly in Florida, Georgia, and the Carolinas.

LUMBERING AND FOREST-PRODUCTS INDUSTRIES

Except for the prairie sections of Texas and Louisiana, and the Florida Everglades, most of this region was originally forested. Accordingly such forest products as lumber and pulpwood have been important. These have been discussed in the previous chapter. The picture in this region is similar to that in the Inland South, with the additional fact that some of the larger pulp mills have tidewater sites, as at Mobile and Houston (fig. 11–5).

Another forest product that is of only minor significance in the Inland South but of major importance in the Southeastern Coast Region is naval stores. These are the tar and pitch that were used before the advent of metal ships to caulk seams and preserve ropes of wooden vessels. When it was discovered that turpentine and resin could be distilled from the gum of southern yellow pine, many new uses were found for these products in paints, soaps, shoe dressing, medicine, and so on.

The normal method of obtaining resin is to slash a tree and let the gum ooze into a detachable cup that can be emptied from

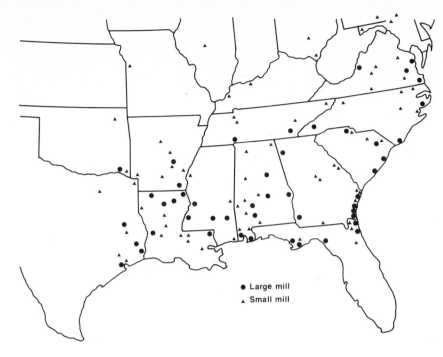

fig. 11–5 Distribution of pulp mills in the southeastern states. Most of the large mills (capacity of more than 1,000 tons per day) are located at tidewater sites in the Southeastern Coast Region, whereas many of the small mills are scattered throughout the Inland South Region (based on 1976 data from the Southern Forest Station, U.S. Forest Service, New Orleans).

● Large mill
▲ Small mill

time to time (fig. 11–6). A more recently developed and popular method is to shred and grind stumps and branches (formerly considered as waste) and put them through a steam-distillation process. A considerable amount of naval stores is also obtained as byproduct from the sulfate process of paper making.

fig. 11–6 A grove of Southern yellow pine slashed to obtain naval stores. The resin, or "gum," oozes downward into the metal cup attached to the tree. In the second photo a worker is chipping the face of a tree with a special tool called a hack. Approximately every two weeks a new "streak" is added to the chipped face. The plastic bottle hanging on the collection trough contains a sulfuric acid solution, which is used to stimulate the flow of gum from the streak.

Extensive forests and high-yielding species of trees permit this region to produce more than half of the world's resin and turpentine. The principal area of production is around Valdosta in southern Georgia and in adjacent portions of northern Florida.

COMMERCIAL FISHING

The total volume of the commercial catch in Gulf waters is greater than that from either Atlantic or Pacific waters of the United States, although the value of the Pacific fishery is considerably higher than that of the Gulf. Two-thirds of the tonnage caught by fishermen of the Southeastern Coast Region consists of menhaden, but their value is comparatively small.

The shrimp fishery is by far the most important of the region. Shrimp are the most valuable variety of ocean product in the United States, and more than half of total national shrimp landings are made at Southeastern Coast Region ports, particularly in Texas and Louisiana. Shrimping is so widespread in this region that almost every estuary and bay has at least one little fishing hamlet and a small complement of shrimp boats (fig. 11-7). Larger port towns and cities, such as Corpus Christi, Pascagoula, and Savannah, are likely to have a more numerous shrimping fleet.

Louisiana leads all other states in volume of fish landings, and Mississippi ranks fifth; menhaden account for the great bulk in both states. In terms of value of catch, Louisiana ranks third and Texas is fourth among the states. Half of the leading fishing ports of the nation are located along the Gulf or South Atlantic coasts, with Cameron, Louisiana, and Brownsville, Texas, as the busiest in the region.

AGRICULTURE

Farming is by no means continuous throughout the region. Large expanses of land have very little arable land, particularly such poorly drained areas as the Dismal and Okefenokee swamps, the Everglades, the coastal flatwoods zone of western Florida and adjacent Alabama and Mississippi, the coastal marshlands of Louisiana, and the drier coastal country between Corpus Christi and the Lower Rio Grande Valley. Although terrain hindrances are nil, agriculture is frequently handicapped by drainage problems (see vignette on next page). Also, soils tend to be infertile; considerable fertilizer, strongly laced with trace elements, must be applied, especially in Florida.

Regional agriculture faces a host of problems: insect pests thrive in the subtropical environment, frost damage is sometimes heavy, marketing is often complex, and overproduction sometimes occurs. A long growing season, adequate moisture, and relatively mild winters compensate, with the result that a considerable quantity of high-quality, and often high-cost, crops is grown.

The grains that are the staple crops of most Anglo-American farming areas are virtually absent in this region. Instead farmers concentrate on growing specialty crops of various kinds. The region's major agricultural role is the output of subtropical and off-season specialties.

one crisis after another for the everglades

Perhaps nowhere in Anglo-America has the basic conflict between wilderness and civilization been brought into sharper focus for a longer period of time than in the semitropical flatlands of southern Florida. The unique ecosystem of the Everglades depends upon a delicate balance of natural factors, the cornerstone of which is a remarkable drainage system that encompasses nearly one-fifth of the state's total area. Natural disasters—floods, hurricanes, and especially droughts—have always posed sporadic dislocations to the Everglades ecosystem, but it is only in the twentieth century that the ultimate threat has appeared. Humanity has developed the means to "tame" the marshlands and put them to more "productive" uses. In doing so it has introduced a continuing series of crises to the area, crises that have engendered an unending controversy between the "developers" and the "protectors" of the sea of grass.

Under normal circumstances there is a steady and reliable flow of water from the Kissimmee chain of lakes into Lake Okeechobee, from which the natural overflow sends a very broad and very shallow sheet of water southward to sustain Big Cypress Swamp and the Everglades before eventually draining into the Gulf of Mexico (fig. 11-a). As more and more settlers were attracted to southern Florida, farms and cities were established and grew apace. The relatively frequent minor, and occasional major, natural floods brought hardships to farmers and urbanites alike, and a number of artificial drainage canals were constructed for flood control purposes and to "improve" the land for agricultural and urban expansion.

As metropolitan Miami, one of the continent's fastest growing cities, burgeoned, truck

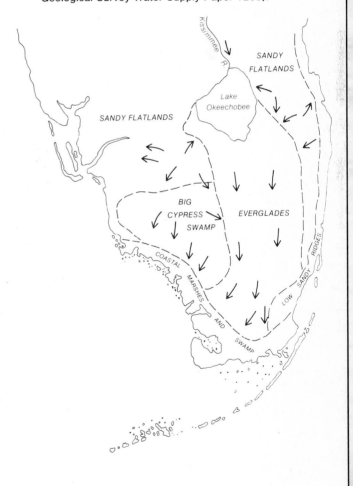

fig. 11-a   The natural drainage pattern of southern Florida is generally southwestward from Lake Okeechobee through the Everglades (after G. G. Parker, U.S. Geological Survey Water Supply Paper 1255).

(Continued)

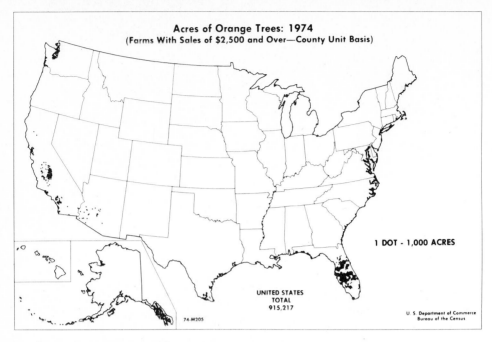

Acres of Orange Trees: 1974
(Farms With Sales of $2,500 and Over—County Unit Basis)

1 DOT - 1,000 ACRES

UNITED STATES
TOTAL
915,217

74-M205

U. S. Department of Commerce
Bureau of the Census

fig. 11-8 Florida is the principal source of oranges in the United States.

Citrus Fruits If any crop typifies both the image and the actuality of specialty production in the Southeastern Coast Region, it is probably citrus (fig. 11–8). Central Florida and the Lower Rio Grande Valley of

fig. 11-b Air boats skimming the watery sawgrass of the Everglades (courtesy Florida Division of Tourism).

farmers and other specialty crop growers of southern Florida were displaced, and the only direction they could move was westward, into the Everglades. Other fringes of the 'Glades were being claimed for industrial purposes, and construction of a huge international jetport was begun virtually in the heart of the original extent of the Everglades. Two highways, the Tamiami Trail and Alligator Alley, were built east-west across the area. Further land development, primarily for residential and second home purposes, was undertaken in Big Cypress Swamp, as a sort of subsidiary of the west coast urban clusters of Fort Myers and Naples (fig. 11-b). Even the Kissimmee River was channeled into a straight-line, stagnant canal.

These varied developments were met with increasing opposition by individuals and groups from many parts of the country, and the "conservation coalition," gaining in strength and po-

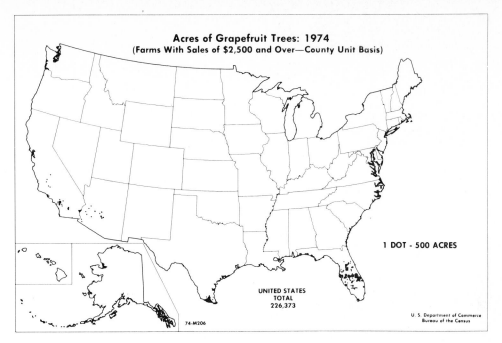

Acres of Grapefruit Trees: 1974
(Farms With Sales of $2,500 and Over—County Unit Basis)

1 DOT - 500 ACRES

UNITED STATES
TOTAL
226,373

U. S. Department of Commerce
Bureau of the Census

74-M206

fig. 11-9 Central Florida is also the principal producer of grapefruit, with the Lower Rio Grande Valley as an important secondary producer.

Texas, two of the four principal citrus areas of the country, are in this region.

Florida is the outstanding citrus producer, supplying about 75 percent of the national grapefruit (fig. 11–9) and orange

litical muscle, succeeded at many points. Everglades National Park was established in 1947, providing complete protection for 1.4 million acres at the lower end of the drainage system. Construction of the jetport was stopped but not before it was half completed (and it is still in use as a training facility). In 1974 the federal and state governments authorized the purchase of more than half a million acres of Big Cypress Swamp to stop piecemeal development and set up a watershed reserve. Authorization to dechannel the Kissimmee River has been granted, although the source of funds for such an immense project is unclear.

The ecological threat, however, persists. Much of the land north and east of Everglades National Park and the Big Cypress Reserve is in private ownership, and pressures for develop-

ment have not abated. These are mostly "upstream" areas in the watershed, and any disruptions in the normal drainage pattern may have serious repercussions in the downstream sections. Moreover, most of the original drainage canals are still functioning, thus cutting off much of the natural southward flow, which is particularly serious in minimum rainfall years.

Future developments will probably be governed by rulings and zonings of local authorities, primarily county commissioners. They must try to strike a reasonable balance between agricultural-industrial-residential needs on the one hand and protection of a complex and fragile ecosystem on the other. Meanwhile, "artificial" droughts have become a frequent occurrence in the Everglades, with the result that both avian and aquatic fauna have been significantly reduced. And the crisis continues.

fig. 11–10 The lake-and-orchard district of central Florida. The orderly geometry of citrus groves is interrupted by the patchy pattern of shallow lakes (courtesy State of Florida, Department of Citrus).

crops, over 60 percent of the tangerine crop, and all of the limes and tangelos. Early Spanish settlers introduced citrus to the state, and Indians propagated it for their own use. "Some of the first commercial groves in nineteenth-century Florida were the result of budding strains on the pruned stock of earlier Indian plantings."[3] The "Big Freeze" of 1894–95 caused a relocation of the industry, for most groves in northern Florida were destroyed, and the northern third of the state was essentially abandoned for citrus. Commercial groves are now mostly in the gently rolling, sandy-soiled lakes district of central Florida (fig. 11–10).

Surface drainage, air drainage,[4] and the warming effect of the lakes are all beneficial in combating frost danger. In addition, oil-burning heaters are employed when the air temperature drops below about 27°F. The land is expensive, the yields are good, and production is increasing.

Consumer demand for oranges and grapefruit continues to mount, but expan-

sion of the main Florida citrus areas is both difficult and costly. Poor drainage to the south and slightly colder temperatures to the north inhibit a latitudinal expansion of the orchard area, and the rapid growth of cities in central Florida continues to displace citrus acreage.

The exacting requirements of modern citrus production make it increasingly practical for farmers, particularly if their holdings are not large, to contract all operations to a production company. Such farmers may never set foot on the land; indeed, many live tens or hundreds of miles away from their orchards. The production company "tends the grove and picks and markets the fruit. The cost of each operation is charged against the farmer's account, and these charges are levied against the profits when the fruit is sold. The grove owner may have no contact whatsoever with his grove other than the annual check."[5] Many growers are members of cooperatives, which usually also have their own production crews and equipment and operate their own processing plants for citrus concentrate.

[3] Edward Higbee, *American Agriculture: Geography, Resources, Conservation* (New York: John Wiley & Sons, Inc., 1958), p. 346.

[4] A 30-foot hill at Avon Park has recorded temperatures as much as 18 degrees higher than those in a "frost pocket" 150 yards away. See Higbee, *American Agriculture: Geography, Resources, Conservation,* p. 348.

[5] John Fraser Hart, "The Changing American Countryside," in *Problems and Trends in American Geography,* ed. Saul B. Cohen (New York: Basic Books, Inc., 1967), p. 69.

Marketing arrangements are often complicated. More than half of all citrus harvested in Florida is now sold as processed products. Canned juices and canned salad are among these, but easily the most important is frozen concentrated juice. There has also been some success in transporting fresh orange juice directly to New York in a glass-lined refrigerated tanker ship. Citrus waste (pulp and peelings) is generally fed to cattle, although the flavoring oil is sometimes removed to be used in the manufacture of table wines and salad oils.

The Texas citrus area is located on the terraces of the Lower Rio Grande delta. Practically all production is based on irrigation water diverted from the river. Severe frost occasionally damages the groves, sometimes so badly that new trees must be planted. On such occasions, the horticulturists usually raise cotton or vegetables for a few years until the groves become reestablished. Seedless pink grapefruit is the specialty of the valley, which in most years produces more than 15 percent of the national grapefruit crop; it also produces about 3 percent of the orange crop. Considerable canning and freezing are done here, as in Florida.

Truck Farming With increasing demands for fresh vegetables, the Southeastern Coast has become one of the major regions for early truck products of the continent. Aside from parts of Southern California and the gardens under glass in the North, nearly all the nation's winter vegetables grown for sale come from this region, particularly from Florida and the Lower Rio Grande Valley. Other commercial vegetable-producing areas are in the vicinity of Corpus Christi in Texas, Dothan in Alabama, Thomasville in Georgia, and Charleston in South Carolina.

Climate is the dominant factor affecting the growth of early vegetables, and soils help to determine the specific locations. In Florida, the best truck crops are produced on muck or other lands having a higher organic content than the sandy soils that characterize much of the state. Vegetable growing in the Lower Rio Grande Valley is largely confined to the alluvial lands of the delta.

The climate in most of the region is suited to the production of early vegetables. In the southern parts of Florida and Texas, some winters have no killing frosts; however, even here an occasional cold spell, or "norther," may sweep down from the interior and kill the more sensitive vegetable crops. Production is circumscribed by economic rather than by geographical conditions. Winter markets can consume only a limited amount of truck crops. Even in the most favored places the growing of winter vegetables is therefore highly speculative, although sometimes highly remunerative.

Sugar Cane Sugar cane growing in the delta country of Louisiana began in 1751, when Jesuits introduced the crop from Santo Domingo. The first successful sugar mill, built on a plantation near New Orleans in 1795, inaugurated the industry in that area. Most Louisiana cane production today is on the fertile soils of the Mississippi delta, where the major environmental problem is a shorter growing season than in the other domestic sugar cane states; consequently both yields per acre and average sugar content are relatively low. Production and harvesting are almost entirely mechanized.

Florida has been a sugar cane producer since 1931, but the output was relatively limited until the 1960s, when the United States ceased buying Cuban sugar. Production is concentrated on the organic soils just south of Lake Okeechobee, where very high yields are attained. These soils, however, oxidize and "evaporate" when exposed to the atmosphere, which causes subsidence at a rate of about twelve inches per decade. This creates major water control problems, and the expanding industry is having to move to sandy soils further from the lake. Even so, Florida cane planting has been on a steadily upward trend for several years, and by the late 1970s nearly 40 percent of the national

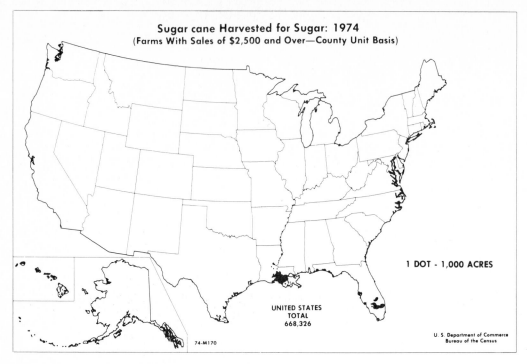

Sugar cane Harvested for Sugar: 1974
(Farms With Sales of $2,500 and Over—County Unit Basis)

1 DOT - 1,000 ACRES

UNITED STATES
TOTAL
668,326

74-M170

U. S. Department of Commerce
Bureau of the Census

fig. 11–11   All sugar cane in the conterminous
states is grown in the Southeastern Coast Region.

fig. 11–12   Florida's sugar cane is normally
burned before it is cut, in order to remove
the dead leaves and to make it easier for the
machete-wielding harvesters to do their job.
Here workers are spreading oil preparatory
to lighting the field. In the background is
smoke from a nearby field that is already
burning (courtesy Florida Division of Tourism).

cane output was from this area (fig. 11–11).
Most of the harvesting is accomplished by
Jamaicans who are flown in to work during
the November-to-April cutting season (fig.
11–12).

The newest sugar cane area is the Lower
Rio Grande Valley of Texas, which had almost a century of commercial cane production until its total demise in the 1920s. The
recent rise in sugar prices, however, tempted
valley farmers to begin planting cane again
in 1973. The results were encouraging, and
acreage has been expanding.

Rice   In colonial times the coastal
areas of South Carolina and Georgia produced large quantities of rice. Although rice
had been grown in Louisiana for more than
a century it did not become an important
commercial crop until after 1880, when the

fig. 11–13 Harvesting rice near Lake Charles, Louisiana.

introduction of harvesting machinery permitted large-scale farming on the prairies of southwestern Louisiana and southeastern Texas.

When the Acadians spread westward along the coast of Louisiana they occupied first the higher, lighter, and more easily drained lands along the streams, leaving unoccupied the heavier prairie soils of the interfluves. These prairie areas, where an impervious claypan underlies the surface, were covered by thousands of shallow ponds that held water after each rain. When these were drained by ditching, they made ideal areas for the cultivation of rice.

The flat terrain permits subdivision of the fields by small levees, a necessity since the field must be covered with about six inches of water during much of the growing period. Heavy rainfall, supplemented by artesian wells and surface streams, provides ample water. With proper drainage the water can be taken from the fields when it is time for mechanical equipment to harvest

the crop or when heavy rains flood the area (fig. 11–13).

Mills, concentrated mainly in Crowley, Lake Charles, and Beaumont, are equipped with complicated machinery for drying, cleaning, and polishing the rice and for utilizing its byproducts. Favorable geographical conditions and complete mechanization enable this region to grow rice at a low per-acre cost.

Despite acreage allotments and marketing quotas, rice production in the United States has more than doubled in the last two decades. Most of the increase is predicated on expanded overseas markets. In most years this country grows less than 2 percent of the world's rice but furnishes more than 20 percent of total world rice exports. The rice-growing area in the Southeastern Coast Region extends from Lafayette, Louisiana, to Matagorda Bay, Texas. About 40 percent of the United States rice crop is grown here, divided about equally between Texas and Louisiana (fig. 11–14).

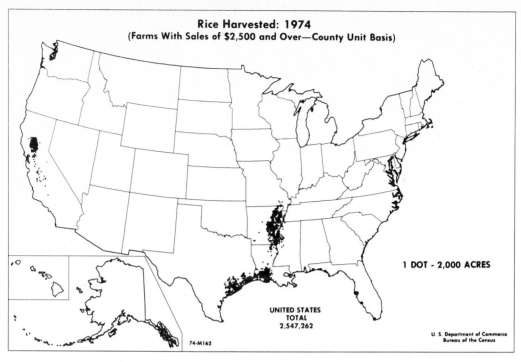

Rice Harvested: 1974
(Farms With Sales of $2,500 and Over—County Unit Basis)

1 DOT - 2,000 ACRES

UNITED STATES
TOTAL
2,547,262

U. S. Department of Commerce
Bureau of the Census

74-M162

fig. 11–14 United States rice production is concentrated along the Texas-Louisiana coast, with secondary centers in eastern Arkansas and the Sacramento Valley of California.

fig. 11–15 The harvested tobacco is bundled in large, loose bales and brought for sale to auction sheds in small towns in southern Georgia and northern Florida. This scene is in Waycross, Georgia.

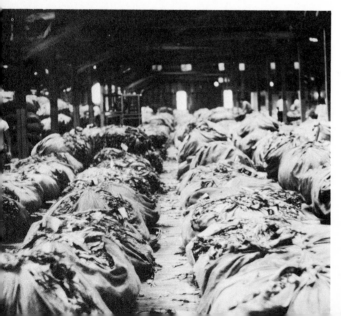

Other Crops Other prominent crops in the Southeastern Coast Region include cotton and grain sorghums in the Lower Rio Grande Valley and the Coastal Bend area (around Corpus Christi) of Texas and tobacco in southern Georgia and northern Florida (fig. 11–15).

THE LIVESTOCK INDUSTRY

The Southeastern Coast Region has been an important producer of beef cattle since French and Spanish colonial times. But after the Great Plains were opened to grazing in the 1870s, the poorer pastures of the Gulf Coast fell into disfavor. For several decades, cattle raising was all but abandoned except in the Acadian French country of southwestern Louisiana, the coastal grasslands of southwestern Texas, and the open range cattle country of northern and central Florida. Through the introduction of new breeds, particularly the Brahman, the cattle industry has expanded in recent years to other parts of the coastal region.

Brahman, or Zebu, cattle (*Bos indicus*) were brought from India to the Carolina coastal country more than a century ago because cattlemen thought they would be better adapted to the hot, humid, insect-ridden area than were the English breeds common in the rest of the country. The oversized, hump-shouldered, lop-eared, slant-eyed, flappy-brisketed newcomer has been a thorough success and is often crossbred to produce special-purpose hybrids (fig. 11–16).

One of these hybrids, the Santa Gertrudis, meticulously developed on Texas's gigantic King Ranch, is considered to be the first "true" cattle breed ever developed in Anglo-America (fig. 11–17). It is five-eighths Shorthorn and three-eighths Brahman. Although there are many purebred Brahmans, as well as Herefords, Santa Gertrudis, and other breeds in the region, most of the beef cattle are of mixed ancestry, and their physiognomy usually reveals the presence of some Brahman inheritance.

One of the most interesting developments in the region has been the rapid rise of the beef cattle industry of peninsular Florida. Today the ranching area extends from the lakes district in the northern part of the peninsula to the lands south of Lake Okeechobee. In this area more than 2 million head of beef cattle are roaming the range. Because of this rapid expansion, Florida now ranks among the leading cattle-raising states of the nation. Livestock markets and packing houses are developing in the state, and sections of Florida, such as the area around Kissimmee where extensive ranches have been cut out of the undergrowth and swamp, are definitely taking on a "western" appearance.

MINERAL INDUSTRIES

Phosphate Rock Florida is Anglo-America's most important producer of phosphate rock, accounting for about 75 percent

fig. 11–16 Brahmas grazing on artificial pastures in central Florida (courtesy Florida Division of Tourism).

fig. 11–17 Santa Gertrudis cattle on a King Ranch pasture.

of the total output. A little hard rock phosphate is dug, but most of the production comes from unconsolidated land-pebble phosphate deposits east of Tampa Bay. There are mines, all open-pit, in three counties (fig. 11–18). Large holes (often ponded because of the high water table), spoils banks, and considerable smoke from the processing plants (a council on air-pollution control has been established) are characteristic landscape features in the mining area. Phosphate mining began in 1888 in Florida, and there are still abundant reserves. Most of the output is used in fertilizer manufacture, but there is considerable export, especially to Japan.

253

fig. 11-18 Phosphate quarries near Lakeland in central Florida.

fig. 11-19 Distribution of salt domes on and near the Gulf Coastal Plain. (After William D. Thornbury, *Regional Geomorphology of the United States* [New York: John Wiley & Sons, Inc., 1965], p. 67. Reprinted by permission.)

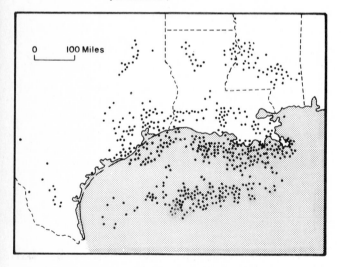

Sulfur Coastal Louisiana and Texas produce about 70 percent of the continent's sulfur. The deposits are found in the cap rock overlying certain salt domes (fig. 11–19); however, most of the domes do not contain sulfur in paying quantities (fig. 11–20). Although sulfur is found at moderate depths 500 to 1,500 feet below ground, commercial exploitation by shaft-mining proved unsuccessful because of danger from cave-in of the overlying sands and gravels. When the Frasch process was perfected in 1900, commercial success was assured and the Gulf Coast soon took first rank among the world's sulfur-producing regions.

The Frasch process is based on the fact that crystalline sulfur melts at 240°F., only slightly above the boiling point of water. Wells are drilled into the deposits on top of the salt plugs (fig. 11–21). Superheated water is pumped into the deposit, and the sulfur is converted into a liquid. Compressed air is used to force the molten material to the surface. The pipes are heated to prevent the sulfur from solidifying until it reaches huge temporary vats on the surface. On being ejected into the vats, the molten sulfur promptly hardens. When the gigantic bins are filled, the sides are stripped off to expose a huge block that can be blasted apart.

The fragments of almost chemically pure sulfur are then loaded into open freight cars by power shovels and hauled to the shipping port to be loaded on coastwise or ocean vessels for the large industrial consuming markets. A considerable quantity of sulfur is shipped by barge up the Mississippi River system to the cities of the interior. A recent innovation, which is becoming more common, is the transport of sulfur to the processing plant in molten form by specially constructed pipelines or boats containing heated cargo tanks.

Less than 10 percent of the 250 known salt domes have been productive by the Frasch process, and it is not anticipated that other productive domes will be discovered on the Gulf Coastal Plain. In offshore waters, however, there undoubtedly are great reserves. The first offshore dome went into production seven miles from the Louisiana coast in 1960. Molten sulfur is taken by heated pipeline to the port of Grand Isle, then transshipped by tanker to Port Sulphur.

Salt The entire region from Alabama westward is dotted with deposits of rock salt. The deposits occur mostly in salt domes of almost pure sodium chloride. Mining is limited to Louisiana and Texas, the two leading salt-mining states in the nation. The reserves are enormous. Although only a few domes are being mined in the region at present, they are yielding great quantities of salt, and none is approaching exhaustion.

The mine usually lies at the top of the salt dome, 600 feet or more below the surface. A shaft is driven down, and large chambers are excavated. Mine props do not have to be used because large supporting columns of salt are left in place. The chambers are sometimes more than 100 feet high. Some salt is extracted in brine solution by a modified Frasch process. Although the Gulf Coast has no monopoly in salt production, it has sufficient reserves to make it an important producer for a very long time. There are many known salt domes (some of them are now producing petroleum or sulfur) where salt can be obtained when needed.

Shells Oyster and clam shells have been used for many years as a road-building material, but the big development in this industry did not begin until the heavy chemical industry started its phenomenal growth in the 1940s. Today one sees large mounds of gray, gravelly material piled up at many industrial establishments; these are oyster shells that have been dredged from the shallow bays along the Gulf Coast. With the nearest source of limestone in Texas more than 200 miles from the coast, oyster shells from dead reefs provide industry with a cheap and abundant supply of lime (fig. 11–22).

Lone Star Cement opened its Houston plant in 1916, using oyster shells in place of limestone, and in 1934 Southern Alkali Corporation of Corpus Christi began using shells as a source of lime for their process.

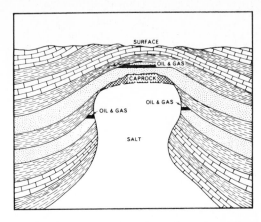

fig. 11–20   Generalized geologic cross-section of a salt dome, showing typical reservoirs of oil and gas.

fig. 11–21   Generalized diagram of the Frasch process. A well is drilled down to the sulfur formation, and three concentric pipes are inserted into the hole. Hot water is forced down one pipe and compressed air down another. The water melts the sulfur and the resulting brine solution is forced back up the third pipe to the surface, where it is stored and allowed to solidify before shipping or is transported as a brine.

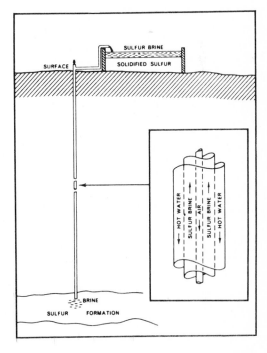

fig. 11-22 Mountains of oyster shells that have been dredged from Matagorda Bay along the Texas coast.

Today shells provide road ballast as well as raw materials for making lime and cement at many coastal factories. The chief dead oyster reefs being dredged today are in Atchafalaya Bay in Louisiana, and in Galveston, Matagorda, and Nueces bays in Texas.

The extraction operation is totally mechanized. Dredges of various sizes suck up the dead oyster shell, mostly from the Virginia oyster (*Crassostrea virginica*), clean it, and expel it onto large barges floating alongside, which in turn transport it to the numerous markets in the coastal area.[6] The devastating nature of a dredging operation causes significant controversy in an area where a number of competing activities are relatively incompatible. Commercial fishermen, sports fishermen, tourists, and nature lovers frequent the same bays as the shell dredgers; petroleum extraction, commercial shipping, and pleasure boating add to the activities in these shallow waters.

There is much dispute about the ecological and economic consequences of reef dredging, and state agencies in both Louisiana and Texas have finally (tardily, some would say) imposed stringent regulations on the dredging industry; furthermore, production trends have been static for the last decade, and there is considerable concern that the supply of this valuable industrial raw material will be unable to meet the growing demand.

Petroleum and Natural Gas The Southeastern Coast Region encompasses most of the area known as the Gulf Coast Petroleum Province, one of the continent's major oil producers. It normally yields about one-fourth of the United States total flow. The oil fields, almost exclusively in association with salt domes, are scattered along the west Gulf Coastal Plain from the mouth of the Mississippi to the mouth of the Rio Grande. Numerous new discoveries are being made, particularly in the shallow coastal margin of the Gulf of Mexico. This province holds the record for the first large gusher and also has the largest number of productive deep wells in the United States, some of which reach depths below 20,000 feet.

Since much crude oil is today transported by pipelines, the Gulf Coast port cities have become the termini of most pipelines from the Gulf Coast and Midcontinent oil provinces. These pipelines have permitted the rapid development of the refining industry along the west Gulf Coast between Baton Rouge and Corpus Christi. Enormous quantities of both crude and refined petroleum are also shipped by tankers to the North Atlantic seaboard.

The continental shelf off the Gulf Coast is broad and shallow, and underlain by geologic structures of the same types as those of the coastal plain. Accordingly salt domes, with their associated petroleum, natural gas, and sulfur, are widespread in the "tidelands," as the shelf has come to be called. Many favorable structures have been discovered geophysically, and numerous wells have been sunk.

Offshore drilling is quite expensive, costing two to five times as much as a conventional dry-land well, largely because of the elaborate, self-contained drilling platforms or vessels that are used—sometimes several dozen miles from the coast. Drilling platforms cost up to $20 million apiece, and

---

[6] Alex Kerr, *The Texas Reef Shell Industry*, Texas Industry Series no. 11 (Austin: Bureau of Business Research, University of Texas at Austin, 1967), p. 3.

drilling rigs operate at a cost of up to $40,-000 per day. About half of all the active offshore rigs and drilling platforms in the world are operating in the Gulf of Mexico (fig. 11–23). In the past most drilling and most well completions were off the coast of Louisiana, in part because of protracted litigation between federal and state governments over the ownership of mineral rights off the Texas coast; however, since 1968 there has been an acceleration of activity in Texas waters.

The Southeastern Coast Region is also a major source of natural gas, which is distributed by pipeline to consumers in many parts of the country. Reserves of gas in the tidelands area are thought to be gigantic, but as yet there is little production of natural gas from the continental shelf because of the high cost of drilling.

manufacturing

In the last four decades industrial expansion in the Southeastern Coast Region has been nothing short of spectacular. New factories have been built by the dozen, many of them large. Employment opportunities have expanded rapidly and accelerated population growth. Many of the plants, however, are highly mechanized and not labor-intensive; thus, the rate of industrial output has been even higher than the growth of manufactural employment.

The region offers many attractions to industrial firms, but the principal locational advantages are (1) large supplies of basic industrial materials, such as petroleum, natural gas, sulfur, salt, and lime (oyster shells); (2) an abundance of natural gas for fuel; and (3) a tidewater location providing cheap water transport rates for bulky manufactured products. Other factors, such as available labor, a growing local market, and local venture capital, are also important, but these are of less overall significance in attracting major industries.

In most parts of the region, the industrial sector is specialized rather than diversified, on the basis of specific resources or

fig. 11–23 Offshore oil drilling platform with conspicuous helipad, in Louisiana water near Grand Isle (courtesy Louisiana Tourist Development Commission).

other locational attractions. The principal types of manufacturing are limited in variety, although often enormous in magnitude.

PETROLEUM REFINING

The basic specialized manufacturing industry of the region is the refining of petroleum. From Pascagoula to Corpus Christi there are numerous nodes of refineries, inevitably connected by a network of pipelines to other industrial facilities as well as to storage tanks and shipping terminals (fig. 11–24). Much of the crude oil is obtained within the region, but a considerable proportion of the refinery input comes from oil fields to the north of the coastal zone and from imported oil. The whole region contains approximately 40 percent of the nation's refinery capacity. The principal refining centers are Houston–Texas City and Beaumont–Port

fig. 11–24 The Humble refinery complex at Baton Rouge, located on the east bank of the Mississippi River. Much of the refinery's output moves by water transport on the river, both by inland waterway barges and by ocean-going tankers (courtesy Humble Oil and Refining Company).

Arthur; each has about 10 percent of the national refining capacity, which is more than twice as much as any other industrial center in the country.

PETROCHEMICAL INDUSTRIES

The demand for aviation gasoline revolutionized petroleum refining and indirectly created many new products industries. Along the west Gulf Coast in the early 1940s, leading oil companies built subsidiary plants to process the byproducts of aviation gasoline. Included were butadiene plants for the manufacture of synthetic rubber, toluene plants for the manufacture of a basic ingredient for trinitrotoluene (TNT), and many others. Recycling plants that "strip" natural gas of gasoline, butane, and other hydrocarbons were also established. Another important industrial product made from natural gas is carbon black, of which about 80 percent is produced by Texas, although not all of this comes from the coastal region. Petrochemical plants are usually located near refineries. Often a complex pattern of pipelines conducts liquid or gaseous products from one plant to another, the finished product of one factory serving as the raw material for another. Petrochemical plants are scattered along the coast from Mobile to Brownsville, but the principal concentrations are in the major refining areas: along the Houston Ship Canal, around Texas City, in the vicinity of Sabine Lake, around Lake Charles, and along the Mississippi River between Baton Rouge and New Orleans.

PLASTICS

Plastics are synthetic resins derived from hydrocarbons; they are complex chemical combinations made from petrochemical products. The recent rapid growth of the plastics industry has made significant inroads into markets that were formerly dominated by metals, wood products, glass, and paper. The world's greatest concentration of plastics manufacturers is situated on the Gulf Coast of Texas and Louisiana, primarily to utilize products from the petrochemicals industry of the region. More than 80 percent of national output of polyethylene and styrene plastics comes from this area. The third significant branch of the industry, vinyl plastics, is more widely distributed over the country.

INORGANIC CHEMICALS

Salt and sulfur—already discussed as major products of the Texas-Louisiana coastal zone—are the principal raw materials for the production of several significant industrial chemicals, notably sulfuric acid and soda ash. Caustic soda and chlorine are other inorganic chemicals produced in huge quantities in the region.

METALLIC INDUSTRIES

For a long time the lack of suitable coking coal prohibited the development of an iron and steel industry along the Gulf Coast, although low-grade brown iron ores from East Texas and ample supplies of scrap in the Gulf Southwest were available. There was also lime from oyster shells. The first plant

was not constructed, however, until 1942 when Sheffield Steel opened a mill on the Houston Ship Channel. This plant has been enlarged several times but produces only a tiny fraction of national output.

The Gulf Coast area is an advantageous site for alumina plants. Most of the United States supply of bauxite comes from northern South America and the West Indies and can be brought directly to the area by inexpensive maritime transport. During the period immediately after World War II several huge alumina facilities were built along the Texas and Louisiana coast, utilizing the abundant nearby supplies of natural gas as a fuel for generating the prodigious amounts of electricity needed to reduce the bauxite ore to alumina. At the present time nearly seven-eighths of national alumina output is from Gulf Coast plants (fig. 11–25). Most

fig. 11–25 Distribution of United States bauxite and alumina supply and aluminum plant capacities, 1973 (thousand short tons of aluminum content). Six of the eight alumina plants in the United States (middle level of diagram) are located in the Southeastern Coast Region.

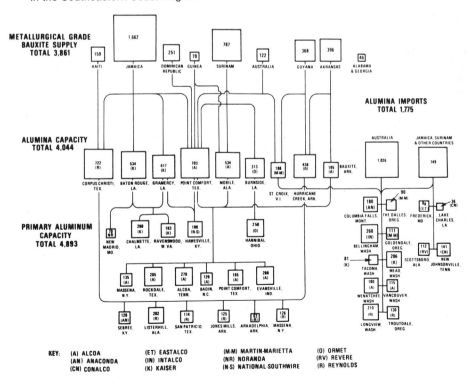

KEY: (A) ALCOA   (ET) EASTALCO   (M-M) MARTIN-MARIETTA   (O) ORMET
(AN) ANACONDA (IN) INTALCO   (NR) NORANDA   (RV) REVERE
(CN) CONALCO   (K) KAISER   (N-S) NATIONAL-SOUTHWIRE   (R) REYNOLDS

BUREAU OF MINES
U.S. DEPARTMENT OF THE INTERIOR

aluminum plants (where alumina is refined into metallic aluminum), however, are located elsewhere; Gulf Coast plants produce only one-eighth of the nation's aluminum.

Numerous other metal industries are located along the coast, primarily because of cheap fuel and cheap water transportation. In practically every case the ore is imported from overseas or from inland domestic sources. The only exception is the magnesium plant of Dow Chemical Company at Freeport, Texas, where metallic magnesium is extracted from salts dissolved in the waters of the Gulf of Mexico.

WOOD-PRODUCTS INDUSTRIES

Sawmills are widely scattered in the forested portions of the region, but pulp and paper production is much more significant in terms of employment and output. Some of the nation's largest mills are located in ports of this region, although much of the pulp-wood supply is obtained from the Inland South Region. Georgia is the leading state in the nation in pulp and paper output; most of its production is from three huge coastal mills.[7]

FOOD-PRODUCTS INDUSTRIES

This prosaic branch of manufacturing has a specialized flair in the Southeastern Coast Region because of the availability of large quantities of a few raw materials and of such port-related industries as coffee mills in New Orleans. Prominent features of many harbors in the region, from North Carolina to Texas, are the local seafood-processing plants, especially those that pack shrimp. Other notable food-processing facilities are fruit and vegetable canning and freezing plants, rice mills, and sugar refineries.

[7] C. S. Ryun, "The Southeast's Booming Paper Industry," *Monthly Review*, Federal Reserve Bank of Atlanta, 54 (September 1969), 113.

urban boom in the space age

No other part of Anglo-America, except Arizona and California, has experienced such notable urban growth in recent years as the Southeastern Coast Region (see table 11–1 for the region's largest urban places). A relative abundance of employment opportunities combines with the attraction of mild winters and a coastal environment to make this a region of rapid, continuing in-migration from other parts of the country. The location of several major space-related facilities in Texas, Florida, Louisiana, and Mississippi has significantly contributed to the boom in the region.

GULF COAST METROPOLISES: HOUSTON AND NEW ORLEANS

Houston and New Orleans are the well-established metropolitan centers of the region, although the former has long since surpassed the latter in terms of both absolute and relative growth. Houston, perhaps more than any city east of the Rockies, epitomizes the story of Anglo-American urban expansion in recent decades, whereas New Orleans is an older city that has grown with unspectacular vigor.

Houston is the largest city in the South, and no city in its size-category has grown at a faster rate in the last 20 years (fig. 11–26). Its image is one of a brash, sprawling, oil-oriented boom town. The urban economy is "vertically integrated," with petroleum refining and distribution at the base and succeeding layers of petrochemicals and metal fabrication—particularly the production of steel pipe and oil-field machinery. Services of various kinds and a bustling port round out the base of the economy.

Houston is one of the busiest ports in the nation, although its traffic is largely coastwise shipment of bulk materials. Its artificial harbor is located at the end of a narrow, dredged, 52-mile channel, which is one of the most dynamic and most dangerous (owing to the great quantity of volatile ma-

table 11–1   Largest Urban Places of the Southeastern Coast Region

name	population of principal city	population of metropolitan area	name	population of principal city	population of metropolitan area
Baton Rouge, La.	294,394	411,300	Lakeland, Fla.	49,705	273,800
Baytown, Tex.	48,191		McAllen, Tex.	48,563	220,700
Beaumont, Tex.	113,696	349,500	Melbourne, Fla.	39,821	232,600
Biloxi, Miss.	46,407	173,400	Miami, Fla.	365,022	1,438,600
Boca Raton, Fla.	42,363		Miami Beach, Fla.	94,063	
Brownsville, Tex.	72,157	169,300	Mobile, Ala.	196,441	401,600
Charleston, S.C.	57,470	371,600	New Orleans, La.	559,770	1,094,400
Clearwater, Fla.	67,069		North Charleston, S.C.*	58,544	
Coral Gables, Fla.*	43,370		North Miami, Fla.*	42,135	
Corpus Christi, Tex.	214,838	297,300	Orlando, Fla.	113,179	585,200
Daytona Beach, Fla.	48,037	209,800	Pasadena, Tex.*	94,670	
Dothan, Ala.	44,256		Pascagoula, Miss.	30,403	105,800
Fort Lauderdale, Fla.	152,959	862,500	Pensacola, Fla.	64,168	267,000
Fort Myers, Fla.	36,170	155,400	Pompano Beach, Fla.*	48,821	
Gainesville, Fla.	72,236	129,600	Port Arthur, Tex.	53,557	
Galveston, Tex.	60,125	182,000	St. Petersburg, Fla.	234,389	
Gulfport, Miss.	43,126		Sarasota, Fla.	47,089	162,600
Harlingen, Tex.	40,423		Savannah, Ga.	110,348	203,100
Hialeah, Fla.*	117,682		Tallahassee, Fla.	83,725	138,700
Hollywood, Fla.*	119,002		Tampa, Fla.	280,340	1,365,400
Houston, Tex.	1,326,809	2,297,300	Texas City, Tex.	40,939	
Jacksonville, Fla.	535,030	700,600	Victoria, Tex.	44,842	
Kenner, La.*	43,781		W. Palm Beach, Fla.	61,471	460,100
Lafayette, La.	75,430	125,300	Wilmington, N.C.	53,818	128,300
Lake Charles, La.	76,087	150,500			

* A suburb of a larger city.

fig. 11–26   The skyline of Houston, Anglo-America's fastest-growing metropolis (courtesy Houston Chamber of Commerce).

fig. 11–27 One of several huge space exploration facilities in the region is NASA's Manned Spacecraft Center in Houston (courtesy Houston Chamber of Commerce).

terials being shipped on a cramped waterway) canals in the world. As the site of the Manned Spacecraft Center of the National Aeronautics and Space Administration, Houston's preeminent place in the space age is assured (fig. 11–27). Nearby elements in the Houston conurbation include residential Pasadena and Baytown, industrial Texas City, and the island port and beach resort of Galveston.

New Orleans is one of those rare Anglo-American cities that is distinguished by uniqueness of character. Its wretched and crowded site between the Mississippi River and Lake Pontchartrain,[8] its splendid location near the mouth of the continent's mightiest river, its remarkable past that encompasses the full span of Southern history, and its unusual French cultural flavor that is

unparalleled south of Montreal combine to set New Orleans apart. In most years its foreign trade is exceeded only by that of New York; indeed, New Orleans depends much more heavily on income from oceanborne commerce than any other major port in the country.[9] Conversely, the industrial base is limited; proportional employment in manufacturing is only half the national average for large cities.

THE BOOM CITIES OF FLORIDA

Florida has experienced several periods of rapid population and economic expansion in its history, but the growth trends of recent years have been unparalleled in continuity and stability. The state's population increase between 1950 and 1976 was exceeded only by California, and its rate of population growth was exceeded only by Nevada. As is commonplace throughout Anglo-America, the growth has been predominantly in urban areas. During the 1970–76 period, nine of the fifteen fastest growing metropolitan areas in the nation were in Florida.[10]

The state's premier metropolis, *Miami*, now sprawls widely from its focus on Biscayne Bay, and the resort suburb of Miami Beach merges imperceptibly northward with Fort Lauderdale. The urbanized zone extends almost uninterruptedly to Palm Beach, which is 50 miles north of the Miami central business district. Miami's rapid recent growth makes it the second largest city in the region, and fourth largest (after Houston, Dallas, and Atlanta) in the South. Its economic orientation is essentially commercial and recreational, but its attraction as a tourist center is on a waning trend, presumably because Miami's large urban area

[8] See Peirce Lewis's list of the ten major environmental handicaps that give New Orleans what is probably the most miserable site of any Anglo-American metropolis in *New Orleans: The Making of an Urban Landscape* (Cambridge, Mass.: Ballinger Publishing Co., 1976), pp. 31–32.

[9] See James B. Kenyon, "Elements in Inter-Port Competition in the United States," *Economic Geography*, 46 (January 1970), 1–24.

[10] David B. Longbrake and Woodrow W. Nichols, Jr., *Sunshine and Shadows in Metropolitan Miami* (Cambridge, Mass.: Ballinger Publishing Co., 1976), p. 24.

has engendered a host of social problems (for example, the highest rate of major crimes in the nation[11]) and lost some of its charm as a tourist goal. No new hotels have been built in Miami Beach in a decade, and there is now a concerted campaign to legalize casino gambling (following Atlantic City's lead) in an attempt to restore the city's image as a swinging resort.

Manufacturing is of relatively minor importance in the economy, and maritime commerce is relatively limited, although increasing. Nevertheless, the city's role as gateway to Latin America is stronger than ever, its airport is one of the nation's busiest for both domestic and international flights, and Miami has displaced New York as the leading United States port of departure for international sea passengers (with nearby Port Everglades ranking third). There are two unusual elements to Miami's demographic structure: it has a higher proportion of older people than any other metropolis, and more than half of the central city's population is of Latino (primarily Cuban) origin.

Florida's other principal urban areas are also growing rapidly, although the rate of increase is greater in the cities of central Florida than in those of the northern part of the state. The *Tampa–St. Petersburg* metropolitan area now has a population of 1.5 million; its diversified economy and busy phosphate port continue to attract many newcomers. *Jacksonville* is one of Florida's oldest cities, but its recent growth pattern has been more erratic than that of cities further south. The burgeoning *Orlando–Winter Park* area of central Florida is the state's major inland metropolis. It has significantly shared in the space boom because of its relative proximity to the Kennedy Space Center on Cape Canaveral, and it is the nearest city to Anglo-America's leading theme amusement park, Walt Disney World, which

records some 20 million visitors annually. The *Lakeland–Winter Haven* area, between Tampa and Orlando, is also growing rapidly; a midstate megalopolis is in the making here, stretching from St. Petersburg to Orlando.

SMALLER INDUSTRIAL CENTERS

There are several small to medium-sized cities that are highly industrialized and represent, in microcosm, the recent economic history of the region. All are ports, and all are significantly dependent on one or more aspects of the petroleum industry.

Baton Rouge, situated on the Mississippi River more than 150 miles from the Gulf, is a veritable beehive of petrochemical activity and oil refining. It also has the second largest alumina reduction works in the nation. *Corpus Christi* is the busy port of the central Texas coast. As such its commercial function is more notable than its manufacturing, although it is the site of a significant concentration of factories, many of which are petroleum-oriented. In the extreme southeastern corner of Texas are the Sabine Lake cities of *Beaumont,* noted for oil refining, rice milling, and wood-products manufacturing; *Port Arthur,* petrochemicals and synthetic rubber; and *Orange,* shipbuilding.

THE OLDER PORT CITIES

Several of the region's older ports have followed the trend of economic and population expansion at a somewhat slower rate. *Charleston* and *Savannah* had glory days during colonial and Confederate times but have experienced limited and erratic growth during most of the past century. More recently their river-mouth harbors have been busy again, their fishing fleets have been active, and their rate of industrial expansion (pulp and paper, shipbuilding, and food-processing) has been impressive.

As the only major Gulf Coast port serving much of the Southeast, *Mobile* has enjoyed a privileged position. It is the ore-import port for the Birmingham steel in-

[11] They were Fort Myers (1), Fort Lauderdale–Hollywood (2), Sarasota (3), West Palm Beach–Boca Raton (6), Pensacola (8), Orlando (10), Tampa–St. Petersburg (11), Bradenton (13), and Tallahassee (15). See *Sales and Marketing Management, Survey of Buying Power,* 119 (25 July 1977).

dustry and serves as the funnel for goods moving in and out of Alabama's inland waterway system. A few major industrial plants—shipbuilding, paper-making, alumina reduction—are notable. Several small cities serve as central places in the Lower Rio Grande Valley, but only *Brownsville* has a deep-water harbor and effectively functions as a port. Urban growth in the valley is related primarily to agriculture, fishing, tourism, and services, rather than to manufacturing or port activities.

ports, waterways, and barges

There are many busy ports in the Southeastern Coast Region. A considerable overseas trade is carried on; most of it is in bulk cargo, of which crude petroleum and fuel oil are by far the leaders. For every major port in the region except Mobile (iron ore) and Tampa (phosphate rock), oil is the principal commodity on a tonnage basis. General cargo tonnage, however, has increased significantly at most ports in recent years. New Orleans is the outstanding port in the region on the basis of foreign commerce handled. Many of the ports tend to be specialized in their trade, such as the busy cotton wharves at Galveston; the bustling rice docks at Lake Charles; the new banana-unloading facilities at Gulfport, Mississippi; and the entirely new lumber and oil port of Georgetown, South Carolina.

A large proportion of the port activity of the region involves coastwise traffic going to other parts of the United States rather than foreign import-export business. Houston's high ranking as a commercial port, for example, is primarily reflective of its domestic trade. Much of the coastwise traffic is carried in barges, large flat-bottomed craft that are usually connected in strings and pushed or pulled by tugs. Barges provide the least expensive form of transportation but can only be used in quiet waters since they are quite susceptible to swamping or capsizing.

The Southeastern Coast Region is particularly well suited to barge traffic because of the large number of canals and other dredged interior channels that are available and because of its direct connection with the Mississippi River waterway system. Flat land and a high water table make the construction of inland waterways in the region relatively inexpensive; thus, an extensive system of interconnected channels is found. Most of the region's important ports are set inland some distance from the open sea and can function as ports only by means of channels that have been dredged along stream courses in the flat coastal plain. Houston, with its dredged Buffalo Bayou, is the prime example of this, but the same process has been carried out in a number of other instances. For the port of New Orleans a second channel has been cut directly east from the city, shortening the distance to the Gulf considerably.

The most remarkable of the region's water routes is the Gulf Intracoastal Waterway, which extends from Brownsville to the Florida panhandle just inland of the coast, utilizing lagoons behind barrier islands where possible and cutting through the coastal plain where necessary. For most of its 1,100-mile length it has only a 12-foot depth; thus, it is designed primarily for barge traffic (fig. 11-28). It was only partially completed by the time of World War II but was particularly useful during that conflict because of the activities of German submarines in the Gulf of Mexico.

The waterway was finally completed in 1949. It is most heavily used in its central portion; two-thirds of total traffic is in the section between Houston and the Mississippi River. Sulfur, cotton, grain, and other bulk goods are important commodities shipped, but by far the most important are petroleum and petroleum products, which constitute nearly two-thirds of the tonnage. Heavy use of the waterway is shown by the fact that nine of the fifteen largest United States seaports (in tonnage) are located along its course.

Of major significance to the Gulf Intracoastal Waterway is its connection with the

Mississippi River system. Barge traffic from the waterway can move into the Mississippi via two major channels in southeastern Louisiana, which means that barges from the Gulf Coast can be towed to the far-flung extremities of the Mississippi navigation system—up the Tennessee, Ohio, or Missouri rivers, and even into the Great Lakes via the Mississippi and Illinois rivers.

The Alabama, Tombigbee, and Black Warrior rivers of the state of Alabama also have been dredged and stabilized to provide navigation systems for barges. A modest amount of traffic utilizes these rivers, mainly between Birmingham and Mobile.

Along the Atlantic Coast is the Atlantic Intracoastal Waterway, which is theoretically analogous to the Gulf Intracoastal Waterway. The former, however, does not have the advantage of tapping a major region of bulk production or of connecting to the Mississippi navigation system; consequently commercial traffic on the Atlantic Intracoastal Waterway is exceedingly sparse, except in a few short reaches. It is used much more extensively for pleasure boating.

A Cross-Florida Canal has long been mooted to join the two Intracoastal waterways. Construction was actually begun in the late 1960s but was halted in 1970 because of anticipated ecological problems and the highly questionable economics of the project.

fig 11–28   Barge tows moving on a busy stretch of the Gulf Intracoastal Waterway near Morgan City, Louisiana (courtesy U.S. Army Corps of Engineers, New Orleans District).

fig. 11–29   Fine beaches are the major natural recreational attractions of the region. This scene is in Crandon Park near the Rickenbacker Causeway in Miami (courtesy Miami-Metro Department of Publicity and Tourism).

recreation

The recreation and tourist industry of the Southeastern Coast Region is a major segment of the regional economy. The mild winter climate is part of the attraction, as is an abundance of shows, amusement parks, and historical sites. It is the coastline and its beaches, however, that draw visitors to the region. There is a greater total mileage of usable beaches in this region than in the rest of Anglo-America combined (fig. 11–29). And, except in the vicinity of the largest cities or principal resorts, the beaches are

fig. 11–30 Hundreds of hotels and thousands of apartment buildings front the ocean almost without interruption from Miami Beach to Fort Lauderdale (courtesy Miami Beach News Bureau).

sand, with the busy coastal highway intervening. Wherever this pattern is interrupted, the string of big homes is replaced by a newer resort or commercial development, as at Biloxi.

Beaches are intermittent and usually located on offshore islands along the South Atlantic coast north of Florida. The most famous resort area is near Brunswick, where each of the three nearby offshore islands has a different use pattern. Sea Island is the classic resort island; its relatively small acreage is devoted to pretentious summer homes, many of which are mansions. Just to the south is St. Simons Island. This is a much larger land mass that shows evidence of sporadic development over a long period of time, ranging from summer homes to modest motels. Of more recent vintage is the development of Jekyll Island; most of this island is maintained as uncrowded stretches of white sand, but in the center is a prominent concentration of modern motels and convention facilities. There are similar developments at Hilton Head and Myrtle Beach in South Carolina. Much of the North Carolina mainland shore is without beaches, but projecting as a curved crescent into the Atlantic are the remarkable sand bar islands of Cape Lookout and Cape Hatteras, with a continuous oceanside beach.

There are many places of historical interest in the region, but by far the most notable are the four urban centers that have preserved the architectural flavor of yesteryear. The Vieux Carré (French Quarter) of New Orleans is the preeminent attraction of this type, and sets the theme—with its Royal Street shops and Bourbon Street night spots—for one of Anglo-America's most distinctive tourist centers (fig. 11–31). Both Savannah and Charleston are cities of similar and unusual historic interest. Their extensive areas of eighteenth and nineteenth century architecture are unmatched elsewhere and are nicely counterpointed by Charleston's waterfront Battery area and Savannah's delightful system of city squares. In northeastern Florida, the Jacksonville–St. Augustine area has maintained a smaller

likely to be both clean and uncrowded—even on a hot Sunday afternoon in August.

The coast of Florida is most heavily used, of course (fig. 11–30). The Atlantic margin of that state consists of an almost-continuous beach from the St. Johns estuary in the north to Biscayne Bay in the south. Beaches are spaced more irregularly on Florida's Gulf Coast but are splendid in quality.

The Texas coast also contains hundreds of miles of beaches, although most of them are on offshore islands and all are not readily accessible. The principal beach resort is Galveston Island, near the Houston conurbation. The Corpus Christi area also has fine beaches, and Padre Island, extending for 100 miles south from Corpus Christi, has the longest stretch of undeveloped beach in the nation.

The Mississippi coastline, from Pascagoula to Bay St. Louis, is one continuous beach and has an interesting pattern of development. In the area from Pass Christian to Ocean Springs, a stretch of some 35 miles, there is an almost unbroken line of lovely old homes set on the beach ridge, a few feet higher than the magnificent stretch of white

fig. 11–31 The distinctiveness of historic French architecture in the Vieux Carré is one of the prime visual attractions of New Orleans (courtesy Louisiana Tourist Development Commission).

but more varied sampling of historic architecture.

In a region where recreation and tourism are big business, it is not surprising that there has been heavy capital investment in constructed or "modified" attractions to which the public is invited for an admission charge. Florida, again, is the leader in such development. Most of the early endeavors were associated with some sort of water show featuring swimmers, skiers, or fish at one of the numerous artesian springs or lakes. More recently the scope of the attractions has broadened and now runs the gamut from specialized commercial museums (circus, vintage car, and so on) to the variety of Walt Disney World.

The tourist industry of Florida is a major source of income. In the southern half of the state it flourishes primarily in the winter, with a secondary smaller peak in summer; in the northern half, business is greatest in the summer. Visitors come from practically every state and many foreign countries, but the majority are urban dwellers from east of the Mississippi and north of the Ohio and Potomac rivers. Avoidance of winter is one of the major stimuli for coming to Florida, in a pattern that had its beginning more than 75 years ago.

The tourist industry in Florida has experienced more than one major setback and is still overextended at times, but is now solidly based and is the most important revenue-producing activity in the state. The principal concentration of resorts is along the southeastern coast, focusing on the extravagant hostelries of Miami Beach, which has the largest concentration of first-class resort hotel accommodations of anywhere in the world and is by far the most visited semitropical beach resort in the conterminous states. Peripheral attractions include Everglades National Park, the various islands of the Keys, and tourist-oriented Seminole Indian settlements.

the outlook

The Southeastern Coast Region remained one of the most backward parts of Anglo-America until almost the beginning of the present century. Prior to 1900 its chief activities were forest exploitation, agriculture, and ranching. The few rundown ports were in need of modernization.

With the discovery of oil at Spindletop and the development of salt, phosphate, lime (oyster shells), and sulfur, the coastal region began to attract industry, even though no major development took place until the 1940s. In this region industry has found a favorable habitat; indeed, few parts of Anglo-America present a brighter outlook for manufacturing than this area that is the world's most extensively industrialized subtropical region.

In the Texas-Louisiana section, industries that are based on petroleum or natural gas for raw materials and fuel undoubtedly will be the leaders of growth; elsewhere in the region industrialization is more varied and less spectacular, although the prospects for paper making seem particularly good.

Petroleum overshadows all other factors in the economy of the western part of the region, however. The national energy deficit encourages expanded exploration and production from the tidelands, despite the high costs of such activities. Nevertheless, the increasing dependence on foreign sources of petroleum furnishes an economic imperative for the establishment of one or two oil superports to handle imported crude. Construction of a superport would be a colossal

undertaking and would cost hundreds of millions of dollars, but it is anticipated that such a facility would provide long-term stimulation of local refinery, pipeline, and petrochemical industries, and furnish a solid base for other transportation and industrial complexes. Gulf coastal waters are too shallow for an onshore superport; thus, construction would undoubtedly take place at locations from 12 to 25 miles at sea, literally out of sight of land.

Conventional port business continues to expand throughout the region, and greatly enlarged facilities, particularly at Houston, New Orleans, and Mobile, are under construction.

Specialized farming will continue to occupy an important place in the economy, led by citrus, sugar cane, and vegetables. Intensification of beef cattle raising is likely, although its areal spread will probably slow down.

The space boom of the 1960s has significantly ebbed, but the period of hardship resulting from the sharp decline seems to have passed, and a steadier but less spectacular era of space-related activities will probably become established at the prominent centers of Cape Canaveral-Titusville in Florida, Houston, and the Bogalusa-Picayune border area of Louisiana-Mississippi.

The attraction of mild winters and outdoor living remains very compelling for northeasterners; thus, people are likely to continue to pour into the region at a rapid rate to visit, to work, or to retire, especially in Florida and the Lower Rio Grande Valley. Rapid population growth and a continually expanding tourist trade will be major elements in the economic and social geography of the region for some time to come. Increasingly too, Florida serves as a way station for tourists on the way to the Bahamas or the Caribbean.

The striking juxtaposition of natural areas and constructed landscapes in this region makes it a prominent place for ecological confrontations. Several major battles have already been joined: the Everglades jetport has been delayed if not cancelled; the Cross-Florida Canal has at least been postponed; "development" plans for Padre Island and Cape Hatteras are being contested; the ramifications of pesticides are being heatedly debated in southern Louisiana; the maintenance of a water supply for the Everglades remains an unresolved issue. In this region the "developers" and the "preservationists" find much cause for conflict, and with the passage of time, the arena of combat is sure to widen as the need for rational land-use plans becomes increasingly pressing.

selected bibliography

CARTER, L. J., *The Florida Experience: Land and Water Use Policy in a Growth State*. Baltimore, Md.: Johns Hopkins University Press, 1975.

DAVIS, DONALD W., "Trainasse," *Annals*, Association of American Geographers, 66 (1976), 349–59.

DILLMAN, C. DANIEL, "Brownsville: Border Port for Mexico and the U.S.," *Professional Geographer*, 21 (1969), 178–83.

DOLAN, ROBERT, "Beach Changes on the Outer Banks of North Carolina," *Annals*, Association of American Geographers, 56 (1966), 699–711.

DOLAN, ROBERT, AND KENTON BOSSERMAN, "Shoreline Erosion and the Lost Colony," *Annals*, Association of American Geographers, 62 (1972), 424–26.

FROST, MELVIN J., "Florida Marshlands to Cattle Ranches: The Changing Landscape," *Ecumene*, 6 (May 1974), 19–24.

HURT, HARRY, "The Boomsday Book," *Texas Monthly*, 4 (October 1976), 136.

JENNA, WILLIAM, *Metropolitan Miami: A Demographic Overview*. Coral Gables, Fla.: University of Miami Press, 1972.

KERR, ALEX, *The Texas Reef Shell Industry*. Austin: University of Texas, Bureau of Business Research, Texas Industry Series 11, 1967.

KNIFFEN, FRED B., *Louisiana, Its Land and People*. Baton Rouge: Louisiana State University Press, 1968.

LEWIS, PEIRCE F., *New Orleans: The Making of an Urban Landscape*. Cambridge, Mass.: Ballinger Publishing Company, 1976.

LONGBRAKE, DAVID B., AND WOODROW W. NICHOLS, JR., *Sunshine and Shadows in Metropolitan Miami*. Cambridge, Mass.: Ballinger Publishing Company, 1976.

MARCUS, ROBERT B., AND EDWARD A. FERNALD, *Florida: A Geographical Approach*. Dubuque, Iowa: Kendall/Hunt Publishing Company, 1974.

MEALOR, W. THEODORE, JR., AND MERLE C. PRUNTY, JR., "Open-Range Ranching in Southern Florida," *Annals*, Association of American Geographers, 66 (1976), 360–76.

PADGETT, HERBERT R., "Physical and Cultural Associations on the Louisiana Coast," *Annals*, Association of American Geographers, 59 (1969), 481–93.

PALMER, MARTHA E., AND MARJORIE N. RUSH, "Houston," in *Contemporary Metropolitan America, Vol. 4, Twentieth Century Cities*, ed. John S. Adams, pp. 107–49. Cambridge, Mass.: Ballinger Publishing Company, 1976.

PSUTY, NORBET P., AND PAUL SANFORD SALTER, "Land-Use Competition on a Geomorphic Surface: The Mango in Southern Florida," *Annals*, Association of American Geographers, 59 (1969), 264–79.

RANDALL, DUNCAN P., "Wilmington, North Carolina: The Historical Development of a Port City," *Annals*, Association of American Geographers, 58 (1968), 441–51.

SALTER, PAUL SANFORD, "Changing Agricultural Patterns on the South Carolina Sea Islands," *Journal of Geography*, 67 (1968), 223–28.

SCHULTZ, RONALD R., AND THOMAS J. CAMARCO, JR., "Migration to and from Southeast Florida, 1965–70," *Southeastern Geographer*, 17 (May 1977), 33–48.

STANSFIELD, CHARLES A., JR., "Changes in the Geography of Passenger Liner Ports: The Rise of the Southeastern Florida Ports," *Southeastern Geographer*, 17 (May 1977), 25–32.

TONER, M. F., "Farming the Everglades," *National Parks and Conservation Magazine*, 50 (August 1976), 4–9.

VANDERHILL, BURKE G., "Traffic Generation on the Apalachicola-Chattahoochee-Flint Waterway," *Southeastern Geographer,* 15 (May 1975), 1–16.

WESTERN, JOHN, "Social Groups and Activity Patterns in Houma, Louisiana," *Geographical Review,* 63 (1973), 301–20.

WOOD, ROLAND, AND EDWARD A. FERNALD, *The New Florida Atlas: Patterns of the Sunshine State.* Tampa, Fla.: Trend Publications, 1974.

ZIEGLER, JOHN M., "Origin of the Sea Islands of the Southeastern United States," *Geographical Review,* 49 (1959), 222–37.

THE ANGLO-AMERICAN HEARTLAND

12

One of the most productive, prosperous, and self-sufficient regions in the world is the northeastern interior of the United States and adjacent southeastern Ontario. This is the Anglo-American Heartland, a broad region with moderately high population density and enormous economic productivity. For example, its population is only two-thirds that of France and Britain combined, but its gross output (industrial, agricultural, and mineral) is more than twice as great.

It is a region with a remarkably favorable combination of physical factors for the development of agriculture. These, in combination with intelligent farm management and the considerable application of inanimate energy, make this the largest area of highly productive farmland in Anglo-America—if not in the world. The Heartland Region is also the industrial core of the continent. Although containing less than one-third of Anglo-America's population, it has well over half of the manufactural output of both countries.

This widespread and well-balanced regional economy provides much of the stability and diversity that have permitted the people of the United States and Canada to enjoy, on the average, the world's highest standard of living. And yet it is not economic muscle alone that gives this region its "heartland" appellation. This is in many ways the "core" region of Anglo-American society. Here are exemplified the ideas, attitudes, and institutions that are most representative of the way of life in Anglo-America. Here the population amalgam is most thoroughly distilled, and the "average" American or Canadian (not, however, the average French-Canadian) is most likely to be found. The region possesses an inordinate amount of political power, at least in part because the American political system has given rural people a greater proportional representation than urbanites in legislative bodies and the rural population is larger here than in other parts of the continent.

The Heartland is the transportation and communication hub of the continent. Its productive lands and relatively level terrain stimulate and make feasible a dense network of highways and railroads. Waterway traffic on the lower Great Lakes and the major Midwestern rivers—Ohio, Mississippi, Missouri, and Illinois—continues to increase. Air transportation among the cities of the region is remarkably dense. Indeed, Chicago is by all odds the leading railway center of the world and has the busiest commercial airport in Anglo-America.

There are some very important parts of Anglo-America that are not located in the Heartland: the great decision-making centers of New York, Washington, and Montreal; the rapidly growing cities of the West and South; the totality of French Canada; and many others. Nevertheless, the role of the Heartland Region in the life of Anglo-America is critically important. In this regard Robert McLaughlin noted, "Had any of America's other regions been detached over the course of history, the United States would not be the nation as we know it—but it would still exist. Without the Heartland, however, the United States would be inconceivable."[1] Wilbur Zelinsky declared the region to be "justly regarded as the most modal, the section most nearly representative of the national average."[2]

The Heartland encompasses a smaller portion of Canada, but that portion (southeastern Ontario) contains such a concentration of wealth, power, and population that it is often regarded as the "norm" of Canadian life and has had a more important policy-making role than any other part of the country.[3] The "Americanism" of southern Ontario has attracted much attention from scholars, as has its cultural affinity with the United States Midwest.[4]

The Anglo-American Heartland, then, is a broad region that encompasses what is generally referred to as the Midwest. It includes, however, somewhat more than the cultural Midwest: western Kentucky and the Nashville Basin are more properly "Southern" in culture, western New York is only marginally Midwestern, and the term is rarely used in southeastern Ontario.

[1] Robert McLaughlin and the Editors of Time-Life Books, *The Heartland* (New York: Time Incorporated, 1967), p. 16.

[2] Wilbur Zelinsky, *The Cultural Geography of the United States* (Englewood Cliffs, N.J.: Prentice-Hall, Inc., 1973), p. 128.

[3] John Warkentin, "Southern Ontario: A View from the West," *Canadian Geographer*, 10 (1966), 157.

[4] See, for example, Andrew H. Clark, "Geographical Diversity and the Personality of Canada," in *Readings in Canadian Geography*, ed. Robert M. Irving (Toronto: Holt, Rinehart and Winston of Canada, 1972), pp. 9–10; and Zelinsky, *Cultural Geography of the United States*, p. 128.

extent of the region

The Anglo-American Heartland occupies only part of the vast interior plain of North America; it is set off from adjoining regions, particularly to the west and north, by imprecise and transitional boundaries (fig. 12–1).

The eastern and southern margins of the region are relatively definite because of land-use contrasts that are associated with physiographic differences. The interior lowlands support more intensive, diversified, and prosperous agricultural activities, as well as more and bigger cities, than do the slopelands of the Appalachians and Ozarks; thus, the regional boundary generally follows the topographic trend from northernmost New York State south and west to the Missouri-Kansas border, with a southerly salient to include parts of western Kentucky and Tennessee.

The northern boundary of the Heartland Region approximately follows the southern edge of the Laurentian Shield, where differences in bedrock geology are accompanied by related vegetation and agricultural variations. On the west the Heartland merges with the Great Plains; scanty rainfall separates the prairie margin from the short-grass country of the plains at about the 98th meridian. Here precipitation is inadequate for the profitable production of unirrigated corn, and this crop tends to be replaced by those that are more drought-resistant. The western boundary of the Heartland Region is generalized as the transition from corn-dominated farming on the east to wheat-grain sorghums-pasture-dominated land use on the west.

The Heartland is by no means the largest region in Anglo-America; several exceed it in areal extent. It has, however, the greatest population of any major region, as well as the largest economic output. Despite the magnitude of these factors it is difficult to subdivide the region in a satisfactory manner, for there is an essential homogeneity of pattern and interdependence of relationship of most elements of geographical signifi-

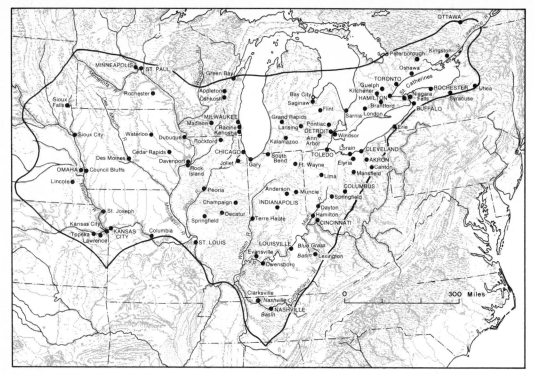

fig. 12–1 The Anglo-American Heartland (base map copyright A. K. Lobeck; reprinted by permission of Hammond, Inc.).

cance. It is, however, possible to delineate meaningful subregions on the basis of limited factors, for example, agriculture.

The Corn Belt is a widely accepted term applied to the core of the Heartland; it is an east-west band extending from central Ohio to eastern Nebraska in which the predominance of corn in the agricultural scene has long been recognized. North of the Corn Belt, and most prominent in Minnesota-Wisconsin-Michigan, is the Dairy Belt. Southeast of the Corn Belt is a tobacco and general farming area. But if subdivision by agricultural pattern is meaningful, on a more general geographical basis it is not, unless a relatively large number of subregions is recognized. Accordingly, we will not be concerned with delimiting subregions.

the look of the landscape

The landscape of the Anglo-American Heartland has a certain similarity of appearance throughout its length and breadth, which is another element of unity in the region. The conspicuous environmental features are absence of slopeland, prevalence of trees, and abundance of small bodies of water. The terrain is flat to undulating throughout and extends to a relatively featureless horizon in all directions. Despite the extensive acreage of cropland and pasture, trees are present in many portions of the region: wide-branching oaks, maples, and other hardwoods in the forests and woodlots, and tall cottonwoods and poplars along the stream courses. Large lakes, with the exception of the Great Lakes, are uncommon, but thousands of small marshes and ponds dot the landscape everywhere north of the Ohio and Missouri rivers.

No other human activity is nearly so conspicuous as agriculture; crops and pastures cover more of the land than does anything else. Appearance, of course, greatly varies with the season. In spring, for example, deep green fields of winter wheat, pale green pastures, and still paler green blocks of oats are just breaking through the earth, and black, brown, and tan, depending on the type of soil, squares of land are plowed and ready to be planted to corn and soybeans.

Of great prominence in the landscape, particularly if viewed from the air, is the rectangularity of areal patterns. Primarily as a result of the systematic rectangular land survey of the eighteenth century, landholdings in most of the region have right-angled boundaries. Thus, the fields and farms appear as a gigantic checkerboard intersected by a gridiron pattern of roads, which mostly cross at one-mile intervals. Modern interstate highways may appear as diagonal scars superimposed on the grid, but the functional roadway network of the rural Heartland is almost as straight and angular as it ever was.

Conspicuous farmsteads dot the patterned rectangles of the farmlands. Although large and pleasant, the farmhouses may suffer in comparison with the architectural gems of New England, New York, eastern Pennsylvania, and Maryland, but the total farmstead is usually large and impressive. The two-story farmhouse, normally ringed with trees, is dwarfed by imposing and generally well-kept outbuildings, such as huge barns, corncribs, silos, machine sheds, dairy buildings, and chicken houses (fig. 12–2).

Villages and small towns occur at regular intervals over the land, delicately sprawling around a road junction or alongside a railway line. They lie flat against the earth, with only a water tower or grain elevator rising above the leafy green trees. Businesses are clustered along one or two

fig. 12–2 A typical Heartland farmstead near St. Cloud, Minnesota.

main streets, but commercial bustle is usually lacking, for most small towns are stagnating or withering anachronisms in an era of metropolitan expansion and transportation ease. The residential sections are characterized by big old homes, sometimes frame and sometimes brick, whose unused front porches look across broad lawns to tree-lined streets (fig. 12–3).

Large and small cities are spaced more irregularly across the region. In contrast to the serenity of the small towns, they are places of constant movement. These are representative Anglo-American cities, sprawling outward around the periphery

fig. 12–3 A quiet residential street in a small Heartland town. This is Fairfield in eastern Iowa.

fig. 12–4 At the upper end of the Heartland urban scale is the metropolis. This is the business heart of Detroit (courtesy Michigan Travel Commission).

and rising upward in the center (fig. 12–4). Above all, the urban centers are foci of activity: hubs of transport routes that converge from all directions with a steady stream of incoming and outgoing traffic.

the physical setting

Few, if any, large regions of the world have a more favorable combination of climate, terrain, and soils for agriculture. J. Russell Smith's classic accolade, "The Corn Belt is a gift of the gods,"[5] also almost equally applies to other parts of the Heartland Region.

TERRAIN

Almost all the Heartland Region is in the vast Central Lowland of Anglo-America. Throughout the lowland the land is mostly level to gently undulating, with occasional steeper slopes marking low hills, ridges, or escarpments. The entire region is underlain by relatively horizontal sedimentary strata, one of the most extensive expanses of such bedrock to be found on earth.[6] These various sedimentaries—mainly limestone, sandstone, shale, and dolomite—are relatively old, mostly originating in Paleozoic time. Their structural arrangement is generally subdued, consisting of broad shallow basins and low domes.

The limited relief and gentle slopes of the region are partly ascribed to the underlying structure, but in large measure are the result of glacial action during Pleistocene time (fig. 12–5). The several ice advances of the last million years had lasting effects, as they leveled the topography from its preglacial profile. There was some planing of hilltops and gouging of valleys, but for the most part ice action in this region was depositional rather than erosional in nature;[7] thus, it was the filling of valleys rather than the wearing down of hills that produced the present land surface. Over most of the region the bedrock has been buried many tens or hundreds of feet by glacial debris; for the Corn Belt section glacial drift is thought to average more than 100 feet in depth. The greater part of the Heartland is therefore indebted in no small measure to the Ice Age for its flat lands and productive soils.

Impaired drainage and loess are two other significant legacies of the Pleistocene in the region. The areas of more recent glaciation, the so-called Wisconsin stage, contain many marshes, bogs, ponds, and lakes because "normal" drainage patterns have not as yet had time to develop since the most recent ice recession (about 8,000 years ago). Beyond (south of) the margin of Wisconsin glaciation there are extensive areas that are mantled with deep deposits of loess, which is fine-textured windblown silt, believed to have originated from the grinding action of ice on rock, which often produces fertile soils.

[5] J. Russell Smith and M. O. Phillips, *North America* (New York: Harcourt, Brace and Co., 1942), p. 360.

[6] Wallace E. Akin, *The North Central United States* (Princeton, N.J.: D. Van Nostrand Company, 1968), p. 8.

[7] William D. Thornbury, *Regional Geomorphology of the United States* (New York: John Wiley & Sons, Inc., 1965), p. 218.

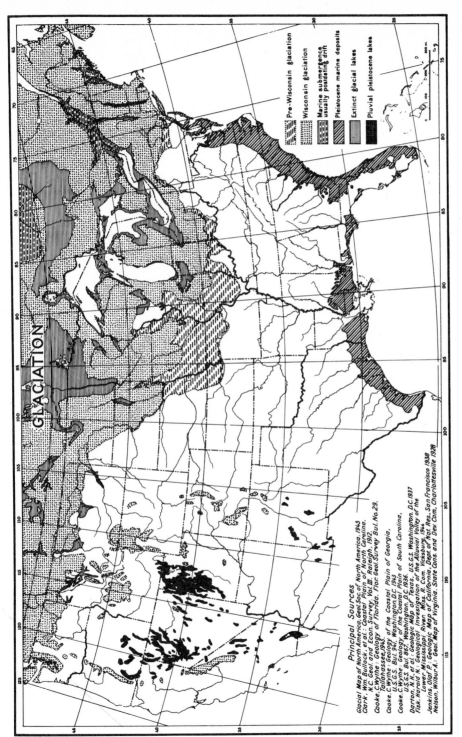

Principal Sources

Glacial Map of North America. Geol. Soc. of North America. 1945
Clark, Wm. Bullock, et al.: Coastal Plain of North Carolina.
  N.C. Geol. and Econ. Survey, Vol. III. Raleigh. 1912.
Cooke, C. Wythe: Geology of Florida. Flor. Geol. Survey Bul. No. 29.
  Tallahassee, 1945.
Cooke, C. Wythe: Geology of the Coastal Plain of Georgia.
  U.S.G.S. Bul. 941. Washington, D.C. 1943
Cooke, C. Wythe: Geology of the Coastal Plain of South Carolina.
  U.S.G.S. Bul. 867. Washington, D.C. 1936.
Darton, N.H., et al.: Geologic Map of Texas. U.S.G.S. Washington, D.C. 1937
Fisk, Harold N.: Geological Investigation of the Alluvial Valley of the
  Lower Mississippi River. Miss. R. Com. Vicksburg. 1944.
Jenkins, Olaf P.: Geologic Map of California. Dept. of Nat. Res. San Francisco 1938
Nelson, Wilbur A.: Geol. Map of Virginia. State Cons. and Dev. Com. Charlottesville 1928

fig. 12–5 Glacial conditions in the United
States and southern Canada during the
Pleistocene Epoch. The continental ice
sheets penetrated further south in the
Heartland Region than anywhere else (map
prepared by Agricultural Research Service,
U.S. Department of Agriculture).

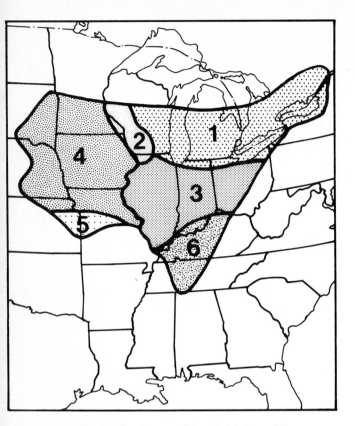

fig. 12-6 Topographic subdivisions of the Heartland: (1) Great Lakes, (2) Driftless Area, (3) Till Plain, (4) Dissected Till Plain, (5) Osage Plains, and (6) Interior Low Plateaus.

There are several relatively discrete topographic sections in the Heartland Region, with characteristics sufficiently distinctive to warrant separate mention (fig. 12-6).

The northeastern part of the region, from the Upper St. Lawrence Valley in Ontario–New York to south-central Wisconsin, is the *Great Lakes* (1) section where large and small lakes dominate the landscape. Two of the Great Lakes are entirely and two are partially within this section, as are thousands of smaller bodies of water. There are many prominent examples of glacial or glaciofluvial deposition: drumlins, eskers, outwash plains, and particularly, the long irregular ridges of terminal moraines. Several significant scarps occur in this section, the

most conspicuous of which is the Niagara Escarpment. Its abrupt cliffs of gray dolomite overlook the gentler glaciated plain between lakes Erie and Ontario, then arc around the north side of lakes Huron and Michigan, and reappear in Wisconsin.

In southwestern Wisconsin and adjacent Minnesota, Iowa, and Illinois lies the *Driftless Area* (2), an unglaciated island in a sea of glacial drift. Missed by the continental ice sheets, it differs topographically and economically from the surrounding territory. Its landscape, consisting mostly of low but steep-sided hills, is similar to the one that existed before the glacier came.

The central portion of the Heartland, from central Ohio to eastern Iowa, is the *Till Plain* (3) section. The terrain varies from extremely flat to gently rolling, the remarkable lack of relief presumably resulting from cumulative deposition of at least three ice advances. Drainage is much better integrated here than in the Great Lakes section, and there are fewer lakes and marshes.

The *Dissected Till Plain* (4) occupies the northwestern portion of the region, extending from Minnesota to Missouri. It is covered with till from earlier glacial advances, and there has been more time for stream erosion to modify the surface; hence there is a greater degree of dissection and a general absence of lakes as well as a lack of terminal moraines.

In the southwestern corner of the Heartland is the *Osage Plains* (5) section that extends from Missouri southwestward into Texas. This is an area that was essentially unaffected by glaciation and is represented by a nearly featureless plain developed on horizontal sedimentary beds.

In the southeastern portion of the Heartland Region is a section known as the *Interior Low Plateaus* (6), although most of the terrain has the appearance of low hill country. This area is structurally and topographically complex, with a series of cuestas, escarpments, basins, major fault lines, and some intrusive vulcanism. Much of the area is referred to as the Highland Rim; it consists mostly of low hills and scarp ridges and has a great many karst features, particularly sinkholes and caverns. There are two famous and fertile basins in this section, the Nashville Basin and the Bluegrass Basin, that are flat lands surrounded mostly by infacing escarpments.

CLIMATE

The region's interior location in the eastern part of the continent results in a humid continental climate that is noted for significant seasonal and abrupt day-to-day changes in weather conditions. Climatic patterns are broad and transitional across the region, since there is relatively uniform relief and no significant topographic barriers. Thus, temperatures and length of growing season increase more or less uniformly from north to south, and precipitation generally decreases from east to west.

Summer is a time of hot days and relatively warm nights. Humidity is generally high, and well over half of the total annual precipitation falls during this season. Thunderstorms are common in summer, and tornadoes are frequent.

Although summer conditions are quite benign for crop growing, winter is generally severe. The cold weather is not continuous, for there are periodic spells of relative warmth with the passing of low pressure centers. But cold fronts are frequent, often accompanied by blizzards and followed by anticyclonic spells of clear and very cold weather. Snow is commonplace throughout the region, although only in the far north does it remain unmelted on the ground for long periods.

The transitional seasons, spring and fall, are usually brief but dramatic, with rapid shifts of temperature and abrupt periods of storminess. Flooding is a perennial natural hazard in spring and early summer, sometimes resulting from heavy spring rains falling on frozen ground but often simply the result of prolonged rain with rapid runoff. In any event, the densely populated flood plains of the region's major rivers are frequently threatened with inundation.

NATURAL VEGETATION

The region's original vegetation consisted of forest and grass. The eastern part was forested. Ohio, Indiana, southern Michigan, southern Wisconsin, and southern Illinois all were a part of the oak-hickory southern hardwood forest, and the Kentucky Bluegrass and the Nashville Basin were a part of the chestnut–oak–yellow poplar southern hardwood forest. The forest near the northern boundary of the region was characterized by conifers on the sandy soils and by magnificent stands of hardwoods on the clay lands. Elsewhere the forest consisted wholly of hardwoods.

Southern Minnesota, all of Iowa, central Illinois, northern Missouri, and eastern Nebraska and Kansas composed the prairie, a vast billowy sea of virgin grass without timber except along the streams. It was tall grass with long blades and stiff stems, growing to a height of one to three feet and frequently six to eight feet. People and horses could be lost in it. The trees growing along the streams were chiefly cottonwoods, oaks, and elms in the western portion, with occasional sycamores and walnuts farther east.

The true prairie extended from Illinois (small patches existed in western Ohio and northern Indiana) to about the 98th meridian, where it was gradually replaced by the short grass of the steppe. The boundaries of the prairie were never sharply defined. They were not the meeting place of two contrasted vegetation belts; rather they were broad mobile zones that moved with pronounced changes in precipitation. Many interesting theories for the origin of the prairie have been advanced, but none as yet has been wholly acceptable to botanists, plant ecologists, and plant geographers.[8]

SOILS

Nowhere else on the continent is there such a large area that combines generally fertile

[8] See James C. Malin, *The Grassland of North America* (Lawrence: University of Kansas Press, 1948), pp. 295–98.

soils with a humid climate. This combination is at its best in the region's core, the Corn Belt. The Bluegrass area and the Nashville Basin are also highly productive. Some of the soils, however, as in central Michigan and central Wisconsin, in the Driftless Area, and in the Highland Rim of Kentucky and Tennessee, are far from rich.

Most of the region is characterized by Alfisols and Mollisols. Although the former develop under deciduous forest in the milder of the humid continental climates, the fact that they are forest soils means that in general they are less productive than the dark-brown to black Mollisols of the prairie. Still, some of the forest soils, such as those in western Ohio and north-central Indiana, yield about as well per acre as the prairie soils. It may be said that forest soils that develop on calcareous till or on limestone, granite, gneiss, and schist are superior to those that evolve from shale and sandstone. All forest soils, however, are permanently leached, acid in reaction, and poor in humus.

The true prairie soils are generally fertile. They develop in cool, moderately humid climates under the influence of grass vegetation and are characterized by a dark-brown to black topsoil underlain by well-oxidized subsoils. Being relatively well supplied with moisture, they are moderately leached and acid in reaction, and they lack a zone of lime accumulation. They are mostly silt loams and clay loams in texture and are derived largely from glacial till.

In summary, much of the eastern portion of the Heartland is dominated by Alfisols, which are gray-brown in color and have subsurface clay accumulation. In the west there is a preponderance of Mollisols, which tend to be black in color and rich in organic matter.

human occupance of the heartland

The Heartland has always been a productive region for goods that were valuable in each period of its history: game, furs, crops, minerals, and factory output. Thus it has been a region that was coveted and struggled over by a diversity of peoples who learned of its riches. Three great nations as well as a dozen major Indian tribes fought for supremacy here, and the early history of the region is punctuated by battles, massacres, wars, and alliances.

Once white settlers were able to overcome the twin barriers of Appalachian topography and hostile Indians, they poured into the Heartland. The Indians, who frequently had fought each other, readily formed defensive alliances—often encouraged by French, British, or American leaders—in opposition to the intruders. But the combination of inferior firepower and lack of immunity to new diseases soon turned the tide against any Indian host, and they were decimated or pushed westward. Then the pageant of settlement spread and intensified, with little bloodshed but much conflict between competing groups.

ABORIGINAL OCCUPANCE

Relatively little is known about the earlier aboriginal inhabitants of the region. Prehistoric Indians occupied many areas for perhaps a century, beginning about 300 B.C. They are generally referred to as "Mound Builders," and just about the only landscape evidence of their presence is the large number of burial mounds and other scattered earthen structures.

At the time of European contact there were many well-organized tribes in what is now the Heartland Region. These were mostly forest dwellers of the Algonkian linguistic group. There were, however, Iroquoian tribes on the northeastern fringe, including the important Hurons in southern Ontario and Siouan tribes (especially the Sioux and the Osage) on the western prairie margin. The forest Indians were semisedentary in pattern, their economy combining hunting with farming (corn, beans, squash, and tobacco). In some areas, as with the Hurons north of Lake Erie, a considerable section of forest was cleared for agriculture, although in most cases such cleared land had again reverted to woodland between the times the Indians were expelled and the white settlers arrived in any numbers.

FRENCH EXPLORATION AND SETTLEMENT

Most of the early explorers and pioneering fur traders in the region were French. During the seventeenth and the early part of the eighteenth centuries, various French individuals and expeditions explored most of the major waterways of the Heartland. They were primarily interested in fur and wanted to monopolize the fur trade; accordingly they helped various Indian tribes to keep colonial settlers east of the Appalachians.

The French made little attempt at colonization, but eventually they founded a number of settlements that were the first towns of the region. Most started out as trading posts, forts, or missions and were located along the Mississippi River, the Wabash River, or near the Great Lakes. Cahokia and Kaskaskia, in what is now Illinois, date from 1699 and became thriving wilderness towns in a short while.[9] Vincennes, on the Wabash River, was founded soon afterward. In 1701 the French established a fort where Detroit now stands, but it was not incorporated as a village for another century. The only original French settlement in southern Ontario that still exists was also on the Detroit River.[10] St. Louis, founded in 1764, was another French trading post; it soon became the principal settlement in the Upper Mississippi Basin.

THE OPENING OF THE MIDWEST TO SETTLEMENT

Britain gained title to most of the present Heartland Region in 1763 by overwhelming the French in Canada. An Indian alliance, led by the Ottawa tribe, immediately was formed to keep the British out of the region. The tribes destroyed eight British forts and laid siege to Detroit. Eventually the siege was raised, but the British government agreed to reserve that part of the continent between the Appalachians and the Mississippi solely for Indian occupance—a highly impractical resolution, considering the sentiment and politics of the time. Within two decades the American colonies had successfully revolted against the Crown, and the new nation inherited control of the trans-Appalachian Midwest by virtue of the surrender of land claims by the states of the Eastern seaboard.

The first Congress of the United States drew up ordinances in 1785 and 1787 to provide for the systematic survey and disposition of lands in the "Northwest Territories"—the territory northwest of the Ohio River—that have proved to be some of the most enduring legislation ever promulgated. A grid system, based on principal meridians and baseline parallels, was staked out to divide the entire area into a township and range pattern, a township to consist of 36 sections of 640 acres (one square mile) each (fig. 12-7). Thus the land could be accurately surveyed and realistically sold on a sight-unseen basis. The result of this surveying system can be seen in the field, land ownership, settlement, and road patterns of most of the Heartland today.

Provision was soon made for a territory to be admitted to the Union as a state, in all respects equal to the original states, as soon as its population reached 60,000. Ohio was admitted under this provision in 1803, although both Kentucky and Tennessee had already become states in the 1790s.

Before the time of the American Revolution, white settlement had begun on a small scale in the Bluegrass portion of Kentucky and parts of Tennessee; these areas attracted a small flood of settlers immediately after the Revolution. There was also a considerable influx into Upper Canada (southern Ontario) at this time, mostly people whose property had been confiscated in New York and other revolutionary colonies; some 10,000 such Loyalists had settled along the upper St. Lawrence and at either end of Lake Erie by 1783.

[9] Akin, *The North Central United States*, p. 43.
[10] Jacob Spelt, "Southern Ontario," in *Canada: A Geographical Interpretation*, ed. John Warkentin (Toronto: Methuen Publications, 1968), p. 340.

fig. 12-7 A range-and-township pattern of land survey was begun in the lands west of the Appalachians in 1785. A rectangular grid system, surveyed from principal meridians and base line parallels, was started in seven rows of townships ("the seven ranges") in eastern Ohio and gradually extended westward. All of the basic survey of the area shown here was completed within half a century. Detail of the range and township pattern in a portion of western Illinois is shown in the second drawing as an example of the whole. The third drawing shows the six-mile-by-six-mile grid of a typical township, with the sequential numbering of the sections.

The Ohio River was a major artery of movement during this period. Fort Duquesne had already evolved into Pittsburgh. Louisville was founded at the falls of the Ohio in 1779. Cincinnati began a decade later and soon became the principal river town.

Ohio did not attract many settlers until the recalcitrant Indians had been dealt with. During the early 1790s several thousand soldiers fought a series of battles with the "lords of the forest," finally achieving a decisive defeat of the Miamis and their allies in 1794. This opened a floodgate of in-migration, and within less than a decade Ohio had enough inhabitants to become a state.[11] Cleveland was founded in 1796. By the War of 1812 there were more than a quarter of a million people in Ohio, although the only places of significant settlement farther west were in southern Indiana and the Mississippi Valley below St. Louis.

WESTWARD EXPANSION

During the War of 1812, Tecumseh, the Shawnee chief, tried to organize a Great Lakes-to-Gulf Indian confederation to fight the United States. He was only partly successful in his mission but did persuade many tribes, from the Creeks in Alabama to the

Township 4N, Range 2E

6	5	4	3	2	1
7	8	9	10	11	12
18	17	16	15	14	13
19	20	21	22	23	24
30	29	28	27	26	25
31	32	33	34	35	36

[11] McLaughlin and the Editors of Time-Life Books, *The Heartland*, p. 51.

Chippewas in the Lake Superior country, to join the alliance. The venture ended in 1813 in a battle in Ontario; Tecumseh was killed, and the confederation collapsed. After the war most of the Heartland Indians were deported west of the Mississippi, where they were assured that the land would be theirs forever.

Settlement in the Heartland had basically flowed from three fountainheads: (1) New England, whose Puritans came by way of the Mohawk Valley; (2) the South, whose frontiersmen broke through the mountains of Kentucky and Tennessee via Cumberland Gap; and (3) Pennsylvania, whose Scotch-Irish and Germans came via Pittsburgh and the Ohio River country as well as by way of Cumberland Gap. Whereas only 1 million Americans were living west of the Appalachians in 1800 (less than 50,000 of this total in Ontario), their numbers had increased by 1820 to 2.5 million, and by 1830 to 3.5 million.

After the War of 1812 settlement rapidly expanded in the forested portions of Indiana and Illinois; these two states were admitted to the Union in 1816 and 1818 respectively. The Driftless Area of Wisconsin attracted settlers because of discoveries of lead ore. The Missouri Valley attracted enough settlement so that Missouri became a state in 1821.

The tide of settlement soon shifted to the southern Great Lakes area. Fort Dearborn (Chicago) was founded in 1816; Toledo, in 1817. The opening of the Erie Canal in 1825 was the harbinger of a reorientation of the regional transportation pattern from north-south along the rivers to an east-west axis, which was furthered by the building of more canals and the beginning of railway transportation in the 1840s. The major flow of settlers was then via the Mohawk corridor (Erie Canal route) from New York and New England.

On reaching the forest-prairie margin, in such areas as northern Illinois and eastern Iowa, the migrant settlers were puzzled by the fact that the land was clothed with grass rather than forest. They were even suspicious, reasoning that soils bearing no timber must be inferior, and for the most part they avoided the prairie.[12]

The pioneers who did settle on the prairie often chose tracts that were contiguous to forest land, which they made the real base of the farm establishment. The taming of the prairie was not easy, for the heavy soil would stick to the iron plows then in use until the plow could not move in the furrow, and many plows broke. The prairie was not really conquered until 1837, when John Deere, a blacksmith living in the tiny village of Grand Detour, Illinois, invented the steel plow. It soon became apparent that the good crop yields of the deep prairie soil would readily pay for the cost of breaking the sod. And so Illinois and Missouri were almost totally settled by 1850, as were southern Wisconsin and southern Iowa.

The more westerly cities in the region were founded at this time: Milwaukee and St. Paul in the 1840s, and Minneapolis and Kansas City in the 1850s. Intensification of settlement proceeded rapidly; southern Ontario, for example, had more than 40 percent of Canada's population by 1861. But as the frontier moved westward beyond the Heartland, there was a continual out-migration following it; if the Heartland was easy to move into, it was also easy to move out of. This was particularly true of the Ontario portion of the region.

IMMIGRANTS TO THE CITIES

After about 1880 there was a greatly increased flow of European immigrants to the Heartland, which continued through the early decades of the twentieth century. By 1920, one-sixth of the region's population was foreign-born. For the most part these immigrants settled in urban areas, often giving them a distinctive ethnic flavor, such as

[12] In 1836 Alby Smith, an Illinois pioneer, lost an election because the voters decided that anyone so stupid as to settle in the prairie should not be entrusted with the responsibilities of public office. See Harlan H. Barrows, "Geography of the Middle Illinois Valley," *Illinois Geological Survey, Bulletin 15* (Urbana: Illinois Geological Survey, 1910), p. 78.

Germans in Milwaukee or Scandinavians in Minneapolis.

In many ways the Heartland has become the true melting pot of Anglo-America. The Midwestern blend of culture, speech, and life style is the one most readily identified as the standard for the United States; in similar fashion southern Ontario represents Anglo-Canada. The large-scale and relatively recent in-migration of blacks, mostly from the Southern states, to Heartland cities furnishes a discordant note to the melting-pot concept. Prejudice and ghetto-ization are commonplace in the region, although there are numerous encouraging examples of racial harmony.

the incredible opulence of heartland agriculture

Although the economy of the region is not primarily agricultural and the regional population is not predominantly rural, the Heartland is easily the preeminent producer of crops and livestock on the continent. Its large expanse of productive agricultural land is unparalleled in Anglo-America, and despite the continuing downtrend in farm numbers and farm population, the level of farm output continues to rise. By far the greatest concentration of agricultural counties in the United States is found in this region; this is less so for Canada.

Throughout the greater part of this region the country appears to be under almost complete cultivation, with four or five farmsteads to each square mile in the eastern portion and two or three in the western portion. The farms are based on the subdivision of sections into half-sections, quarter-sections, and 40-acre plots. Corn, winter wheat, soybeans, oats, and hay are almost universal crops. Tobacco and fruits are locally important, and much land is in pasture. The region not only grows tilled crops but also supports the densest population of cattle and swine in Anglo-America.

SYSTEMS OF FARMING

Mixed farming characterizes most of the region, with a major emphasis on corn in nearly all parts. Corn has long been granted pride of place for the best land because of its high yields (in terms of both volume and value) and because of its lesser tolerance for variations in weather and soil quality than the other grains. Most other midlatitude grains, however, are also widely grown in the region, as are several oil seed crops, a great variety of vegetables, a few deciduous fruits, and a handful of specialty crops. In addition, cattle, hogs, sheep, and poultry, the principal midlatitude meat animals, are raised in great quantity.

This variety of crops and livestock is produced in several farming systems. The traditional Midwestern agricultural operation is a *general farm* in which both grains and meat animals are raised; such farms are usually not large, are normally family operated, and typically involve a small or medium-sized feedlot as the cornerstone of the operation. *Cash grain farms* are particularly prominent in the central part of the Corn Belt and are dependent on growing corn, soybeans, and feed grains for sale. Widely scattered over the region are *livestock farms,* in which cattle, swine, or chickens are fed or grazed to the almost total exclusion of crop-growing. In the northern part of the region and around the larger cities are numerous *dairy farms,* which yield fresh milk for urban consumption or supply dairy factories that make processed milk products, butter, or cheese. *Specialty crop farms* emphasize the intensive growing of one or more nongrain crops, usually tobacco, vegetables, or fruits.

FARM OPERATIONS

Production per acre and per work-hour has been increasing steadily throughout the region. Annual yields are such that the average farmer now produces enough food to supply five dozen people. This has been made possible by the increased use of a host of techniques and equipment, most of them involving the substitution of capital for labor. More and more the operation of even a small farm requires an investment base of hundreds of thousands of dollars.

Machinery The Heartland farmer today is essentially a machine tender and a power user. In addition to such ordinary machinery as tractors and trucks, there are all sorts of other mechanized equipment, such as combines, corn pickers, seeders, high-wheeled platforms for detasseling corn, sprayers, mechanical hay balers, hydraulic loaders, manure spreaders, flame weed killers, push-button-operated auger feeders, liquid manure handlers, automatic conveyor-belt feed dispensers and egg gatherers for poultry houses, and potato dig-and-bag machines. In Illinois and Iowa, for example, there is an average of more than two tractors per farm, and three-fourths of all farms in these states have mechanical corn pickers. Mechanization, by making it profitable to farm on a larger scale, is a major cause of the increasing size of farms. It takes larger acreages to cover the first high cost of machinery and at the same time keep production costs low. In turn, machinery encourages new farming methods.

Fertilizer The Heartland was originally extremely fertile, but many decades of cropping have been depleting the soil of its plant-food reserves. Corn normally requires more fertilizer than any other major crop on the continent. Hence, the farmers are using fertilizers in ever-growing quantities, and it is understandable that nearly 40 percent of all farmland fertilizer in the nation is applied in the Heartland Region.

Pesticides Farmers are engaged in a constant battle against insects and plant diseases, and their attacks on these pests become ever more sophisticated, even as the pests themselves develop immunities to the chemical weapons. A continuing stream of new and complex pesticides is being used, and the techniques and equipment for dispensing the sprays and mists and powders are also continually being refined. This is not to say that there will not be occasional severe crop losses, but in general no other large agricultural region in the world is so thoroughly under control from an entomological standpoint. Since the mid-1960s there has been growing apprehension concerning the effect of pesticides on the ecosystems of the continent, particularly in regions of high agricultural productivity where pesticides tend to be relied on most heavily. The resulting furor—exaggerated by those who would totally eliminate all pesticides and those who deny any harmful effects at all from chemical applications—has led to a searching scrutiny of the entire pesticide question, philosophy as well as technique. The most controversial of the common pesticides, DDT, has now been banned, and a more balanced pattern of pesticide usage is likely to result.

Plant Breeding Improved varieties of plant seeds have also contributed significantly to increased crop yields. Plant breeders develop hybrid seeds that give vigor or resistance to disease, tolerance of cold or drought, or simply higher yields. Most farmers buy new seed every year, usually from large companies whose sole business is developing and growing crop seeds.

Supplemental Irrigation The artificial watering of crops has long been an accepted necessity in much of western Anglo-America, but only in recent years has irrigation become important in the East. Average annual precipitation is adequate for most midlatitude crops east of the Missouri River, but variations from the average, as well as seasonal fluctuations, have resulted in decreased vigor of growth and on occasion even in crop failures. Supplemental irrigation can eliminate these hazards. Sprinkler irrigation, using lightweight aluminum pipes, is widespread; the most common sprinkler system, called center pivot (discussed in chapter 13), has spread very rapidly since the early 1970s and now accounts for nearly half of the total irrigated acreage in the region.

Drainage In most parts of the Heartland, particularly in the northeast and in the northwest, there are drainage problems. These areas, generally on old glacial lakebeds or till plains, normally did not require complete reclamation, as in many coastal zones. But the establishment of artificial drainage as an adjunct to a deficient natural system of surface and internal soil drainage has been one of the surest methods of increasing cultivated acreage and yields.

Specialization Changing technology has made crop diversification and rotation less necessary in the region. The trend to specialize more and diversify less is especially pronounced on the better lands, particularly involving a concentration on corn and soybeans at the expense of hay crops and small grains. Traditional Corn Belt farmers grew crops that could be sold for cash or fed to livestock. Depending on the crop-livestock price ratio, they could shift from marketing grain to marketing meat, or vice versa. But more recently farmers have tended more to be either cash-grain farmers or livestock feeders, without fluctuating from one to the other.[13] There is also a decrease in animal diversification. Horses are mostly gone except in racehorse-breeding areas such as the Kentucky Bluegrass. Poultry is mostly a thing of the past on general farms; chickens and turkeys are concentrated on specialty farms. There is even a consolidation trend in hog raising.

FARM MANAGEMENT

An interesting and significant characteristic of agriculture in the Heartland Region is the persistence of the family farm. The concept

[13] John Fraser Hart, "A Map of the Agricultural Implosion," *Proceedings,* Association of American Geographers, 2 (1970), 71.

of the relatively small family farm has been one of America's traditional and cherished virtues. Increasingly in recent years, however, the structure of agriculture has been changing; there are many references to "corporate farming," "farm firms," and "agribusiness." The dynamic trends of Anglo-American farming since World War II emphasize the "industrial" aspects of agriculture. Although only 10 percent of United States farms can be classed as corporate farms, they produce 40 percent of the total value of farm products that are marketed.

Within the Heartland Region, however, corporate farming is much less significant than elsewhere. Family farms continue to dominate the agricultural scene not only in terms of farm numbers and area but also in total and proportional output. Corporate farming is less than half as notable in the Heartland as it is in the Inland South and has less than one-sixth the significance that it does in California.

This general situation prevails in all aspects of Heartland agriculture. For example, perhaps the most prominent trend in livestock feedlots in the United States is their increasing size. But in the Heartland, which is by far the largest cattle-feeding region, very few large-scale feedlots have been developed, and the great majority of all feedlot operations involve only a few dozen animals.

CROPS

Despite this tendency toward specialization, the Heartland is the classical region of mixed crop-and-livestock farming in Anglo-America. The mixture, however, mostly involves grains and hay crops, with a decided emphasis on products that can be used as feed for livestock.

Corn Corn (maize) thrives under the favorable conditions of hot, humid summer weather; fertile, well-drained, loamy soils; and level to rolling terrain. No other country has this favorable combination of growing conditions over such a wide territory; thus the United States produces about 40 percent

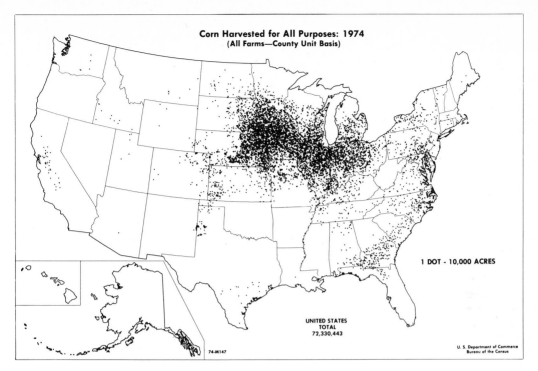

Corn Harvested for All Purposes: 1974
(All Farms—County Unit Basis)

1 DOT - 10,000 ACRES

UNITED STATES
TOTAL
72,330,443

U. S. Department of Commerce
Bureau of the Census

74-M147

fig. 12–8 Corn is the great American cereal, and the Heartland grows the bulk of it. The Corn Belt subregion alone produces nearly one-half the national total.

of the world's corn, most of which is grown in this region (fig. 12–8).

Corn-growing techniques have changed significantly since World War II. Up until that time it was planted in a "checkrow" (equally spaced in two directions) or other broadly spaced pattern, generally without fertilizer and normally rotated on at least a three-year cycle with other crops such as winter wheat, oats, and clover. Under those circumstances, Corn Belt yields averaged 35 to 40 bushels per acre. Genetic and agronomic technological changes have made crop rotation and diversification less necessary, and today corn is seldom grown in a rotational cycle in this region.[14] The seeds, furthermore, are planted in much greater numbers in more closely spaced rows, and there is heavy application of fertilizer and herbicide chemicals. The resulting yields in many areas are more than 150 bushels per acre; for the Corn Belt as a whole, the average yield in most years is nearly 100 bushels per acre.[15]

The principal corn-growing areas are still in the heart of the Corn Belt, from central Indiana to western Iowa; this section also achieves the highest average yields (fig. 12–9). Development of higher-yielding, short-season, vigorous corn hybrids has permitted the expansion of corn into drier country westward and colder country north-

[14] Walter M. Kollmorgen, "Farms and Farming in the American Midwest," in *Problems and Trends in American Geography*, ed. Saul B. Cohen (New York: Basic Books, Inc., 1967), p. 82.

[15] Donald D. Durost and Warren R. Bailey, "What's Happened to Farming," *Contours of Change*, Yearbook of Agriculture, 1970 (Washington, D.C.: Government Printing Office, 1970), p. 3.

fig. 12–9 A typical Corn Belt scene in summer is a luxuriant field of corn with a farm woodlot in the distance and rain clouds gathering overhead (courtesy Illinois Department of Agriculture).

fig. 12–10 Even in the bleakness of winter the prominence of crop-growing, particularly corn, is clear. This scene is in southeastern Wisconsin.

ward. This has not caused an acreage increase in the United States, but in southern Ontario it has resulted in a doubling of acreage in the last two decades and a spreading of corn northward in the province. Corn continues as the dominant crop in most of the Heartland; it occupies more than twice as much acreage as any other crop in the Corn Belt (fig. 12–10). About 75 percent of all grain corn grown in the United States is in the Heartland[16]; the comparable figure for Canada is 97 percent.

In much of the core of the Corn Belt, especially Illinois and Iowa, most of the harvested corn is sold as grain. In most other parts of the region, a large share of the corn is fed to livestock—cattle, hogs, and some sheep—in the nearby area and often on the same farm where the corn is grown. In the cooler and more moist portions of the Heartland the corn is often cut while still green and is stored as ensilage for stock feed.

Soybeans Soybeans were introduced into the United States as early as 1804 but became a major crop only during the 1920s and reached really high acreage levels since the 1930s. Probably the greatest stimulus came when it was recognized that soybeans could be processed for oil.

The soybean, a shallow-rooted legume, is a heavy feeder on plant food elements in the surface soils. It is popular because it yields a heavy crop of beans; is valuable for meal and oil; makes good hay, silage, and pasturage; has few diseases; and is not attacked by pests.

The major soybean belt is approximately coextensive with the Corn Belt (fig. 12–11). The crop's climatic and soil requirements are about the same as for corn. Of the region's crops, only corn brings in more money.

No crop in twentieth century Anglo-America has experienced such expanded production as the soybean. The United

[16] Fully half of all United States grain corn is grown in the three states of Iowa, Illinois, and Indiana.

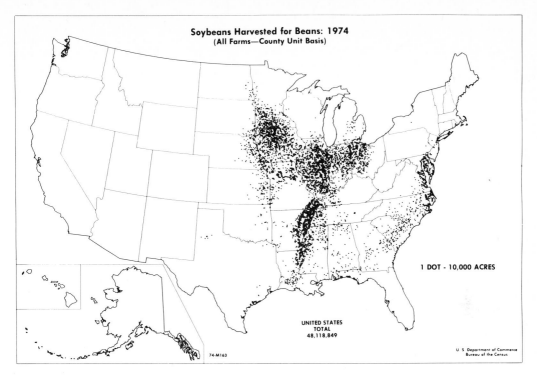

Soybeans Harvested for Beans: 1974
(All Farms—County Unit Basis)

1 DOT - 10,000 ACRES

UNITED STATES
TOTAL
48,118,849

74-M163

U.S. Department of Commerce
Bureau of the Census

fig. 12–11 The United States is the world's leading producer of soybeans, and the Heartland is its outstanding growing region.

States is now the world's leading producer (75 percent) and leading exporter (90 percent) of soybeans. Soybeans are second only to corn as a source of cash farm income to American farmers and are usually the leading agricultural export of this country. Although the most rapid recent production growth rate has been in the Inland South, the Heartland Region is still the main source of soybean output (fig. 12–12). Nearly two-thirds of national production is in the Heartland; the four leading states are Illinois, Iowa, Indiana, and Missouri. Export demand continues to grow apace; about one-third of total United States production is shipped abroad, particularly to Japan.

Oats Oats were long the second most widely grown crop in the Heartland, but in recent years they have been noticeably sur-

fig. 12–12 A contoured soybean field in central Illinois (courtesy USDA Soil Conservation Service).

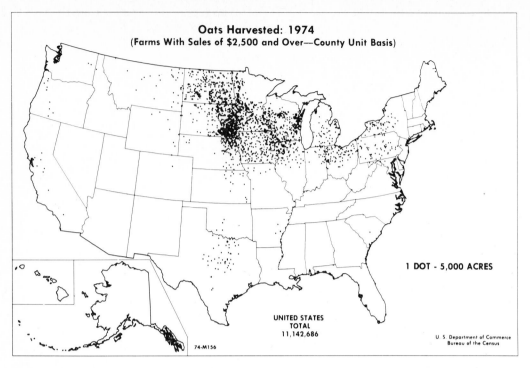

Oats Harvested: 1974
(Farms With Sales of $2,500 and Over—County Unit Basis)

1 DOT - 5,000 ACRES

UNITED STATES
TOTAL
11,142,686

U. S. Department of Commerce
Bureau of the Census

74-M156

fig. 12–13 Oats are a crop that is widely grown
in the more humid parts of the United States
and are of major importance in the Heartland.

passed by soybeans; nevertheless, the region remains the most important oats-growing area in Anglo-America (fig. 12–13). Unlike other small grains, oats do not compete with corn during seeding, harvesting, and threshing. Oats are seeded in the spring before work on the corn crop begins and are cut in summer when corn cultivation is about over. Thus, the farmer is kept busy throughout most of the summer.

Oats, often used as a "nurse crop" for clover, alfalfa, and timothy, are grown primarily as feed for livestock. Oats are fed mostly on the farms where produced. This results from the crop's low value per unit of bulk and its limited industrial uses, which discriminate against its entering trade channels. Only about 3 percent of the crop is utilized for human consumption.

The huge acreage in oats in this region results from the crop's high feed value and

the fact that no other small grain fits so well into the labor-use pattern. Major production is in the northwestern portion of the Heartland; Minnesota, the Dakotas, and Wisconsin are the principal producing states. There has been a considerable decline in oats production over the last decade or so, particularly in the Corn Belt portion of the region but also in Ontario.

Winter Wheat An important cash crop is winter wheat. Most of the acreage is in the southern half of the region, in the southern Corn Belt and the tobacco and general farming subregions. Wheat is a secondary crop over the greater part of the region because it is less restricted in its range of adaptation. It is produced to equalize the seasonal distribution of labor, being seeded in autumn after corn cultivation is over and threshed in early summer. Winter wheat also helps to control erosion during the winter months. It is, moreover, planted to provide a "nurse crop"; when sown with hay, its quick growth shields the young hay plants from the blistering summer sun. The grain is cut sufficiently early to allow the root systems of grass to withstand the succeeding winter.

Although most Canadian production of winter wheat is in southern Ontario, it constitutes only 5 percent of the total Canadian wheat crop. In recent years, wheat acreage has been steadily declining in Ontario; principal production is in the extreme southwestern area near Lake St. Clair.

Alfalfa The legume alfalfa is well adapted to the region, especially to the prairie portion where winter rainfall is less abundant and the soils less leached and therefore higher in calcium. It thrives best on soils rich in lime. The crop has greatly increased in importance in the Corn Belt and the Dairy Belt since 1920, even in the eastern part of the Heartland. When grown in such areas, however, due consideration must be given to soil conditions, especially to the availability of phosphates and to drainage.

Since alfalfa is harvested several times each season and recovers quickly after cutting, the per-acre yield exceeds that of any other hay crop. In the short-summer dairy portion of the region, alfalfa becomes a very significant crop. Wisconsin, for example, grows almost as much alfalfa as corn. In most years, Wisconsin and Minnesota vie with California as the leading grower of alfalfa.

Other Hay Crops Numerous other crops are also planted for hay production— the so-called tame hays. None approaches alfalfa in acreage or output, but their combined total in the region is approximately double that of alfalfa. *Clover, timothy,* and *clotim mixtures* are the most widespread types of tame hay after alfalfa. Emphasis on hay production is greatest in the cooler and more moist northern portions of the region, with the largest acreage in Ontario.

Tobacco Two of the most important tobacco-growing areas in Anglo-America lie in northern and central Kentucky and in northern Tennessee. Southern Wisconsin and southwestern Ontario also are impressive producers.

The Bluegrass Basin of Kentucky is the most important tobacco-growing area in the Heartland Region. The limy soils, high in phosphorus, are among the best in Anglo-America. In the Inner Bluegrass, although more than 90 percent of the land is improved and has been producing for generations, little soil depletion has occurred. Maximum yields of burley tobacco are obtained on the silt loams and level to undulating terrain. Burley tobacco is also grown under almost identical conditions in the Nashville Basin. Originally this light, aromatic, air-cured leaf was grown for use in plug chewing tobacco but is now blended with other tobaccos in the manufacture of cigarettes.

Dark-fired tobacco, the leaves of which are cured by the use of smoldering sawdust smoke, is grown on the fertile rolling lands of the Pennyroyal District on the Highland Rim. In this area tobacco is the pivot crop, and around it revolves the whole system of farming. The more progressive farmers employ a four-year rotation in which tobacco is followed by wheat, hay (frequently the legume lespedeza), and corn. On a national basis, Kentucky is second only to North Carolina in tobacco growing; Tennessee usually ranks fifth among the states.

Although tobacco is generally not considered an important Canadian crop, it is the leading one in several counties bordering on Lake Erie, particularly around Norfolk. Tobacco is the most valuable cash crop in Ontario.

Fruit The commercial growing of fruit is not a widely distributed enterprise but is concentrated in definite localities. Tree fruits, more exacting in climate than in soil requirements, frequently suffer from extremes of temperature; hence, the best-suited areas are those with a minimum of danger from late spring and early fall frosts,

notably peninsulas, hillsides, and the leeward sides of lakes. This tempering effect of
a large body of water has given rise to a fruit
belt on the eastern shore of Lake Michigan,
where peaches and cherries are of great importance, and on the southern shore of Lake
Erie, where grapes, peaches, and apples are
dominant crops.

The Niagara Peninsula in Canada, ben-
efiting from the same climatic principle, is
famous for fruits, particularly grapes and
peaches. The narrow lake plain between
Hamilton and the Niagara River is one of
only two major areas in Canada where
tender fruit crops can be produced. Its location in the most rapidly growing area of
Canada makes available a ready market,
but urban and industrial expansion in the
so-called Golden Horseshoe have caused
fruitlands to be subdivided at a rapid rate.
More than half of the original area has now
been lost to urban use, and the rapid attrition continues.

THE LIVESTOCK INDUSTRY

The Heartland concentrates on growing
feed for livestock rather than on food for
people. In few areas elsewhere in the world is
the system of farming based to such a large
extent on livestock. From two-thirds to
three-fourths of the income from Corn Belt
farms comes from livestock, a situation in
sharp contrast with that in most other outstanding agricultural areas.

The farmers here have several possible
choices for the utilization of their corn; accordingly certain roughly defined areas of
corn use have arisen. The "cash-grain" area
(central Illinois, parts of northern Iowa, and
to a lesser extent, parts of northern Ohio and
Indiana) sell corn as grain to industry; this is
possible in part because of low freight rates
to nearby cities. Obviously swine and beef
cattle are relatively less important here than
elsewhere in the Corn Belt. In the eastern
Corn Belt swine and dairy cattle predominate, although some beef cattle are also
raised (fig. 12–14). Fresh milk finds a ready
market in the large cities. In the western

fig. 12–14 The greatest concentrations of
cattle occur where there is an overlap of
Corn Belt beef cattle with dairy cattle from
the Hay and Dairy Belt (right).

Corn Belt (western Iowa and eastern Nebraska) both beef cattle and swine are
important.

Beef Cattle Beef cattle are most numerous in the central and western parts of
the region—the old prairie portion—for,
unlike swine, they are essentially grass
eaters. Contrary to the common notion that
the range states provide only the grazing
and breeding lands, and the Corn Belt the
fattening areas, the fact is that about two-
thirds of the animals slaughtered within the
Corn Belt are bred in it.

Feeding is a major agricultural enterprise in the western part of the region, the
animals being carried through the winter on
hay and other home-grown feeds and fattened on corn. There are more cattle on feed
in Iowa than in any other state; Nebraska
ranks next. Most cattle feedlots in this region are relatively small, fattening less than
100 animals annually. This is in marked
contrast to the situation in other regions,
particularly in the West, where there is a
strong trend toward ever-larger feedlots.

Swine Of all domesticated animals,
swine most efficiently and rapidly convert
corn into meat. Spring shoats, for example,
are ready for market in approximately eight
months. During the feeding period, they
gain in weight from one to one and one-
fourth pounds per day. Two-thirds of the
swine in the United States are raised in this
region, where the density is about four times
the average for the rest of the country (fig.
12–15). Where swine are most numerous,
corn is cheapest and therefore can move to
market advantageously in the concentrated

fig. 12–15 The distribution of hogs (right) bears
a close relationship to the distribution of
corn (see fig. 12–8).

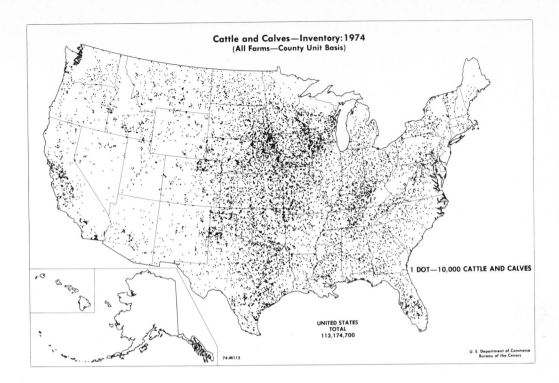

Cattle and Calves—Inventory: 1974
(All Farms—County Unit Basis)

1 DOT—10,000 CATTLE AND CALVES

UNITED STATES
TOTAL
113,174,700

74-M115

U. S. Department of Commerce
Bureau of the Census

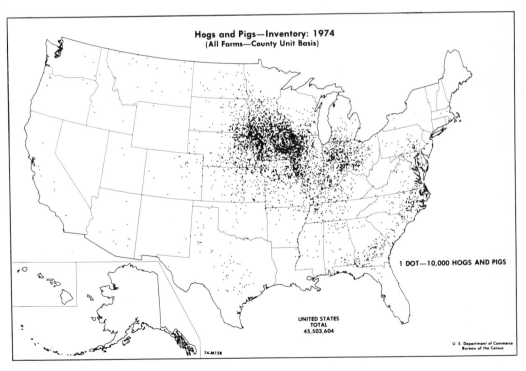

Hogs and Pigs—Inventory: 1974
(All Farms—County Unit Basis)

1 DOT—10,000 HOGS AND PIGS

UNITED STATES
TOTAL
45,503,604

74-M128

U. S. Department of Commerce
Bureau of the Census

form of live or slaughtered animals (fig. 12–16). It is much more economical to ship one pound of hog than five pounds of grain (roughly the quantity required to produce one pound of live weight).

The generally smaller farms in the eastern part of the region often emphasize pork rather than beef production, since swine require less space than cattle. Even so, the largest numbers of swine are found where there is the greatest production of corn; thus Iowa has twice as many hogs as the second-ranking state, Illinois.

Dairy Cattle Dairying is widespread in the Heartland but is dominant only in the northern part of the region and around the major cities (fig. 12–17). In Wisconsin and Minnesota the principal products are manufactured items—butter, cheese, evaporated milk, dried milk—to combat the high cost of

fig. 12–16 Much of the corn grown in the Heartland is used to fatten livestock, particularly hogs. This scene is in southern Wisconsin.

fig. 12–17 The principal concentrations of dairy cattle are in a northern belt extending from Minnesota to New England.

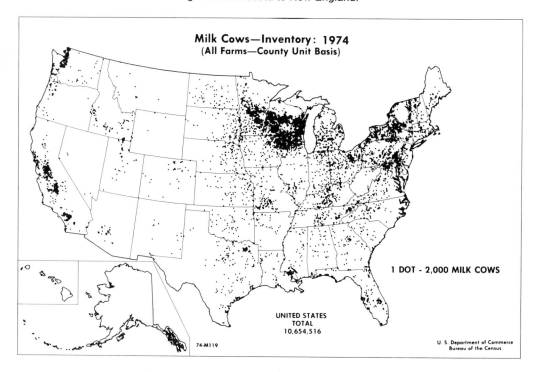

Milk Cows—Inventory: 1974
(All Farms—County Unit Basis)

1 DOT - 2,000 MILK COWS

UNITED STATES
TOTAL
10,654,516

74-M119

U. S. Department of Commerce
Bureau of the Census

shipping fluid milk. Dairy farms tend to be relatively small and often involve marginal land that is not well suited for crop farming but is satisfactory for pasture. Many dairy farmers now also raise and fatten dairy animals for sale as beef; this has to some extent replaced the secondary raising of hogs on dairy farms, which was a traditional activity.

THE NATIONAL GOVERNMENT AND THE FARMER

In both Canada and the United States, agriculture, that "last stronghold of free enterprise," has become ever more dependent on the government. Within the last four decades a bureaucracy of astounding magnitude has evolved, doing many noble things for the farmer but enmeshing agriculture in an endless series of quotas, regulations, and artificial conditions.

Direct government influence on farming comes about in many ways and is somewhat different in the two countries. The geography of agriculture, however, is most likely to be affected by the following practices:

Cost Sharing of Conservation Practices Interested farmers can obtain from the government advice, plans, and technical assistance for soil conservation. Also, the government pays approximately half the cost of establishing certain conservation practices on their land. In addition, they can take some acres out of cultivation and receive direct payments for not growing crops. All these measures have been beneficial for overused and eroded land. But, at the same time, the high productivity of intensified farming on the better-cultivated land has offset the tendency toward decline in total production that would be an anticipated effect of conservation practices.

Farm Credit The United States and Canadian governments make loans to their qualifying farmers who cannot obtain credit from conventional sources.

Crop Insurance The governments have set up crop insurance agencies to indemnify farmers for crop losses due to "acts of God."

Acreage Allotments and Marketing Quotas Most major crops are now grown under some sort of allotment and quota system, whereby maximal acreages are designated for each year's harvest.

Price Supports Several basic agricultural commodities in both countries achieve what amounts to a guaranteed sale on the basis of federal price supports, regardless of national or international market conditions. These provisions were softened in the early 1970s, which, with a strong international market, permitted the disposal of most of the astronomical crop surpluses that had accumulated in both countries.

Direct Payments to Farmers The price-support program did not succeed either in holding down overproduction or bolstering farm income; thus, it was superseded by a complex system of direct payments to producing farmers. By the early 1970s these payments in the United States reached almost $4 billion annually and amounted to almost one-fourth of all realized net farm income. Later in the decade, however, the amount and proportion of these payments had been significantly reduced.

Export Controls In a highly fluctuating pattern the two governments sporadically impose export controls on certain basic commodities.

What to do about the complex federal farm programs (which have been grossly oversimplified in this brief discussion) is enigmatic. Friend and foe alike agree that they are too big, too all-pervading, and too expensive. And yet neither Republicans nor Democrats nor Conservatives nor Liberals nor Social Crediters nor Independents have been able to devise a scheme for getting government out of agriculture without wrecking the farm economy.

minerals

Although relatively inconspicuous in this region of remarkable agricultural and industrial output, mining is also an important enterprise in many localities.

COAL

Coal deposits are widely distributed, and one of the nation's leading provinces, the Eastern Interior, is in this region. The Eastern Interior Province is second (although distantly) only to the Appalachian Province as a coal producer. Illinois is the fourth ranking coal state, with about 10 percent of total national output. Mines in western Kentucky and southern Indiana together yield slightly more coal than Illinois, and their output is increasing. In most years Muhlenberg County in Kentucky produces nearly twice as much bituminous coal as any other county in the nation. Most of the coal in the Eastern Interior Province is obtained from strip mines.

PETROLEUM AND NATURAL GAS

Important oil and gas reserves have been tapped in Michigan, Ohio, Indiana, Kentucky, and Illinois. Production is scattered, however, and the region as a whole yields only 2 percent of the total United States output; about half of this comes from Illinois.

The only oil and gas of any consequence in eastern Canada are found in this region, somewhat scattered in extreme southern Ontario. Oil output amounts to less than 1 percent of the national total, but further modest discoveries are anticipated. The proportion of the national output of natural gas is somewhat higher.

LIMESTONE

In south-central Indiana, in the Bedford-Bloomington area, are the famous limestone quarries that supply a superior limestone used in buildings throughout the East and Midwest. About three-fifths of the dimension (block) limestone of the country comes from these quarries. The building stone business is declining, however, for it suffers in competition with cheaper concrete, brick, and lumber.

SALT

Salt occurs widely in Anglo-America, but major deposits are in the vicinity of the southern end of Lake Huron. Michigan is one of the leading states and Ontario is the leading province in salt output of their respective countries. The salt is obtained in the solid form by underground digging and in the dissolved state by the modified Frasch process. There are several mines in Michigan, but the principal output is actually beneath metropolitan Detroit. The Ontario mines are at Goderich, Watford, Sarnia, and Windsor.

heartland manufacturing

Despite the unparalleled opulence of agriculture in the Heartland, the economic well-being of the region is much more dependent on industrial prosperity. No other part of the United States or Canada has such a concentration of factories or of industrial employment. In fact, a major portion of the American Manufacturing Belt is encompassed within the Heartland Region.

THE AMERICAN MANUFACTURING BELT

The American Manufacturing Belt is a broad zone of industrial-urban concentration in parts of northeastern United States and adjacent southern Ontario and Quebec (fig. 12–18). As in most of Anglo-America, manufacturing here is clustered in and near large cities.

Within the roughly shaped parallelogram that describes the boundaries of this belt is found more than 60 percent of the factory production of the United States and 70 percent of that of Canada. Included are 13 of the 20 largest industrial centers of the United States and 5 of the 8 largest in Canada.

Although referred to as a belt, the actual factory distribution is spotty and occupies only a small fraction of the land. Here the concept of a belt involves the relative

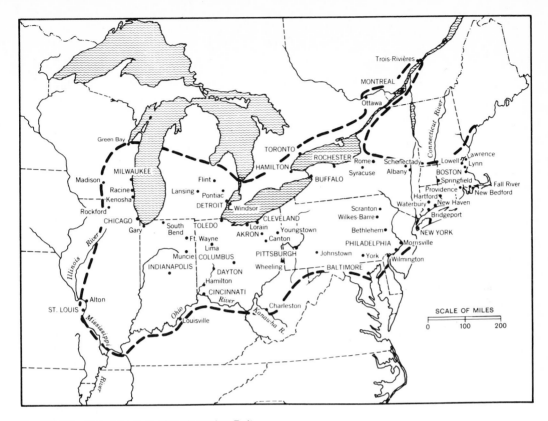

fig. 12–18 The American Manufacturing Belt.

continuity of significant industrialization from one urban node to the next in the broad area extending from Portland and Baltimore on the East Coast to Green Bay and St. Louis in the Midwest; most of the land, however, is in nonindustrial usage. In short, there are large expanses of meager manufactual activity among numerous centers of industry.

The pattern of secondary industry varies significantly in different portions of the American Manufacturing Belt. In order to gain more than a very generalized understanding of the belt, it is necessary to subdivide it into districts (fig. 12–19). Four of these districts and a portion of four others lie outside the Heartland Region and have been discussed in previous chapters.

Generally speaking, the more westerly districts of the American Manufacturing

Belt have been those that have experienced the most rapid recent industrial growth, although their rates of expansion have been anything but uniform. It is these districts that are in the Heartland Region and provide the principal industrial components to its economy.

Central New York The Mohawk Valley and the Ontario Plain occupy the great water-level route from Troy to Buffalo and are traversed by the main line of the Penn-Central Railway, the New York State Barge Canal, Interstate Highway 90, and the Thomas E. Dewey Thruway.

The district contains many cities. The first arose in response to the stimulus of the Erie Canal, built in 1825; the later ones arose near a series of short railroads that paralleled the river and canal. Later these

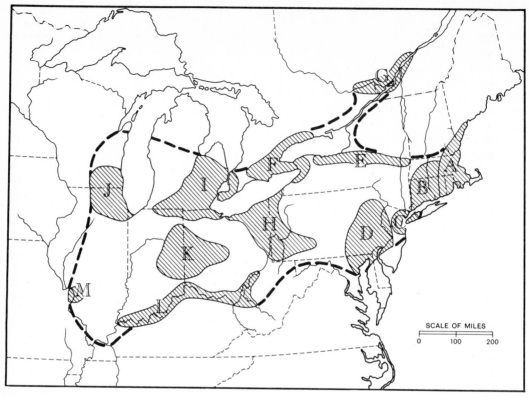

fig. 12-19   Principal manufacturing districts:
(A) Southeastern New England,
(B) Southwestern New England,
(C) Metropolitan New York,
(D) Philadelphia-Baltimore district,
(E) Central New York, (F) Niagara Frontier,
(G) Middle St. Lawrence district,
(H) Pittsburgh-Cleveland district,
(I) Southern Michigan automotive district,
(J) Chicago-Milwaukee district,
(K) Inland Ohio–Indiana district,
(L) Middle Ohio Valley, and (M) St. Louis district.

lines were consolidated, and the area became one of the major traffic arteries of Anglo-America. Factories sprang up all along the route. Each city tends to specialize in several products: *Rochester* makes cameras, electrical machinery, optical goods, and men's clothing; *Rome,* copper and brass; and *Syracuse,* machinery and alkalies.

The Niagara Frontier   This subregion lies between Lake Ontario and Lake Erie in western New York and adjacent Ontario. It is complicated by the international boundary that, as a result of the tariff, plays a vital role in causing manufacturing to be more important on the Canadian side than it would be otherwise.

The power from Niagara Falls is widely used on both sides of the border and has played an important part in the development of chemical, metallurgical, and other industries. Because of the international border, there are two industrial capitals: Buffalo on the United States side, and Toronto on the Canadian.

The industrial structure of the district is undergirded by two great concentrations of basic iron and steel manufacturing. At Lackawanna, a northern suburb of Buffalo, is a major steel facility that was relocated from a crowded site in eastern Pennsylvania in 1900, and clustered around the harbor of Hamilton is more than half of all Canada's steel making. As in other Lower Lake cities these locations are economical meeting places for coal, iron ore, and fluxing limestone, and the finished steel can be shipped conveniently by waterway, rail, or truck to much of eastern Anglo-America.

Flour milling has long been the symbolic industry of Buffalo, and the city still ranks as one of the world's leading milling centers. The total industrial structure of the district, however, is quite diversified, especially on the Canadian side. The automotive industry is well established in the Niagara Frontier, with many parts factories and a few assembly plants in Toronto, Hamilton, and Buffalo. Electrochemical and electrometallurgical facilities have been established on both sides of the border to utilize Niagara Falls power. Fabricated metals (especially in Buffalo) and agricultural machinery (particularly in Toronto) are also products of note.

Canada's leading industrial center is *Toronto*, which ranks twelfth among the major manufacturing cities of Anglo-America. *Buffalo* ranks nineteenth. *Hamilton* has only one-third as much industrial output as Toronto, and yet is the third largest Canadian manufactural center.

The Pittsburgh - Cleveland District

The Pittsburgh-Cleveland district is the continent's outstanding producer of iron and steel. It is also a leading producer of metal products in their secondary and tertiary stages—fabricated metals and machinery. Some other industries, such as rubber and glass products, are important, but predominantly this is a district of metalworking.

The area is strategically located for heavy industry since it lies between Lake Erie on the north, over whose waters move millions of tons of iron ore and limestone, and the productive Northern Appalachian coal field on the south. Here, too, is one of Anglo-America's leading markets for iron and steel.

Three of the largest steel-making centers in Anglo-America are in this district: Pittsburgh, second; Youngstown, third; and Cleveland, tenth. Typically the mills are of medium size, are several years or even decades old, may suffer from congestion and lack of space, and are nearly always located beside a river or stream. These valley sites provide water for cooling, flat land for building, and access to transportation facilities.

Motor vehicle manufacturing and assembly are a major industry in this district; automotive output here is second only to that of the Southern Michigan district. The industry is a major employer in Cleveland but is proportionately even more significant in Lorain and Youngstown.

Related to the automotive industry is the long-lived rubber industry of the Akron area. The manufacture of rubber in Akron, predicated on the original work of B. F. Goodrich, has been carried on for more than a century, but its principal prosperity has been due to the automotive industry's need for tires. In the last few years the Akron rubber industry has declined significantly, but much of the slack has been taken up by rising employment in plastics industries, attracted to Akron because of some manufacturing similarity with rubber-making (they both involve polymer chemistry) and the availability of skilled workers.

Other major manufacturing industries in the district are mostly producers of durable goods that use steel as an important component of their product: fabricated metals, machinery of various kinds, machine tools, and electrical machinery.

The Southern Michigan Automotive District

The automobile-manufacturing district contains the heart of the world's automotive industry. This industry dominates the district much more than steel dominates the Pittsburgh-Cleveland district. It includes, besides the metropolitan areas of *Detroit* and *Windsor*, the inner and outer rings of cities. Included in the semisuburban inner ring are *Pontiac, Ann Arbor, Ypsilanti,* and *Monroe.* Included in the outer ring are nine cities in the orbit of Detroit's great industry: *Port Huron, Bay City, Saginaw, Flint, Owosso, Lansing, Jackson, Adrian,* and *Toledo.*

The Automotive Industry The automotive industry has made Detroit the most heavily industrialized major city in Anglo-America.[17] Within Detroit are more than 40 large automotive parts factories and almost a dozen assembly plants.

Throughout southeastern Michigan and adjacent parts of Ohio and Indiana there are dozens of cities, towns, and even villages that are functionally tied to Detroit because they have one or several factories producing items for the automotive industry. Many of these outlying centers are even more dependent on this single industry than is Detroit. Flint is the prime example. Not only is it the most industrialized small city in Anglo-America (nearly 50 percent of its labor force works in factories), but it is also the second largest automobile-producing city on the continent and the most specialized manufacturing center in the nation (more than 80 percent of its manufacturing is for the automotive industry).

Detroit became the first great automobile center "by the accident of being the hub of a circle within which were located the pioneers of the industry."[18] Henry Ford developed an automobile cheap enough for almost every family; he adapted the assembly line to the industry; and he introduced standardization and interchangeable parts to the industry and thereby made mass pro-

duction possible. Ford was not, however, the innovator of modern mass production. The credit for this achievement goes to Eli Whitney. Ford, moreover, raised the necessary capital among local bankers rather than on Wall Street. He and the alert local capitalists were largely responsible for the rise of automobile manufacturing in Michigan.

Geographic and economic conditions have justified the selection of Detroit as the automotive center. The industry had to be strategically located with respect to steel. In the American Manufacturing Belt is concentrated more than 80 percent of the finished-steel-producing capacity of the United States. Besides having locally made steel, Detroit's automotive industry has easy access to the steel mills at South Chicago, Gary, Cleveland, Lorain, and Buffalo.

But the automobile industry has been decentralized toward both coasts, to Canada, and overseas. Thus it has been following the twin principles of modern relocation: first, regional plants, and second, production in well-balanced communities where labor efficiency is high.

The Canadian motor-vehicle industry, which is mainly centered at Windsor and Oshawa in Ontario, is the most important industry in this province. As in the United States, however, factories in many widely scattered cities and towns provide the innumerable parts. Some of these devote such a large part of their total industrial output to the automobile that they may justifiably be termed "automobile cities."

The Chemical Industry So important is the automotive industry in this area that it overshadows the manufacture of chemicals, which is also an impressive enterprise. Most of the chemical plants, drawing on huge deposits of salt that underlie Detroit, are located down the Detroit River from the Rouge or just beyond the northern edge of the city.

Sarnia, situated where Lake Huron empties into the St. Clair River, is an outstanding Canadian chemical manufacturing center. Oil refining, based on local petroleum, got its start late in the nineteenth cen-

---

[17] Approximately 34 percent of all employed people in Detroit work in factories. Comparable figures for other metropolises are Cleveland, 31 percent; Philadelphia, Pittsburgh, and Chicago, 27 percent each; Los Angeles, 25 percent; New York, 21 percent; and Boston, 20 percent.

[18] John A Piquet, "The Factor of Plant Location in Automobile Production," *Industrial Management,* 68 (November 1924), 297.

tury and has expanded considerably since then, first with pipelined oil from Ohio and more recently with the completion of a pipeline to bring in vast supplies from Alberta. The local refineries, as well as nearby salt deposits, stimulated the attraction of petrochemical, synthetic rubber, plastics, fertilizer, and other types of chemical factories.

Iron and Steel   Although Detroit is the largest steel-consuming center in the United States and enjoys every advantage of other Lower Lake cities for the economical assembly of raw materials at the blast furnaces, the city produces only one-fourth as much steel as the Chicago area. Production expansion has been predicted for a long time, but only in the last few years has it come about. The rate of production increase in Detroit recently has been the fastest among Anglo-American steel centers, and it is now the fourth leading producer of steel on the continent (fig. 12–20).

The Chicago - Milwaukee District

The Chicago-Milwaukee district occupies the western and southwestern shores of Lake Michigan from Gary to Wauwatosa and includes satellite towns and cities extending a short distance inland. Heavy industry predominates. The fountainhead of all manufacturing is the great primary iron and steel industry at the southern end of Lake Michigan, from which fan out in all directions— although mostly to the west and north—the many industries that utilize steel. This district may well be considered as the western outpost of both the primary and the secondary iron and steel industries of the continent.

Other major industrial enterprises produce electrical machinery, farm equipment, railway rolling stock, automobiles, apparel, oil, and beer. Food processing, printing, and publishing are also notable.

Most manufacturing in Wisconsin and Illinois is confined to this district. *Chicago* is the second largest industrial center on the continent, and *Milwaukee* ranks eleventh. Smaller centers of note include *Rockford, Joliet, Racine,* and *Kenosha.*

fig. 12–20   A steel mill in Detroit, with ore boats at the unloading docks (courtesy Detroit Department of Public Information).

Iron and Steel   Chicago-Gary, one of the outstanding manufacturing areas of the world, is strategically located for making iron and steel: iron ore and limestone can be brought directly to the blast furnaces by lake carrier, and coal is not far distant in central and southern Illinois, although most coking fuel is brought from West Virginia and Kentucky by rail or by the combination of rail and lake carrier. This district has the best balance between production and consumption of any iron and steel area in the United States. Its output of steel is greater than that of the entire United Kingdom and almost as much as that of West Germany.

Further expansion of steel making to the east, around the southern tip of Lake Michigan, is projected. A major conflict of interests has developed between industrialists who want to use the sandy lake margin for factories and conservationists who would prefer to have the area reserved for recreational purposes.

Machinery and Metal Fabrication
Although this district is justly famous for its primary steel industry now and its meatpacking industry in the past, its prominent types of manufacturing today—

301

whether measured by employment or by value of production—are machinery output and metal fabrication. Chicago is the continent's leading center in the fabrication of metals, that relatively prosaic heavy industry in which primary metal (mostly sheets, bars, and rods of steel) is shaped and fashioned into pipes, screws, wire, beams, cans, and other products of specific utility.

For the district as a whole and Chicago in particular, however, machinery production is the leading type of manufacturing. Electrical machinery, such as communication equipment, radio and television sets, electronics equipment, electric lighting and wiring equipment, is particularly notable. This is the largest single industry in the district. Nonelectrical machinery is also produced in great quantity, particularly metalworking, construction, and industrial machinery.

Milwaukee In its industrial structure Milwaukee is a sort of miniature Chicago, encompassing a broad range of manufacturing types but with emphasis on machinery and other metal-using industries. The distinctive industrial specialty of the city, however, is brewing.

The Industries of the Rock Valley On the fringe of the district is the Rock Valley of southern Wisconsin and northern Illinois. The leading products of the valley are metal goods, machinery, hardware, machine tools, and automotive equipment, although some furniture, textiles, and foods are also manufactured. The cities that contribute most to production are Rockford, Beloit, Madison, Janesville, Sterling, and Freeport.

Considering the valley's prominence industrially, it is surprising to note the paucity of local raw materials, absence of an important local source of coal and hydroelectric power, lack of a substantial encircling market, and merely average transport facilities.

The big advantages are imaginative and inventive management, a labor supply with the disposition and talent for manufacturing, a location near enough to Eastern markets to prevent prohibitive transport costs, an early start in that the factories were built

to supply the local market and were based on local water power and local timber resources, and the advantages inherent in small cities. Wages are slightly lower than those paid for the same work by Eastern competitors. The first of these factors is indisputably the most important; nearly half of the larger factories can be traced directly to local inventions.

Inland Ohio–Indiana District This district is situated between the Great Lakes and the Ohio River; thus it can draw on both for transportation but suffers in cost by being adjacent to neither. It lies between the coal fields to the east and the productive farmlands to the west. Its industries are diversified, including machine tools, cash registers, refrigerators, soaps, meat, tobacco, iron and steel, beer, shoes, radios, and clothing. The most intensely industrialized part is the Miami Valley from Springfield to Hamilton. Indianapolis is the major center in the western part; Dayton and Columbus, in the eastern.

Miami Valley Within the valley there are today several cities with a long industrial history and considerable production. They early supplied commodities for use in the prosperous farming hinterland, but the real stimulus to manufacturing was the building of the Miami and Erie Canal in the 1820s. *Dayton* is the largest industrial center in the valley. It specializes in machinery production, particularly refrigerators, cash registers, accounting equipment, and machine tools. *Hamilton* is famed for its output of paper and paper-making machinery as well as pig iron; *Middletown* has a large primary steel industry; and *Springfield* is a diversified machinery center.

Other Industrial Cities Elsewhere in the district, manufacturing complexes are found only in isolated cities. Indianapolis and Columbus, the two largest, are landlocked localities that have prospered because of an early start at the crossing of surface transportation routes. *Indianapolis* is a diversified industrial center, with an emphasis on metalworking factories. Food processing, especially meatpacking and flour milling, are also important. *Columbus* is not primarily an industrial city, but its factories have prospered because of its central location, its skilled labor force, and the strong impetus given to local metalworking firms by the establishment of a large aircraft factory during World War II. Smaller industrial cities in the district include *Fort Wayne, Muncie,* and *Lima.*

Middle Ohio Valley

One of the more dynamic manufacturing districts in the world extends for 500 miles along the valley of the Ohio River. The district benefits by its river location, but cheap water transportation is only one of the factors that has attracted many large industrial enterprises in the last few years.

The availability of large, reliable supplies of coal from nearby mines is an important consideration. The seasonal vagaries of hydroelectricity have caused many industrialists to consider again coal as a power source, and the Ohio Valley has a plentiful supply. In addition, earlier the valley had an abundance of land at reasonable prices, although now flat land is more expensive. In general, there is also a greater surplus of suitable labor in and near the district than in any comparable portion of Anglo-America.

Within the Heartland portion of the district are two older established industrial centers that have shared in the new boom. *Cincinnati,* largest city in the valley, has added electrical equipment to the machine tools, auto parts, and aircraft engines that were its previous stock in trade. Also, its basic steel industry has expanded considerably in recent years. *Louisville* is famous for its distilleries, cigarette factories, and chemical plants, but its principal recent growth has been in machinery production, which is dominated by General Electric's Appliance Park, a 1,000-acre complex of diversified household-appliance manufacture.

St. Louis District

The St. Louis district lies mostly in Missouri but partly in Illinois. The largest urban center between Chicago and the Pacific Coast, *St. Louis* is a commercial and transportation hub and one of the ten leading industrial centers in Anglo-America. It exerts a strong influence in the Middle Mississippi Basin. Its industrial structure is more diversified than that of any other city except Philadelphia, although the most important growth industries of the last two decades have been aircraft and automotive. Since about 1970 there has been virtual stagnation in manufacturing in the area.

Despite its importance in manufacturing, St. Louis is essentially a commercial city. Its strategic location on the high west bank of the Mississippi River, a short distance below the mouth of the Missouri, has since early days enabled St. Louis to dominate much of the river trade. Later the city became an outstanding railway center, and today it ranks second only to Chicago.

The metropolitan district, which includes East St. Louis, Alton, Belleville, and Granite City, contributes heavily to the nation's total output of shoes, automobiles, beer, meat, electrical equipment, airplane engines and accessories, chemicals, drugs, furs, glass, refined petroleum, and iron and steel. About 75 percent of the factories and plants are in the city and its Missouri suburbs; the remaining 25 percent are on the Illinois side of the river.

HEARTLAND MANUFACTURING OUTSIDE THE AMERICAN MANUFACTURING BELT

West and southwest of the American Manufacturing Belt, several large and medium-sized cities function as isolated nodes of industrial concentration. As might be anticipated, the bulk of the manufacturing in these urban areas is oriented toward agriculture, either by using farm products as raw materials or by producing items for sale to farmers.

Meatpacking is probably the principal type of food processing, following the well-established trend of decentralization toward the source of raw materials—in this case toward the areas of cattle and hog raising.

Omaha has displaced Chicago as the premier slaughtering center of the continent (fig. 12–21), and other meatpacking localities of prominence include South St. Paul, Sioux City, Waterloo, St. Joseph, and Kansas City.

Flour milling is the other outstanding food-processing activity in the region, part of the wheat coming from the Heartland but most of it coming from the Great Plains to the west. Minneapolis and Kansas City have maintained major milling enterprises for decades; they normally rank just behind Buffalo in national statistics.

The farm populace also serves as a market. Major manufacturing centers of farm machinery are Minneapolis, the Tri-Cities (Davenport–Rock Island–Moline), Des Moines, Waterloo, and Kansas City. Nashville is an important producer of farm fertilizer.

Diversified manufacturing, primarily for the wholesale markets, is also characteristic of Minneapolis–St. Paul, Kansas City, and Nashville.

transportation

The extensive and busy Heartland Region is well served by transportation facilities. Gentle relief and the lack of topographic barriers made the construction of surface transport lines relatively easy, partly accounting for the dense networks of roads, railways, and pipelines in the region. In addition, the two outstanding natural inland waterway systems of Anglo-America, the Great Lakes and the Mississippi River drainage, are largely within the region, and numerous canals have at one time or another helped to augment the waterway transport system.

RAILWAYS

The first railroads in the Midwest were not built as competitors to navigable waterways but as links connecting them. The rapid extension and improvement of the railway facilities after 1850, however, profoundly changed agriculture and revolutionized the whole course of internal trade. By 1860, railroads had triumphed over inland waterways, and since then port rivalries have been expressed in the competition of the railroads serving them. Railroads, by spanning the great interior with a network of steel rails, also stimulated the growth of cities and the development of manufacturing.

The present railway network is dense, but its major flow is east-west. The main lines principally connect the eastern metropolises of New York, Philadelphia, and Toronto-Montreal with the major Midwestern hubs of Chicago and St. Louis. The principal north-south traffic is associated with the Mississippi Valley axis of Chicago–St. Louis–New Orleans.

Since World War II there has been a long-term downtrend in railway usage in the Heartland, as over most of Anglo-America. Passenger traffic is now very limited, and there are strenuous efforts to revive passenger use of the railways, particularly by the federally supported Amtrak system. Many short lines have been abandoned, and there has been considerable consolidation of trackage. The role of the railroad today, more than ever before, is to take bulk commodities, particularly mineral and agricultural products, on long hauls. Most of the short-haul freight business, as well as a considerable amount of long-haul traffic, has been lost to truckers.

ROADS

The truck and the automobile have revolutionized transportation in the twentieth century almost as much as the railway did in the nineteenth. Motor trucking operations benefit from low capacities, high speed, and flexibility of route; therefore they can provide frequent shipments at relatively low cost. Their principal advantage over railroads is on short hauls, although they can often compete on intermediate and even long hauls. Most major railway companies have organized piggyback operations (hauling loaded trailers on flat cars) to add flexi-

bility to and reduced handling charges in their competition with truck lines.

Most parts of the Heartland are well served by highways and roads, for both long-distance and local travel. Several major toll roads were built in this region in the 1940s and 1950s in an effort to speed cross-country traffic and alleviate congestion around cities. More recently, however, the idea of toll roads has been virtually abandoned because of the construction of the national interstate highway system, which was essentially completed in 1978 (42,000 miles at a cost of $70 billion). All of the large and most of the medium-sized cities in the nation are connected by this system, normally with a four-lane, divided, controlled-access type of highway. A large portion of the new roadway system is located in the Heartland Region.

INLAND WATERWAYS

Rivers, lakes, and canals have been and, in many cases, continue to be of considerable importance for transportation in the Heartland Region.

Rivers Rivers were the principal routeways of pioneer days and were used whenever possible in preference to the hard and slow overland routes. Their chief advantages as highways were low cost and convenience. Many a stream that now seems too small or shallow for transportation was very extensively used, and many a settlement would have died out had there been no stream over which to float products to market. Almost all large western communities in the period from 1800 to 1850 were located on the Ohio or the Mississippi.

The Detroit, Ohio, Mississippi, Illinois, St. Lawrence, and Missouri are the principal commercial rivers of the Heartland.

The Detroit River The Detroit River, which drains Lake St. Clair into Lake Erie, is 28 miles long and 0.5 mile to 3 miles wide. A shoal that formerly blocked its entrance from Lake St. Clair has been cut through. About three-fourths of the tonnage moving down the lakes passes through the Detroit River, and this is more than the combined total tonnage that normally moves through the Suez and Panama canals.

The Ohio River The channel of the Ohio River was not navigable during the droughts of late summer until the federal government established a permanent nine-foot stage with a system of four dozen dams that back the water into a succession of lakes deep enough for navigation. Locks permit boats to get around the dams.

The Ohio accordingly has become one of the continent's leading carriers of water-borne freight. Thousands of commodious barges, shackled in tows, are propelled over the river at all seasons except for several days in spring when the water is too high or in winter when ice is hazardous. The tonnage is several times greater now than it was at the height of the steamboat period. Bulk products compose 95 percent of the total freight: coal, coke, ore, sand and gravel, stone, grain, pig iron, and steel. Increasing quantities of gasoline are also being shipped.

The recent industrial boom along the Ohio Valley has further stimulated river traffic. Some problems, however, are becoming clearer. The 46 dams on the Ohio are several decades old, and their locks are not big or fast enough to move the barge traffic with dispatch at peak times. Cross-river traffic flow is also slow; there are few bridges, so that ferries must be used. Water pollution, in spite of the good work of the Ohio River Valley Water Sanitation Compact, and a growing scarcity of flat land may slow the pace of expansion, but new plant investment is measured in billions of dollars, an indication that expansion will continue. Construction has begun according to a master plan that calls for the reduction of the number of dams and locks on the river by 60 percent, which will result in longer pools and considerable saving of time for the carriers.

The Mississippi and Missouri Rivers Barge traffic is also significant on these two rivers of the western Heartland. Minneapolis is the head of navigation on the Mississippi, and Sioux City is the effective head of navigation on the Missouri. There is a number of flood-control and power-generation dams on the two rivers, with locks to let the barges pass through. Most traffic on this system is from St. Louis southward.

The Illinois River The principal function of navigation on the Illinois River is to connect the Great Lakes with the Mississippi system. The upper course of the Illinois has been dredged and channeled to connect with the port of Chicago and Lake Michigan via the Chicago Sanitary and Ship Canal, which, as its name implies, provides transportation for both barges and sewage.

Canals Although most proved inadequate, particularly because they were closed by ice for several months each year, canals nevertheless played a vital role during the decades when people depended primarily on inland water transportation. Canals were built to connect natural waterways. Two of the most important merit attention.

The Welland Canal Most important in this region is the Welland Canal, built to avoid Niagara Falls and to connect Port Colborne on Lake Erie with Port Weller on Lake Ontario. Constructed in 1829, it was a tortuous ditch with 25 locks. Nevertheless it did a tremendous business.

Unfortunately the large lake carriers, which constitute about 90 percent of the ships on the lakes, could not navigate the canal; cargoes had to be unloaded at Port Colborne, the Canadian terminal harbor 25 miles west of Buffalo, and placed aboard smaller ships. These required about 16 hours to make the canal trip, against 4 hours today. The greater economy and efficiency attained by larger lake vessels led to a desire to enlarge the canal; the work was begun in

fig. 12-22 Buffalo is a major transshipment point at the junction of land and water transport routes. Its function in grain storage and milling can also be noted here (courtesy Buffalo, New York, Area Chamber of Commerce).

1913 and completed in 1931. The canal was remodeled and enlarged again in the 1950s.

New York State Barge (Erie) Canal This canal, which connects Lake Erie with the Hudson River, was opened in 1825. It follows the Mohawk Gap and the Ontario Plain, the only practical route through the Appalachian barrier. The opening of this canal, perhaps more than any other single factor, provided the stimulus to make New York City the greatest port on the Atlantic coast. The Erie was financially successful, and for many years it was the busiest inland waterway in the world.

In 1875, however, it was surpassed by the railway. Tolls were abolished in 1883, but this was only a temporary solution. By 1895 the tonnage fell to 3.5 million as against 19 million for the competing railroad. The solution appeared to be a larger canal. Its construction was undertaken, and the New York State Barge Canal was completed in 1918. It followed the route of its predecessor most of the way. It is 353 miles long from Buffalo to Waterford (near Troy) on the Hudson. Little traffic was generated, however. Traffic has been increasing in recent years, but only slowly.

The Great Lakes The Great Lakes are the most valuable system of inland waterways in the world. For 1,700 miles they extend in an east-west direction and connect the rich and productive interior hinterland with the markets and ports of the East. The shores of the lakes are dotted with great industrial and commercial cities (fig. 12–22).

The Great Lakes have been open to oceangoing traffic ever since the Welland Canal was built, but only for small vessels. The completion of the St. Lawrence Seaway in 1959 changed that (see vignette below).

the urban system
of the heartland

In no other major region of Anglo-America is there such regular development of an urban hierarchy as in the Heartland (see table 12–1 for a listing of the region's largest urban places). The concept of city and hinterland is prominently displayed in most parts of the region, and there is a "nested hierarchy" of at least half a dozen levels of magnitude from metropolis to village. The almost classical regularity of the pattern in the Corn Belt and the western margins of the region is interrupted by three major factors that counterpoint the scheme:

1 The Great Lakes, which constrict the areal pattern, provide an important func-

the st. lawrence seaway

After decades of speculation, discussion, controversy, and planning, the governments of Canada and the United States finally reached an agreement in 1954 that authorized the construction of the St. Lawrence Seaway project. The basic plan was to enlarge the existing navigation facilities that circumvented the falls and rapids on the St. Lawrence River above Mont-

fig. 12-a   The Welland Canal, which bypasses Niagara Falls, is one of the busiest canals in the world. Here a lake carrier is being locked through (courtesy Ontario Ministry of Industry and Tourism).

real and to improve the waterways connecting the various Great Lakes.

Most Seaway construction was undertaken along the St. Lawrence River between Montreal and Lake Ontario. Canals and locks were built to bypass rapids and dams in this stretch of the river. The Welland and Sault St. Marie canals were also deepened and augmented (fig. 12-a). The Seaway was officially opened in 1959, although some ancillary construction (particularly the deepening of connecting channels near Detroit and the dredging of channels at several other ports) was not completed until 1964. The final result was an inland waterway that extends 2,342 miles from the western end of Lake Superior to the Atlantic Ocean, with a uniform minimum depth of 27 feet (fig. 12-b). This provides direct access for medium-sized oceangoing vessels to some five dozen Great Lakes ports. In addition, a considerable amount of hydroelectricity is generated at riverside plants in New York and Ontario.

The basic purpose of the project was to open the Great Lakes' regional economy to world markets by a direct ocean transport route. An important secondary consideration, from the Canadian viewpoint, was to enhance transportation between Great Lakes ports and East Coast ports.

Total ship movements on the lakes have increased by more than 400 percent since the Seaway was opened. The first decade saw many problems, however, and traffic generational connection with overseas regions and stimulate urban development on lakeshores to an unusual degree.

2 Major deposits of economic mineral resources (coal and petroleum) distort the pattern with regard to the distribution of smaller cities and towns.

3 The presence of an important international boundary essentially divides the pattern into two separate systems, one of which has a significant influence on the other.

It would require a detailed analysis of the economic base and function of each individual city to determine its exact position in the hierarchy, and even then the position would depend on the stated limits of the scheme. Here we can note only some of the major components and guess about the position of individual cities:

1 Although the economic influence of New York City is felt to some extent throughout the region, particularly in the

---

tion was significantly lower than anticipated. During the 1970s, traffic volume increased to a level that was not far below projections.

The principal disappointment has been the lack of general cargo, for the basic pattern of commodity flow on the lakes has not been altered. The Seaway is essentially a limited bulk cargo waterway, with iron ore, grain, and coal accounting for 85 percent of all freight carried. Canadian ore is brought up the Seaway from Sept Îles, and American ore is taken down the waterway from the Lake Superior deposits. Both United States and Canadian grain (primarily wheat) is carried down the lakes and out the Seaway for export overseas. Coal is

shipped in both directions on the lakes, but mostly upbound. General cargo movement has actually been on a declining trend. This is due in part to the rapid proliferation of containerized shipping over the world; the Seaway is still not deep enough for large containerships.

In its first two decades of operation, the Seaway has been most important as a route for trade within Canada, for trade between Canada and the United States, and for export of grain from both countries. Toronto and Chicago have thus far been the ports that have benefited most from the Seaway, at least in part because they have been most active in redesigning their port facilities to take advantage of the opportunities.

(Continued)

fig. 12-b Compressed diagram of the Great Lakes–
St. Lawrence Seaway System, showing dams and locks.

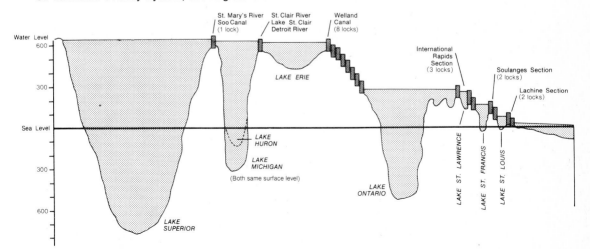

fig. 12–23 Toronto, its skyline punctuated by the tallest structure on the continent, is one of three subregional metropolises in the Heartland Region (courtesy Ontario Ministry of Industry and Tourism).

eastern portion, *Chicago* is clearly the dominant metropolis. Its position as the wholesaling center and transportation hub is an obvious indicator of its primacy in any hierarchical urban system for the Midwest.

2 Subregional metropolises, at the second level of magnitude, would probably be represented by Toronto, Detroit, and St. Louis. *Toronto's* sphere is essentially limited to the Ontario portion of the Heartland, but as one of the two primate cities of Canada, it serves many of the same functions as Chicago (fig. 12–23). *Detroit* would probably be a major subregional metropolis even without the automobile industry because of its outstanding situation on a strategic isthmus alongside the principal waterway of the continent; the addition of the automotive industry adds another major dimension to its significance. *St. Louis* is a more straightforward example of the hierarchical pattern, serving as the principal gateway city for much of the midcontinent.

3 The third level of the hierarchy should probably include such major industrial cities and Great Lakes ports as *Cleveland, Buffalo,* and *Milwaukee,* as well as such sectional gateway cities as *Cincinnati* (fig. 12–24), *Minneapolis–St. Paul,* and *Kansas City.*

4 The fourth level should probably include cities of major intrastate influence, such as *Ottawa, Hamilton, Rochester, Columbus,*

The Seaway project was an expensive endeavor for its day; total cost was in excess of $1.3 billion. The original plan was for the users to pay the cost of construction. Tolls on the 16 locks of the Seaway were established so that anticipated traffic would produce enough revenue to cover operating and maintenance costs, as well as interest on loans, and for the repayment of capital costs over a 50-year period. Revenues have been less than projected, and despite several increases in toll charges, there is insufficient income to meet all interest charges, not to mention reducing the capital indebtedness. A separate Seaway corporation in each country manages the operation. The United States corporation had its interest forgiven by the federal government and is slowly repaying capital costs. In Canada, however, accumulated interest had mounted to almost $1 billion by the late 1970s.

If the Seaway is questionable from an economic standpoint, it has been a singular success politically: two nations have collaborated on a peacetime venture of great magnitude and great complexity. Moreover, the waterway is operationally viable. Despite high costs, commerce has been augmented and the economy of many parts of the Heartland has been stimulated.

table 12–1 Largest Urban Places of the Heartland Region

name	population of principal city	population of metropolitan area	name	population of principal city	population of metropolitan area
Akron, Ohio	251,747	668,200	Flint, Mich.	174,218	520,100
Anderson, Ind.	69,486	138,100	Florissant, Mo.*	70,465	
Ann Arbor, Mich.	103,542	256,400	Fort Wayne, Ind.	185,299	374,600
Appleton, Wis.	59,182	285,200	Gary, Ind.	167,546	640,400
Arlington Heights, Ill.*	70,019		Grand Rapids, Mich.	187,946	567,600
Aurora, Ill.*	76,955		Green Bay, Wis.	91,189	172,400
Battle Creek, Mich.	43,338	182,400	Guelph, Ont.	66,431	
Bay City, Mich.	47,215	119,700	Hamilton, Ohio	66,469	244,100
Bloomington, Ill.	41,509	116,600	Hamilton, Ont.	308,845	525,222
Bloomington, Ind.	48,955	90,800	Hammond, Ind.*	104,892	
Bloomington, Minn.*	79,210		Independence, Mo.*	111,481	
Brampton, Ont.*	102,743		Indianapolis, Ind.	714,878	1,147,400
Brantford, Ont.*	66,385		Jackson, Mich.	43,994	147,100
Buffalo, N.Y.	407,160	1,327,200	Joliet, Ill.	74,401	
Burlington, Ont.*	104,133		Kalamazoo, Mich.	79,542	265,200
Cambridge, Ont.*	71,798		Kankakee, Ill.	27,961	95,800
Canton, Ohio	101,852	488,300	Kansas City, Kans.	168,153	412,000
Cedar Rapids, Iowa	108,998	166,300	Kansas City, Mo.	472,529	875,200
Champaign, Ill.	58,398	163,400	Kenosha, Wis.	80,727	123,100
Chicago, Ill.	3,099,391	6,982,900	Kettering, Ohio*	69,949	
Cicero, Ill.*	63,444		Kingston, Ont.	59,804	
Cincinnati, Ohio	412,564	1,384,500	Kitchener, Ont.	130,866	269,828
Clarksville, Tenn.	51,910	143,700	LaCrosse, Wis.	49,082	85,100
Cleveland, Ohio	638,793	1,975,400	Lafayette, Ind.	48,894	112,800
Columbus, Ohio	535,610	1,077,000	Lakewood, Ohio*	65,395	
Council Bluffs, Iowa	58,660		Lansing, Mich.	126,805	447,000
Davenport, Iowa	99,941	369,300	Lawrence, Kans.	50,887	
Dayton, Ohio	205,986	836,900	Lexington, Ky.	186,048	292,700
Dearborn, Mich.*	98,986		Lima, Ohio	51,372	211,600
Dearborn Heights, Mich.*	79,239		Lincoln, Nebr.	163,112	185,400
			Livonia, Mich.*	114,881	
Decatur, Ill.	89,604	427,300	London, Ont.	234,968	264,639
Des Moines, Iowa	194,168	331,300	Lorain, Ohio	84,907	268,700
Des Plaines, Ill.*	55,828		Louisville, Ky.	335,954	891,700
Detroit, Mich.	1,335,085	4,444,700	Madison, Wis.	168,196	309,900
Dubuque, Iowa	61,754	93,900	Mansfield, Ohio	56,916	130,400
East St. Louis, Ill.*	57,929		Milwaukee, Wis.	665,796	1,426,400
Eau Claire, Wis.	47,852	122,100	Minneapolis, Minn.	378,112	2,027,500
East Lansing, Mich.*	50,425		Mississauga, Ont.*	246,746	
Elgin, Ill.*	59,754		Muncie, Ind.	78,329	129,200
Elyria, Ohio	52,474		Muskegon, Mich.	44,176	177,600
Erie, Pa.	127,895	271,700	Nashville, Tenn.	423,426	753,100
Euclid, Ohio	63,307		Niagara Falls, N.Y.	80,773	
Evanston, Ill.*	76,665		Niagara Falls, Ont.	69,450	
Evansville, Ind.	133,566	287,500	Oak Lawn, Ill.*	62,317	
Farmington Hills, Mich.*	54,124		Oak Park, Ill.*	59,773	
			Omaha, Nebr.	371,455	572,900

* A suburb of a larger city.

(Continued)

table 12-1 (*Continued*)

name	population of principal city	population of metropolitan area
Oshawa, Ont.	106,002	133,959
Oshkosh, Wis.	59,182	
Ottawa, Ont.	291,088	668,853
Overland Park, Kans.*	81,013	
Owensboro, Ky.	50,788	81,200
Parma, Ohio	98,883	
Peoria, Ill.	125,983	351,100
Peterborough, Ont.	59,077	
Pontiac, Mich.	76,027	
Racine, Wis.	94,744	175,900
Rochester, Mich.	56,211	88,500
Rochester, N.Y.	267,173	971,200
Rockford, Ill.	145,459	270,900
Roseville, Mich.*	58,141	
Royal Oak, Mich.*	79,191	
Saginaw, Mich.	86,202	226,800
St. Catherines, Ont.	121,657	298,129
St. Clair Shores, Mich.*	85,934	
St. Cloud, Minn.	40,621	150,700
St. Joseph, Mo.	77,679	99,700
St. Louis, Mo.	524,964	2,369,500
St. Paul, Minn.	279,535	
Sarnia, Ont.	54,859	
Sioux City, Iowa	85,719	120,200
Sioux Falls, S.Dak.	73,925	100,100
Skokie, Ill.*	67,674	
South Bend, Ind.	117,478	279,000
Southfield, Mich.*	75,978	
Southfield, Ill.*	87,418	179,500
Springfield, Ohio	77,317	182,200
Sterling Heights, Mich.*	86,932	
Syracuse, N.Y.	182,543	647,800
Taylor, Mich.*	76,626	
Terre Haute, Ind.	63,998	171,000
Toledo, Ohio	367,650	781,400
Topeka, Kans.	119,203	178,300
Toronto, Ont.	611,171	2,753,112
Troy, Mich.*	55,169	
Utica, N.Y.	82,443	334,900
Warren, Mich.	172,755	
Waterloo, Iowa	77,681	134,500
Westland, Mich.*	92,689	
Windsor, Ont.	192,683	243,289
Wyoming, Mich.*	57,918	
Waukesha, Wis.	56,514	
West Allis, Wis.*	69,084	

* A suburb of a larger city.

Dayton, Indianapolis, Louisville, Nashville, and *Omaha.*

5 Succeeding levels in the hierarchy would successively enumerate smaller urban centers with successively less extensive fields of influence.

the outlook

The importance of this region to Anglo-America cannot be overstated. It includes a large share of the population and economic power of the United States, and it encompasses that relatively small part of Ontario that provides much of the economic and political leadership of Canada. Thanks to benign nature and enterprising people, the Heartland generally has had a prosperous past; its future should be similarly bright.

Although the farmers of the region occasionally suffer from the caprices of nature—drought, flood, tornado, hail, freezes, insect pests—agricultural problems are much more associated with marketing than with production. Free-market prices tend to be soft and erratic, and only the continuance of considerable government support, as distasteful as this is to all concerned, is likely to keep the farm economy viable. Current trends of fewer farms, larger farms, decreasing acreage, and increasing yields will probably continue—at least in the short run. The levels of accumulated crop surpluses may fluctuate from time to time, partly as a result of the international market and partly with changes in federal agricultural policies. Without strict government controls, however, continually increasing yields are virtually assured. The late 1970s, for example, saw all-time record yields of corn, soybeans, wheat, and hogs in the region, in each case surpassing records that had been established less than half a decade earlier.

But the tempo of the Heartland is geared to the city, not to the rural areas. Continuing urban-industrial expansion is now the norm in the United States and Canada, and this region is typical of the pattern. Economic indicators may glisten at more spectacular rates in some other areas such as the Gulf South, Texas, California, and British Columbia, but the Heartland will continue to be a region of solid economic vigor.

This is not to say that there will not be stagnation, poverty, and problems from place to place and from time to time. Certain districts will prosper more than others. Chicago should maintain and strengthen its primacy owing to its market and transportation advantages; Detroit's steel industry is likely to expand even more to accommodate the local market; metropolitan Toronto seems favored by growing markets and increased Seaway traffic; the Ohio Valley's coal-triggered boom should continue for some time. Overall, the region is blessed with many economic advantages. But there will be setbacks and erratic advances. Generally the economic future is bright for the world's largest and most productive agricultural-industrial region.

Economic and population growth nowadays, however, is not the unabashed delight that it once was. More urbanites mean more crowding, and more growth means more growing pains. The happiness quotient is not always a function of the stock market. Polluted air and polluted waterways are now also common in the Heartland. Even the vast expanse of Lake Erie is often so foul that its waters are unfit for swimming, much less for municipal water supply. Ecological and social problems can be expected to multiply along with population and economic growth.

fig. 12–24 A view across the Ohio River to Cincinnati, the principal metropolis of the Middle Ohio Valley. This bridge, built in the 1860s, was the first span across the Ohio River (courtesy Ohio Development Department).

selected bibliography

ABLER, RONALD, JOHN S. ADAMS, AND JOHN R. BORCHERT, *The Twin Cities of St. Paul and Minneapolis.* Cambridge, Mass.: Ballinger Publishing Co., 1976.

AKIN, WALLACE E., *The North Central United States.* Princeton, N.J.: D. Van Nostrand Company, Inc., 1968.

ALEXANDER, CHARLES S., AND NELSON R. NUNNALLY, "Channel Stability on the Lower Ohio River," *Annals,* Association of American Geographers, 62 (1972), 411–17.

BAINE, RICHARD P., AND A. LYNN MCMURRAY, *Toronto: An Urban Study.* Toronto: Clarke Irwin & Co., Ltd., 1970.

BANNISTER, GEOFFREY, "Population Changes in Southern Ontario," *Annals,* Association of American Geographers, 65 (1975), 177–88.

BERRY, BRIAN J. L., ET AL., *Chicago: Transformations of an Urban System.* Cambridge, Mass.: Ballinger Publishing Company, 1976.

BLUMSTEIN, J. F., AND B. WALTERS, eds., *Growing Metropolis: Aspects of Development in Nashville.* Nashville, Tenn.: Vanderbilt University Press, 1975.

BORCHERT, JOHN R., AND DONALD P. YAEGER, *Atlas of Minnesota Resources and Settlement.* St. Paul: Minnesota State Planning Agency, 1969.

BURGHARDT, ANDREW F., "A Hypothesis about Gateway Cities," Annals, Association of American Geographers, 61 (1971), 269–85.

CARLSON, ALVAR W., "Specialty Agriculture and Migrant Laborers in Northwestern Ohio," Journal of Geography, 75 (1976), 292–310.

CHAPMAN, L. J., AND D. F. PUTNAM, The Physiography of Southern Ontario. Toronto: University of Toronto Press, 1966.

CLARK, W. A. V., "Migration in Milwaukee," Economic Geography, 52 (1976), 48–60.

CUTLER, IRVING, Chicago: Metropolis of the Mid-Continent (2nd ed.). Dubuque, Iowa: Kendall/Hunt Publishing Company, 1976.

———, The Chicago Metropolitan Area: Selected Geographic Readings. New York: Simon and Schuster, 1970.

———, The Chicago-Milwaukee Corridor. Evanston, Ill.: Northwestern University, Department of Geography, 1965.

DACK, W. L., "Canada's Steel Industry Expands in a Big Way," Canadian Geographical Journal, 91 (October 1975), 32–41.

DAVIS, ANTHONY M., "The Prairie-Deciduous Forest Ecotone in the Upper Middle West," Annals, Association of American Geographers, 67 (1977), 204–13.

DEAN, W. G., ed., Economic Atlas of Ontario. Toronto: University of Toronto Press, 1969.

DEAR, MICHAEL, AND ANDREW F. BURGHARDT, "How Is Hamilton Coping with Growth?" Canadian Geographical Journal, 93 (October–November 1976), 22–31.

EHRHARDT, DENNIS K., "The St. Louis Daily Urban System," in Contemporary Metropolitan America, Vol. 3, Nineteenth Century Inland Centers and Ports, ed. John S. Adams, pp. 61–107. Cambridge, Mass.: Ballinger Publishing Company, 1976.

ELFORD, JEAN, "The St. Clair River: Centre Span of the Seaway," Canadian Geographical Journal, 86 (January 1973), 18–23.

———, "What Lake Tankers Mean to Central Canada," Canadian Geographical Journal, 88 (May 1974), 24–31.

GENTILCORE, LOUIS, ed., Ontario. Toronto: University of Toronto Press, 1972.

GREGOR, HOWARD F., "The Large Industrialized American Crop Farm: A Mid-Latitude Plantation Variant," Geographical Review, 40 (1970), 151–75.

HART, JOHN FRASER, "Field Patterns in Indiana," Geographical Review, 58 (1968), 450–71.

———, "A Map of the Agricultural Implosion," Proceedings, Association of American Geographers, 2 (1970), 68–71.

———, "The Middle West," Annals, Association of American Geographers, 62 (1972), 258–82.

HART, JOHN FRASER, AND RUSSEL B. ADAMS, "Twin Cities," Focus, 20 (February 1970), 1–11.

HART, JOHN FRASER, AND NEIL E. SALISBURY, "Population Change in Middle Western Villages: A Statistical Approach," Annals, Association of American Geographers, 55 (1965), 140–60.

HELLER, CHARLES F., ELDOR C. QUANDT, AND HENRY A. RAUP, Population Patterns of Southwestern Michigan. Kalamazoo, Mich.: Western Michigan University, Institute of Public Affairs, 1974.

JOHNSON, HILDEGARD BINGER, Order upon the Land: The U.S. Rectangular Land Survey and the Upper Mississippi Country. New York: Oxford University Press, 1976.

KARAN, PRADYUMNA K., Kentucky: A Regional Geography (2nd ed.). Dubuque, Iowa: Kendall/Hunt Publishing Company, 1976.

KERR, DONALD, AND JACOB SPELT, The Changing Face of Toronto. Ottawa: Department of Mines and Technical Surveys, Geographical Branch, 1965.

KIANG, YING-CHENG, "Recent Changes in the Distribution of Urban Poverty in Chicago," Professional Geographer, 28 (1976), 57–61.

KINGSBURY, ROBERT C., An Atlas of Indiana. Bloomington, Ind.: Indiana University, Department of Geography, 1970.

LANGMAN, R. C., Poverty Pockets: The Limestone Plains of Southern Ontario. Toronto: McClelland and Stewart, Ltd., 1975.

MATHER, COTTON, ET AL., Upper Coulee Country. Prescott, Wisc.: Trimbelle Press, 1975.

MAYER, HAROLD M., AND THOMAS CORSI, "The Northeastern Ohio Urban Complex," in Contemporary Metropolitan America, Vol. 3, Nineteenth Century Inland Centers and Ports, ed. John S. Adams, pp. 109–79. Cambridge, Mass.: Ballinger Publishing Company, 1976.

MAYER, HAROLD M., AND RICHARD C. WADE, Chicago: Growth of a Metropolis. Chicago, Ill.: University of Chicago Press, 1969.

MOSS, M. R., "Forest Regeneration in the Rural-Urban Fringe: A Study of Secondary Succession in the Niagara Peninsula," Canadian Geographer, 20 (1976), 141–57.

NELSON, RONALD E., *Illinois: Land and Life in the Prairie State.* Dubuque, Iowa: Kendall/Hunt Publishing Company, 1977.

POWLEDGE, FRED, "Profiles: Louisville, City in Transition," *The New Yorker* (9 September 1974), 42–83.

RAITZ, KARL B., "The Wisconsin Tobacco Shed: A Key to Ethnic Settlement and Diffusion," *Landscape*, 20 (October 1975), 32–37.

RAITZ, KARL B., AND E. COTTON MATHER, "Norwegians and Tobacco in Western Wisconsin," *Annals*, Association of American Geographers, 61 (1971), 684–96.

RAUP, HALLOCK F., AND CLYDE SMITH, *Ohio Geography: Selected Readings.* Dubuque, Iowa: Kendall/Hunt Publishing Company, 1973.

ROBINSON, ARTHUR H., AND JERRY B. CULVER, *The Atlas of Wisconsin.* Madison: University of Wisconsin Press, 1974.

SANTER, RICHARD A., *Michigan: Heart of the Great Lakes.* Dubuque, Iowa: Kendall/Hunt Publishing Company, 1977.

SIMMONS, JAMES, "How Much Growth Can Toronto Afford?" *Canadian Geographical Journal*, 92 (March–April 1976), 4–11.

SINCLAIR, ROBERT, *The Face of Detroit: A Spatial Synthesis.* Detroit, Mich.: Wayne State University, National Council for Geographic Education, United States Office of Education, 1970.

SINCLAIR, ROBERT, AND BRYAN THOMPSON, "Detroit," in *Contemporary Metropolitan America, Vol. 3, Nineteenth Century Inland Centers and Ports,* ed. John S. Adams, pp. 285–354. Cambridge, Mass.: Ballinger Publishing Company, 1976.

SMITH, PETER C., AND KARL B. RAITZ, "Negro Hamlets and Agricultural Estates in Kentucky's Inner Bluegrass," *Geographical Review*, 64 (1974), 217–24.

SOMMERS, LAWRENCE M., ed., *Atlas of Michigan.* Grand Rapids, Mich.: William B. Eerdmans Publishing Company, 1977.

SPELT, JACOB, *Toronto.* Don Mills, Ont.: Collier-MacMillan Canada, 1974.

————, *Urban Development in South-Central Ontario.* Toronto: McClelland & Stewart, 1972.

SWAIN, HARRY, AND E. COTTON MATHER, *St. Croix Border Country.* Prescott, Wisc.: Trimbelle Press, 1968.

WALKER, D. F., AND J. H. BATER, eds., *Industrial Development in Southern Ontario.* Waterloo, Ont.: University of Waterloo Press, 1974.

WARKENTIN, JOHN, "Southern Ontario: A View from the West," *Canadian Geographer*, 10 (1966), 157–71.

WARREN, K., *The American Steel Industry 1850–1970: A Geographic Interpretation.* New York: Oxford University Press, 1972.

YEATES, MAURICE, *Main Street: Windsor to Quebec City.* Toronto: MacMillan Company of Canada, 1975.

ZAKRZEWSKA, BARBARA, "Valleys of Driftless Areas," *Annals*, Association of American Geographers, 61 (1971), 441–59.

13

THE
GREAT
PLAINS

The Great Plains Region as recognized in this volume corresponds roughly with the Great Plains physiographic province that has been described by many geomorphologists and geographers.[1] On the basis of land-use and cropping patterns the extent of this region has been extended somewhat to the south to include ranching and irrigated farming country in south-central Texas and to the northeast to encompass the agricultural area of the Red River Valley (fig. 13–1). The entire eastern boundary of the region varies somewhat from the physiographic boundary, again on the basis of land-use patterns.

The problem of delimitation of the regional boundaries of the Great Plains has been discussed in some detail in chapter 5. In summary, the western boundary is marked fairly abruptly by the rise of the frontal ranges of the Rocky Mountains; the northern boundary represents the southern

margin of the boreal forest; and the eastern boundary is transitional between the extensive wheat-farming systems to the west and corn-and-general-farming systems to the east.

the changing regional image

This is a vast interior plains region whose unpredictable climate and dramatic weather have defied man's accurate assessment. This has resulted in fluctuating patterns of land use and economic well-being but has never changed the region's basic role as a quantity producer of selected agricultural and mineral resources for the continent.

The Great Plains Region contains some of the best soils and potentially most productive farmlands of Anglo-America; yet crop failures have alternated with crop surpluses, and accelerated soil erosion is commonplace. Relatively deep, dark-colored soils, which contain a considerable amount of organic matter and lime, are widespread. These soils, low relief, and much summer sunshine combine to provide several of the necessary ingredients for productive agriculture, but erratic precipitation, sometimes ill-advised farming practices, and the vagaries of market are inhibitory factors. Average annual precipitation is on the minimal

[1] See, for example, Wallace W. Atwood, *The Physiographic Provinces of North America* (Boston, Mass.: Ginn & Company, 1940); Nevin N. Fenneman, "Physiographic Divisions of the United States," *Annals*, Association of American Geographers, 18 (1928), 261–353; Charles B. Hunt, *Natural Regions of the United States and Canada* (San Francisco, Calif.: W. H. Freeman & Company, 1973); and William D. Thornbury, *Regional Geomorphology of the United States* (New York: John Wiley & Sons, Inc., 1965).

317

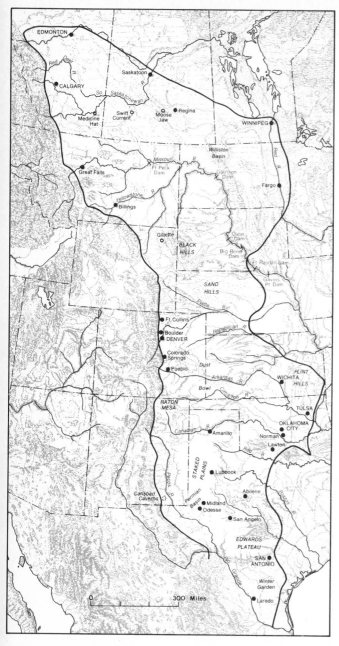

fig. 13–1 The Great Plains Region (base map copyright A. K. Lobeck; reprinted by permission of Hammond, Inc.).

side for crop production, and its usefulness is further limited by considerable fluctuations from the average in any given year, by the cloudburst nature of much of the rain, and by spring floods caused by rapid snowmelt and heavy showers.

In the past an expanding international market for wheat, and occasionally for other crops, has persuaded farmers to attempt cultivation of land that should not have been plowed. This has resulted in crop failures and soil abuse, most notably in dust bowl conditions. In a subhumid to semiarid region such as this, the dangers of accelerated soil erosion are great, and wind erosion, in particular, has left its mark on extensive areas. The history of the region is thus marked by occasional monumental crop failures, although in recent years bumper crops have resulted in stupendous surpluses.

Within the region relatively few people are engaged in the primary production of relatively few products, but their output is tremendous. The total farm and ranch population of the region is only a small percentage of the Anglo-American total; yet well over half of the continent's annual output of wheat, grain sorghums, barley, rye, flax, mohair, and potash originates in the region. In addition there is notable production of cotton, cattle, wool, petroleum, and natural gas. The gathering, storage, transportation, and sometimes processing of these products are major activities in the region and employ a large number of people, although there are marked seasonal fluctuations. Ultimately the great majority of the output leaves the region for most of its processing, as well as for final disposition to consumers.

Although the cities are growing and many of the villages are stagnating, there is a strong rural orientation to life. As in the rest of Anglo-America, increasing urbanization is characteristic of the Great Plains. Many of the small towns and villages, however, do not show marked growth tendencies (fig. 13–2); the larger cities are the growth centers. Overall, even though the majority of the populace is urban, primary produc-

fig. 13–2 The characteristic Great Plains landscape
consists of extensive cropland (strip-cropped wheat
here) and pasture, dotted with small towns that
are marked by tall grain elevators. This is
Cowley, Alberta (Alberta Government photo).

tion has always been such a significant
backbone of the economy that rurally
oriented viewpoints, values, opinions, and
judgments are often prevalent.

The character of the region encompasses
a curious mixture of the drab and the grandiose. Flat land, endless horizons, blowing
dust, colorless vistas, withering towns, and
workaday tasks emphasize the former. But
many facets of the Great Plains scene are on
an heroic scale: sweeping views, dramatic
weather, natural calamities, stupendous production, staggering problems, and immense
distances.

In the past the Great Plains stereotype
was a vast land of dry, treeless plains,
sparsely settled and mainly given over to the
raising of cattle. But technological change
has come to this region as it has to most
of Anglo-America. Improved dry-farming
techniques, the development of large-scale
irrigation enterprises, expanded oil and
gas output, the establishment of miltary

bases in the region, and the rapid growth of
significant urban-industrial nodes have
combined to reshape the distinctive image
of the Great Plains.

the physical setting

It is convenient to think of the physical geography of the Great Plains as being uniform, the flat land engendering basic
homogeneity in other physical aspects.
There is some validity to this concept of
broad regional unity in terms of gross patterns; in any sort of detailed consideration of
the region, however, there is a quite notable
variety of contrasts—in physical as well as in
cultural geography. The words applied by
two geographers to the Oklahoma panhandle are relevant to the entire region:

*Within this area means are insignificant, averages mis-
leading, and generalizations are often invalid. Flat*

319

plains alternate with dissected semibadlands; bitter cold and snow vie with blistering heat and dust; fertile calcareous soils contrast with sterile blow sand; bounteous grain yields alternate with crop failures; huge ranches compete with small subsistence farms; emigration meets immigration.[2]

TERRAIN

The region has the basic topographic unity of an extensive plains area (fig. 13–3), but in detail the plains character is only true in the broadest sense owing to significant variations from area to area. The underlying structure is a broad geosyncline composed of several basins separated by gentle arches, the surface bedrock consisting mostly of gently dipping sedimentary strata of Cretaceous and Tertiary age. The surface expression is an extensive plain that is highest in the west and gradually descends to the east at an average regional slope of about 10 feet per mile.[3] Near the western margin the plain

is in some places more than 6,000 feet above sea level; at the eastern edge the average altitude is less than 1,500 feet. There are great aprons of alluvial deposits near the Rocky Mountain front and along the major river valleys, and glacial deposits thinly cover the surface north and east of the Missouri River.

There are several prominent physiographic subdivisions that can be recognized on the basis of their landform associations. From south to north, these include:

1 The Rio Grande Plain is flattish throughout, with some incised river valleys.

2 The Central Texas Hill Country consists of a broad crescent of low but steepsided hills that form the dissected margin of the Edwards Plateau on its eastern and southern sides and somewhat to the north. Associated features include an eroded dome of Precambrian rocks and a number of large fault-line springs that discharge around the edge of the hills.

3 The High Plains section of the Great Plains occupies most of the area from the Edwards Plateau northward to Nebraska. Much of it is extraordinarily flat, except where crossed by one of the major eastwardflowing rivers. The surface rock is mostly a thick mantle of Tertiary sediments. The extreme flatness is partly a result of a concentration of carbonates (caliche) in a "cap rock" layer that resists erosion and is partly due to surface formations that are sandy and thus highly porous. In both cases water erosion is at a minimum, except along the escarpmentlike edges of the cap rock and where certain rivers, particularly the Canadian and Red, have cut down through the resistant surface. In west Texas and eastern New Mexico is the Llano Estacado ("Staked Plains") where there are some 30,000 square miles of almost perfect flatness, essentially unmarked by stream erosion. The Edwards Plateau, extending southeastward from the Llano Estacado, is geologically different but topographically identical.

4 The longitudinal valley of the Pecos River is a gentle trough lying below the level

[2] Arthur H. Doerr and John W. Morris, "The Oklahoma Panhandle—a Cross-Section of the Southern High Plains," *Economic Geography*, 36 (January 1960), 70.

[3] Thornbury, *Regional Geomorphology of the United States*, p. 288.

of the Llano Estacado and is characterized by karst features and gravel-capped terraces.

5 The Raton Mesa section along the New Mexico–Colorado border consists of a series of mesas and buttes supported by basalt flows, along with a few cinder cone volcanoes.

6 The Colorado Piedmont is an irregularly shaped zone extending along the Rocky Mountain front from the Arkansas Valley to the Platte Valley where much of the Tertiary alluvium has been eroded, causing the surface to be lower than the High Plains to the east. Topography here is strongly controlled by stream dissection.

7 The Nebraska Sand Hills cover much of the western and central portions of that state. The area is a maze of sand dunes and ridges that rise to several hundred feet in height and are separated by numerous small basins.

8 The Unglaciated Missouri Plateau occupies most of the northern Great Plains north of Nebraska and south of the Missouri River. There is considerable variety to the topography, but most is gently undulating. There are conspicuous badlands in South Dakota, North Dakota, and Montana, as well as notable outliers of the Rocky Mountains (fig. 13–4).

9 The Glaciated Missouri Plateau section, north and east of the Missouri River, demonstrates many features of glacial origin on its surface, particularly moraines and ponds.

10 The Lake Agassiz Basin encompasses the valley of the Red River of the North, as well as much of southern Manitoba and eastern Saskatchewan. Lake Agassiz was the largest of the late Pleistocene ice marginal lakes, and its ancient lake bed is extremely flat and deeply floored with silty clay. Several dozen beach lines are identifiable.

In the northwestern portion of the Great Plains, several isolated ranges are offset from the Rocky Mountains. Although most are topographically and geologically related to

fig. 13–4 Irregular terrain is also widespread in the region. Most difficult to traverse are the extensive badlands, which occur in various locations. This section is in western Nebraska (Union Pacific Railroad photo).

the Rockies, their outlying position makes them a part of the Great Plains Region. The largest and most conspicuous of the outliers is the Black Hills; others are shown in figure 13–5.

DRAINAGE AND HYDROGRAPHY

There is generally good drainage throughout the region, with some significant exceptions. Much of the area north and east of the Missouri River is dotted with small lakes and marshes, which is generally the result of Pleistocene glacial deposition. Drainage in the Nebraska Sand Hill area is also irregular, with many small basins and pockets that do not have exterior drainage outlets.

The basic stream-flow pattern of the region is from west to east; the rivers rise in the Rocky Mountains and flow down the regional slope to join the Mackenzie, Hudson Bay, Mississippi, or Gulf of Mexico systems. The only two significant variants from this pattern are the Red River of the North, which flows northward into Lake Winnipeg, and the Pecos River, which flows generally southward to become a tributary of the Rio

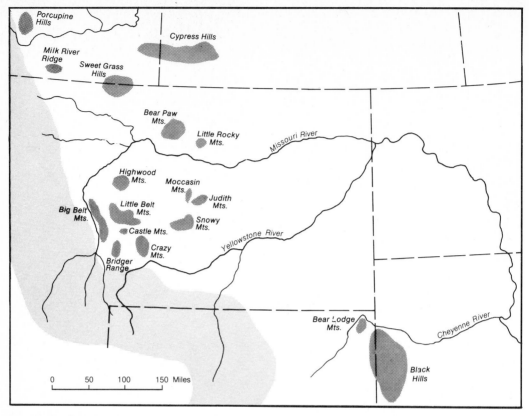

fig. 13–5 Principal mountain outliers in the northern Great Plains. The extensive shaded area on the left represents the Rocky Mountains.

Grande. Most of the principal river valleys are conspicuous as narrow strings of irrigated agriculture, denser rural settlement, and urban clusters.

Large or medium-sized natural lakes are virtually unknown in the region. A number of large reservoirs have been constructed, however, and more are planned. The most prominent are those along the Missouri River, where there is now little free-flowing water from eastern Montana to northeastern Nebraska.

CLIMATE

In such a latitudinally extended region there is considerable variation in climate, particularly in temperature. The essential characteristics, however, are clear-cut: moisture conditions are subhumid to semiarid, with evaporation usually exceeding precipitation; there are pronounced seasonal extremes; and there is much drama and violence in day-to-day weather conditions (fig. 13–6).

The climate of the Great Plains is continental; precipitation ranges from 15 inches in the northwest to 35 in the southeast and varies greatly from year to year. There are periods of dry years, when the westerly margins become almost desertic. The growing season varies from about 120 days in the north to about 300 days in the south. Summers are normally very hot, although the duration of high temperatures is much shorter in the northern part of the region than in the southern.

fig. 13-6 The region is famous for its dramatic weather. Here a thunderstorm builds up on the plains of southern Alberta.

Winters are bitterly cold[4] and dry and therefore very hard on such perennials as cultivated hay and fruit trees. The differences in temperature between winter and summer are so great as to give this region the distinction of having one of the greatest ranges of any region in Anglo-America.

Precipitation is the most important climatic factor of the Great Plains. The rainfall is less than 20 inches annually throughout most of the area (hilly and mountain regions excepted), and it has wide year-to-year variations. In a humid area an annual variation of approximately 15 inches would not be significant; but here, where the average is less than 20, a downward fluctuation of only a few inches may be disastrous for agriculture. Wet and dry years tend to run in periods of varying lengths and intensities. Since instrument records first became available, there have been four major drought periods in the Great Plains; they were roughly two decades apart, with the mid-points in 1892, 1912, 1934, and 1953.[5]

The high evaporation, ranging from 68 inches in southwest Texas to 37 inches in northern Montana, results from high wind velocities and a maximum of sunshine. These factors also reduce precipitation effectiveness.

Summer winds are so hot and dry and those of winter so biting and cold that most farms have trees planted as a windbreak to reduce surface wind velocities. In the western part of the region, however, from Colorado northward, the winter weather is sporadically ameliorated by *chinook* winds. These warming, drying, downslope winds from the Rockies bring periods of relative mildness that are a welcome relief to both people and livestock.

The Great Plains has the highest incidence of hail of any region in Anglo-America. The crop-destroying nature of the ice pellets is so intense that hail insurance is important to most farmers, particularly in the northern portion.

[4] Steffanson, the last of the great Arctic explorers, has been quoted as saying that if you can live in Winnipeg you can live anywhere in the Arctic, as regards winter discomfort. See George Jacobsen, "The Northern Urban Scene," in *Canada's Changing North*, ed. William C. Wonders (Toronto: McClelland and Steward Limited, 1971), p. 292.

[5] John R. Borchert, "The Dust Bowl in the 1970s," *Annals*, Association of American Geographers, 61 (March 1971), 2.

fig. 13–7 After a blizzard this northeastern Colorado rancher scatters hay to his cattle (Union Pacific Railroad photo).

Above all, this is a region of violent weather conditions and abrupt day-to-day or even hour-to-hour weather changes. The horizon may be flat and dull in the Great Plains, but the skies are often turbulent and exciting. Cold fronts, warm fronts, tornadoes, thunderstorms, blizzards, heat waves, hail storms, and dust storms are all part of the annual pageant of weather in this region (fig. 13–7).

SOILS

The soils of the wheat belts, among the most fertile in Anglo-America, are mostly Mollisols. They have a lime zone, a layer of calcium carbonate a few inches or a few feet beneath the surface within reach of plant roots. Because of the scanty rainfall, these soils have not had the lime leached from them. Their fertility—when combined with greater rainfall—makes them the most productive, broadly distributed soils in the world, although there is less humus than in the grassland soils to the east. They are characterized by being dark-colored, rich in organic matter, well supplied with chemical bases, and usually containing a subsurface accumulation of carbonates, salts, and clay.

In drier localities Entisols and Aridisols are dominant, particularly in eastern Colorado, Wyoming, and Montana and in western Nebraska. These soils contain little organic matter and are either dry and clayey or dry and sandy, although their level of natural fertility is generally high.

NATURAL VEGETATION

Between the forests on the east and the mountains on the west lie the prairies and the steppe. The prairie, whose grasses attain a height usually of 1 to 3 feet, characterizes areas with 20 to 25 inches of precipitation in the north and 35 to 40 inches in the south. Merging with the prairie on the semiarid fringe to the west is the steppe, whose grasses are of low stature and where rainfall is less than 20 inches.

The native vegetation of the semiarid grazing portion of the Great Plains is dominantly short grass, with grama and buffalo grasses most conspicuous. Before the introduction of livestock in the latter half of the nineteenth century, luxuriant native grasses (mainly western wheat grass) covered extensive areas. Overgrazing and extension of wheat farming into unsuitable areas reduced thousands of square miles to a semidesert.

The entire region is not grass-covered, of course. The isolated upland enclaves are mostly forested, primarily with Rocky Mountain conifers, plus aspen and willow. The largest forest area is in the Black Hills, but tree cover is also dominant in the Raton Mesa area, the so-called Black Forest between Colorado Springs and Denver, portions of the Nebraska Sand Hills, most of the Montana mountain outliers, and almost every hill in the southern Prairie Provinces. A scrubby cedar woodland also covers much of the central Texas hill country and some of the cap-rock escarpment faces in that same state.

The major stream valleys of the region are usually marked by a narrow band of riparian timber, nearly all of which consists of cottonwood, willows, poplars, and similar deciduous species.

During the past century there has been a massive invasion of much of central and southern Texas by a deep-rooted, scrubby tree called mesquite (*Prosopis juliflora*); it is native to the area but has greatly expanded its range, presumably as the result of overgrazing, short-term climatic fluctuations, and cessation of recurrent grassland fires.[6] This has significantly reduced the grazing forage and has encouraged ranchers to undertake stringent control campaigns, involving poisons, burning, and especially uprooting with heavy equipment.

In the last century, junipers (*Juniperus* spp.) have similarly expanded their range over more than 25 million acres of what had been mostly grassland in central and western Texas. There are nine species of these hardy, scrubby, fragrant conifers—which are often inaccurately referred to as "cedars"—in the southern plains. Although useful for fence posts and as a source of oil to add an aroma to household detergents, junipers, like mesquite, are generally considered to be pastoral pests.

[6] David R. Harris, "Recent Plant Invasions in the Arid and Semi-Arid Southwest of the United States," *Annals*, Association of American Geographers, 56 (September 1966), 408–22.

WILDLIFE

The Great Plains Region was the principal habitat of the American bison, with an estimated 50 million of these magnificent beasts occupying the region at the coming of the white man. Once white penetration of the region got under way in earnest, practically all the vast herds were exterminated in less than a decade (fig. 13–8)

Other hoofed animals—pronghorn antelope, deer, elk, and mountain sheep—were also common. They suffered a lesser fate than the bison, mostly being pushed into the mountains to the west as settlement advanced.

Although this is a subhumid region, furbearers were numerous along the streams. Beaver, muskrat, mink, and otter attracted the trappers and fur traders, who were, with the exception of a few explorers, the first whites to penetrate the region.

A tremendous number of small, shallow marshes and ponds dot the glaciated terrain of the Dakotas and Prairie Provinces. These poorly drained areas provide an excellent muskrat habitat and are used as summer breeding ground for myriads of waterfowl

fig. 13–8 Several herds of bison are maintained under quasi-wild conditions in the region. The largest numbers are found in Custer State Park in the Black Hills of South Dakota.

fig. 13–9 The "duck factory" of the northern plains consists of tens of thousands of small ponds and marshes. This is Beaverhill Lake in central Alberta (Alberta Government photo).

(fig. 13–9). It is estimated that about half of all the ducks in North America breed in these ponds of the northern Great Plains.[7]

Several exotic species have been introduced to this region, generally to provide more prey for hunters. Most important by far is the ring-necked pheasant (*Phasianus colchicus*), which has become well-established in every state and province from Colorado and Kansas northward. Because of the money spent by nonresident hunters, pheas-

ant hunting has become so important to the economy of South Dakota that it is one of the prime economic and political factors in that state.

sequent occupance of the great plains

The human saga of the Great Plains, with its varied stages of occupance and settlement and its diversified attempts at satisfactory and profitable land use, is a dramatic and interesting one. Only a few of the highlights are recounted here, with emphasis on the sequential occupance of the region.

The Plains Indians occupy a special place in Anglo-American history because of their relationship to the Wild West era and their midcontinent position athwart the axis of the westward flow of empire. At the time of European contact, the Indians of the Great Plains consisted of about two dozen major tribes, most of which were scattered in small semisedentary settlements over a particular territory. Their livelihood was based partly on hunting, especially buffalo, and partly on farming, particularly corn; their chief avocation was combat with other tribes; and one of their major problems was lack of transportation over the vastness of the plains.

By the middle of the eighteenth century essentially all the Plains Indians had obtained horses, and most had become expert in their use. They became much more mobile, much more effective as hunters, and much more deadly as warriors. Some tribes—such as the Dakota (Sioux) and Blackfeet in the north, and the Comanche and Apache in the south—became very powerful and for many years exerted a strong influence over parts of the region. Their dominance was eventually challenged and overthrown, however, in part by Eastern tribes that were displaced to the plains by whites; in part by the virtual extermination of bison, the principal food supply; but mainly by the overwhelming superiority of white soldiers and settlers.

The last stronghold of Indians in the

---

[7] David A. Munro, "The Prairies and the Ducks," *Canadian Geographical Journal*, 75 (July 1967), 3.

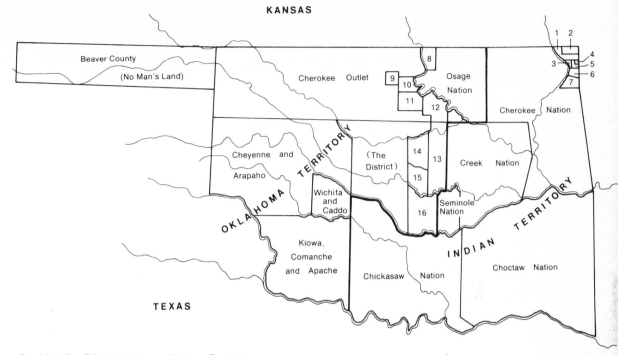

fig. 13-10 Tribal divisions of Indian Territory
and Oklahoma Territory, generalized for the late 1800s:
(1) Peoria, (2) Quapaw, (3) Ottawa, (4) Modoc, (5) Shawnee,
(6) Wyandot, (7) Seneca, (8) Kansa, (9) Tonkawa, (10) Ponca,
(11) Oto and Missouri, (12) Pawnee, (13) Sauk and Fox,
(14) Iowa, (15) Kickapoo, and (16) Potawatomi and Shawnee.
(From *A Guide to the Indian Tribes of Oklahoma*, by Muriel H. Wright.
Copyright 1951 by the University of Oklahoma Press.)

Great Plains was the Indian Territory established between Texas and Kansas (fig. 13–10). Displaced tribes from the Southeast were settled there in the early 1800s, and Midwestern and Plains tribes were relegated there after the Civil War. Eventually Indian Territory became Oklahoma, and all its reservations were dissolved.

The first significant movement of white settlers into the region came from the south, from Mexico. Very early in the eighteenth century Spanish settlers moved north of the Rio Grande, following missionaries who had come to the Tejas Indians in 1690. Their major bastion in this region was San Antonio, founded in 1718 (the same year that New Orleans was founded by the French).

For several decades, Spanish and later Mexican settlers trickled into what is now southern Texas. They were soon joined by Anglos, who were attracted by Mexico's initially generous land-grant policies. Most of the early Anglo settlement of Texas, however, was to the east of the Great Plains Region.

The first white settlers in the central and northern plains were not slow to follow the explorers and fur traders of the early nineteenth century, but most of the major early parties were moving across the region to Oregon, Utah, and California. In the meantime the prairies of the eastern part of the region were being occupied by farmers who moved out of the forested Midwest, the major thrust being into Kansas. The west-

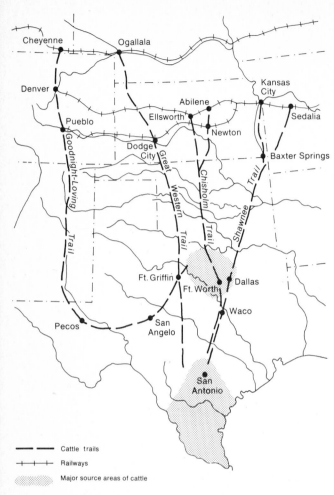

stock enterprise that lacked only one significant factor, a market. This problem was soon solved by trail driving the cattle northward to railheads in Missouri and Kansas. Trail driving started in 1866 and lasted for barely two decades, long enough to establish an enduring legend. During this period much of the northern plains area was also stocked by Longhorns that were overlanded to Wyoming and Montana from Texas.

The open-range trail drives were soon replaced by established ranches, which were made possible by the use of barbed wire for fencing and windmills to augment water supply. A vast cattle kingdom of large ranches soon spread the length and breadth of the Great Plains, with sheep introduced into some areas.

Railways provided the next catalyst to settlement. It was hoped that they would accelerate all phases of development of the region, but as it turned out, their main function was to provide access to markets for the products of the plains. The railways received huge land grants and sold much of the land to settlers.[8] But only in the Canadian portion of the region did the railway, the Canadian Pacific, actually colonize; the others merely sold land.

The flood tide of settlement in the Great Plains was most prominent in the last three decades of the nineteenth century. During the 1870s Nebraska's population more than tripled to nearly half a million; Kansas reached the million mark early in the 1880s. The Great Plains were "tamed," the age of the farmer began, and the frontier moved westward to other regions.

There was only a slight increase in cattle on the plains after 1890. The encroachment of the wheat farmer curtailed the amount of land available for cattle ranches, and overgrazing on the drier western parts still further reduced the area.

After 1910 several new influences made themselves felt in the region. The develop-

fig. 13–11 Major cattle trails and railways of the southern plains during the trail-driving era, from the 1860s to 1880s.

ward flow of settlement into the region was soon in full swing, to be interrupted only partially by the Civil War.

After the war the cowboy era came to the Great Plains. The extensive diamond-shaped area of south Texas, between San Antonio and Brownsville, was the home of literally millions of wild Longhorn cattle and thousands of wild Mustang horses (fig. 13–11). To the penniless returning Confederate soldiers who were hard-working enough, here was the raw material of a live-

[8] The Union Pacific, for example, received 20 square miles of land for every mile of track laid.

ment of the tractor, combine, and other power machinery made feasible the planting and harvesting of a much larger acreage of land. Numerous drought-resistant crops, especially wheat and the grain sorghums, were planted on the plains. The high prices during both world wars resulted in further expansion of the wheat area, and many overstocked and overgrazed native pastures were plowed up and planted.

ERRORS MADE IN SETTLEMENT

It is always easy to see errors after they are made. Settlers coming into the region homesteaded quarter-sections, the amount permitted the head of a family in accordance with the Homestead Act of 1862. They plowed up the grass on land that was unsuitable for cultivation. They soon learned that they could not make a satisfactory living growing wheat on 160 acres, especially in the western margin. A family needed more land here than in humid regions where intensive methods were practicable.

In 1904 the Kincaid Act increased to 640 acres the amount of land that could be homesteaded in western Nebraska, and in 1909 the Enlarged Homestead Act established the 320-acre homestead over a large area. But even these enlarged homesteads, including those made possible by the Stockraising Homestead Act of 1916, proved to be little more than gestures in the right direction. The great weakness of all these acts was that they did not fit conditions west of the 100th meridian and 20-inch rainfall line. The desire for small farms within semiarid Anglo-America was tenacious but untenable. In 1934 and 1935, all remaining unreserved and unappropriated public lands in the United States were withdrawn from homesteading by the federal government.

Possibly the biggest mistake of all was made during the first world war when the price of wheat skyrocketed, and it was every farmer's patriotic duty to feed the Allies and win the war. This meant growing wheat and more wheat. Millions of acres that had never been anything but grazing land were attacked with tractor-drawn plows and seeded with wheat. Improved machinery enabled large amounts of power per person to be employed in crop production. The increase in wheat acreage took place mostly as a western extension outside the so-called Winter Wheat Belt.

The yield was favorable at first, for the soil was fertile, rains were plentiful, and there was much moisture in the subsoil. Farmers grew wheat year after year. Before long, however, the soil-binding quality of the humus became depleted by continuous cropping. Livestock were turned in to graze the poorly developed crop, and their hoofs pulverized the ground. Then in the spring of 1934, winds began to blow the soil. Great clouds of dust swept eastward from this land largely devoid of anchoring vegetation. Thus the nation paid a high price for having grown wheat on grazing land. And yet that is what might be expected from a people who had inherited the idea that in America land is practically unlimited and soil is inexhaustible.

The Dust Bowl at its greatest extent covered 16 million acres. During the months December to May, the blow season, fine fertile soil particles were whisked hundreds of miles away forming "black blizzards." The heavier particles remained as drifts and hummocks. Sand dunes attained heights of 20 feet. The atmosphere was choked with dust; in some areas people had to put cloth over their faces when going out of doors. The vegetation in the fields was coated and rendered inedible for cattle, and whole groups of counties became almost unlivable.

The Dust Bowl has been shrinking, however, because of greater and better-distributed rainfall, the regrassing of extensive areas, and the erosion-preventive measures or new farming techniques of the Soil Conservation Service and other federal and state organizations. New techniques, including contour plowing and strip cropping, have been devised to utilize all the rain that falls.

contemporary population of the great plains

A current map of population distribution would show a fairly open and regular pattern, generally decreasing from east to west. In detail the irrigated valleys stand out as distinct strings of denser occupance. The topographically unfavorable areas, such as the Sand Hills and various badlands and mountain outliers, are quite barren of population.

There is considerable ethnic homogeneity to the population of the Great Plains. Most of the people are of European origin, and the vast majority is Anglo-Saxon. Asians are almost nonexistent in the populace, and blacks are a smaller minority than in any other major region of the United States. In the Dakotas, for example, less than 0.5 percent of the population is black.

The principal ethnic "minority" consists of Hispanos, who are prominent in portions of Texas, New Mexico, and Colorado. The major concentration is in southern Texas, where more than half of the citizenry of San Antonio (second largest city in the region) is of Hispanic extraction.

There is a varied European ethnic mix in the Canadian portion of the region. The only concentration of French Canadians in western Canada is found in the St. Boniface suburb of Winnipeg, but Ukrainians and other Eastern Europeans are prominent in many parts of the Prairie Provinces.

Indians are a significant proportion of the population in Oklahoma, where more than 100,000 citizens of Indian extraction represent some 36 tribes. There are large Indian reservations in South Dakota and Montana. The Blood Reserve in Alberta is the largest in Canada.

The most significant characteristic of the population of the Great Plains, however, is probably its urbanity. Despite the prominence of a rural way of life in most of the region, the population is estimated to be nearly 70 percent urban.

crop farming

Although crop growing does not occupy so much acreage as livestock raising, it is the most conspicuous use of the land in the Great Plains. The close-knit precision of the rows of irrigated cotton in the Texas High Plains, the gargantuan linearity of strip-cropped wheat in central Montana, and the immense cultivated circles serviced by "walking" sprinkler irrigators in western Kansas are representative of the grandiose geometry of Great Plains farming that is obvious even to the traveler jetting 40,000 feet above the region (fig. 13–12).

Despite the fact that the region had an "historic position on the margins of both moisture and accessibility for crop agriculture in the eastern half of the continent,"[9] the natural advantages for growing certain kinds of crops are not to be denied. Flat land and fertile soil combined with some sort of water source make this a region of prodigious production for grains, oilseeds, and some irrigated crops. Wheat is the keystone on which fortunes are made and governments are elected, but active efforts toward diversification have also brought significance to other crops.

The region as a whole is characterized by a mixture of intensive and extensive farming. Irrigated vegetables, sugar beets, and cotton typify the former; wheat, other

fig. 13–12 The geometrical precision of strip-cropped wheat near Great Falls, Montana.

[9] Borchert, "The Dust Bowl in the 1970s," p. 1.

small grains, and oilseeds, the latter. Storage, transportation, and processing facilities are conspicuous in every farming area—cotton gins here, sugar mills there, and grain elevators looming on the flat horizon in every town.

WHEAT FARMING

Wheat is widely grown throughout the United States and Canada, but the two most important areas are the Winter Wheat Belt in Kansas, Nebraska, Colorado, Oklahoma, and Texas; and the Spring Wheat Belt in the Dakotas, Montana, western Minnesota and the Prairie Provinces (fig. 13–13).

The two wheat-growing areas are not contiguous. Between them (in southern South Dakota and northern Nebraska) is a belt where little wheat is grown. Much of this is Sand Hill country, a disordered ar-

rangement of grass-covered slopeland that is unsuited to cultivation.

The Winter Wheat Area The typical farm in the Winter Wheat Belt is large—it has to be. The size is greater in the western than in the eastern part. In central Kansas, the heart of the area, farms approach 1,000 acres. Windbreaks on the windward sides of many farmsteads are conspicuous features of the landscape. Windbreaks offer, among other advantages, protection from the cold, dry northwest winds of winter and the hot southwest winds of summer.

The seasonal rhythm of winter wheat cultivation begins with planting in late summer or fall. The seeds germinate, and growth begins. By the time winter sets in, the green wheat seedlings have raised their shoots several inches above the ground. Winter is a period of dormancy, but the shoots can begin growth with the first warm

fig. 13–13   The Winter Wheat Belt is centered on Kansas, and the Spring Wheat Belt focuses on North Dakota.

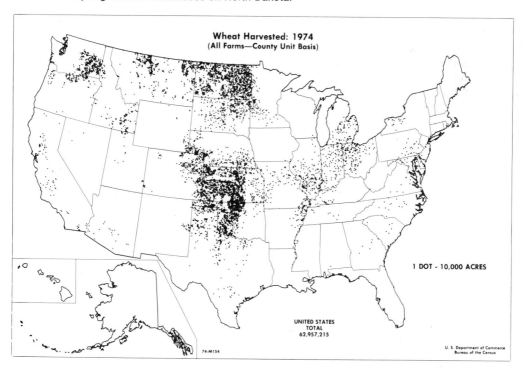

Wheat Harvested: 1974
(All Farms—County Unit Basis)

1 DOT - 10,000 ACRES

UNITED STATES
TOTAL
62,957,215

74-M154

U. S. Department of Commerce
Bureau of the Census

fig. 13–14 Harvesting winter wheat on the High Plains of western Texas (courtesy USDA Soil Conservation Service).

days of spring. The crop is ready for harvesting by late May or early June in the southern part of the region, and even in Montana it can normally be harvested before August (fig. 13–14).

Winter wheat is increasingly being cultivated in the northern part of the Great Plains Region because, where it can survive winter, it generally gives larger and more valuable yields than does spring wheat. Improved varieties of seed are more tolerant of cold weather and allow a northward shift. Today hardly any spring wheat is grown in eastern Wyoming. In South Dakota spring wheat is still the leader, but winter varieties are rapidly gaining in favor. In the plains area of Montana there is actually more winter than spring wheat grown, and even in southwestern Alberta there is increasing cultivation of winter wheat.

The Spring Wheat Area Only in North Dakota, western Minnesota, and most of the Prairie Provinces does spring wheat still hold undisputed sway. Spring wheat is planted as soon as the ground thaws and dries in late spring or early summer. It grows during the long days of summer, and the harvest takes place in August, September, or occasionally October. Unlike winter wheat, which is cut and threshed in a single combined operation, spring wheat normally is harvested in two steps. The stalks are first cut and raked into long windrows, where they are left for a few days to dry out. Spring wheat usually contains so much moisture that it would mildew in storage if not dried first. After drying, it is safe to collect and thresh the wheat.

Dry Farming versus Irrigation Most wheat in the Great Plains Region is grown under natural rainfall conditions. One of the great advantages and attractions to wheat growing is that it is capable of producing a plentiful harvest on a minimum of rainfall. In some parts of the region, satisfactory yields are obtained where the annual rainfall is only 11 inches.

In order to maximize the effectiveness of the scanty precipitation, it is characteristic for wheat farmers, particularly those in the western part of the region, to utilize special "dry-farming" techniques. The simplest and most widespread of these techniques is stripcropping, in which strips of wheat are alternated with strips of fallow land. Care is taken to see that nothing grows on the fallow strips; the year's rainfall is thus "stored" in the soil of those strips so that it can be utilized the next year when the fallow strips are cropped and the cropped strips left fallow. One of the most distinctive landscape patterns in the Great Plains is the expansive crop-and-fallow stripping of dry-farmed wheat areas. The strips are usually oriented north-south, which is at right angles to the prevailing westerly winds, in order to minimize damage from wind erosion.

A relatively small proportion of the Great Plains wheat crop is irrigated. Where irrigation is practiced, yields are much higher. A farmer who has irrigation resources available, however, is likely to grow more valuable crops than wheat, for one of the virtues of wheat is its relative productivity without irrigation.

Harvesting Problems To equalize the seasonal distribution of labor is difficult, particularly in a monocultural region. In the early days of wheat growing labor was scarce, especially during harvest; accordingly, migratory workers, tempted by substantial wages and a relatively short working period, poured into the area. They started in Texas and Oklahoma, where the harvest begins in early June, and moved northward at the rate of about 100 miles a week. They arrived in Nebraska in early July and in the Dakotas in August. Some of them went on to the Prairie Provinces, where the harvest begins in September. Labor of this kind was expensive, but when the kernels are ripe, wheat must be harvested, threshed, and put under cover before rain falls.

Migrant workers have been important in wheat harvesting for many decades. They operate as custom-combining crews, working northward throughout the long summer and returning to their homes and families, usually in Texas, for the winter. After World War II there was a decided decline in custom combining, as wheat farmers had accumulated sufficient wealth and land to make it feasible for most of them to own their own combines. Since the mid-fifties, however, federal wheat acreage controls have caused a swing back to custom combining. Some 16,-000 men work as combine crews, following the northward harvest trail. More than one-third of the total wheat crop is combined by migratory crews; the proportion is twice as great in much of the Winter Wheat Belt.

Sidewalks and Suitcases Extensive wheat growing lends itself easily to absentee ownership. If no livestock are kept on the farm, a resident operator is not needed. Work needs to be done only at seeding and harvest times, and even this can be custom contracted. Special terminology has therefore come into being to identify certain types of wheat farmers. A "sidewalk farmer" lives and works in a nearby town but can drive to the farm when there is work to be done there. A "suitcase farmer" is likely to live farther away, perhaps in another state, and pay only occasional visits to the wheat property. Sometimes the suitcase farmer owns land in both Winter and Spring wheat belts, migrating back and forth with machinery at planting and harvesting times.

Transportation of Wheat Since the population in this region is so small and wheat production is so great, the bulk of the crop is shipped elsewhere, except for the surplus that ordinarily goes to nearby newly constructed storage bins. Accordingly, wheat regions must have good transport facilities. The crop is first carried by truck from the farm to one of the many small country elevators distributed throughout the wheat belt alongside the railroads (fig. 13–15). From there it goes by rail to some large primary market. Getting the grain to elevators before rains set in has long been a major problem, necessitating the bringing in of freight cars by the tens of thousands.

In the United States the wheat is taken from the elevators to larger primary markets by rail. That which is destined for domestic consumption continues via train to the milling centers. Export wheat is normally shipped from Great Lakes ports during the summer season of navigation. Some is also exported year-round from Atlantic coastal cities, and barge traffic down the Mississippi for transshipment on oceangoing vessels

fig. 13–15 The relative importance of small Great Plains towns is often shown by the number of grain elevators present. Brownville, Alberta, is a five-elevator town (courtesy Canadian Pacific Railway).

In addition to wheat, there are several other grains and some oilseeds that are important crops in the extensive farming system of the Great Plains. All are grown under irrigation in some instances, but the great bulk of their production is under natural rainfall conditions.

Grain Sorghums With the exception of production in southern Texas, most of the grain sorghums of the United States are grown in the winter wheat area on the High Plains of Texas, Kansas, Nebraska, and Oklahoma (fig. 13–16). These drought-resistant crops, introduced from semiarid parts of Africa, have grown in importance in the southwestern part of the area, where they are being used for fodder and as a binder crop in strip and terrace cultivation. In dry years, grain sorghums produce a partial crop for feed and cover even when the wheat withers and dies. They have been known to grow on as little as 10 inches of annual rainfall; moreover, the stubble stands erect against the wind and thereby reduces erosion.

The principal use of grain sorghums is for stock feed. Some are considered to be 90 percent as good as corn for feeding and fattening. The more important types of sorghums grown on the High Plains include the milos, the kafirs, feterita, darso, and hegari. They provide a good substitute for wheat and for cotton in areas of questionable water availability and have replaced corn in parts of Nebraska and Kansas.

Severe acreage limitations were imposed on sorghum planting during the 1960s, as sorghums had become second only to wheat as a surplus crop. Even so, the spectacular expansion of sorghum cultivation since World War II has made it an outstanding crop in the southern Great Plains (fig. 13–17). In Texas and Nebraska wheat and grain sorghum acreages are approximately equivalent, and even in Kansas there is one-third as much acreage in sorghums as in wheat. In west Texas grain sorghums are the

from Gulf ports accounts for further exports.

The Prairie Provinces ship most of their wheat from field to country elevator, nearly 6,000 of which dot the Canadian Prairie. Elevators occupy railway sidings, and many small towns consist of little else. A large part of the grain moves to Winnipeg for grading, whence it is hauled to Thunder Bay for shipment by lake carrier to Montreal or Buffalo.

The grain is exported to Europe from Montreal, St. John, and Halifax; from Buffalo it goes to New York City for transshipment. An appreciable quantity of wheat from the Prairie Provinces is exported from Vancouver as well as from Victoria and Prince Rupert via the Panama Canal to Europe or across the Pacific to the Orient. Some also travels over the Hudson Bay Railway to Churchill for subsequent export to Europe. Much of the United States spring wheat goes to Minneapolis, which is the leading terminal storage center. Some also moves via lake carrier to Buffalo.

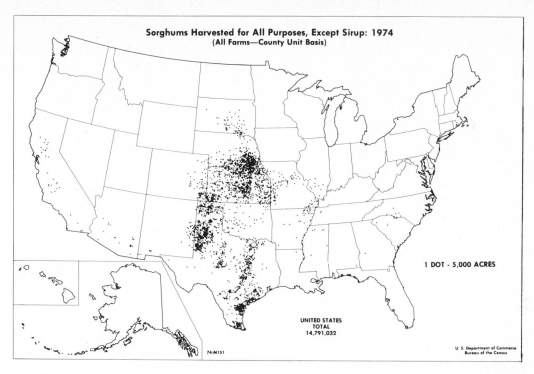

Sorghums Harvested for All Purposes, Except Sirup: 1974
(All Farms—County Unit Basis)

1 DOT - 5,000 ACRES

UNITED STATES
TOTAL
14,791,032

74-M151

U. S. Department of Commerce
Bureau of the Census

fig. 13-16 The growing of grain sorghums is
mostly in the Winter Wheat Belt, with special
concentration in the Texas High Plains.

fig. 13-17 Grain
sorghums on the
High Plains of west
Texas, near
Brownfield.

second most important source of farm crop income, after cotton.

Small Grains The northern plains constitute Anglo-America's major producing areas of barley and rye, and rank a close second to the Heartland as a producer of oats. The strong emphasis on crop diversification in the Prairie Provinces has resulted in a doubling of barley acreage in the last decade, although barley production has recently decreased on the United States side of the border (fig. 13–18). Oats continue as a widely raised secondary crop in the subregion. Rye is less important than the other two, but its output is on an upward trend. The greatest concentration of production of all three of these feed grains is in the Lake Agassiz Plain of North Dakota, Minnesota, and Manitoba.

Oilseeds The northern plains have long been the stronghold of flax production in Anglo-America; 95 percent of the United States crop and 99 percent of the Canadian crop are grown there (fig. 13–19). The crop is grown almost exclusively for its seed, from which linseed oil is extracted. There has been a spectacular increase in rapeseed production in the Prairie Provinces in the last few years; for example, acreage more than doubled between 1969 and 1971. Rapeseed is achieving much wider world acceptance as an edible oil, strongly competing with soybean oil; most of the Canadian crop is exported as oil. Soybean production is also increasing in the northern plains, almost entirely in the Red River Valley of the Dakotas and Minnesota.

IRRIGATION AGRICULTURE

The first irrigation project to be established on the Great Plains dates from 1870, when the Greeley Union Colony developed a large

fig. 13–18 Barley is grown mostly in the northern plains, especially in the valley of the Red River of the North.

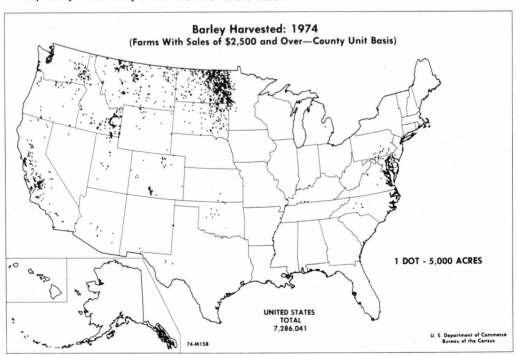

Barley Harvested: 1974
(Farms With Sales of $2,500 and Over—County Unit Basis)

1 DOT - 5,000 ACRES

UNITED STATES
TOTAL
7,286,041

U. S. Department of Commerce
Bureau of the Census

74-M158

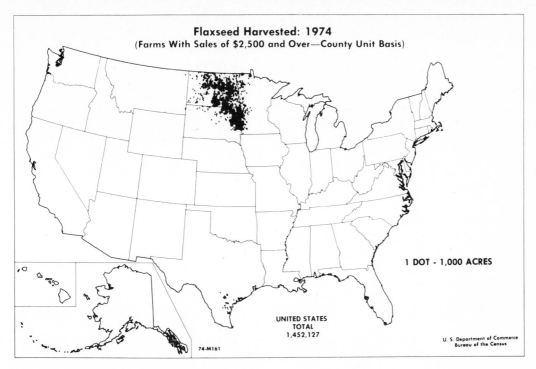

Flaxseed Harvested: 1974
(Farms With Sales of $2,500 and Over—County Unit Basis)

1 DOT - 1,000 ACRES

UNITED STATES
TOTAL
1,452,127

U. S. Department of Commerce
Bureau of the Census

74-M161

fig. 13–19 Flax is almost exclusively a product
of the northeastern portion of the Great
Plains.

tract of land in northern Colorado by using water from the South Platte and Cache la Poudre rivers.

Irrigation farming is now widespread in the region and has been developed in a variety of ways. Most spectacular have been the large-scale government projects developed by the federal Bureau of Reclamation in the United States and by various national and provincial authorities in Canada. The largest single scheme in the Great Plains is the Colorado–Big Thompson Project in northeastern Colorado, which depends primarily on transmountain diversion of water from the western slope of the Rocky Mountains to the valley of the South Platte River where more than 600,000 acres are irrigated. Also particularly notable are the projects associated with the six huge dams of the Pick-Sloan Plan on the upper Missouri River.

A great deal of irrigation in the region, however, is not related to such giant schemes but involves smaller local projects or individual farms that have their own water sources, often from wells. Many different types of irrigation are practiced. In sprinkler irrigation, by far the most popular in recent years, the water is sprayed on the land from lightweight aluminum pipes that can be shifted from place to place manually or move automatically in response to motors or piston drive. Of the various sprinkler irrigation techniques, the dominant recent development in the region is the center pivot (see vignette on next page).

The Major Irrigated Crops The length of the growing season within this region varies from more than 280 frost-free days in the Winter Garden and Laredo districts of south Texas to less than 120 in

337

northern Montana and southern Canada. The most widely grown crop is *alfalfa*, which is the basic hay crop throughout the West. Alfalfa occupies the largest acreage of any irrigated crop from southern Colorado northward.

The Winter Garden and Laredo areas of southern Texas produce early *Bermuda onions*, *spinach,* and other *winter truck crops*. On the several irrigated areas of the Pecos Valley in southern New Mexico, cotton and alfalfa are the dominant crops; *peanuts* and *grain sorghums* are also important.

Probably the outstanding irrigated area in the region is the Texas High Plains section in the vicinity of Lubbock, where *cotton*

---

center pivot, a remarkable irrigation innovation

One of the most striking and conspicuous changes in the farm landscape of Anglo-America has been the rapid recent proliferation of huge circular fields, resulting from the introduction and spread of center pivot irrigation systems. These irrigated circles are most numerous and widespread in the Great Plains but are also relatively common in parts of the Pacific Northwest, the Upper Lakes States, and the far Southeast. The presence of these great circles signals a significant change in the overwhelming rectangularity that has characterized the American farm landscape since its original agricultural occupance; most of this rectangularity was basically predetermined by the public land survey of the National Land System, dating from 1785. The regularity of the circular patterns, the abruptness of their introduction, and the rapidity of their diffusion are clear indications that more is involved than a simple change in field shape. This striking metamorphosis of agricultural geometry represents a technological innovation that has been described as the most significant mechanical development in farming since the introduction of the tractor.[a]

A center pivot system consists of a self-propelled (usually powered by electricity or a hydraulic mechanism), elevated (six to nine feet above the ground) pipe that is anchored at a pivot point in the center of the area to be irrigated. It moves in a circular arc and dispenses water, which is fed into the system at the pivot, by means of sprinkler heads that are scattered at intervals along the pipe (fig. 13-a). The system can be programmed to move at a variety of speeds and can apply liquid fertilizers and pesticides at predetermined rates along with the water.

The vast majority of all center pivot systems is designed to irrigate a quarter section (160 acres) of land. Both small and larger systems are in use, however; some are designed to cover as little as five acres, and some to fit a full section (640 acres).

The most significant advantage of center pivots is a saving in labor, as they are virtually push-button operations that allow the irrigator to handle up to ten times as much acreage as conventional irrigation systems. In addition, they are extremely efficient water users, can be employed on undulating land without the ne-

fig. 13-a A typical center pivot irrigation system in an alfalfa field in central Kansas (courtesy Valmont Industries, Inc.).

[a] William E. Splinter, "Center-Pivot Irrigation," *Scientific American*, 234 (June 1976), 90.

is the principal source of farm income. When the potentialities of the High Plains area for cotton production became known, the acreage rapidly increased; by the close of World War I, it had developed into a great cotton-growing area. At first practically all the crop was grown by dry-farming methods, but in time much of the cotton area was irrigated by means of shallow wells. This has changed the appearance of the area from a land of ranches and extensively cultivated cotton and grain sorghums to one of intensive cultivation of cotton through irrigation methods.

Since most of the water for irrigation in the South Plains area comes from wells

cessity of leveling it, and are effective on sandy soils, which are difficult to irrigate by other means. The most significant drawbacks to center pivot systems are the large initial investment and the fact that the "corners" of a quarter section (approximately 27 acres out of 160) are not reached by the water.

Invented in Colorado in 1949 and first marketed in Nebraska in 1952, center pivots were slow to catch on. By the early 1970s, however, their popularity had become phenomenal, particularly in the Great Plains (fig. 13-b). By 1978 more than 10 percent of the irrigated land in Anglo-America was under center pivot, a tenfold proportional increase since 1970. In the Great Plains, center pivots were in use on nearly one-fourth of all irrigated land by 1978. Table 13-a shows salient statistics and rank-

(Continued)

fig. 13-b   In many parts of the Great Plains the traditional rectangularity of the landscape is increasingly being modified by the gigantic circles of center pivot irrigation systems. This is a U2 photograph of north-central Nebraska (courtesy University of Nebraska Remote Sensing Unit).

drilled into water-bearing sands that have no large surface outcrop and since this area lies within a region of low rainfall, the underground water source is being rapidly depleted; in the mid-1970s the water table was dropping at an average rate of more than two feet per year.[10] There are some 71,000 wells in the area. These once-shallow wells now have an average depth of more than 150 feet, and the natural gas that is used as a source of power to pump the water to the surface is now five times as costly as it was in the early 1970s. Despite prodigious yields of

[10] Alan M. Young, "Irrigated Agriculture— Higher Costs Dampen Economy of Texas High Plains," *Review*, Federal Reserve Bank of Dallas, (July 1977), p. 9.

cotton, grain sorghums, and wheat, the high cost of pumping water has accelerated a reversion to dry-land production on a sizable acreage in the area.

The Arkansas Valley in eastern Colorado and western Kansas is noted for sugar beets, feed grains, alfalfa, and *cantaloupes*.

In northeastern Colorado, associated with the Colorado–Big Thompson Project and the South Platte River, is the second outstanding irrigated area in the Great Plains. The chief specialty crop is *sugar beets*, but a great variety of other crops is also grown, and Weld County (the Greeley area north of Denver) is a national leader in total value of agricultural output. Vegetables, dry beans, corn, alfalfa, and feed grains also occupy large acreages.

---

ings for the Great Plains states and provinces. The greatest concentrations of center pivots are in Nebraska, Kansas, eastern Colorado, and the Texas High Plains (fig. 13-c).

Most of the center pivots in the region obtain their water from wells. Only in the Prairie Provinces and Montana is the water primarily from surface sources.

The high cost of center pivot systems and

the high yields that result from their use encourage farmers to concentrate on growing crops that provide the greatest financial return per acre. The principal result has been a vast increase in acreage devoted to corn, which is by far the leading crop grown on irrigated circles in the Great Plains. In the northwestern part of the region (North Dakota, Wyoming, Montana, and Alberta), corn ranks second in center pivot

table 13-a The Importance of Center Pivot Irrigation in Great Plains States and Provinces, 1976

state	center pivot acreage	center pivot ranking	total irrigated acreage	total irrigated ranking	center pivot as percent of irrigated acreage
Nebraska	1,762,900	1	6,301,000	2	28%
Kansas	727,000	2	3,032,000	5	24%
Texas*	520,000	3	8,700,000	1	6%
Colorado*	500,000	4	3,100,000	3–4	16%
New Mexico*	150,000	5	1,070,000	7	14%
South Dakota	150,000	6	296,000	10	51%
Oklahoma	141,000	7	941,000	8	15%
Wyoming	78,000	8	1,830,000	6	4%
Alberta	68,000	9	940,000	9	7%
North Dakota	56,000	10	103,000	11	54%
Montana	33,000	11	3,100,000	3–4	1%
Saskatchewan	10,000	12	80,000	12	13%
Manitoba	1,000	13	4,000	13	25%

Data Source: "1976 Irrigation Survey," *Irrigation Journal*, 29 (November-December 1976), 23–29; and personal communication with irrigation authorities in the various states and provinces.
Note: These data refer to the entire state or province and are not restricted to the Great Plains portions.

The rapid expansion of cattle feedlots and dairying in northeastern Colorado in the last few years has stimulated production of feed grains. Much *corn* is grown under irrigation, and most of it is cut green for silage. A lack of permanent storage facilities has necessitated innovation in the provision of temporary storage. Three-row cutting machines grind up the entire cornstalk and disgorge it into trucks, which take it to dugout pits (usually cement-lined) where the ground-up corn is simply piled and covered with a sheet of black plastic, weighted down with old tires, until it is needed for feeding.

North of the Platte irrigation is less distinctive but no less widespread. Most river valleys in the northern plains have irrigated sections along their flood plains; about 1 million acres is irrigated in Alberta, for example, almost all within the drainage area of the South Saskatchewan River. Throughout the northern plains hay crops occupy the bulk of the irrigated acreage, with a considerable share devoted to grains (particularly wheat), sugar beets, and potatoes.

livestock raising

The Great Plains Region has long been famous for its range livestock industry. Some of the world's largest, best-run, and most productive ranches are located here. Both beef cattle and sheep are widespread, and in some cases both species are raised on the same ranch. By and large, however, the bet-

acreage to alfalfa, and in Texas it ranks third behind wheat and grain sorghums; elsewhere in the Great Plains corn is clearly the leading center pivot crop.

Although obviously popular and marked by continually expanding adoption, conventional center pivots pose the nagging perplexity of corners where the water cannot reach. This objection is met in part by the placement of a "big gun" sprinkler at the end of the pipe, which is activated only as the corners are approached. A more sophisticated solution to this problem was introduced by several center pivot manufacturers in the late 1970s, with the addition of a sweep arm that swings out to bring water to the previously unirrigated portions. Most users, however, are content with the original center pivots, contending that the circular systems are so efficient and productive on 133 acres that they more than compensate for the 27 acres that are missed.

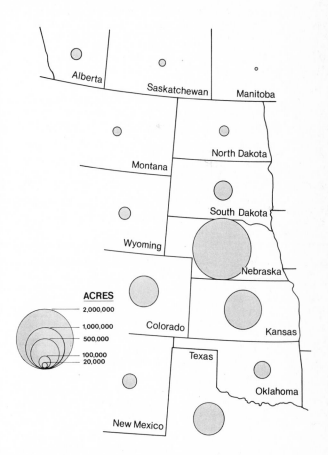

fig. 13-c Distribution of acreage watered by center pivot systems in the Great Plains, 1977. The greatest popularity of center pivot technology has been in the southern part of the region, but there has been rapid recent adoption in the northern areas as well (data obtained through mail questionnaire survey).

fig. 13-20 A cattle round-up in southern Saskatchewan (courtesy National Film Board of Canada).

ter lands are utilized by cattle; sheep tend to be restricted mostly to rougher, drier, or otherwise less suitable country. Cattle are distributed relatively uniformly over the region, although densities decrease northward and westward (fig. 13–20). Sheep are much more irregularly scattered, with the principal concentration being in the central Texas hill country and Edwards Plateau; lesser concentrations are in eastern Wyoming and adjacent parts of South Dakota and Montana. These four states produce more than 40 percent of all Anglo-American wool.

Summer grazing is mostly on natural grasses, although there is increasing replacement with more nutritive artificial pastures. The most noted natural grasslands of the region are probably in the so-called bluestem belt: the Flint Hills of eastern Kansas and the Osage Hills of northeastern Oklahoma. In winter, however, artificial feeding—mostly with hay—is necessary over much of the region because of the long period of snow cover.

CATTLE FEEDLOTS

By far the most dynamic recent development in the livestock industry of the Great Plains has been the rapid proliferation of cattle feedlots. In the past nearly all the range cattle were shipped out of the region, usually to the Corn Belt, for fattening. More recently the feedlot capacity of the Great Plains has expanded phenomenally, and thus beef production has been vertically integrated in the region, from raising on the range through fattening in feedlots to slaughtering in local packing houses.

The Chicago–St. Louis axis of the "beef belt" has now shifted considerably westward and can be considered as being oriented along an Omaha-Amarillo line. Feedlot operations are widespread in Nebraska and Kansas but are particularly prominent in west Texas and northeastern Colorado; furthermore, many of the new feedlots are highly mechanized and have very large capacities. In the Texas Panhandle, for example, more than 1 million cattle can be accommodated at one time on large feedlots; feedlot capacity in the three principal counties of northeastern Colorado is more than half a million.

There are many reasons for the rapid growth of the feedlot industry in the region. Some of the more important include the development of high-yielding grain sorghums, expanded irrigation, improved feedlot technology, the economies of scale in dry-lot confinement feeding, improved transportation, and westward decentralization of meatpacking operations.

ANGORA GOATS

The hill country of central Texas yields more than 95 percent of the nation's mohair. Goat ranching is similar to sheep ranching, except that goats, being browsing animals, can subsist on pastures not good enough for sheep. Most of the pasture land used by Angora goats is in the brush country where scrub oak and other small trees and shrubs supply browse (fig. 13–21). A severely depressed world market during most of the 1970s caused a reduction of about 60 percent in the number of goats kept in Texas, but a strengthening of prices late in the decade sparked an upturn.

mineral industries

Some of the most flamboyant history in the region revolved around the discovery (1874) and the production of gold in the Black Hills. The Homestake Mine is now the only one in operation in the area, but its production is so great that it makes South Dakota the leading state in gold output.

It is, however, the nonmetallic minerals that are the mainstay of the region's mineral industry.

PETROLEUM

Because of its extensive size and because most of it is underlain with sedimentary

fig. 13–21 Angora goats in the central Texas hill country.

rocks that may contain oil, the Great Plains Region has many producing oil fields. Among the 14 states and provinces with portions included in this region, only Minnesota lacks significant production.

Nearly half of all Texas petroleum production—amounting to one-sixth of the national output—is from west Texas fields, particularly the Permian Basin. Major yields are also obtained in parts of Oklahoma and Kansas; in the increasingly prolific fields of Wyoming, particularly the Elk Basin; in scattered Montana localities; in the Williston Basin of North Dakota; and in the skyrocketing production areas of Alberta and Saskatchewan.

Oklahoma is an example of a state with a long-term productive petroleum industry that has declining future prospects. There are some 90,000 oil and gas wells scattered over 72 of the state's 77 counties. There are even 18 oil wells on the state capitol grounds in Oklahoma City, about half of which are still producing. But finding oil is becoming more difficult, and producing it is becoming more expensive all the time. There are only about half as many drilling rigs operating in Oklahoma now as there were a few years ago, and wells that are completed are more often deep than shallow and consequently much more costly to develop.

In the last three decades there has been a continually increasing flow of oil from the

Prairie Provinces, primarily from Alberta (more than 80 percent of Canadian output) and westernmost Saskatchewan. Pipelines have been built eastward to the head of Lake Superior at Duluth and on to Sarnia and Toronto, southward to Montana, and westward across the Rocky Mountains to Vancouver. The provincial governments, rather than individual landholders, own most of the mineral rights; thus, sales of crude oil undergird a large share of the provincial budgets and account for the fact that Alberta has had the most prosperous and stable economy in Canada for some years.

NATURAL GAS

The Prairie Provinces are also prominent producers of natural gas, particularly Alberta whose output is four-fifths of the Canadian total. Natural gas is also a major product from Wyoming, Kansas, Oklahoma, and west Texas; the Panhandle field of the last three states is the largest producer of natural gas in the world. In the middle and late 1970s an outstanding new field was being developed in the Laredo area of southern Texas, with indications that it might eventually equal the Panhandle field in output.

HELIUM

The major helium-producing area in the world is located within the Panhandle gas fields. Originally helium was used mostly as a lifting gas for dirigibles, but now it has a multitude of atomic, spacecraft, medical, and industrial uses (particularly for helium-shielded arc welding). Of the 12 plants in the United States producing helium, 11 are in the Great Plains Region. The long-range helium outlook is for increasing demand and decreasing supply.

COAL

It has long been known that there were enormous deposits of relatively low grade bituminous and lower grade lignite coal in the northern Great Plains, but they were largely unexploited until the energy crisis of the 1970s. Although some mining has been carried on for decades in such places as Montana's Judith Basin and lignite has been extracted in southeastern Saskatchewan for almost a century, it is only in the last few years that coal mining has abruptly begun to change the landscape, economy, and life style in parts of the Plains.

Most of the coal deposits are extensive and near the surface, and are therefore strip mined. The deleterious environmental consequences of strip mining are well known, and the problems of heavy water use and revegetation of the spoils banks and mining scars continue to mount.

The abrupt and ambitious plans for mining in Wyoming, Montana, and the Dakotas have occasioned unprecedented economic and population growth, and enormous growing pains. Land values have skyrocketed. Sleepy villages have become bustling boom towns (Gillette, Wyoming, for example, experienced a fivefold population increase in eight years), and "instant" towns have sprouted, with the help of acres of mobile homes, on the barren steppe (for example, the population in Colstrip, Montana, grew from 0 to 3,000 in two years).

Coal reserves in the area are stupendous, topped by Campbell County in northeastern Wyoming; it has only one town but is underlain by more coal than is found in all but four countries in the world. Frantic development of various growth nodes in the northern Plains can be expected to continue for an indefinite period.

POTASH

The world's two largest suppliers of mineral potash are located at opposite ends of the Great Plains Region. Near Carlsbad, New Mexico, on both sides of the New Mexico–Texas boundary, are extensive deposits of polyhalite and sylvite, which have been a major source of potash for many years.

Within the last two decades, however, production has begun from the world's largest known body of mineral potash in southern Saskatchewan. Ten mines are in operation between Saskatoon and the Manitoba border; nine are conventional shaft mines, and one solution mine of the Frasch type extracts potash brine from more than a mile below the surface. These are high-cost operations because much of the overlying rock is so waterlogged that the area around the shafts must be kept permanently frozen or made watertight by other methods. About one-fifth of total world output now comes from these Saskatchewan deposits.

SULFUR

The only significant production of sulfur outside the Gulf Coast salt-dome area is in west Texas, just south of Carlsbad. Sulfur brine is extracted by the Frasch process, and the solution is transported by a continuous shuttle of unit-sulfur trains more than 900 miles to the major sulfur port of Galveston.

the ebb and flow of urbanization in the great plains

The Great Plains is a region that exemplifies many of the contemporary trends of Anglo-American geography, and not the least of these is shown in the pattern of urbanization. Here, better than in any other region, is demonstrated the decay of the small town in juxtaposition with the rapid growth of larger urban centers.

WITHERING TOWNS

Proportionally, no other region has as many small towns that have registered population declines during the last two census periods (fig. 13–22). In part this results from the changing economy of the Great Plains, but in large measure it reflects the specialized origin of many of the towns.

Originally, numerous Great Plains towns were established along the advancing tentacles of westering railway lines. The situation is most prominent in the Prairie Provinces, where settlement did not significantly precede the railways and the urban pattern was preconceived and superimposed on the land, but it is shown to some extent throughout the region because a large share of the towns grew up along the east-west railway routes. With regard to the prairies, the scheme has been described as follows:

The building of the railways accompanied or preceded settlement. Settlement in advance of the railway merely anticipated the railway already projected or under construction, and such towns as were built were usually established in anticipation of the line passing through them. When thwarted, these settlements were frequently moved across the prairie to sites adjoining the line. . . . The distance between the towns was determined by the economic distance for hauling grain at a time when local transportation was horse-drawn. Whenever possible, the railway companies brought production areas to within 10 miles of their lines and, by placing elevators and sidings 7 to 10 miles apart, created a maximum hauling distance of 12 to 15 miles, the upper limit depending on the location and direction

fig. 13–22 Many small towns in the region are stagnating or dying. For example, more than half of the commercial buildings fronting the town square in Paducah, Texas, are now empty.

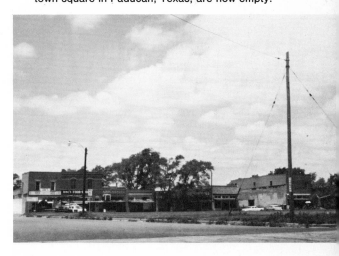

table 13-1 Largest Urban Places
of the Great Plains Region

name	population of principal city	population of metropolitan area
Abilene, Tex.	96,459	128,400
Amarillo, Tex.	138,743	152,000
Arvada, Colo.*	74,254	
Aurora, Colo.*	118,060	
Billings, Mont.	68,987	97,400
Bismarck, N. Dak.	38,378	
Boulder, Colo.	78,560	
Brandon, Man.	34,481	
Calgary, Alta.	457,828	457,828
Casper, Wyo.	41,192	
Cheyenne, Wyo.	46,677	
Clovis, N. Mex.	31,734	
Colorado Springs, Colo.	179,584	291,900
Denver, Colo.	484,531	1,404,300
Edmonton, Alta.	542,800	542,800
Englewood, Colo.*	35,870	
Enid, Okla.	48,030	
Fargo, N. Dak.	56,058	128,200
Fort Collins, Colo.	55,984	120,900
Grand Forks, N. Dak.	41,909	
Grand Island, Nebr.	33,304	
Great Falls, Mont.	60,860	84,700
Greeley, Colo.	47,362	107,700
Hutchinson, Kans.	40,925	
Lakewood, Colo.*	120,350	
Laredo, Tex.	76,998	78,100
Lawton, Okla.	76,421	102,900
Lethbridge, Alta.	46,048	
Lubbock, Tex.	163,525	196,700
Medicine Hat, Alta.	32,263	
Midland, Tex.	62,950	69,700
Midwest City, Okla.*	50,105	
Minot, N. Dak.	32,790	
Moose Jaw, Sask.	31,884	
Norman, Okla.	59,948	
Odessa, Tex.	84,476	98,800
Oklahoma City, Okla.	365,916	752,900
Pueblo, Colo.	105,312	125,400
Rapid City, S. Dak.	48,156	648,100
Red Deer, Alta.	31,723	
Regina, Sask.	147,529	148,965
Roswell, N. Mex.	37,980	
Salina, Kans.	38,960	
San Angelo, Tex.	66,099	74,800
San Antonio, Tex.	773,248	977,200
Saskatoon, Sask.	132,291	132,291
Stillwater, Okla.	33,870	
Tulsa, Okla.	331,726	585,800
Wichita, Kans.	264,901	382,500
Winnipeg, Man.	553,148	570,725

* A suburb of a larger city.

of the roads. These transshipment centres became the distributing points for supplies, e.g., agricultural implements, coal, lumber and general merchandise. . . . The result of this method of settlement is that the towns are arranged along the railway like beads on a string. They appear, heralded by elevators, as regularly as clockwork. . . . Frequently, the names as well as the sites of the towns were chosen by the railway companies since there were few existing place names to recognize. This task, too, was executed with characteristic dispatch. One solution was simply to arrange the names in alphabetical order down the line as, for example, on the Grand Trunk railway, which runs from Atwater, Bangor, Cana, to Xena, Young, and Zelma.[11]

With the decreasing importance of railway transportation, most such towns no longer have any functional significance and are left to decay. Other towns that grew up along roads and highways have been subsequently bypassed by new interstate or interprovincial highway construction, and they, too, have become anachronistic and stagnant.

BURGEONING CITIES

More auspiciously located market towns, located further apart and with a more diversified economic function, have prospered at the expense of the smaller places; thus railway division points, separated from one another by 100 miles or so, have been able to maintain their vigor by expanding their functional hinterland. Even division points that were sited more or less arbitrarily by the railway companies have been growth nodes, for example, Moose Jaw, Swift Current, Medicine Hat, and Calgary along the Canadian Pacific.

The larger urban centers of the Great Plains Region are few and far between (see table 13–1 for a listing of the region's largest urban places). Their prosperity in each case represents an extensive trading territory or a local area of high productivity. In almost every instance their recent rate of population growth has been higher than the national average.

[11] Ronald Rees, "The Small Towns of Saskatchewan," *Landscape*, 18 (Fall 1969), 30.

Denver is by far the largest city in the region; it is the commercial and distributing center for much of the plains, as well as for an extensive portion of the Mountain West. In addition to being the state capital, it is a major regional center for federal offices and has a rapidly increasing industrial component. Although situated on the plains, it is the tourist gateway to the mountain recreation areas of the Southern Rockies.

The other large urban centers of the southern plains have significant functional differences. *San Antonio* is the oldest city in the region; it is the principal commercial city of southern Texas and is surrounded by an unusually large number of military bases. *Oklahoma City* and *Tulsa* are both prominent in the petroleum industry; the former's larger size is at least partly related to its role as a governmental and financial center. *Wichita* has a prosperous agricultural hinterland, but its special claim to fame is as an aircraft manufacturing center.

The northern plains in the United States have no large cities. Apparently the overlapping hinterlands of Denver, Minneapolis, and Seattle have militated against metropolitan growth in this subregion.

The metropolitan pattern of the Prairie Provinces is still evolving. *Winnipeg* achieved early subregional dominance on the basis of its splendid gateway location at a river crossing at the apex of an extensive, fan-shaped potential hinterland in the prairies.

fig. 13–23 Despite having seemingly endless land over which to sprawl, the cities of the Great Plains are marked by a notable vertical dimension as well. This is the city center of Edmonton, hard by the banks of the North Saskatchewan River (Alberta Government photo).

But Winnipeg never became the primate city of the Prairie Provinces, indicating that a peripheral location can perhaps be a handicap despite its gateway opportunity. After World War II, *Edmonton* (fig. 13–23) and *Calgary* rapidly became the focus of the western prairies. Curiously, the centrally placed cities of *Regina* and *Saskatoon* have always been the smallest of the prairie metropolitan areas (fig. 13–24).

fig. 13–24 The urban hierarchy of the Canadian Prairies.

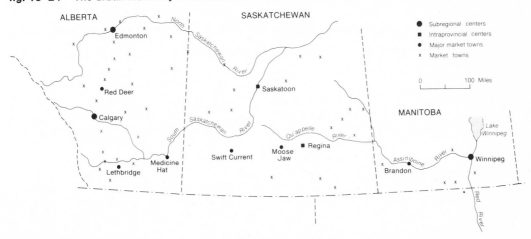

a transit land

The Great Plains Region has served primarily as a transit land. Most of the freight and passenger traffic passes through the region en route to and from the Pacific Coast; thus the transportation lines of the region show a predominance of east-west railways, highways, and airways. The only important north-south traffic flows along the western edge, at the foot of the Rocky Mountains, where there are some significant population clusters. The cities of this western margin, such as Roswell, Pueblo, Colorado Springs, Denver, Cheyenne, Billings, Great Falls, Calgary, and Edmonton, serve both the Great Plains and the Rocky Mountains, although they are all located in the former region.

Despite the rapid growth of the larger urban areas of the Great Plains, the historic pattern of transportation—through rather than to—has been maintained. The major interstate and interprovincial highways continue to have an east-west orientation, and flow patterns are predominantly latitudinal.

limited tourism

The Great Plains Region, with its extensive area of level to gently rolling lands and its continental climate of hot summers and very cold winters, offers few attractions for the tourist. Hence it is not important as a resort region, despite the fact that each summer it is crossed by throngs of tourists seeking a vacation in the mountains to the west. Three areas within the region, however, are of significance: the Black Hills, the Carlsbad Caverns, and the hill country of southwestern Texas.

Of these areas, the most scenic and most important is the Black Hills. With forest-clad mountains, the attractive Sylvan Lake area, Wind Cave National Park, Custer State Park and its abundant wildlife, and Rushmore Memorial, the Black Hills area annually attracts hundreds of thousands of tourists.

In southeastern New Mexico, in an area where the surface of the land is harsh, lies the world-famous Carlsbad Caverns National Park with its extensive subterranean caves. As one of the most popular tourist attractions of Anglo-America, it is visited by great numbers of people each year. The area, however, does not encourage the tourist to stay long; in most cases, it is visited for a short time by persons on their way to other resort centers.

Several cities on the western margin of the Great Plains have become important summer tourist centers because they are gateways to the mountains beyond. Colorado Springs, Denver, Cheyenne, and Calgary are particularly notable in this respect.

Hunting and fishing activities are limited in this region, with two important exceptions: the central Texas hill country contains one of the largest and most accessible deer herds in Anglo-America, and the introduced pheasant population of the central and northern plains is a leading hunter's quarry from Colorado northward.

the outlook

Agricultural maladjustment has been the ruination of many people in the Great Plains. All too often the sod has been broken on marginal land that should have stayed in grass. In spite of bleak chapters in its history, however, the region can boast of fertile farms, impressive ranches, and mushrooming cities.

Agricultural prosperity in the future will be in part determined by activities and controls of the two national governments. In general, however, there will be decreasing wheat acreage and increasing wheat yield. The fluctuating world market for wheat provides a built-in uncertainty for a region heavily oriented toward a single crop, which cannot be dissipated by anything short of agricultural or other economic diversification.

Approaches toward crop diversification are being made: grain sorghums and various irrigated crops in the south, corn and soybeans in the east, barley and oilseeds in the north, and improved pastures in many localities.

The wheat industry of the northern plains, particularly in Canada, faces other major adjustments. Recent technological changes in milling make it possible to use a much higher proportion of less expensive soft wheat for bread flour (75 percent now in comparison to 25–40 percent in the past); most spring wheat is hard and relatively costly so the shift in demand to more soft wheat will have a major impact in the Prairie Provinces. Further, millers now require much closer quality control in the protein content of wheat, a factor that has been largely ignored in Canadian wheat marketing in the past. In the future Canadian wheat will surely have to be graded on a protein basis, which will require further adjustments for farmers.

Irrigation promises to expand throughout the region, partly as the result of large government reclamation projects, partly through the more intensive use of local waters by individuals and groups, and partly through the continuing adoption of sprinkler technology, especially center pivot. Ill omens on the irrigation horizon relate to falling water tables and rising energy costs. The cost squeeze resulting from these two trends is likely to cause significant land use and cropping changes in the Texas High Plains, and the general effect eventually may be inhibitory on center pivot expansion throughout the region.

Farms will continue to become larger as small operators sell their land and large farmers consolidate their holdings. The complexity of farm ownership will probably increase, with more part-owners, absentee owners, and nonagricultural investors.

The energy resources of the region will likely be the foci of frenzied development. Petroleum and natural gas exploration and production, particularly in Alberta and Wyoming, will be prominent, but the major areas of activity will probably relate to proliferation and expansion of coal strip mines, involving all the states and provinces of the northern Plains.

The pace of economic activity will be much more intense in some areas than others. The prosperity of Alberta is based on rising petroleum revenues, good grain income, and further industrial expansion in the so-called forward linkages of processing between crude oil and gas on the one hand and final consumer products on the other; it is likely to set a pace unmatched by any other state or province. Other conspicuous growth areas will probably be west Texas, the Colorado Piedmont, and parts of Wyoming.

Prosperity can be expected to wax and wane, but the region will maintain its essential character. The landscape will be dominated by a mixture of extensive and intensive agriculture, with notable centers of mineral activity; the population will never be very dense except in a few urban areas; and it will always be an important transit land, lying as it does across all transcontinental routeways.

selected bibliography

BARR, BRENTON M., ed., *Calgary: Metropolitan Structure and Influence,* Western Geographical Series, Vol. 11. Victoria: University of Victoria Department of Geography, 1975.

BEATY, CHESTER B., *The Landscapes of Southern Alberta: A Regional Geomorphology.* Lethbridge, Alta.: University of Lethbridge, Department of Geography, 1975.

BLAINE, RICHARD P., *Calgary: An Urban Study.* Toronto: Clarke Irwin, 1973.

BORCHERT, JOHN R., "Climate of the Central North American Grassland," *Annals,* Association of American Geographers, 40 (1950), 1–39.

———, "The Dust Bowl in the 1970 s," *Annals,* Association of American Geographers, 61 (1971), 1–22.

CHAKRAVARTI, A. K., "The June–July Precipitation Pattern in the Prairie Provinces of Canada," *Journal of Geography,* 71 (1972), 155–60.

DAVIES, W. K. D., AND G. T. BARROW, "A Comparative Factorial Ecology of Three Canadian Prairie Cities," *Canadian Geographer*, 17 (1973), 327–53.

DORT, W., AND J. K. JONES, eds., *Pleistocene and Recent Environments of the Central Great Plains.* Lawrence: University of Kansas Press, 1970.

FARNEY, DENNIS, "The Last of the Tallgrass Prairie," *Defenders*, 50 (1975), 308–16.

FIDLER, V., "Cypress Hills: Plateau of the Prairie," *Canadian Geographical Journal*, 87 (September 1973), 28–35.

HARRINGTON, LYN, "Medicine Hat: The Town That Was Born Lucky," *Canadian Geographical Journal*, 80 (April 1970), 126–33.

HARRIS, DAVID R., "Recent Plant Invasions in the Arid and Semi-Arid Southwest of the United States," *Annals*, Association of American Geographers, 56 (1966), 408–22.

HEWES, LESLIE, *The Suitcase Farming Frontier: A Study in the Historical Geography of the Central Great Plains.* Lincoln: University of Nebraska Press, 1973.

LAATSCH, WILLIAM G., "Hutterite Colonization in Alberta," *Journal of Geography*, 70 (1971), 347–59.

LAUT, PETER, *The Geographical Analysis and Classification of Canadian Prairie Agriculture.* Winnipeg: University of Manitoba Department of Geography, 1974.

LAWSON, MERLIN P., KENNETH F. DEWEY, AND RALPH E. NEILD, *Climatic Atlas of Nebraska.* Lincoln: University of Nebraska Press, 1977.

LEHR, J. C., "The Sequence of Mormon Settlement in Southern Alberta," *Albertan Geographer*, 10 (1974), 20–29.

LONSDALE, RICHARD E., ed., *Economic Atlas of Nebraska.* Lincoln: University of Nebraska Press, 1977.

MCINTOSH, CHARLES B., "Forest Lieu Selections in the Sand Hills of Nebraska," *Annals*, Association of American Geographers, 64 (1974), 87–99.

MATHER, E. COTTON, "The American Great Plains," *Annals*, Association of American Geographers, 62 (1972), 237–57.

MOSLEY, M. P., "Evolution of a Discontinuous Gully System," *Annals*, Association of American Geographers, 62 (1972), 655–63.

MOWERS, CLEO W., "Lethbridge, Alberta," *Canadian Geographical Journal*, 84 (May 1972), 140–51.

MUNRO, DAVID A., "The Prairies and the Ducks," *Canadian Geographical Journal*, 75 (July 1967), 2–13.

NELSON, J. GORDON, *The Last Refuge.* Montreal: Harvest House, 1973.

NKEMDIRIM, L. C., AND P. W. BENOIT, "Heavy Snowfall Expectation for Alberta," *Canadian Geographer*, 19 (1975), 60–72.

NORTH, MARGARET E. A., *A Plant Geography of Alberta: An Interpretation Based on the 1965 Vegetation Map,* University of Alberta Studies in Geography, Monograph 2. Edmonton: University of Alberta, Department of Geography, 1976.

OETTING, R. B., "How the Garrison Dam Project Affects Canada," *Canadian Geographical Journal*, 95 (October–November 1977), 38–45.

REES, RONALD, "The Small Towns of Saskatchewan," *Landscape*, 18 (1969), 29–33.

RICHARDS, J. H., "Is Lake Diefenbaker Justifying Its Planners?" *Canadian Geographical Journal*, 91 (December 1975), 22–31.

RICHARDS, J. H., and K. I. FUNG, eds., *Atlas of Saskatchewan.* Saskatoon: University of Saskatchewan, 1969.

RIDDELL, W. A., "Potash: New Wealth for Saskatchewan," *Canadian Geographical Journal*, 89 (September 1974), 16–23.

RILEY, ROBERT B., "Notes on the Northern Plains," *Landscape*, 21 (1977), 38–47.

SCHKADE, LAWRENCE L., CHARLES T. CARK, AND CHARLES A. PIEPER, *Midland-Odessa: An Analysis of the Economic Base for Urban Development.* Austin: University of Texas, Bureau of Business Research, 1965.

SIMS, JOHN, AND THOMAS FREDERICK SAARINEN, "Coping with Environmental Threat: Great Plains Farmers and the Sudden Storm," *Annals*, Association of American Geographers, 59 (1969), 677–86.

SINCLAIR, GORDON, "Cities and Towns of Manitoba," *Canadian Geographical Journal*, 81 (August 1970), 54–63.

SMITH, P. J., "Edmonton and Calgary: Growing Together," *Canadian Georgraphical Journal*, 92 (May–June 1976), 25–33.

———, ed., *The Prairie Provinces.* Toronto: University of Toronto Press, 1972.

TIESSEN, H., "Mining Prairie Coal and Healing the Land," *Canadian Geographical Journal*, 90 (January 1975), 29–37.

TILLER, JAMES WEEKS, *The Texas Winter Garden:*

Commercial Cool-Season Vegetable Production. Austin: University of Texas, Bureau of Business Research, 1971.

UNIVERSITY OF ALBERTA, DEPARTMENT OF GEOGRAPHY, *Atlas of Alberta.* Edmonton: University of Alberta Press/University of Toronto Press, 1969.

VOGELER, INGOLF, and TERRY SIMMONS, "Settlement Morphography of South Dakota Indian Reservations," *Yearbook,* Association of Pacific Coast Geographers, 37 (1975), 91–108.

WATTS, F. B., "The Natural Vegetation of the Southern Great Plains of Canada," *Geographical Bulletin,* 14 (1960), 24–43.

WEIR, THOMAS R., ed., *Maps of the Prairie Provinces.* Toronto: Oxford University Press, 1971.

WILLIAMS, JAMES H., AND DOUG MURFIELD, eds., *Agricultural Atlas of Nebraska.* Lincoln: University of Nebraska Press, 1977.

WOTJIW, L., "The Climatology of Hailstorms in Central Alberta," *Albertan Geographer,* 13 (1977), 15–30.

ZIEBER, G. H., "The Dispersed City Hypothesis with Reference to Calgary and Edmonton," *Albertan Geographer,* 9 (1973), 4–13.

14

THE
ROCKY
MOUNTAINS

The Rocky Mountain Region encompasses the great cordillera of the western interior of Anglo-America. It is one of the conspicuous highlands of the world, rising between the flatness of the interior plains and the irregular topography of the intermontane West. It is a region of steep slopes, rugged terrain, and spectacular scenery; of extensive forests, abundant wildlife, and deep snows; and of sparse settlements, decaying ghost towns, and busy ski trails. Mine output has long been notable, forest products are significant in some areas, and there are scattered pockets of productive agriculture. The chief functions of the region, however, are as a place for outdoor recreation and as a source of water for most of the rivers of the West.

extent of the region

The Rocky Mountain Region, as recognized in this book, includes the lengthy extent of the Rockies from New Mexico to the Yukon Territory as well as the various mountains, valleys, and plateaus of interior British Columbia. This latter section is included within the Rocky Mountain Region because its patterns of vegetation, occupance, land use, and economic activities are much more like those of the Rockies than like those of either the Intermontane Basin and Plateau Region to the south or the North Pacific Coast Region to the west.

As thus delimited, the eastern boundary of the Rocky Mountain Region is marked by the break between the Great Plains and the Rocky Mountains (fig. 14–1). From central New Mexico to northern Alberta the mountains rise abruptly from the flatlands, except in central Wyoming where the Wyoming Basin merges almost imperceptibly with the Great Plains. The western boundary, which marks the transition from the Rocky Mountain Region to the Intermontane Region, is fairly distinct in the southern and middle sections. In much of British Columbia, however, the demarcation between the interior mountains and plateaus to the east and the Coast Mountains to the west consists of an indefinite transition zone, particularly in north-central British Columbia where the Omineca and Skeena mountains provide a "bridge" across the interior plateaus to connect the Coast Mountains with the Rockies. The northern boundary of the region is also transitional, except where the broad lowland of the middle Liard River Valley makes an abrupt interruption in the topographic pattern.

353

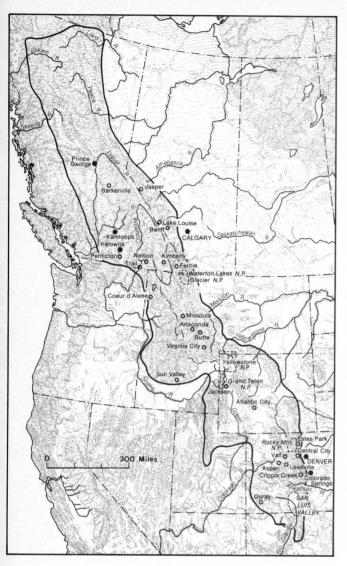

fig. 14–1 The Rocky Mountain Region (base map copyright A. K. Lobeck; reprinted by permission of Hammond, Inc.).

origin of the rocky mountains

During the Cretaceous Period most of the area of the Rocky Mountain Region and of the Great Plains was covered by a shallow sea that extended from the Gulf of Mexico to the Arctic Ocean. At the close of that pe-

riod, the Rocky Mountain area was uplifted and the waters drained off. Sediments with a thickness of perhaps 20,000 feet were involved in this first great uplift.

A long period of erosion accompanied and followed this early uplift, during which time much material was removed from the summits and deposited in the basins. During the later Tertiary Period the Rocky Mountains were subjected to another period of uplift, accompanied by considerable volcanic activity and followed by still another period of leveling. The region's master streams, flowing over sediments that had buried the mountain roots, established courses that they continued to hold after they cut into older rocks, forming major gorges and canyons through many ranges. In the more recent uplifts many of the ranges have been raised so high that erosion has stripped away much of the sedimentary cover, exposing the ancient Precambrian rocks (usually granitic) of the mountain core. The sedimentaries that originally extended across the axis of the uplifts are now mostly found as uptilted edges on the flanks of the ranges or as downfolded or downfaulted basins within the mountain masses.

The geologic history varies from range to range, but overall this is a region of crustal weakness and young mountains; consequently the relief is great and slopes are steep. In many areas, however, there are fairly extensive tracts of land at high elevation—10,000 to 11,000 feet in much of the Colorado Rockies, for example—which apparently represent old erosion surfaces that have been uplifted without significant deformation and appear as gently rolling upland summits or accordant ridge crests. These smooth upland surfaces are often referred to as peneplains or pediplains, but there is considerable dispute among geomorphologists as to their origin.[1]

[1] For a discussion of peneplanation versus pediplanation, see W. W. Atwood and W. W. Atwood, Jr., "Opening of the Pleistocene in the Rocky Mountains of the United States," *Journal of Geology*, 46 (1938), 239–47; William D. Thornbury, *Regional Geomorphology of the United States* (New York: John Wiley & Sons, Inc., 1965), 328–29.

Essentially all the high country was severely reshaped by glaciation during the Pleistocene Epoch. In more southerly latitudes, abrupt U-shaped valleys, broad cirques, and horn peaks are the most prominent results of mountain glaciation; further north the glacial features are more complex, since the mountain glaciers were larger and some continental glaciation also impinged on the ranges.

In terms of geomorphic association and geographical proximity, the Rocky Mountain chain can be subdivided into five principal sections (fig. 14–2):

1 the Southern Rockies, mostly in the state of Colorado

2 the Middle Rockies, primarily in Utah and Wyoming

3 the Northern Rockies, in Montana and Idaho

4 the Columbia Mountains, in southeastern British Columbia

5 the Canadian Rockies along the Alberta–British Columbia boundary

It goes without saying that the entire region is not mountainous. There are many valleys and some extensive areas of relative flatness. But mountains are everywhere on the horizon, and true mountain country almost universally dominates the landscape. The most extensive nonmountainous area is the so-called Wyoming Basin, which represents an extension of Great Plains topography into the Rocky Mountains in southern and central Wyoming. This "basin" is topographically quite heterogeneous, varying from alluviated plains to badlands to steep hills.

Scattered about in the Southern Rockies is a large number of relatively flat-floored basins, generally called *parks,* that are mostly not timbered and present a distinct change in landscape from the surrounding mountainous terrain. The largest of these is the San Luis Valley. Other notable basins include South Park, Middle Park, and North Park, and there is a host of smaller parks.

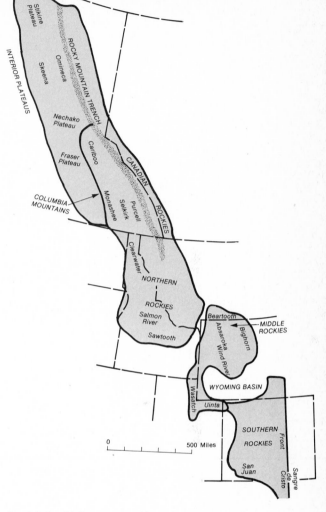

fig. 14–2   Major geomorphic units of the Rocky Mountain Region.

North of Wyoming the circular basin is much less common; more distinctive landscape features in this subregion are long linear valleys of structural origin. The most conspicuous of these is the Rocky Mountain Trench, which extends for 1,000 miles from the vicinity of Montana's Flathead Lake to the Liard Plain in northeastern British Columbia.

fig. 14-3 The frontal ranges of the Southern Rockies rise
abruptly to great heights. This is a northward view along
the Sangre de Cristo Range in southern Colorado,
with the open expanse of the San Luis Valley (to the left)
and the Great Plains (off the photo to the right). Several of the
snow-spangled peaks in this range exceed 14,000 feet in elevation.

major geomorphic subdivisions

THE SOUTHERN ROCKIES

The Southern Rockies include a series of
linear ranges that extend from north-central
New Mexico northward into southern Wyoming, as well as a number of mountain
masses in central and western Colorado that
are less orderly in arrangement. The frontal
ranges rise abruptly from the western edge
of the Great Plains with just a narrow foothill zone that consists mostly of uptilted sedimentary strata, often in the form of
hogback ridges. In southern Wyoming these
mountains are called the Laramie or Snowy
ranges, in most of Colorado they are simply
named the Front Range, and in southern
Colorado and northern New Mexico they
are known as the Sangre de Cristo Mountains (fig. 14-3).

The origin of these frontal ranges is
complex, involving huge batholithic intrusions, erosion of the sedimentary cover, further uplift, perhaps peneplanation, and

extensive alpine glaciation. The general pattern of the present topography is a high-altitude subdued upland, with peaks up to
14,000 feet standing above the rolling upland surface and deep canyons trenching it.

Just west of the frontal ranges is an interrupted line of the four large-size basins
previously mentioned, extending from Wyoming to the New Mexico border. The origin
of these extensive "parks" is varied, but all
four are flat-floored and broad.

The ranges of central and western Colorado are generally similar in appearance
and height to the frontal ranges. Their patterns are much more amorphous, however,
and there are significant variations in both
structure and origin. The most complicated
highland mass is the San Juan Mountains in
southwestern Colorado.

The Southern Rockies reach the greatest altitudes of the entire Rocky Mountain
cordillera, although greater local relief is
found in some parts of the Middle Rockies.
There are no low passes through the Southern Rockies. These ranges functioned much

more significantly as a barrier to transportation than did the ranges farther north in the region.

THE MIDDLE ROCKIES

The Middle Rockies include the mountains of western Wyoming, northern Utah, and adjacent parts of Idaho and Montana. Three major separate ranges are involved:

1 The Uinta Range in Utah is the only significant range in the entire cordillera that extends east-west rather than north-south. It is a broad and massive range and is less rugged than the others.

2 The Wind River Mountains in western Wyoming encompass some of the most rugged granitic wilderness that can be found. It is a little-known area characterized by steep slopes and high relief. It was heavily glaciated in the past and still contains more than 60 living glaciers, constituting a greater total ice area than all other United States Rocky Mountain glaciers combined.[2]

3 The Bighorn Mountains of north-central Wyoming are a massive range rising between the Great Plains on the east and the Bighorn Basin on the west. There is a steep eastern slope, a broad subdued upland surface, ramparts of higher glaciated country, another broad subdued upland, and a less rugged western slope.

To the west of these three major units is a series of smaller ranges extending from central Utah to northern Wyoming, arranged with a conspicuous north-south linearity. The most massive is the Wasatch Range, which rises fairly gently on the eastern side but whose precipitous western face—the Wasatch Front—is unexcelled in the conterminous states in its combined height and steepness. North of the Wasatch several relatively small ranges reach into west-central Wyoming and culminate in the majestic Grand Tetons, whose block-faulted

[2] Stephen F. Arno, "Glaciers in the American West," *Natural History,* 78 (February 1969), 88.

and glaciated eastern scarp presents an even more spectacular face than the Wasatch Front (fig. 14-4).

Also a part of the Middle Rockies is the broad, jumbled mountain mass that makes up the Absaroka Range in Wyoming and the Beartooth Mountains in Montana. These are fairly rugged and steep-sided but with no discernible pattern and no notable crest line.

The lava plateau of Yellowstone Park and the north-trending valley of the upper Yellowstone River provide a relatively complete break between the Middle and Northern Rockies, although this breach had no transportational significance in the history of the West.

THE NORTHERN ROCKIES

The Northern Rockies occupy essentially all of western Montana and central and northern Idaho. The eastern half consists of a number of discrete linear ranges separated

fig. 14-4 The spectacular eastern fault scarp of the Grand Tetons rises abruptly to glaciated peaks above the flat floor of Jackson Hole.

by broad, flat-bottomed, structural valleys. It is almost ridge-and-valley topography on a grand scale. Some of the mountains are exceedingly rugged, but altitudes are lower than in the Middle and Southern Rockies.

The western portion of the Northern Rockies is a massive jumble of mountains that is almost patternless. Nearly all the land is in slope with many deep, narrow river valleys. Generalized nomenclature refers to the southern part as the Salmon River Mountains and the Sawtooth Mountains; most of the northern section is considered to be part of the Clearwater Mountains. The Sawtooths are the highest and most rugged, but no part is easily crossed by transportation routes. Two large natural lakes, Coeur d'Alene and Pend d'Oreille, are found in the extreme north, where continental glaciation occurred.

THE COLUMBIA MOUNTAINS

The Columbia Mountains occupy an area in southeastern British Columbia that is quite broad in the south but tapers northward until it pinches out at about the latitude of Edmonton and Prince George (54° N.L.). There are four major ranges: the north-south trending Purcell, Selkirk, and Monashee ranges in the south, and the knot of the Cariboo Mountains in the north. Unlike most of the Canadian Rockies, these mountains are largely composed of crystalline rocks. The narrow north-south trenches among the ranges are mostly occupied by long, beautiful bodies of water such as Kootenay Lake and Lake Okanagan.

THE ROCKY MOUNTAIN TRENCH

In many ways, the most remarkable topographic feature of the entire cordillera is the Rocky Mountain Trench. It is a valley that extends in a direct line from Montana almost to the Yukon Territory with regular box-like sides. Its exact origin is uncertain and variable, although parts are clearly related to faulting.[3] The trench bottom is flat to rolling and even hilly in spots, with four

low drainage divides between major north- and south-flowing streams. Eleven rivers, including the upper reaches of both the Columbia and the Fraser, occupy some portion of the trench. Recently constructed dams now impound two immense reservoirs in the trench: Williston Lake behind W. A. C. Bennett Dam on the Peace River and McNaughton Lake behind Mica Dam on the Columbia River.

THE CANADIAN ROCKIES

Along the Alberta–British Columbia border is a lengthy northern continuation of the cordillera known as the Canadian Rockies. Although these are not so high as the Middle and Southern Rockies, there is great local relief, and the ranges are more rugged and steep-sided. There was alpine glaciation during the Pleistocene, with extensive present-day mountain glaciers and even some upland icefields—the largest is the Columbia Icefield—from which lengthy glaciers extend downvalley.

The mountains are composed mostly of conspicuously layered sedimentary rocks that have been uplifted and, in some cases, extensively folded and faulted. Ridges and valleys are more or less uniform in altitude and tend to parallel one another for long stretches in a general northwest-southeast trend. These ranges provide some of the most spectacular scenery of the continent (fig. 14–5).

INTERIOR PLATEAUS AND MOUNTAINS OF BRITISH COLUMBIA

The interior section of British Columbia consists of an extensive area of diversified but generally subdued relief. The Fraser Plateau in the south and the Nechako Plateau in the center are characterized by moderately dissected hills, occasional mountain protuberances, and a few large en-

[3] J. Lewis Robinson, "The Rocky Mountain Trench in Eastern British Columbia," *Canadian Geographical Journal*, 77 (October 1968), 132.

fig. 14-5 The jagged peaks of the Canadian Rockies are world famous. This is the Sunwapta Valley in Jasper National Park.

trenched river valleys. Most notable of these entrenchments are in portions of the Fraser and Thompson valleys and in the Okanagan Trench with its series of beautiful lakes.[4]

North of the Nechako Plateau is a relatively complicated section of mountains and valleys—the Skeena Mountains to the west and the Omineca Mountains to the east—that flattens out into a series of dissected tablelands, the Stikine Plateau, in the far north. The Stikine country is underlain by lava and surmounted by several volcanic peaks.

vertical zonation: the topographic imperative

In a landscape dominated by slopes and considerable relief, the nature of other environmental elements is significantly dic-

---

[4] The spelling of this name differs in Canada and the United States. In the former it is "Okanagan"; in the latter, "Okanogan."

tated by the topography; thus climate and vegetation are most markedly affected by altitude, and secondarily by exposure and latitude. Within the Rocky Mountain Region are found some of the classic examples of vertical zonation in vegetation patterns, with major variations occurring in short horizontal distances because of significant vertical differences.

CLIMATE

The paradox of the Rocky Mountain climate is that summers tend to be semiarid and winters are relatively humid. Summer is a time of much sunshine, even though there may be a characteristically brief thundershower each afternoon. Windiness, generally low humidity, and sunshine quickly evaporate the rainfall, partially negating the effectiveness of the precipitation. Summer is therefore a time of relative dryness; after the main runoff of the melting snowpack has subsided, dust is much more characteristic than mud on the mountain slopes, except in the Canadian portion of the region where the summers are rainier.

The inland location of this region means that the prevailing westerly winds have had to pass over other mountains before reaching the Rockies and that part of their available moisture was dropped there. The western slopes of the high country may receive a considerable amount of summer rain, since the forced ascent squeezes out more moisture from the westerlies. But the lowland valleys, parks, and trenches of the region may experience almost desert-like conditions. Hence, the center of Colorado's San Luis Valley receives only six inches of moisture annually, and Challis, on Idaho's Salmon River, records seven inches; Ashcroft, in the Thompson River Canyon, with seven inches, is probably the driest nonarctic locality in Canada.

The low temperatures of winter make dry weather seem less dry because the precipitation that does fall is normally in the form of snow, and once it is on the ground it

fig. 14–6 The irresistible effect of wind shear on tree growth near the timberline is clearly shown in this Colorado scene. Branches are able to sprout and survive on these subalpine firs only on the direct leeward side of the tree trunks.

may not melt until spring, even in the valleys. Storm tracks are also shifted southward in winter, with the result that stormy conditions are more numerous and frontal precipitation is more commonplace. Usually snow lies deep and long over most of the region, particularly at higher altitudes.

The general pattern, then, is that the lower elevations are quite dry, but with increasing altitude there is increasing precipitation up to some critical level (generally between 9,000 and 11,000 feet) above which there is once again a decreasing trend. West-facing slopes normally receive more rain and snow than comparable levels on east-facing slopes because the prevailing winds are from the west and make their forced ascent on that side. Also, south-facing slopes receive more direct sunlight than north-facing ones, which makes for more rapid evaporation on the former and reduces the effectiveness of the rainfall or snowmelt that is received.

NATURAL VEGETATION

The region is basically a forested one with coniferous species predominant, but there are many areas in which trees are absent. All the valleys and basins in the Southern and Middle Rockies and some in more northerly localities are virtually treeless except for riparian hardwoods along stream courses. A sagebrush association is common throughout the Wyoming Basin and in many of the lower parks and valleys as far north as southern British Columbia. The higher valleys and basins are more likely to be grass covered.

At the other altitudinal extreme, on the mountaintops, trees are also normally absent. These higher elevations have the low-growing but complex plant associations of the alpine tundra (fig. 14–6). Thus, on many mountain ranges of the region there is a double tree line: one at lower elevation that marks the zone below which trees will not grow because of aridity, and one at higher elevation above which trees cannot survive

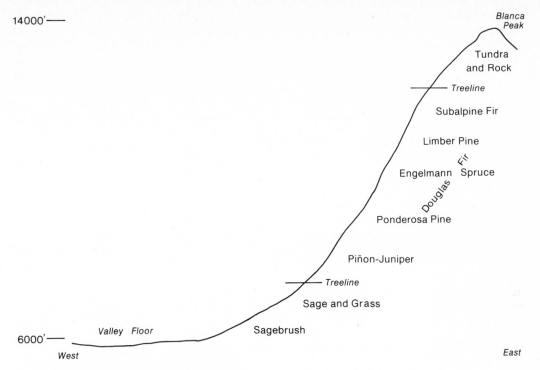

14000'—

Blanca
Peak

Tundra
and Rock

—— *Treeline*

Subalpine Fir

Limber Pine

Engelmann Spruce

Fir

Douglas

Ponderosa Pine

Piñon-Juniper

—— *Treeline*

Sage and Grass

Sagebrush

Valley Floor

6000'—

West

East

fig. 14–7 Schematic diagram of vegetation zonation on the western side of the Sangre de Cristo Range in southern Colorado. The lower treeline is an adjustment to aridity; the upper treeline reflects low summer temperatures and a short growing season.

because of low temperatures, high wind, and short growing season.

The relationship of altitude to latitude is shown quite clearly by the variation in elevation of the upper tree line in the Rocky Mountains (fig. 14–7). At the southern margin of the region, at 36° N.L. in New Mexico, the upper timberline occurs between 11,500 and 12,000 feet above sea level. This elevation progressively decreases northward: about 9,500 feet at 45° in Yellowstone Park; about 6,000 feet at 49° at the international border; and about 2,500 feet at 60° at the northern extremity of the region near the Yukon border. Exposure, drainage, and soil characteristics influence the details of this

pattern, but the general principle is clear-cut.

The varying elevation of the upper tree line represents only one facet of the broader design of vertical zonation in vegetation patterns. As a result of abrupt altitudinal changes in short horizontal distances, various plant associations tend to occur in relatively narrow bands or zones on the slopes of the ranges. An example of the zonation pattern in the Southern Rockies can be seen in the accompanying transect up the west slope of the Sangre de Cristo Range from the San Luis Valley of Colorado. In other localities the speciation might vary, and all the zones would be shifted downhill in more northerly latitudes. The principle of vertical zonation is nevertheless ever present in the Rockies; only the details vary.

the opening
of the region
to settlement

Except in the extreme southern part of the region that was penetrated by the Spaniards at the end of the sixteenth century, the first white men to see the Rocky Mountains were French fur traders who sporadically worked their way up the Great Plains rivers during the eighteenth century. Beginning in the late 1700s, there were several significant exploring expeditions in various parts of the region; some were government-sponsored, and others were backed as commercial ventures.

Alexander Mackenzie was the first explorer of note to cross the Rockies; he did so in 1793 by penetrating the Peace River Valley in the far north of the region. The Lewis and Clark Expedition of 1803–4 made its way up the Missouri River and crossed the Northern Rockies on the way to the mouth of the Columbia. While Lewis and Clark were still encamped on the Pacific shore, Simon Fraser, who was affiliated with the North West Company as was Mackenzie, established the first trading post west of the Rockies, at Fort McLeod on a tributary of the Peace River.

Other significant early explorations included those of Lieutenant Zebulon Pike in the Southern Rockies in 1806–7; of David Thompson, who discovered the source of the Columbia River in 1807 and established a trading post, Kootenay House, there; and of Major Stephen Long in 1820 in Colorado.

In the meantime fur trapping and trading became a way of life throughout the region, with large periodic trading rendezvous at such places as Jackson's Hole at the eastern base of the Grand Tetons in Wyoming and Pierre's Hole in eastern Idaho. This colorful period, however, did not last long because the value of beaver fur declined in the 1840s, following changes in the style of men's hats. From that time until the discovery of gold in the late 1850s, the Rocky Mountains served only as a barrier to the westward movement, and pioneers pushed through the lowest mountain passes as rapidly as possible on their way to the Oregon Territory or to California.

The discovery of gold in 1849 at Sutter's Fort in the newly acquired California Territory created a mad rush of gold seekers coming from all parts of the world, many of whom braved the natural hardships and Indian dangers in the overland crossing of the continent. In crossing the Rocky Mountains, some prospected for gold in the stream gravels and found traces of the precious metal. Although most seekers of gold went on to California, many returned within a few years to prospect further in the numerous mountain gulches.

It was not until 1859, however, that gold in paying quantities was found in the Rocky Mountains. At almost the same time a gold rush began to Central City, Colorado, and another to the western flanks of the Cariboo Mountains in British Columbia. By the early 1860s the Cariboo gold fields had the largest concentration of people in western Canada; and Barkerville, center of the find, was the largest western town north of San Francisco. By the early 1870s Central City had grown to become the largest urban center in the Rocky Mountain Region.

Within a short time more people had settled in the mountain country than in all its previous history. Practically every part of the region was prospected, and many valuable mineral deposits were found, especially in the Southern Rockies. Boom towns sprang up in remote valleys and gulches of the high country, and this in turn led to the development of a series of narrow-gauge railroads, built at great expense per mile, for hauling out gold ore. As the higher-grade ores became exhausted, production declined

fig. 14–8 Remnants of hundreds of ghost towns still exist in the region. This is Zincton in the Columbia Mountains of British Columbia.

in these camps; in time most of them became ghost towns (fig. 14–8).

Lumbering and logging, grazing activities, irrigation agriculture, and the tourist trade brought additional population to the mountains, but none was so significant in the early peopling of the region and in bringing its advantages to the attention of the rest of the country as was gold mining.

the mining industry

Wherever rich mineralized zones were found, mining camps developed. Colorado was especially important, with its Central City, Ouray, Cripple Creek, Victor, Leadville, Aspen, Georgetown, and Silver Plume. Wyoming and New Mexico were relatively insignificant, but farther north there were major discoveries around Virginia City in southwestern Montana, in the vicinity of Butte and Anaconda, in the Coeur d'Alene area of northern Idaho, and in the Kootenay and Cariboo districts of British Columbia. Although gold was the mineral chiefly sought, valuable deposits of silver, lead, zinc, copper, tungsten, and molybdenum were also found.

MINING TODAY

The Rocky Mountains is a highly mineralized region. Only four leading districts are, however, discussed here:

1 Leadville, Colorado—gold, silver, lead, zinc, and molybdenum

2 Butte, Montana—copper, silver, lead, and zinc

3 Coeur d'Alene, Idaho—gold, silver, lead, and zinc

4 Kootenay, British Columbia—lead and zinc.

The Leadville District One of the oldest and most important mining areas of the Rocky Mountain Region is located at Leadville, in a high mountain valley near the headwaters of the Arkansas River at an elevation above 10,000 feet (fig. 14–9). Following the discovery of gold in the Central City area in 1859, prospectors searched the numerous mountain valleys of practically all highland Colorado. In the spring of 1860, placer gold was found in California Gulch near Leadville. News of the discovery immediately spread, and by July of that year more than 10,000 people were in the camp.

363

fig. 14-9 Leadville, Colorado, was a mining town that experienced several periods of notable prosperity and now continues as a shadow of its former self. The mine dumps in the foreground are clear evidence of past economic history. Mount Massive in the background is the second highest peak in the entire Rocky Mountain cordillera, but its 14,418-foot peak is not particularly prominent because even the valley bottoms in this area are more than 10,000 feet above sea level (courtesy Colorado Department of Public Relations).

In 1874 silver-lead mining began, and gold soon ceased to be the dominant metal. Within the next five years 10 million ounces of silver and 66 million pounds of lead were produced with a total value of nearly $15 million. Zinc, although discovered in 1885, was unimportant until after the close of the nineteenth century. In 1902 the zinc output exceeded that of lead, and in 1903 that of silver.

The Leadville area continues as an important mining district, producing all its former metals as well as molybdenum and tungsten.[5] The molybdenum comes from Anglo-America's highest major mining complex (11,000 feet) at Climax, which is 13 miles northeast of Leadville and is the

world's largest producer of this valuable ferro-alloy ore.

The Butte-Anaconda District In western Montana is located a major copper-mining district that is normally the second most prolific producer in the nation. The Anaconda Copper Company, which owns the mining properties at Butte and the large smelter at Anaconda, dominates Montana copper production and also produces most of its silver, gold, lead, and zinc.

The large hill on which Butte is built is honeycombed with mine tunnels that have produced more than $2 billion worth of metal within the more than 100 years of operation, giving it the name "The Richest Hill on Earth." For a long time the smelter was located at Butte, but injurious fumes from its stacks destroyed so much vegetation in the city that it was removed to Anaconda,

[5] Lake County (Leadville) is the leading United States producer of these two last-named metal ores.

23 miles to the west. The Anaconda smelter, once famous for having the world's tallest smokestack (585 feet), throws the fumes high into the air. Since the smelter's removal from Butte, the city has had some success in growing trees and grass.

The district has always been famous for its deep shaft mines, but since the mid-1970s all output has been from open-pit operations.

The Coeur d'Alene District This mining area, one of the richest of the Rocky Mountains, lies in northern Idaho. There are 24 active mines in the district, yielding major outputs of silver, lead, zinc, and antimony, as well as some copper, gold, and miscellaneous byproducts. Since Coeur d'Alene became active in 1884, minerals to the value of more than $2 billion have been extracted from its mines.

The lead, silver, and zinc ores of the Coeur d'Alene district are so complex that effective recovery has been difficult. The gravity process used before 1922 was extremely wasteful because of the almost identical weights of lead and zinc. In 1922 the selective-flotation process was introduced, which made possible the extraction of the metals through their varying affinities to oils and chemicals after the ores had been ground to a fine powder. The concentrates are smelted in the district or elsewhere in the Pacific Northwest.

The Pine Creek area, lying to the east of the city of Coeur d'Alene, is one of the oldest mining areas of northern Idaho. Difficulties of access and the complexity of the ores made development very costly, however. In recent years new techniques have been perfected to economically separate the components of the complex ores, and a network of modern roads has been built to the various mines to make them accessible to the large zinc reduction plant and smelter at Kellogg, only a few miles away.

Northern Idaho is the nation's leading producer of silver and antimony, and normally ranks second in lead and fifth in zinc.

The Kootenay District In the southeastern corner of British Columbia lies an important lead- and zinc-mining district. Most of the ore comes from the great Sullivan mine at Kimberly.

Concentrates from the Kootenay district as well as from other parts of western Canada and some foreign sources are treated in the Consolidated Mining and Smelting Company refinery at Trail, which is one of the world's greatest nonferrous metallurgical works (fig. 14–10). Its principal

fig. 14–10 One of the largest metal refining complexes on the continent is found adjacent to the Columbia River at Trail, British Columbia (courtesy British Columbia Department of Travel Industry).

products are lead, zinc, silver, gold, phosphate, and lesser minerals.

Unfortunately, nuisance emanations from the smelter smokestacks at Trail have caused problems with international ramifications. For years Trail was pervaded by an unpleasant odor, and the vegetation on the surrounding hillsides was killed by the toxic atmospheric pollution. Also the smelter fumes were wafted southward down the Columbia Valley into Washington State, where natural vegetation and fruit orchards were damaged and soils became hyperacid. Several lawsuits were successfully prosecuted against the company as a result. During the last two decades expensive treatment units have been installed to cleanse the fumes, with favorable results.

Other Recent Developments Although for several decades the mining industry had been gradually declining in the Rocky Mountain Region, in recent years there has been a considerable upsurge with the evidence of more valuable deposits still to be discovered. Recent major developments include a huge open-pit iron mine at the southern end of the Wind River Range in Wyoming (Atlantic City), great expansion in the mining of phosphate rock in southeastern Idaho, open-pit bituminous coal mining in southwestern Wyoming, trona (soda ash) and expanded petroleum and natural gas operations in the Wyoming Basin, several copper and molybdenum mines in central British Columbia, and remarkable expansion of coal mining in the Crow's Nest Pass–Fernie area of the Alberta–British Columbia border and the eastern foothills of the Rocky Mountains in Alberta.

These latter developments result from huge contracts with the Japanese steel industry, which will absorb most of the expanded production. Specially built unit coal trains make the 1,400-mile round trip from Crow's Nest Pass to the ports of Vancouver and Roberts Bank in three days.

Future mining developments in the Rocky Mountains will almost surely be based on large-scale corporate enterprise and will be organized around existing settlements or new planned communities. The ghost town, the abandoned mine shaft, and the dilapidated miner's hut located deep in the mountain fastness provide mute romantic reminders of a picturesque phase in the occupance of the Rocky Mountain Region.

forestry

Although there has long been small-scale local cutting of timber for mine props, firewood, cabin construction, and other miscellaneous purposes, large-scale commercial forestry has been restricted to certain sections of the Rocky Mountain Region, particularly the northern half. For example, less than 2 percent of the total United States timber cut is from the Southern and Middle Rockies, whereas nearly 10 percent comes from the Northern Rockies. Large sawmills and pulp mills operate at several localities in western Montana and northern Idaho.

The traditional logging area of western Canada has been coastal British Columbia, but in recent years increasing timber supplies have come from the interior of the province. Sawmilling has become a major activity at such places as Fernie, Cranbrook, Nelson, Golden, and McBride. Pulping, although growing, is much more limited, but there are large mills at Prince George, Kamloops, and Castelegar.

Douglas fir is the most sought-after species and constitutes the largest cut. Pines of various kinds are also important. The ponderosa pine is the most valuable, but the lodgepole is being used more and more, especially for pulping, even though it is a small-diameter tree. Spruce are also valuable. Most of the larger logging operations are operated on a clearcutting basis.

agriculture
and stock raising

In any consideration of Rocky Mountain agriculture and ranching, it must be remembered that the region consists mostly of forested or bare rocky slopes. The occasional level areas are utilized for irrigation farming, dry farming, or ranching, and thus attain an importance out of proportion to their size.

When the Spaniards settled in the Santa Fe area of the Southern Rockies at the beginning of the seventeenth century they were primarily prospecting for gold and silver. Finding little mineral wealth, they soon turned to ranching in the broad basins of the upper Rio Grande Valley. From Spain they received large land grants in the San Luis Valley, and for the next two centuries the area was dominated by "cattle barons." After the close of the Mexican War and the annexation of this territory by the United States, the large land holdings were broken up. Because of semiaridity, ranching has remained the principal occupation of the San Luis Valley, although considerable acreages are irrigated for farming. Owing to the high altitude (above 7,000 feet) and the resulting short growing season, the crop options are limited.

Although originally profitable, wheat yields have declined, and potatoes now constitute the main cash crop (fig. 14–11). There is also a considerable amount of truck farming, based on the hot sunny summers and abundant irrigation water from artesian wells. Migratory farmworkers do most of the harvesting.

Ranching began much later in the valleys and basins to the north, for this land remained unexplored and unoccupied by white men until trappers and prospectors entered the mountains. In time, each grassy plot in the Middle and Northern Rockies was homesteaded and turned into a ranch. Many areas, however, have been given over to dry farming or to irrigation agriculture. As is the case elsewhere, the best lands were the first to be cultivated, and the poorest and most inaccessible ones remained in pasture. In the Northern Rockies and in the higher mountain valleys where frosts are common even during summer, ranching has remained the major activity (fig. 14–12). Both cattle and sheep are raised widely in the region, but the latter have declined con-

fig. 14–11 Potatoes growing in the San Luis Valley, with the Sangre de Cristo Range rising in the background (courtesy Colorado Department of Public Relations).

fig. 14–12 Beef cattle grazing in a "park," or mountain valley, in southwestern Colorado, with the high country of the San Juan Mountains behind (courtesy Colorado Department of Public Relations).

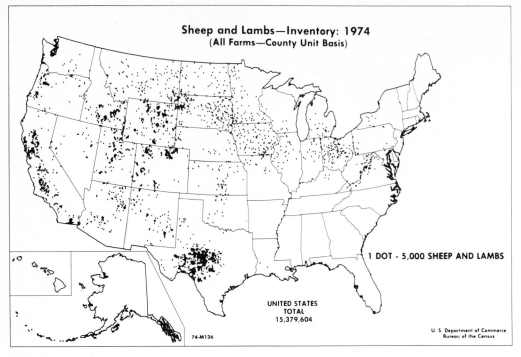

Sheep and Lambs—Inventory: 1974
(All Farms—County Unit Basis)

1 DOT - 5,000 SHEEP AND LAMBS

UNITED STATES
TOTAL
15,379,604

74-M136

U. S. Department of Commerce
Bureau of the Census

fig. 14–13 Sheep are raised in many parts of
the United States, but particularly in the West.

siderably in importance in recent years (fig. 14–13).

The Forest Service, through its permit system, cooperates with ranchers by allowing them to pasture sheep and cattle within the national forests, but it also attempts to see to it that the land is neither overstocked nor overgrazed. This *transhumance* (the driving of grazing animals to high mountain pastures in summer and back to lower valleys in winter) is almost universal throughout the Rocky Mountain Region.

IRRIGATION AGRICULTURE

The establishment of mining towns throughout the Rocky Mountain Region, which were isolated from the agricultural areas to the east, made it profitable to withdraw some of the more favored valleys and basins from pastures and plant them to wheat and other staple crops. High prices

and a great demand also stimulated the production of vegetables by irrigation. Wherever water could be diverted for irrigation, additional land was placed under cultivation (see vignette on next page).

At first all irrigation projects were either privately developed or under state supervision, but ultimately the United States Bureau of Reclamation established several projects within the region. One of the most interesting of these is the Uncompahgre Project in southwestern Colorado. Surplus waters from the Gunnison River—along which there is little land suited to irrigation—were diverted through a mountain range via a six-mile tunnel to the broad, flat, semiarid valley of the Uncompahgre River, thus making it irrigable.

The basic crop throughout the region is hay. Irrigated valleys yield valuable supplies of alfalfa and other hay crops for winter feeding of livestock. Some specialty crops are also grown: pinto beans and chili peppers in New Mexico, miscellaneous vegetables in Colorado and Utah, sugar beets and grains in Idaho and Montana, fruits around Flathead Lake and in some of the Kootenay valleys, and wheat in the Kootenay River Valley and around Cranbrook. But hay occupies the principal cultivated acreage almost everywhere.

The most notable irrigated valley in the Rocky Mountain Region, and one of Canada's most distinctive specialty crop areas, occupies the long narrow trench of the Okanagan Valley. Extending north for 125 miles from the international border, the valley is only three to six miles wide except where it broadens a bit into tributary valleys in the north. Large lakes occupy most of the valley floor, and farming is limited to the adjacent terraces. Irrigation is necessary in the desert-like conditions (annual rainfall, 9 inches, and temperatures up to 110°) of the southern part of the valley, but general farming can be carried on under natural rainfall in the north (precipitation, 17 inches).

A variety of field crops, feed crops, and vegetables is grown, but fruit growing is the distinctive activity in the valley. The

fig. 14-14   The Okanagan Valley, western Canada's premier fruit-growing area. Shown here are Lake Osoyoos, the town of Osoyoos, and orchards (darker areas) covering most of the valley bottom lands (courtesy British Columbia Department of Travel Industry).

Osoyoos section in the south is said to produce the earliest fruits in Canada (fig. 14-14). Apples are the major crop (about one-third of Canada's total output), but the

water storage and diversion

The Rocky Mountain Region is sometimes spoken of as the "mother of rivers" because so many of the major streams of western Anglo-America have their headwaters on the snowy slopes of the Rockies. This water-collecting function is generally considered to be one of the two leading economic assets (tourism is the other) of the region. From the Rocky Mountains the Rio Grande and Pecos flow to the south; the Arkansas, Platte, Yellowstone, Missouri, South Saskatchewan, North Saskatchewan, Athabasca, Peace, and Liard flow to the east; and the Stikine, Skeena, Fraser, Columbia, Snake, Green, and Colorado flow to the west.

The capriciousness of river flow has long been recognized, and the alternation between flood and low-water stages has been deplored.

Dam-building is the chief tool to smooth these imbalances of flow and make the waters more "usable" for various purposes. In the past, most "development" of Rocky Mountain rivers has been deferred to downsteam locations, particularly in the Great Plains and Intermontane regions. But more recently dam-building has come to the high country, modified in some cases by wholesale water-diversion schemes.

The principle of transmountain diversion is that "unused" water, generally from western slope streams, is taken from an area of surplus by means of an undermountain tunnel to an area of water deficit, normally on the eastern slope of the Rockies or in the western edge of the Great Plains. Potential western-slope users are compensated for this loss by the building of

(Continued)

valley is particularly noted as one of only two areas in the nation that has a sizable production of soft fruits—peaches, plums, pears, cherries, and apricots. In recent years there has been a significant increase in the acreage devoted to vineyards; these are almost exclusively under contract to British Columbia wineries. There are more than 3,500 fruit farms in the valley, with an average size of about ten acres; the smaller orchardists have trouble making a living from fruit farming alone.

the tourist industry

The major role of the Rocky Mountain Region is probably in providing an attractive setting for outdoor recreation. The tourist industry is undoubtedly the most dynamic segment of the regional economy.

SUMMER TOURISM

With its high rugged mountains, spectacular scenery, extensive forests, varied wildlife,

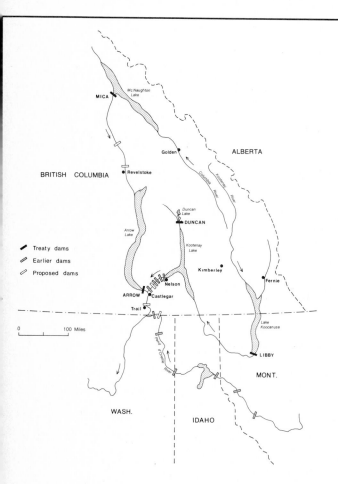

fig. 14-a The upper Columbia River area and its dams.

storage dams there to catch and hold flood-stage flow for later release when the river is low.

The first major transmountain diversion scheme was the Colorado–Big Thompson Project, which was initiated in the early 1950s and has been discussed in chapter 13. Since then, several other major schemes have been completed or started in the Southern Rockies, primarily to benefit the large population concentration on the Colorado Piedmont. The municipal water supplies of both Denver and Colorado Springs have been augmented by diversions from central Colorado streams. The Fryingpan River is tapped between Aspen and Glenwood Springs for diversion to the headwaters of the Arkansas, whence it will provide municipal water for Pueblo and expanded irrigation supplies farther downstream in the Great Plains. The Chama Project is providing diversion from the watershed of the San Juan River to the upper Rio Grande in northern New Mexico.

Until the decade of the 1960s, there had been almost no dam building in the Canadian portion of the region except for five small hydroelectric dams along the lower Kootenay River to supply power to the huge smelter at Trail. In 1964, however, the United States and Canada ratified the Columbia River Treaty, which provided for the construction of four major dams (fig. 14-a). The basic purposes of the dams are to control floods and to permit increased power generation at United States dams downstream on the Columbia by provid-

and cool summer temperatures, the Rocky Mountain Region is a very popular summer vacationland. The location of the region between the Great Plains on the east and the intermontane and Pacific coastal areas on the west places it directly across lines of travel. Nearby flatlanders flock to the mountains for surcease from the summer heat of Dallas, Kansas City, or even Denver. And people come from greater distances to sample the scenic delights of Banff (more than 3 million tourists per year) or Yellowstone (175,000 visitors in a midsummer week, a number equal to nearly half of Wyoming's resident population).

The development of specific resort centers depended on accessibility; thus the first resorts were those sponsored by the railroads. Others were developed after highways were built through the region. Only where some unusual natural or scenic feature presented itself were resort hotels and lodges built in remote places.

Throughout the Rockies there are

---

ing release water at low-water periods. The following are the four dams of the project:

1 Duncan Dam is on the Duncan River between Duncan Lake and Kootenay Lake. Its 120-foot height enlarges the area of Duncan Lake by about 200 percent.

2 Keenleyside Dam was built on the Columbia at the southern end of Lower Arrow Lake. Its 170-foot height has raised the level of the Arrow lakes by 40 feet, making them into a 100-mile long reservoir.

3 Mica Dam was completed at the Big Bend of the Columbia River in 1973. It is 700-feet high and backs up a two-pronged Rocky Mountain Trench reservoir for 85 miles on the Columbia and 60 miles on the Canoe River. This is the only one of the three Canadian dams at which large-scale power generation is planned.

4 Libby Dam has been built on the Kootenay River in northern Montana. It is included in the treaty because half of the 80-mile long reservoir (Lake Koocanusa) is in Canada.

The financial arrangements provide that the United States pay in advance for the increased power; that money was used to build the Canadian dams. Future power generation, part of which is legally Canada's, will mostly be sold to the United States.

An even more grandiose scheme has been constructed on the upper reaches of the Peace River near Finlay Forks, British Columbia. The W. A. C. Bennett Dam backs up a reservoir for 70 miles on the Peace and another 170 miles on two major tributaries, the Finlay and the Parsnip rivers. It is 680 square miles, the largest artificial lake on the continent. The ultimate capacity for hydroelectricity generation is one of the largest in the world (more than 2.3 million kw). There is no nearby market for this power, so 600 miles of extra high-voltage transmission lines have been erected to conduct the electricity to the lower Fraser Valley and Vancouver, the largest population concentration in western Canada.

The long, narrow, structural valleys of the Columbia Mountains and the Rocky Mountain Trench are thus increasingly filled with reservoirs.

As with most major development projects, the environmental ramifications of these dam-reservoir schemes are enormous. For almost all of them, however, no environmental impact studies were made prior to construction, and mitigative efforts were either minimal or nonexistent. The inevitable result has been major loss of critical wildlife habitat,[a] flooding of streams needed for fish spawning, destruction of waterfowl nesting areas, and fluctuating water levels that exposed naked tree stumps and eroding shorelines where there had been forested valleys. Some economic benefits are undeniable, but the environmental degradation is awesome.

[a] For example, a post-construction inventory of the country around McNaughton Lake on the Columbia River showed a 70 percent decline in deer, moose, and bear populations.

places of interest for tourists, with spectacular scenery as the principal attraction. Many of the outstanding scenic areas have been reserved as national parks, which generally function as the key attractions of the region. The following are seven of the most popular tourist areas in the region, in terms of numbers of visitors.

New Mexico Mountains The southernmost portion of the Rocky Mountains, located in northern New Mexico, is not particularly rugged or spectacular and consists mostly of pleasant forested slopes. Its summers, however, are considerably cooler than those of the parched plains of the Southwest. It is an area with a rich historical heritage that is manifested in the pervasive Indian and Hispanic character of the cultural landscape. As a result the narrow twisting streets of nearby Santa Fe (the principal focal point of the area, although not actually located within the Rocky Mountain Region) are jammed with visitors' vehicles during the

summer. The Taos area is a center for dude-ranch and youth-camp activities, and Red River has developed into a year-round tourist resort.

Pikes Peak Area Colorado Springs is a city of the Great Plains, but its site is at the eastern base of one of the most famous mountains in Anglo-America. Pikes Peak, with a summit elevation of 14,110 feet, is far from being the highest mountain in Colorado, but its spectacular rise from the plains makes it an outstanding feature (fig. 14–15). The surrounding area contains some of the most striking scenery (Garden of the Gods, Seven Falls, Cheyenne Mountain, Cave of the Winds, Rampart Range) and some of the most blatantly commercial (Manitou Springs) tourist attractions in the region. Few tourists visit the Southern Rockies without at least a brief stop in the Pikes Peak area, as the overcrowding of even the unusually wide streets of Colorado Springs gives eloquent evidence.

fig. 14–15   Pikes Peak is probably the most famous mountain in Anglo-America. It is seen here beyond the Gateway Rocks of vertically tilted sandstone hogbacks in the Garden of the Gods near Colorado Springs (Union Pacific Railroad photo).

Denver's Front Range Hinterland
The Front Range of the Southern Rockies rises a dozen miles west of Denver, and the immediate vicinity provides a recreational area for the residents of the city as well as for visitors from more distant places. Denver maintains an elaborate and extensive group of "mountain parks," which are actually part of the municipal park system. There are thousands of summer cabins to be rented; many streams to be fished; deer, elk, mountain sheep, and bear to be hunted; dozens of old mining towns to be explored; and countless souvenir shops in which to spend money.

Rocky Mountain National Park Following many years of agitation by the people of Colorado for the establishment of a national park in the northern part of the state to preserve the scenic beauty of that section of the continental divide, a rugged area of 400 square miles was reserved by Congress in 1915 as Rocky Mountain National Park (fig. 14–16). It includes some of the highest and most picturesque peaks, glacial valleys, and canyons of the region, as well as extensive forested tracts that provide protection for native wildlife. This park, one of the most accessible in the country, may be

fig. 14–16 National Parks of the United States.

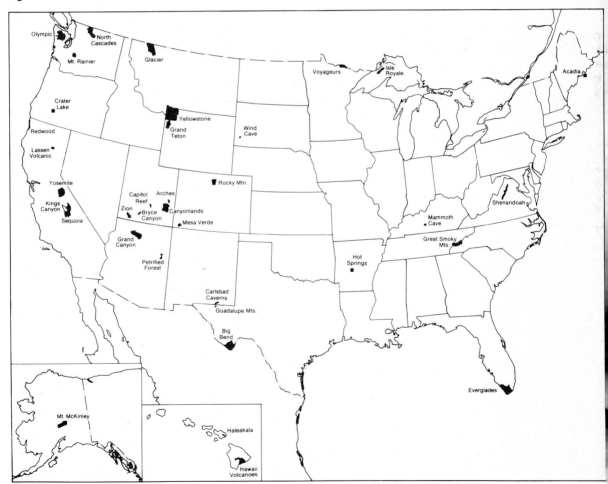

reached by excellent highways from either the east or west.

Spectacular Trail Ridge Road traverses the park, connecting the tourist towns of Grand Lake and Estes Park, and reaches an elevation of 12,185 feet. Automobile touring is the principal activity in the park, but hiking, climbing, and trail riding are also popular.

Yellowstone–Grand Teton–Jackson Hole In the northwestern corner of Wyoming is an extensive forested plateau of which one 3,500-square-mile area has been designated as Yellowstone National Park. It was established in 1872 as the first national nature preserve in the United States. It is lacking in spectacular mountains but contains a huge high-altitude (elevation 7,700 feet) lake, magnificent canyons and waterfalls, and the most impressive hydrothermal displays—geysers, hot springs, fumaroles, hot-water terraces—in the world (fig. 14–17). A few miles to the south is Grand Teton National Park, a smaller and more recently reserved area that encompasses the rugged grandeur of the Grand Teton Mountains, a heavily glaciated fault block that rises abruptly from the flat floor of Jackson Hole. Jackson Hole was an early fur-trappers' rendezvous that is now the winter home of the largest elk herd on the continent.

The Tetons are particularly attractive to hikers and climbers; Yellowstone is a motorists' park. The ubiquitous moose and a great variety of other species of wildlife add to the interest of the area. In spite of its relatively remote location and the short time that it is open, the Yellowstone–Grand Teton country annually attracts more than 2.5 million visitors.

fig. 14–17 The unique attraction of Yellowstone Park is its unrivaled assemblage of hydrothermal features, particularly geysers. Here Old Faithful performs in its reliably spectacular fashion.

Waterton-Glacier International Peace Park Glacier National Park in Montana and Waterton Lakes National Park in Alberta are contiguous and have similar scenery. The mountains are typical of the Canadian Rockies, with essentially horizontal sediments uplifted and massively carved by glacial action. The area is a paradise for hikers, climbers, horseback riders, and wildlife enthusiasts, and contains one of the most spectacular automobile roads on the continent, the Going-to-the-Sun Highway that traverses Glacier Park from east to west.

The Canadian Rockies The most magnificent mountains in the region are found west of Calgary and Edmonton on the Alberta–British Columbia boundary. The national park system of Canada was started in 1885, when a small area in the vicinity of the mineral hot springs at Banff was reserved as public property (fig. 14–18). The famous resorts of Banff, Lake Louise, and Jasper were developed by the two transcontinental railways, and the Canadian Pacific and Canadian National are still major operators in the area. Today there are four na-

fig. 14–18 The national parks of Canada.

tional parks and four provincial parks with a contiguous area totaling nearly 11,000 square miles, probably the largest of heavily visited nature recreational areas in the world. Heavily glaciated mountains, abundant and varied wildlife, spectacular waterfalls, colorful lakes, deep canyons, the largest ice field in the Rockies, and luxurious resort hotels characterize the area.

WINTER SPORTS

The region possesses superb natural attributes for skiing, and ever-increasing numbers of skiers are being attracted to the Rocky Mountains during the period of heavy snows. High elevation assures a long period of snow cover; many areas can provide skiing from Thanksgiving to mid-May. Because the winter storms have lost much of their moisture by the time they reach the Rockies the snow is often of the fine, powdery variety preferred by skiers. And there is

fig. 14–19 One of the busiest ski areas in the Rockies is Winter Park, due to its relative closeness to the major population center of Denver. Note the western entrance to Moffat Tunnel (a railway tunnel) in the background (Union Pacific Railroad photo).

an abundance of different degrees of slopeland to accommodate all classes of skiers.

In the past the region was relatively remote from large population centers, and few skiers came to the Rockies. To some extent this is still true, but many regional ski areas, especially in the Southern Rockies, have experienced a rapid increase in the number of users. Nearby populations have grown, and skiers travel much greater distances to ski than they did in the past. About 20 percent of the citizens of Colorado are skiers, and about 67 percent of the users of ski areas in the state are local people. In the other large winter sports areas of the region, about 50 percent of the users are nonresidents.

There are three basic types of ski areas depending on their clientele: vacation, weekend, and single-day. Many of the famous older ski resorts are of the vacation variety, and may have more remote locations because the skiers will stay several days and are willing to put in more travel time and money to get there. The most heavily used ski areas in the region are mostly of the vacation variety: Taos Ski Valley in New Mexico, Aspen and Snowmass in Colorado, Jackson Hole and Snow King in Wyoming, and Sun Valley in Idaho.

Weekend and single-day ski areas must be located near population centers to be profitable. Consequently the greatest concentration of such areas in the Rockies is in the Front Range near Denver, where Berthoud Pass, Winter Park, Arapaho, Loveland Basin, and other developments attract large numbers of short-term visitors (fig. 14–19). A smaller but even more concentrated group of ski areas is found in the Wasatch Range just east of Salt Lake City; some of these, such as Alta and Snowbird, are actually reached by city bus lines.

Some ski areas are sufficiently diversified and sufficiently accessible to attract a combination of both long-term and short-term visitors. The prime example of this in the Rocky Mountain Region is Vail, a relatively new but highly developed and promoted area on the main transcontinental highway west of Denver. Vail has 11 lifts that can carry more than 10,000 skiers per hour and has more skiers each year than any other area in the region. Banff, in the Canadian Rockies, has a similar pattern of visitation on a smaller scale.

Almost all winter sports areas in the United States portion of the region are located on National Forest land, which is leased from the Forest Service by the promoters. Provisions of the leases give the Forest Service right of approval of the rates charged, which presumably has a lot to do with the fairly uniform price scale that prevails in most areas.

FISHING AND HUNTING

No other generally accessible region in Anglo-America provides such a variety of faunal resources to tempt the hunter and fisherman. The fishing season normally lasts from May until September, with various species of trout as the principal quarry. Only diligent artificial stocking can maintain the resource in the more accessible lakes and streams where overfishing is rampant. The hunting season lasts from August to December in various parts of the region. The list of legal game is extensive, running the gamut from cottontail rabbit to grizzly bear and from pronghorn antelope to mountain goat. In an average year more than a quarter of a million big game animals and two dozen hunters are killed in this region.

PROBLEMS

The flocking of visitors to these high-country scenic areas is a mixed blessing. By its very nature, a pleasurable outdoor experience can be ruined by overcrowding of people and overdevelopment of facilities to cater to the crowds. The national parks and other prime scenic attractions of the Rockies are rapidly becoming centers of controversy between the advocates of wilderness preservation on one hand and developers on the other. Important, precedent-setting decisions are now being made. Should a complete summer-winter resort town site be constructed at Lake Louise? Should the roadway system of Yellowstone Park be converted to one-way traffic? Do we want national parks, or national parking lots?

transportation

Like the Great Plains, the Rocky Mountains have been a major barrier to east-west travel. The early trails across the Rockies either passed around the southern end in New Mexico or crossed through the Wyoming Basin between the Southern and Middle Rockies. The first "transcontinental" railroad, the Union Pacific, used the Wyoming Basin route. Railroad surveying parties explored all possible routes, but in the end only nine lines succeeded in completely crossing the mountain barrier. Two of these, the Southern Pacific and the Santa Fe, were built through New Mexico, south of the mountains. Only the Denver and Rio Grande Western crossed through the highest part of the Rocky Mountains by way of Tennessee Pass (elevation 10,202 feet). Later, with the completion of the six-mile Moffat Tunnel, it succeeded in reaching the western slope by a shorter and lower route. Three "transcontinental lines," the Northern Pacific, the Great Northern, and the Milwaukee Road, crossed the mountains in Montana.

In Canada, only two lines were built: the Canadian Pacific to the south and the Canadian National farther north. Only these two are true transcontinental railways in that they link ports on opposite coasts, the Pacific ports of Vancouver and Prince Rupert with the Atlantic ports of Montreal, Halifax, Saint John, and Sydney. Primary Canadian Pacific service crosses the Rockies at the relatively low Kicking Horse Pass between Banff and Yoho, and then descends through the famous spiral tunnels in its westward route. Secondary service is over the more southerly Crow's Nest Pass route.

fig. 14–20 The carving of transport routes through the Rockies was often difficult, slow, and expensive (courtesy Canadian National Railways).

The route of the Canadian National Railway traverses the northerly but low-level Yellowhead Pass (fig. 14–20).

Highway development later followed similarly, but the two southern routes and the one through the Wyoming Basin carry most of the traffic. Highways in the Canadian Rockies suffer from two difficulties that are uncommon south of the border: their routes are interrupted in several places by long, narrow lakes that occupy the structural trenches of the subregion; and every winter finds avalanches damaging or destroying sections of the highway, and thus much summer maintenance and repair work are inevitably necessary.

Canada's most ambitious road-building program was the Trans-Canada Highway. Completed in 1963 and extending from St. John's in Newfoundland to Victoria in British Columbia, it is reputed to be the longest unbroken stretch of roadway ever built by one country (although the Cabot Strait and the Strait of Georgia are too wide to be bridged and so must be crossed by automo-

bile ferry). The most expensive and difficult section of the highway to construct was that crossing the Rockies, where many tunnels were cut and costs in some segments reached $1 million per mile.

settlement nodes

This is virtually a cityless region. No urban place in the Rocky Mountains has as many as 60,000 people, and only Missoula, Kelowna, Kamloops, and Prince George have more than 25,000 (see table 14–1 for a listing of the region's largest urban places). Modest population concentrations are mostly associated with major lumbering, pulping, and mining-smelting activities or with agricultural valleys. The greatest concentration of population in the entire region is in the Okanagan Valley, where a dense farming population is clustered around the three small urban centers of Kelowna, Penticton, and Vernon in an area that is also popular with summer vacationers.

During the busy tourist season the population of some resort towns is swelled to many times normal size. Estes Park in Colorado, Jackson in Wyoming, and Banff in Alberta are prime examples of this.

the outlook

Permanent settlements in the region are based mostly on mining, forestry, limited agriculture, and tourism. Farming and ranching are developed almost to capacity and cannot be expected to change to any great extent. Logging activities have also probably reached their limit, except in British Columbia where further expansion can be anticipated.

Mining undoubtedly will experience fluctuating fortune in different areas, but most future mineral activity will be focused on energy resources, rather than on metals as in the past. Coal-, petroleum-, and uranium-oriented boom towns will grow rapidly, especially in Wyoming.

The overall rate of population growth in

the region was three times the national average in the 1970s, and the trend is likely to continue.

The dynamic future of the Rocky Mountains appears to be intimately associated with that seasonal vagabond, the tourist. Natural attractions are almost limitless; recreational developments on government lands have been accelerated by the National Park Service, the Forest Service, and other federal, state, and provincial agencies; and improvements in transportation facilities and accommodations are being made haphazardly but continually. The unprecedented growth currently characterizing tourism is expected to continue, although the national petroleum shortage will probably diminish the growth rate.

How will it be possible to reconcile the pressures of relentlessly expanding tourism with the maintenance of an environment that visitor and resident alike can enjoy? This is the basic and crucial question for the Rocky Mountain Region. Thousands of other questions are corollary to it. Should a new national park be created in the Wind River Range? Should a half dozen new ski areas be established in the Wasatch? Should another dam be built on the Green River? Should the Trans-Canada Highway be

widened through Lake Louise and Yoho? Should commercial exploitation of the oilshale deposits of western Colorado and southern Wyoming be undertaken? The Rocky Mountains are a region of remarkable aesthetic appeal; effective use without destructive abuse requires Solomonic wisdom.

table 14-1   Largest Urban Places of the Rocky Mountain Region

name	population of principal city	population of metropolitan area
Bozeman, Mont.	19,847	
Butte, Mont.	23,476	
Coeur d'Alene, Idaho	17,879	
Cranbrook, B.C.	13,310	
Durango, Colo.	11,771	
Kalispell, Mont.	14,457	
Kamloops, B.C.	57,241	
Kelowna, B.C.	50,111	
Missoula, Mont.	29,569	
Penticton, B.C.	21,017	
Prince George, B.C.	58,292	
Rock Springs, Wyo.	17,773	
Vernon, B.C.	17,162	

selected bibliography

ARNO, STEPHEN F., "Glaciers in the American West," Natural History, 78 (1969), 84–89.

CALDWELL, HARRY H., ed., Idaho Economic Atlas. Moscow: Idaho Bureau of Mines and Geology, 1970.

CANTWELL, ROBERT, "Blueprint of Disaster," Sports Illustrated, 44 (23 February 1975), 34–41.

CARLSON, A. V., "Seasonal Farm Labor in the San Luis Valley," Annals, Association of American Geographers, 63 (1973), 97–108.

CROWLEY, JOHN M., "Ranching in the Mountain Parks of Colorado," Geographical Review, 65 (1975), 445–60.

FOSCUE, EDWIN J., AND LOUIS O. QUAM, Estes Park: Resort in the Rockies. Dallas, Tex.: Southern Methodist University Press, 1949.

GAILIUN, JEFFREY, "Requiem for the Red Desert?" The Living Wilderness, 40 (July–September 1976), 36–46.

HARRINGTON, LYN, "The Columbia Icefield," Canadian Geographical Journal, 80 (June 1970), 202–5.

HARRINGTON, ROBERT F., "Prince George: Western White Spruce Capital of the World," Canadian Geographical Journal, 77 (September 1968), 72–83.

IVES, JACK D., ET AL., "Natural Hazards in Mountain Colorado," Annals, Association of American Geographers, 66 (1976), 129–44.

McKECHNIE, N. D., "The Mineral Industry in British Columbia," *Canadian Geographical Journal,* 78 (March 1969), 76–89.

McPHERSON, J. J., "Landforms and Glacial History of the Upper North Saskatchewan Valley, Alberta, Canada," *Canadian Geographer,* 14 (1970), 10–16.

O'BRIEN, BOB R., "The Future Road System of Yellowstone National Park," *Annals,* Association of American Geographers, 56 (1966), 385–407.

PROVINCE OF BRITISH COLUMBIA LANDS SERVICE, *The Atlin Bulletin Area.* Victoria: Queen's Printer, 1967.

————, *The Fort Fraser–Fort George Bulletin Area.* Victoria: Queen's Printer, 1969.

————, *The Kamloops Bulletin Area.* Victoria: Queen's Printer, 1970.

————, *The Okanagan Bulletin Area.* Victoria: Queen's Printer, 1968.

————, *The Quesnel-Lillooet Bulletin Area.* Victoria: Queen's Printer, 1968.

ROBINSON, J. LEWIS, "The Rocky Mountain Trench in Eastern British Columbia," *Canadian Geographical Journal,* 77 (1968), 132–41.

SHEEHAN, PATRICIA, *Social Change in the Alberta Foothills.* Toronto: McClelland and Stewart Ltd., 1975.

SLAYMAKER, H. O., AND H. J. McPHERSON, eds., *Mountain Geomorphology: Geomorphological Processes in the Canadian Cordillera,* British Columbia Geographical Series 14. Vancouver: Tantalus Research Ltd., 1972.

STENTON, JEAN E., "A Critical Look at Canada's National Parks," *Canadian Geographical Journal,* 79 (December 1969), 180–91.

TRENHAILE, A. S., "Cirque Elevation in the Canadian Cordillera," *Annals,* Association of American Geographers, 65 (1975), 517–29.

————, "Cirque Morphometry in the Canadian Cordillera," *Annals,* Association of American Geographers, 66 (1976), 451–62.

THE INTERMONTANE BASINS AND PLATEAUS

15

The Intermontane Basin and Plateau Region occupies the western interior of the United States. As the term *intermontane* implies, it primarily encompasses the vast expanses of arid and semiarid country between the Rocky Mountain cordillera on the east and the major Pacific ranges (Sierra Nevada and Cascade) on the west (fig. 15-1).

The boundary of the region is relatively clear-cut in most sections, for there are prominent geomorphic units that are usually associated with obvious land-use changes. In only three areas is the regional boundary indistinct:

1 The complexity of hills, valleys, and low mountains near the international border between north-central Washington and south-central British Columbia defies simple separation of the Intermontane, Rocky Mountain, and North Pacific Coast regions. For convenience here, the main demarcation between the Intermontane Region to the south and the Rocky Mountain Region to the north is considered to coincide approximately with the international border.

2 In northwestern Colorado there is an east-west transition from Rocky Mountains to Intermontane Region that is broad and indistinct.

3 In Southern California there is a very clear environmental boundary between the desert portion of the Intermontane Region and the various Transverse and Peninsular mountain ranges of the California Region. But the spillover of urban population from the Los Angeles basin into the Palm Springs area of the Colorado Desert and the Antelope Valley section of the Mojave Desert is so pronounced, and the resultant functional connection of these two areas with the Los Angeles metropolis is so strong, that it seems clear to the authors that these two areas should be considered as part of the Southern California conurbation and thus as part of the California Region. The boundary of the Intermontane Region is therefore drawn east of these two areas.

The vast extent of the Intermontane Region and its topographic diversity have led some regionalists to consider it as several regions rather than one. For this book, however, it is felt that a single regional designation is warranted. The three prominent subregions that are identified in figure 15-1 include the Columbia Plateau in the north; the Colorado Plateau, occupying parts of four states, in the eastern portion of the region; and the Basin-and-Range section, the largest subregion, extending in a crescent from southern Oregon to western Texas.

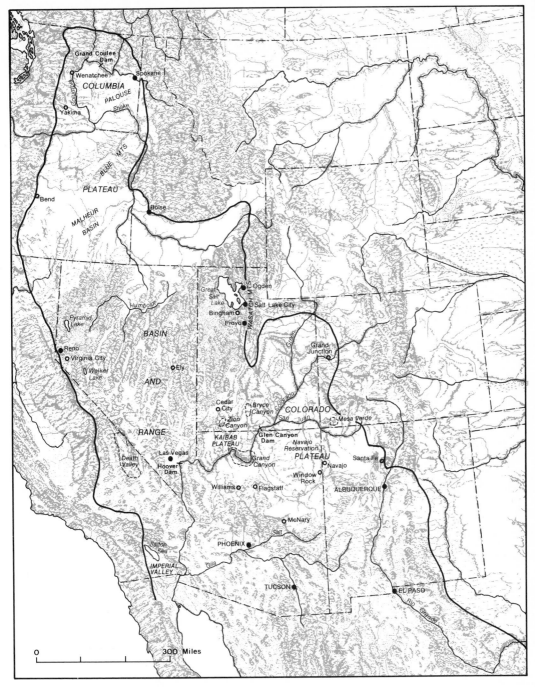

fig. 15-1 The Intermontane Basin and Plateau Region (base map copyright A. K. Lobeck; reprinted by permission of Hammond, Inc.).

assessment of the region

In broad generalization, this can be thought of as a sparsely populated region whose vast extent, relatively isolated inland location, rugged but varied terrain, and paucity of fresh water make it best suited to serve the nation as a limited source of primary resources and as a recreation ground.

Where people have attempted economic endeavor in this region, the bulldozer has been their instrument, the cloud of dust their symbol, and a drastically altered and "tamed" landscape the result. Where humanity is found in any numbers, there are the ordered fields of an irrigated farming development, the giant amphitheater of an open-pit copper mine, the massive wall of a major dam, the extensive runways of a military airfield, or the bright lights of a gambling town.

The region's economy is based partly on primary production, especially from irrigated agriculture, pastoralism, and mining, and partly on such tertiary activities as tourism and government expenditures. Where water is available for irrigation and where the land is sufficiently level, intensive farming prevails as an oasis type of development. Sheep and beef cattle are grazed widely throughout the region, usually on extensive ranches, and the region in general is well endowed with economic mineral resources. Most of the feeding and slaughtering of the livestock, the refining of the ores, and the marketing of both is done outside the region. It is significant that the great majority of land in the region is still in the public domain, and government expenditures for management, development, construction, and exploitation are a major contribution to the local economy.

The scenic beauties and other recreational attractions of this region are distant from major population centers of the nation, but tourists and other recreationists visit the region in ever-increasing numbers, and their spending provides an important part of the region's economic base. The historical movement of population in the region has been from east to west, generally *across* rather than *into*. The region served as a barrier to westward expansion and only incidentally as a goal for settlement.

In recent years this pattern has been modified. The interior West still serves in part as a transit region, but more and more it is the chosen destination of automobile nomads. Tourists, hunters, skiers, and other recreationists visit the region for a few days or weeks of vacation, and increasingly people are settling on a long-term or permanent basis, particularly in the sunny southern section.

If there is an eternal verity for the Intermontane Region, it is scarcity of water. The simple fact that evaporation exceeds precipitation throughout the region is critical to all forms of life. John Wesley Powell, the most notable explorer of the inland West, probably said it best: "All the great values of this territory have ultimately to be measured to you in acre-feet."

topographic variety

There is a great deal of topographic variety in the Intermontane Region. Each of the three subregions has its distinctive geomorphic personality, which can be easily recognized and described.

THE COLUMBIA PLATEAU

The Columbia Plateau lies between the Cascade Mountains on the west and the Rocky Mountains on the east and north, and grades almost imperceptibly into the Basin-and-Range section to the south. Although called a plateau, which popularly suggests a rather uniform surface, the area has quite varied relief features of mountains, plateaus, tilted fault blocks, hills, plains, and ridges. In general, this intermontane area is covered with basalt lava flows that originally were poured out over a nearly horizontal landscape and interbedded with a considerable quantity of silts that were deposited in extensive lakes. After the outpouring of the sheets of lava and the deposition of the lake beds, the surface of much of the region was strongly warped and faulted so that the present surface of the lava varies from a few hundred feet above sea level to nearly 10,000 feet in elevation.

In central Washington, steep-sided, flat-floored, streamless canyons, eroded by glacial meltwater floods following Pleistocene glaciation, cut the plateau into a maze known as the *channeled scablands*. In eastern Washington is the rolling Palouse hill country, deeply mantled with loess.

In northern Oregon is an irregular pattern of faulted and folded mountains, generally referred to as the Blue and Wallowa mountains. Southeastern Oregon and southern Idaho have variable terrain, ranging from the lava-covered flatness of the Snake River Plain in southeastern Idaho to the irregular basins and hills of the Malheur Basin in south-central Oregon to the spectacularly deep canyons of the lower Snake drainage.

THE COLORADO PLATEAU

This enormous area consists of several strongly differentiated parts but has sufficient unity to justify separation from adjacent subregions. It stretches outward from the Colorado River and its tributaries in Colorado, Arizona, New Mexico, and Utah. The greater part consists of a series of flattish summit areas slightly warped or undulating as a result of earlier crustal movements and interrupted by erosion scarps in the eastern portions and fault scarps in the western parts. Physiographically the area is distinguished by the following:

1 All the subregion except the bottoms of canyons and the highest peaks has an elevation of 4,000 to 8,000 feet. Some high plateau surfaces reach 11,000 feet, and there are a few mountain ranges that have still higher peaks.

2 Hundreds of remarkable canyons thread the canyon lands of southeastern Utah, northern Arizona, and the Four Corners country in general. These make this subregion the most dissected and difficult to traverse part of the country.

3 Numerous arroyos, which cut some parts of the subregion into mazes of steep-sided chasms, are dry during most of the year but filled from wall to wall during the rare rains.

4 Mesas, flat-topped islands of resistant rock, rise abruptly from the surrounding land (fig. 15–2).

The basic topographic pattern might be described as mesa-and-scarp, that is, flat summits bordered by near-vertical cliffs. Some of the summit areas, such as the Kaibab Plateau in northern Arizona and Mesa Verde in southwestern Colorado, are remarkably extensive. The scarps, too, sometimes extend to great lengths; the Book Cliffs of Colorado-Utah, for example, are more than 100 miles long.

Throughout the Colorado Plateau subregion the land is brilliantly colored, particularly in the exposed sedimentary surfaces of the scarp cliffs. The Painted Desert of northern Arizona, which is badlands terrain, is especially noted for its rainbow hues, but throughout the mesa-and-scarp country the landscape is marked by colorful rocks and sand.

fig. 15–2 The landscape of the Colorado Plateau subregion is dominated by vertical cliffs and flat-topped plateaus and mesas, as shown here at the western edge of Mesa Verde in southwestern Colorado.

To the northwest, west, southwest, south, and southeast of the Colorado Plateau, from southern Oregon to western Texas, is a vast expanse of desert and semidesert country that has notable physiographic similarity. Throughout this extensive area the terrain is dominated by isolated mountain ranges that descend abruptly into gentle alluvial piedmont slopes and flat-floored basins (fig. 15–3).

The mountain ranges are characteristically rough, broken, rocky, steep-sided, and deep-canyoned. They tend to be narrow in comparison with their length, distinctly separated from one another, and often arranged in parallel patterns. Although their origins are somewhat diverse, most consist of tilted and block-faulted masses of previously folded and peneplained rocks. The canyons and gullies that drain them are waterless most of the time, harboring intermittent streams only after a rain.

Near the base of the mountains there is normally an abrupt flattening out of the slopes. As the streams reach the foot of the mountains, their gradient is sharply decreased so that they can no longer carry the heavy load of silt, sand, pebbles, and boulders that they have brought down from the highlands, and considerable deposition takes place. (Although the streams flow only intermittently, they are subject to violent floods and the amount of erosion they can accomplish is tremendous.) This piedmont deposition generally occurs in fan- or cone-shaped patterns (called alluvial fans) that become increasingly complex and overlapping (piedmont alluvial plains) as the cycle of erosion progresses.

The fans become increasingly flatter at lower elevations and eventually merge with the silt-choked basin floors. The basins themselves frequently are without exterior drainage. Shallow lakes, mostly intermittent, may fill the lowest portion of the basins. They are saline because they have no outlet and because the streams that feed them, like all streams, carry minute amounts of various salts. As the lake waters evaporate, the salts become more concentrated; the complete disappearance of the water leaves an alkali flat or salt pan.

There are several large and relatively permanent salt lakes in the subregion, particularly lakes Walker and Pyramid in Nevada and Great Salt Lake in Utah (fig. 15–4). The latter expands and contracts according to the variation in precipitation in the mountains, its water source, and according to the rate at which irrigation water is drawn off. It is a shrunken remnant of prehistoric Lake Bonneville, a great body of fresh water that was as large as present Lake Huron. Although Lake Bonneville and other Pleistocene lakes in the region disappeared thousands of years ago, old beach lines still remain strikingly clear on the sides of the mountains. The highest shoreline lies about 1,000 feet above Great Salt Lake.

There are only a few permanent streams in the region, and they generally can be classified as "exotic" because the bulk of their water supply comes from adjacent regions. Most conspicuous are the Rio Grande and the Colorado rivers. The latter and its left-bank tributary, the Gila, provide a significant amount of water for irrigation and for domestic use. The Salton Basin in south-

fig. 15–3 The Basin-and-Range subregion consists mostly of alternating mountains and valleys in parallel arrangement. This is the Toiyabe Range in central Nevada (courtesy Nevada Highway Department).

fig. 15-4 The renowned buoyancy of Great Salt Lake is its principal attraction for swimmers. Less attractive are the salt flies that abound, and the salt itches that result. In the background the slopes of the Oquirrh Mountains are partially blotted out by the fumes from the nonferrous metal smelter at Garfield.

eastern California was partially flooded in 1906 when attempted irrigation permitted the Colorado River to get out of control. The river was reestablished in its original channel the following year, but the Salton Sea still exists as a permanent reminder of the incident.

an arid,
xerophytic environment

The greater part of the region is climatically a desert or semidesert, and the vegetation shows a variety of xerophytic (drought-resisting) characteristics.

CLIMATE

Moisture is the most critical element of the climate. On the basis of precipitation-evaporation ratios, there are four moisture realms: (1) the subhumid, (2) the semiarid, (3) the moderately arid, and (4) the extremely arid.

The *subhumid* portion of the region occurs only in limited highland areas, mostly in Washington and Oregon. More precipitation on the upland slopes and less evaporation because of lower summer temperatures result in a climate that shows little evidence of precipitation deficiency. Winters are long and cold; summers are short and cool. Precipitation is concentrated in summer or is evenly distributed.

The *semiarid* climate is typical of most of the Columbia Plateau. Precipitation ranges from 10 to 20 inches per year and falls chiefly in late autumn, winter, and spring.

The *moderately arid* climate, characteristic of most of the Great Basin, has periodic rainfalls that are fairly regular although limited and during which vegetation bursts into life and the water table is replenished. The precipitation at Elko, Nevada, a typical station, is 9 inches. The frostless season varies from 100 to 180 days.

In the *extremely arid* climate the rainfall is episodic, coming largely in summer at irregular intervals and usually as cloudbursts. The Mojave-Gila Desert exemplifies this type. Its annual precipitation is less than 5 inches, too little even for grazing. Almost the entire annual rainfall may come in a single downpour lasting but a few moments. So much water falls so quickly that little can penetrate the soil.

The diurnal range of temperature throughout the region is high. The days are generally hot to very hot in summer, but radiational cooling in the dry atmosphere decreases the temperature rapidly at night except at low elevations in the southern part of the region, which has the highest summer nighttime temperatures to be found in Anglo-America. In winter the nights are usually quite chilly, following daytime temperatures that may be relatively mild or even warm.

NATURAL VEGETATION

In such a large area and in one varying so greatly in landforms, marked differences in

387

the natural vegetation occur. On the whole, however, low-growing shrubs and grasses predominate.

Forests Ponderosa pine and Douglas fir forests are mostly confined to the higher elevations where the rainfall is relatively heavy. Where precipitation is somewhat less, forest is replaced by woodland, a more open growth of lower trees, particularly piñon and juniper.

Grasslands More extensive than might be supposed, grasslands characterize the uplands of southeastern Arizona, New Mexico, and the Columbia Basin. Mesquite grass grows where temperatures are high, evaporation excessive, and annual precipitation low. Short grass characterizes large areas in the high plateaus of New Mexico and Arizona, as does bunchgrass in the Columbia Plateau. The noxious cheat grass is almost everywhere.

Desert Shrub Xerophytic plants dominate in the deserts. *Sagebrush,* the principal element in the vegetation complex of the northern part of the region, grows in pure stands where soils are relatively free from alkaline salts. It is especially abundant on the bench lands that skirt mountains and on the alluvial fans at the mouths of canyons. *Shadscale,* a low, gray spiny plant with a shallow root system, grows on the most alkaline soils but never in dense stands. Much bare ground lies between the plants. It is especially prominent in Utah and Nevada.

Greasewood, bright green in color and occupying the same general region as sagebrush and shadscale, grows from one to five feet in height and is tolerant of alkali. *Creosote bush,* dominating the southern Great Basin as sagebrush does the northern, draws moisture from deep down under the surface. Creosote bush is a large plant, attaining a height of 10 to 15 feet.

Within the last century a number of woody plant species have greatly expanded their range in the arid and semiarid Southwest, mostly at the expense of grassland communities. As in the southern Great Plains, *mesquite* has occupied the greatest area of new territory, particularly in the Rio Grande and Tularosa valleys of New Mexico, and the Colorado, Gila, Santa Cruz, and San Pedro valleys of Arizona.[1] There has also been considerable expansion of the acreage of native *juniper* and introduced *tamarisk,* the latter having extensively colonized islands and sand bars along most southwestern rivers, especially the Colorado and its tributaries.

Various types of *cacti* are widespread in the more arid portions of the region, especially in Arizona. The giant saguaro, symbol of the desert, is most prominent, although many smaller species of cactus are more numerous (fig. 15–5).

---

[1] David R. Harris, "Recent Plant Invasions in the Arid and Semi-Arid Southwest of the United States," *Annals,* Association of American Geographers, 56 (1966), 409.

fig. 15–5 A ground squirrel, perched on a rock, surveys a cactus-studded landscape southwest of Tucson.

FAUNA

In spite of considerable barrenness and scarcity of water, the Intermontane Region has a surprisingly varied fauna. It was never an important habitat for bison, but the plains-dwelling American antelope, or pronghorn, is still found in considerable numbers in every state. In the mountains and rough hills other ungulates are notable, including deer, elk, desert mountain sheep, feral burros (particularly in California and Arizona), feral horses (especially in Nevada, Utah, and Oregon), and javelinas (in Arizona).

Furbearers are common only in forested portions of the northern half of the region. Most predators (coyote, fox, cougar, and bobcat) are systematically poisoned and becoming increasingly scarce. The relatively few rivers and lakes provide important nesting and resting areas for migratory waterfowl.

settlement of the region

The pre-European inhabitants of the Intermontane Region were extraordinarily varied. Most of the Indian tribes in the northern part of the region eked out a precarious existence as seminomadic hunters. Yet in the arid Southwest were developed some of the highest stages of Indian civilization to be found in Anglo-America, mostly in the form of sedentary villages based on self-contained irrigated farming. These settled tribes, the Pueblos, Hopis, Zuñis, and Acomas, were islands of stability in an extensive sea of nomadic hunting and raiding tribes, most notably Apaches and Utes.

THE ARRIVAL OF THE SPANISH

The Spanish, the first European arrivals, were brought to the area by tales of great wealth. They pushed up the Rio Grande and conquered central New Mexico almost four centuries ago and, exploring widely,

ruled most of the Southwest for more than two hundred years. The major early Spanish settlements were in the Socorro–Albuquerque–Santa Fe–Taos area in the Upper Rio Grande Valley, with another important concentration in the El Paso oasis. Many decades later and at a much lower level of intensity they occupied that part of southern Arizona called *Pimería Alta,* mostly in the Santa Cruz Valley as far north as Tucson.

The Spaniards left an indelible influence on the history of the Southwest as well as on American civilization. Their livestock formed the basis of the later American cattle and sheep industry, and their horses gave mobility to the Indians, the importance of which can hardly be overestimated. Small Spanish settlements and trading posts such as Albuquerque housed most of the Caucasian population of the Southwest until the middle of the nineteenth century.

ANGLO-AMERICAN EXPLORERS AND TRAPPERS

British and American explorers began to filter into the region in the early nineteenth century. Lewis and Clark entered the Pacific Northwest in 1804–5. The Astorians were active in 1811–13. Smith penetrated the Great Basin in 1826; and Wyeth, the Pacific Northwest in 1832–33. Bonneville in 1832 and 1836 traded furs and casually explored the area drained by the Bear River. Fremont, in 1845–46, entered the Salt Lake Basin by way of the Bear River, becoming the first white man to examine it systematically. These are but a few of the many who explored the region.

Trapping, a powerful incentive to exploration, was the main object of many of the men who explored the West in the early nineteenth century. The trappers were a special breed—self-reliant, solitary, largely freebooters—who strove to outwit their rivals, to supplant them in the good will of the Indians, and to mislead them in regard to routes. They lasted until fashion suddenly switched from beaver to silk for men's hats. The trappers were then through; nevertheless, they left an indelible stamp on the region's history.

It was the Canadians rather than the Americans who were in control of the Northwest from 1813 until 1846. The intense rivalry between the Hudson's Bay Company and the North West Company ended with amalgamation in 1821. Although many American names are associated with it, no American fur company was dominant in the northern part of the Intermontane Region for any length of time. The "Snake Country" was the great zone of conflict between the Americans and the Hudson's Bay Company.

THE FARMER INVASION

The outstanding example of farmer invasion was the Mormon migration to Salt Lake Basin in 1847. The Mormons had trekked from Ohio, Missouri, and Illinois to escape persecution and to find a sanctuary where they might maintain their religious integrity. To accomplish this, they felt impelled to establish themselves on the border of the real American Desert. The agricultural fame of the Deseret colony was soon known far and wide.[2] Utah is the only state in the Union that was systematically colonized. The leader, Brigham Young, sent scouts into every part of the surrounding area to seek lands suitable for farming. He personally selected the colonists, who were of sufficient number to build forts against Indian attacks and construct dams and canals for irrigation. He located all farm-villages near streams, for the colonists depended on water for their very existence.

Before long all the arable land had been acquired. Scouts were then sent outside Utah to seek new irrigable lands; thus Mormons made the first permanent settlement in Idaho and were the first Anglo-Saxons to arrive in the Grand Canyon country.

[2] *Deseret* is a word from the Book of Mormon, meaning honeybee and symbolizing the hard work necessary for the success of their desert settlements. The Mormons organized the State of Deseret, but it was not accepted by Congress, which later formulated the Territory of Utah.

THE CALIFORNIA GOLD RUSH

Following the explorers, trappers, and farmers came the gold seekers of 1849. So large was the movement that it led to the establishment of trading posts and stations where the migrants rested and refreshed themselves. The Salt Lake Oasis especially became a stop for the weary and exhausted. Farther west the wagon trains rested in Carson, Walker, and Mono basins. Important in the route through Nevada was the Humboldt River:

This is the paradox of the Humboldt, that it was almost the most necessary river of America, and the most hated. Americans came this way to stand on the mountain passes and look far upon the Pacific; Americans came back. Emigrant and immigrant came this way, Mormon and miner and soldier, Pony Express and Overland stage, Overland telegraph and Pacific Railroad, cattleman and sheepman, highway and airline. Indians fought for life in the river bottoms while the West went mad as the Comstock poured out its bonanzas on the heights. . . . The Humboldt was a way, a means; few settled here until they had to, until greener lands were occupied.[3]

Other precious-metal discoveries had a significant influence on early settlement. Outstanding were the silver lodes of western Nevada, dating from 1859.

THE GRAZIERS

Most of this region was favorable for the grazier. For some years after the Spaniards came, cattle raising was almost the only range industry, although Navajo Indians and Mexican colonists herded some sheep. Northward in Utah and Idaho as well as in the Oregon Country cattle raising held sway in nonfarming areas. In fact the Columbia grasslands were major cattle-surplus areas for many years and shared the stocking of the Northern Great Plains ranges with Texas.

In Utah the self-sufficing Mormons raised sheep for homespun, and as early as

[3] Dale L. Morgan, *The Humboldt* (New York: Farrar & Rinehart, Inc., 1948), p. 16.

the 1850s nearly every farmer possessed a few head.

In the 1870s and early 1880s bands of Spanish and French Merino sheep were driven into the Southwest from California, furnishing a fine short-staple wool in sharp contrast to the coarse long wool of Navajo sheep. Transhumance was practiced; in Arizona the cool northern mountains were used from May until August, then the flocks were moved to the lower desert ranges. Late spring found them once more in the mountain pastures.

Most parts of the range in this enormous region were overgrazed. This situation in Utah was typical; after only 35 years of use, the best pasture grounds showed scarcely a trace of the originally abundant grass and browse. By the turn of the century every locality west of the Wasatch Mountains showed the effects of overgrazing.

SPREAD OF SETTLEMENT IN THE SOUTHWEST

The movement of people into the Southwest was erratic and variable, and extended over a long period of time. Least noticed but fundamentally very important was the gradual influx of Hispanos.

The gradual contiguous spread of Hispano colonists during the nineteenth century is a little-known event of major importance. Overshadowed in the public mind and regional history by Indian wars, cattle kingdoms, and mining rushes, this spontaneous unspectacular folk movement impressed an indelible cultural stamp upon the life and landscape of a broad portion of the Southwest. It began in a small way in Spanish times, gathered general momentum during the Mexican period, and continued for another generation, interrupted but never really stemmed until it ran head on into other settler movements seeking the same grass, water, and soil.[4]

In the latter part of the nineteenth century the influx of Anglos from Kansas, Colorado, California, and especially Texas was the major force in the region, quickly dominating both the economy and the political pattern. Mining camps and pastoral enterprises were particularly prominent, but the coming of the two major east-west railroad corridors—a northerly one through Albuquerque and Flagstaff, and a southerly route through El Paso and Tucson—signaled the beginning of a more diversified economy and the growth of urban nodes.

ERRORS MADE IN SETTLING ARID AMERICA

The Spaniards who settled in this region, which was not fundamentally different from their Meseta, knew how to cope with its problems, and as a result, Spanish colonization was relatively successful. The Anglo-Saxons, on the other hand, encountered a distinctly new type of habitat, for they came from lands of ample rainfall. Even the federal government blundered. Its laws had been framed for humid and not for arid and semiarid land; accordingly, the Homestead Act's gift of 160 acres, adequate for the humid East, was inadequate for the arid region. Said Paul Sears, "a family might starve to death in the grazing country on a farm of one square mile, while a quarter or even an eighth of that would mean comparative comfort in the beautiful valley of Virginia."[5] Only after the pioneer, through trial and error, had learned certain lessons did the government change the size of the homestead unit from 160 to 320 acres. But this amount was inadequate for stock farming in the arid West. Investigators estimated that a family could support itself on 640 acres; thus, after considerable agitation on the part of congressmen from the western states, the Stock-Raising Homestead Act was passed in 1916, allowing a family 640 acres.

That close settlement was pushed well beyond safe limits is proved by the hundreds of abandoned homesteaders' shacks. The history behind nearly every one is the same. Land was offered for settlement to people

[4] D. W. Meinig, *Southwest: Three Peoples in Geographical Change, 1600–1970* (New York: Oxford University Press, 1971), p. 30.

[5] Paul B. Sears, *Deserts on the March* (Norman: University of Oklahoma Press, 1935), p. 208.

who had never lived in a dry region and hence knew nothing of its problems. Time after time people settled where they could not possibly make a living. In many instances they tried to grow crops totally unsuited to the climate. These people were not to blame so much as their government, which should have determined the true character of the land before it was settled. It is significant that in 1878 Major John W. Powell, in reporting to Congress, pointed out that for parts of the West there was need for a special land policy that would allot 2,500 acres to each family.

Within a century after the formation of the United States government, the Director of the Census announced that there was no longer a frontier. In 1935 the Homestead Policy, which really had long been obsolete, was brought to an end.

land ownership
in the intermontane region

A striking feature of the geography of the intermontane West is the large amount of land that is in the public domain. In the 11 western states more than half of the land is owned by the federal government.[6] And in the Intermontane Region, the proportion is much higher than that. For example, in Utah, Arizona, and Nevada, the three states that are almost wholly within the region, more than 75 percent of the land is owned by either federal or state government.

The basic reason that so little land is in private ownership is that nonirrigated agriculture is impractical over most of the region. The historical pattern of occupance is also important. The two principal categories of public land are national forests, which include the great majority of all forest land in the region, and Taylor grazing lands, which were withdrawn from homesteading and are reserved for seasonal grazing use. Also notable in the region are Indian and military res-

[6] East of the Mississippi River only Florida and New Hampshire have as much as 10 percent of their land in federal ownership.

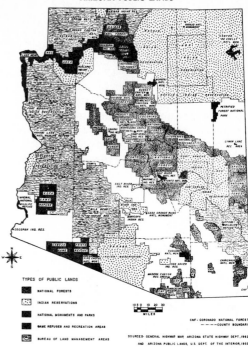

ARIZONA PUBLIC LANDS

fig. 15–6 In Arizona, as throughout the Intermontane Region, there are five principal categories of federal lands, although one category, Indian reservations, is held in trust and is not managed like other public lands (courtesy *Arizona Review*, University of Arizona College of Business and Public Administration [June 1965]).

ervations. An example of the complexity of public land ownership is seen for Arizona in figure 15–6.

the contemporary population:
varied and rapidly increasing

What population there is in the intermontane West congregates mostly in "islands" where (1) precipitation is adequate, (2) water is available for irrigation farming, (3) ore deposits permit commercial mining, or (4) transportation routes converge. In the entire region only seven cities have 100,000 or more inhabitants: Phoenix, El Paso, Tucson, Albuquerque, Salt Lake City, Spokane, and Las Vegas. The principal nonmetropolitan population concentrations are in the lower Salt River Valley in Arizona, the Imperial Valley of southernmost California, along the western Wasatch Piedmont in Utah, at various places along the Snake River in Idaho, and along the middle Columbia Valley in central Washington.

This is a region of considerable population movement—migration into, out of, within, and across. Statistics from the second five years of the 1960s in Arizona emphasize this restless mobility. During that half decade, more than 300,000 people moved into the state, and nearly half that many moved out of the state. And of the Arizonans who lived in the state throughout the five years, only half occupied the same dwelling in 1970 that they did in 1965.

The net rate of population growth, however, has been very rapid in the southern part of the region, and less so in the north. Nearly 1.2 million inhabitants were added to the regional total between 1970 and 1976. Nevada's population gained 25 percent, and Arizona's 28 percent, during the six-year period.

There are three significant and readily identifiable "minority" elements in the contemporary population of the Intermontane Region. All three represent subcultures that are more prominent here than in any other region in the United States. There is a Mormon culture realm centered in Utah, an Hispanic-American borderland along the southern margin of the region, and Indian lands covering vast areas, particularly in Arizona and New Mexico.

MORMON CULTURE REALM

As the earliest white settlers in the central part of the Intermontane Region, Mormons (members of the Church of Jesus Christ of Latter Day Saints) have dominated the human geography of the Deseret area for a century and a quarter. Their cohesive and readily distinguishable culture is manifested in various social patterns, in economic organization and development, and in certain

fig. 15–7 The Mormon culture realm. (Reproduced by permission from the *Annals of the Association of American Geographers,* Volume 55, 1965, p. 214, D. W. Meinig.)

aspects of settlement.[7] Today most Mormons, like most other Anglo-Americans, are urbanites; nevertheless, distinctive cultural characteristics set them apart and set their realm apart as a cultural subregion.

Figure 15–7 displays the Mormon cul-

---

[7] The "classic" Mormon town was a small, nucleated settlement with large lots, extraordinarily wide streets, a network of irrigation canals alongside the streets, relic agricultural features, unpainted barns, and houses of Greek Revival style constructed of bricks. Such settlements were totally unique in western Anglo-America but actually represented a re-creation of the "New England nucleated village and the persistence of nineteenth century structures and . . . patterns in the twentieth century" (Richard H. Jackson, "Religion and Landscape in the Mormon Cultural Region" [unpublished manuscript, 1977]). Small towns in which these characteristics persist today are relatively rare and occur in remoter parts of the Mormon culture realm.

ture realm as recognized in Meinig's definitive study.[8] The *core* is that intensively occupied and organized section of the Wasatch oasis that focuses on Salt Lake City and Ogden; it is the nodal center of Mormonism. The *domain*, which encompasses most of Utah and southeastern Idaho, includes the area where Mormonism is dominant but with less intensity and complexity of development. The *sphere* is defined as an area in which Mormons live as important

[8] D. W. Meinig, "The Mormon Culture Region: Strategies and Patterns in the Geography of the American West, 1847–1964," *Annals,* Association of American Geographers, 55 (June 1965), 191–220.

nucleated groups enclaved within Gentile (non-Mormon) country.

HISPANIC-AMERICAN BORDERLAND

Along the southern margin of the Intermontane Region, from the Imperial Valley in California to the Pecos River in Texas, there are concentrations of varying intensity of Hispanic people. Their presence is numbered in the millions. Their proportional size is so great that they are in the majority in some towns and counties, including El Paso, the third largest urban center of the region.

---

opportunities and problems for the navajos

Of all the large Indian tribes of the subcontinent, it is the Navajos who have led the way in adapting to a capitalistic society while still maintaining their cultural and tribal integrity. To achieve this they have had wise leaders, but they also have the immeasurable advantage of valuable natural resources to exploit. The massive and abrupt effort to establish Navajo lands as a functional part of modern America, without loss of the traditional Navajo culture, has been fraught with problems; the effort continues, and the complexities compound.

The Navajo Reservation of Arizona, New Mexico, and Utah is the largest (15 million acres) on the continent, and the Navajo tribe is also the largest (more than 150,000 people) and fastest growing.[a] The reservation is a sun-

[a] Almost two-thirds of the reservation Navajos live in the Arizona portion, with about one-third in the New Mexico portion and the remainder in Utah. In addition there are some 20,000 "off-reservation" Navajos who occupy lands east and southeast of the main reservation in New Mexico. And, as with most other tribes, there is a continuing drift of Navajos to the cities, particularly to Los Angeles, Flagstaff, and Gallup, but also to San Francisco, Denver, Albuquerque, Dallas, Chicago, and elsewhere.

scorched, windblown, water-sculptured land of high plateaus, flat-topped mesas, deep canyons, and sandy washes. The climate is arid to semiarid, water is scarce, and much of the land is marginal for any productive usage.

When the Navajos first turned to the raising of livestock, the range was in good condition. But with increasing population more animals were needed, and with more livestock came overgrazing. This has diminished the carrying capacity of the range, and erosion has attacked it, gashing it with gullies and seaming it with arroyos. Still, until recently pastoralism was the dominant occupation of the Navajos. Their mixed flocks of sheep and goats range widely over the reservation, usually tended by women or children (fig. 15-a). For the men, however, other means of employment are increasingly available.

Federal grants in 1950 and 1958, primarily for roads and other public works, stimulated the Navajo economy, but it was discoveries of minerals in payable quantities that changed the basis of Navajo life. Uranium, helium, coal, petroleum, and natural gas are now being extracted from various parts of the reservation, and the Navajo Tribal Council has a multimillion-dollar annual budget with which to work.

The legacy of Hispanic settlement in the Southwest is long and notable. Architecture, settlement patterns, language, and cookery are but a few of the more prominent elements of this heritage.[9] The continuing high rate of immigration from Mexico and the rapidity of increase among Hispanic-Americans assure that this portion of the Intermontane Region will maintain its Hispanic subculture indefinitely.

[9] For more details on the concept of an Hispanic-American borderland, see Richard L. Nostrand, "The Hispanic-American Borderland: Delimitation of an American Culture Region," *Annals*, Association of American Geographers, 60 (1970), 638–61.

LAND OF THE INDIAN

More than in any other large portions of Anglo-America outside the Subarctic, the intermontane West is the land of the Indian. Some 200,000 Indians of various tribal affiliations are scattered over the region, although predominantly in Arizona and New Mexico. There are several large Indian reservations in the northern portion of the region: Colville and Yakima in Washington, Warm Springs in Oregon, Pyramid Lake and Walker River in Nevada, and Uintah and Ouray in Utah. It is around and south of the Four Corners country that Indian lands are most prominent, however. The Navajo Reservation (see vignette below)

The tribe founded a large forest products company and a huge sawmill in the new town of Navajo. And industrial facilities have been attracted to or near the reservation, providing more employment opportunities for the rapidly growing population. Tourist facilities have also been expanded, and there has been a revival of tribal crafts, such as weaving and silversmithing, to catch the tourist trade.

One of the great strengths of the Navajos is the all-powerful Tribal Council, an administrative body that provides centralized decision making, from its headquarters at Window Rock, on all important aspects of reservation life. Although there are varied political factions among the Navajos, with acute power struggles from time to time, the supremacy of the council is virtually absolute, and it commands widespread support of its actions.

A major and longstanding problem is the acrimonious relationship between the Navajos and their closest Indian neighbors, the Hopis. Some 6,500 Hopis occupy a reservation that is virtually in the center of, and completely surrounded by, the Navajo Reservation. Most of the Hopis live in agricultural villages that are situated on three high mesas. They are much more farming-oriented than the Navajos, but

(Continued)

fig. 15-a Traditional activities continue in Navajo lands. The typical mixed flock of goats and sheep is tended by young girls and dogs (courtesy Arizona State Department of Economic Planning and Development).

is by far the largest, but there also are extensive reservations for the various Apache tribes, the Papagos, the Hualapais, and the Utes. In addition there are many smaller reservations in the Intermontane Basin and Plateau Region; some of them are densely populated, particularly the Pueblo reservations in north-central and northwestern New Mexico.

In general the Indians of the Intermontane Region are economically poor, socially deprived, and politically inactive. On reservations they have usually maintained cohesive tribal identities, although their livelihood is often near or below the poverty level. Those who have left the reservation—as all Indians are free to do—often find that adjusting to life in a harsh Anglo world is difficult. "Evidence of the heavy human cost of forced culture contacts is still readily apparent in any of the bordering towns: high rates of minor social disorders—drunkenness, brawling, petty thievery; a vagrant population of derelicts adrift between two cultures; discrimination against and exploi-

tation of the Indians in residence, commerce, education, and work."[10]

There are, however, many pleasant exceptions to this generally depressing picture. Many off-reservation Indians have made the adjustment to living in Southwestern cities, as the rapidly growing Indian populations of Los Angeles, Phoenix, and Albuquerque attest; furthermore, economic and social conditions on many reservations have been improving rapidly. The Apaches of the Fort Apache, San Carlos, and Mescalero reservations have developed prosperous logging industries and have shrewdly organized outdoor recreational advantages to attract tourists. The 30,000 Pueblo Indians have mostly been able to adjust to the pressures of modern civilization because their ancestral lands have been legally restored to them, and each Pueblo village is thus surrounded by a protective girdle of farmland that reinforces its insularity.

[10] Meinig, *Southwest: Three Peoples in Geographical Change, 1600–1970*, p. 116.

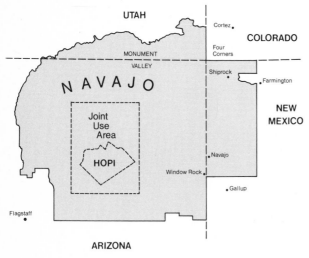

fig. 15-b The Navajo and Hopi reservations of the Four Corners country.

UTAH

Cortez

COLORADO

Four
Corners

MONUMENT

VALLEY

Shiprock

Farmington

N A V A J O

NEW
MEXICO

Joint
Use
Area

HOPI

Navajo

Window Rock

Gallup

Flagstaff

ARIZONA

the Hopis, too, engage in extensive pastoralism with sheep and goats on and around their mesas. There are many facets to the Navajo-Hopi dispute, but it centers around the use of grazing lands. Each tribe claims land that is used by the other, and much stock that has strayed beyond disputed boundaries has been confiscated by both Navajo and Hopi police who patrol the disputed areas. A 1,800,000-acre Joint Use Area has been established as a sort of buffer zone around the 600,000-acre Hopi Reservation, but the problem is far from solved (fig. 15-b).

Much more visible to outsiders are the problems associated with the exploitation of energy resources, particularly coal. During the 1960s the Tribal Council signed several long-term contracts with mineral and utility companies for the mining and transport of coal and the construction of power-generating facilities to utilize the coal. Although the Navajos receive large sums of money for the leases and royalties involved, many think that inadequate value

the water problem

The limitations imposed by paucity of water are felt throughout the Intermontane Region. Limited rainfall makes use of stream water desirable, but rivers are scarce and often located in deep gorges, making their water relatively inaccessible. Well water has been obtained in some areas, but the principal hope for increasing the natural water supply of the region has always been river catchment and diversion.

In this region, as in other parts of the West, the federal government has not hesitated to become "enlisted on the side of The People vs. The Desert" by building dams and blocking the rivers to create tiny islands of moisture availability in the sea of aridity.[11] Flood control and irrigation have been the twin purposes of most river development projects in the region, although some dams

[11] Walter Prescott Webb, "The American West: Perpetual Mirage," *Harper's Magazine*, 214 (May 1957), 28.

are more specifically designed to provide an urban water supply or generate hydro-electricity.

THE DAMMED COLUMBIA

Of all the rivers in North America, the annual flow of the Columbia is exceeded only by the Mississippi and the St. Lawrence. The Columbia, however, has a steeper gradient and therefore has the greatest hydro-electric potential on the continent. The Columbia's average runoff is about ten times that of the Colorado, but only one-third that of the Mississippi. Along its 740-mile course in the United States, the Columbia descends 1,290 feet; it has now been so completely dammed that only 157 feet of this "head" is still free-flowing.

Beginning with Rock Island Dam in 1929–31, 11 dams have been built along the Columbia in Washington and Oregon. Except for Grand Coulee, the dams are primarily for hydroelectricity generation and navigation on the lower Columbia. Grand

is being obtained for the resources given up and the environmental deterioration that results. The coal is strip mined, and thousands of acres of admittedly poor grazing land are lost as a result. The coal is used to generate electricity and to produce coal gas in several large plants that spew enormous amounts of conspicuous pollutants into the heretofore pristine air of the Four Corners country. The electricity and gas produced are transported outside the region, mostly to Southern California, for sale. Probably the most serious problem, however, is the great deal of water that is required for these operations. Ultimately, water is the most critical of all resources in the arid reaches of the Navajo Reservation, and the long-term commitment of this precious commodity, as specified in the contracts, may cause problems in the future.

These controversies notwithstanding, there is now a relative affluence among the Navajos that was previously unthinkable. The general standard of living has risen significantly,

much better schooling is available, the roadway network has been upgraded, and there is a greater variety of economic activity. Poverty is far from being abolished, of course, and the high birth rate practically assures a relatively high rate of unemployment. Opportunities for Navajos are greater than ever before, however. Indeed, the Navajos are becoming a political force of significance for the first time. Just prior to the 1974 gubernatorial elections in Arizona and New Mexico, the Tribal Council reached an agreement with the AFL-CIO whereby the latter would train some 1,400 Navajos in various building trades in return for a concerted effort by the former to turn out a massive block vote for Democratic candidates. Approximately 20,-000 Navajos voted in that election, 90 percent for Democrats. Democratic governors were elected in both states, by a margin of about 4,000 votes in each case. Thus, the Navajos now have both political and financial muscle, and their opportunities may finally be greater than their problems.

Coulee is a dam of superlatives. It houses the largest hydroelectric power plant in the world; impounds the sixth largest reservoir, F. D. Roosevelt Lake, in the United States; is the fifth highest dam in the nation; and is designed to irrigate more than 1 million acres.

Several other dams have been built on tributaries of the Columbia, particularly the lower Snake (for hydroelectricity and navigation) and several short streams issuing from the Cascade Mountains (for irrigation).

THE UPPER SNAKE

About a dozen major dams have been constructed along the upper Snake River and its tributaries, mainly in southern Idaho. Several are federal dams for irrigation, and others were built by private power com-

panies to generate electricity. Water storage and diversion in this area began before the turn of the century, and some of the most extensive irrigation projects in the nation are included.

THE CONTINUING CONTROVERSY OF THE COLORADO

Although there are many rivers in Anglo-America that carry more water, the Colorado is particularly important because it is the only major river in the driest part of the subcontinent. The river flows for 1,400 miles, its drainage basin encompassing about one-twelfth of the area of the conterminous states. Seven states and Mexico clamor for the use of the Colorado's waters.

The first major dam in the Colorado watershed was Roosevelt Dam on the Salt River near Phoenix, which was begun soon after Congress passed the Reclamation Act of 1902 authorizing the Department of the Interior to establish large-scale irrigation projects. Before long it was realized that basin-wide planning was needed for efficient use of the waters of the basin. The Colorado River Compact was finally hammered out, taking effect in 1929; its main provision apportioned the use of Colorado River water between the Upper Basin states (Colorado, Wyoming, Utah, and New Mexico) and the Lower Basin states (Arizona, Nevada, and California) on a fifty-fifty basis.

Later emendations provided a share for Mexico and subdivided the Upper Basin total among the four states involved. The Lower Basin states, however, could not agree on division of their share, and complex litigation finally ended with the Supreme Court subdividing the Lower Basin allotment.

Several major problems persisted, not the least of which was the fact that the Colorado River was bankrupt; the various agreements called for an annual use of 3 million more acre-feet than the river normally carried. Four dams, starting with the mammoth Hoover Dam (fig. 15–8), have been

fig. 15–8 Reservoirs have flooded many of the canyons of the Intermontane Region. This is Lake Mead behind Hoover Dam (courtesy Nevada Highway Department).

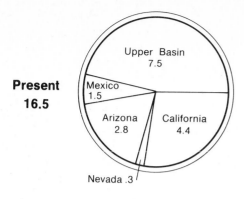

**Present
16.5**

Upper Basin
7.5

Mexico
1.5

Arizona
2.8

California
4.4

Nevada .3

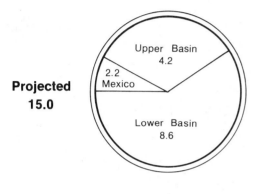

**Projected
15.0**

Upper Basin
4.2

2.2
Mexico

Lower Basin
8.6

(Amounts in millions of acre feet)

fig. 15–9 The present and projected allotment of Colorado River water.

built along the lower course of the Colorado for a variety of purposes but particularly to stabilize the river's flow and provide maximum usage in California and Arizona.

The $2-billion Colorado River Basin Project was authorized in the 1960s for the construction of seven major dams in the Upper Basin and the completion of the Central Arizona Project. Further modifications and agreements resulted in a more realistic reallotment of the river's water (fig. 15–9). Satisfaction is not widespread, however, and more controversy and further litigation are in the offing.

agriculture

Although agriculture is the dominant economic enterprise throughout the greater part of this region, only a fraction (3 percent in Utah, for example) of the total land area is in farms, and little of this is actually in crops. Moreover, this picture will not change greatly in the future because of (1) aridity, (2) alkaline, rocky, or poorly drained soils, (3) rugged terrain, and (4) remoteness from efficient and cheap transportation and from large markets.

DRY FARMING

Dry farming is the growing of crops with water-conserving methods. Usually only a single crop is grown in two years, the crop being alternated with summer fallow. In the Palouse, many farmers fallow only one year in three. Fallowing is one device for conserving moisture by eliminating weeds and retarding evaporation.

The proportion of the region actually being dry-farmed is small indeed. That the area is so small is significant. Dry farming is highly uncertain, except in the Palouse, because the Intermontane Basins and Plateaus frequently have years of drought followed by periods when the precipitation is well above average. With more rainfall, dry-land crop production flourishes and is accordingly pushed farther into the more arid sections; then in the following period of less rainfall, the farmers blame the drop in production of these expanded areas on the lack of rainfall instead of on their poor judgment.

The Columbia intermontane area of eastern Washington and Oregon is one of the most noted dry-farming areas on the continent and is a major world wheat region. Most of the crop is dry-farmed, although along the eastern margin some is grown by customary farm methods. At any one time about half the cultivated land is in fallow, and wheat constitutes essentially the only crop in areas of less than 18 inches annual precipitation. In the more moist parts, peas, lentils, barley, oats, clovers, alfalfa, and grass may be grown in rotation with wheat; thus the area is almost a one-crop region, and the yield per acre and the price per bushel for a given year are vital regional indexes of prosperity.

Both spring and winter wheat are grown in the parts of this area best suited to it. Some spring wheat is grown in the winter wheat area when a dry autumn has prevented the germination of winter wheat or when snowfall is so light and winter temperatures so low as to have killed the planting of the winter variety. As in other parts of the United States, spring wheat is rapidly being displaced by winter wheat.

The Palouse country of eastern Washington and adjacent rolling lands in north-central Oregon are the nation's most productive wheat area. Whitman County, just north of the Snake River in southeastern Washington, is by far the leading wheat-producing county in the United States, primarily because of the very high yields that average 65 to 75 bushels per acre. The bulk of the output is soft white winter wheat, which is used mostly for pastry, crackers, and cookies rather than for bread. More than three-quarters of the output is normally exported, particularly to Japan and India.

A crop that has become extremely important since 1929, when seed was first planted in the foothills of the Blue Mountain area of eastern Oregon and Washington, is peas. In this former checkerboard area of wheat fields and summer fallow, peas now occupy considerable land on slopes of the Blue Mountains between 1,400 and 3,400 feet in elevation.

Unlike the Blue Mountains district, which concentrates on green peas, the Palouse district raises dry peas and lentils. Peas fit in as an alternate crop with wheat instead of leaving the land in fallow. The area has cool temperatures and adequate rainfall, highly favorable physical conditions for the crop. Also, the same equipment is used as for wheat. Production of the crop is mostly concentrated in the eastern edge of the Palouse counties. This area is now the most important dry pea area in the United States, and the Blue Mountains district grows more green peas than any other district in the country.

There are no other major areas of dry-land farming in the region. Scattered patches of dry-land wheat are found in Idaho, Oregon, and Washington. Dry beans are raised without irrigation in central New Mexico, southwestern Colorado, and southeastern Utah, where there is sufficient summer rain.

IRRIGATION FARMING

The importance of irrigation farming to the Indians and Spaniards has been pointed out. The Mormons in Utah were the first Anglo-Saxons to practice it on a large scale on this continent and by this means transformed an inhospitable desert into a productive oasis. Since 1847, when the first pioneers entered Salt Lake Valley, irrigation has been practiced wherever water was available. In the dry lands it is the water of the stream rather than the land itself that has value; hence whoever controls the water controls the land.

Since irrigation is restricted to the smoother and less sloping terraces and to alluvial belts along rivers and since the total amount of water is definitely limited, it is obvious that most of the Intermontane Basins and Plateaus—probably more than 95 percent—can never be irrigated. Even so, there are now more than 14 million acres under irrigation in the region; Idaho, with more than 4 million irrigated acres, is the leader.

Oases The principal irrigated areas are (1) the Imperial Valley, (2) the Salt River Valley, (3) the Rio Grande Project, (4) Colorado's Grand Valley, (5) the Salt Lake Oasis, (6) the Snake River Plain, (7) the Columbia Plateau Fruit Valleys, and (8) the Columbia Basin Project (fig. 15–10).

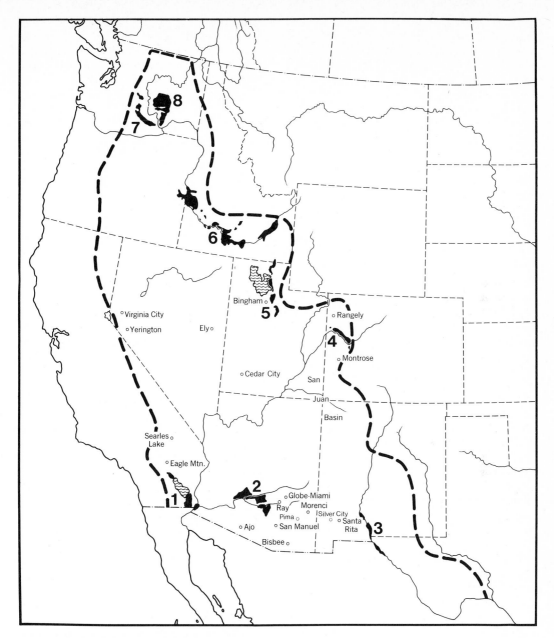

fig. 15–10 Major irrigated areas and mining
towns in the Intermontane Region:
(1) Imperial Valley, (2) Salt River Valley,
(3) Rio Grande Project, (4) Colorado's Grand Valley,
(5) Salt Lake Oasis, (6) Snake River Plain,
(7) Columbia Plateau Fruit Valleys,
and (8) Columbia Basin Project.

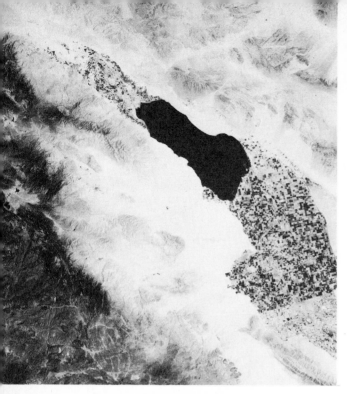

fig. 15–11 Probably the most famous space image of Anglo-America is this scene in Southern California and adjacent Mexico. The checkerboard pattern of intensive, irrigated agriculture south (Imperial Valley) and north (Coachella Valley) of the Salton Sea contrasts strongly with the surrounding barrenness of desert basins and mountains. The international boundary shows as an east-west line at the south end of the Imperial Valley; its abruptness is caused by a different intensity of land use in Mexico, as well as seasonal differences in planting and harvesting practices (Landsat image).

The Imperial Valley This hot, flat, below-sea-level valley at the southern end of the Salton Sea is an extremely productive agricultural area that is watered from the Colorado River via the All-American Canal (fig. 15–11). It produces a remarkable variety of crops, ranging from high-value iceberg lettuce (which dominates the winter market in the United States) to mundane alfalfa (up to seven cuttings a year). It is a major producer of sugar beets and cotton, but its most valuable output is beef from

cattle that are fattened in the area before marketing.

The 470,000 irrigated acres of the Imperial Valley yield about 750,000 acres of crops each year as a result of the widespread adoption of double-cropping. A great deal of labor is required on most farms, and the area is heavily dependent on migratory workers.

Two smaller but equally intensively cultivated irrigation areas are near the Imperial Valley. The *Coachella Valley,* at the northern end of the Salton Sea, grows a variety of crops, but the bulk of farm income is earned from the four-level agricultural pattern of carrots, vineyards (mostly table grapes), grapefruit (California's principal area), and dates (leading source in the nation). The *Yuma Valley,* on both sides of the Colorado River just above its crossing into Mexico, is similar to the Imperial Valley in its crop pattern, except for a recent major emphasis on citrus growing (especially oranges) that is being crowded out of Southern California by urbanization.

The Salt River Valley First of the major irrigation projects undertaken by the Bureau of Reclamation and one of the most economically successful in Anglo-America is that in the Salt River Valley. Twentieth-century engineers built near the inner margin of the desert of south-central Arizona the large Roosevelt Dam, which has converted the upper valley into Roosevelt Lake and has turned the lower valley into a great producer of citrus fruits, truck crops, alfalfa, and cotton. The site chosen was the narrow canyon of the Salt River, just below the junction with Tonto Creek about 75 miles east of Phoenix.

Oranges and grapefruit are grown in large quantities, and safflower is becoming a very popular crop. In addition, the Phoenix area has become one of the outstanding cattle feedlot centers west of the Corn Belt.

Short-staple cotton is the chief cash crop (fig. 15–12). It is grown under irrigation on relatively large properties. Costs are high—Arizona has the highest cost irrigation of any state—but so are yields.

An infestation of pink bollworm has caused sporadic distress in the area, but the outstanding problem is water. Only a portion of the irrigation water comes from storage and diversion. More than half of Arizona's irrigation water is obtained from wells, and increased pumping has caused the water table to drop alarmingly. No other state utilizes such deep wells, on the average, as Arizona, and each year new wells must be drilled deeper. In some localities the water table is several hundred feet below the surface, and pumping is no longer feasible.

The Rio Grande Project The Middle Rio Grande Valley, which is above and below El Paso, constitutes one of the oldest irrigated areas on the continent, having been developed by pre-Columbian Indians (fig. 15–13). Three centuries of Spanish dominance did not materially change the systems or extend the area "under the ditch." When the land became part of the United States, some improvements were made by private capital. Since the federal government did not own any land in the area, it was not interested in development even after the passage of the Reclamation Act in 1902. More and more water was diverted from the Rio Grande, and it became a dry stream immediately below El Paso. As a result, the Juarez Valley, a considerable part of the total irrigated area, was rapidly reverting to desert, and the Mexican government threatened suit unless their lands were provided with water and again made irrigable.

After considerable negotiation, Elephant Butte Dam in southern New Mexico was constructed and a treaty signed guaranteeing the Juarez Valley 60,000 acre-feet of water a year delivered to the head of the International Diversion Canal. The Rio Grande Project then developed rapidly under federal auspices. Today it contains some 175,000 acres. At first it produced fruits and alfalfa almost exclusively, and then shifted to continuous cotton cultivation as the major agricultural enterprise. But farm income from cotton declined by about 70 percent during the 1960s; higher produc-

fig. 15–12 Acres of bales and mountains of seed mark the premises of one of the nation's largest cotton gins at Phoenix.

tion of hay and feed grains for cattle fattening, pecans, eggs, and milk has only partially offset the loss.

An area income growth program called GAIN (Greater Agricultural Income Now) has been formulated by the Agricultural Extension services and Agricultural Experiment stations of the two states to foster the streamlining and diversification of farming in the three-county area.

fig. 15–13 The Rio Grande Valley is an irrigated ribbon throughout most of its traverse of New Mexico. This view looks upstream just north of Albuquerque.

Colorado's Grand Valley In west central Colorado there are several major irrigated areas that utilize water flowing westward from the Rocky Mountains in rivers such as the Colorado and the Gunnison. Most notable is the Grand Valley project near Grand Junction. Many different field crops, such as corn, small grains, alfalfa, sugar beets, potatoes, and vegetables, are grown. The area's reputation, however, is based on its fruit crop, which is primarily peaches but also includes other orchard fruits and grapes. Intensive feeding of cattle and sheep is also common.

Salt Lake Oasis The valley of the Great Salt Lake, one of the most favored spots in the entire West, was settled by the Mormon Church, which claimed a vast territory extending from the Sierra Nevada to the Rockies and from Oregon to Southern California. Brigham Young carefully picked leaders and families and sent them to definite locations; by means of these outpost colonies, based on irrigation farming, he systematically colonized Utah.

The area occupied by the Oasis today virtually coincides with that occupied in 1857, ten years after the arrival of the Mormon pioneers. Some irrigated areas have been added as a result of surface water brought from outside the watershed and, to a lesser extent, from ground water. For the most part, these have not changed the map of irrigated land very much.

The lofty Wasatch Mountains tower above the Oasis on the east; from their snow-clad slopes comes the life-giving water for the valleys below. The greater part of Utah is rugged; hence, the levelness of the area at the foot of the Wasatch and the depth of its fertile soils are additional reasons for the concentration of settlement in the Salt Lake Oasis. This, the heart of Utah, contains about three-fourths of the state's inhabitants.

At the mouth of almost every stream canyon, as it emerges from the Wasatch, is located a city or village girdled by green fields and adorned by orchards and shade trees. Each town is separated from its neighbors by five to ten miles of field, orchard, or pasture. Both north and south of the Oasis, where there is less water, the towns and irrigated farms lie at greater intervals.

Crops are so diversified that farms resemble gardens; yet three-fourths of the cropped land is devoted to sugar beets, wheat, and hay (primarily alfalfa). Most farmers concentrate on those products that give a high return per acre and can be sold locally.

The Snake River Plain Another important series of oases in this region is in the Snake River Plain. As compared with the Salt Lake Oasis, it lacks the productive nearby mines and possesses little focal quality with respect to transportation. It supports more than one-half the population of Idaho. From the Grand Tetons, two forks of the Snake River come into this area, pouring their waters through head gates into canals. The irrigable land totals more than 4 million acres and is increasing each year. The basic Idaho crops are potatoes, hay, and sugar beets. Idaho normally produces twice as many potatoes as Maine, the second-ranking state (fig. 15–14). It is second only to California in sugar beet output. Lesser acreages are devoted to wheat, dry beans, fruits, and vegetables.

The three principal irrigation projects are the Minidoka in southeastern Idaho, and the Boise and Owyhee in southwestern Idaho and adjacent southeastern Oregon. The most dynamic irrigation developments in the West in recent years, however, have been extensive, mostly privately financed operations relying on electric or gas-operated pumps in various locations in the Snake River Plain. The water is pumped from 400 to 600 feet from wells, or a comparable vertical rise from the Snake River.

Development of very large, privately financed irrigated farms on virgin sagebrush land is inducing striking changes in landscape morphology. . . . The new farms

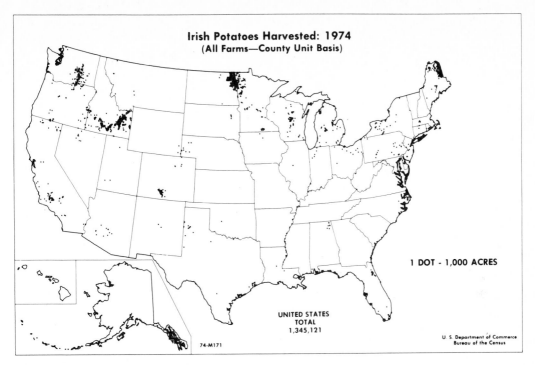

fig. 15-14 The major potato-growing areas of the United States are the Snake River Plain, the valley of the Red River of the North, and the Aroostook Valley.

are distinct in social and spatial organization from existing farms in the area; the latter are smaller, require less capital, frequently occupy federal reclamation projects, and are family-oriented. New developments are located on lands previously considered too high and too dry for economic development; improved irrigation technology, coupled with reduced investor risk-perception, is resulting in conversion of blocks of over ten square miles of sagebrush to potatoes within six months.[12]

More than 10,000 pumps were in operation by the early 1970s, and it is anticipated that the irrigated acreage in southern Idaho and

[12] David Lawrence Smith, "Superfarms vs. Sagebrush: New Irrigation Developments on the Snake River Plain," *Proceedings*, Association of American Geographers, 2 (1970), 127.

southeastern Oregon might be doubled before the expansion ceases.

Columbia Plateau Fruit Valleys In the rain shadow of the Cascade Mountains lies a series of disconnected oases: the Yakima, Hood River, Wenatchee, and Okanagan valleys. This is Anglo-America's famous apple growing area. Most of the irrigated land is in fruit, chiefly apples (fig. 15-15). Washington is by far the leading apple growing state, normally yielding more than one-third of national output. Moreover, production appears to be on a long-term upward trend. Other important crops are alfalfa, asparagus, dry beans, grapes, hops, peppermint, potatoes, sugar beets, and vegetables, as well as soft fruits.

The Yakima Valley ranks high in agri-

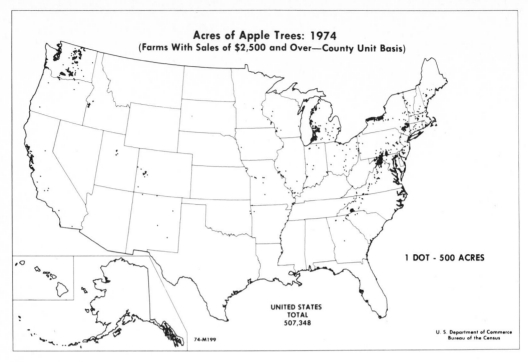

Acres of Apple Trees: 1974
(Farms With Sales of $2,500 and Over—County Unit Basis)

1 DOT - 500 ACRES

UNITED STATES
TOTAL
507,348

74-M199

U. S. Department of Commerce
Bureau of the Census

fig. 15-15 The central part of Washington is by far
the leader in United States apple production.

culture in the state of Washington, in the Intermontane Region, and nationally. A quality product, national advertising, and national and international markets are responsible; yet this prestige has been attained solely by irrigation from the Yakima River and its tributaries, which are in a region receiving only 7.5 inches of precipitation per year, less than one-third of which falls during the growing season.

In the public mind, Yakima and fruit are synonymous despite the great importance of open field crops. Most orchards are planted on slopes to benefit from air drainage. Apples occupy more land than any other fruit crop, although pears are very important. These two crops are grown mostly in the Upper Valley (upstream from Union Gap, a few miles southeast of the city of Yakima), and apricots, cherries, grapes, and peaches in the Lower Valley (downstream from Union Gap). There is less land favored by air drainage in the Lower Valley so that

field crops—row crops (asparagus, corn, hops, peppermint, potatoes, and sugar beets), alfalfa, and small grains—are important. The animal industries, involving cattle and sheep, have also attained prominence in recent years. Many bands of sheep are grazed in the Cascade Mountains in summer and fed during winter in the valley. Much hay, grain, and pasture are available.

The Columbia Basin Project (Grand Coulee Dam) During the Pleistocene Epoch the course of the Columbia River was obstructed by ice, forcing the river to cut a new channel in the state of Washington, some 150 miles from the Canadian border. When the ice receded northward, the dam disappeared and the river resumed its former course, leaving the old channel abandoned. It is now known as the Grand Coulee.

In 1933 the federal government began construction of the Grand Coulee Dam, one

406

of the largest concrete dams in the world, aiming to create a new agricultural frontier and make irrigable some 1,200,000 acres of semiarid land in the Big Bend area of south-central Washington. The Grand Coulee Dam was built on the Columbia River 92 miles west and north of Spokane, and just below the head of the Grand Coulee. Here granite is exposed on both banks. Behind the dam lies Lake Roosevelt, a 151-mile-long storage reservoir, impounding nearly 10 million acre-feet of water.

By the late 1970s about half of the projected acreage had been brought under irrigation, serviced for about seven months each year by water flowing through nearly 4,000 miles of canals (the irrigated fields are between 25 and 125 miles south of Grand Coulee Dam). More than 5,500 farms are in operation, growing some 60 crops, particularly alfalfa, sugar beets, potatoes, beans, other vegetables, and grapes. As more land is being brought under irrigation each year, the agricultural pattern is still developing. The most recent major development is the introduction of center pivot systems to disperse the water. Washington has a greater acreage under center pivot irrigation than any state outside the Great Plains, and the principal concentration of this activity is in the Columbia Basin Project (fig. 15–16).

pastoralism

In this region of rough terrain, light rainfall, sparse vegetation, and poor soils, most of the land (if it is to be used at all) must serve as range for livestock. Probably not more than 4 percent of the land between the Rockies and the Sierra Nevada–Cascades is in crops.

Pronounced differences in elevation cause differences in precipitation and in vegetation, which in turn are reflected in the seasonal utilization of the range. Mountain pastures are strictly summer pastures; deserts are utilized mostly in winter, when snowfall provides water for sheep and occasionally for cattle. Oasis pastures and feedlots are caring for more and more animals in winter.

The establishment of federal grazing

fig. 15–16 Circular irrigation on a grand scale, a multiplicity of center pivot systems near Moses Lake in central Washington (courtesy Valmont Industries, Inc.).

fig. 15–17 Cowboys and cattle on the sagebrush plains of eastern Oregon.

districts by the enactment of the Taylor Grazing Act of 1934 had a significant effect on the pastoral pattern of the region. This legislation put an end to unrestricted grazing on public lands, and it has helped to stabilize the balance between forage resources and numbers of stock. Ranchers may lease portions of a grazing district for seasonal use. It is up to the Bureau of Land Management, the administering agency, to harmonize the carrying capacity of the range with the economic realities of the ranchers (fig. 15–17).

SHEEP

This region has been one of Anglo-America's leading sheep raising areas since late in the nineteenth century. Because sheep do well on rugged land and over a wide range of climatic conditions, their production has been relatively successful in the arid West; furthermore, they relish the shrubby and wheaty types of forage that horses and cattle do not favor.

Ranches handling sheep are nearly always located near streams or perennial water holes. A person with a couple of dogs can manage and keep in good condition about 3,000 sheep. The herder is constantly with the flocks, directing grazing, preventing sheep from straying, and protecting them against wild animals. The herder is aided by a camp tender, who brings supplies and moves camp. The sheep are raised for both wool and mutton, with the former predominating.

CATTLE

Although beef cattle can graze on rough land and sparse vegetation, as a rule they are raised in areas of better forage. In summer they are usually driven into areas of abundant grassland in the mountains. In winter they are either taken to valley ranches and fed hay or are shipped to feedlots for fattening.

Like other parts of the West, in the last few years the Intermontane Region has experienced a rapid increase in cattle feedlots. It has become a big business in the Phoenix area, in the Imperial Valley, in the Yuma Valley, and in several parts of Utah, southern Idaho, and central Washington. Scarcity of feed grains is a problem that is partially solved by utilizing grain sorghums, beet pulp, and cottonseed meal. Feedlot development in the intermontane West has reached nothing like its scale in the Corn Belt, the Great Plains, or California's Central Valley, but it has become a very substantial producer of goods, buyer of goods and services, and employer for the region.

There is a high proportion of large feedlots, especially in Arizona. There is also a high proportion of non-British breeds in the feedlots. In most other parts of the country the British breeds, especially Hereford and Angus or crosses of these breeds, are the usual ones placed on feed. In Arizona, as well as in California and increasingly in the High Plains, there is often a dominance of other breeds, especially Brahmas, Brahma crosses, and "Okie" cattle. Okies are mixed-breed beef cattle that include some dairy but no noticeable Brahma or Charolais blood; their mottled coloring reflects their mixed ancestry.

mining

From the Wasatch to the Sierra Nevada and from Canada to the Mexican border, the region is dotted with communities located solely to tap the mineral resources. These communities enjoy rapid growth as long as the mines produce but decline precipitously and become ghost towns once the ores are worked out or relative price changes make mining unprofitable.

In several of the states, particularly Nevada, prospecting for minerals was the major factor in settlement and early development. Moreover, the total value of minerals mined during the history of the Intermontane Region still is said to be greater than that of any other single product of the region.

MAJOR DISTRICTS IN UTAH

Bingham, lying in a canyon of the same name in a low basin range about 30 miles southwest of Salt Lake City, is one of the world's best-known and most profitable mining ventures. Historically it is important because the first mining claim in the state of Utah was staked out there in 1863. Although several other metals are obtained as byproducts, copper is the principal basis of mining here, and this is the leading single source of copper in the country. Great electric shovels are tearing down an enormous mountain of low-grade ore, about 0.6 percent metallic copper. The mountain is girdled with levels of terraces, tracked, and completely electrified. Laden ore cars are delivered to the mountain base, made into

trains, and transported to concentration mills and then the smelter at Magna. The Bingham operation is around-the-clock, seven days a week. With more than 7,000 workers, it is the largest nongovernmental employer in Utah.

Iron ore has been mined in the *Cedar City* area for more than a century, but only in recent decades has it been a major producer. Six open-pit mines in Iron County yield ore for steel mills in Utah, Colorado, and California.

SOME MINING COMMUNITIES IN NEVADA

In 1859 silver was discovered in Nevada, a state differing from others in the West in that its economic life and very existence have been derived from mining. From 1875 to 1877, Nevada produced more gold and silver than all the rest of the United States combined. Near the western border of the desert lies *Virginia City,* formerly the greatest silver-mining camp of all time and a rip-roaring prodigy of the wildest days of the West. The industry has now declined, and Virginia City owes its continued existence to the tourist business.

The *Ely* district, lying in eastern Nevada in the heart of the parched Great Basin, is the principal copper-mining area of Nevada. Its porphyry ores are very much like those at Bingham, the copper being disseminated in veins so small that crushing fails to separate the metal from the gangue. The mines lie 140 miles south of Cobre on the Southern Pacific Railroad to which they are connected by the Nevada Northern Railway. The unproductive desert in the intervening land exerts a tremendous charge against the mines. This is in marked contrast to the situation at Bingham, which is close to the productive agricultural lands of the Salt Lake Oasis and hence benefits from transportation built and supported largely by farming.

There are several other important copper mines in Nevada, particularly at *Yerington.* But the greatest value of mineral production from the state is gold, which is extracted from a number of lode mines as well as being obtained as a byproduct in copper mining. Nevada normally produces more gold than any other state except South Dakota.

SOME ARIZONA MINING DISTRICTS

The mines of Arizona furnish the bulk of the state's railway tonnage and support a large proportion of the state's population. Arizona is the first state in copper production, yielding about two-thirds of the national total. Since 1858 Arizona's mines have produced in excess of $4 billion in metals, approximately 87 percent of which was copper. Some of this copper is rich ore, although there is also much of the lower grade type. As elsewhere in the region, copper mining requires heavy capital investments. Arizona prospers and suffers according to the price of copper. The exploitation of gigantic supplies in Chile, Peru, Africa, and Canada results in the periodic closing down of high-cost producing mines in Arizona.

There are 14 major open-pit mines in the state, as well as about 30 shaft mines and several leaching operations, all producing copper. *Morenci,* in the eastern part of the state, is the home of Arizona's largest copper mine. A low-grade ore body, it had been

fig. 15–18 The big copper smelter at Douglas, Arizona, with its smoke plume drifting southward into Mexico.

known for a long time but could not be worked profitably before modern technology. Now it is the second largest copper producer in the United States, annually yielding about half as much ore as the famous mine at Bingham, Utah. Open-pit mining is utilized, gigantic electric shovels removing the ore and dumping it into trucks and trains.

Arizona's other outstanding copper producers include the frequently expanding underground mines at *San Manuel,* and open pits at *Ray, Ajo, Pima, Bisbee, Tucson* and in the *Globe-Miami* district. Almost all the copper operations also yield significant quantities of other metals, especially gold, silver, and molybdenum.

Much of the processing of Arizona ore is done within the state (fig. 15–18). Each major mine has a concentrator nearby. The concentrate is smelted at eight localities within Arizona and is further refined electrolytically at Inspiration, El Paso, and several coastal locations between New York and Baltimore.

OTHER MAJOR NONENERGY MINING DISTRICTS

A variety of minerals is mined at many different localities in the Intermontane Region, but only a few others are of major significance.

Most of New Mexico's copper is produced in the *Santa Rita–Silver City* area of Grant County. Recently several new mines have been opened, and output has increased so rapidly that New Mexico is now the third-ranking state (after Arizona and Utah) in copper production.

The second most important iron district in the West is at *Eagle Mountain* in California's Mojave Desert. Most of the ore dug from the open-pit mine goes to the Kaiser steel mill in nearby Fontana; also there are sporadic contracts for ore export.

Several places in the intermontane deserts yield salts of one kind or another, but the principal production locality is at *Searles Lake* in California's San Bernardino County. The lake is a remnant of an inland sea and has a salt deposit 12 square miles in size containing a crystal mass whose surface is firm and compact. Brine is pumped from wells sunk in the lake, and surface deposits are also scraped off. Two chemical plants at opposite ends of the lake accomplish the primary processing. Many products result, but most important are boron, bromine, and potash.

ENERGY MINERALS

Coal This region is fairly well endowed with coal. Among the states included, Utah ranks first in reserves, in production, and in the importance of coal in a state's total economy. There has been production for several decades in Carbon and Emery counties, an area with extensive reserves in which mining is increasing annually.[13] Both coals with high heating value and lower grade coals with more environmentally acceptable low sulfur contents are produced.

Coal output has also been expanding in the Four Corners country, with mines in Arizona, New Mexico, and southern Utah. Most of the production is utilized by thermal electric generating plants or coal gasification plants (fig. 15–19). These facilities are heavy users of precious water resources and create an abundance of obvious air pollution.

Petroleum Although the map of oil lands in this region is expanding and the amount of drilling is increasing, the Intermontane Region contributes less than 2 percent of the national output. Principal production comes from the *Rangely* field in northwestern Colorado, several fields in the *Uinta Basin* of northeastern Utah, and the

fig. 15–19 Electricity transmission lines are conspicuous landscape features in several parts of the Intermontane Region, particularly in the Four Corners country. This scene is near Cameron, Arizona.

San Juan Basin in southeastern Utah and northwestern New Mexico. The last-named area has experienced remarkable development in the last decade, with pipelines to California and Gulf Coast refineries providing excellent market outlets.

Oil Shale Some day oil shale will serve as a great source of petroleum. It is widely scattered over that part of the region in Utah south of the Uinta Mountains, in adjacent west-central Colorado, and in southern Wyoming (partly outside the Intermontane Region). Actually these shales contain not petroleum but kerogen, which can be converted to crude oil by heating. At present it costs more to distill a gallon of gasoline from shale than to refine or polymerize it from crude oil; however, continuing research will doubtless make it possible to utilize the oil shales in the future. Total reserves in this area are incredibly large, estimated to be equivalent to 2 trillion barrels

[13] Price, the largest town in Carbon County, was chosen by the *Wall Street Journal* as the community in the United States with the greatest potential growth in the coming decade, because of its surrounding coal reserves. See Deon C. Greer, "Perceptions of Utah," in *Perceptions of Utah: A Field Guide*, ed. Deon C. Greer (Washington, D.C.: Association of American Geographers, 1977), p. 3.

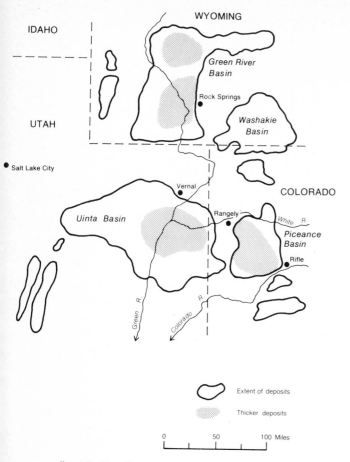

IDAHO

WYOMING

Green River
Basin

● Rock Springs

Washakie
Basin

UTAH

● Salt Lake City

Vernal ●

COLORADO

Uinta Basin

Rangely ● White R

Piceance
Basin

● Rifle

Green R

Colorado R

⬭ Extent of deposits

⬤ Thicker deposits

0   50   100 Miles

fig. 15–20 Principal deposits of oil shale in the West.

of crude oil (fig. 15–20). Nevertheless, potential production problems are awesome. Immense amounts of water would be needed to cool the hot kerogen vapors and to remove the gangue (the spent shale after it has been crushed and roasted), and the volume of useless overburden and gangue to be disposed of would be considerably greater than that produced in any previous mining operation.

Uranium The history of uranium mining in the United States is one of remarkable ebbs and flows. The frantic boom of the early 1950s and the great decline of the late 1950s have been followed in the late 1970s by another major boom. About half of the nation's uranium is found in a 100-mile strip

of northeastern New Mexico, centering on the town of Grants. There is scattered production elsewhere in New Mexico, as well as in western Colorado and eastern Utah.

forestry

Forests are generally absent from this region, except on the higher mountains and in the north, so logging is not a major activity. Only two areas are notable: central Arizona, and the intermontane fringe areas in Oregon, Washington, and Idaho.

The high plateaus and mountains of the Mogollon Rim country and the San Francisco Peaks of Arizona are clothed with forests of ponderosa pine, Douglas fir, and other coniferous species. Much of the area is within the boundaries of national forests or Indian reservations, and logging practices are generally quite good. Exploitation is limited mostly to a few large timber-cutting operations and their associated sawmills, although a pulp mill has been brought into operation. Arizona logging and milling centers are at Flagstaff, Williams, and McNary.

A considerable amount of relatively open forest is found around the margins of the Intermontane Region in the three northern states. The principal species involved is ponderosa pine. Logging here is usually on a small scale, except in a few instances, such as at Bend and Burns, Oregon, which are major pine sawmilling centers.

tourism

The Intermontane Region is one of the most scenic in America; within it are Bryce Canyon, Zion, the Grand Canyon, Cedar Breaks, Utah's Canyonlands, Monument Valley, the Petrified Forest, the Painted Desert, Death Valley, Hell's Canyon on the Snake River, and the Columbia River Gorge. Fortunately the United States government has preserved most of these scenic beauties in its systems of national parks, monuments, and forests.

THE GRAND CANYON OF THE COLORADO

The Grand Canyon, a colossal chasm 250 miles long, 10 to 12 miles wide, and more than 1 mile deep, is too gigantic for the human mind to encompass. It is the world's choicest exhibit of erosion—the result of cutting and grinding of fast-flowing mud- and rock-laden water, abetted by frost, wind, and rain. It presents the world's most ·exposed geological timetable; the mile of rock from bottom to rim represents a period estimated at 700 million years. The whole panorama is a riot of colors from the mineral stains and mineral salts originally in the sediments. To be appreciated, the canyon should be seen in the sunlight, in the moonlight, during a rain, and in cloudy weather. No color film, no brush, no pencil—no matter how inspired—can reproduce what one sees, and word pictures are completely inadequate.

BRYCE CANYON NATIONAL PARK

Bryce Canyon in south-central Utah is a significant amphitheater. No other national park appears so fantastic; its bizarre forms are slender, dainty, bulky, or grotesque, and they are of many colors, but essentially pink, red, white, orange, and purple. The tall and erratically carved stone spires also tell a story of erosion.

ZION NATIONAL PARK

Lying a short distance from Bryce is Zion National Park, consisting of a narrow meandering canyon with vertical walls 1,000, 2,000, and 2,500 feet high with a maze of side canyons. The towering walls are banded with white and many shades of red and are considered by some to be one of the most inspiring sights in the world. The canyon is entered through a long tunnel. The Virgin River occupies the bottom of the valley.

OTHER TOURIST ATTRACTIONS

This region of colorful and spectacular scenery has an almost unlimited number of natural attractions. Many of them, however, are difficult to reach, and most tourists invest only a limited amount of time in sightseeing off the beaten track. Consequently, various constructed attractions, which almost invariably are reached by excellent roads, draw considerable attention from visitors to the region.

Many ancient *cliff dwellings* and cliff-dwelling ruins are to be found in the Southwest. The most elaborate and best interpreted of these are in Mesa Verde National Park in southwestern Colorado (fig. 15–21). Many others are preserved (and sometimes restored) in national monuments in Arizona and New Mexico. The present-day *Indians,* with their traditional culture and handi-

fig. 15–21 The most extensive and most famous cliff dwellings in the nation are in Mesa Verde National Park in southwestern Colorado. This is Cliff Palace (courtesy Colorado Department of Public Relations).

crafts, also draw visitors from other regions. The Navajo Reservation and several of the Pueblo villages attract the largest crowds.

There are many *historic towns* in the region, remnants of that romanticized and immortalized period in American history, "the Old West." Some of these, such as Bisbee, Tombstone, and Jerome in Arizona or Virginia City in Nevada, have capitalized on their heritage and built up a steady trade in historically minded tourists.

The remarkable history of *Mormonism* in Utah and the continued importance of Salt Lake City as headquarters of the Mormon Church are compelling tourist attractions. Various edifices and monuments in and around Salt Lake City are visited by hundreds of thousands of visitors annually.

Although Nevada has a colorful past, its present is in many ways even more flamboyant. As the only state that has systematically utilized *gambling* as a major source of revenue, the development of games of chance in Nevada has reached amazing proportions. Every town in the state has its cluster of "one-armed bandits," but Las Vegas (fig. 15–22) and Reno are by far the chief centers. As added attractions, these cities also specialize in glamorous entertainment, quick marriages, and simple (although not speedy) divorces.

Originally Reno was the leader in the gambling-entertainment business of Nevada, but it has long since been surpassed by the extraordinary development of Las Vegas, which is strongly abetted by its ready accessibility to the large population of the Los Angeles conurbation. The attraction of Las Vegas has been summarized as follows:

Sprawling across the barren valley from which it sprang, Las Vegas shimmers in the heat, a surreal shrine to the gods of opulence and good fortune who dwell in its Greco-Roman-French provincial-ponderosa-riverboat-neo-neon palaces, where they exact tribute from the reverent who travel hence on missions of

fig. 15–22   Las Vegas at night. The flamboyance of gambling casinos and the relatively inexpensive power of nearby Hoover Dam combine to give Fremont Street the brightest lights in the Intermontane Region. In a three-block frontage there are some 43 miles of neon and more than 2 million light bulbs.

homage and seduction. Condemned by some for its outrageous success of excess, ignored by others who seek their pleasure in smaller measure, Las Vegas is the most persuasive monument ever erected to man's inconsolable yearning for a wild weekend.[14]

Major highways enter "Vegas" from four directions, but many visitors come by air (some 4.5 million a year). About 35 million tourists visit Nevada each year, which is 25 times the number who travel to Hawaii. The greatest majority focus on Las Vegas as the center of attraction.

Engineering feats always seem to hold great interest for tourists, and the three great *dams* of the region are prime attractions. Grand Coulee Dam is particularly noted for its power plant, and Hoover Dam for its boating facilities on Lake Mead. Glen Canyon Dam and its extensive Lake Powell are rapidly becoming the boating center of the Southwest, despite their great distance from population centers.

specialized southwestern living

The rapid population growth of the southern part of the Intermontane Region in recent years, matched only by Florida and Southern California, is an obvious tribute to sunshine and health. Many modern Americans feel that sunny mild winters and informal outdoor living provide sufficient satisfaction to counteract the problems of moving to a distant locality, even if that locality is characterized by scorching summers. Sufferers from respiratory afflictions also derive some real and some imagined health benefits from the dry air of the Southwest.

In Arizona, southern Nevada, southern New Mexico, and southeastern California particularly, the ordinary summer tourist is

[14] "Vegas and Tahoe: Nonstop Superesorts," *Playboy,* 17 (March 1970), 105.

a relatively minor element in comparison with the frequent winter visitor, the new resident eagerly anticipating opportunity in a growing community, and the retired couple content to spend their last years in sunny relaxation. It is on these three groups that the social and, to a considerable extent, the economic structure of the Southwest is turning. The significance of these groups is demonstrated nowhere quite as pointedly as in the growth of suburban Phoenix. Scottsdale, on the northeast, is a semiexclusive residential and resort suburb whose luxury hotels and elaborately picturesque shops and restaurants are geared specifically to the winter visitor. Deer Valley, on the north, is a sprawling desert community scattered with large factories and ambitious subdivisions for the migrant from the eastern states. Sun City, on the northwest, is a specifically planned retirement community without facilities for children but with abundant amenities for senior citizens. Litchfield Park, on the west, is a grand design for a totally planned community in which last year's cotton fields will give way to next decade's city of 100,000 people.

Another facet of Southwestern living is the rise of the mobile home park. Throughout Anglo-America the mobile home is a sign of the times, but in the southern Intermontane Region it is a way of life. Mobile home parks are widespread, both as semipermanent installations in urban areas and as temporary expedients in "boom" districts that tend to be rurally located. Trailer homes are not self-sufficient; they must cluster where they can get water, electricity, and sewers. Mobile home communities are now a transient but basic element of the cultural landscape and consist of several dozen, or even several hundred, trailers parked side by side on small lots that focus on the cement block building housing the toilets, laundromat (the central social institution), and manager's office. The amount of landscaping depends on the permanency of the residents, but tricycles and portable gas tanks abound.

table 15–1 Largest Urban Places of the Intermontane Basin and Plateau Region

name	population of principal city	population of metropolitan area
Albuquerque, N. Mex.	279,401	387,700
Boise City, Idaho	99,771	137,200
Bountiful, Utah*	30,358	
El Paso, Tex.	385,691	414,700
Glendale, Ariz.*	65,671	
Idaho Falls, Idaho	37,042	
Las Cruces, N. Mex.	40,336	
Las Vegas, Nev.	146,030	332,500
Mesa, Ariz.*	99,043	
North Las Vegas, Nev.*	37,476	
Ogden, Utah	68,978	
Orem, Utah*	35,584	
Phoenix, Ariz.	664,721	1,217,500
Pocatello, Idaho	40,980	
Provo, Utah	55,593	169,300
Reno, Nev.	78,097	145,200
Richland, Wash.	29,543	102,300
Salt Lake City, Utah	169,917	783,800
Scottsdale, Ariz.*	77,529	
Sparks, Nev.*	31,639	
Spokane, Wash.	173,698	304,000
Tempe, Ariz.*	84,072	
Tucson, Ariz.	296,457	441,200
Yakima, Wash.	49,264	153,700

* A suburb of a larger city.

suburbia in the sun: the southwest's rush to urbanism

The extremely rapid population expansion of the southern part of the Intermontane Region is primarily manifested in the burgeoning of cities and extensive urban sprawl (see table 15–1 for a listing of the region's largest urban places). The spectacular growth of Southwestern cities in the last three decades is readily apparent:

city	1940 population	1976 population	percentage increase
Albuquerque	35,449	279,401	688%
El Paso	96,810	385,691	298%
Las Vegas	8,422	146,030	1634%
Phoenix	65,414	664,721	916%
Tucson	36,818	173,698	705%[15]

If the magnitude of recent Southwestern urban growth has been remarkable, it is the character and form of this growth that has been even more eye-catching. The "urban culture," as Meinig called it, includes many people who are well beyond the continuously settled urban zones. Seemingly rural countryside is often dominated by "essentially urban people scattered about in satellite towns, housing tracts, resorts, and homesteads, all in close functional and cultural connection with metropolitan areas by high speed highways and individual or commuter air services."[16]

The cities themselves have also developed in different fashion, with unusual patterns of settlement, population, and business activity (fig. 15–23). An astute observer of the scene has summarized the development as follows:

Their physical structure is looser than in older cities; their average density is low, they consist mostly of detached single-family houses or garden apartments, they expand rapidly at their edges, and they often enclose a crazy-quilt pattern of unbuilt-upon land. Not even the slum areas, backward as they might be, approach traditional urban densities. Mass transportation is inadequate or nonexistent. . . .

These cities have not only grown to maturity in the time of the automobile, they live by the automobile—and

[15] In contrast, the major cities of the northern part of the region have grown at a leisurely pace, more representative of the national average:

city	1940 population	1976 population	increase
Salt Lake City	149,934	169,917	13%
Spokane	122,001	173,698	42%

[16] D. W. Meinig, "American Wests: Preface to a Geographical Interpretation," *Annals,* Association of American Geographers, 62 (1972), 175.

fig. 15–23 The central business districts of most of the larger intermontane cities were revitalized and metamorphosed by ambitious and imaginative building projects during the 1970s. This is Phoenix (courtesy Arizona Office of Tourism).

it is for the most part a pleasant and convenient way of life. Traffic jams are rare; parking, if not always well designed, is at least plentiful and inexpensive. Because of the automobile, the strip has often long ago replaced downtown as a center of business. Not just a competitor of the central core, it has become the vital economic area—if not in terms of quantity of money handled, then certainly in terms of daily shopping activity.[17]

Many of the "new" cities have been condemned by urban planners; they are different and do not resemble the "old" and great cities of the world. They lack the important attributes of high population and building density and a centric orientation.

But downtown in these new cities is not the same downtown that we remember from other places and times. To revitalize or preserve a downtown that contains excellent stores and restaurants, museums and schools as well as banks and offices, a downtown that is served by an adequate or expandable rapid-transit system, and that has an emotional meaning to the people of a city is one thing. Creating a downtown in an area having no good stores and few good restaurants, no cultural or education facilities, an area in which even the movie theaters are second-rate with the cinerama-size screens located in the suburbs, where the only unique

facilities are more old and cheap office space, bank headquarters, and the bus and railroad stations, a downtown located in a city of a density too low to support mass transit, in a city whose inhabitants' nostalgic memories are of a downtown in a far-off place that they have left—this is a very different matter.

. . . This new form of urban structure . . . is a result of increasing affluence and mobility, vastly improved communication, greater flexibility of transportation, and the increased importance of amenity in residential, commercial and site location. . . .

What is happening [in Southwestern cities] . . . is precisely what is happening in the megalopolises of the eastern and western seaboard and the urban regions of the midwest—with one important difference. In the latter areas the new developments take place over, around or between strong and still vital industrial urban forms, forms which both dampen and distort the growth of radically new patterns. In the Southwest, where no such strong earlier forms exist, the new forms, as yet neither fully developed or understood, can at least be seen more clearly and studied for what they are or want to become.[18]

The new pattern is emerging, and the cities of the Intermontane Region are inevitably caught up in it. Where and how it will end is unclear, but that it will continue indefinitely is a certainty.

[17] Robert B. Riley, "Urban Myths and the New Cities of the Southwest," *Landscape*, 17 (Autumn 1967), 21.

[18] Ibid., p. 23.

the outlook

People have accomplished much in this restrictive environment. No one can stand on the steps of the State Capitol Building at Salt Lake City and gaze at the green island that is the Oasis without being impressed. Nevertheless, there is a limit to what human beings can accomplish against a stubborn and relentless nature. Since water, which means life, is scarce and much of the terrain is rugged, the greater part of the region is destined to remain one of the emptiest and least used on the continent.

Agriculture should become more important, but the development of further large reclamation projects is unlikely, simply because most feasible dam sites in the region have already been developed (except at very controversial locations in the Grand Canyon). Irrigated crop acreages will undoubtedly expand most in central Washington and southern Idaho, but modest expansions will be widespread, particularly in Oregon and Arizona, and often associated with center pivot technology.

Livestock raising will probably increase. More feeding will be carried on, both at local ranches and at centralized feedlots. Hay and sorghum feeding will continue to dominate, but grains, often brought into the region, will increase in importance. More attention will be paid to breeding, too, with improved Hereford and Angus strains in the north, and more emphasis on Santa Gertrudis and Charolais in the south.

Mining is an industry of fluctuating prosperity in the region and will continue to be so. Copper, the most important commercial intermontane mineral, has an unstable market and suffers from antagonistic labor relations. Uranium, the most dynamic intermontane mineral, is in undersupply, and intensive exploration is in progress. The best growth prospect is in coal, but monumental environmental problems are inhibitory factors.

Manufacturing will continue to grow rapidly in a few urban places. Although such localities are limited, they are the population centers and continued industrial growth will be impressive in the overall economy. It is a measure of the stability of the current population growth that industrial expansion is keeping pace.

Tourism in this region, as in most, is bound to expand. Summer is tourist time in the northern three-fourths of the Intermontane Basins and Plateaus; winter visitors are more important in the southern portion. An abundance of natural allurements, a variety of constructed attractions, and improving transportation routes combine to assure a steady flow of tourists.

Population growth in the northern half of the region picked up speed in the 1970s. While it does not match the phenomenal growth rates of some portions of the southern intermontane area, it will probably continue at a substantial rate. The southern, or sunbelt, portion of the region will continue to grow apace. Mild winters, few clouds, dry air, informal living patterns, and the mysterious attraction of the desert will continue to exert their magnetic effects on dissatisfied, snow-shovel-weary citizens of the northern states.

This migration-fostered population growth will probably become overextended at times, outstripping a sound economic base. Generally, however, it is likely to grow with soundness, for capital will accompany people in the migration. Water may be a long-run limiting factor, but in the short run it is no barrier; urban growth is often at the expense of irrigated agriculture, and the former uses less water than the latter.

The southern Intermontane Region, then, is in functional transition from desert to metropolis. Today one can find smog in Phoenix that would make a Los Angeleno proud, traffic jams in Albuquerque that would do credit to Chicago, and tension-induced psychiatric treatments in Salt Lake City that would be suitable for New York. Indeed, the "new" cities of the interior West are already embarking on imaginative urban renewal projects to revitalize their downtowns. The developments are most striking to Tucson and Albuquerque, but almost every city of note from Spokane to El Paso has made at least a start on a mall-

fig. 15–24 A splashy modern park is the centerpiece around which downtown Albuquerque has been rebuilt.

park-fountain complex in association with sparkling modern high-rise buildings in the heart of the central business district (fig. 15–24).

Progress will manifest itself in this region in a nodal fashion. The rural areas will never fill up, but the urban centers will continue to grow.

selected bibliography

BARR, JAMES L., AND DAVID E. PINGRY, "The Central Arizona Project: An Inquiry into Its Potential Impacts," *Arizona Review*, 26 (April 1977), 1–49.

BEHEIRY, SALAH A., "Sand Forms in the Coachella Valley, Southern California," *Annals*, Association of American Geographers, 57 (1967), 25–48.

CAMPBELL, CHARLES E., "Some Environmental Effects of Rural Subdividing in an Arid Area: A Case Study in Arizona," *Journal of Geography*, 71 (1972), 147–54.

CARLSON, A. W., "Long-Lots in the Rio Arriba," *Annals*, Association of American Geographers, 65 (1975), 48–57.

CHAPPELL, JOHN E., JR., "Passing the Colorado Salt," *Geographical Magazine*, 46 (1974), 568–76.

COOKE, RONALD U., AND RICHARD W. REEVES, *Arroyos and Environmental Change in the American South-West*. London: Oxford University Press, 1976.

DUNBIER, ROGER, *The Sonoran Desert: Its Geography, Economy, and People*. Tucson: University of Arizona Press, 1968.

DURRENBERGER, ROBERT W., "The Colorado Plateau," *Annals*, Association of American Geographers, 62 (1972), 211–36.

FRANCAVIGLIA, RICHARD V., "The Mormon Landscape: Definition of an Image in the American West," *Proceedings*, Association of American Geographers, 2 (1970), 59–61.

GIBSON, LAY J., AND RICHARD W. REEVES, "Functional Bases of Small Towns: A Study of Arizona Settlement," *Arizona Review*, 19 (1972), 19–26.

GILBREATH, KENT, *Red Capitalism: An Analysis of the Navajo Economy*. Norman: University of Oklahoma Press, 1973.

GREEN, CHRISTINE, AND WILLIAM SELLERS, *Arizona Climate*. Tucson: University of Arizona Press, 1964.

HUNDLEY, NORRIS, JR., *Dividing the Waters*. Berkeley: University of California Press, 1966.

———, *Water and the West: The Colorado River Compact and the Politics of Water in the American West*. Berkeley: University of California Press, 1975.

JAEGER, EDMUND C., *The California Deserts*. Stanford, Calif.: Stanford University Press, 1965.

McINTIRE, ELLIOT G., "Changing Patterns of Hopi Indian Settlement," *Annals*, Association of American Geographers, 61 (1971), 510–21.

McKNIGHT, TOM L., "The Feral Horse in Anglo-America," *Geographical Review*, 49 (1959), 506–25.

———, "Manufacturing in Arizona," *University of California Publications in Geography*, 8 (1962), 289–344.

MEINIG, D. W., *The Great Columbia Plain—An Historical Geography, 1805–1910.* Seattle: University of Washington Press, 1968.

————, "The Mormon Culture Region: Strategies and Patterns in the Geography of the American West, 1847–1964," *Annals,* Association of American Geographers, 55 (1965), 191–220.

————, *Southwest: Three Peoples in Geographical Change, 1600–1970.* New York: Oxford University Press, 1971.

MORRIS, JOHN W., *The Southwestern United States.* New York: Van Nostrand Reinhold Company, 1970.

NOSTRAND, RICHARD L., "The Hispanic-American Borderland: Delimitation of an American Culture Region," *Annals,* Association of American Geographers, 60 (1970), 638–61.

PEASE, ROBERT W., "Modoc County, A Geographic Time Continuum on the California Volcanic Tableland," *University of California Publications in Geography,* 17 (1965), 1–304.

PEW, THOMAS W., "Last Squeeze on the Colorado," *Defenders,* 50 (1975), 302–5.

REEVES, RICHARD W., AND LAY JAMES GIBSON, "Town Size and Functional Complexity in a Disrupted Landscape," *Yearbook,* Association of Pacific Coast Geographers, 36 (1974), 71–84.

RILEY, ROBERT B., "Urban Myths and New Cities of the Southwest," *Landscape,* 17 (1967), 21–23.

RUHE, ROBERT V., "Landscape Morphology and Alluvial Deposits in Southern New Mexico," *Annals,* Association of American Geographers, 54 (1964), 147–59.

SELLERS, WILLIAM D., AND RICHARD H. HILL, *Arizona Climate, 1931–1972.* Tucson: University of Arizona Press, 1974.

SMITH, COURTLAND L., *The Salt River Project: A Case Study in Cultural Adaptation to an Urbanizing Community.* Tucson: University of Arizona Press, 1972.

SMITH, DAVID LAWRENCE, "Superfarms vs. Sagebrush: New Irrigation Developments on the Snake River Plain," *Proceedings,* Association of American Geographers, 2 (1970), 127–31.

THOMAS, JOHN L., ed., *Reclamation and Use of Disturbed Land in the Southwest.* Tucson: University of Arizona Press, 1977.

VALE, THOMAS R., "Forest Changes in the Warner Mountains, California," *Annals,* Association of American Geographers, 67 (1977), 28–47.

WHEELER, SESSONS S., *The Nevada Desert.* Caldwell, Idaho: Caxton Printers, 1971.

THE CALIFORNIA REGION

16

fig. 16-1 The California Region (base map copyright A. K. Lobeck; reprinted by permission of Hammond, Inc.).

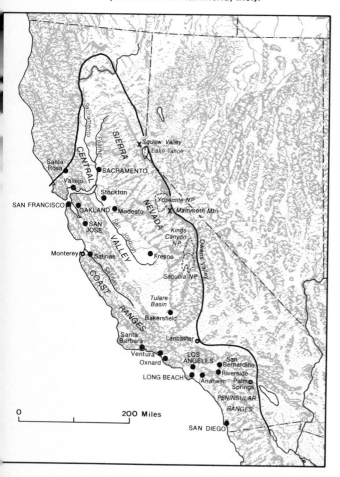

Although one of the smallest major regions in Anglo-America, the California Region is also the most diverse. This diversity is shown in almost every aspect of the region's physical and human geography, from landforms to land use and from soil patterns to social patterns.

The region's location in the southwestern corner of the conterminous states has been a major long-range determinant of its pattern and degree of development (fig. 16-1). The location is remote from the area of primary European penetration and settlement of Anglo-America and from the heartland of the nation that emerged after colonial times. Adjacency to Mexico has been significant from early days, even though the region is relatively distant from the heartland of that country too. The region is well positioned for contact across the Pacific, but the Pacific has always been the wrong ocean for significant commercial intercourse. California has thus been denied ready access to the core regions of the United States and Mexico, and even to the Pacific Northwest, by pronounced environmental barriers (mountains and deserts). This has had an important effect on the population and economic development of the region; it is remarkable that it has not had an even greater effect.

The California Region encompasses most of the settled parts of the state, excluding only the northern mountains (north Coast Ranges, Klamath Mountains, Southern Cascades), the northeastern plateaus and ranges, and the southeastern deserts except the Antelope Valley and Palm Springs areas, which are functionally integrated with the Southern California conurbation and are therefore considered to be part of this region. The region, then, is essentially a California region and includes the intrinsic California.[1] More than 97 percent of the inhabitants of the most populous state, numbering about 21.5 million persons in the late 1970s, reside within this region.

The great variety in Californian geography encourages the delineation of subregions. There are many Californias, and despite significant overall aspects of regional unity, variations in patterns of physical landscape, population distribution, and land use characterize the four major subregions:

1 Southern California, from Santa Barbara down the coast to San Diego, and interiorward to San Bernardino and Riverside, with the two desert "spillover" sections of the Antelope Valley to the north and the Palm Springs area to the east

2 the Central Valley, which encompasses both the Sacramento and San Joaquin valleys, and the large area of interior drainage of the Tulare Basin

3 the Sierra Nevada

4 the Central Coast ranges and valleys, including the San Francisco Bay Area

the california image: benign climate and landscape diversity

The image of the region is synonymous with the image of the California life style. This is the never-never land of contemporary

American mythology: it is focused on Hollywood, Disneyland, and the Golden Gate; flavored with equal parts of glamour and smog; and populated by a mixture of sunbronzed beach lovers and eccentric night people.

That the actuality is less exciting than the image is of small consequence. The facts that most Californians live in the same sorts of suburban tract homes as other Anglo-Americans, watch the same television shows, vote for the same political candidates, and complain about the same taxes are convenient to overlook. For the California life style has been sugarcoated, packaged, and marketed to the world as a thing apart, a destiny with a difference.

There is, to be sure, some substance to the image. This arises in part from the relatively late development of the region's urban economy; in part from the boom-and-bust psychology and flamboyant nature of some of the staple industries, for example, gold mining, oil drilling, real estate promotion, motion picture industry, aircraft and spacecraft production; in part from the unusual natural endowments of this southwestern corner of the country; and in part from its residents, people who are drawn from every corner of the globe and who come seeking an elusive opportunity that they failed to find in their homeland and that they expect to find in California.

Of utmost importance, both physically and psychologically, is the regional climate. This is the only portion of the continent with a dry summer subtropical climate, generally called "mediterranean." Its basic characteristics are simple and appealing: abundant sunshine, mild winter temperatures, absolutely dry summers, and relatively dry winters. No other type of climate is so conducive to outdoor living.

And the diverse characteristics of the California outdoors multiply the opportunities and expand the appeal of the region. High mountains are adjacent to sandy beaches and dramatic sea cliffs; dense forests rise above precipitous canyons that open into fertile valleys. Nearby to the east is the compelling vastness of the desert, and to the

---

[1] Richard Logan, a leading California geographer, emphasizes the "atypical" characteristics of the northeastern, northwestern, and southeastern portions of the state by referring to them as "unCalifornia."

south is the charm of a different culture in a foreign land. And yet there is much more to the regional character than a flamboyant image, a benign climate, and a diverse landscape.

The California Region is outstanding in agriculture, significant in petroleum, unexcelled in aerospace and electronics, important in design, trend-setting in education, innovative in urban development, and increasingly significant in decision making. It is also the world champion in air pollution, the national leader in earthquakes and landslides, preeminent in both traffic movement and traffic jams, and the destination of a population inflow that has been unparalleled in the history of the continent.

population: sensational growth, abruptly decelerating

The keynote of the geography of the California Region during most of this century has been the rapid growth of its population. The rate of natural increase (excess of births over deaths) has been just average, but the trend of net in-migration (excess of in-migrants over out-migrants) has been nothing short of sensational.

From 1941 to 1964 California's population increased at an annual average rate of 4 percent per year, more than twice the national rate. During this period there was a *net* addition to the state's population of one person every 71 seconds, day and night, for 23 years. More than half of this increment was ascribed to in-migration; thus the state's population tripled in three decades, reaching nearly 20 million in 1970. In order to cope with such growth, state and local authorities had to create a gigantic infrastructure of services, facilities, and institutions. For example, it was necessary to open two new and fully equipped elementary schools every week for two-and-one-half decades to accommodate the increase in school-aged children.

Such growth was applauded by many people but was increasingly being decried by others. There was widespread realization that "crowding destroys the values that the people who crowd in came to seek."[2] How long before California's fertile valleys would consist of a single gigantic slurb (formless suburb), and the vaunted freeway system would become the site of a monumental, immovable traffic jam?

Beginning in 1965, the pattern changed suddenly with a downturn in migration. From a net in-migration of 320,000 in 1964, the rate declined to a net gain of 100,000 in 1969 and of only 25,000 in 1971. At the same time there was a decline in the rate of natural increase, paralleling a similar slowdown throughout the nation. The result was that the net growth of the state's population decreased from an annual average of more than half a million in the early 1960s to a low of only 150,000 in 1972.

Since that year the growth rate has once again picked up, averaging approximately 300,000 annually during the mid-1970s, which is by far the largest numerical increase of any state. Approximately one-third of the population increment of the 1970s is due to net in-migration, and the majority of this now comes from foreign countries rather than other states.

Certain other population trends also bear on the matter. For example, the people of the region are extraordinarily restless and shift more often than the populace of any other major region. In San Francisco, for example, two out of five families move *every* year, which is twice the national rate; in Los Angeles, one family in two moves annually.[3] The ethnic mix of the region's population is also changing. The black population continues to increase rapidly, although this rate has also decelerated in the last few years; 7 percent of all Californians today are black, in comparison with less than 2 percent in 1940. Other nonwhites, primarily the Japa-

[2] Raymond F. Dasmann, *The Destruction of California* (New York: The Macmillan Company, 1965), p. 207.

[3] Neil Morgan and the Editors of Time-Life Books, *The Pacific States* (New York: Time Incorporated, 1967), p. 86.

nese, Chinese, and Filipinos, are also increasing absolutely and proportionally, constituting 2 percent of the state population in 1940 but 5 percent in 1977. The Hispanic populace is increasing almost as dramatically and is now about 20 percent of the state total, not counting illegal Mexican aliens who probably number more than 1 million.

The history of settlement in California has always been characterized by a continuous movement in numbers and space. The present patterns seem to be only a shifting phase in the constantly changing situation.

One facet of the population pattern that has not changed is urbanization, the dominant theme in the region (see table 16–1 for the region's largest urban places). Only two other states exceed California in proportionate urban population. The prospects and problems accompanying urban growth and urban sprawl are enormous.

water: spatial disharmony and the complexities of diversion

California receives sufficient rainfall as a state, but the moisture does not fall in the right places at the right time and in the right amounts to be very useful to the population (fig. 16–2). Comparing a map showing distribution of water availability with one showing population distribution, it immediately becomes apparent that people have not settled in accord with the pattern set by nature. The northern third of the state, much of which is outside the California Region, receives 70 percent of the annual average runoff, but the southern two-thirds of the state have almost 80 percent of the water need on the basis of population and land-use patterns. Also, the bulk of the runoff is in winter and spring, often in the form of floods.

The principal problem is to get water from where there is too much to where there is not enough. Strenuous efforts have been made to accomplish this, and construction expenditures have amounted to more than

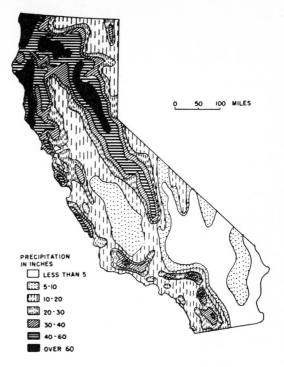

PRECIPITATION
IN INCHES
- LESS THAN 5
- 5-10
- 10-20
- 20-30
- 30-40
- 40-60
- OVER 60

fig. 16–2 Map of California showing average annual precipitation. Southern California generally suffers from moisture deficiency, but the northern part of the state is sometimes troubled by too large a surplus.

$10 billion in major projects alone. The result has been the establishment of the most extensive and sophisticated water storage and delivery systems in the world. A listing of the larger projects exemplifies the magnitude of these systems:

1 Los Angeles Aqueduct—diversion from Owens Valley and Mono Valley to Los Angeles, 300 miles

2 Hetch Hetchy Aqueduct—diversion from upper Tuolumne drainage to San Francisco area, 140 miles

3 Mokelumne Aqueducts—diversion from upper Mokelumne drainage to East Bay area, 100 miles

4 Colorado River Aqueduct—diversion from Colorado River to Los Angeles and San Diego areas, 250 miles

5 Central Valley Project—diversion

425

table 16-1   Largest Urban Places of the California Region

name	population of principal city	population of metropolitan area	name	population of principal city	population of metropolitan area
Alameda*	72,017		Norwalk*	86,826	
Alhambra*	60,715		Oakland	330,651	
Anaheim	193,616	1,936,616	Oceanside*	56,003	
Arcadia*	46,697		Ontario*	63,140	
Bakersfield	77,264	343,700	Orange*	82,157	
Baldwin Park*	45,712		Oxnard	86,506	438,100
Bellflower*	51,145		Palo Alto*	52,277	
Berkeley*	110,465		Pasadena*	108,220	
Buena Park*	61,840		Pico Rivera*	51,495	
Burbank*	86,001		Pomona*	82,275	
Carson*	78,671		Redondo Beach*	62,400	
Cerritos*	43,153		Redwood City*	54,160	
Chula Vista*	75,497		Richmond*	69,713	
Compton*	75,143		Riverside	150,612	1,223,400
Concord*	95,114		Rosemead*	41,514	
Costa Mesa*	76,058		Sacramento	260,822	880,100
Daly City*	72,741		Salinas	70,438	265,000
Downey*	85,812		San Bernardino	102,076	
El Cajon*	60,404		San Diego	773,996	1,587,500
El Monte*	67,698		San Francisco	664,520	3,128,800
Escondido*	49,815		San Jose	555,707	1,173,400
Fairfield*	50,264		San Leandro*	66,953	
Fountain Valley*	52,377		San Mateo*	77,878	
Fremont*	117,862		San Rafael*	45,219	
Fresno	176,528	445,600	Santa Ana*	177,304	
Fullerton*	93,692		Santa Barbara	72,125	279,600
Garden Grove*	118,454		Santa Clara*	82,822	
Glendale*	132,360		Santa Cruz	36,807	151,500
Hawthorne*	53,953		Santa Monica*	92,115	
Hayward*	92,802		Santa Rosa	65,087	245,600
Huntington Beach*	149,706		Seaside*	36,886	
Inglewood*	86,610		Simi Valley*	70,086	
Lakewood*	81,802		South Gate*	56,560	
La Habra*	43,037		South San		
La Mesa*	42,587		Francisco*	48,947	
Livermore*	49,850		Stockton	117,600	299,400
Long Beach	335,602		Sunnyvale*	102,462	
Los Angeles	2,727,399	6,944,900	Thousand Oaks*	55,523	
Modesto	83,540	223,800	Torrance*	139,776	
Montebello*	46,665		Vallejo	70,681	277,600
Monterey Park*	49,179		Ventura	63,441	
Mountain View*	55,143		Walnut Creek*	46,321	
Napa	46,557		West Covina*	75,783	
National City*	44,289		Westminster*	66,758	
Newport Beach*	61,853		Whittier*	72,059	

* A suburb of a larger city.

from Sacramento Valley to San Joaquin
Valley

6 California Water Project—diversion
from Sacramento Valley to San Joaquin
Valley and various coastal locations in central and Southern California (fig. 16–3)

Yet even these are not enough. Despite
immense costs and remarkable efficiency in
intrastate water diversion, the burgeoning
cities and thirsty farmlands of the region
have an almost insatiable demand for water.
Feasible sources for further storage-diversion
are limited, and strident opposition based
on both environmental and economic objections is increasingly powerful. Moreover, the
drought years of the mid-1970s exposed the
Achilles heel of the water diversion syndrome. Below-normal precipitation over an
extended period of time undermines the
whole concept; if there is inadequate water
to store, diversion is at best inefficient and at
worst impractical. Even some normally
well-watered portions of Northern California experienced critical water shortages in
1975–78; indeed, most of semiarid Southern
California actually fared better than the
north, as their extensive storage-distribution
systems were more adjustable to the deficiencies of precipitation.

The water future of the California Region is problematical. There is hope that desalinization of seawater will eventually
provide for the water needs of the region,
but this is still too costly a process for the immediate future. Under "normal" weather
conditions lack of water should not inhibit
sustenance and growth, although the profli-
gate consumption of the past will be increasingly intolerable. The specter of future
drought years is an implacable reality, however, and the ingenuity of planners and politicians may be tested to the utmost.

settlement of the region

The region's physical and cultural diversity
is further reflected in its sequential occupance pattern. The prominent waves of In-

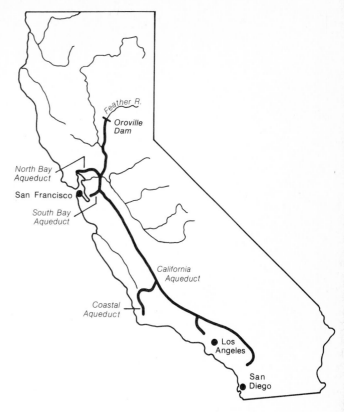

fig. 16–3   The California Water Project is the
most recent and the most ambitious of the
long-range diversion schemes in the state.

dian, Spanish, Mexican, and Anglo settlers
have been more recently augmented by an
influx of blacks and Asians.

CALIFORNIA INDIANS

In contrast to the prosperous and attractive
way of life in the region today, the aboriginal inhabitants found California to possess
limited resources of value to them, and thus
they had restricted livelihood opportunities.
Essentially they were hunters and gatherers,
and the basic foods for most of the tribes
were either seafoods or plants that gave
seeds and nuts that could be ground into
flour and then boiled as gruel or baked into
bread.

427

Tribal organization was loosely knit and generally involved small units. Often just a dozen or so families, perhaps related in some sort of patriarchal lineage, would form a wandering band. There were few large tribes or strong chiefs, and internecine warfare was the exception rather than the rule. This made it possible for California to support a relatively high density of Indian population in comparison with most other parts of the country. It is estimated that at the time of the European discovery of this continent, perhaps one-tenth of all Anglo-American Indians lived in what is now the California Region.

fig. 16–4 Early settlements in California. During the late eighteenth and early nineteenth centuries all of the non-Indian settlements in California were along or near the coast.

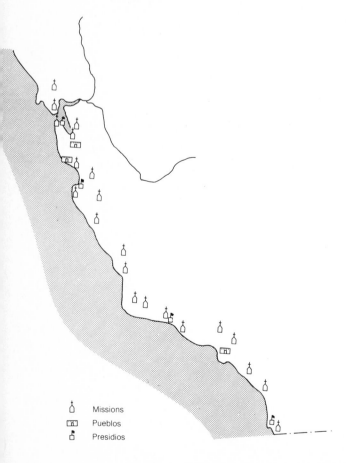

Missions
Pueblos
Presidios

There was considerable linguistic, cultural, and economic diversity among the Indians, within the constraints of their rather limited resources. Most, however, could be classed as relatively primitive and were easily degraded on contact with a more advanced culture. Thus, California Indians tamely gave way to white occupance of the region and left few marks on the landscape to signal their passing. And yet all the earliest recorded history of California revolved about them, and the entire pre-Anglo period was shaped by Indian relations.

THE SPANISH MISSION PERIOD

The European "discoverer" of the region was Rodriguez Cabrillo, on a maritime mission from Mexico in 1542. Following this expedition there was a long era of occasional exploration, but more than two centuries passed before there was any attempt at colonization of Alta California by the Spaniards. California seemed to offer little attraction to the adventurous, gold-seeking conquistadors. Renewed interest was stimulated not by the possibilities of the region itself but by the rapid advance of Russian domination of the Pacific Coast south from Alaska. Although Spain considered the whole California area economically worthless, it wanted a buffer state to prevent possible Russian encroachment on the more valuable colony of Mexico.

The first of Spain's famous missions in California was founded in 1769 at San Diego, and within three years an irregular string of missions, both in protected coastal valleys and directly on the coast, had been established as far north as Monterey. Eventually 21 continuing missions were established, the last in 1823 (fig. 16–4). The purpose of the mission system was to hold the land for Spain and to Christianize the Indians. This was accomplished by settling the nearby Indians at each mission to carry on a completely self-sufficient, sedentary crop-growing and livestock-herding existence. Each of the missions garnered an attached population of from 500 to 1,500 Indians.

The basic results of the system were that

some 25,000 Indians were "civilized", at least that many and probably more were exterminated by the inadvertent introduction of exotic diseases, a variety of European plants and animals was introduced to the region, and a number of settlement nuclei and transportation routes was established.

Two other types of settlements, *presidios* and *pueblos,* were established during the mission period. Four presidios were set up as army posts for protection against Indians and pirates; each developed as a major settlement nucleus (San Diego, Monterey, San Francisco, and Santa Barbara). Pueblos, also four in number, were planned farming villages; Los Angeles and San Jose survived as future major cities.

The missions generally reached the height of their prosperity in the 1820s in spite of problems with fire, flood, earthquake, and unbelievers. The mission-presidio-pueblo system, however, did not succeed in attracting many settlers to California. Land grants were few, small, and allotted mostly to retired soldiers.

THE MEXICAN PERIOD

Mexico, including California, achieved independence from Spain in 1822, and the missions were gradually secularized. This resulted in the rapid alienation of the land into private ownership, neglect of property and buildings, and lapsing of the mission Indians into degraded poverty or demoralized frontier life. The Mexican government embarked on a large-scale scheme of land grants to individuals; within only a few years most of the land from Marin and Sonoma counties (just north of San Francisco Bay) southward along the coast was held in *ranchos.*

Ranchos quickly replaced missions as the focus of life in California. They were mostly self-sufficient cattle empires, with beef as the chief food and hides and tallow as the principal exports. Towns were few, small, and far apart. Los Angeles was the largest; Monterey was the capital and the chief seaport. Most of the inland portion of the region remained unsettled, except for a few ranchos in the Central Valley.

THE EARLY ANGLO-AMERICAN PERIOD

California Territory was annexed to the United States at the end of the Mexican War in 1848. By a remarkable coincidence, gold was discovered in the Sierra Nevada foothills only two months before the peace treaty was signed. The impact of gold discovery was sensational. The total population of California in 1845 was about 5,000, of whom less than 8 percent were Anglo-Americans. Half a decade later the population had reached nearly 100,000, of whom 90 percent were Anglos.

The gold boom caused a rapid growth of towns in the Mother Lode country. Such places as Grass Valley, Auburn, Hangtown, Columbia, and Sonora became instant towns that were eclipsed in a few years as their mines declined. Sacramento and Stockton, located on the valley floor below the foothills, benefited from their riverside sites that gave them commercial advantages for a more stable economy. Sacramento was chosen the state capital in 1854, providing further stability and diversification.

It was San Francisco, however, that prospered most as a result of gold. Its population of 800 almost vanished in the first rush to the gold fields. Its outstanding location soon gave it ascendancy, however, and in a short time it was the largest city in western Anglo-America. The population increased to 35,000 in two years and was more than 50,000 in 1860 despite having been leveled by fires five times during that period. The population of California was 380,000 by then.

Los Angeles at that time had less than 5,000 people; the influence of the gold strike had been much less significant in the "cow counties" of Southern California. Most of the land was devoted to cattle raising, and except for the pueblo of Los Angeles and settlements around a few presidios and missions, there were no towns at all.

The demand for beef rapidly accelerated. Herds from Mexico and Texas were driven to California. Many of the ranchos were broken up to accommodate more people; the settlers were almost entirely Anglo-Americans except for the Chinese who came to the gold fields. Ranching became more intensive; and crop farming, especially wheat and barley in the Central Valley, began to be important for the first time.

THE BEGINNINGS OF THE COMMERCIAL-INDUSTRIAL ERA

The first California land boom started slowly but grew abruptly in the 1880s. The boom spread from Los Angeles to San Diego and Santa Barbara and was felt over much of the region. The population of Los Angeles County tripled to 100,000 in that decade. Separate colonies, based on irrigation farming of specialty crops, were founded in many places. There were orange colonies at Anaheim, Pasadena, Riverside, and Redlands; grape colonies in the Fresno area; and other varied colonies in different parts of the San Joaquin Valley.

The availability of "transcontinental" railway connections provided access to distant markets and proved to be a major solution to marketing problems. The first transcontinental line, from Omaha to San Francisco, was completed in 1869, and a railway was extended from San Francisco to Los Angeles in 1876.

Irrigated agriculture spread and intensified rapidly in the Los Angeles lowland, in the numerous coastal valleys, and in the Central Valley. Agricultural progress was accelerated by the development of refrigerated railway cars, canning and freezing of produce, improved farm machinery, pumps and pipes for irrigation and drainage, and the beginnings of agribusiness enterprises.

Industrial growth began with petroleum discoveries toward the end of the nineteenth century. The emergence of the motion picture business was a major catalyst, both physical and promotional, to economic and population growth and to urban expansion. Manufacturing was stimulated during World War I and experienced a phenomenal growth during World War II.

The present occupance and land-use pattern of the region, however, was basically in existence by the early years of the twentieth century. Changes since that time have mostly involved the extension of irrigated acreage in lowland areas and the never-ending sprawl of the cities.

southern california

This is the smallest of the four subregions of the California Region, but it is one of the most intensively developed areas in all Anglo-America. It occupies a relatively narrow coastal zone and includes the east-west trending Transverse Ranges on the north, the north-south trending Peninsular Ranges on the east, and the sprawling desert spillover zones of the Antelope Valley and Palm Springs (fig. 16–5).

fig. 16–5 The northwestern portion of the Southern California metropolis as seen from a satellite. The Los Angeles–Long Beach–Anaheim complex shows in the lower right corner. Northwesterly up the coast is another urban area, Oxnard-Ventura. In the upper left of the photo, across the Transverse Ranges from Los Angeles, is the Tulare Basin portion of the San Joaquin Valley with its intricate agricultural pattern; particularly notable are the huge square fields in the dry bed of Buena Vista Lake. In the upper right is the "high desert" portion of the Mojave, which includes a patchy pattern of irrigated farming and urban spillover (Landsat image).

Approximately half of the areal extent of this subregion consists of very steep-sided mountains and hills, some of which rise to heights above 10,000 feet. The strikingly parallel patterns of both the Transverse and the Peninsular ranges indicate a strong association with crustal movements of folding, faulting, and warping. The ranges tend to be both rugged and rocky with thin soils and generally sparse, usually bushy vegetation cover.

Enclosed by the mountain perimeter on the north and east and by the waters of the Pacific on the west are various lowlands, valleys, and coastal terraces where most of the people live and most of the economic activities take place. The only large extent of flat land is the Los Angeles lowland, which is wide at its coastal margin and tapers inland until it pinches out about 60 miles to the east. In several places the lowland is interrupted by prominent hills, partially subdividing it into separate valleys.

Much of the lowland is covered with extensive coalescing alluvial fans formed of material washed down from the mountains. These fans slope from altitudes of 1,000 to 2,000 feet at the base of the mountains, to 300 to 500 feet a few miles away. The streams forming these fans are broad, stony washes, becoming surface streams only during times of flood. They provide, however, an important supply of ground water for the area's large-scale irrigation development and for domestic use.

Farther south, in Orange and San Diego counties, the lowland is replaced by a series of slightly elevated coastal terraces, frequently interrupted by abrupt arroyos that sometimes divide the gently-sloping terraces into separate sections locally called "mesas."

The coastline of Southern California is marked by low shelving beaches at points where the deltaic plains reach the ocean, alternating with elevated beaches and bold promontories where the mountain spurs approach the coast. From 25 to 90 miles offshore lie several mountainous islands, presently little developed but definitely a part of the region.

The climate is a true mediterranean type, having a marked seasonal rhythm of rainfall. The precipitation—10 to 20 inches in the lowlands—comes almost entirely during the winter season. Desert conditions with a maximum of sunshine prevail during the summers. Winters are mild and summers are hot, although near the Pacific Ocean the summer temperatures are modified by cool sea breezes and frequent fogs. The high percentage of sunshine, even during the winter rainy season, has attracted tourists as well as many important industries. Southern California vies with Arizona and Florida in selling climate to the people of the rest of the continent.

The natural vegetation in this foothill and valley area consists largely of chaparral up to elevations of 3,000 to 5,000 feet, with annual and perennial grasses forming much of the understory. The floors of the interior valleys are dotted with large oaks and covered with grasses that are green in winter and spring and golden the rest of the year. On the higher slopes, where the rainfall is greater and snow frequently occurs in winter, extensive stands of conifers attract general recreation seekers in summer and skiers in winter.

THE SOUTHERN CALIFORNIA METROPOLIS

The development of a Southern California megalopolis has long been anticipated but has not yet eventuated despite the rapid growth and incredible sprawl of cities in the area. The urban assemblage is an extensive one: the east-west axis from Palm Springs to Santa Barbara is 170 miles; the north-south extent from Lancaster, in the Antelope Valley, to the Mexican border is approximately the same distance; and the southeast-northwest coastal frontage from San Diego to Santa Barbara covers more than 200 miles. Urbanization is by no means complete within these dimensions. Massive hills and even a few mountain ranges are encompassed; urban areas are restricted mostly to the lowlands and valleys except where favored hill slopes are being carved and terraced for residential construction.

Characteristics of the Urban System Urban Southern California consists of a "loosely knit complex of people, commerce, and industry—all fused in a single system by a highly developed freeway network, a common technology, a common economic interest, and by numerous other shared values."[4] Los Angeles is the major center, and its name serves as a toponymic umbrella for most of the urban system; however, Los Angeles cannot properly be classified as the focus of the metropolis, for this sprawling urban complex really has no focus. Its development has been polynuclear, and with each passing year the other nuclei become proportionately stronger and more self-contained.

The Los Angeles–Long Beach node is the largest and most prominent; the other major nuclei, in descending rank-order of population, are Anaheim–Santa Ana–Garden Grove, San Diego, Riverside–San Bernardino, Oxnard-Ventura, and Santa Barbara. All these nodes are interrelated within the subregional economy and within the general sphere of Los Angeles influence,

but they are also essentially separate entities that dominate their own cluster of lesser cities. Separating the major nodes is a mixture of nonurban land, attenuated and irregular string-street commercial development, and low-density residential sprawl.

The complexities of the polynuclear pattern are varied. Important commercial centers, for example, are not limited to central business district locations but are widely dispersed over the metropolis. A visual indication of this dispersion is provided by the relatively large number of localities—more than a dozen—where there are concentrations of high-rise commercial buildings. Although Southern California skyscrapers do not rise so high as those in many Eastern cities, their clustering is much more thoroughly disseminated, which has a markedly different effect on traffic patterns and subregional economic relationships.

The Economic Base The Southern California economic structure is highly diversified, as with most metropolises, but it has certain distinctive elements. Most notable is perhaps the major role played by certain types of manufacturing in this area, the third largest manufacturing district of the continent. Ever since the early years of World War II, the local economy has been significantly geared to defense production. Shipbuilding was once an important facet of this, but the aircraft industry, which has now developed into the *aerospace* industry, has always been dominant (fig. 16–6).

[4] Richard E. Preston, "Recent Changes in the Size and Form of the Southern California Metropolis," in *California, 1970: Problems and Prospects,* ed. David W. Lantis (Chico, Calif.: Association of American Geographers, 1970), p. 83.

fig. 16–6 Large aerospace factories are widespread in Southern California. This is the Rockwell International plant in Anaheim (courtesy Rockwell International).

Southern California has been the world's leading aircraft manufacturing center since the 1930s and maintains that distinction today in aerospace, despite the recent development of spacecraft production facilities in other parts of the country. Roughly one-third of the subregion's total manufactural employment is in aerospace.

The economic dangers of such heavy reliance on federal procurement expenditures has long been realized, and the harsh reality of curtailed defense spending in the late 1960s and early 1970s put a major crimp in the Southern California economy for the first time since the depression of the 1930s. Even so, aerospace production persists as the leading industry of the subregion. The huge windowless plants of the prime contractors are invariably located adjacent to an airport—Los Angeles International, Santa Monica, Long Beach, Burbank, Palmdale, San Diego's Lindbergh Field—but the numerous subcontracting firms are widespread over the subregion.

Other notable or distinctive types of manufacturing in Southern California include electronics; sports clothes; furniture, particularly outdoor furniture; automobile assembly; fish canning; rubber products, especially tires; and petroleum refining.

The most distinctive major economic activity in the subregion, however, is the *motion picture and media entertainment industry*. Hollywood was the birthplace and long-time capital of movie making and is still a focal point, although there has been decentralization of the major studios and network production facilities, particularly to Culver City and the San Fernando Valley.

The original studios were attracted to Southern California by the sunny mediterranean climate and the great variety of scenery to be found within the immediate area: mountains, deserts, subtropical vegetation, and seascapes. Early photography required good sunlight, and before the advent of sound films, most pictures were taken in the open. This required periods of protracted sunlight with a minimum of rain that might damage the equipment. Today most movies and television films are staged in studios,

and since a large part of the lighting effect is artificially produced, Southern California sunshine is no longer a controlling factor. Nevertheless, the industry is firmly entrenched here because of the early concentration of talent, skills, and reputation.

The Population Mix The spectacular long-run population growth of Southern California has slowed a bit in the most recent years but is still impressive. The subregion's population grew by 2.8 million (to 11,650,000) in the decade of the 1960s, which is a million more than the population increment of the New York–northeastern New Jersey and Chicago–northwestern Indiana consolidated areas combined. The 1976 population of the Southern California subregion (12.5 million) was larger than that of 48 of the 50 states.

During most of the twentieth century the populace of Southern California has had a surprisingly homogenous character, despite the attraction of in-migrants from all over the country. Numerous local communities of retired Iowa farmers, Oklahomans, or displaced Texans or Chicagoans could be noted. A relatively large Hispanic minority and localized pockets of Orientals constituted the only notable elements of heterogeneity.

Within the last three decades, however, there has been a remarkable upsurge of in-migration of ethnic minority peoples, most particularly since 1960. The proportion of blacks and Hispanic-Americans in the subregional population mix has increased dramatically, and an even greater percentage gain has been registered by Asians and American Indians, although their total numbers are much smaller than the blacks or the Chicanos.

All these groups have tended to settle in relatively concentrated, ghettoized areas. The major clusters by far are in Los Angeles, where blacks occupy the area south and southwest of the central business district (Watts, Willowbrook, Compton); Chicanos live to the east (Boyle Heights, East Los Angeles); and Chinese agglomerate to the north (New Chinatown). These ethnic ghettos

fig. 16-7 Los Angeles contains the most complete and complex system of freeways in the world. Shown here is a simple interchange between the Santa Monica and Harbor freeways.

"exhibit a high incidence of low income, unemployment, low educational attainment, and deficient tax revenues. Amid the sea of material prosperity that is Greater Los Angeles, [these] communities are islands of neglect."[5]

The Changing Urban Pattern For many years the form and pattern of urban areas of Southern California in general, and Los Angeles in particular, have been acclaimed as unique, their development diverging from that of other Anglo-American metropolises. The most conspicuous abnormalities have included a lack of focus on the central business district, emphasis on detached single-family housing, low population density, and overwhelming dependence on the automobile for local transportation (fig. 16-7). More recently, however, the distinctiveness of Southern California urbanism has been significantly muted. This reflects, in part, the fact that the older cities of Anglo-America have been exhibiting some of these same characteristics—declin-

ing CBD focus, increasing urban sprawl, greater dependence on automobiles—in their recent development.

More pertinent to Southern California, however, is the fact that opposite tendencies have become apparent within the subregion. Population density is increasing, multifamily housing is expanding rapidly, and CBDs are developing "new" central functions. In short, a centripetal trend is setting in. In and around the principal urban cores of Southern California, multifamily housing units, often high-rise, are now being constructed in greater numbers than are single-family detached units. Rising land costs and an expanding population are (perhaps inevitably) producing a housing and business profile, and possibly an overall urban profile, that is increasingly similar to cities in the East and Midwest.

These centripetal tendencies are particularly prominent in Los Angeles but can also be seen in San Diego, Santa Monica, Long Beach, Santa Barbara, and even Pasadena. The functional complexity of the CBD increases. There is no intensification of the commercial function, but there is an increasing focalization and centralization of

[5] Ibid., p. 108.

corporate headquarters, financial services, government offices, and cultural facilities. Furthermore, population and building densities are increasing in residential areas, owing to high-rise apartments, smaller subdivisions, and other factors. By the mid-1970s, for example, suburban Los Angeles had a population density comparable to that of suburban Chicago or Philadelphia.

The Southern California metropolis, long a harbinger of things to come in urbanism, has thus lost much of its distinctiveness. "In varying ways the urban area has evolved into a reasonably 'average' metropolis."[6] This is not to say that uniformity has set in but merely that some tendencies have been changed and even reversed.

There are still many unique and perhaps futuristic characteristics to the urban pattern and life style of Southern California.

[6] Howard J. Nelson and William A. V. Clark, *The Los Angeles Metropolitan Experience: Uniqueness, Generality, and the Goal of the Good Life* (Cambridge, Mass.: Ballinger Publishing Company, 1976), p. 24.

Where else does one find such a conspicuous example of cellular urban development on a polynuclear framework, spatially integrated by a highly developed (and developing) freeway system, and seemingly capable of indefinite expansion? Where else can one find a meticulously detailed plastic Matterhorn rising 146 feet above the floor of Disneyland, only to be topped by the $21-million, 230-foot-high scoreboard of a nearby baseball stadium, which is in turn overshadowed by the 250-foot fluorescent cross of a neighboring drive-in church?

Specialized Urban Problems All large urban areas are beset with problems of various kinds, and the Southern California metropolis is no exception. There are, however, certain specialized problems that are particularly notable in Southern California, owing to the local environment and to the extraordinary sprawl.

Smog Perhaps the most infamous nuisance in Anglo-America is the Southern California smog (see vignette below).

smog, pollution in the balmy air

The public's mental image of California is varied, but if only a half dozen key words are selected to epitomize the region, it is likely that one of them would be "smog." Indeed, it is probable that smog vies with overpopulation as the principal snake in the California Garden of Eden.

Smog is a complex phenomenon that is difficult even to define. In simplest terms it is air pollution that both impairs visibility and has an adverse effect on the health of plants and animals, including humanity. Air quality can be affected by a great many different kinds of pollutants, but the principal constituents of the region's infamous smog—oxidizing photochemical smog—are ozone (O_3), nitrogen oxides (NO_x), carbon monoxide (CO), and sulfur dioxide (SO_2); ozone is normally the most conspicuous cause of the problem. Smog strongly affects our vision and smell, and if it is severe enough it can even be tasted and its residues can be felt on surfaces. Besides its eye-watering, lung-searing, nostril-burning characteristics, it is also a health hazard and a vegetation toxicant.

Smog is by no means a peculiarly California phenomenon, but the term first came into prominent usage there, and Los Angeles has for more than three decades been the undisputed smog champion of the world. Other portions of the California Region are not nearly so smog-prone as the Southern California metropolis, although no urban area in the region is smog-free. The principal cities of the Central Valley, particularly Bakersfield, are significant centers of air pollution. In the Bay Area, on the other hand, there is considerable variation. San Francisco is an almost smogless city, primarily because of its high degree of windiness, whereas San Jose, at the poorly ventilated
(Continued)

Unstable Earth The Southern California metropolis is situated squarely atop one of the most geologically active portions of Anglo-America. The area is seamed in profusion by faults, and earthquakes are felt, sporadically and unpredictably, from time to time. Some of the tremors have had spectacular and tragic results (the San Fernando quake of 1971 killed 64 people and caused more than half a billion dollars worth of property damage), but despite a high public consciousness of the potential danger, only a miniscule proportion of homeowners carry earthquake insurance.

Other kinds of earth slippages, on a much smaller scale, occur with greater frequency. The steep hills and unstable slopes of the subregion often afford spectacular views but precarious building sites. Every year there are dozens of small slumps and slides, and a few unfortunate residents

"move down to a new neighborhood," whether they want to or not.

Flood and Fire The relatively small amount of precipitation falls almost entirely in the winter. As it flows down the steep hill slopes into urban areas, which are so extensive that they are inadequately supplied with storm drains, destructive floods and mud slides often result. During the rainless summers, on the other hand, forest and brush fires are ever imminent. The tangled chaparral, chamisal, and woodland vegetation of the abrupt hills and mountains that abut and intermingle with the urbanized zones is readily susceptible to burning. Only carefully enforced fire precautions, a network of fire breaks and fire roads, and efficient suppression crews are able to hold down the damage. And where burning strips away vegetation in the summer, flooding

---

southern end of the bay, experiences considerable air pollution.[a]

The frequent high level of smogginess in Los Angeles is due primarily to the unique physical characteristics of the metropolitan site. The Los Angeles lowland is sandwiched between desert-backed mountains and a cool ocean. At this latitude there is persistent sub-

[a] During the 1966–76 decade Los Angeles averaged about 150 days per year in which peak hour ozone levels exceeded the federal air quality standard; in San Jose the annual average was about 45 days, and in San Francisco the average was 4 days.

sidence of air from upper levels, which acts as a stability lid over the lowland, inhibiting updrafts and keeping vertical air motions at a minimum (fig. 16-a). Significant horizontal air motion is also limited by the combination of hot desert, high mountains, and cool waters, with the result that Los Angeles has a much lower average wind speed than any other major metropolitan area in Anglo-America. Local winds—land and sea breezes, mountain and valley breezes—help to break the stability from time to time, but the most prominent characteristic of the air over the metropolis is its relative lack of movement. This stagnant condition en-

fig. 16-a A typical late summer inversion lid over the Los Angeles lowland. Air pollutants are trapped below the lid (marked by the shallow cloud layer), with clear skies above.

becomes even more likely in the following winter.

NONURBAN ACTIVITIES

Although most of the population of this subregion is urban and the vast majority of all jobs is in urban-related activities, there are three prominent nonurban activities that are intensively developed and contribute significantly to the area's economy.

Agriculture Agriculture has been an outstanding activity in Southern California ever since the first irrigated colonies were established in the nineteenth century. Grains and beans have been grown extensively without irrigation, but nearly all significant farm production has been dependent on artificially supplied water. Most of the alluvial fans and lowlands in the subregion have been farmed at some time. In recent years, however, urban sprawl has crowded out many farmers, and subdivisions have replaced orchards and fields at a rapid rate. The principal farm products are milk, citrus fruits, truck crops, horticultural specialties, and subtropical specialties.

Citrus production was concentrated in Southern California for many decades, but urbanization of the orange groves has caused a major shift to other areas, particularly the San Joaquin Valley. Orange County, between Los Angeles and San Diego, is still an orange-growing area, but it is also the most rapidly urbanizing county in the nation. The Ventura area, between Los Angeles and Santa Barbara, has always been the leading lemon-growing locale in the United States and, despite some urban-caused displacement of groves, continues to have that distinction.

ables the air pollution to build up with annoying frequency.

Many varieties of pollutants are scattered into the stagnant air from factory smokestacks, electricity generation, human lungs, and especially automobile exhausts. By the late 1970s it was calculated that 90 percent of all pollutants emanated from moving sources, primarily automobiles and trucks.

To combat this menace a bewildering variety of local, state, and federal regulations and regulatory bodies have been established, with a great deal of overlap and redundancy. Federal regulations (the Clean Air Act and its amendments) generally control auto emission standards throughout the nation except in California, where state regulations, which are more stringent than the federal ones, prevail. The history of air pollution control is a continuing story of the balance between the rate of reduction in allowable emissions from polluting sources and the growth rate in the number of emission sources (largely vehicles).

Stationary sources of pollution are now thoroughly controlled in Southern California, and increasingly rigorous auto emission standards are being phased in almost every year.

The result is a continuing improvement in air quality in the Los Angeles Basin. The peak years of air pollution were in the late 1950s. In 1958–59, for example, the all-time high in ozone incidence was reached, with 329 days in which state air quality standards were not reached; by 1974–75 the number of such incidences was less than 200, and the trend continues downward. First stage smog alerts were proclaimed 17 times in 1955–56, but none has been proclaimed since 1972.[b]

Smog is by no means conquered, but almost all measures of air quality in the Los Angeles Basin are on an upward trend. It should be noted, however, that such improving conditions are either absent or are much less pronounced in the downwind (eastern) portions of the basin, such as the Riverside–San Bernardino area and in those parts of the Southern California metropolis where rapid population growth is significantly increasing the number of sources of emissions (as in Orange County).

[b] Los Angeles Department of Environmental Quality, *State of the Environment 1977* (Los Angeles: Department of Environmental Quality, 1977), pp. 20–21.

Various kinds of *truck crops* and *vegetables* are widely grown in the subregion, with the principal concentration on the Oxnard Plain near Ventura. Horticultural specialties, such as flowers and flower seeds, and subtropical specialties, such as avocados and macadamia nuts, are particularly notable in San Diego County.

Dairying is another highly intensive and productive agricultural enterprise in Southern California. The large local population provides a major market for dairy products, particularly fluid milk. The more than 800 dairy herds totaling 100,000 cows, of which more than half are in Los Angeles County, produce more milk than those of any other county in the nation. It is mostly "dry-lot" dairying, which means it is done on small land units that are not large enough to produce feed or to use as pasture land for the herds. Well over half a million tons of alfalfa are brought into Los Angeles County annually from the San Joaquin and Imperial valleys to feed the cows. The value of the land, however, increasingly becomes so great that the dairy owners cannot afford not to sell. Consequently each year finds fewer dry-lot dairy farms in the urbanized areas, more dairies moving out to less-developed districts to the east of the coastal zone, and more milk being brought in from outside the subregion.

Commercial Fishing Major fishing grounds extend from Southern California waters southward to Peru and westward to Hawaii. Most fish are brought to the ports of Los Angeles (San Pedro), which is home base for the largest commercial fishing fleet in the country, and San Diego.

Tuna is by far the most important catch of Southern California fishermen, although anchovies (for fish meal, oil, and bait), mackerel, and bonito are also significant. California is the second-ranking state in both volume and value of commercial fishery landings. San Pedro is the leading United States fishing port, and San Diego ranks among the ten leaders.

In recent years the tuna fleet has been the only segment of the United States fishing industry to excel, despite continuing difficulties with the 200-mile territorial waters restrictions of Latin American nations and major changes in fishing techniques and gear.[7] Problems with porpoises, however, are now providing much greater obstacles for the industry. Nearly all the tuna catch is accomplished by large, modern purse seiners with electronic gear for finding the fish. The fishing boats home in on a school of porpoises feeding on tuna; the porpoises are "rounded up" by motorboat, which also concentrates the tuna beneath them. The boat sets the purse seine, and both tuna and porpoises are taken. The porpoises are released, but the mortality rate is so high that a federal law has been enacted that severely limits the number of porpoises that may be netted. Tuna fishermen have had difficulty with this restriction, and the tuna catch is declining.

Petroleum and Natural Gas The Southern California subregion contains some of the most productive oil fields on the continent and, despite its small areal extent, yields more than 5 percent of total United States crude oil production. Although initial discoveries in the area date from 1875, the big oil boom came in the early 1920s with the bringing in of major fields at Huntington Beach, Signal Hill, and Santa Fe Springs.

Four of the ten leading oil fields in the United States, in terms of cumulative production, are in Southern California. The Wilmington Field is second only to the fabulous East Texas Field in output, the Huntington Beach Field ranks sixth, Long Beach is seventh, and Ventura is tenth.

Probably the most interesting geographical aspects of the Southern California fields are those concerned with land utilization. In general, oil fields have been brought in on lands having little surface value. In the Los Angeles Basin, however, much of the land was being used intensively before oil

---

[7] Tom Alexander, "American Fishermen Are Missing the Boat," *Fortune*, 84 (September 1973), 196.

was discovered. Although some of the fields are in brush-covered hill lands, many are either in irrigated agricultural lowlands or in crowded urban territory. Those along the Pacific Coast compete with bathing beaches and in some cases have been forced out into the water. Nowhere else have oil wells had such keen competition for surface rights.

In the Wilmington and Huntington Beach fields, oil and gas wells are spaced closer together than they are anywhere else in the world. In some instances, derrick legs almost overlap. This, in part, is caused by wasteful exploitation, a result of small surface-land ownership plots, but in most cases it is an expression of whipstocking, or directional drilling. Modern drilling techniques allow wells to be drilled at any angle from a single location, so that much offshore drilling can be whipstocked from dry land.

There are large known and suspected reserves of petroleum in the Southern California offshore waters, but exploitation was very limited until 1965, when the city of Long Beach sold the first major leases to oil companies. Several hundred new wells have been drilled since then, most of them whipstocked from four islands that have been built in Long Beach harbor. The wells have been totally camouflaged by a covering of pastel shielding, and the artificial islands have been made as attractive as possible by the planting of palm trees, creation of waterfalls, and night lighting.

Offshore drilling is more expensive in Southern California than it is in the Gulf of Mexico because the producing horizons are deeper. Furthermore, there have been several costly and controversial leaks—most notably in the Santa Barbara Channel—that resulted in protracted litigation and stringent regulation. In spite of that, the reserves of this offshore area are among the largest in Anglo-America, and expanded exploitation will undoubtedly continue.

Another problem, unique in its magnitude, has arisen from oil drilling in the Long Beach area. The long-continued removal of oil from the Wilmington Field resulted in remarkable land subsidence, causing the surface to sink as much as 30 feet in some places and doing untold damage to constructional and engineering features in the Long Beach harbor area and in downtown Long Beach. An extensive water-flooding project was initiated in 1959 to replace the oil with seawater pumped down into the producing formations. Nearly 2 billion barrels of water were injected before the subsidence was stabilized. The project will continue as long as oil is extracted in the area.

FUN IN THE SUN

The Southern California subregion, with its mild and sunny climate, is an American "Riviera." Southern California offers the tourist mountains, beaches, citrus groves, Disneyland, and Hollywood. These draw visitors from all parts of the continent and the world; more than 10 million out-of-state people visit the subregion annually.

At first Southern California attracted people largely during the mild winter season. Although summers are relatively cool near the beaches, the inner parts of the Los Angeles Basin often record high temperatures. The winter season is a festive occasion, with many pageants and entertainments, climaxed by the "Tournament of Roses" and the famous Rose Bowl football game at Pasadena on New Year's Day.

Generally speaking, the natural attractions of the subregion (mountains, beaches, islands) are the haunts of local residents on vacation; the constructed attractions draw the out-of-state visitors. Disneyland, for example, has become a tourist goal that ranks with the Grand Canyon, Yellowstone Park, and Niagara Falls in popularity. Movie and television studios are always swarming with visitors, and such specialized commercial spots as Knott's Berry Farm, Marineland, and Sea World are nationally famous.[8]

[8] Disneyland, Knott's Berry Farm, and Universal Studios receive more visitation than any other commercial attractions in Anglo-America except Walt Disney World in Florida. 1977 attendance figures were Walt Disney World, 12.8 million; Disneyland, 10.5 million; Knott's, 3.8 million; and Universal, 3.2 million. No other such attraction in the country exceeded 2.6 million in attendance.

the central valley

The Central Valley subregion consists of a broad trough lying between the Sierra Nevada and the Coast Ranges, averaging about 50 miles in width and more than 400 miles in length. It is outstanding agriculturally, yielding nearly two-thirds of the total value of production of all farms and ranches in the California Region.

THE NATURAL ENVIRONMENT

Structurally the valley is synclinal, having been warped downward when the Sierra Nevada and the Coast Ranges were uplifted. The long period of erosion that followed this uplift caused the trough to be filled by great quantities of sand, silt, and gravel washed down from the mountains. In places the alluvium has a known thickness of more than 2,000 feet.

The valley is divided into three drainage basins: the Sacramento Valley in the north; the San Joaquin Valley in the middle section; and the Tulare Lake Basin, an area of interior drainage, in the extreme south. (In common usage, however, the San Joaquin Valley is extended southward to include the Tulare Basin.)

The Sacramento River flows south through the northern half of the Central Valley, and the San Joaquin flows north through the southern half (fig. 16–8). They converge near San Francisco Bay and empty into the Pacific Ocean through the only large break in the Coast Ranges. Their delta originally comprised a maze of distributaries, sloughs, and low islands. It has now been diked and canalized and is one of the state's leading truck-farming and horticultural areas.

Climatically the area has mild winters with occasional rains and dry hot summers. Lying between the Coast Ranges and the Sierra Nevada, most parts suffer from a deficiency of rainfall. The precipitation decreases rapidly from more than 30 inches in the north to less than 6 inches in the extreme south. Nearly all rain falls in the winter.

The soils in the Central Valley consist of immature alluvial materials deposited by the torrential flood waters of the rivers. Continuous deposition of alluvium has prevented most of the valley soils from attaining mature profiles; nevertheless, it is the alluvial fans that serve as the foundation for productive agriculture.

In the southern part of the valley near Tulare Lake, alkaline conditions make large areas unsuited to irrigation agriculture, although several thousand acres have been reclaimed by an elaborate system of pumps and drainage ditches that impound the flood waters for irrigation during the dry season. Along the lower course of the Sacramento–San Joaquin rivers, some land is waterlogged and hence is unsuited to cultivation. On the whole, however, most of the Central Valley is covered with rich alluvium.

fig. 16–8 Drainage pattern of the Sierra Nevada and Central Valley.

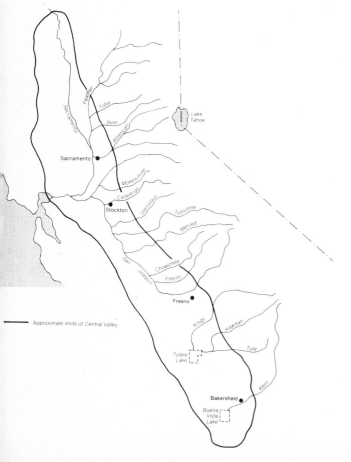

Because of the low rainfall nearly all the Central Valley was originally grassland with tall grasses and scattered oaks in the better-watered northern section and bunchgrass and desert vegetation in the drier southern part. The largest area of open grassland in the state lies along the edge of the Central Valley.

AN AGRICULTURAL CORNUCOPIA

Although many other states harvest greater acreages of crops than California, throughout the past half century total value of farm products sold has been higher in California than in any other state (fig. 16–9). Fertile soil, abundant sunshine, supplies of irrigation water, a long growing season, and careful farm management result in high yields of high-value products. California produces essentially all the national output of almonds, artichokes, dates, figs, lemons, nectarines, olives, persimmons, and pomegranates. In addition, the state is by far the nation's leading grower of apricots, asparagus, avocados, boysenberries, broccoli, brussels sprouts, cantaloupes, carrots, cauliflower, celery, chili peppers, garlic, grapes, lettuce, lima beans, onions, peaches, pears, plums, prunes, spinach, strawberries, tomatoes, and walnuts.

By almost any measure, California is the leading agricultural state. For example, it produces more than 40 percent of the national total of fresh fruits and vegetables, which is more than the combined total of the next three ranking states. With 2 percent of the nation's farms, it earns nearly 10 percent of gross national farm receipts. Many valleys and lowlands contribute to this agri-

fig. 16–9 Gross farm income is higher in the California Region than in any other. The Central Valley concentration is particularly marked.

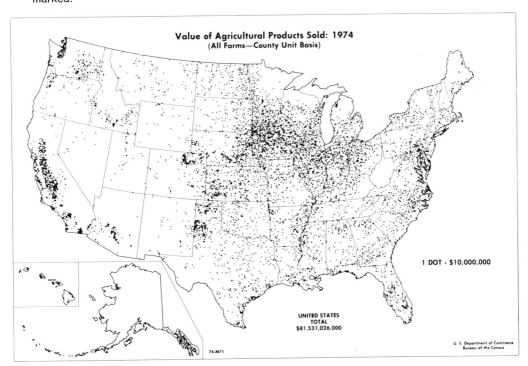

Value of Agricultural Products Sold: 1974
(All Farms—County Unit Basis)

1 DOT - $10,000,000

UNITED STATES
TOTAL
$81,531,026,000

U.S. Department of Commerce
Bureau of the Census

74-M71

cultural cornucopia, but easily the major area of production is the Central Valley.

Irrigation in the Central Valley Early agricultural enterprises in the subregion mostly concentrated on beef cattle, wheat, or barley, all of which could be grown without irrigation. It was only after the irrigation potential began to be exploited in the 1880s that the true worth of the area began to become apparent. Prior to that time the courts of California had upheld the doctrine of riparian rights for the waters of the valley, which allowed the owners of land bordering streams to have full use of the flow, unimpaired in quality and undiminished in quantity. This doctrine, designed for a humid country, was unsuited to a land where the chief use of water was to be for irrigation, which inherently would diminish the quantity and change the quality of the water.

The "prior appropriation" doctrine, widely accepted in other western states, allows consumptive use in full measure by the earliest users on a "first-come, first-served" basis. This doctrine was also considered inadequate for California, and a combination policy was devised whereby riparian users were limited to the amount reasonably required for beneficial use, with provision for diverting the surplus. Following the peak year of grain production in the Central Valley (1885), irrigation steadily increased. The irrigated lands of the valley now represent more than two-thirds of the total for California.

The following two major projects are the important irrigation plans for the Central Valley:

The Central Valley Project, which transfers water from the surplus north to the deficient south, is the subregion's major irrigation scheme. Its two main purposes are to supply water to the dry southeastern San Joaquin Valley and Tulare Basin and to prevent salt-water encroachment in the delta area. The principle of operation is that surplus Sacramento River water is stored and then diverted by canal to the middle course of the San Joaquin River, where it replaces upstream San Joaquin water that has been diverted to the dry lands southward.

The California Water Plan is similar and supplementary to the Central Valley Project. Water from Sacramento River tributaries is stored and diverted to the San Joaquin Valley and Tulare Basin, where it is being used to expand irrigated acreage on the drier western side of these lowlands.

These two major projects, in addition to subsurface pumping from ever-deeper wells, provide the Central Valley with a tremendous amount of available water. Complete integration and totally effective utilization of water supply is very difficult but has been more closely approached in this subregion than in most other irrigated areas in the world.

Agricultural Pattern of the Valley Generally speaking the crops grown in the valley are adapted to topographic, edaphic, irrigation, and drainage factors rather than to latitude. Irrigation water comes from the Sierra Nevada, so the eastern side of the valley is easier to irrigate, and consequently, it was irrigated earlier and is more productive. Extension of irrigation canals to carry pumped water to the western side of the valley is being increased. Seepage from upper level irrigation has caused alkali accumulation in the "trough" (lowest part of the valley) to such an extent that several hundred thousand acres have reverted from cultivation to grazing usage.

A traverse of the San Joaquin Valley from east to west would show the following land-use cross section:

1 nonirrigated grain (wheat and barley) and cattle pastures in the eastern foothills

2 oranges, lemons, and other frost-sensitive crops (irrigated) in the sheltered foothill basins (fig. 16–10)

3 irrigated deciduous fruits, nuts, grapes, vegetables, potatoes, and cotton on the upper slopes of the alluvial fans

fig. 16–10   Orange orchards in a sheltered cove on the eastern side of the San Joaquin Valley.

4 irrigated cotton, alfalfa, and dairy farms on the lower alluvial fan slopes

5 irrigated rice, cotton, sugar beets, and asparagus, and nonirrigated pasture in the trough (fig. 16–11)

6 irrigated cotton and grain or nonirrigated pasture and grain on the west side, with rapid increase of irrigated citrus, deciduous fruits, and vines from the new west side canal

7 poor grazing in the dry western foothills

The land-use pattern is less varied but also less predictable in the Sacramento Valley. The major differences are that vineyards, citrus, and cotton are missing, and rice and sugar beets are much more important.

Agricultural Products The leading crop and livestock products of the Central Valley are many and varied.

For some time, *cotton* has been the most valuable crop of both the subregion and the region. Hot summers, flat land, availability of irrigation water, fertile soil, and lack of rain at picking time are highly favorable to cotton growing. The output is high in both yield and quality; in most years, Central Valley cotton is sold for several cents per pound more than the government price support level.

fig. 16–11   Flooded rice fields in the lowest part of the San Joaquin Valley.

The second most valuable of California crops is *hay,* and its production is widespread in this subregion, which is almost invariably under irrigation. Alfalfa is by far the leading variety; it is grown for hay, seed, meal, and pasture, and is a principal legume for soil improvement. The long growing season allows five to eight cuttings annually.

California produces about nine-tenths of the national output of *grapes,* which rank third among the state's valuable crops (fig. 16–12). Although some valleys in Southern California and the Bay Area concentrate on vineyard production, the great majority of regional output is in the Central Valley and particularly in the San Joaquin section. Raisin, table, and wine grapes are all grown, with the greatest concentration of all three in the Fresno area. The industry's major problem in recent years has been availability and cost of labor.

Citrus fruits, almost exclusively oranges and lemons, are increasingly significant in the Central Valley owing to orchard displacement from Southern California. Lemons are mostly grown in protected "coves" along the western foothills of the Sierra Nevada, whereas oranges are much more widespread throughout the southern two-thirds of the subregion. Orange acreage has been rapidly increasing in the eastside area north of Bakersfield and in westside areas served by the new westside canal.

Vegetables are widely grown in the valley. Tomatoes are most important and rank as the fifth most valuable crop of the region (fig. 16–13). Asparagus is also notable, especially in the muck soils of the delta.

California ranks second only to North Dakota in total *barley* production, which is both dry-farmed and irrigated. Barley greatly exceeds wheat in acreage in the Cen-

fig. 16–12 California, especially the Central Valley, produces most of the nation's grapes.

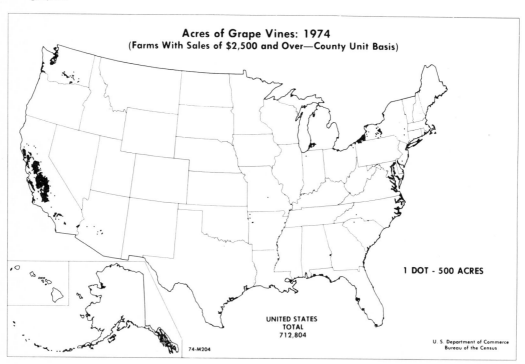

Acres of Grape Vines: 1974
(Farms With Sales of $2,500 and Over—County Unit Basis)

1 DOT - 500 ACRES

UNITED STATES
TOTAL
712,804

74-M204

U. S. Department of Commerce
Bureau of the Census

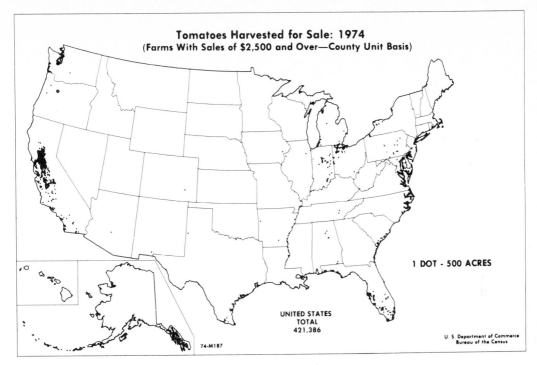

Tomatoes Harvested for Sale: 1974
(Farms With Sales of $2,500 and Over—County Unit Basis)

1 DOT - 500 ACRES

UNITED STATES
TOTAL
421,386

74-M187

U. S. Department of Commerce
Bureau of the Census

fig. 16–13 The delta area and adjacent parts
of the Sacramento and San Joaquin valleys
grow the majority of the nation's tomatoes.

tral Valley, mainly because it yields more per acre to offset the price advantage of wheat. Most of the crop is used as livestock feed, although about one-fourth of the output is malted for beer production.

California is by far the leading state in *sugar beet* output. Sugar beets are widespread, especially in the delta area and the southern portion of the Sacramento Valley.

Rice is a major crop in the Sacramento Valley and in some parts of the San Joaquin Valley. The farmers are monocultural specialists. Land preparation and harvesting are completely mechanized, and seeding and fertilization are accomplished from low-flying airplanes.

In addition to citrus, *tree crops* of various kinds are important specialties in various parts of the Central Valley. Peaches are by far the most widespread; this subregion grows more than half the national total, but most of the output is canned rather than marketed fresh. Other notable tree crops in the valley include apricots, olives, figs, almonds, and walnuts.

Livestock of various kinds are produced or fattened in abundance in the Central Valley. Beef cattle, dairy cattle, and sheep are pastured and fed on locally grown alfalfa and barley. The valley is the nation's leading area of turkey raising and one of the leaders in production of chicken eggs. Beef is actually the chief source of farm income in the subregion, and milk ranks second.

Industrialization of Agriculture The open, relatively level floor of the Central Valley and the relative scarcity of farm labor stimulate the wide employment of labor-saving machinery. Because of the climate and the kinds of crops grown, the problems are not precisely like those in other

445

agricultural areas. Californians, however, are noted for their versatility in solving peculiar crop problems through the use of special inventions.

The combined harvester-thresher was being used on the big Central Valley farms as early as the 1880s. During World War II, when field labor was particularly scarce, a number of "dirt farmers" in the Central Valley developed machinery adapted to their own special products. One farmer developed a machine for shaking walnuts off the trees. Another device is the sloping catching-frames, placed under the trees for collecting and delivering the fruit to field boxes. Vacuum and brush pickups even gather the nuts from the ground. Other contributions include a green-asparagus harvester, tomato-picking aids, a mechanical apricot-cutter, a hay-making machine that lifts hay to the wagons, a sugar-beet harvester, a hay-bale shredder, and a weed cutter. Pneumatic shears are used for pruning. Onions are harvested by machine. One machine sorts adobe lumps from beans. A mechanical sugar-beet thinner electronically zeroes in on a single plant and then activates knives that cut down any adjoining plants that are too close. More than 200 mechanical grape-harvesting machines are now being used in the valley.

Probably in no other part of Anglo-America has farming "progressed" from a way of life to an industrial enterprise to such an extent as it has in the Central Valley. The farm family is by no means a thing of the past, but increasingly it is being replaced by the farm corporation that controls huge acreages with carefully calculated large-scale efficiency. Sometimes the corporation owns its own machinery; some farms, for example, have as many as 50 mechanical cotton pickers that cost $15,000 to $30,000 each. In other instances the corporation owns nothing but the land, with the farm manager subcontracting the entire crop-growing operation: planting is done by one firm, cultivation by another, spraying by an airplane contractor, and harvesting by a crew of migratory workers.

Central Valley farming is thus a mixture of big business and agriculture. In most years, four of the six leading agricultural counties in the United States, as measured by value of farm products sold, are Central Valley counties.

CROP PROCESSING

Because harvested fruits and vegetables may rapidly deteriorate, most processing of these items tends to be done near the fields where they are grown. Consequently, the Central Valley carries on a great deal of processing of various kinds of agricultural products: cotton ginning, cotton-oil processing, flour milling, beet-sugar refining, canning and freezing of fruits and vegetables, meat packing, rice milling, almond processing, drying of raisins and other fruits, and wine making.

PETROLEUM AND NATURAL GAS

The San Joaquin Valley petroleum district, comprising more than 25 fields, was more productive in the past than it is today. There are considerable quantities of known reserves of both oil and natural gas, however, and there have been some extensions of production in recent years. Bakersfield is the headquarters of the oil industry in this subregion.

THE URBAN PATTERN

Urban places are dotted with relative uniformity over the established agricultural sections of the Central Valley. The eastern portion and the central "trough" have, therefore, a hierarchical scattering of small and large market towns. The drier western portion, where until recently agriculture has been insignificant, has a much more open urban network, and the towns are mostly associated with a crossroad location or petroleum production.

The largest city of the Central Valley, *Sacramento*, is the commercial center for the northern third of the subregion. Its commercial function is almost overshadowed by the administrative importance of being the capital of the most populous state. There is also a significant amount of manufacturing in Sacramento, particularly aerospace production.

In the San Joaquin Valley are three prominent urban centers, spaced equally apart. *Fresno,* in the center, is the largest, but *Stockton* and *Bakersfield* are of the same magnitude and rapidly growing.

the sierra nevada

From some points of view, the Sierra Nevada is the least important of the four subregions. Population is much smaller than elsewhere, and economic opportunities are fewer. Mining, logging, grazing, and recreation are the leading occupations. Of these, mining is declining in importance. Transportation is a big problem, particularly in winter.

THE NATURAL ENVIRONMENT

The Sierra Nevada is an immense mountain block 60 to 90 miles wide and 400 miles long. It was formed by a gigantic uplift that tilted the block westward. The eastern front is marked by a bold escarpment that rises 5,000 to 10,000 feet above the alluvial-filled basins of the Intermontane Region to the east; this escarpment marks one of the most definite geographical boundaries on the continent (fig. 16–14). The western slope, although more gentle, is deeply incised with river canyons and has been greatly eroded by glaciers, forming such magnificent

fig. 16–14   The abrupt eastern escarpment of the Sierra Nevada, as seen from Owens Valley. Mount Whitney is the peak in the center of the photograph.

fig. 16–15 The long western slope of the Sierra Nevada contains spectacular canyons that were carved by Pleistocene glaciers. This is Yosemite Valley.

canyons as those of the Yosemite and Tuolumne (fig. 16–15).

The summits of the Sierra Nevada have suffered severe glacial erosion and consist of a series of interlocking cirques. Complex faulting, mountain glaciation, and stream erosion account for most of the details of the mountain mass. Some of the block-faulted valleys contain lakes, the most noted of which is Lake Tahoe; smaller but often spectacularly sited lakes occupy some of the glaciated valleys.

The long western slope of the range contains many magnificent glaciated valleys in which the glacial debris was completely washed away by the subsequent meltwater and deposited in the Central Valley. On the abrupt eastern slope, however, drier conditions resulted in less ice and less melting, with the result that glacial till accumulated in great moraines and now often enclose lovely alpine lakes. The high country of the Sierra Nevada still contains some 70 glaciers, all small, including the southernmost

in North America (Palisade Glacier at 37° N.L.).

The Sierra Nevada, because of its great elevation and because it presents a formidable barrier to the rain-bearing winds from the Pacific Ocean, has its heaviest precipitation on the western slope; this flows down into the Central Valley and provides it with water for irrigation. The eastern, rainshadow side is comparatively dry. Although some rain falls during the summer, the maximum precipitation comes as snow during the winter season (fig. 16–16). The western slope receives the heaviest snowfall of any part of the United States, the average being more than 400 inches a year. Heavy snows tend to emphasize the barrier nature of the Sierra Nevada and have caused great expense to transportation lines operating across them.

Vertical zonation is the dominant feature of the vegetation pattern, but there are many variations attributable to bedrock and soil differences, to the effects of fire, and to

fig. 16–16 The Sierra Nevada is normally deeply inundated with snow every winter. Here a snow-blower clears the road in Giant Forest of Sequoia National Park.

sunny versus shady slopes. Proceeding up-slope from west to east, the Central Valley grassland extends to approximately 1,500 feet, with a mixture of oak trees scattered throughout. A mixed woodland and chaparral association—mostly oaks and pines, and prominently including the live oak—reaches to 4,000 or 5,000 feet. A mixed forest of conifers extends from about 5,000 to about 10,-000 feet; its composition varies from place to place, and there is some admixture of hardwoods and brush (especially manzanita). In general the lower portion of this forest is more open and is dominated by pines, especially ponderosa; this is also the zone that contains the giant Sequoia trees, scattered in half a hundred discrete groves spread over a horizontal distance of 225 miles. Firs, especially red and white, are dominant in the middle portions of the forest belt, and the lodgepole pine association is most prominent in the higher areas.

A subalpine forest of increasingly stunted trees, mostly high altitude conifers, occupies the zone from 10,000 to 11,000 feet. Above about 11,000 feet trees can no longer grow except as stunted stragglers in protected sites, and alpine meadows and bare rock dominate the landscape. This general pattern is repeated in abbreviated fashion on the steep eastern face of the range; however, abrupt slopes, thin soils, and lack of moisture produce a modified appearance in most areas.

THE ECONOMY

Water Water is the great resource of the subregion, but its economic impact is in the surrounding lowlands rather than in the Sierra Nevada. The significance of the west-ward-flowing rivers for irrigation in the Central Valley has already been discussed. In addition, the three major California metropolises tap Sierra Nevada water for their municipal supplies: San Fancisco uses stored Tuolumne River water from Hetch Hetchy Reservoir; the East Bay Area has reservoirs on the Mokelumne River; and Los Angeles diverts water from the Owens River and Mono Valley on the eastern slope of the Sierra. Hydroelectric generating facilities are also maintained on each of these aqueducts by the operating agency and on various Sierra Nevada streams by utility companies serving a score of California and Nevada towns and cities.

Forestry Logging and lumbering began with the development of mining. For a long time the chief uses for wood products were as mine props, railroad crossties, and construction timber for dwellings and other buildings in the mining camps. Logging operations in those days were extremely wasteful, and doubtless much more timber was destroyed through fire and careless logging methods than was actually utilized.

449

With the development of the national forests, much of the formerly cut-over and burned-over land was withdrawn from logging activities, although a large part still remains in the hands of major lumber companies. The establishment of the national forests in the Sierra Nevada was partly to reestablish forest stands for future lumbering industries but chiefly to protect the watersheds of the numerous streams that provide waters for irrigation, domestic use, and power. These national forests also serve as important recreational centers for the entire region and provide summer pastures for a large range-livestock enterprise.

Since the snows in the mountains are extremely heavy, most logging activities are confined to the summer months. When logs can be moved out of the forests they are brought to such lumber towns as McCloud and Weed, where they are converted into lumber.

The forest-products industries of the Sierra Nevada are of much importance to the subregion, but they occupy a place of lesser significance in the national scene. California is the second-ranking state in lumber production, but most of its output is from the forests in the northern part of the state.

Mining The extraction of minerals is mostly a thing of the past in the subregion. An occasional mine is still in operation, but practically no large mines are now working. The major activity of the past was in the Mother Lode gold country, on the western side of the range between Mariposa and Placerville. Throughout this section are reminders of better days, when an active mining economy dominated the subregion. Ghost and semighost towns are common, as are the remnants of mills, smelters, cyanide tanks, and tailings piles.

Grazing Cattle ranches are situated in a number of lower valleys of the range. In some cases they provide permanent grazing in grassland and woodland plant associations. Most grazing in the subregion, however, is restricted to summer transhumance.

Both cattle and sheep are brought into the high country for summer grazing, primarily under permit on national forest land.

Recreation The great extent of the Sierra Nevada; their height, deep canyons, waterfalls, fish-laden streams and lakes, forests, historical interests, good roads, and heavy winter snows at well-developed ski resorts; and the tremendous nearby urban population have made the mountains a great attraction for tourists and vacationists. In the Sierra Nevada are located three of the nation's most famous national parks: Sequoia, Kings Canyon, and Yosemite. All are noted for their magnificent groves of giant Sequoia trees, spectacular glaciated valleys, waterfalls, and wildlife. Another particularly scenic area is Lake Tahoe, which nestles in a large pocket between the double crest of the Sierra Nevada.

Most visitors to the subregion come in summer, but there is some year-round use. Hunters, primarily seeking deer, come in the fall; skiers flock to such booming centers as Squaw Valley, Lake Tahoe, and Mammoth Mountain in winter; and fishermen are attracted in late spring.

TRANSPORTATION

Transportation routes within the Sierra Nevada nearly all trend in a northeast-southwest direction, for this is the trend of the long western canyons that provide means of access. These canyon floors have relatively gentle gradients but are narrow. In many cases there is not room for both road and railroad on the same side of the stream, so that they exchange sides at the same spot. North-south transportation is virtually impossible in the main portion of the range, except by foot, horseback, ski, or snowshoe. The High Sierra is so rugged that no road crosses it between Tioga Pass (in Yosemite National Park) and Walker Pass, a distance of over 160 miles.

A few important rail lines cross the northern portion of the Sierra, as at Donner Pass, utilizing many tunnels to maintain an acceptable grade. Disruption of service by rock slides and snow avalanches, as well as by occasional furious blizzards, is to be expected every winter. There are elaborate protection devices (such as snow- and rocksheds and fences) and warning devices (such as overhead wires that give an electric signal when broken by falling rock or sliding snow).

Roads are built into the subregion only at great cost, with considerable difficulty, and with notable scarring of the land. Bridges, culverts, and tunnels are common. In many instances the valleys are so narrow that the roads must be built hundreds of feet up on the slopes.

POPULATED AREAS

Population is sparse in the Sierra Nevada, but it increases dramatically during the summer tourist season. The principal area of permanent population is the Mother Lode country, where the larger towns have an air of commercial bustle, especially in summer. The smaller towns, however, are mostly decadent and semiabandoned. There are crowded resort and tourist settlements around the shores of Lake Tahoe. The major congested area, however, is on the floor of Yosemite Valley in summer, where the transient seasonal population is almost overwhelming.

the central coast and bay area

The Central Coast subregion extends from the Transverse Ranges of Southern California northward to northern Sonoma County beyond San Francisco Bay (fig. 16–17). It is sandwiched between the Central Valley on the east and the Pacific Ocean on the west. Included within the subregion are the several parallel ranges and valleys that constitute the Coast Ranges and the only significant topographic break in the ranges, the complex of bays and rivers that focuses on San Francisco Bay.

fig. 16–17 California's Central Coast.

THE NATURAL ENVIRONMENT

The central Coast Ranges consist of three parallel groups of ranges that are strikingly linear in arrangement and are separated by longitudinal valleys of similar trend. The topography is structurally controlled, with prominent fault lines—of which the San Andreas is the most conspicuous and famous—tilted fault blocks, and some folding of the predominantly sedimentary strata (fig. 16–18). The "grain" of the topography is at a slight angle to the coastline, so most of

451

fig. 16-18 This originally straight sidewalk down a residential street in Hollister provides dramatic evidence of movement along the San Andreas Fault.

the valleys are truncated by the ocean, with a barrier bar across the mouth of the resulting bays. The nearly even crests of the ranges average 2,000 to 4,000 feet above sea level and are notable barriers to the westerly sea breezes.

The coastline is generally steep and rocky. There are few bays or other indentations. Offshore currents are strong, and the combination of rugged land and active water is spectacular.

On the whole, the subregion is characterized by mild winters with some rain, and rainless summers, with great heat in the interior while the coastal area is cooled by the sea and frequent fog. The Coast Ranges receive more moisture than the Central Valley and are somewhat cooler in summer, but since few of the summits exceed 2,000 feet in elevation, they do not get the heavy precipitation of the Sierra Nevada. Certain portions, however, such as the Santa Cruz Mountains, receive moderately heavy rainfall.

Along the coast a distinctive variation of the Central California climate exists in what is known as the Fog Belt. This area is characterized by mild winters and cool summers, with a prevalence of fog; the maximum temperature often occurs in the autumn, after the fog has disappeared. Rainfall comes largely during the winter season.

The pattern of natural vegetation is exceedingly mixed. A forest association, mostly coniferous with a conspicuous number of coastal redwoods, is prominent north of San Francisco Bay but dwindles rapidly south of the bay. An extensive oak-grassland association is dominant in drier inland sections, and chaparral is the principal cover over the remainder of the subregion.

AGRICULTURE

Environmental conditions vary so widely within the subregion that there is much agricultural specialization. Generally speaking, the lower reaches of the valleys are intensively cultivated under irrigation, whereas the upper portions of the valleys and the hill slopes are usually devoted to the raising of nonirrigated grains and to cattle and sheep ranching. The major concentrations of agriculture, as well as population, are found in the principal valleys or in bay-fringing coastal lowlands.

Santa Ynez Valley The southernmost farming area in the subregion is in the long and fairly narrow valley occupied by the Santa Ynez River, which widens toward its lower (western) end where it is called the Lompoc Valley. The area had a large farming colony dating from the 1870s, and crop patterns have changed through the years. In the irrigated Lompoc section, vegetables and flower seeds (the nation's leading producer) are principal products; cattle ranching dominates the upper portion of the valley.

452

Santa Maria Valley This "valley" is actually a deltaic plain. It is more compact in its development than the Santa Ynez Valley and has a considerably greater agricultural output, primarily vegetables, strawberries, beef, and milk.

San Luis Bay Area Around the margin of San Luis Bay are a series of gentle slopes and terraces that are partially irrigated from wells. Dairying is the principal activity, with fluid milk being shipped to both Los Angeles and San Francisco.

Salinas Valley This is a famed area of outstanding agricultural produce, both in quantity and in diversity. The lower portion of the valley, with its long growing season, adequate irrigation water, and absence of temperature extremes, produces a great variety of vegetables, especially such items as lettuce (half of the nation's summer lettuce) and artichokes and brussels sprouts (which have only a limited temperature tolerance). Lettuce is more valuable in this area than the next five leading crops combined (fig. 16–19).

The middle part of the valley is devoted to mixed farming, with many different crops as well as livestock. The upper part of the valley is essentially a grazing area, although poultry and almonds are specialties of significance, and there are extensive new plantings of wine grapes.

Pájaro Valley This small valley and the associated coastal lowland on the north side of Monterey Bay have been intensively cultivated for many decades. This area is a leading apple producer but also specializes in strawberries, brussels sprouts, and other vegetables.

Santa Clara Valley This broad lowland is the southern portion of the trough occupied by San Francisco Bay. In the same way that the Salinas Valley has been called the "Salad Bowl," the Santa Clara Valley has often been referred to as the "Fruit Bowl" because of its prodigious output of tree fruits, grapes, and strawberries. Prunes,

fig. 16–19 Harvesting lettuce in the Salinas Valley (courtesy Southern Pacific Company).

apricots, pears, and cherries are grown in profusion, and the sun-drying of prunes and apricots has long been a landscape feature in the area (fig. 16–20). In addition, considerable acreage is planted to truck crops, flowers, and walnuts; milk, eggs, and beef are also produced in quantity.

fig. 16–20 Harvesting prunes in the Santa Clara Valley.

During the last two decades there has been a rapid displacement of agriculture by the urban sprawl of San Jose and other cities. Santa Clara County is second only to Orange County in rate of growth among populous American counties; thus there is a continuing shift of farm activities from the Santa Clara Valley westward, southward, and particularly eastward into the Central Valley.

Santa Rosa Valley North of the Bay Area is the broad fertile lowland of Sonoma County, called the Santa Rosa Valley. Dairy farms occupy most of the rural land, and fluid milk for San Francisco is the principal product. The area was once known as the nation's "egg capital," but acreage devoted to poultry has significantly declined, although eggs are still second only to milk as a source of farm income. Fruits, especially prunes, apples, and grapes, are the other major products of the valley.

Napa Valley This small valley is world famous for its wines (fig. 16–21). Most of the wineries are family operations on a relatively small scale, concentrating on quality wines rather than on quantity production. Fruit growing and dairying are other activities of note in the valley.

THE URBAN SCENE

The remarkable urban metropolis that has grown up around San Francisco Bay had its antecedents in the Gold Rush period but has reached its present form and significance in association with the rapid population expansion of the last few decades. The bayside location has been an outstanding economic advantage from earliest days. As the best large natural harbor on the West Coast, it served as the nation's funnel to the Pacific, serving an extensive western hinterland but especially oriented toward first the Mother Lode Country and later the Central Valley.

San Francisco was the largest city in the western United States from the time of the gold rush until World War I and served as the dominant focus of the Bay Area metropolis until well after the Golden Gate and Oakland Bay bridges were completed in the 1930s; indeed, San Francisco is still "The

fig. 16–21 A terraced vineyard in the rolling hills of the Napa Valley, north of San Francisco (courtesy Wine Institute).

fig. 16–22 San Francisco's new skyline from the east (San Francisco Visitor Bureau photo).

City" to most people in Northern California (fig. 16–22).

Since World War II, however, the metropolitan focus has become much more diffused (fig. 16–23). The metropolis has become noncentric; the three generalized foci of development are San Francisco, the East Bay district, and San Jose, around each

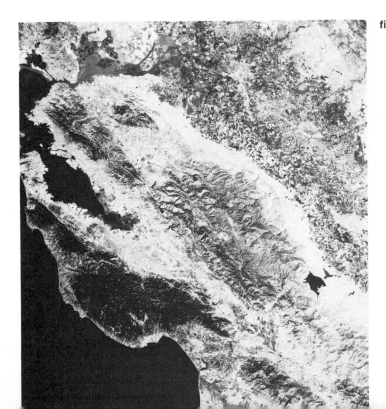

fig. 16–23 The San Francisco Bay from above. The cities of San Francisco, Oakland, San Jose, and others cluster around the margins of this huge coastal indentation. The Coast Ranges trend northwest-southeast across the scene, with the clear trace of the San Andreas Fault entering the picture from the lower right corner. In the upper right is the intensively farmed central part of the Central Valley. The dark waters of San Luis Reservoir, a major storage component of the California Water Plan, appear in the Diablo Range at lower right (Landsat image).

fig. 16–24 The Golden Gate Bridge is a famous landmark in San Francisco. It is a critical (and spectacular) element in the transportation network of the Bay Area.

of which further diffused growth has taken place.[9] The movement of workers and commuters is not predominantly from the periphery to a "core" but rather from one outlying area to another.

San Francisco itself is a place of charm and variety and usually ranks very high on lists of favorite cities for people all across the country (fig. 16-24). The beauty of its setting (sloping streets readily providing extensive bay or ocean views) combines with the unusual nature of its weather patterns (brisk breezes and the alternation of brilliant sunshine and moving fog), the rich diversity of its culture, and the cosmopolitan life style to make it one of the few cities in Anglo-America with a valid claim to urban uniqueness.

Its economic base is also unusual, primarily in the relatively limited role of man-

ufacturing (San Francisco is one of the least industrialized cities—proportional to its size—in the nation) and the heavy dependence on government employment (San Francisco is second only to Washington in number of federal employees). Further distinction is provided by a style of residential development that is different from other western cities. Most homes are packed next to one another; the tall, narrow, white, stucco row houses are set close to the street, with a tiny backyard, miniscule frontyard, and no sideyard. Population density is significantly higher in San Francisco than in any city west of Chicago.

The East Bay area consists of a number of separate but adjacent communities, with Oakland as the largest political entity. This is a very heterogenous urban complex with several important commercial cores, many affluent residential hillsides, prominent black ghettos, major port facilities (the port of Richmond greatly outranks the port of San Francisco in total tonnage because of the volume of petroleum shipments, and Oakland, the third largest container port in

[9] For a discussion of the development of the East Bay as a separate focus and the concept of a noncentric metropolis, see James E. Vance, Jr., *Geography and Urban Evolution in the San Francisco Bay Area* (Berkeley: Institute of Governmental Studies, University of California, 1964).

the world,[10] surpassed San Francisco in general cargo handling as long ago as 1965), notable counterculture complexes, and an endless horizon of middle-class subdivisions.

San Jose is the focal point of South Bay urban sprawl. This Santa Clara County area is in the midst of a phenomenally rapid transition from an agricultural and food-processing economy to one based on durable goods manufacture (San Jose has a greater share of its work force employed in factories than any other major city in the region) and related urban services. The rapid outward spread of urban sprawl has triggered much controversy with regard to both the philosophy and practicality of maintaining large green spaces around mushrooming metropolises.

Concern about urban sprawl has been only one of many catalysts that has led to innovative changes in social attitude and life style. As Southern California has been a trend setter in recent years, so the Bay Area may be destined to make a major impact on American society in the near future. In the words of one observer,

Here seems to be the most concentrated awareness of many national problems and concern for solutions or alternatives. From here has come the main impetus of the new environmental consciousness. . . . Here, certainly, is the major hearth of the "counter-culture" which has mounted a comprehensive critique of American society and markedly influenced national patterns of fashion, behavior, and attitudes. . . . Although national in scope, the impact of such movements is regionally varied, and their prominence and power in [the Bay Area] serves to set that . . . diverse metropolitan area apart from other Western regions, reinforcing earlier cultural distinctions.[11]

One of the most interesting developments in the geography of the Bay Area in recent years has been the construction of the first stage of one of the newest, most innovative, and costliest rapid-transit systems in Anglo-America. The Bay Area Rapid Transit (BART) system was designed to serve nine counties but has been reduced to three counties in actual construction (fig. 16–25).

[10] Jean Vance, "The Cities by San Francisco Bay," in *Contemporary Metropolitan America: Nineteenth Century Ports*, ed. John S. Adams (Cambridge, Mass.: Ballinger Publishing Company, 1976), p. 235.

[11] D. W. Meinig, "American Wests: Preface to a Geographical Interpretation," *Annals*, Association of American Geographers, 62 (1972), 182.

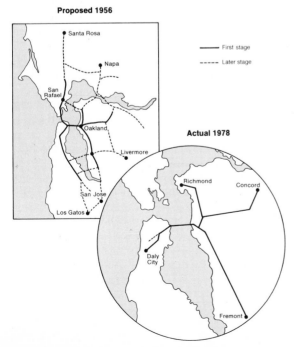

fig. 16–25 The Bay Area Rapid Transit (BART) system, as proposed and actual.

Oakland is the focus of the system, which began operation in 1972, but the eight-minute under-bay ride between Oakland and San Francisco carries the greatest number of passengers. There are three dozen stations in this first stage of the system; one-third are in San Francisco, and the remainder on the East Bay side. It is not likely that BART will solve the metropolitan transportation tangle of the Bay Area, but it is an ambitious step that has generated world-wide attention.

TOURISM

Tourism is a business of considerable importance in the subregion. San Francisco and the coast are the two areas of major attraction. San Francisco is a city of beauty and charm unexcelled in Anglo-America. Its hill-and-water site, its cosmopolitan air, and its many points of scenic and historic interest have given it an international reputation as a place to visit.

The central coast is stirringly beautiful when not fogbound and is a favorite holiday area, particularly for Californians. Principal interest focuses on the Monterey Peninsula, where spectacular scenery, marine fauna (sea lions, sea otters, water birds), and a reputation for glamour (Monterey, Carmel, Big Sur, Pebble Beach) exist in close conjunction.

the outlook

The future of this region, which includes all but the wettest and driest parts of California, seems bright. Blessed in climate—possibly the most highly publicized in the world—as well as in the bases for a thriving agriculture, and with a rich heritage in forests, minerals, and scenic attractions, California has long experienced an absolute population growth greater than any other state. In every population census since 1920 California has outstripped all other states. Even the sharp in-migration downturn of the late 1960s and early 1970s did not pro-duce a major change in this pattern; net in-migration is on the upswing again, with 1977 bringing the highest totals for any year since 1966. In fact, during the 1970–77 period California again added more population than any other state.

Year after year California ranks as the leading agricultural state, and many of its counties are in the vanguard in national standing. More and more the agriculture of this region will be devoted to the production of specialized fruit and truck crops and to dairy products. General farming will shrink to small proportions. Displacement of farmland by urban sprawl seems to be a permanent feature of the land-use pattern of the region. Pressure to subdivide farm acreage undoubtedly will intensify and expand, particularly in Southern California and the Bay Area. The Central Valley will continue to be the principal recipient of displaced agriculture, although increased irrigation and intensified farming will also be experienced in various coastal valleys. A spread of sophisticated, water-conserving irrigation techniques can be anticipated. California already contains nearly half of Anglo-America's drip irrigation acreage, primarily in tree crops, and more will undoubtedly be added. Center pivot technology, so popular in most other irrigation states, has been little adopted in California but is likely to become much more widely used in the near future. In drought years, however, overall irrigated acreage can be expected to decline, with a shift to such dry-farmed field crops as barley and wheat.

The expansive sprawl of urbanization will continue its steady march in the region. Its most conspicuous impact should be in the coastal zone between Los Angeles and San Diego, where the ambitious planned development of the huge Irvine Ranch and many lesser individual schemes will eventually result in an unbroken conurbation except for the Camp Pendleton Marine base in San Diego County. Other major growth areas will be in the hills and valleys between the San Fernando Valley and Ventura, in the desert margin of the Antelope Valley, in the Santa Clara lowland, and in the Concord–Walnut Creek area east of the Berkeley Hills.

The recent decline in the region's leading manufacturing activity, aerospace, has ended, but the industry is still heavily dependent upon government expenditures and thus has an uncertain future. Aerospace manufacturers are increasingly diversifying into consumer and commercial electronics production as a hedge against this problem.

From the broad economic viewpoint, the region has been an important trend setter for the nation, and its shift to a sequence of slower growth thus has implications for the broader national economy as well as for its own future. California has declined in economic importance relative to the rest of the nation since the mid-1960s, but it still generates about one-ninth of total national income and would be among the world's ten largest countries in personal income if it were a nation in itself.

Continued, if slowed, population growth and accompanying urban expansion are predictable, at least in the near future. In the long run, the outlook is different. There must be a limit to frantic urban expansion. Probably the potential urban and industrial water problem can be solved by desalinization of seawater; but smog, transportation difficulties, urban crowding, energy problems, and the sheer mass of humanity may combine to destroy the "California way of life" and, with it, the principal reasons for continued long-term growth.

selected bibliography

ARREOLA, DANIEL D., "The Chinese Role in Creating the Early Cultural Landscape of the Sacramento–San Joaquin Delta," *California Geographer,* 15 (1975), 1–15.

BAILEY, HARRY P., *The Climate of Southern California.* Berkeley: University of California Press, 1966.

BANHAM, REYNER, *Los Angeles: The Architecture of the Four Ecologies.* New York: Harper & Row, Publishers, 1971.

BLAND, WARREN R., "Seasonal and Spatial Patterns of Air Pollution in Los Angeles County," *Yearbook,* Association of Pacific Coast Geographers, 36 (1974), 25–34.

———, "Smog Control in Los Angeles County: A Critical Analysis of Emission Control Programs," *Professional Geographer,* 28 (1976), 283–89.

BURCHAM, L. T., "Ecological Significance of Alien Plants in California Grasslands," *Proceedings,* Association of American Geographers, 2 (1970), 36–39.

CLARK, W. A. V., "Myth and Reality in Los Angeles: The Future of a Metropolitan Area," *New Zealand Journal of Geography,* 58 (1975), 1–9.

CROWLEY, WILLIAM K., "Grapes Conquer Prunes: Vineyard and Winery Expansion in Sonoma County, California," *California Geographer,* 17 (1977), 11–24.

DASMANN, RAYMOND F., *The Destruction of California.* New York: The Macmillan Company, 1965.

DAVIS, RAYMOND, "Ravaged San Francisco Bay," *Defenders,* 50 (1975), 289–99.

DURRENBERGER, ROBERT W., ed., *California: Its People, Its Problems, Its Prospects.* Palo Alto, Calif.: National Press Books, 1971.

DURRENBERGER, ROBERT W., AND ROBERT B. JOHNSON, *California: Patterns on the Land* (5th ed.). Palo Alto, Calif.: Mayfield Publishing Co., 1976.

FELTON, E. L., *California: Many Climates.* Palo Alto, Calif.: Pacific Books, 1965.

FIELDING, GORDON J., "The Los Angeles Milkshed: A Study of the Political Factor in Agriculture," *Geographical Review,* 54 (1964), 1–12.

GREGOR, HOWARD F., "Spatial Disharmonies in California Population Growth," *Geographical Review,* 53 (1963), 100–22.

HARRIES, KEITH D., "Ethnic Variations in Los Angeles Business Patterns," *Annals,* Association of American Geographers, 61 (1971), 736–43.

HORNBECK, DAVID, "Mexican-American Land

Tenure Conflict in California," *Journal of Geography,* 75 (1976), 209–21.

LANTIS, DAVID W., ed., *California, 1970: Problems and Prospects.* Chico, Calif.: Association of American Geographers, 1970.

LANTIS, DAVID W., RODNEY STEINER, AND ARTHUR E. KARINEN, *California: Land of Contrast.* Dubuque, Iowa: Kendall/Hunt Publishing Company, 1977.

MACDIARMID, JOHN MACLEOD, "The State Water Plan and Salinity Control in the Sacramento–San Joaquin Delta of California," *Yearbook,* Association of Pacific Coast Geographers, 37 (1975), 39–54.

MASON, PETER F., "The Distribution of Air Pollution in California: A Study in Spatial Interaction," *Journal of Geography,* 73 (1974), 30–37.

MEDDERS, STANLEY, "California's Channel Islands," *National Parks and Conservation Magazine,* 49 (October 1975), 11–15.

NELSON, HOWARD J., "The Spread of an Artificial Landscape over Southern California," *Annals,* Association of American Geographers, 49 (1959), 80–100.

NELSON, HOWARD J., AND W. A. V. CLARK, *The Los Angeles Metropolitan Experience: Uniqueness, Generality, and the Goal of the Good Life.* Cambridge, Mass.: Ballinger Publishing Company, 1976.

PARSONS, JAMES J., "Corporate Farming in California," *Geographical Review,* 67 (1977), 354–57.

PIERCE, R. M., AND S. D. BRUNN, "The Classification and Regionalization of California Politics," *California Geographer,* 15 (1975), 16–24.

PRESTON, RICHARD E., "The Changing Form and Structure of the Southern California Metropolis," *California Geographer,* 12 (1971), 5–20.

PRYDE, PHILIP R., ed., *San Diego: An Introduction to the Region.* Dubuque, Iowa: Kendall/Hunt Publishing Company, 1976.

RICHARDSON, ROBERT T., "The Coming of Summer in Coastal Southern California," *Yearbook,* Association of Pacific Coast Geographers, 37 (1975), 63–76.

SCOTT, FRANK, "California Gold Mining Landscapes," *California Geographer,* 12 (1971), 38–44.

SHLEMON, ROY J., "The Quaternary Deltaic and Channel System in the Central Great Valley, California," *Annals,* Association of American Geographers, 61 (1971), 427–40.

TYNER, GERALD E., "The Historical Development of California's Herb Industry," *California Geographer,* 16 (1976), 43–52.

VANCE, JAMES E., JR., "California and the Search for the Ideal," *Annals,* Association of American Geographers, 62 (1972), 185–210.

VANCE, JEAN, "The Cities by San Francisco Bay," in *Contemporary Metropolitan America, Vol. 2, Nineteenth Century Ports,* ed. John S. Adams, pp. 217–307. Cambridge, Mass.: Ballinger Publishing Company, 1976.

VAN KAMPEN, CAROL, "From Dairy Valley to Chino: An Example of Urbanization in Southern California's Dairy Land," *California Geographer,* 17 (1977), 39–48.

VANKAT, JOHN L., "Fire and Man in Sequoia National Park," *Annals,* Association of American Geographers, 67 (1977), 17–27.

WILCOCK, D. N., B. P. BIRCH, AND L. M. CANTOR, "Changing Attitudes to Water Resource Development in California," *Geography,* 61 (1976), 127–36.

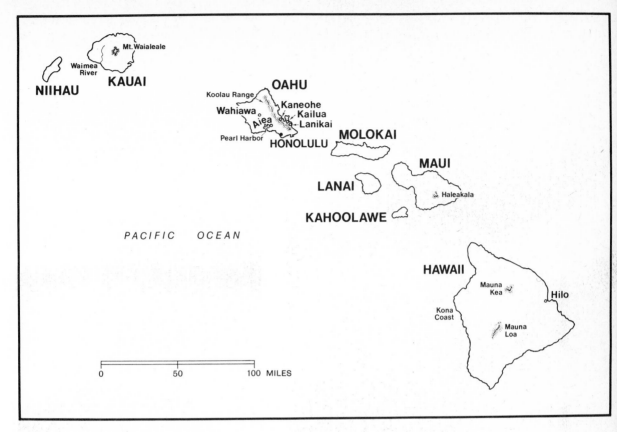

fig. 17–1　The Hawaiian Islands Region.

traordinarily massive mountain; the volume of Mauna Loa above its sea-floor base is estimated to be 125 times greater than that of California's Mount Shasta.

Vulcanism has continued to the present; there are two major active volcanoes on "the Big Island" (Hawaii) and several smaller areas of geothermal activity. Periodic lava flows are actually expanding the area of the Big Island, forming new peninsulas on the southeast coast. A single eruption of Kilauea in 1960 added 500 acres of new land to the island. Lava ejections from the northeast rift zone on Mauna Loa's flank pose a continuing potential danger for Hilo, the island's largest city. Some 24 flows have entered the present area of Hilo in the last 2,000 years,

and it is predicted that an average of one flow per century can be expected to penetrate Hilo in the future.

Coralline limestone has been uplifted in a few places to form flattish coastal plains of modest size. In addition there are submerged fringing coral reefs that partially but not completely surround most of the islands. Coral sand has frequently been washed up to form beaches in bays that are sheltered between rocky lava headlands.

SURFACE FEATURES

The islands are all dominated by slopeland, and most are distinctly mountainous. Sheer cliffs, called *pali,* and rugged, steep-sided

463

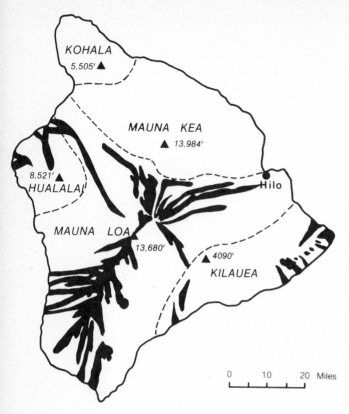

fig. 17-2   Shield volcanos of the Big Island, showing the extent of major lava flows within historic time.

fig. 17-3   The abrupt cliffs of Nuuanu Pali on the windward side of Oahu.

canyons provide the most abrupt changes in elevation. Flat land is scarce, even around the coastal fringes.

The Big Island was formed by the overlapping union of five gently sloping volcanic cones (fig. 17-2), of which Mauna Kea and Mauna Loa are the highest and most massive. None of the three northern cones has erupted in the last one and a half centuries, but both Kilauea and Mauna Loa are sporadically active; the latter is reputed to be the world's most active volcano, averaging a lava outbreak every three years. There are a few short rivers on the northern and eastern sides of the island, some of which drop into the sea as waterfalls over sheer cliffs.

Maui is composed of two volcanic complexes separated by a narrow lowland isthmus. The extinct volcano Haleakala (elevation 10,032 feet) towers over the eastern part of the island. Its gigantic eroded summit depression, which resembles a giant caldera but is not, contains several dormant cinder cones and other volcanic forms. The West Maui Mountains are much lower but are rugged.

Oahu comprises two mountain ranges separated by a rolling plain. The Waianae Mountains parallel the west coast, and the more extensive Koolau Range parallels the east coast. The Nuuanu Pali of the latter range is one of the most spectacular terrain features in Anglo-America, its sheer cliffs descending from cloud-shrouded peaks to a fertile coastal fringe (fig. 17-3). The lowland between the mountains is abruptly dissected by deeply incised, steep-sided gorges in several places, and at its southern end is the embayment of Pearl Harbor, one of the largest and finest harbors in the North Pacific. Honolulu's two conspicuous natural landmarks, Diamond Head and Punchbowl, are the stumps of extinct volcanoes.

Kauai is completely dominated by Mount Waialeale, which rises to 5,170 feet in the center of the island. Heavy rainfall results in numerous short rivers plunging coastward, often cutting deep canyons, of which Waimea Canyon is the most spectacular. The coastal fringes have little flat land, with the steep Na Pali of the northwest coast prohibiting the building of a complete circumferential roadway.

Kahoolawe, a barren hilly island with a maximum elevation of nearly 1,500 feet, is uninhabited and used only as a military firing-range target. Lanai is also hilly. The long, narrow island of Molokai consists of a rugged mountain mass on the east and a broad sandy plateau on the west. Niihau consists of a moderately high tableland in the center, with low plains at either end of the island.

CLIMATE

In its basic characteristics, the climate of the Hawaiian Islands is controlled by three factors:

1 Its subtropical location in a vast ocean accounts for generally mild equable temperatures and an abundance of available moisture.

2 The northeast trade winds blow almost continually across the islands during the summer but are less pronounced, although persistent, during the winter (fig. 17–4).

3 The terrain's height and orientation are the major determinants of temperature and rainfall variations.

The dominance of the trade winds throughout the region means that usually there are some clouds in the sky, the humidity is relatively high on the average, temperatures are mild to warm, there is some

fig. 17–4 The trade wind precipitation pattern on Oahu. Similar situations prevail on the other larger islands of Kauai, Maui, and Hawaii. (Diagram 1 from *Hawaii: A Natural History* by Sherwin Carlquist. Copyright © 1970 by Sherwin Carlquist. Used by permission of Doubleday & Company, Inc.)

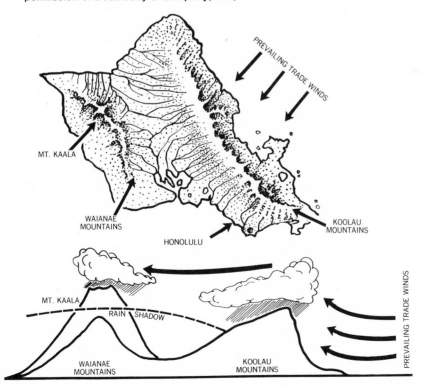

wind movement that hastens evaporation, and showers of brief duration are to be expected with some frequency.

The most striking aspect of the climate is the variation in rainfall from place to place. In general, a windward (essentially northeast in this region) location receives considerably more precipitation than does a leeward one. As moisture-laden air rises over a topographic barrier, it expands and cools and becomes incapable of retaining all the moisture it contains; rainfall results. As the same air descends the lee side of a mountain, it contracts and becomes warmer and can hold more moisture; thus rainfall is unlikely. Specifically it can be seen that the higher mountains receive most rain on the northeast flanks at moderate elevations of 2,000 to 4,000 feet, while the lower mountains receive most rain along or near the crest line.[2] This difference is the result of the movement of the onshore trades that blow *over* the lower mountains but *around* the higher ones.

This windward-leeward relationship results in extraordinary rainfall variations within short horizontal distances. A weather station on the northeast slope of Mount Waialeale on Kauai (said to be the rainiest spot on earth) records an average of 476 inches of rain annually, but 15 miles away at Kaumakani the average is only 20 inches. Variations of the same order of magnitude also occur on Oahu, Molokai, Maui, and Hawaii. Only the three small and relatively low-lying islands do not have similar situations. Within the urbanized area of Honolulu it is possible to choose a building site with a 93-inch average rainfall or one with a 25-inch average only five miles away.[3]

Temperatures are uniformly mild. Honolulu's January average of 72°F., is close to its July average of 78°F., and the highest temperature ever recorded in the city is only 88°F., in comparison with an absolute minimum of 57°F. Only in locales of great altitude do temperatures drop markedly below the mild range; for example, the Mauna peaks of the Big Island are sometimes snow-covered.

SOILS

Heavy rain and steep slopes have been the principal determinants of soil development. In general, the slopelands have only a thin cover of soil, and the flattish lands have deep soil development. Most of the mature soils are lateritic by nature, having been leached by percolating water. The average soil in agricultural areas is red in color, moderately fertile, and relatively permeable, so that irrigation is often necessary even in places of considerable rainfall.

BIOTA

The Hawaiian chain is the most remote group of high volcanic islands in the world—remote from any continent or from any other islands of appreciable size. This isolation engendered a native flora and fauna that was not only limited in variety but also exhibited many unusual characteristics. To cite but two prominent examples among many:

1 More so than in any other area in the world, many Hawaiian plant groups have developed arborescence, an evolution of growth form from small nonwoody plants into large shrubs, even trees.[4]

2 There is an exceptionally high proportion of flightless insects.

The fragility of island ecosystems is well known, and Hawaii is a classic example of this principle. More than 95 percent of the biotic species that originally were endemic to Hawaii were found nowhere else in the world; and yet within a relatively short time the vast majority was exterminated, significantly endangered, or thoroughly displaced.

[2] David I. Blumenstock, "Climate of Hawaii," *Climates of the States,* U.S. Weather Bureau Publication (Washington, D.C.: Government Printing Office, 1961), p. 8.

[3] Loyal Durand, Jr., "Hawaii," *Focus,* 9 (May 1959), 2.

[4] Sherwin Carlquist, *Hawaii: A Natural History* (Garden City, N.Y.: The Natural History Press, 1970), p. 139.

The statistics are overwhelming: "24 of the 69 species of birds known from Hawaii are extinct, and another 26 are either rare or endangered. Both native species of mammals—the hoary bat and the monk seal—are endangered, and half the native land mollusks are extinct. A partial list of endangered insects contains over 250 entries; the list of endangered plants includes 227 species."[5] This situation is mostly the result of man's carelessness or indifference and of the introduction of exotic plants and animals that have often proliferated at the expense of the native biota.

Mild temperatures and abundant precipitation provide conditions for lush vegetation. The better watered areas are noted for thick growth of tropical trees and shrubs. Most of the areas of thick forest, however, have been denuded by commercial logging or overgrazing. In areas of intermediate rainfall the flora often reflects more arid conditions, because the highly permeable volcanic soil permits water to percolate rapidly to great depths—frequently beyond the reach of plant roots. Xerophytic plants characterize such areas. The introduction of exotic plants has been particularly characteristic of this region, so that now a large proportion of the total vegetative cover represents earlier imports.

Animal life has always been limited on the islands. Native fauna was mostly restricted to insects, lizards, and birds. The most conspicuous wildlife today consists of feral livestock (livestock that has reverted to the wild). Tens of thousands of feral sheep, goats, and pigs roam the islands, and there are considerable numbers of feral cattle, dogs, and cats. These animals destroy many plants and other animals and are a major nuisance in some areas, particularly on the Big Island. But they provide an important recreational resource for sports hunting. Other exotic species, such as mouflon, axis deer, and mongoose, are also present in some profusion.

[5] Warren King, "Hawaii: Haven for Endangered Species?," *National Parks and Conservation Magazine*, 45 (October 1971), 9.

population

EARLY INHABITANTS

Little is known of the pre-Polynesian inhabitants of the Hawaiian Islands, except that they are reported to have been short in stature and peaceful by nature. Presumably they were either destroyed or assimilated by waves of Polynesian settlers, the first of which is thought to have arrived from the western Pacific between 750 and 1000 A.D. After several hundred years of isolation, there was another great Polynesian immigration in the fourteenth and fifteenth centuries, followed by a second lengthy period of insular seclusion.

These people have been known through recent history as Hawaiians and are characterized by bronze skin, large dark eyes, heavy features, and dark-brown or black hair. Although their social and community life was intricately complicated by restrictions and regulations, making a living was relatively simple. They had domesticated pigs and chickens and a variety of cultivated food plants. Fruits and a vegetables were common, but dietary staples were fish and poi (the cooked and pounded root of the taro plant).

EUROPEAN PENETRATION

The islands were officially discovered by Captain James Cook of England in 1779; however, it is thought that a Spanish captain named Gaetano had been there more than two centuries previously, and still other seafarers may have touched the islands before Cook. It is clear, nevertheless, that Cook's visit opened up the "Sandwich Islands," as he called them, to the world. Before long the islands became important bartering, trading, and refreshment stops for merchant vessels of England, France, Spain, Russia, and the United States and for whalers and pearlers of many nationalities.

British influence was strong for many years, but few colonists were attracted. Missionaries from New England arrived during the 1820s, and these dedicated people became very influential by the 1840s. Moderate but increasing numbers of United States settlers migrated to the islands during the nineteenth century.

OTHER IMMIGRANTS

Asiatics came and were brought to Hawaii in considerable numbers during the last half of the nineteenth century, usually in response to a need for cheap labor. The first Chinese were brought to work on the sugar plantations in 1852. The Japanese began to arrive in 1868, first as fishermen blown off course and later as plantation workers. In spite of restrictions, Japanese immigration greatly exceeded that from any other country. The first Filipino sugar workers came in 1906, and many more were brought in during succeeding years. Other immigrants came from Korea, Samoa, other Pacific islands, and Portugal's Atlantic islands (Azores and Cape Verde).

THE CONTEMPORARY MELTING POT

The present population of the islands is much more complex and varied than that of any other region in Anglo-America (fig. 17–5). All ethnic groups have intermarried, particularly in recent decades. Pure Hawaiians are almost nonexistent today, composing less than 1 percent of the total population. Part-Hawaiians are sixteen times as numerous. Japanese have intermarried the least with other groups; only about 15 percent of their marriages have been intermarriages.

Hawaiian society is increasingly open and has an unusual degree of social and economic mobility. Although there are visible cracks in the region's widely acclaimed racial harmony, Hawaii still stands as Anglo-America's most successful melting pot. Caucasians (called *haole*), mostly from mainland Anglo-America, have been significantly outnumbered by Japanese in the past, but in the last few years a large *haole* influx has made Caucasians the most numerous element in the region's population, nearly 30 percent of the total. The Japanese make up about 27 percent of the mix; Hawaiians and part-Hawaiians, about 18 percent; Filipinos, sparked by rapid immigration in recent years, about 10 percent; and the Chinese, about 4 percent. One out of every 10 persons currently residing in the Hawaiian Islands is an alien.

fig. 17-5 The historic pattern of ethnic change in Hawaii. The decline of the Hawaiian component and the rapid growth of the Caucasian and Asian elements are conspicuous.

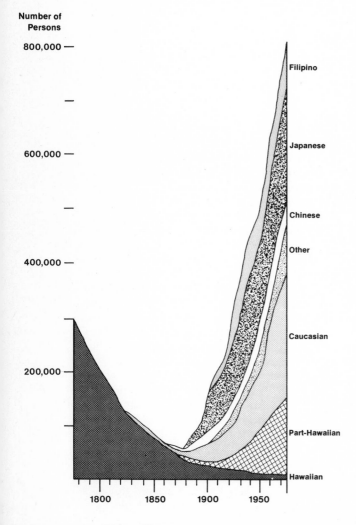

Number of Persons

centuries of political change

Throughout this region's early history the islands were politically fragmented. Various kings and chiefs ruled different islands and parts of islands with a sporadic pattern of warfare and change. The uniting of the region under one ruler was accomplished by Kamehameha I, but it required 28 years of war, diplomacy, and treachery. In 1782, he began a bloody civil war on the Big Island that lasted for nine years. Later he conquered Maui and Molokai and overwhelmed Kalanikupule's army to seize control of Oahu. The other islands came under his rule by 1810.

Six kings and a queen successively carried on the monarchy after Kamehameha's death in 1819. The first constitution was promulgated during the reign of Kamehameha III, and the kingdom became a constitutional monarchy. Most of the influential Hawaiians became increasingly interested in some sort of liaison with Britain, but a location near the United States and increased trade with California (sugar, rice, and coffee) in the 1850s and 1860s, as well as the establishment of regular mail service with San Francisco, foreshadowed the manifest destiny of annexation by the United States. The monarchy declined after 1875, and Queen Liliuokalani was deposed in 1891.

An American immigrant served as president of the interim republic until annexation was completed in 1900. For Hawaii the basic motive for annexation was to increase trade, especially in sugar; and for the United States, to secure a major Pacific naval base. In spite of much agitation for statehood, the islands remained a territory for nearly six decades. In 1959 Hawaii was admitted as the fiftieth state.

the hawaiian economy: specialized, lively, erratic

Economic opportunities have always been limited in the region because of its insular position and lack of natural resources. Although bauxite and titanium have been discovered, no mineral deposits have ever provided a significant income. Commercial fishing has been only partially successful. Logging of sandalwood was once very important and formed the basis of a thriving trade with the Orient, but the stands of sandalwood have long since been depleted. Consequently the basic economic activity of the region has nearly always been agriculture.

Although only one-tenth of the land is arable, the soil is generally productive, there is no danger of frost, and natural rainfall and abundant ground water provide sufficient moisture. The first foreign cash crop was tobacco, which flourished during the first half of the nineteenth century and then faded out. During the Gold Rush period in California, foodstuffs of various kinds were exported to the West Coast. This trade was significant to the Hawaiian economy for only about a decade and then virtually ceased. The provisioning of whalers and other ships bolstered the production of local crops from the 1820s until the 1870s, but that also declined. Eventually it became evident that the best hope for agriculture was to specialize in growing subtropical crops for the mainland market.

The growing of specialized plantation crops carried the brunt of the regional economy for a long time. Nevertheless, the role played by federal government expenditures, primarily for the construction and maintenance of military facilities, has been, until recently, the single largest component of the economy for many decades. In recent years the relative significance of agriculture has declined, and the importance of tourism has soared. The latter, however, is an inherently erratic producer of income, for it is extremely influenced by the ebbs and flows of the national economy. It is one of the first activities to show the deleterious effect of a recession, however slight, on the mainland.

SUGAR

Since the 1870s, sugar has been the leading crop of the region (fig. 17–6). Sugar cane

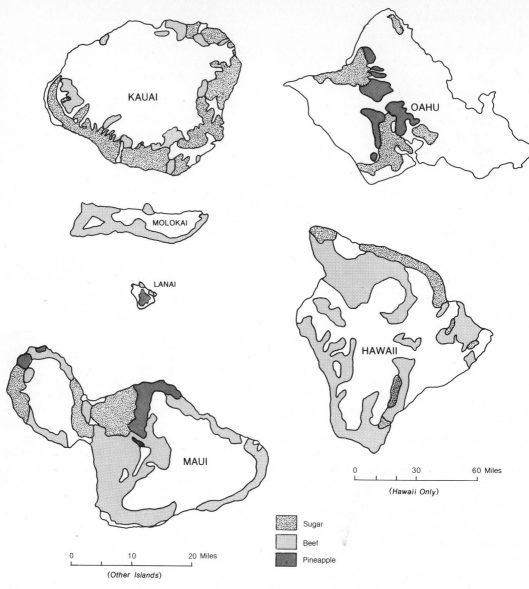

KAUAI

OAHU

MOLOKAI

LANAI

HAWAII

0   30   60 Miles

(Hawaii Only)

MAUI

Sugar

Beef

Pineapple

0   10   20 Miles

(Other Islands)

fig. 17–6 Land-use pattern of the principal islands. The prominence of sugar, beef, and pineapple is striking.

was grown in Hawaii long before the first Europeans came, but the first successful plantation was not established until 1835, on Kauai. Irrigation came into use about two decades later. The scale of operations has always been large, primarily because

of the inherited pattern of feudalistic landholdings.

There are now about two dozen large sugar ranches, or plantations, that produce some 95 percent of the crop; in addition there are about 300 small, independent pro-

fig. 17-7 Loading harvested cane on a truck for transport to a sugar mill (courtesy Hawaii Visitors Bureau).

ducers, mostly on the Big Island, who operate on a much smaller scale by contract through the plantations (fig. 17-7). Most of the refining, which is done in California, and all the marketing of the raw sugar is handled by a producers' cooperative, the California and Hawaiian Sugar Corporation.

The region ordinarily produces more than one-third of total United States sugar output. The principal cane-growing areas are on the north coast of the Big Island, in the lowland of Maui, in several places on Oahu, and around the coastal margin of Kauai. On both sugar and pineapple plantations the majority of workers today are Filipinos.

Hawaiian cane growers average three to five times the output per acre of cane farmers on the mainland. Despite these extraordinarily high yields, however, the Hawaiian sugar industry is in economic distress. Production costs are high and continually rising, and the distance to the mainland market is a major handicap.

PINEAPPLE

The pineapple presumably was introduced from Tahiti about 1800, but there was no real commercial production until about 1890. The industry became notable after Dole's development of improved varieties in 1903, and Ginaca's invention of a mechanical peeling, coring, and slicing machine 10 years later.

There are less than a dozen plantations, and their large size facilitates mechanization. After the fields have been shaped and contoured by earth-moving equipment, other machines lay spaced strips of special mulch paper that retains moisture and retards weed growth. Slips are planted on open soil alongside the paper. Spraying, fertilization, irrigation, and hormone application are accomplished by mobile equipment that swings booms 50 to 65 feet long over the field. The fruit is picked by hand and placed on boom conveyor belts that take the pines to trucks (fig. 17-8). These then distribute the fruit to the canneries.

fig. 17-8 Harvesting pineapples on Maui (courtesy Hawaii Visitors Bureau).

fig. 17-9 A small papaya plantation on rocky, volcanic soil (courtesy Hawaii Visitors Bureau).

Before World War II the region supplied about 80 percent of total world production, but strong competition from lower cost producers in the Philippines, Taiwan, and other places had reduced this proportion to only about 30 percent in the late 1970s. Two of the four islands (Kauai and Molokai) where pineapple was prominent are no longer producers, and even on Oahu and Maui pineapple acreage has declined. For a while it appeared that the region might lose the industry entirely, but the situation seems to have stabilized.

OTHER CROPS

Until recently coffee was the third most valuable crop but has been declining under the pressure of rising production costs. Almost all coffee farms are concentrated in a narrow strip along the Kona (southwest) coast of the Big Island. Most are small holdings owned and operated by farmers of Japanese ancestry.

During the last two decades several previously unimportant crops have expanded significantly. Horticultural specialties, such as potted plants, cut flowers, and lei flowers, have been notable, but particularly striking has been the rise of papaya (fig. 17-9) and macadamia nut output. The bulk of the cultivation of these specialty crops is on the Big Island.

CATTLE

Cattle are the principal domestic livestock in the region, and ranches occupy more than three-quarters of the agricultural land. Most ranches are large—one is reputed to be among the five largest in Anglo-America—and concentrate on the raising of beef cattle. Grain feeding is uncommon, and although some hay is produced, generally the animals subsist on pasturage. Nearly all the meat is consumed on the islands, but this satisfies less than one-half of the local demand for beef. Hides are exported. Cattle ranches are most notable on the Big Island but also occupy much of Maui and Molokai, and the entire island of Niihau is owned and operated as a single ranch.

FISHING

Although fish has been a major staple in the diet of the islanders since ancient times, commercial fishing rarely has been of great significance. The early Hawaiians had a professional class of fishermen; they also raised favorite varieties of food fish in ponds. Today native fishing skills have largely disappeared.

Most commercial fishing in the region is carried on by people of Japanese extraction. There are only about 600 active fishermen, and most fishing is done from Oahu, although catches are landed at all six of the larger islands. Tuna makes up about 60 percent of the total catch. Most of it is canned locally, and some Japanese tuna is also imported for packing. The other principal fish caught are scad, snapper, and marlin. Generally speaking, the fishery resource is underexploited; however, labor difficulties, competition with mainland tuna packers, and problems in catching bait fish are inhibitory factors.

The most rapidly expanding sector of and the largest source of income for the Hawaiian economy has been tourism. Beaches, climate, scenery, ceremonies, hospitality, and a trans-Pacific crossroads location are the major assets. These items are exploited by one of the most thorough and best-organized publicity efforts anywhere; the renown of a holiday in Hawaii is worldwide.

Much of the business life of the region is geared to the visitor. Companies that cater to sleeping, eating, entertainment, and transportation services are continually expanding their operations. Well over half of the tourists come from mainland United States, and nearly 40 percent are from California. Packaged tours have increased considerably and add significantly to total tourist trade. A notable recent trend has been the rapid proliferation of Japanese tourists to the islands, now almost equaling visitors from California.

Hawaii is the major stopping point for trans-Pacific passengers. The great majority of all passenger ships and planes crossing the Pacific call at Honolulu. It is unrivaled as the major terminal city within the entire Pacific Basin, excluding the marginal centers of California, Japan, and Australia. Summer is the busiest season, with June decidedly the peak month. A smaller secondary peak occurs in December and January.

The Waikiki area of Honolulu is the unquestioned center of island tourism (fig. 17–10). It contains more than half of the region's hotel rooms and is a seething hive of restaurants, elegant shops, sparkling beaches, and fashionable sunburns. Most visitors, however, also manage to see some other parts of the region. Two interisland air carriers offer frequent and convenient service among the six larger islands, and it is estimated that more than three-fourths of the visitors go to at least one other island in addition to Oahu. The volcanic features of the Big Island and the exceptional scenic beauty

fig. 17–10 Waikiki, with its 250 resort hotels and apartment hotels, is the tourist hub of Hawaii (courtesy Hawaii Visitors Bureau).

of Kauai are the principal attractions among the "outer islands." A second international airport for the region was opened in 1969 at Hilo on the Big Island, making outer island visitation even easier and more attractive.

The frantic expansion of tourism that characterized the 1960s slowed considerably during the early 1970s. More recently, however, visitation is on another pronounced upswing. The annual number of visitors to the region is now four times as large as the permanent population, and nearly one-sixth of the total comes from Japan. For all its dynamism, however, tourism is an uncertain industry.

FEDERAL GOVERNMENT EXPENDITURES

The second largest generator of wealth in the islands is the federal government. Because of the strategic value of its mid-Pacific location, Hawaii contains some of the nation's largest military bases. It is the headquarters for the U.S. Pacific Command and the administrative center for the Pacific operations of each of the three individual services.

table 17–1 Largest Urban Places of the Hawaiian Islands

name	population of principal city	population of metropolitan area
Aiea*	12,560	
Hilo	26,353	
Honolulu	324,871	704,500
Kailua*	33,783	
Kaneohe*	29,903	
Pearl City*	19,552	
Schofield Barracks City	13,516	
Wahiawa	17,598	
Waipahu*	22,798	

* A suburb of a larger city.

Approximately one out of every five members of the region's labor force, including military personnel, is employed by the federal government, mostly in military establishments. The U.S. Armed Forces annually spend more than $1 billion in the islands; however, in every year since 1975 the volume of federal nonmilitary spending has been even greater than that figure, primarily because of the vast increase in direct health, education, and welfare benefit payments.

urban primacy: a one-city region

No region in Anglo-America is so thoroughly dominated by a single city as Honolulu dominates the Hawaiian Islands (table 17–1). Not only does it contain most of the region's population—some 79 percent of the total—but also it has the great preponderance of all economic, political, and military activities.

There has been a long-continued drift of population from the outer islands in general and rural areas in particular to Honolulu. Since 1930 outer island population has been on a declining trend, which only recently has been slightly reversed. Oahu's share of the Hawaiian population total has grown from just over half in 1930 to more than four-fifths in the 1970s. Honolulu's population continues to boom, whereas other parts of the region show only irregular and sporadic growth (fig. 17–11).

Despite its exotic location, Honolulu is much like other rapidly growing Anglo-American urban areas and exhibits both the best and the worst of urban patterns and trends. There are many delightful residential areas, and a variety of parks and beaches provide almost unparalleled recreational opportunities. Transportation routes, however, are congested, and some Honolulu traffic jams would be impressive in cities twice its size. The cost of living is high, most people cannot afford to own their own homes, unregulated high-rise construction

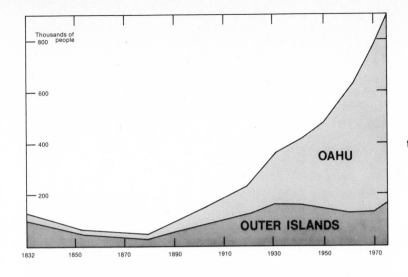

fig. 17–11 Historic population trends. The population growth of Oahu has been spectacular in recent decades, whereas the population of the outer islands has fluctuated very little through the years.

has blighted the most cherished views of Waikiki and Diamond Head,[6] and the city's

[6] Not until 1971 was a height limit restriction (350 feet) enforced for Honolulu.

raw sewage still pours undiminished into the blue Pacific. Urban sprawl is extensive, although constricted by the steep slopes of the Koolau Range (fig. 17–12). The extent of the urbanized area has rapidly spread east-

fig. 17–12 Honolulu's urban sprawl has encompassed much of the leeward coast of the island as well as jumping across the Koolau Range to occupy much of the Kaneohe lowland.

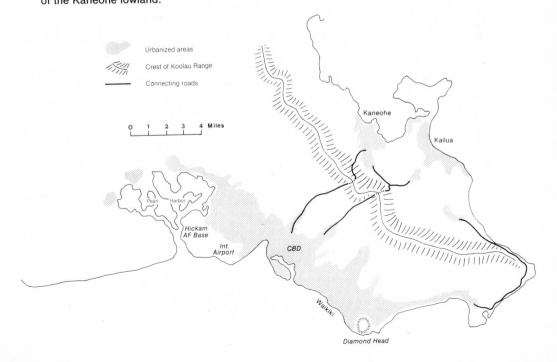

ward toward Koko Head and westward partially to surround Pearl Harbor, and has jumped the Koolau Range to encompass the shores of Kaneohe Bay on the east coast.

problems and prospects

Its unique environment and location in comparison with the mainland of the United States have helped to engender in Hawaii an unusual pattern of economic-social-political relationships that have significant effects on the geography of the region. Overshadowing all else in recent years has been the high rate of population growth (see vignette below).

DEVELOPMENT VERSUS PRESERVATION

A prominent and continually escalating controversy in the region revolves around the desirability and propriety of development. Development in the Hawaiian context mostly involves the building of resort complexes. Many of the projects are in the already supercrowded environs of Waikiki, but increasingly the emphasis is on the construction of condominium-hotel resorts, with their associated infrastructure of roads and golf courses, in remoter locations on Oahu and in the outer islands (fig. 17–13).

The number of hotel rooms in the region increased from 5,000 in 1960 to nearly

overpopulation in paradise

In 1972 the Senate of the state of Hawaii formally proposed that in-migration, from other states or from foreign countries, be limited by law. This was a clearly unconstitutional resolution, but it served as an obvious warning that the toleration of overcrowding in Hawaii was reaching its limit. Since that time a number of other measures has been introduced in both the Hawaiian Senate and House of Representatives relating to population and migration questions. In 1977, the governor of the state kicked off a campaign to amend the United States Constitution to permit a state to limit the number of new residents it accepts. These were not capricious gestures on the part of politicians; they emphasize the seriousness with which Hawaii's burgeoning population is viewed.

On the face of it, the population growth rate in the region is not overwhelming. In the decade from 1967 to 1977 Hawaii experienced an annual increase of 2.1 percent.[a] Six other states had higher rates than that. It was, however, nearly 2.5 times faster than that of the na-

tion as a whole. In 1973 the population of Hawaii reached 860,000, its highest point in history, exceeding the World War II peak although the latter was almost half composed of military personnel stationed in the islands. By 1978 the population of the region exceeded 900,000 and was growing at a rate of 2.5 percent per year. Nearly 40 percent of the increment is due to net in-migration, and more than half of that fraction consists of immigrants from foreign countries, especially the Philippines.

The burgeoning population is largely focused in Honolulu, and it is there that the unpleasantness of overcrowding has an almost smothering effect. In portions of the Ala Moana–Waikiki census tract the population density exceeds 60,000 people per square mile. Although such numbers would not be unusual on Manhattan Island or in Chicago's Loop, they represent an abrupt shattering of any image of tranquil Hawaii. And the concomitant deterioration of the quality of life shows clearly.

[a] "Population Growth in the United States and Canada," Statistical Bulletin, Metropolitan Life Insurance Co., 58 (April 1977), 7.

As the new arrival drives through the city en route to the tropical hotel beside a palm-fringed shore that he has been promised by his travel agent, he

fig. 17–13 Large new resorts line the Kaanapali coast of Maui (courtesy Hawaii Visitors Bureau).

finds himself trapped in traffic with heavy trucks and cement mixers, nauseated by gasoline fumes at every red-light intersection, beset by high-rise buildings on all sides, and generally overwhelmed by the sound and sight of construction and congestion everywhere.[b]

Vehicular congestion is a particular nuisance. Whereas the region's population has doubled in the last quarter century, the number of motor vehicles has tripled. Hawaii has fewer miles of streets than the District of Columbia, for example, but nearly twice as many cars.

Another disturbing aspect of the population increase is the escalating welfare load. Nearly 10 percent of the total population is on welfare, and welfare costs have accelerated ninefold in the most recent decade. Sample studies show that only 30 percent of the welfare cases are Hawaii-born; most represent relatively recent in-migrants. The high cost of living in Hawaii is generally unanticipated by

[b] Charles F. Gallagher, "The Finite Fiftieth State," North American Series, American Universities Field Staff, 1 (July 1973), 1.

potential immigrants, whether they are foreigners or mainlanders.

Although crowding, congestion, pollution, staggering welfare costs, and related problems are by no means restricted to Hawaii, they pose a particularly menacing situation in a region that is both insular and isolated. Hawaii has limited resources and a finite land base, but the crux of this whole complex of problems is that this region, unlike any other in Anglo-America, must face the problems alone, without feasible interaction with neighboring regions or states. A mainland region can supplement its own resources by bringing products in from elsewhere; water or gas or electricity can be obtained by pipeline or transmission line. This option, of course, is unavailable for Hawaii. Ships and planes can move goods into and people out of the region to alleviate the situation, but for Hawaii even these normal flows are greatly complicated by cost and distance.

Palliatives, such as land-use restrictions and zoning, have been instituted, but these do not get to the root of the matter. Overpopulation can only be solved by some sort of limitation on growth. Yet freedom of interstate (and international) migration is a cherished Ameri-

(Continued)

50,000 in 1978, but tourism continues to grow at an annual rate of about 12 percent; thus, the demand for more rooms and facilities appears to be unabated. Can the fragile environment of the island state withstand such pressures?

Hawaii was the first state to enact a statewide land-use plan, and many areas have local regulations that strictly control zoning, building heights, parking, landscaping, and building design. Still, it would appear that without an agonizing reappraisal of land-use plans and more regulatory safeguards, the charm of uncluttered beaches and valleys, not to mention the perpetuation of local life styles, may be dissipated or destroyed by the ambitious schemes of land developers, highway lobbies, and construction unions.

At any given time the list of major projects underway is breathtaking, for example, Boise-Cascade's "dream city" on the Big Island, the Maui Land and Pineapple Company's multimillion dollar resort at Fleming Beach, a 500-acre development near Wailuku, Sheraton's hotel-condominium complex on Molokai, Hemmeter's $80-million resort along Maui's Kannapali Beach; the roster of outer island schemes is almost endless. Meanwhile, on Waikiki practically every rooftop is the resting place for a construction crane. It is abundantly clear that the demand for more hotel rooms and second homes continues. But it is equally clear that careful planning for controlled growth was never more necessary.

LAND OWNERSHIP

One of the most unusual aspects of Hawaiian geography is the system and pattern of land ownership. Approximately 42 percent of the total land area is under government control. This is a much smaller proportion than obtains in many states west of the Mississippi, but furthermore, another 47 percent is held by a mere 70 estates, trusts, and other large owners. Less than 11 percent of the land is therefore subject to general private ownership. Many plans have been advanced, particularly by the state legislature, to enable individuals to obtain small parcels of land. As a result the number of farms is increasing and the average farm size is decreasing, both in direct opposition to the trends on the mainland. More than half of the farms in Hawaii are now less than ten acres in size.

Homesteads have proliferated on Molokai, Hawaii, and Oahu, but generally the land is in large estates. Traditionally these estates do not pass freely to heirs; instead, trusts of various kinds are set up to administer them. This has resulted in "freezing" the ownership, and the land is leased in large blocks rather than being sold. Two-thirds of the private land in the islands is owned by ten major estates. Such a situation is not inherently unsavory, but the long-range effect may prove deleterious to economic growth as well as to social and political conditions.

UNIONISM

Because of its economic dependence on two main crops and its insular location some distance from the mainland, the region is particularly susceptible to pressure exerted by organized labor. Approximately one-fourth of the labor force belongs to organized unions, the largest and most influential by far being the International Longshoremen's and Worker's Union (I.L.W.U.). This organization began its phenomenal rise to power

---

can principle that is clearly upheld by the Constitution.

Hawaii has long been noted for its activist, liberal stance on socioeconomic issues. Now, however, the authorities face the necessity of considering some very repressive and conservative approaches to population limitation. What is the best way to react to the immutable problem of overpopulation in a fragile island environment, exacerbated by the region's unique position with relation to mainland United States and, increasingly, to Asia?

during World War II, beginning with the pineapple industry and spreading to several other phases of the economy. Today it is probably the most powerful organization of any kind in the islands. In the past, the economy has been severely strained by pineapple strikes, and a shipping strike in 1949 almost throttled the region. Unbridled unionism, then, is another uncertain factor in regional prosperity.

TRANSPORTATION

Here, as for other islands far removed from the mainland, the problem of transportation is always notable. The islands depend on imports from the mainland, and the region's economy depends on exports to the world. Because the region consists of a group of islands, the physical matter of moving people and goods from one place to another within the region can be intricately complicated. Factories in Honolulu must have materials that originate on the other islands, and citizens of the outer islands need goods produced in or shipped through Honolulu.

Most tourists arrive by air, but the shipment of food and other commodities is handled by surface transport, which is slow, expensive, and subject to disruption by labor disputes, weather, and other factors. The problem of transportation is one of the immutable facts of life in the region.

the outlook

Perhaps in no other region are the hazards and the potentials so clear-cut. From an economic standpoint there is cause for concern, but there is also reason for optimism. The sugar industry is well established, but it is caught in a cost-price squeeze that portends an increasingly precarious existence. The future for pineapples has also been dark, but increased sales of fresh pineapples have provided an added dimension to its market, and problems in other producing areas may provide a time of stability in the Hawaiian industry.

Much lip service is given to agricultural diversification, but an estimated 80 percent of all foodstuffs and other raw materials consumed or processed in the islands must still be brought from the mainland, including over half the beef. Hawaii is self-sufficient in no important commodity other than sugar. Undoubtedly there will be continued expansion of beef, poultry, pork, dairy, and vegetable production, but it is questionable that such expansion can even keep up with population growth.

Hawaii's cost of living is significantly higher than that of any other state except Alaska, and the state budget is strained in many directions. The unemployment rate has been at a high level for some time, even though such occupations as garment workers and coffee harvesters are in short supply. Manufacturing in general shows some prospects for growth but primarily in fields that are not basic to the total economy, that is, those that supply goods for the Hawaiian market.

As agriculture declined in recent years, the tourist boom has taken up much of the economic slack in this resource-poor region, and it is tourism that is the brightest hope for the future. The mobility of Americans seems to know no bounds, and the appeal of the islands appears to grow with time. But as the exotic quality of Hawaii tarnishes under the increasing burden of tourists, as the relative cost of air travel is lowered, and as the lure of the South Pacific and the Far East grows, it is possible to visualize Hawaii as less of a destination and more of a way station to more distant vacation spots. The cloudiest aspect of Hawaiian tourism, however, is the simple fact that it is the first industry hurt in a recession on the mainland.

It is questionable whether government expenditures will remain at such a high level in the future. Hawaii is essentially a garrison state with an economy that is largely artificial and hence precarious. Decreased military spending in the near future is unlikely, but substantial reductions in the long run could be expected.

From a social standpoint, Hawaii has been an American showcase for racial assimilation. Continued intermarriage will probably blur individual ethnic strains into a more widespread Hawaiian blend.

The region's population should grow faster than the national average because of a relatively high birth rate and continued in-migration of people attracted by the prospect of island living. Greatly expanded urbanization is likely, particularly on Oahu, where Greater Honolulu, along with its extended suburbs of Lanikai-Kailua-Kaneohe, will spread north and south on both sides of the Koolau Range.

Hawaii's ancient motto is "The life of the land is perpetuated in righteousness." But how is it possible to preserve righteousness toward the land in a tropical island milieu that is being overwhelmed with the incessant pressures of civilization? The delicate balance between an economy dependent on boom-growth tourism and the maintenance of a pleasant environment and attractive life style to lure tourists is an almost imponderable dilemma.

selected bibliography

ARMSTRONG, R. WARWICK, ed., *Atlas of Hawaii.* Honolulu: University Press of Hawaii, 1973.

BRYAN, E. H., JR., *The Hawaiian Chain.* Honolulu: Bishop Museum Press, 1954.

CARLQUIST, SHERWIN JOHN, *Hawaii: A Natural History.* Garden City, N.Y.: Natural History Press, 1970.

EARICKSON, ROBERT J., AND BRIAN J. MURTON, "Preferred Environments and Spatial Behavior in an Area of Rural-Urban Transition: The Kona Coast," *Proceedings,* Association of American Geographers, 2 (1970), 52–55.

FOSBERG, F. R., "The Deflowering of Hawaii," *National Parks and Conservation Magazine,* 49 (October 1975), 4–10.

GAGNE, W. C., "Hawaii's Tragic Dismemberment," *Defenders,* 50 (1975), 461–70.

JUVIK, JAMES O., AND DOUGLAS J. PERRIRA, "Fog Interception on Mauna Loa, Hawaii," *Pro-

ceedings,* Association of American Geographers, 6 (1974), 22–25.

KAY, E. ALISON, ed., *A Natural History of the Hawaiian Islands: Selected Readings.* Honolulu: University of Hawaii Press, 1972.

KING, WARREN, "Hawaii—Haven for Endangered Species?" *National Parks and Conservation Magazine,* 45 (1971), 9–13.

LIN, GONG-YUH, "Secular Trends of Hawaiian Rainfall," *Proceedings,* Association of American Geographers, 8 (1976), 12–14.

MACDONALD, GORDON A., AND AGATIN T. ABBOTT, *Volcanoes in the Sea: The Geology of Hawaii.* Honolulu: University of Hawaii Press, 1970.

MCDOUGALL, HARRY, "Volcanoes of Hawaii," *Canadian Geographical Journal,* 80 (June 1970), 208–17.

THE NORTH PACIFIC COAST

18

The North Pacific Coast Region occupies the northwestern coastal fringe of Anglo-America, extending latitudinally for more than 2,000 miles from northern California to south-central Alaska (fig. 18–1). Nowhere does it reach more than 250 miles interiorward from the coast, and over most of the region its inland penetration is less than 200 miles.

The attenuated, coast-hugging shape of the region is due largely to the topographic pattern. The major mountain ranges of far western Anglo-America are oriented parallel to the coastal trend, lying directly athwart the prevailing currents of midlatitude atmospheric movements and severely restricting the longitudinal penetration of oceanic influences. The interior (eastern and northern) boundary of the region is thus approximately coincidental with the crest of the principal mountains: the Cascade Range in the conterminous states, the Coast Mountains in British Columbia, the St. Elias Mountains in the Yukon Territory, and the Wrangell and Alaska ranges in Alaska. The southern margin of the region is just north of the San Francisco Bay Area conurbation in California, and the western extremity is in the Alaska Peninsula where forest is replaced by tundra.

Such coastal proximity ensures that the influence of the sea is pervasive throughout the region, although it is somewhat subdued in such sheltered lowlands as Oregon's Willamette Valley and Vancouver Island's eastern coastal plain. Human activities and the physical environment are significantly affected by the maritime influence, which is most conspicuously reflected in climatic characteristics. Winters are unusually mild for the latitude, and summers are anomalous in their coolness.

The most memorable climatic characteristics are associated with moisture relationships. Abundant precipitation, remarkably heavy snowfalls in the mountains, high frequency of precipitation, considerable fogginess, and the widespread and relatively continuous occurrence of overcast cloudiness produce a climatic regime that, although not extreme, is exceedingly drab.

Another prominent characteristic of the North Pacific Coast Region is that its natural resources occur in limited variety but often in great quantity. In partial consequence of this, the economy of the region is not diversified but is dependent on specialties of production; furthermore, the limited resource base is a continual arena of controversy. The exploitation and development of the resources frequently involves major conflicts of interest. How to dam the rivers for hydroelectricity generation without ruining the salmon fishery? How to exploit the timber resources without despoiling the unparalleled scenery? How to develop the

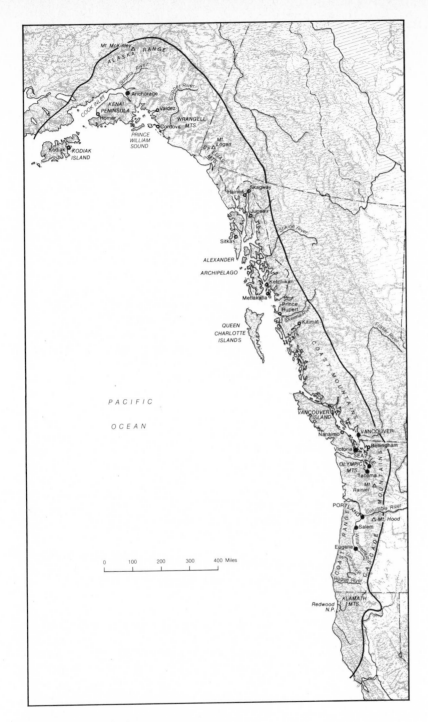

fig. 18–1 The North Pacific Coast Region
(base map copyright A. K. Lobeck;
reprinted by permission of Hammond, Inc.).

national parks for visitor convenience without destroying the wilderness?

This is a region in which the people have had to live with remoteness—which is a joy to some but despair for others. The North Pacific Coast is remote from the heartland of both nations and is separated by significant topographic barriers from all external population centers. Access to the interior is limited to a relatively few routes, and north-south connections are difficult. No railroad runs along any part of this coast, and no highway is found along most of the British Columbia and Alaska coastline. This difficulty of access and connectivity has been a significant deterrent to economic growth, resulting in high transportation costs for goods brought into the region and in one of the continent's highest cost-of-living indexes.

Another effect of remoteness has been psychological, a provincialism of attitude that rivals the more celebrated parochialism of Texans, Californians, New Englanders, French Canadians, or Southerners.[1] But this aspect of the regional character is changing as improved communications tend to smooth out regional differences throughout Anglo-America.

the terrain:
steep and spectacular

The entire region is dominated by mountains. These vary in height from the comparatively low coastal ranges of northern California, Oregon, and Washington, to the higher ranges of the Cascade Mountains with their superb volcanic peaks, and to the great alpine ranges of western Canada and Alaska surmounted by Mount McKinley (elevation 20,300 feet), the highest peak on the North American continent.

[1] A classic example of this attitude was the headline in the *Vancouver Sun* a few years ago when a severe blizzard had disabled major highways, both railway lines, and all wired communications extending east from Vancouver. The headline read, "Canada Cut Off."

The general topographical pattern consists of three very long landform complexes, northwest-southeast in trend and generally parallel to one another throughout the region. The westernmost zone comprises low mountains that become higher, more rugged, and more severely glaciated toward the north. Just to the east is the longitudinal trough that is prominent from Oregon to the Yukon. The easternmost zone consists of complex mountain masses surmounted by spectacular volcanic peaks in the south and extensive ice fields in the north.

COASTAL RANGES

The coastal ranges within the United States portion of this region are a series of somewhat distinct mountain areas. They include the Coast Ranges of northern California, the Klamath Mountains that tie these ranges to the southern Cascades, the Coast Range of Oregon and Washington, the Olympic Mountains of Washington, the Vancouver Island Mountains, the Queen Charlotte Ranges, and the mountains of the Alexander Archipelago in southeastern Alaska.

California's northern Coast Ranges have the same parallel ridge-and-valley structure as those of the central coast of the state. The topography is strongly controlled by structure, with folding and faulting dominant. Ridge crests are even, if discontinuous; slopes are generally steep.

The Klamath Mountains mass appears as a complicated and disordered complex of slopeland. It is wild and rugged country extending inland to connect with the southern part of the Cascade Range. Peaks reach to almost 9,000 feet, and much of the high country was heavily glaciated in Pleistocene time.

The Coast Range of Oregon and Washington has relatively low relief; crest lines average about 1,000 feet in elevation, with some peaks another 1,000 feet above that. North of the Columbia River the range is much more subdued. Unlike the California Coast Ranges, it is crossed by a number of prominent transverse river valleys—notably those of the Columbia, Rogue, and Umpqua rivers.

The Olympic Mountains are a massive rugged area of high relief and steep slopes. Although their highest peak (Mount Olympus) is less than 8,000 feet, heavy snowfall has given rise to more than 60 active glaciers in the range. The margins of the Olympic Mountains are abrupt and precipitous, particularly on the east side.

The Strait of Juan de Fuca, which separates the Olympic Peninsula from Vancouver Island, provides a broad passage across the coastal mountain trend. Most of Vancouver Island is composed of a complex mountain range that descends steeply to the sea on the southwestern side, where the coastline is deeply fiorded and embayed. This range, too, has been heavily glaciated and contains a number of active glaciers, although its maximum elevation is less than 7,500 feet.

The mountains of the Queen Charlotte Islands and the Alexander Archipelago are relatively low and less rugged. Farther north, the coastal mountains unite with the inland ranges in the massive and spectacular knot of the St. Elias Range.

INTERIOR TROUGH

Between the Cascades to the east and the Olympic and Coast ranges to the west lies the structural trough of the Willamette Valley and Puget Sound. The trough was formed by the sinking of this land mass at the time the Cascades were elevated. In glacial times, a large lobe of ice advanced down Puget Sound and was instrumental in shaping the basin that holds that body of water. Today the Willamette Valley is a broad alluvial plain, 15 to 30 miles wide and 125 miles long; the Puget Sound lowland is somewhat smaller in area, since a large part of it has been submerged. North of Puget Sound the structural trough persists as the Strait of Georgia and Queen Charlotte Strait, which becomes a continuous waterway (the "Inside Passage") almost to the Yukon Territory.

INLAND RANGES

The Cascade Range, extending from Lassen Peak in northern California to southern British Columbia, is divided into a southern and a northern section by the deep gorge of the Columbia River. The relief features of the southern part are predominantly volcanic in origin, with a subdued and almost plateau-like crest on which several conspicuous volcanic cones have been superimposed. From south to north, prominent peaks are Mount Lassen, most recently eruptive volcano in the conterminous states; the 14,162-foot Mount Shasta; Mount Mazama, whose caldera is now occupied by Crater Lake, the deepest body of water in Anglo-America; The Three Sisters (fig. 18–2); Mount Jefferson; and the 11,225-foot Mount Hood.

fig. 18–2 The Three Sisters are volcanic cones superimposed on the main crest of the Cascade Range. This view is from the east, with the Deschutes River in the foreground (courtesy Oregon State Highway, Travel Section).

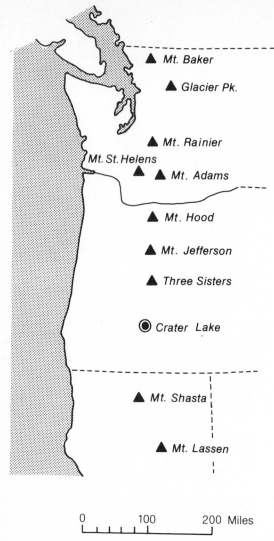

fig. 18–3 The major peaks of the Cascade Range.

Alaska) are in the north Cascades; more than 40 are on Mount Rainier alone.[2]

North of the international boundary the ranges that correspond to the Cascades are known as the Coast Mountains. They average 100 miles in width, are nearly 900 miles in length, and have been severely eroded by mountain icecaps and glaciers. Deep canyons of the Fraser, Skeena, Stikine, and Taku rivers have cut across the range, forming features similar to the Columbia Gorge. These mountains plunge directly down to the coast without a fringing lowland, where they are incised by a remarkable series of long fiords and inlets. The high country contains innumerable glaciers and some ice fields that are hundreds of square miles in extent (fig. 18–4).

Inland from the Gulf of Alaska, where Alaska, the Yukon Territory, and British Columbia come together, is the ice-and-rock wilderness of the St. Elias Mountains. This mountain fastness contains Canada's highest peak, Mount Logan (19,850 feet), as well as giving rise to the most extensive glacier on the continent, Malaspina. These are the highest coastal mountains in the world and contain more than a dozen peaks that are higher than any in the conterminous states or elsewhere in Canada (fig. 18–5).

West and northwest from the St. Elias massif the mountain trend again bifurcates. Along the coast is the long, remarkably rugged, and heavily glaciated Chugach Range, which eventually gives way to the less extensive but equally rugged Kenai Mountains. The inland ranges include the massive Wrangell Mountains and the Alaska Range, which is the continent's highest, culminating in Mount McKinley.[3] The Alaska Range is crescent-shaped, with its western extrem-

The northern Cascades are granitic rather than volcanic and are much more rocky and rugged. Surmounting the mass of the range are five prominent, old, ice-capped volcanoes: Mount Adams, Mount St. Helens, Mount Rainier, Glacier Peak, and Mount Baker (fig. 18–3). Heavy snowfall and cool summers combine to produce extensive glaciation. About half of the active glaciers in the United States (outside

[2] Glaciers have developed wholly within the forest zone in some parts of the North Cascades, a phenomenon that apparently does not occur elsewhere in the Northern Hemisphere. See Stephen F. Arno, "Glaciers in the American West," *Natural History,* 78 (1969), 86.
[3] There is a strong campaign underway to restore the old Indian name *Denali* to Mount McKinley.

fig. 18–4 There are dozens of high mountain ice fields in this region. The Juneau Ice Field, pictured here, straddles the Alaska–British Columbia border for nearly one hundred miles.

fig. 18–5 Anglo-America's most spectacular corner, the St. Elias–Malaspina area of Alaska and the Yukon Territory. The shaded areas represent glaciers and ice fields.

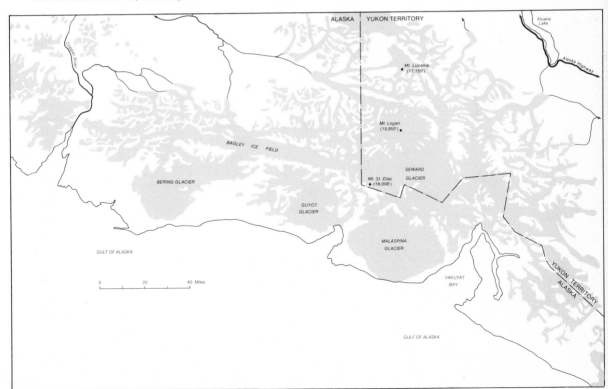

ity terminating at the base of the Alaska Peninsula. Between the Alaska Range and the Kenai Peninsula is the only extensive lowland in the northern part of the region; about half of it is occupied by the broad bay of Cook Inlet, and the remainder comprises the valleys of the Susitna and Matanuska rivers.

climate:
moist and monotonous

The North Pacific Coast Region has a temperate marine climate in which the downwind relationship with the ocean markedly ameliorates the temperature. High summer temperatures are virtually absent, and only highland localities have low winter temperatures with any frequency.

Precipitation is characteristically abundant, but this factor is sharply modified by altitude and exposure. In general there is a fairly even seasonal regime in the north but a decided winter maximum in the south. During the winter gigantic cyclonic storm systems, which migrate eastward across the Pacific basin, bring simultaneous rains for 1,000 miles north and south along this coastal region. Mountainous terrain influences the areal distribution of precipitation, southwest slopes receiving copious rainfalls and northeast sides receiving scant ones. The southwest flank of the Olympic Mountains, saturated in winter, has an average annual precipitation of 150 inches, the maximum for the conterminous United States. In contrast, the northeast side of these mountains (only 75 miles away) has an annual rainfall of 16 inches, which without the aid of irrigation is too little to support even good pastures. The northwestern corner of Vancouver Island records 250 inches annually and is considered to be the wettest spot in continental Anglo-America. Snow accumulates to great depth, especially on exposed mountain slopes; some localities experience annual snowfalls in excess of 80 feet.

Modified by the terrain, the east-west precipitation pattern falls into four easily recognizable belts:

    1 the coastal strip, with abundant rainfall and little snow

    2 the windward side of the coastal ranges, with excessive precipitation

    3 the leeward side of the coastal mountains and the interior trough, with only a moderate rainfall and sporadic snows

    4 the western slope of the Cascades in the United States and Coast Mountains in Canada, with nearly 100 inches of precipitation—mainly winter snows

The winter season is cloudy, monotonously damp, and protected from chilling continental winds by a double barrier of mountains to the east. Summer—the dry season—is characterized by mild temperatures, light surface winds, coastal fogs, and low clouds. Throughout most of the region the average number of clear days each year is less than 100; Juneau, for example, records only 45.

the world's
most magnificent forests

Except in some of the interior valleys, the heavy precipitation throughout this region makes it a land of forests. In the northern California Coast Ranges the dominant tree is the redwood, and within this area may be found some of the most magnificent forests of the world. Along the coasts of Oregon and Washington and in the Cascade Mountains the Douglas fir is dominant, constituting one of the major lumber trees of the continent (fig. 18-6). Other trees within this area are western hemlock, western red cedar, and Sitka spruce. In the Canadian section, Douglas fir is the most valuable species, followed by hemlock. In southeastern Alaska, the Sitka spruce is the leading tree. The forests of this region are almost exclusively coniferous.

A marked contrast in natural vegetation

fig. 18–6 The North Pacific Coast is a region of big trees. This mammoth Douglas fir began growing more than 1,000 years ago. It has a breast-height diameter of nearly 16 feet, reaches 210 feet into the air, and is estimated to contain 105,650 board feet of usable lumber (courtesy Crown Zellerbach Corporation).

exists between the Willamette Valley of Oregon and Puget Sound area of Washington. In the former, the barrier nature of the Coast Range tends to produce a light summer rainfall; in the latter the rainfall is slightly heavier in summer because the gaps in the Coast Range allow more rain-bearing winds to enter from the Pacific. The cooler temperature of the Puget Sound area also causes it to be somewhat more humid. As a result, the native vegetation of the Puget Sound area was a dense stand of giant Douglas fir trees with limited expanses of prairie; the Willamette Valley's original vegetative cover apparently was largely prairie grass, although some scholars believe that the original prairies were artificially generated and maintained by deliberate annual fires set by the Indians.[4] This contrast of vegetation types at the time of European contact profoundly influenced the settlement of the two areas.

Much of the region, particularly in the north, is above the treeline; in such areas alpine tundra, rock, and ice constitute the ground cover.

occupance of the region

The aboriginal inhabitants of the North Pacific Coast Region consisted of a great variety of Indian tribes: small tribes of Algonkian speakers in northern California; various Chinook groups in the Columbia River area; Salishan, Nootka, Kwakiutl, Bellacoola, and Tsimshian in British Columbia; and the redoubtable Haida and Tlingit in southeastern Alaska. From the Indian standpoint, this was a region rich in resources: salmon and other seafoods in great quantity, berries in profusion in summer, and great forests of useful trees. The Indians built impressive buildings of evergreen planks, fashioned large dugout canoes from

[4] For example, see Carl L. Johannessen et al., "The Vegetation of the Willamette Valley," *Annals*, Association of American Geographers, 61 (June 1971), 302.

the native cedars, and particularly in the north, became skilled woodcarvers—with giant totem poles as their most lasting achievements.

The Chinooks and Bellacoolas did considerable trading with the encroaching whites, but for the most part the Indians of the region had minimal effect on European penetration and settlement, with the important exception of the Tlingits in the north. The Tlingits were proud, well-organized, and resourceful, and for several decades they exerted both political and economic hegemony in the Alaska panhandle area, controlling trade between the more primitive Athabaskan Indians of the interior and the European mercantile interests. But even the Tlingits were soon swept aside in the flurry of prospecting and settlement.

Today in the southern part of the region Indians are insignificant in numbers. In north coastal British Columbia and southeastern Alaska, however, they are still relatively numerous and constitute much of the work force in fishing, canning, and forestry. Annette Island, near Ketchikan, is an Indian reservation, and the Tsimshian village of Metlakatla is probably the most prosperous Indian community in Alaska.

EARLY EXPLORATION

The voyages of Vitus Bering between 1728 and 1742 led to the advance of Russian trappers and fur traders southward along the Alaskan coast. In 1774, the Spaniard Juan Perez sailed as far north as latitude 55°. Another important voyage was that of the English Captain Cook in 1778, who explored the coast between latitudes 43° and 60°N. and further complicated the claims to this strip of coast. In 1792 a New England trading vessel reached the mouth of the Columbia River and established the fourth claim to the region. Thus, by the end of the eighteenth century Spain, Russia, Great Britain, and the United States had explored and claimed in whole or in part the Pacific Coast of North America from San Francisco Bay to western Alaska.

Permanent Spanish settlements were never established north of San Francisco Bay, but by 1800 Russia was entrenched on Baranof Island in southeastern Alaska and had its seat of colonial government at Sitka. Further settlements were made to the south,[5] but agreements were signed with the United States and Great Britain in 1824 and 1825 limiting the Russians to territory north of the 54°40' parallel. Spain abandoned its claim to all land north of the 42nd parallel. This left the Oregon country—between the Spanish settlements in California and the Russian settlements in Alaska—to the United States and Great Britain.

British claims were based partly on the voyages of Captain Cook but more on the explorations of the Hudson's Bay Company, which had sent expeditions into the area via the Saskatchewan River, the Selkirk Rockies, and the Columbia River. The claims of the United States were based primarily on the discovery of the mouth of the Columbia River by an American sea captain and later on the explorations of Lewis and Clark, who reached the coast in 1805 via an overland route.

LATER SETTLEMENTS

Spain made no further attempts at colonization in the North Pacific, and Russia was content to establish additional settlements in southeastern Alaska north of the 54°40' parallel. Great Britain and the United States, however, became active in the settlement of the disputed territory between Spanish and Russian America. Following the Lewis and Clark expedition, the American Fur Company in 1810 established a trading post at Astoria, at the mouth of the Columbia, but this settlement was seized by agents of the Hudson's Bay Company during the War of 1812. British forts on the lower Columbia dominated the area until

---

[5] In 1803 the Russians even established a settlement, Fort Ross, at the southern tip of the North Pacific Coast Region in what is now California's Sonoma County. Their agricultural efforts failed and fur trapping was soon unprofitable, so the settlement was abandoned.

1818, when an agreement was reached for joint occupance by English and American traders.

At first the only Americans who reached this far-off land were a few trappers and traders, but in the early 1830s New England colonists came overland via the Oregon Trail, and soon a mass migration began. The great trek along the Oregon Trail took place in the early 1840s. These pioneers, determined to establish a Pacific outlet for the United States, had the slogan "Fifty-four forty or fight." Most of them located in the prairie land of the Willamette Valley of Oregon, and by 1845 there were 8,000 Americans in the Oregon country. In the settlement of the "Oregon Question" in 1846, the United States got the lands south of the 49th parallel (except for Vancouver Island) and Great Britain got the land between there and Russian America. The final status of the San Juan Islands, now a part of the state of Washington, was not decided until 1872.

THE PACIFIC COAST OF CANADA

Victoria was chosen as a settlement site by the Hudson's Bay Company in 1843, but there was little activity in the British part of this region until the great Cariboo gold rush that began in 1858. Victoria prospered as the transshipment point and funnel for the British Columbia gold fields in the same way that San Francisco did for the California mining areas. In the 1850s two other settlements were founded in southwestern British Columbia: Nanaimo on Vancouver Island had the only tidewater coal field on the North American Pacific coast, and New Westminster in the lower Fraser Valley became the mainland commercial center. British Columbia joined the Canadian confederation as a province in 1871, but there was little population or economic growth until the arrival of the transcontinental railway in 1886 and the founding of Vancouver as its western terminus. Within a decade of its origin, Vancouver had surpassed Victoria as the largest city in western Canada (population 25,000).

THE TRANSFER OF ALASKA

After furs became depleted in the 1840s, the Russians began to lose interest in their far-off American possession. Although they had leased or sold some of their posts to the Hudson's Bay Company, they were loath to sell Alaska to Great Britain because of the Crimean War and therefore offered it to the United States. The purchase was made in 1867 for the sum of $7.2 million, or less than two cents per acre. Except for a few fur trappers, however, citizens of the United States showed little interest in this vast northern territory until the end of the century when gold was discovered in the Klondike district of Canada and at Nome, Alaska.

THE COMING OF THE RAILROADS

The Puget Sound country was still remote from populous centers of the continent, and until the completion of the Northern Pacific Railroad in 1883, its only outlet for bulky commodities of grain and lumber was by ship around Cape Horn. Between 1840 and 1850 a number of small sawmills were erected in the area to export lumber to the Hawaiian Islands and later to supply the mining camps of California. The Canadian Pacific Railway reached its Vancouver terminus in 1886; in 1893 the Great Northern completed its line across the mountains to Puget Sound; and some time later the Chicago, Milwaukee, St. Paul and Pacific Railroad built into the region. Meanwhile the Union Pacific established direct connection with Portland, and the Southern Pacific linked Portland with San Francisco. These rail connections made possible the exploitation of the great forest resources, which became important about the beginning of the present century and contributed also to the industrial development and urban growth of that part of the region. Not until 1914 was the other Canadian transcontinental railway, which was originally called the Grand Trunk Pacific and is now the Canadian National, completed to its terminus at Prince Rupert.

INFLUENCE
OF THE KLONDIKE GOLD RUSH

When gold was discovered in the Klondike in 1897 and at Nome in 1898, a stampede began that closely rivaled the California rush of 1849. It was a long, hard, dangerous trip; the most direct route to the Klondike field was by ship through the Inside Passage from Seattle to Dyea and later Skagway, thence over Chilkoot Pass or White Pass to the headwaters of the Yukon River, and finally by riverboat or raft about 500 miles downstream to Dawson. When gold was found in the beach sands at Nome, the trip was made entirely by ship, but in each case Seattle profited by being the nearest port having railroad connections with the rest of the United States.

ETHNIC GROUPS

Between 1900 and 1920, more than 100,000 European immigrants—Scandinavians, Germans, Finns, Swiss, and Hollanders—came to the Puget Sound area and the lower Columbia River Valley. In addition to the Europeans, an equal number of Americans of European parentage came from the immigrant colonies earlier established in the Corn Belt, the Upper Lakes States, and the northern Great Plains. Some immigrants were attracted to western Washington and Oregon by the climatic similarity of the area to northwestern Europe, but most of them migrated across the continent in search of new land and new opportunities.

Because the Willamette Valley had been previously occupied, the wave of north European migrants moved into the lowlands of western Washington. The Bellingham Plain, the Skagit Delta, and certain minor valleys west of the Cascades attracted Scandinavians, Germans, and Hollanders, noted for their dairying, poultry raising, and bulb growing. The Tillamook area of western Oregon more than a century ago attracted Swiss dairymen, who laid the basis for the most profitable cheesemaking industry in the western United States.

The fishing industry at Astoria is dominated by Finns and Norwegians, who own and operate the fleet. The Ballard district of Seattle—base of a large fishing fleet, a large mill, and most of the tug fleet—has the greatest concentration of Scandinavians in the North Pacific Coast Region. North of the Columbia River, Scandinavian groups constitute a larger percentage of the population than anywhere else in the United States except in Minnesota.

SOUTHERN ALASKA

Settlement has significantly expanded and intensified in the older centers of the region, that is, the Willamette Valley, Puget Sound lowland, lower Fraser Valley, and the Victoria area. The most spectacular relative growth in recent decades, however, has been in the Cook Inlet area of south coastal Alaska. Anchorage and its immediate hinterland, the Matanuska Valley and the Kenai Peninsula, have attracted a great many settlers from various parts of the United States. Nearly half of the people of Alaska live within 25 miles of Anchorage.

wood products industries:
big trees, big cut,
big problems

The North Pacific Coast Region, with its temperate marine climate, contains the most magnificent stand of timber in the world. The trees decrease in size from the giant redwoods of northwestern California and the large Douglas firs and western red cedars of Oregon, Washington, and British Columbia to the smaller varieties of spruce, hemlock, and fir along the coast of Alaska. Originally probably 90 percent of the region was covered by these great forests.

The Douglas fir has a greater sawtimber volume than any other tree species on the continent, the size of the individual trees and the density of the stand being exceeded only by Sequoias and redwoods. Douglas fir attains its best development in western Oregon, Washington, and British Columbia, and constitutes about half of both the sawtimber volume and cut of this region. Sawlog-size trees range in diameter from 16 to more than 100 inches, and the average per-acre volume is about 60,000 board feet. Douglas fir is marketed throughout the world, the wood being widely used for structural timbers, flooring, doors, factory lumber, piling, ties, and plywood. Western hemlock, redwood, Sitka spruce, western red cedar, and white fir are other major commercial species in the region.

The North Pacific Coast Region has long been dominant in lumber production on the continent, and in recent years its share has increased. It is also a leader in pulp and paper, plywood, particleboard, and logs for export. British Columbia, for example, with the bulk of its production in this region, normally yields more than 70 percent of all Canada's lumber output. Oregon, California, and Washington are the three leading states in lumber production, with about 19 percent, 15 percent, and 11 percent, respectively, of the national cut. Oregon also leads the nation in output of logs, plywood, and particleboard. Washington vies with Georgia as the leading pulp and paper state.

LOGGING OPERATIONS

The lumber industry of the continent has been migratory. As each timbered district was depleted, the industry was forced to move to a locality more remote from the consuming centers. When the lumber industry came from the Lakes States and later from the South to the Pacific Northwest, it moved into the last timbered frontier. Today this region and the South together produce most of the forest products of the continent. Not only does distance from market affect the industry in this region, but also the gigantic size of the trees, particularly the

fig. 18-7 Felling a big tree. The faller nears the completion of a back cut, and the tree is just beginning to fall. The plastic wedges at the left edge of the cut help tip the tree in the proper direction (courtesy Western Wood Products Association).

Douglas fir, has forced the development of many new logging methods (fig. 18-7).

Nearly all timber harvesting in this region has long been done by the clearcutting technique, in which every tree in a designated section of an area is removed but none is removed from surrounding sections until later years. A typical acreage may be divided into 70 sections, with one section being clearcut each year and immediately afforested. At the end of the seventieth year

all sections will have been cut, and the first section, now supporting a mature, even-aged stand, is ready for harvest again (fig. 18–8).

Today the logging industry is highly mechanized. Giant diesel-powered tractors or bulldozers "snake" the logs out of the forest. These are then hauled by large trucks or by rail to the sawmills or to streams where they can be floated to the mills. In British Columbia the common system of logging is the "skyline," which utilizes two strong spar trees, several hundred yards apart, with a cable fastened between them high above the ground. A traveling carriage runs along the cable, or skyline, and from it a steel cable is fastened to the logs. The logs, with one end elevated, are dragged to the head spar tree. By the use of skylines, logs can be taken from mountainous forests more cheaply than by any other method.

In remoter locations more imaginative techniques are sometimes used for log removal. Helicopter transport is increasingly popular. A long cable attached to a hovering copter is fastened to three or four big logs, and the helicopter quickly whisks them over intervening hills to a collection depot, where the logs are uncoupled while the copter hovers (fig. 18–9). In some cases tethered, helium-filled balloons give logs an airborne ride out of difficult terrain.

The majority of the timberland in the region is government owned. In the United States the Forest Service is the principal administering agency; it conducts regular timber sales and tries to cooperate with the forest products companies in coordinating the areas of operation for both efficient utili-

fig. 18–8   Forest regeneration in the Pacific Northwest. The three photos were taken from virtually the same location in 1940, 1955, and 1970. The logging camp building lower right in the first photo can be seen in the other two photos as well (courtesy Weyerhaeuser Company).

zation and sustained yield production. Similar management is carried out on both provincially and federally owned timberlands in British Columbia.

Most of the privately owned timberland in the region is either owned outright by major forest products corporations or is leased by them. Many large tracts have been organized into tree farms for perpetual forestry production.

CONSERVATION CONTROVERSIES

Despite a generally good record of forest conservation policies, the logging interests in the North Pacific Coast Region have long been the subject of attack for despoiling the environment. Much ill will is engendered by the technique of clearcutting because it is perceived differently by different people.[6]

To the forest products manufacturer, clearcutting is the cheapest and most efficient method to cut down timber and open the way for intensive new growth of certain species. To the professional forester, it is an effective tool of scientific management of a renewable resource. To the wildlifer, it creates new kinds of habitat which attract greater numbers and varieties of wildlife. To the outdoors enthusiast, it jars the serene landscape with stripped, ravaged surfaces that in some areas cause soil erosion and water pollution. To the ecologist, the single-species of tree-growth . . . that follows clearcutting can be more vulnerable to pests or fire than a diversified, multiaged forest.[7]

The principle of clearcutting is considered by most foresters as being a sound silvicultural practice in stands of big, shallow-rooted trees such as the Douglas fir (fig. 18–10); nevertheless, it is a practice that

[6] The principal disputes about clearcutting are taking place outside the North Pacific Coast Region. Prior to the 1960s there was very little clearcutting carried on in other parts of Anglo-America. The practice is now widespread, however, from Texas to Newfoundland, and in those eastern areas the arguments in its favor are much less persuasive.

[7] "Clearcutting Moves into Congress," *Conservation News*, National Wildlife Federation, 41 (1 May 1976), 10.

fig. 18–9 Logs can be airlifted by helicopters from difficult sites without the necessity of building haul roads. A suspended log can be seen at the bottom center of the photo, as it is being lowered to a collection yard (courtesy Western Wood Products Association).

fig. 18-10 This photograph of irregular clearcut areas in Cascade Mountain foothills near Olympia, Washington, shows the proper approach (courtesy Western Wood Products Association).

fig. 18-11 This clearcutting of immense proportions, far from prying eyes in the back country of central Oregon, is a questionable approach.

lends itself to abuse in many instances (fig. 18-11).

The most acrimonious forest conservation controversy in the region involves redwood logging in northwestern California. The coast redwood (*Sequoia sempervirens*) is the world's tallest tree and grows nowhere else but in California's north Coast Ranges and the Klamath Mountains. It is also the principal lumber tree of the second-ranking lumber state, and more than 80 percent of redwood stumpage is found on private land.

After years of wrangling, a Redwood National Park was finally established in the late 1960s, but it is relatively small in size and considered by many people to be an inadequate preserve. Accelerated logging also continues in the area, in part to forestall plans for expanding the park. Some of the logging is clearly handled in a responsible fashion, but there is increasing evidence that careless or hurried logging is causing unnecessary violence to the environment in many places.

The economy of the local area is heavily dependent on logging, and a cutback would undoubtedly cause short-run economic hardship. In the long run, however, it is likely that increased tourist revenue would more than offset the slump, and an outstanding natural treasure would not have been needlessly despoiled.

Another focal point of controversy is in the Alaskan panhandle, where the Forest Service is auctioning off timber stands in Tongass National Forest. Despite the guidelines under which this government agency operates, there is considerable criticism that timber harvesting is being permitted in reckless fashion, without adequate survey and planning.

FOREST-PRODUCTS INDUSTRIES

Although most of the large sawmills of the region have always been at coastal locations, in the early days of the industry there were many small sawmills on remoter, landlocked sites. As time passed the trend was to phase out the small mills and concentrate activities at ever-larger sawmills situated either on tidewater or at strategic inland locations (fig. 18–12).

A prominent pulp and paper industry has also developed in the region, particularly in recent years. Although a considerable quantity of pulp is shipped out of the region, local paper mills are consuming an increasing quantity in the manufacture of kraft paper and newsprint.

Big corporations and huge mills are characteristic of the wood products industries in this region. Vertical and horizontal integration of production facilities is commonplace. This enables many economies of scale and more efficient utilization of each log.

fig. 18–12 A huge sawmill, with its log pond, on the Olympic Peninsula of Washington.

Logs are sorted and graded at the camps and towed to the mill in which the log will be best utilized. The largest go to plywood mills, better grades of Douglas fir and hemlock to sawmills; cedar is used for shingles and siding; small diameter logs are cut into lumber at gangmills; and pulp-grade logs go either to the kraft pulp or newsprint mills. Further, the bark-free woodwaste from sawmills and plywood mills is chipped and is sent, as a raw material, by barge to the kraft pulp mills.[8]

Integration of logging, transportation, processing, and manufacturing operations is widespread in western Oregon and Washington but is most notable in the Strait of Georgia area of British Columbia, where functional interconnection in terms of both areal space and corporate organization is tightly knit.

ECONOMIC TRENDS

As one of the major income generators of the region, the forest products industry is critical to economic well-being. In the late 1960s and early 1970s the lumber industry experienced a severe slump, occasioned by a continentwide decline in housing construction. Housing provides the market for nearly half of all lumber output, and the decrease in housing demand, particularly for single-family homes, was rapidly felt in the lumber industry. Continued expansion in pulping, and particularly in plywood production, helped to soften the blow, but overall, the wood products industries of the region began the decade of the 1970s in a severe recession.

This industrywide decline would have been even more serious if it were not for the increasing role of Japanese purchases of logs, lumber, and other wood products. Japanese capital has been infused in several Canadian and Alaskan forestry enterprises, and Alaskan lumber mills now ship more than 90 percent of their output to Japan. Whether or not the Japanese market will be as significant in the future is conjectural, but its short-run impact is very favorable.

A strong resurgence of home-building in the United States in the late 1970s provided a much-needed stimulus to the forest products industries of the region. This development, however, also emphasized the precarious economic balance of this industry that is so critical to the North Pacific Coast Region.

[8] J. Lewis Robinson and W. G. Hardwick, "The Canadian Cordillera," in *Canada: a Geographical Interpretation,* ed. John Warkentin (Toronto: Methuen Publications, 1968), p. 455.

agriculture: sparse and specialized

The North Pacific Coast is still largely in timber, relatively little of the land being suited to agriculture. Dairying, the dominant farming activity of the region, accounts for a large part of the agricultural land being in pasture (fig. 18–13). Hay and oats occupy more than half of the land in crops.

Some of the more important agricultural areas that contain most of the crop land are (1) the Umpqua and Rogue River valleys of southwestern Oregon, (2) the Willamette Valley, (3) the Cowlitz and Chehalis valleys and the lowlands around Puget Sound in Washington, (4) the Bellingham Lowland, (5) the lower Fraser Valley of British Columbia, (6) southeastern Vancouver Island, and (7) the Matanuska Valley of Alaska. Of these, the Willamette Valley, having more than 2 million acres in crop lands, is by far the largest and best developed.

AGRICULTURE IN OREGON AND WASHINGTON

The older settled parts of the Willamette Valley and the Puget Sound lowlands present an agricultural picture of a mature cultural landscape such as can be found in few places in the West. The Willamette Valley has miles of fruit farms that grow prunes, cherries, berries; hop fields; fields of wheat and oats; excellent pastures; and specialized farms that produce commercial grass seeds or mint (for the oil). The Willamette Valley, occupied by farmers of the third or fourth generation on the same farms, is the old, long-settled, prosperous heart of Oregon that grows most of the fruit, berry, vegetable, and grain crops of the North Pacific Coast Region. Dairying is the principal occupation, but diversified horticultural and general farms are also common.

In the Puget Sound lowlands, where considerable land is diked or drained, are the region's best dairy and pasture lands. Market gardening is an important agricul-

fig. 18–13 A spring scene in Oregon's Hood River Valley, with Mount Hood towering above pasture and blooming pear trees (courtesy Oregon State Highway, Travel Section).

tural activity that has increased in ratio with the growth of the large urban centers. Vegetables are grown in this area for the local urban markets, but the surplus is shipped to other parts of the United States. The quick freezing of field peas has caused a marked expansion in pea acreage.

The lower flood plains and deltas of four medium-sized rivers, often collectively referred to as the Bellingham Plain, occupy most of the eastern fringe of Puget Sound north of Seattle. Dairy farming is the principal rural activity in this area, but there is a major concentration of green pea cultivation; many kinds of vegetables and various berries are also grown here.

AGRICULTURE IN BRITISH COLUMBIA

Most of the agricultural areas of British Columbia are concentrated on the flood plain and delta of the Fraser River or on southeastern Vancouver Island. In these areas general mixed farming and dairying are carried on; there are also many specialty crops such as fruits, berries, vegetables, and flowering bulbs. The leading agricultural industry of the Lower Fraser Valley is the production of whole milk for the Vancouver market. Pasture occupies the largest proportion of the farm land (fig. 18–14).

Other important agricultural activities include horticulture, especially berries; poultry and beef cattle raising (increasing); and hops. Major farm problems in the valley include small and uneconomic farm size, too little summer rain—the annual average is 70 inches, but dry summer periods often cause crops to wilt—occasional floods, and inadequate seasonal labor supply.

The southeastern lowlands of Vancouver Island contain about 50,000 acres of cultivated land. Temperatures are similar to those of the Fraser Delta, but the rainfall is considerably lower. In addition to dairying, poultry raising, and the cultivation of fruits and vegetables, this area has specialized in the growing of spring flowers such as daffodils and narcissi for the eastern Canadian

fig. 18–14   A pastoral landscape in the Fraser River Valley east of Vancouver (courtesy British Columbia Department of Travel Industry).

markets. Many of the farms are marginal, and Vancouver Island is not even self-sufficient in dairy products.

THE MATANUSKA VALLEY OF ALASKA

The Matanuska Valley, a fairly extensive and well-drained area of reasonably fertile silt-loam soils, lies at the head of Cook Inlet inland from Anchorage. Nearly two-thirds of Alaska's cropland acreage is in the valley, but this comprises less than 200 farms. Grasses, barley, and oats are the chief crops, mostly destined for dairy cattle feed. In recent years, most agricultural production has been on a declining trend, including milk, which accounts for about half of total farm income in the area. Even though more than 90 percent of Alaska's food must be brought in from elsewhere, production costs are so high and crop options are so limited that the agricultural future of the Matanuska Valley is uncertain.

the ups and downs of commercial fishing

The North Pacific Coast is one of the major fishing regions of the continent and ranks, in total catch, with the banks fisheries of the North Atlantic. The bulk of the catch comprises only a few varieties of fish, but they are taken in tremendous quantities, and the contribution of the industry to the total economy of the region is a major one. By far the most significant fishery in the region is that involving salmon (see vignette below).

Although salmon are the commercially dominant fish in North Pacific waters, large quantities of halibut, herring, albacore tuna, and bottom fish (especially cod and flounders) are also caught. In addition, a gigantic shellfish industry has developed in recent years.

Halibut, by far the most important of the other true fish and one of the standard food fishes of America, is a large deep-sea flounder that weighs up to 400 pounds. Unlike salmon, halibut live and spawn in deep waters. The eggs then rise to near the surface and drift with the currents. The small fish, when hatched, work toward the shallow waters near the shore. Halibut spawn more than once in their life cycle and do not enter fresh-water streams. They are caught in deep water either with baited hooks or by power-trawling. After many years of declining halibut catches, this American-Canadian fishery was strictly regulated on a quota basis and has been stabilized at a productive level. In an average year a little more than half the catch is from British Columbia waters, and most of the remainder from Alaskan waters.

Although oysters, crabs, and other shellfish had been taken commercially for a long time in regional waters, only in the last two decades has an outstanding shellfishery de-

the saga of the salmon

The Pacific salmon is the second ranking commercial fish in Anglo-America. In terms of value it is the leader in Canada and ranks second only to shrimp in the United States. It is by far the most important fish caught in Alaska, the leading fishing state, and British Columbia, the leading fishing province.

Because of its remarkable life cycle, vast numbers, and susceptibility to entrapment and depletion, it is both a major resource of the region and a focal point of controversy and dispute. There are five species of Pacific salmon: chinook (*Oncorhynchus tshawytscha*), coho (*O. kisutch*), sockeye (*O. nerka*), pink (*O. gorbuscha*), and chum (*O. keta*). All five species are anadromous, that is, they spend most of their life in the ocean but migrate up freshwater streams to spawn. Only a few weeks or months

veloped. This was stimulated primarily by greatly increased catches of king crabs in the Gulf of Alaska. These demersal giants weigh up to 25 pounds and may have a "claw spread" of 6 feet. They are caught in baited crab pots or taken by trawling; packaging is accomplished at tidewater plants in Alaska (particularly at Kodiak), British Columbia, and Washington, and the frozen packages are marketed mostly in the eastern United States. After a drastic decline—apparently due to overfishing—in the late 1960s, the king crab fishery seemed to stabilize as one of the most productive on the continent (fig. 18–15).

Other varieties of shellfish have also been taken in increasing numbers in North Pacific coastal waters in recent years. Most notable have been Dungeness crabs off California and Oregon and snow crabs in Alaskan waters. Also outstanding has been the growth of the Alaskan shrimp fishery, which now is larger than that of either Louisiana or Texas.

power generation

Because of the mountainous terrain and heavy rainfall, the region has one of the greatest hydroelectric potentials of any part of Anglo-America. Some of the potential was developed early; Victoria, for example, had electric street lights in 1882, just one year after Edison's developments in New

fig. 18–15 Unloading king crabs at Kodiak (courtesy Alaska Travel Division).

after being hatched, salmon fingerlings swim downstream to the sea. They spend from one to five years in salt water before returning to their place of birth (up the same river, the same tributary, and the same creek) to spawn. After the female lays eggs in the stream gravel and the male fertilizes them, the adults die.

During the time they are in the ocean, salmon must face the normal hazards of the sea and a modest pressure from oceangoing fishermen. It is only after the spawning instinct begins to govern their behavior that they cluster in immense numbers and become liable to almost total entrapment. As salmon congregate in estuaries and bays at the mouths of rivers and particularly as they begin to move upstream in singleminded response to the urge to propagate, it is relatively easy to capture entire

(Continued)

York, and a commercial hydroelectric power plant in 1895, two years after the first such plant at Niagara Falls.[9] Some large facilities were established to provide power to the Trail smelter shortly after the turn of the century, but Grand Coulee and Bonneville dams were the first major projects on the United States side of the border.

Most of the major power-generating facilities are in association with dams situated to the east of the North Pacific Coast Region, particularly on the Columbia River and some of its tributaries. In addition, the continent's largest atomic-generating plant

[9] Ibid., p.459.

---

runs by the use of nets, seines, and fishtraps.

In addition to the potential for overfishing, the concentration of migrating fish (both adults moving upstream and fingerlings going downstream) in rivers opens the danger of severe depletion owing to damming. Although mature salmon are incredibly persistent and tenacious in swimming up rapids and jumping over small obstructions in rushing streams, it requires only the smallest of dams to totally prohibit their upstream progress. In most cases where dams have been built on salmon rivers, fish ladders or other kinds of artificial passageways have been constructed at great cost to enable the migrating fish to bypass the dams (fig. 18-a). Such schemes are sometimes very successful but not always.

Damming on the Columbia River, the principal salmon river in the conterminous states, has a continuing adverse effect. Fish ladders permit salmon to pass around low dams like the Bonneville, but high dams, such as Grand Coulee, are apparently impassable. Even more serious is the staggering mortality rate among fingerlings, which must either cascade over the spillways or be sucked through the turbines as they move downstream to the sea. There are now eleven major dams on the Columbia River; it has only a single 50-mile stretch of free-flowing water in its entire 750-mile length between the Canadian border and the Pacific Ocean. More than half of the natural spawning area of the Columbia Basin has been denied to anadromous fish by dams on the Columbia and its tributaries (fig. 18-b).

fig. 18-a A fish ladder to Bonneville Dam. This ladder is more than 1,300-feet long and allows salmon and other fish to bypass the dam by jumping from pool to pool, each pool being about one foot higher than the one before. The dam is shown in the background, with the Columbia River boiling up through outlets (courtesy Oregon State Highway, Travel Section).

The conflict of interests between advocates of hydroelectricity generation and salmon fishermen is probably the principal long-term cause of disharmony in the region. It is becoming increasingly clear that the two resources are virtually incompatible and that one can be developed only at the expense of the other. In the United States, the dam builders seem to have the upper hand; in Canada, the fishermen are more in control. Further conflict on both sides of the border is assured in the future.

is adjacent to the Columbia at Hanford, Washington. The availability of "firm" power has been greatly enhanced by the Columbia River Treaty, whereby water stored behind Canadian dams can be released at low water periods and thus diminish seasonal fluctuations in stream flow and power generation.

The principal markets for Columbia Basin power have been the large cities of Washington and Oregon, and major aluminum factories, most of which are in the North Pacific Coast Region. The rapid recent increase in generation capacity has led to a search for new markets and the establishment of intertie facilities that link the

Regardless of damming controversies and such problems as those caused by stream pollution, the saga of the salmon represents one of the most blatant examples of fishery mismanagement imaginable. Here is one of the most valuable fishery resources in the world, a resource that can be exploited at relatively low cost, that readily lends itself to sustained yield management, and that has a strong market demand that can be translated into high prices for the product. In rational economic terms, this should lead to a stable and prosperous fishing industry. What has happened, however, is just the opposite: the history of the salmon industry consists of alternations of sporadic bursts of expansive prosperity and long, dragging periods of economic hardship.[a]

The resource is not constrained by property rights, and almost anyone can become a commercial salmon fisherman with a moderate investment in equipment and licenses. As a result the fishery has mostly consisted of a frantic scramble to take fish quickly before someone else takes them. Although increasingly complex fishing regulations were introduced in both Canada and the United States, they were planned primarily to ensure sufficient escapement so that the salmon stocks could be maintained; to accomplish this most regulations were specifically designed to reduce the efficiency of vessels and gear, which had some biological merit but was economically disastrous.

[a] James A. Crutchfield, "The Fishery: Economic Maximization," in *Pacific Salmon: Management for People*, Western Geographical Series, Vol. 13, ed. Derek V. Ellis (Victoria: Department of Geography, University of Victoria, 1977), p. 5.

This has resulted in wasteful duplication of capital and labor in an industry that was already overdeveloped. Moreover, the total take of salmon has been declining. In the late 1970s,

(Continued)

fig. 18-b Major streams of the Columbia Basin that are inaccessible to salmon due to dams. (After Ed Chaney, "Too much for the Columbia River Salmon," *National Wildlife*, 8 [April–May 1970], 20).

electric systems of 11 western states in the largest electrical-transmission program ever undertaken in the United States.[10] Thus, the circular cycle continues: build more dams to supply more power and then seek new markets requiring more power that call for more dams, and so on.

the limited benefits of mining

Until the discovery of gold in the Klondike and in the beach sands at Nome—both areas outside this region—little interest was shown in minerals because the mountains of the North Pacific Coast seemed poor in metallic wealth and the dense vegetation discouraged systematic exploration. Even as late as 1880, some years after the United States purchased Alaska, the annual gold production of that territory amounted to only $20,000.

[10] Yvonne Levy, "Aluminum: Past and Future," *Monthly Review Supplement,* Federal Reserve Bank of San Francisco (1971), p. 45.

Various discoveries of gold, silver, lead, and copper have led to moderate flurries of mining activity in southern Alaska in the past, but practically all the operations are of historical interest only. Even the huge gold mine at Juneau, with its nearly 100 miles of tunnels and shafts and said to be the world's largest low-grade gold mine, has been shut down for three decades. Considerable prospecting, especially for copper, continues in southeastern Alaska.

In the Canadian portion of the region there is moderate but increasing production of iron ore and copper as well as some gold, silver, and coal. The largest mines are on Vancouver Island, but there are also some in the Queen Charlottes and on Texada Island. Most of the output from all the mines is exported to Japan, and Japanese capital is behind much of the recent development.

alaska's "other" petroleum

Most of the attention, excitement, and controversy of Alaskan petroleum development has been focused on the North Slope pro-

---

the salmon catch in North Pacific coastal waters was less than half what it was in the peak years earlier in this century.

More enlightened approaches to management have been followed in recent years, and there are indications that it may be possible to have both biological and economic stability in the salmon fishery. Starting in 1968, Canada led the way with an innovative change in management strategy that phased in a program of both limiting and reducing the number of licensed fishermen and boats in the industry. Alaska, with a more complex situation, followed suit in 1973. More recently Washington has adopted a similar, but less comprehensive, program. There are still many burdensome regulations that restrict the efficiency of the fishermen, for maintenance of a sustained yield

resource must still be the keystone to any management program. Nevertheless, at least a start has been made at balancing harvesting capabilities with resource productivity.

Still another scheme has been introduced in British Columbia that may have far-reaching effects. It is a federal program of "Salmonid Enhancement," introduced in 1975 with the long-range goal of restoring Pacific salmon to their nineteenth-century levels of abundance. Principal emphasis is planned in environmental engineering, with a focus on construction of spawning channels, hatcheries, and fishways. Such things have been done, on a piecemeal basis, in both Canada and the United States in the past. It is hoped that the integrated nature of this program will produce both more salmon in the waters and more income for fishermen.

ducing area and the pipeline corridor, which are largely outside the North Pacific Coast Region. Within the region, however, are two other areas of petroleum interest.

Alaska's first commercial oil field was brought into production in 1957 on the Kenai Peninsula. Output of both oil and gas increased continually until the 1970s, when it leveled off at about 75 million barrels; slowly declining output is expected in the future. Much of the production is actually from beneath the waters of Cook Inlet, where high tides and frequent ice make drilling both difficult and costly. Each of the permanent drilling platforms in Cook Inlet—of which there are about 20—cost some $15 million to construct, a figure amounting to twice the original purchase price of Alaska. Within just over a decade Alaska became the seventh-ranking state in petroleum production.

Major oil companies have recently expressed tangible interest in developing offshore oil fields in the Gulf of Alaska by paying nearly $600 million in 1976 to buy the first offshore leases (southwest of Yakutat) that were offered for sale. The area of these initial leases is considered by petroleum experts to be the most promising Anglo-American offshore location still unexploited. Exploitation, however, will be far from easy. The waters of the Gulf are tumultuous at best and supremely hazardous during frequent winter storms. Moreover, these coastal waters are some of the most biologically prolific in the world, and the potential environmental damage from oil spills or leaks is a major point of contention. Industry spokesmen assert, however, that they possess the technology to operate safely and effectively in the Gulf. Time will tell.

urbanism: major nodes and scattered pockets

Most residents of the North Pacific Coast Region—even the Alaskan portion—are

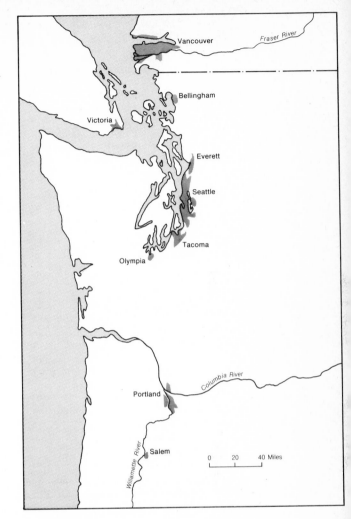

fig. 18-16   Metropolitan complexes of the Pacific Northwest.

urban dwellers. There are five prominent metropolitan nodes and a number of smaller cities and towns, many of which exist in relative isolation (fig. 18–16 and table 18–1). An interesting feature of this region is the relatively high population density on the Canadian side of the border, in contrast with that on the United States side (fig. 18–17).

505

table 18-1 Largest Urban Places of the North Pacific Coast Region

name	population of principal city	population of metropolitan area
Anchorage, Alaska	161,018	254,700
Bellevue, Wash.*	65,365	
Bellingham, Wash.	41,789	
Bremerton, Wash.	37,206	
Corvallis, Oreg.	38,502	
Eugene, Oreg.	92,451	241,200
Everett, Wash.	48,371	
Medford, Oreg.	32,577	
Nanaimo, B.C.	39,655	
New Westminster, B.C.*	37,171	
North Vancouver, B.C.*	31,207	
Portland, Oreg.	356,732	1,081,900
Salem, Oreg.	78,168	207,100
Seattle, Wash.	487,091	1,411,700
Springfield, Oreg.*	33,432	
Tacoma, Wash.	151,267	409,800
Vancouver, B.C.	396,563	1,135,774
Vancouver, Wash.	47,742	
Victoria, B.C.	60,407	212,466

* A suburb of a larger city.

BURGEONING METROPOLITAN CENTERS

With a metropolitan area population exceeding 1 million, *Portland* is the dominant commercial center of the lower Columbia and Willamette valleys. The city's dual harbor facilities, part on the Willamette River and part on the Columbia, are among the most modern in the nation. Bolstered by the transshipment of grain and ores that are barged down the Columbia, Portland's ocean freight business is approximately equal to that of Seattle. Wood products and food processing dominate the industrial structure.

Seattle is the focus of a highly urbanized zone that fronts the eastern shore of Puget Sound from Bellingham and Everett on the north to Tacoma and Olympia on the south. Seattle itself is located on a hilly isthmus between the sound and Lake Washington, which gives it a constricted central area in contrast to the sprawling suburbs to the north and south. The deep and well-protected harbor requires no dredging, and Seattle has long been a major Pacific-oriented port as well as the principal gateway to Alaska.

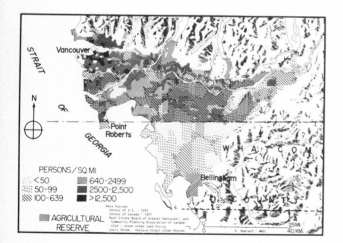

fig. 18-17 Urban pressures at the international border. The relatively high population density on the Canadian side of the border contrasts markedly with the density on the United States side. As a result, there is heavy Canadian investment in land in Washington's Whatcom County, for second homes and recreational purposes. (From Gerard F. Rutan, "The Ugly Canadian: Canadian Purchase and Ownership of Land in Whatcom County, Washington," *The Social Science Journal*, 14 [January 1977], 8. Reprinted by permission.)

fig. 18-18 The Boeing facility that manufactures 747s at Everett, north of Seattle (courtesy The Boeing Company).

Since the 1920s the Boeing Company has been the mainstay of the city's economy, although its employment has fluctuated wildly with defense contracts, ranging between 50,000 and 100,000 over the past decade (fig. 18–18). Wood products and shipbuilding are other major industries in the metropolis. The population of the extended metropolitan area approximates 2 million.

Vancouver overcame its early rivalry with Victoria for economic dominance of British Columbia and has grown to become Canada's second-ranking port, although the tardy development of container facilities caused the loss of considerable business to Seattle (a major container-handling port) during the late 1960s and early 1970s. As the principal western terminus of Canada's transcontinental transport routes, it is clearly the primate city of western Canada as well as the nation's fourth largest industrial center (fig. 18–19). The recent development at Roberts Bank, 25 miles to the south, of a bulk products superport that is primarily for exporting coal and ores to Japan has added to the city's urban primacy.

fig. 18-19 Looking north over Vancouver, showing portions of the central business district and harbor, as well as North Vancouver and Grouse Mountain (courtesy British Columbia Department of Travel Industry).

fig. 18–20 The British Columbia Parliament Building abuts the inner harbor of Victoria (courtesy British Columbia Department of Travel Industry).

fig. 18–21 Alaska panhandle urbanism.

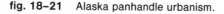

Victoria, British Columbia's capital, is the second largest city in the province. It is perhaps the continent's most attractive city and experiences Canada's mildest climate, which makes it a major goal for tourists and retired people (fig. 18–20).

Anchorage is by far the largest city in Alaska, with about one-third of the state's population and nearly half of its employed workers. It has been the dominant growth center for both population and economic activity in the state. Despite oil to the south, farming to the north, and its role as an international air-transport hub, the city's economy is primarily dependent on government, especially military, activities.

URBANIZATION IN ISOLATION: THE CASE OF THE ALASKA PANHANDLE

In the long stretch of coastland between Vancouver and Anchorage, most urban places are isolated and remote. Only the dual towns of *Prince Rupert* and *Kitimat,* on the north coast of British Columbia, have useful surface transport connections with the rest of the continent; the former is a railway terminus and fishing port, and the latter is one of the world's largest aluminum refining localities.

In the Alaska panhandle are seven small urban centers that exist in remarkable isolation in an area of magnificent scenery and persistent rain (fig. 18–21). Only the two northernmost, *Haines* and *Skagway,* have land transport connections with the rest of the world; the other five, *Ketchikan, Wrangell, Petersburg, Juneau* (fig. 18–22), and *Sitka,* are all situated either on islands or on mountain-girt peninsulas; yet the narrow streets of these hilly towns are crowded with autos. All have highly specialized economies, mostly oriented toward commercial fishing or forestry. In recent years their accessibility has been greatly enhanced by the establishment of the Alaska Marine Highway System, an efficient and frequent ferry service connecting the panhandle towns with Prince Rupert, Vancouver, and Seattle.

fig. 18–22   Juneau is nestled at the foot of the mountain front on the shore of Gastineau Channel. A bridge connects Juneau with the town of Douglas on Douglas Island (left foreground). The mass of light-colored material in the channel just south (this side) of Juneau is waste rock from the famous Alaska-Juneau gold mine (courtesy Alaska Travel Division).

Juneau's principal claim to fame, the fact that it is the state capital, is now presumably a temporary distinction. The voters of Alaska, in statewide referendums in 1974 and 1976, decreed that the capital would be shifted to a much more accessible site 70 miles northeast of Anchorage, where a new planned city would be built. The cost of such an endeavor, however, will be astronomical, and the timetable for the move is still indefinite.

spectacular scenery

The North Pacific Coast is perhaps the continent's most scenic region and is hailed as one of its most desirable outdoor recreation areas.[11] Remoteness from large population

[11] The scenery, however, is frequently shrouded in fog, mist, or rain. The famous Seattle weather forecast still pertains: "If you can see Mount Rainier, it's going to rain; if you can't, it is raining."

fig. 18–23 Mount Rainier on a rare cloudless day.

centers and the inaccessibility of many of the scenic spots, however, have retarded the development of tourism. Improved transport by road, air, and ferry have significantly stimulated the tourist business.

The section south of the international border is best developed, with five magnificent national parks (fig. 18–23); one of the finest combined scenic-and-sandy coastlines in the world, the Oregon coast (fig. 18–24); splendid forests; and a plenitude of accessible winter sports areas. The Canadian section and the Inside Passage of southeastern Alaska rank among the world's most scenic areas, with their spectacular mountains, glaciers, and fiords. In south coastal Alaska, however, is found the continent's most magnificent landscape, thousands of square miles of ice and rock and forest, culminating in the grandeur of Mount McKinley National Park.

In a region of such scenic splendor, it is to be expected that land-use controversies are frequent and ecological confrontations numerous. Such problems occur on many fronts but have been most publicized with regard to three public-use areas: Redwood National Park, North Cascades National Park, and Kenai National Moose Range.

The redwoods controversy has been discussed. To reiterate, the establishment of Redwood National Park came about only after bitter and acrimonious debates among

fig. 18–24 The magnificent Oregon coast, an alternation of fine beaches and rocky headlands. This scene is looking southward, near Port Orford.

many people and organizations. The greatest gain has been the assured preservation of significant groves of redwoods. The continuing controversy revolves around the possibility of enlarging the park and the suitability of logging practices in the redwood forests in general.

The establishment of North Cascades National Park just south of the Canadian border also followed very lengthy discussion between those wanting total preservation of that environment and those seeking exploitation of forest and mineral resources in the area. The park is now a fait accompli, but debate continues about its proper development for tourist use.

In the Kenai National Moose Range the issues are more precisely defined. How much petroleum exploration and exploitation should be permitted in the heart of the only major preserve for the continent's largest hoofed mammal? The obvious economic benefits of oil production have carried the day in this controversy, but stringent regulations have been set down to protect the environment in general and the moose habitat in particular. After early problems, the behavior of the oil seekers has become much more acceptable, which shows that some accommodation should be possible between resource exploitation and the preservation of wilderness values.[12]

[12] Dr. J. S. Tener of the Canadian Wildlife Service, reported as follows after examining drilling sites on the Kenai Peninsula:

One of the things that impressed me most about the Kenai operation was the cleanliness of the industrial sites, i.e., oil wells, storage sheds, and drilling rigs. I was able to examine a number of them and there was not a single piece of paper, tin can, cardboard, or other garbage anywhere in sight. Each site was unobtrusive as was possible to make it and by that I mean a very minimum amount of disturbance of the surrounding terrain was apparent. Equally impressive was the fact that in spite of the oil wells, the streams flowing immediately adjacent to them and the surrounding lakes were free of pollution. The water was clean and contained the usual biota. Seismic lines cut through the timber stopped about one hundred yards from manageable streams and lakes so that a canoeist travelling through has no evidence of undue geophysical activity. [Quoted in Ian McTaggart Cowan, "The Ecology of the North: Knowledge Is the Key to Sane Development," *Science Forum*, 7 (February 1969), 7.]

the vital role of ferries in the region

Highways and railways, the more prosaic forms of transportation, are well established from the Fraser Valley southward despite topographic hindrances. In the northern two-thirds of the region, however, both road and rail routes are mostly limited to lines extending inland from the ports of Prince Rupert, Skagway, Haines, Cordova, Valdez, Seward, and Homer. Air transport thus becomes very important throughout the region.

As in no other part of Anglo-America, ferries play a specialized and vital role in the transportation network of this region. There are four important ferry systems, each basically independent of the others:

1 Ferries provide subsidiary service in the Puget Sound area, mostly radiating from Seattle, but also with interisland service in the San Juan Islands.

2 The British Columbia provincial government maintains an excellent ferry network in the Strait of Georgia, interconnecting mainland and Vancouver Island ports (fig. 18–25). In addition a newly estab-

fig. 18–25 Ferries are critical to transportation in Alaska, British Columbia, and Washington. Shown here is a marine ferry boat on the Inside Passage between Vancouver and Prince Rupert (courtesy British Columbia Department of Travel Industry).

lished "sea-bus" system provides frequent commuter service across Vancouver harbor from suburban North Vancouver to the central business district.

3 The Alaska panhandle ferry system has been mentioned. It serves both the medium-sized and smaller centers of the panhandle with increasing frequency. In the near future there are plans to connect this system with the Prince William Sound system, across the open waters of the Gulf of Alaska.

4 Alaska's other ferry system connects the ports of Prince William Sound, the Kenai Peninsula, and Kodiak Island.

In all these ferry systems the emphasis is on passenger traffic, including roll-on and roll-off facilities for automobiles and trucks. Most freight is carried by regular oceangoing vessels or tug-propelled barges.

the outlook

The characteristics and relative significance of the North Pacific Coast Region are not likely to change much in the near future. It will continue to be a region of specialized economy, Pacific Ocean orientation, magnificent scenery, and conservation controversy.

The forest industries, long outstanding in the economy, can be expected to expand in terms of area (especially in southeastern Alaska), product diversification (more emphasis on plywood, particleboard, and pulp-paper), and scale of corporate enterprise.

Agriculture will become even more specialized than it is today, although dairying should be unrivaled as the principal farm activity throughout the region.

The commercial fishing industry will probably be characterized by considerable fluctuation in the annual catch of the various species. Year-to-year variations in the availability of fish reflect both natural factors and the erratic results of overexploitation. The fishermen have demonstrated remarkable versatility and resiliency in the past, shifting with great rapidity from an overfished species to an underutilized one. As fish processing and marketing facilities develop a similar measure of versatility, the entire industry will become more stabilized. Problems of overexploitation and conflicts of interest, however, will continue to cloud the scene, particularly in regard to salmon.

Commercial ties with Asia in general and with Japan in particular will undoubtedly grow rapidly. The bustling Japanese economy should provide a significant market for the quantity products of the North Pacific Coast's primary industries and the products from the continental interior that are shipped from the region's ports. A continuation of the high level of Japanese capital investment in the region is to be anticipated.

The established urban areas of the southern portion of the region will probably be the major centers of population and economic growth. Most of the region, however, will remain largely a wilderness, dominated by a few extractive industries and continually beckoning Anglo-Americans for all forms of outdoor recreation.

selected bibliography

"Admiralty—Island in Contention," *Alaska Geographic*, 1, no. 3 (1973), entire issue.

ANDRUS, A. PHILLIP, ET AL., "Seattle," in *Contemporary Metropolitan America, Vol. 3, Nineteenth Century Inland Centers and Ports*, pp. 425–500. Cambridge, Mass.: Ballinger Publishing Co., 1976.

BAKER, MARY L., "Heart of B.C.: The Strait of Georgia Region," *Canadian Geographical Journal*, 92 (January–February 1976), 28–35.

BEATTY, ROBERT A., "Pacific Rim National Park," *Canadian Geographical Journal*, 92 (January–February 1976), 14–21.

BISH, ROBERT L., ET AL., *Coastal Resource Use: Decisions on Puget Sound.* Seattle: University of Washington Press, 1975.

BROWNING, R. J., "Fisheries of the North Pacific," *Alaska Geographic,* 1, no. 4 (1974), entire issue.

CAREY, N. G., "Queen Charlottes: Recovery, Rediscovery," *Canadian Geographical Journal,* 89 (October 1974), 4–15.

ELLIS, DEREK V., ed., *Pacific Salmon: Management for People,* Western Geographical Series, Vol. 13. Victoria: University of Victoria Department of Geography, 1977.

FORWARD, CHARLES N., "Parallelism of Halifax and Victoria," *Canadian Geographical Journal,* 90 (March 1975), 34–43.

———, ed., *Residential and Neighbourhood Studies in Victoria,* Western Geographical Series, Vol. 5. Victoria: University of Victoria Department of Geography, 1973.

FOSTER, HAROLD D., ed., *Victoria: Physical Environment and Development,* Western Geographical Series, Vol. 12. Victoria: University of Victoria Department of Geography, 1976.

GASTIL, RAYMOND D., "The Pacific Northwest as a Cultural Region," *Pacific Northwest Quarterly,* 64 (1973), 147–62.

HALEY, DELPHINE, "Puget Sound at the Crossroads," *Defenders,* 50 (1975), 317–25.

HARDWICK, WALTER G., *Vancouver.* Toronto: Collier-MacMillan of Canada, 1974.

HAYES, DEREK W., "Fog and Cloud in British Columbia," *Canadian Geographical Journal,* 83 (December 1971), 200–203.

HIGHSMITH, RICHARD M., JR., ed., *Atlas of the Pacific Northwest: Resources and Development.* Corvallis: Oregon State University Press, 1968.

JOHANNESSEN, CARL L., ET AL., "The Vegetation of the Willamette Valley," *Annals,* Association of American Geographers, 61 (1971), 286–302.

KELLOGG, J. E., "A Tale of Two Ports: Seward and Whittier, Alaska," *Journal of Geography,* 75 (1976), 454–58.

LEVY, YVONNE, *Aluminum: Past and Future.* San Francisco, Calif.: Federal Reserve Bank of San Francisco, Monthly Review Supplement, 1971.

LOY, WILLIAM G., ET AL., *Atlas of Oregon.* Eugene: University of Oregon Press, 1976.

MARTS, M. E., AND W. R. D. SEWELL, "The Conflict Between Fish and Power Resources in the Pacific Northwest," *Annals,* Association of American Geographers, 50 (1960), 42–50.

MINGHI, JULIAN V., "The Conflict of Salmon Fishing Policies in the North Pacific," *Pacific Viewpoint,* 2 (1961), 59–84.

MOULTON, BENJAMIN, "Agriculture in the Kenai," *Professional Paper 7,* pp. 24–32. Terre Haute, Ind.: Department of Geography and Geology, Indiana State University, 1975.

POWERS, RICHARD L., ET AL., "Yakutat: The Turbulent Crescent," *Alaska Geographic,* 2 (1975), entire issue.

"Prince William Sound," *Alaska Geographic,* 2, no. 3 (1975), entire issue.

PROVINCE OF BRITISH COLUMBIA LANDS SERVICE, *Lower Coast Bulletin Area.* Victoria: Queen's Printer, 1970.

———, *Vancouver Island Bulletin Area.* Victoria: Queen's Printer, 1970.

ROBINSON, J. LEWIS, "How Vancouver Has Grown and Changed," *Canadian Geographical Journal,* 89 (October 1974), 40–48.

———, "Nanaimo, B.C.," *Canadian Geographical Journal,* 70 (May 1965), 162–69.

———, ed., *British Columbia.* Toronto: University of Toronto Press, 1972.

ROBINSON J. LEWIS, AND WALTER G. HARDWICK, *British Columbia: 100 Years of Geographical Change.* Vancouver: Talonbooks, 1973.

ROSS, W. M., AND M. E. MARTS, "The High Ross Dam Project: Environmental Decisions and Changing Environmental Attitudes," *Canadian Geographer,* 19 (1976), 221–34.

STEED, GUY P. F., "Intrametropolitan Manufacturing: Spatial Distribution and Locational Dynamics in Greater Vancouver," *Canadian Geographer,* 17 (1973), 235–58.

THEBERGE, J. B., "Kluane: A National Park Two-thirds Under Ice," *Canadian Geographical Journal,* 91 (September 1975), 32–37.

———, "The Mighty Wilderness of Kluane," *International Wildlife* (March–April 1975), pp. 40–47.

WAHRHAFTIG, CLYDE, *Physiographic Divisions of Alaska,* Geological Survey Professional Paper 482. Washington, D.C.: Government Printing Office, 1965.

19

THE
BOREAL
FOREST

Anglo-America's largest region sprawls almost from sea to sea across the breadth of the continent at its widest point, in subarctic latitudes. The Boreal Forest Region is primarily a Canadian region, occupying almost half of that nation's areal extent, although it also encompasses the Upper Lakes States and central Alaska in the United States.

It is a region of rock, water, and ice, but particularly of forest—interminable, inescapable forest (fig. 19-1). The forest extends for hundreds of miles over flattish terrain with relatively little variation in either appearance or composition. Its very endlessness accords a feeling of monotony in some people. Edward McCourt, in describing a traverse in western Ontario, emphasized this point:

In Canada there is too much of everything. Too much rock, too much prairie, too much tundra, too much mountain, too much forest. Above all, too much forest. Even the man who passionately believes that he shall never see a poem as lovely as a tree will be disposed to give poetry another try after he has driven the Trans-Canada Highway.[1]

This is a region in which nature's dominance has been but lightly challenged by

[1] Edward McCourt, *The Road Across Canada* (Toronto: Macmillan of Canada, 1965), p. 110. By permission.

fig. 19-1   The Boreal Forest is a region of trees and water. This scene is in central Quebec (courtesy Government of Quebec, Tourist Branch).

humanity. The landscape is largely a natural one, and people are only sporadic intruders. A map showing distribution of population, superimposed on a map indicating regional boundaries, shows the area's relative emptiness. Maps of soils and climate show *why* there is a paucity of human beings. Much of this region consists of the Canadian Shield, a land of Precambrian crystalline rock, rounded hills almost devoid of soil, fast-flowing rivers, and innumerable lakes, swamps, and muskegs. Long, cold winters characterize most of the region; its amazingly short growing season makes agriculture relatively unimportant. From boundary to boundary, most of the inhabitants are engaged overwhelmingly in *extractive* pursuits.

Most Anglo-Americans have never seen this region, and the vast majority will never set foot in it. And yet it is a region that has enriched the autochthonous literature and folk music of both countries; the sagas of Paul Bunyan, the stories of Jack London, the poetry of Robert Service, and many other literary contributions have brought the "North Woods" into public consciousness. This is particularly true in Canada, where the forest syndrome has played a major role in the conception of the Canadian character. Subarctic expert William Wonders pointed out this emotional attachment:

Forest, rock, water—these are the elements which exert a near-irresistible call for most Canadians. Even if most of the year is spent in a very different setting, the traditional northern ingredients are sought out for rest and relaxation. Though they may live to the south of it and rail against its harshness, many Canadians probably find in the Subarctic the "emotional heartland" of their nation.[2]

The boundaries of the Boreal Forest Region are nowhere clear-cut but can easily be

[2] W. C. Wonders, "The Forest Frontier and Subarctic," in *Canada: A Geographical Interpretation,* ed. John Warkentin (Toronto: Methuen Publications, 1968), p. 477.

conceptualized (fig. 19–2). The northern margin is the tree line, which separates the Subarctic (Boreal Forest Region) from the Arctic (Tundra Region). As with most such vegetation boundaries, the idea of a line is misleading; the interfingering of forest and tundra is very complex, and the northern margin of the region is a transition zone rather than a line. This northern floristic boundary is further reinforced by its approximate coincidence with the 50°F. July isotherm and its almost absolute separation of Indian (to the south) and Eskimo (to the north) settlements.

The region's southern boundary is more complicated and should be conceptualized as follows. In the east it is approximately coincidental with the limit of close agricultural settlement north of the St. Lawrence and Ottawa rivers. Across southeastern Ontario it follows the southern margin of the Canadian Shield. It crosses northern Michigan and central Wisconsin and Minnesota as a transition zone separating essentially agricultural land on the south from essentially forest land on the north. From western Minnesota to western Alberta the boundary coincides with the change from prairie landscape to forest landscape. In western Canada and Alaska the boundary is largely determined by topography; the mountainous terrain of the Rockies and the North Pacific Coast Region ranges mark the southern limits of the Boreal Forest Region in this part of the continent.

The eastern (Labrador) and western (Alaska) margins of the region are generalized as separating the zones of coastal settlement from the almost unpopulated interior, with the added distinction of a forest-tundra ecotone in western Alaska.

a harsh subarctic environment

From a human viewpoint, the natural environment of the Boreal Forest Region is a harsh one. It is a land dominated by winter,

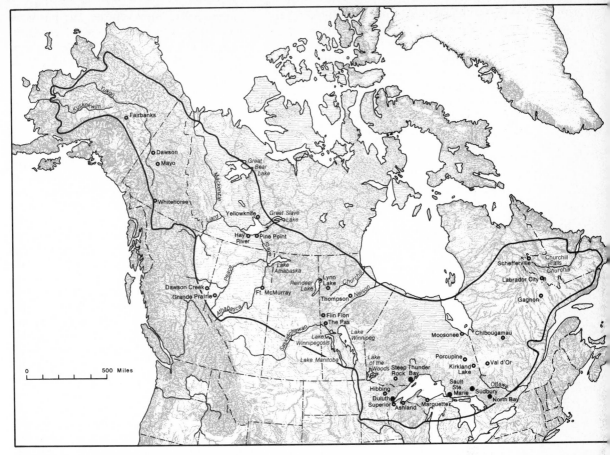

fig. 19-2 The Boreal Forest Region (base map copyright A. K. Lobeck; reprinted by permission of Hammond, Inc.).

and the winter temperatures are the most severe to be found on the continent. The surface is frozen for many months, and during the summer poor drainage inhibits land transportation. The rocky forested landscape, with its filigree of lakes and rivers, was so inhospitable that Canadian settlement expansion was delayed and deflected. The Canadian Shield stood as a barrier between eastern and western Canada, denying the nation the strength and vigor that come with geographical and political unity. Thin soils, poor drainage, hostile climate, and pestiferous insects have made penetration and settlement anywhere in the region a difficult and expensive undertaking.

TERRAIN

The eastern two-thirds of the region is underlain largely by the Canadian Shield, a vast, gently rolling surface of ancient crystalline rocks that has been scraped and shaped by the multiple glaciations of the Pleistocene Epoch. In Labrador and Quebec are several sprawling ranges of mountains and hills that reach elevations exceeding 4,000 feet. The southern edge of the Shield in Quebec is marked by the spectacular and complex Laurentide Escarpment; other less obtrusive scarps occur in other parts of that province. Elsewhere on the Shield the topography is more gently undulating and eleva-

517

tions are mostly well under 2,000 feet. The remarkable sameness of terrain over vast expanses of the Shield can be explained by the constancy of rock types; more than 80 percent of the surface consists of predominantly gneissic granitic rocks.[3]

Scouring by Pleistocene ice sheets remolded the surface and removed most of the preexisting soil. Drainage was totally disarranged, bare rock was left exposed on most of the upland surfaces, and glacial and glaciofluvial debris was deposited in countless scoured valleys. In some places the accumulation of glacial debris and deposits on the floors of old glacial lakes has mantled the underlying Precambrian rocks to considerable depth, most notably in the large lowland surrounding James Bay, in the so-called Clay Belt on the Quebec-Ontario border, and in the Lake St. John lowland.

To the west of the hardrock Shield is a broad lowland of vast extent that is underlain by softer sedimentary materials. It has been built up by deposition of sands and silts washed off the Rockies and the Shield. Consisting for the most part of a plain with scattered hilly districts, it is almost as poorly drained as the Shield, with the result that water features (rivers, lakes, muskegs) are

[3] J. Brian Bird, *The Natural Landscapes of Canada* (Toronto: Wiley Publishers of Canada Ltd., 1972), p. 136.

fig. 19–3 The dominant landscape elements in the region are endless forests and lots of water. This is Lesser Slave Lake in northern Alberta.

commonplace. Some of the largest rivers (Mackenzie, Slave, Athabaska, Saskatchewan) and lakes (Great Bear, Great Slave) in Anglo-America are found here (fig. 19–3). Most of the sedimentary plain, sometimes referred to as the forested northern Great Plains, drains northward to the Arctic Ocean via a complicated hydrographic system dominated by the Mackenzie River.

In the Yukon Territory the region encompasses an area of more complicated geology, greater relief, and greater variety of landscape. There are several rugged mountain ranges and deeply incised plateau surfaces.

In central Alaska the drainage basin of the Yukon River occupies the broad expanse of land between the Alaska Range to the south and the Brooks Range to the north, widening ever more broadly westward. The lower basin of the Yukon and the equally extensive basin of the Kuskokwim River to the south consist of broad, flat lowlands that are quite marshy in summer.

HYDROGRAPHY

Water is abundant in most of the region during the summer, chiefly as a result of glacial derangement of drainage patterns and the fact that the subsoil is at least partly frozen over much of the region, thus preventing downward percolation of surface moisture. There are

water bodies of every conceivable shape and size, from small ponds to some of the largest lakes in the world. [Water] spills from one to the next in swift, dashing streams and sweeps along in major rivers which reach such proportions that in the case of the Mackenzie, the width of its lower reaches is measured in miles. Rapids and falls are common features on almost all rivers.[4]

Lakes are so numerous that parts of the Shield might almost be described as water with occasional land.

Most rivers originate within the region and flow outward from it: some to the At-

[4] Wonders, "The Forest Frontier and Subarctic," p. 474.

lantic via the Great Lakes–St. Lawrence system; some in a centripetal pattern into Hudson Bay; some directly from Quebec or Labrador into the Atlantic; and some to join the Mackenzie, Yukon, or Kuskokwim systems in their path to the Arctic Ocean or the Bering Sea. Only in the so-called Nelson Trough area of northern Manitoba are there rivers that flow *across* the region; the Nelson and Churchill systems originate in the Rocky Mountains and Great Plains to the west before flowing eastward into Hudson Bay.

Swamps and marshes are also widespread as is that peculiar northern feature, muskeg (poorly drained flat land covered with a thick growth of mosses and sedges). These severely inhibit overland transportation and provide an extensive habitat for the myriad of insects that swarm over the region during the brief summer.

CLIMATE

In so enormous an area, important differences of climate from north to south or east to west might be expected, but actually the differences are relatively slight. Everywhere the climate is continental; this is mainly the result of interior location, great distance from oceans, and the barrier influence of the cordilleras, all of which keep out the moderating effects of the Pacific Ocean.

This continentality is the dominating feature of the Shield's natural environment. Winters are long, dark, and bitterly cold. Temperatures occasionally drop to 60° below zero over most of the region, and in the northwest readings of less than –70° have been recorded.

The region is saved from recurrent glaciation only by the warmth of summer; summer temperatures are generally mild, but the long daylight hours sometimes produce decidedly hot weather. The transition seasons are short but stimulating. Spring is characterized by a high degree of muddiness, which makes it the most difficult season for overland transportation.

Precipitation is relatively light over most of the region but is quite effective because evaporation is scanty. Summer is the period of precipitation maximum; the entire landscape is covered with snow throughout the winter. In the east, Quebec and Labrador, precipitation totals are much higher. Drought is virtually unknown there.

SOILS

Soils of the region are characteristically acidic, severely leached, and poorly drained. Spodosols, Inceptisols, and Histosols predominate. Where farming is carried on, it is invariably in an area of more productive soil, generally a clay-based soil that has been derived from glacial lake sediments.

PERMAFROST

Roughly half of the surface area of Canada and about three-fourths of that of Alaska is underlain with permafrost, or permanently frozen subsoil (fig. 19-4). In the zone of continuous permafrost the *active layer* (that part that freezes in winter and thaws in summer) of the soil is only 1.5 to 3 feet in depth.[5] Be-

[5] R. J. E. Brown, "Permafrost Map of Canada," *Canadian Geographical Journal,* 76 (February 1968), 57.

fig. 19-4   The southern limit of permafrost in Anglo-America (after Brown and Thornbury).

——— Southern limit of continuous permafrost

– – – Southern limit of discontinuous permafrost

neath that is the permafrost layer, which is usually several hundred feet thick and has been measured to depths of 1,300 feet in both Canada and Alaska.[6] In the zone of discontinuous permafrost various factors contribute to the presence of sporadic unfrozen conditions; where permafrost occurs, the layer is much thinner and the overlying active layer may be more than 10 feet in depth.

The presence of permafrost creates many engineering difficulties. Although providing a solid base for supporting structures (buildings, roadbeds, railways) when frozen, permafrost readily thaws when its insulating cover is removed and then loses its strength to such a degree that it will not support even a light weight; this results in buckling and displacement of any structure built on it. Various engineering techniques have been developed to overcome these difficulties; most important is to remove the insulating cover (vegetation, surface soil) several months before actual construction begins, thus allowing permafrost conditions to stabilize to a new equilibrium.

NATURAL VEGETATION

The distinctive natural vegetation of the Shield is coniferous forest with a deciduous admixture. From south to north the trees become smaller, those in the extreme north being small and scraggly. In this region of slow growth the trees never reach great heights, although they are normally close-growing except where interrupted by bedrock or poor drainage.

The boreal forest is often referred to as *taiga;* a similar expanse of northern continental forest extends across Eurasia in similar latitudes. Conifers, growing in relatively pure stands, dominate the plant associations of the taiga. The principal species are white spruce, black spruce, tamarack, balsam fir, and jack pine. Associated with the dominant coniferous species is a small group of hard-

woods that is quite widespread; most notable are white birch, balsam poplar, aspen, black ash, and alder. In the southern part of the region, especially in the Great Lakes area, hardwoods are more common, as are pines.

Fire is a prominent ecological force in the Boreal Forest Region, often burning thousands of square miles before it is finally quenched; moreover, the incidence of fire in the taiga has greatly increased in recent years.[7] Burned areas regenerate only very slowly in these subarctic latitudes. Hardwood species, especially birch and aspen, attain their greatest areal extent as an initial replacement for the conifers after a forest fire; they are eventually superseded by conifers as the climax association becomes reestablished.

NATIVE ANIMAL LIFE

Native animal life was originally both varied and abundant; the variety is still great, although abundance has considerably diminished. Furbearing animals have had the greatest geographical and economic influence because of the trapping carried on by natives and outsiders alike. The beaver, distributed throughout the region, has been the most important species, but also notable are the muskrat, various mustelids (ermine, mink, marten, otter, fisher, and wolverine), canids (wolf and fox), the black bear, and the lynx. Another significant group is the ungulates. Woodland caribou occupy most of the region, and vast herds of barren-ground caribou spend the winter in the taiga. Moose and deer are also found, as well as forest-dwelling bison.

Bird life is abundant and varied in summer, when vast hordes of migratory birds, especially waterfowl, come to the region to nest. Only a handful of avian species, however, winters in the Boreal Forest Region.

Insects are superabundant in summer. For two or three months of the year mosqui-

[6] J. Brian Bird, *The Physiography of Arctic Canada* (Baltimore, Md.: Johns Hopkins Press, 1967), p. 40.

[7] Ian McTaggart Cowan. "The Ecology of the North: Knowledge Is the Key to Sane Development," *Science Forum,* 7 (February 1969), p. 6.

toes, black flies, no-see-ums (biting midges), and other tiny tormentors rise out of the muskeg and the sphagnum moss in veritable clouds and make life almost unbearable for people and animals alike.

the occupance

THE INDIAN

Before the arrival of the white man, the Boreal Forest Region was occupied by widely scattered bands of seminomadic Indians. Algonkian speakers, particularly Crees and Ojibwas, were in the eastern portion, and various Athabaskan-speaking tribes lived in the west. The material culture and economy of these widely dispersed tribes were quite uniform, presumably reflecting the homogeneity of the taiga environment. They were hunters and fishermen, depending primarily on the wandering caribou for their principal food supply. The relative scarcity of inhabitants was due to a warlike social tradition and to the fact that hunting and trapping always preclude a dense population, since they entail the great disadvantage of uncertainty. Life was therefore precarious, poverty extreme, and starvation not uncommon.

With the coming of white men, trapping for furs became important. Many Indian women, particularly Ojibwas and Crees whose hunting territory was where most of the fur trade was carried on, intermarried with whites, especially in the earlier years of contact. The offspring of such unions are called *Metis*. They normally acquired a cultural background similar to that of the Indians and lived like Indians. The prevalence of Metis is such that today there are relatively few full-blooded Indians among the tribes of the taiga.

WHITE PENETRATION AND SETTLEMENT

Over most of the Boreal Forest Region, the evolution of white settlement has been associated with exploitive activities: trapping, mining, and forestry. Only in relatively limited areas and under often marginal conditions has settlement on broader scale or greater diversity been attempted.

In the eighteenth and early nineteenth centuries, furs were almost the only stimulus to white penetration of the region. By the middle of the nineteenth century, however, lumbermen were actively at work on the southern margin of the taiga and especially in the Upper Lakes States. At about the beginning of the present century exploitive activities were accelerated, with the initiation of pulping, hydroelectricity generation, and large-scale mining. Although Lake Superior iron ores were being mined as early as the 1850s and there were other isolated mineral discoveries in the region before 1900, mining in the region is largely a twentieth century activity.

The agricultural frontier advanced into the Boreal Forest Region only slowly and hesitantly. Initial farming settlement consisted mostly of a northward overflow from the lower St. Lawrence Valley. Pioneer farmers pushed into various sections of northern Michigan, Wisconsin, and Minnesota, more or less concurrently with logging in those areas. More intensive agricultural settlement came later in the Clay Belt. Still later, the farmlands of Alaska's Tanana Valley were settled. Finally about the time of World War I, the Peace River block began to be occupied with some intensity.

White settlement of the Boreal Forest can thus be seen as a push from the east and the south, primarily motivated by a search for furs, timber, and ores. Agrarian colonies came later and often persisted on the economic margin. Urban settlement has been sporadic, and for the most part, urban prosperity has depended on either the stability of mineral output or some specialized transportation function.

PRESENT POPULATION

Most of the population of the Boreal Forest Region is located on its southern fringe, and nowhere is there a significant density. The few nodes of moderate density are associated with some sort of economic opportunity, such as farming in the Peace River district or mining in northern Minnesota.

The population of the region is about 4 million, amounting to less than 2 percent of the Anglo-American total; the 2 million inhabitants of the Canadian portion of the region are only 9 percent of that nation's populace.

Indians and Metis constitute a significant proportion of the total; this is less so on the southern margin of the region, although even in Wisconsin and Minnesota there is a considerable number of Indians. Their rate of natural increase is very high; in Canada the Indians and Metis are the fastest growing ethnic group in the nation, increasing at a rate of about 3 percent per year.

the economy

Most of the Boreal Forest Region remains economically undeveloped, but that portion lying immediately north of the St. Lawrence River and around Lake Superior is now partially opened up, and small but increasing numbers of people are finding their way into other parts of the region, especially the Mackenzie Valley. In most areas the economy is based on a single exploitive activity, but in three widely separated portions of this vast region a broader development pattern has unfolded, resulting in a more diversified economic base, a higher density of settlement, and a more stabilized, although not necessarily prosperous, economy.

AREAS OF BROADER DEVELOPMENT

Before considering the more typical exploitive industries of the Boreal Forest Region, we will turn our attention to the areas of broader development.

The Upper Lakes Area Surrounding lakes Superior and Huron are parts of northern Michigan and Wisconsin, northeastern Minnesota, and southern Ontario that are functionally focused on the Great Lakes waterway, along which are transported vast quantities of the area's ore output (fig. 19–5). The long-established mineral and transportation industries of the Upper Lakes provide a stable base for the most diversified subregional economy in the entire Boreal Forest Region.

Mining The Upper Lakes area has a limited variety of mineral resources, but they occur in tremendous quantities. Southwest and northwest of Lake Superior lie the continent's largest and most favorably located iron ores. On Michigan's Keweenaw Peninsula are long-mined but diminishing copper deposits. On the west shore of Lake Huron are valuable beds of metallurgical limestone.

Mining is the outstanding economic enterprise in this subregion today. Billions of tons of red hematite ore have been found and mined in the Lake Superior district. The area, which accounts for 85 percent of United States production, comprises eleven counties (three in Minnesota, five in Michigan, and three in Wisconsin). Minnesota alone contributes nearly two-thirds of the total. Based on the Mesabi Range, the greatest body of iron ore in the world, were built the extensive American iron-ore and lake-shipping businesses and, indirectly, most of the steel manufacturing of the Lower Great Lakes area (fig. 19–6). Today, in order to send high-grade ore down the lakes, the lower quality ores must first be sent to beneficiation plants that upgrade the ores by screening, crushing, washing, and concentrating them.

Taconite is a dense, hard rock containing only 25 to 35 percent iron and a considerable amount of impurities. The iron oxide is finely dispersed in the silica and firmly held by it. Since there are billions of tons of taconite in the Lake Superior area, the perfection of an economic method of extracting this iron oxide has been a high-priority job.

Taconite and a similar but nonmagnetic ore called jasper (mostly found in the Michigan iron ranges) are now being mined, con-

fig. 19-5 The Upper Lakes area.

fig. 19-6 An open-pit mine on the Mesabi Range.

fig. 19-7　A taconite beneficiation plant at Hoyt Lakes, Minnesota (courtesy Erie Mining Company).

centrated, and pelletized in large volume. Beneficiation, although expensive, produces a concentrate that is about two-thirds iron and that will yield more pig iron with less blast-furnace cost than will other ores (fig. 19-7). More than half of the Lake Superior iron-ore output is now taconite and jasper.

Pelletization is only the final stage of a complex process of beneficiation for low-grade iron ore, involving the concentration of iron content into small, hard pellets. All three of the Upper Lakes States have en-

fig. 19-8　A typical ore dock (at Marquette, Michigan), with an ore train slowly moving into position to dump.

acted tax laws that are favorable to the long-range development of low-grade ores, particularly by means of large pelletization plants. A "pellet boom" has revitalized the declining mineral economy of the area; it has even revived ore production in Wisconsin, where it had been moribund for several years.

About 140 miles northwest of the head of Lake Superior and relatively near the international boundary lies Canada's Steep Rock mine. This is the second largest iron-mining operation in Canada, accounting for about 15 percent of national output.

Ore from the area's mines is loaded into rail cars, which are assembled into trains and taken to the various Lake Superior ore ports. The trains move onto the loading docks that jut out into the lake like huge peninsulas and dump their ore into "pockets," from which it can be dropped through hatches into the holds of lake vessels (fig. 19-8). The lake carriers operate a busy one-way traffic, carrying a vast tonnage of ore across Lake Superior, through the Soo Canals, and down to the Lower Lakes ports (fig. 19-9). The return trip is often without cargo, despite lower rates offered for up-bound freight. In most years the ore-shipping season on the lakes is about ten months long, beginning in April and being closed by ice in January or February. In both 1975 and 1976, however, icebreakers were able to keep shipments moving year-round from some ports, and it is likely that there will at least occasionally be twelve-month shipping seasons again in the future.

Logging　The Upper Lakes area had Anglo-America's largest and densest stand of white pine. The mass exploitation of this resource began after the Civil War. By 1870, Michigan ranked first in the production of lumber, and reached its peak in the decade from 1880 to 1890. Whereas in 1890 these three lake states produced 35 percent of the nation's total, by 1910 they could not supply their own needs. Today they produce only 3 percent, the bulk consisting of hardwoods.

Fishing　Fishing was a flourishing enterprise in lakes Huron, Michigan, and Superior, antedating lumbering and mining. Whitefish and lake trout in 1880 made up 70 percent of the catch. Since then they have steadily declined as a result of overfishing, depredation by the destructive sea lampreys, destruction of immature fish, the fouling of waters by city sewage and industrial waste, and changing physical conditions in the lakes.

Particularly heartening in recent years has been the establishment of effective lamprey control. The sea lamprey is an adaptable, anadromous, parasitic, eel-like species that has moved up the St. Lawrence and into the Great Lakes from the Atlantic Ocean. It destroys fish by attaching itself to them with its sucker mouthparts and feeding on them. After essentially wrecking the lake trout and whitefish fishery of the Lower Lakes, it then moved into the Upper Lakes. Fishery technicians, however, developed a method of controlling the menace. A selective poison is spread in upstream lamprey spawning grounds, and electric gates are installed at the stream mouths with the current turned on during times of lamprey migration into and out of the lakes. It is an expensive and difficult program, but one that is yielding positive results.

An unusual addition to the recreational and commercial fishery of the Great Lakes is the coho salmon. In the late 1960s young salmon were deliberately released in Michigan streams, and in short order they established their anadromous life cycle in the Upper Lakes. A large niche in the lakes ecosystem was unoccupied, and the coho filled this vacuum and occupied a place in the food chain without much competition to native species. Such exotic introductions must be approached with great care, but the early results of the coho experiment seem to be very positive.

Farming Although a great deal of land in the northern part of the Upper Lakes States was cleared for farming, most of it was only of marginal value. Short growing season, lack of sunshine, poor drainage, and mediocre soils combine to produce very limited areas for prosperous

fig. 19-9 An ore boat being locked through the Soo Canal at Sault Ste. Marie (courtesy Michigan Travel Commission).

crop growing or animal husbandry. Dairying is the principal farm activity in the area, and grains and root crops are cultivated.

Farming is somewhat more prosperous on the Canadian side, where pockets of good soil are utilized and the poor areas have not been settled. For example, in the Rainy River district north of Minnesota, farms average 50 to 100 acres cleared and produce good crops of oats, hay, and flax. The chief source of agricultural income is from the sale of livestock and livestock products.

Urban Activities This portion of the Boreal Forest Region has several important urban nodes, each of which is a lake port of significance. Duluth-Superior is the funnel at the western end of the Great Lakes waterway on the United States side of the border; Thunder Bay performs an analogous function on the Canadian side. The twin cities of Sault Ste. Marie, Ontario, and Sault St. Marie, Michigan, are at the crossroads of the east-west water route and the north-south land route of the Upper Lakes. The former city is also one of Canada's leading iron and steel manufacturing centers.

The Clay Belt The so-called Clay Belt of the Quebec-Ontario borderland actually

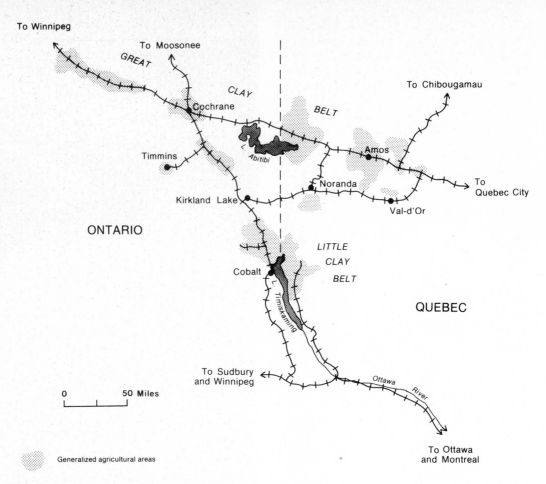

To Winnipeg

GREAT

To Moosonee

CLAY

BELT

To Chibougamau

Cochrane

Timmins

L. Abitibi

Amos

Noranda

To Quebec City

Kirkland Lake

Val-d'Or

ONTARIO

LITTLE

CLAY

BELT

Cobalt

L. Timiskaming

QUEBEC

0   50 Miles

To Sudbury
and Winnipeg

Ottawa River

Generalized agricultural areas

To Ottawa
and Montreal

fig. 19–10   The Clay Belt.

consists of two areas: the Great Clay Belt, which extends about 100 miles both east and west from Lake Abitibi; and the Little Clay Belt, which occupies a more restricted area northeast and northwest of Lake Timiskaming (fig. 19-10). Although some of the more productive soils are clay derivatives from glacial lake sediments, much of the soil development is from glacial and lacustrine deposits that contain only minor clay elements.[8]

Agricultural settlement in the area is all

a product of this century. Many immigrants from overseas came into the Ontario portions, whereas most settlers on the Quebec side of the border were French-Canadians who moved from the more closely settled portions of Quebec.

Agriculture in the area was fostered from early days by mineral discoveries. Silver and cobalt ores were discovered in 1903, and the town of Cobalt became the mining center. A major gold discovery in 1909 soon evolved into the Timmins-Porcupine complex. A second locale of high-grade gold deposits, around Kirkland Lake, began to be developed two years later. Several dozen mines were opened in the next two decades,

[8] For more details on this topic and the resulting confusion, see J. Lewis Robinson, *Resources of the Canadian Shield* (Toronto: Methuen Publications, 1969), pp. 99–106.

mostly producing gold. The mines provided a local market for farm products, and this enabled farmers to achieve some stability of production despite the high cost of their operations and the limited cropping possibilities.

Most of the mines closed down after World War II, and farming became an increasingly profitless occupation. There has been a continued decline in farm acreage, farm population, and the number of full-time farmers. Only a relatively few farmers today can survive without some other source of income. Dairying is the principal activity, along with some production of oats, barley, and hardy vegetables.

There was a mining rejuvenation in the 1960s, with the development of zinc, copper, and silver ores near Porcupine and the opening of a large iron ore mine at Kirkland Lake. Agriculture, however, continues to be marginal in the area. Even in the Ontario portion, the majority of the farmers are now French-Canadians, and the bulk of the farm population is on the Quebec side of the border. Total population in the Clay Belt is now about 350,000.

The Peace River District In the northwestern part of Alberta and adjacent British Columbia is an enclave of black soil and grassy parkland that has some 25,000 square miles of potentially cultivable land (fig. 19–11). This is Canada's northernmost

fig. 19–11 The Peace River district.

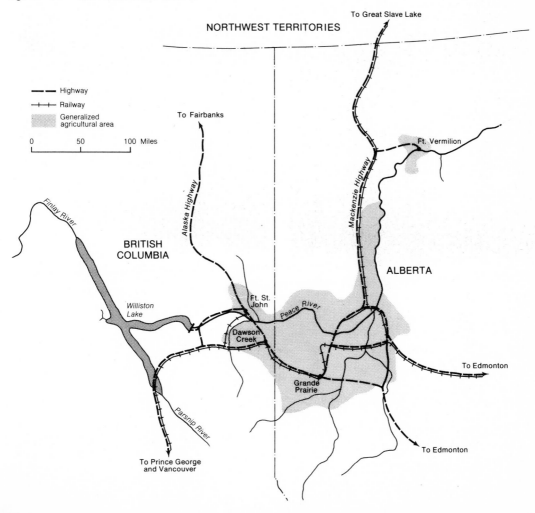

fig. 19–12 Threshing spring wheat on a Peace River farm near Dawson Creek (courtesy British Columbia Department of Travel Industry).

area of satisfactory commercial agriculture. The Peace River district was first entered by settlers as long ago as 1879, but it was only sparsely occupied until well into the twentieth century, particularly after a rail line was laid from Edmonton to Grande Prairie in 1916.

Mixed farming is characteristic, with an

fig. 19–13 An Indian sets a trap in northern Manitoba (courtesy Hudson's Bay Company).

emphasis on cash grains (especially barley) in the older areas, and livestock (particularly beef cattle and hogs) in the newer ones. In recent years there has been a phenomenal increase in rapeseed production, a continuing increase in barley, and an accompanying decrease in both wheat and oats (fig. 19–12).

Completion of a Vancouver railway connection in 1958 gave the Peace River farmers access for the first time to the markets of southern British Columbia. This improved transportation has accounted for a considerable increase in production of feed grain for sale to ranchers west of the Rocky Mountains and for an acceleration of forestry exploitation.

The district is no longer an area of frontier farming. Even though the pioneer fringe of agriculture is being pushed slowly northward toward Great Slave Lake, commercial agriculture is now an accomplished fact. Much of the clearing of land is associated with improvement of already existing farms.

Lumber and pulp are being produced in increasing volumes, primarily from white spruce and lodgepole pine. Petroleum exploration is continuing, and several fields are now in production. Improved transportation by road and rail have stimulated growth, and the larger towns of the district are rapidly expanding.

FAUNAL EXPLOITATION: HUNTING AND TRAPPING

In the past both Indians and Metis led seminomadic lives, depending on wildlife and fish for subsistence and sometimes trapping as a sideline for trading. Within the taiga today there is still a moderate number of these activities, but nomadism is a thing of the past. The introduction of modern arms and ammunition has had the predictable effect of making it easier to kill game at first, but the deer, moose, and caribou that once supplied most of the meat have now been greatly depleted.

Until recent years, trapping was a major source of income for many of the native inhabitants of the region (fig. 19–13). Within the last three decades, however, its importance has continued to decline, and in many areas trapping has almost completely disappeared. The availability of wage labor and government social service payments has taken away much of the incentive for the trapper to spend long, hard weeks in the wilderness. For example, a recent survey of the lower valley of the Liard River in the Northwest Territories, where trapping has long been a major activity, showed that trapping provided only between 7 and 28 percent of total income in the half dozen settlements in the district.[9] The general result is that former hunters and trappers become increasingly clustered in permanent settlement centers. "There, ill-equipped for the modern world, the inheritors of a shattered culture, many lose their independence and pride and often . . . encounter discrimination."[10]

Despite the mounting disinterest in trapping it is unlikely that it will disappear; wage labor is uncertain, and trapping can be a source of supplemental income. Moreover, some areas are unusually productive of furs and provide a relatively high sustained yield, particularly muskrat in the Mackenzie delta and beaver in the James Bay district.

Federal and provincial government programs to bolster the wild fur industry have been promulgated, especially in Manitoba. The establishment of a Registered Trapline System brought order to a previously chaotic endeavor. Controlled harvesting of muskrats on "fur rehabilitation blocks" has brought both stability and increased productivity in various flood plain and delta areas. Other programs are aimed at trapper training, trapline development grants, and fur marketing improvements.

FUR FARMING

The raising of furbearing animals for pelting got its start on Prince Edward Island about

1887 and in Quebec in 1894. Found to be an excellent adjunct to agriculture because of being largely winter work, it was usually practiced by farmers. It was a major commercial activity on Prince Edward Island for several decades but is practically gone from there today. The fur-farming trend in Canada, however, is decidedly upward. The proportion of the pelt value from fur farms of the total pelt value (wild and farmed) has steadily increased from about 35 percent in the late 1940s to more than 60 percent today.

Foxes, mainstay of the early fur farmers, are rarely raised today. Mink farms make up more than 90 percent of the total farms, and chinchillas most of the remainder. Fur farms are found in every region and every province of Canada, but they are characteristic of the Boreal Forest Region, with Ontario as the leading producer.

FORESTRY

Logging and lumbering started early in the accessible edges of the Boreal Forest Region, although only in the Upper Lakes area was there intensified exploitation. Once lumbering got under way in any locale it was usually only two or three decades before the entire stand had been cut-over, the loggers moved on, and the settlements were abandoned or stagnated.

The pulp and paper industry came later and has continued as a prominent activity in many parts of the region, although it, too, is concentrated on the southern margin. This is Canada's leading industry; the nation is second only to Sweden as an exporter of pulp and produces nearly half of all the world's newsprint. Much of the industry is controlled by United States capital.

Cheap power is an important factor in the location of pulp plants, as is shown by their distribution. A string of mills (all water-driven) lines the southern edge of the forest from the mouth of the St. Lawrence to Lake Winnipeg. Further west in the region sawmills and pulp mills are usually large, but they are fewer in number and much more scattered in distribution.

[9] G. M. Higgins, *The Lower Liard Region: An Area Economic Survey* (Ottawa: Industrial Division, Department of Indian Affairs and Northern Development, 1969), p. 217.

[10] Wonders, "The Forest Frontier and Subarctic," p. 504.

fig. 19–14 Loggers use long-handled peaveys to guide floating logs to an outlet of Lake of the Woods near Kenora, Ontario.

Logging depends on snow in this region of long, cold winters. The cutters begin their work in autumn because the logs must be moved out while the ground is frozen. Tractors pull the sleds laden with logs to rivers where the cut is piled awaiting the spring thaw and the freshets, which transport the logs by the hundreds of thousands to downriver mills. River driving is an economical method of transporting logs (fig. 19–14).

COMMERCIAL FISHING

In the last three decades, commercial fisheries have developed in several of the large lakes of the western taiga. The industry is on a small scale compared with oceanic fishing but adds measurably to the local economy. It is a year-round activity, but emphasis is on winter ice-fishing and gill-netting. Nets are set in winter with the aid of an ice jigger, a simple machine that walks along the undersurface of the ice.[11] Transportation is significantly simplified during the cold months when tractor trains can reach the remoter lakes over frozen ground that would be suddenly impassable in summer.

[11] J. G. Hunter, "Fisheries Research Board Studies in Canada's Arctic," *Canadian Geographical Journal,* 82 (March 1971), 104.

Great Bear Lake is too deep, cold, and barren to provide a commercial fishery, but Great Slave Lake has an expanding industry centered at Hay River. Whitefish and lake trout are caught, primarily for export to the eastern United States. Lake Winnipeg has been a major fishing ground, but commercial operations were suspended in the early 1970s because of mercury poisoning in the lake's fish.

Several of the other large lakes in the region support commercial fishing on a regular basis, and a recent summer innovation, pulse fishing, has made it economically feasible to conduct concentrated fishing operations on small lakes without overutilizing the resource. Pulse fishing involves rotational use of small lakes, that is, heavy fishing for one season followed by no fishing at all for 5 to 7 years; this also allows for economical use of portable ice-making and refrigerated fish-holding facilities.

MINING

Mineral industries have been the mainstay of the regional economy throughout most of its history. Mining has formed the basis for most of the urban settlements. Today the outstanding significance of mining continues despite the fluctuating fortunes that accompany variations in local supply and worldwide demand. The hardrock barrenness of the Shield provides an unfavorable basis for agriculture but abundant opportunities for mineralization in economic quality and quantity. Also, the sedimentary formations of the northwest are favorable for hydrocarbon accumulation.

Ore bodies are erratically distributed over the region, but on the basis of relative location several mining districts can be recognized.

Labrador Trough Ore bodies had been known in the Labrador Trough—which extends from near the estuary of the St. Lawrence northward to Ungava Bay—for decades before exploitation was finally initiated in the mid-1950s (fig. 19–15). This development became the most exciting mineral activity in Canada since Alberta's Leduc oil field was brought in.

Transportation was the big problem until the completion of the initial railway. So difficult is the terrain that during construction, bulldozers and other heavy equipment, food, supplies, and people had to be flown into the area. The 360-mile-long railway follows the winding Moisie River for part of the way from the mines at Schefferville to Sept Isles on the shore of the Gulf of St. Lawrence. The cost of the railway averaged in excess of $100,000 per mile.

There are now four principal mining centers in the district. *Schefferville*, at the end of the long railway from the major ore port of Sept Isles, is on the Quebec-Labrador border and is the largest of the centers. *Labrador City–Wabush*, further south on the same border, is connected by spur to the same railway line. *Gagnon*, further southwest in Quebec, is connected by a 200-mile rail line to the new port of Port Cartier on the St. Lawrence. Output of iron ore from these three localities is destined almost entirely for steel mills in the United States. Farther east are the massive ilmenite (titanium) deposits of *Lac Allard*, which are railed 25 miles to Havre-St.-Pierre for shipment.

fig. 19–15 The Labrador Trough mining area.

Sudbury–Clay Belt District Considering the magnitude of the Shield, this is a district of rather closely spaced mining activity. Many metals are recovered, but mostly nickel, copper, and gold.

Modern mining began in Canada after the discovery of the Sudbury nickel-copper ores in 1883. It is decidedly the outstanding metal-mining area in Canada, producing one-third of the world's supply of nickel and considerable amounts of copper, silver, and cobalt. Both open-pit and shaft mining are employed, and most of the smelting is carried on within the area. Although no metal-mining center can be considered as being permanent, Sudbury certainly approaches the goal of permanency. It has tremendous reserves and a relatively steady market.

In the Clay Belt country straddling the Ontario-Quebec boundary is a major gold-copper zone that extends from Timmins on the west 200 miles to Val d'Or on the east. Most of the gold mines are now closed; however, other base metal production has been expanding in the Clay Belt.

Two hundred miles northeast of Val d'Or is the still developing mining complex of Chibougamau. Lead, zinc, copper, silver, and gold are produced from nearly a dozen mines, the area being served by new rail connections with both the Clay Belt and the Lake St. John lowland.

At Elliott Lake, on the north shore of Lake Huron's North Channel, is situated one of the world's largest known deposits of uranium ore. After a booming few years of production, the mines were shut down in the mid-1960s for lack of market. Production has begun a slow recovery since then.

Western Ontario District This is a district of widely dispersed mines. Gold, the principal mineral produced, has a history of fluctuating output. Siderite iron ore has been dug at Michipicoten since 1899; production has increased in recent years as low-grade ores became more valuable. New copper-zinc-silver mines were recently opened in the vicinity of Manitouwadge.

Western Manitoba District Although copper-zinc ore was discovered in 1915 at Flin Flon, exploitation was not begun until a rail line was built from The Pas in 1928. Flin Flon, a well-established center, is a major copper producer and also yields considerable zinc, gold, and silver.

Other producing centers are located northeast of Flin Flon and north of the railway line to Churchill. Lynn Lake yields nickel and copper. Snow Lake produces gold and copper. But the outstanding development is at the planned town of Thompson, a

"Second Sudbury" 200 miles northeast of Flin Flon, which began producing nickel in 1961. It is the world's second largest nickel producer.

Isolated Mining Centers At several other localities in the region are more isolated mines. The following are the most significant:

1 The Pine Point mines on the south shore of Great Slave Lake are a major new source of lead and zinc. The Great Slave Lake Railway was extended east to serve the mines, and production continues to increase.

2 Gold has been produced from the north side of Great Slave Lake since 1935, when the town of Yellowknife was founded. Several mines are in production, although output has decreased in recent years.

3 The fabulous gold mines of the Klondike district of the Yukon Territory are now a thing of the past; even the last gold dredge in the area ceased operation in 1966. But base metal production in the vicinity continues, particularly from silver-lead-zinc mines near Mayo.

Hydrocarbons In the northwestern part of the region there are vast possibilities for production of mineral fuels. Coal of inferior quality is widespread in central Alaska, but the small population, lack of manufacturing, and limited railroad mileage keep production low. It is, however, important locally because transportation costs are high and the winters bitterly cold. Most of the coal mined in Alaska is from the Healy River Field not far from Fairbanks. Ladd and Eielson Air Force bases are the principal consumers of the coal.

Significant production of oil and gas has thus far come only from the Peace River district, where the Rainbow and Zama Lake oil fields are being intensively developed (fig. 19–16).

For many years it has been known that the tar sands of the Athabaska area, 250 miles northeast of Edmonton, contained a fabulous petroleum potential. The recover-

fig. 19–16 A newly developed oil area on the edge of the Peace River district, Alberta.

able reserves are estimated to be more than six times greater than the total reserves of conventional crude oil on the entire continent. Complex technological requirements and extraordinary capital investment costs have deterred development, despite the expenditure of nearly $1 billion to date. A small refinery has been in production since 1967 at Fort McMurray, but its operation is still not breaking even. Both federal and provincial (Alberta) governments have had to agree to share costs with a consortium of petroleum corporations to keep the next stage of development from foundering. The project is continuing on a massive scale, and the population of Fort McMurray has burgeoned from less than 1,000 to nearly 20,000 (fig. 19–17). The ultimate economic success of the venture seems virtually assured, although ecological and political (native land claims) objections are becoming increasingly strident.

PRODUCTIVE WATER USAGE

Hydroelectricity is the principal source of electric power in Canada, accounting for about 70 percent of the total. More than half of the installed hydroelectric-generating capacity of the nation is within the Boreal Forest Region. Hydroelectric power facilities have been critical to the success of most of the pulp milling, mining, smelting, and refining that take place within the region. In addition, a great deal of power has been transmitted southward for use in southern Quebec, southern Ontario, the prairies, southwestern British Columbia, and even the United States.

The continually increasing demand for power has led to the near maximal development of hydroelectric power sources on the tributaries to the St. Lawrence in Quebec and Ontario,[12] with the greatest development on the Ottawa, St. Maurice, and Sa-

[12] Wonders, "The Forest Frontier and Subarctic," p. 499.

fig. 19–17 The tar sands boom town of Fort McMurray on the Athabasca River (Alberta Government photo).

guenay rivers. Now that long-distance, high-voltage power transmission technology has been perfected, it can be anticipated that there will be still further extension of hydroelectric development to the more remote sections of the region.

There are presently four major development schemes under construction, or recently completed, each of which is a great distance from the ultimate market for the power:

1 The Churchill Falls project in Labrador, which delivered its first power in 1972, is the largest construction undertaking in Canadian history. Most of its power is utilized in southern Quebec.

2 In 1973 the government of Quebec initiated construction of a massive scheme; when completed it will produce twice as much electricity as Churchill Falls. It involves the diversion of three rivers, construction of four dams, several powerhouses, three airports, a seaport, 600 miles of highway, and various railway trackage, at an estimated cost of $12 billion. Much of the power will probably be marketed initially in the northeastern United States.

3 In northern Manitoba a complex scheme is under construction on the Nelson River, supplemented by a large diversion from the Churchill River, that will presumably supply all that province's power needs until the end of the century and provide a surplus for export.

4 The Peace River project in British Columbia, now in operation, sends most of its power to the Vancouver area, nearly 600 miles away.

AGRICULTURE

Despite the unattractiveness of the Boreal Forest Region for agriculture, farmers were settling along the edge of the Shield in Quebec and Ontario by the middle of the nineteenth century. Farming settlements were attempted in many places, generally reaching a peak of expansion in the 1930s. Since that time there has been more contraction than expansion in the farming frontier, with the notable exception of the Peace River district. Farm population and farm numbers have been declining in most places, but the development of larger and more efficient farms has meant a rise in productivity in some instances.

The Clay Belt and Peace River district, the only real agricultural areas, have been previously discussed. Otherwise, farming is scattered and marginal, with a few minor concentrations in places such as the Tanana Valley near Fairbanks and the delta of the Saskatchewan River near The Pas, Manitoba. "Frontier" farming is characteristic, emphasizing dairy cattle, hogs, hay, oats, and root crops.

subarctic urbanism: administrative centers and unifunctional towns

Although cities are scarce in the Boreal Forest Region, intimations of increased urbanism can be recognized (see table 19–1 for a listing of the region's largest urban places). The population continues to cluster, as bush-dwellers settle in small settlements and residents of small settlements move to larger centers. The availability of wage-labor opportunities and the advantage of having a stable mailing address for government social service checks provide the major attractions, but the well-recognized amenities of town life are inducements in the Subarctic just as they are in Megalopolis.

Most of the urban places in the region are essentially unifunctional, depending largely on a single type of economic activity for their livelihood. In some cases they are heterogeneous bush towns that have grown up haphazardly around a mine, a mill, or a transportation crossroads. The modern mining towns, however, are planned communities, designed for a specific size.

Two of the three largest urban centers in the region, Duluth-Superior and Thunder Bay, are Lake Superior ports whose well-being is intimately associated with the ship-

table 19–1   Largest Urban Places of the Boreal Forest Region

name	population of principal city	population of metropolitan area	name	population of principal city	population of metropolitan area
Bemidji, Minn.	11,438		Pembroke, Ont.	14,722	
Chibougamau, Que.	10,443		Prince Albert, Sask.	28,240	
Dawson Creek, B.C.	10,316		Rouyn, Que.	17,479	
Duluth, Minn.	93,971	259,500	Sault St. Marie, Mich.	15,807	
Escanaba, Mich.	14,708		Sault Ste. Marie,		
Fairbanks, Alaska	29,920		Ont.	79,090	
Fort McMurray, Alta.	15,139		Sudbury, Ont.	96,038	155,013
Grande Prairie, Alta.	17,471		Superior, Wis.	30,038	
Hibbing, Minn.	16,123		Thompson, Man.	17,083	
Kapuskasing, Ont.	12,542		Thunder Bay, Ont.	110,288	117,988
Kenora, Ont.	10,361		Timmins, Ont.	44,010	
Kirkland Lake, Ont.	13,486		Traverse City, Mich.	19,637	
Labrador City, Nfld.	11,877		Val-d'Or, Que.	20,479	
Marquette, Mich.	23,078		Virginia, Minn.	11,588	
North Bay, Ont.	50,819		Wausau, Wis.	33,549	
Owen Sound, Ont.	19,223		Whitehorse, Y.T.	13,045	

ping of bulk products on the Great Lakes (fig. 19–18). The twin cities of Sault Ste. Marie, Ontario, and Sault Ste. Marie, Michigan, have a crossroads function, although the big steel mill in the former center provides another dimension to its economy. Sudbury is an example of a mining-smelting town that has grown into a subregional commercial center. Smaller mining or mining-smelting centers, such as Thompson (fig. 19–19), Hibbing, or Schefferville, are more clearly unifunctional.

It should be noted that income from government sources, in the form of both

fig. 19–18   Canada's lakehead port, Thunder Bay, is marked by an array of huge shoreline grain elevators (courtesy Ontario Ministry of Industry and Tourism).

fig. 19–19 Thompson, Manitoba, is a planned city in the bush (courtesy Manitoba Department of Industry and Commerce).

transportation: decreasing remoteness and increasing accessibility

Transportation difficulties have long been bemoaned as the principal deterrent to economic prosperity in the region. With increasing technological sophistication, however, it is now clear that mere remoteness is no longer a major handicap. If the economic prize is sufficiently promising, transportation can be provided.

Early transport in the region was by canoe in summer and by dog team and sledge in winter. The maze of waterways with only short portages enabled the canoe to go unbelievable distances, and the accumulation of snow because of the absence of thaws in winter made sledging relatively easy.

Water transport became notable from the earliest days of European penetration of the region, utilizing the long rivers, large lakes, and intricate network of streams. For example, the Quetico area (that part of Ontario and Manitoba between Lake Superior and the edge of the prairie) was traversed by a varied flotilla of watercraft, and "during certain periods, the volume of traffic made this one of the busiest regions of interior North America."[14]

The Yukon and Mackenzie rivers were heavily used waterways, and the latter is still used by barges. Many other rivers and lakes had, and have, considerable usage, but the Great Lakes are by far the major waterway of commercial importance. Their traffic consists almost entirely of bulk products—iron ore, grain, and limestone downbound, and coal upbound—although considerable St. Lawrence Seaway shipping traverses the Huron-Michigan route destined for Chicago.

Canada's two transcontinental railway lines cross the Shield through southern On-

wages and social service payments, also significantly contributes to the local economy for many urban places in the region. Whitehorse and Yellowknife have become territorial capitals, whereby their economy has profited. Many other towns in the region also serve as modified administrative centers, with district or subdistrict offices of various government agencies headquartered there. Often the economic base for small, subarctic settlements can be summarized as "government-supported economy supplemented by trapping." There continues to be questioning of the wisdom of diffusing the administrative infrastructure into communities that no longer have a viable economic base and thus perpetuating stagnant communities that often have serious economic and social problems.[13]

[13] William C. Wonders, "The Canadian Northwest: Some Geographical Perspectives," *Canadian Geographical Journal,* 80 (May 1970), 164.

[14] Bruce M. Littlejohn, "Quetico Country: Part I," *Canadian Geographical Journal,* 71 (August 1965), 41.

tario, providing critical transport links for the nation and encouraging mineral and forestry exploitation. Two rail lines were built across the region to Hudson Bay, reaching Churchill in 1929 and Moosonee in 1932. Most other railway construction in the region was designed as feeder lines to connect mining localities with the outside world: the Labrador Trough lines, Chibougamau, the Clay Belt, the various Manitoba mining centers, and most recently the Great Slave Lake Railway to Pine Point.

In the far northwest are two railway routes of different origin. The *White Pass and Yukon Railway* was built in 1898 during the feverish boom days of the Klondike. It is 111 miles long and extends from Skagway over White Pass to Whitehorse. The *Alaska Railroad*, extending 470 miles from Seward to Fairbanks, was built by the United States government to help develop and settle interior Alaska. It was completed in 1923. This route has greatly stimulated mining in its tributary area, and in turn mining supplies the larger part of the traffic.

The relatively few miles of roads and highways in the region are being rapidly expanded. The Upper Lakes area and Clay Belt have been fairly well served for years, but only recently has roadway construction been accelerated elsewhere. The *Alaska Highway,* extending 1,500 miles from the Peace River district to Fairbanks, has been an important connection since its construction in 1941–42; it is an all-weather road, but only the portion within Alaska has been surfaced (fig. 19–20). The *Mackenzie Highway* is a 650-mile link from the Peace River district to Great Slave Lake, extending as far north as Yellowknife.[15] Elsewhere in the region more roads are built each year. For example, an all-weather road will soon be

fig. 19–20   The Alaska Highway is one of the outstanding roadways of the Boreal Forest Region. The portion in Alaska has been completely paved (courtesy Federal Highway Administration).

completed down the length of the Mackenzie Valley to its delta, and a connection to the Mackenzie delta from the Yukon Territory is scheduled for completion soon. Furthermore, roads usable only in winter have been bulldozed to provide seasonal access in many remoter localities.

Perhaps the most important development in the history of the region was the introduction of the airplane in about 1920. It has revolutionized communications and accelerated the pattern of economic and social progress. There are increasing networks of scheduled airline service, particularly in the Mackenzie Valley and central Alaska, and nonscheduled bush-pilot flying is significant. Light aircraft can be equipped with pontoons, skis, nosewarmers, and other devices to permit operation into almost any area in both summer and winter. The use of the slower but more flexible helicopter has further benefited the region.

A much more recent form of transportation in the region is the long-distance pipe-

[15] The completion of an all-weather road to Yellowknife allowed the price of perishable groceries to drop by nearly 50 percent overnight, a clear indication of the economic effect of reasonable transportation in the more remote parts of the region. See Wonders, "The Canadian Northwest: Some Geographical Perspectives," p. 157.

line. Pipeline development within the last decade has generated more acrimony than any other issue in a period of notable controversies (see vignette below).

tourism

The recreational activities of the region are of two principal types: brief winter and summer visits from nearby population centers, and more extensive expeditions involving considerable travel.

A number of major population centers lies just beyond the southern margin of the region, and short-term visitors from these areas constitute the major component of tourism in the Boreal Forest Region. The Upper Lakes area is within driving distance from many Midwestern cities, whose summer weather is sufficiently uncomfortable to urge "North Woods" vacations on its populace. Thus, many Detroiters visit northern Michigan; people from Chicago and Milwaukee go to northern Wisconsin; and Twin Cities residents travel to the Minnesota north country.

A similar situation prevails for urbanites in southern Canada. Principal areas of attraction include the Laurentides Park area, particularly for the people of Quebec City; the Central Laurentians, favored for skiing as well as summer activities, especially by Montrealers; Algonquin Park near Toronto, notable for fishing and canoeing; the lake country of southern Manitoba and Riding

pipeline controversies and realities

Product pipelines are not unprecedented in the Boreal Forest Region; there have been several in the Upper Lakes area for some years, and a few others in scattered localities. It was not until the decade of the 1970s, however, that long-distance pipeline construction was undertaken amid unending controversy and expenditures of unprecedented magnitude.

After considerable prospecting in various areas, exploratory drilling in 1968 confirmed the existence of a truly immense reserve of petroleum (possibly 50 billion barrels) and natural gas (perhaps 300 trillion cubic feet) on the "North Slope" (the Arctic Ocean coastal plain, in the Tundra Region) of Alaska, focusing on Prudhoe Bay. Before production could begin, however, the problem of transportation had to be solved. After considering various alternatives it was decided that the most feasible plan would be to build a pipeline across the state to the Gulf of Alaska, whence the products could be moved by tanker to national markets. Accordingly, an 800-mile route was surveyed from Prudhoe Bay via Fairbanks to the port of Valdez on Prince William Sound (fig. 19-a). A consortium of oil companies formed the Alyeska Pipeline Service Company to build the Trans-Alaska Pipeline System (TAPline); a three-year construction schedule was designed, and $100 million worth of 48-inch diameter pipe was unloaded in Valdez.

Actual construction, however, was delayed for nearly five years because of protracted litigation in the courts over two major issues: native land claims and potential environmental degradation. The land claims were satisfied in 1971 by congressional action (discussed under "Some 'New' Northern Concerns"). The environmental objections were not abated until 1974, after exhaustive environmental impact assessments had been made and extensive measures undertaken to mitigate the pipeline's deleterious effects on vegetation, permafrost, caribou migrations, anadromous fish movements, marine life in Prince William Sound, and a host of other ecological considerations.

Actual construction began as soon as court approval was received in 1974. At working peak some 24,000 people were laboring 12 hours per day, 7 days a week. The urgency for quick completion was occasioned by frustration at the long enforced delay and by the fact that most of the work was financed by loans, with interest costs running to more than $1.75

(Continued)

Mountain National Park, for Winnipeg; Prince Albert National Park near Saskatoon; and Elk Island National Park, a wildlife preserve within picnicking distance of Edmonton.

The abundant fish and wildlife resources of the taiga are major attractions for hunters on both sides of the international boundary. They make long trips, frequently by air, to fish in remote lakes for trout, whitefish, pike, perch, and muskie, and to hunt moose, caribou, bear, and deer.

some "new" northern concerns

Within the last few years in northern Anglo-America several problems that were pre-viously either unknown or quiescent have had remarkable impact. They are not restricted to the Boreal Forest Region but are largely confined to it. Two of the most pressing are summarized here.

NATIVE LAND CLAIMS

The native inhabitants—Indian, Eskimo, Aleut, and Metis—of the North have emerged from decades of relatively unobtrusive docility to assert, with increasing stridency, claims for much greater control of their own social, economic, and political destiny. These claims focus particularly on land rights and have been unusually effective in attracting attention in both Ottawa and Washington because they have arisen at

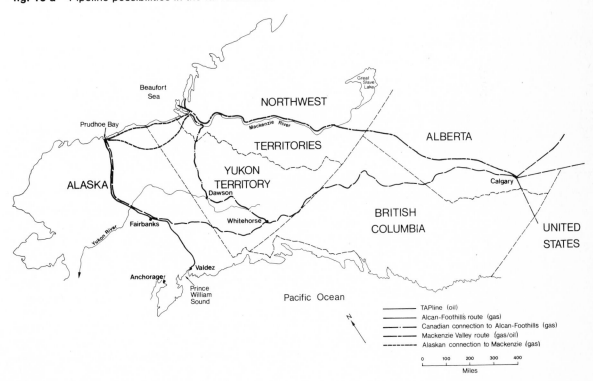

fig. 19-a   Pipeline possibilities in the far Northwest.

least partially in direct opposition to previously discussed energy developments.

Judge Berger stated with reference to the Mackenzie Valley:

[*Our*] *society has refused to take native culture seriously. European institutions, values and use of land were seen as the basis of culture. Native institutions, values and language were rejected, ignored or misunderstood and . . . [we] had no difficulty in supposing that native people possessed no real culture at all. Education was perceived as the most effective instrument of cultural change: so, educational systems were introduced that were intended to provide the native people with a useful and meaningful cultural inheritance, since their own ancestors had left them none.*[16]

Native peoples constitute the bulk of the permanent population in northern Anglo-America, and a large part of the white population is temporary. Thus it seems logical that the future of the North should be determined to some degree by its permanent residents. This is the underlying thought behind native claims.

Thus far there have been two major "settlements" of such claims:

Alaskan Land Claims Representatives of the Alaskan native populace (Indian, Eskimos, and Aleuts) banded together to form the Alaskan Federation of Natives, which instituted law suits claiming native ownership of three-fourths of the state's 375 million acres of land. Congress, goaded by the fact that the litigation prevented TAPline construction, passed the Alaska Native Claims Settlement Act in 1971, remanding to Alaska's estimated 50,000 native people the title to 44 million acres of land (equivalent in area to the state of Washington) and a cash settlement of nearly $1 billion. To implement the settlement, Alaska was divided into 12 regions, with a native regional corporation established in each. The regional corporations and approximately 250 village corporations were allowed to select acreage, pro-rated on the basis of popula-

[16] *Northern Frontier, Northern Homeland: The Report of the Mackenzie Valley Pipeline Inquiry*, Vol. 1 (Ottawa: Minister of Supply and Services Canada, 1977), p. xviii.

million *per day*. Upon completion in 1977 the TAPline had the distinction of being not only the most controversial but also the most costly (nearly $8 billion) privately financed construction job in national history.

Initial flow began in 1977, but it was another year before the planned capacity of 2 million barrels per day was reached. Practical success has now been achieved, and there are obvious economic benefits for both the region and the national energy shortage. The endeavor, however, has been a mixed blessing. Despite efforts to soften the environmental impact, there are many degredational results. Moreover, the effects of enormous temporary population influx, dislocation of traditional economy, graft, crime, inflation, alcoholism, and many other social problems may be overwhelming in the long run.

As ambitious as the TAPline is, all of its superlatives are likely to be surpassed in the near future by the next subarctic long-distance pipe-line, which will be designed to bring natural gas from Alaska's North Slope and Canada's Mackenzie delta and Beaufort Sea areas to consumers in the conterminous states and southern Canada. Several different routes for such a transportation system have been proposed, and detailed studies of engineering and economic feasibility, as well as social, economic, and ecological impacts, have been completed.

Most of the early support was for a route up the Mackenzie Valley from the delta, where it would be fed by an extension from Prudhoe Bay that followed either a coastal or an interior route. A Canadian government-appointed board of inquiry recommended, however, that a Mackenzie Valley pipeline be postponed for a decade to allow sufficient time for a just settlement of native land claims and that no feeder line ever be built across the northern Yukon from Alaska because of the environmental and social damages that would result.

tion, to which they would have full title. The ultimate aim of this settlement appears to be the provision of land and capital resources for local economic development.

James Bay Land Claims Some 10,000 natives (mostly Cree Indians and some Eskimos) who inhabit the area affected by the James Bay hydroelectric project agreed in 1975 to accept a provincial-federal bequest of $225 million and a monopoly of hunting, fishing, and trapping rights on 65,000 square miles of land in return for relinquishing their claim to 400,000 square miles of northern Quebec.

Native claims are also being made in other parts of northern Canada, most notably in the Mackenzie Valley and delta, where some 11,000 Indians (or Dene, as they refer to themselves), 1,500 Metis, and 2,500 Eskimos reside. Native desires in this area are more complex and embrace more than simple land claims. They reject settlement along the Alaskan or James Bay lines and are seeking protection for their land-based native economy, ownership of subsurface as well as surface land rights, control of native education, and some measure of native self-government. Their aspirations are to avoid assimilation into general Canadian society by maintaining a high degree of distinct cultural identity. The Canadian government has thus far categorically rejected the idea of separate native government in the Northwest Territories, and it seems clear that the satisfaction of Mackenzie Valley native claims will be more complicated than those previously described.

THE DISPOSITION OF ALASKAN PUBLIC LANDS

At the time Alaska became a state, most of its land was owned and controlled by the federal government. The statehood act allowed the selection of 104 million acres (about 29 percent of the total) for state government ownership, and the Alaska Native Claims Settlement Act granted 44 million acres to native corporations. Of the exten-

Three other Canadian boards of inquiry examined alternate routes and made their recommendations; the United States government also considered various proposals. Finally, late in 1977, the two governments agreed upon the tentatively named "Alcan-Foothills" route, which would follow the TAPline corridor from Prudhoe Bay to Fairbanks and the Alaska Highway from Fairbanks to Alberta, from which branches would distribute gas to eastern Canada and the United States. A subsequent feeder line would be built from the Mackenzie delta to Whitehorse (along the route of the Dempster Highway) so that Canadian gas could be pumped into the system. The most prominent consideration in selection of this routing is obviously the fact that a transportation corridor is already in existence for almost the entirety of the planned system. This simplifies the construction work, but more importantly, it localizes most environmental, social, and economic impacts to areas where disruptions already have taken place, thus minimizing the negative aspects of construction.

The trunk pipeline will extend for nearly 3,000 miles in Alaska and Canada alone and will certainly be the largest single private energy project in history. The estimated cost is $10 billion, but the actual expenditure may greatly exceed that figure (the TAPline cost nearly eight times its original estimate). It is planned that the main line will be in operation by 1983.

By the time the Alcan-Foothills system is under construction, it is likely that other pipeline projects will at least be in a definitive planning stage. For example, transportation of Canadian petroleum from the Beaufort Sea and High Arctic islands will be a logical necessity before long. Thus the proliferation of terrestrial routeways, with their associated positive and negative effects, across the Boreal Forest Region becomes increasingly significant.

sive remaining area of unreserved public land, Congress has required itself to specify areas suitable for incorporation into the four federal systems of conservation reserves: national parks, national forests, wildlife refuges, and wild and scenic rivers (fig. 19–21). These "national interest lands" are temporarily referred to as d-2 lands, after the section of the pertinent legislation.

Five major proposals are now before Congress, each containing detailed designations of which land should be in each category. These proposals range from as few as 67 million acres to as many as 106 million acres. Most of the plans include a core of 3 to 6 new national parks, 4 to 6 new national monuments, 3 new national forests, about 12 wildlife refuges, up to 24 wild rivers, and 2 or 3 national reserves (a new category somewhat similar to national parks). Further complexities involve the specification of wilderness areas within each system, regulation of hardrock mineral development, control of oil and gas leasing, and the delicate question of subsistence hunting and fishing. Exhaustive hearings have examined the multiple facets of this issue, and the bill that will finally result has been characterized by some as the most important natural resource legislation of the century.

fig. 19–21 Existing and proposed reservations of national interest lands in Alaska.

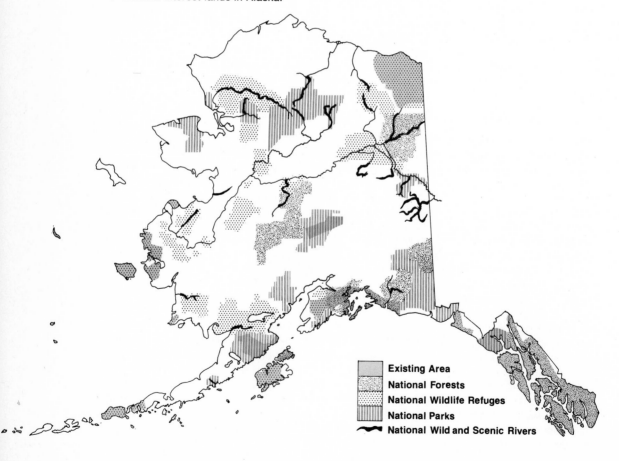

	Existing Area
	National Forests
	National Wildlife Refuges
	National Parks
	National Wild and Scenic Rivers

the outlook

The Boreal Forest Region is primarily an empty area, so far as human occupancy is concerned, and logically will remain so. It represents, however, the northern frontier, and so long as there are frontiers, there will be people trying to push them back. Yet today many parts of the region are emptier than they were 50 or 100 years ago, as bushdwellers increasingly congregate in larger, permanent settlements.

The region's population is youthful. The Yukon Territory has a smaller proportion of old people than any Canadian province, and Alaska has a smaller proportion than any of the other 49 states. This preponderance of young adults results in a high birth rate; the Yukon's is the highest in Canada, and Alaska's is the highest in the United States. But the population is not a stable one. There is considerable seasonal fluctuation, with a summer peak and a winter ebb.

Many people come into the region for temporary summer jobs and then leave at the end of the season. Even many of the year-round residents, attracted by high wages in "hardship" posts, have come to the region on a temporary basis. But with rapidly improving transportation facilities, population stability should increase. In particular, the increasing mileage of roads makes it possible for residents to go "outside" fairly easily and thus encourages them to remain in the region on a permanent or long-term basis.

Economic and demographic stability should also be improved in the Upper Lakes area by the long-term prospects for iron mining. The combination of taconite, pelletization, and enlightened tax laws mean that the Lake Superior iron ranges should continue to be productive for several more decades.

For the region as a whole, mineral industries have been and will continue to be the keystone to the economy. More major ore deposits will undoubtedly be found and developed. It is unlikely that there will ever be a second Sudbury, but more Scheffervilles and Thompsons are certainly to be anticipated.

Large-scale energy developments—oil and gas exploration and production, oil sand development, pipeline projects, and dam building—will dominate the scene in many areas. The ramifications of these major projects are far-reaching and long-lasting.

The role of native peoples should become increasingly significant in most parts of the region. Their political power is increasing, and financial settlements of native claims are providing them with some economic leverage for the first time. Still, a high proportion of the native population will continue to be socially and economically disadvantaged.

As with so many "wilderness" regions, there will be an increasing emphasis on tourism and recreation. Genuine tourists will begin to appear where now only fishermen and hunters go. There is only a short time-lag in Anglo-America between the completion of any fairly negotiable road and the appearance of motels, trailer camps, picnic tables, roadside litter, and new money.

selected bibliography

ALVEY, JOHN, "The Nelson: Manitoba's Own River," *Canadian Geographical Journal*, 78 (1969), 2–11.

BARR, LORNA, "Nawapa: A Continental Water Development Scheme for North America," *Geography*, 60 (1975), 111–19.

BERKES, FIKRET, "James Bay: The Coastal Fishery of the Cree Indians," *Canadian Geographical Journal*, 93 (December 1976– January 1977), 60–65.

BONEFANT, C., "Resurgence of the Caribou in Quebec," *Canadian Geographical Journal*, 89 (August 1974), 48–51.

BORCHERT, JOHN R., AND DONALD P. YEAGER, *Atlas*

of Minnesota Resources and Settlement. Minneapolis: University of Minnesota Department of Geography, 1968.

BROOK, G. A., AND D. C. FORD, "Nahanni Karst: Unique Northern Landscape," Canadian Geographical Journal, 88 (June 1974), 36–43.

BROWN, L. CARSON, "The Golden Porcupine," Canadian Geographical Journal, 74 (1967), 4–17.

———, "Kirkland Lake—50 Golden Years," Canadian Geographical Journal, 79 (1969), 2–15.

———, "Ontario's Mineral Heritage," Canadian Geographical Journal, 76 (1968), 80–101.

BROWN, R. J. E., Permafrost in Canada. Toronto: University of Toronto Press, 1970.

———, "Permafrost Map of Canada," Canadian Geographical Journal, 76 (1968), 56–63.

BRYSON, REID A., Airmasses, Streamlines, and the Boreal Forest. Madison: University of Wisconsin Press, 1966.

FORD, DEREK C., "The Extraordinary Landscape of South Nahanni," Canadian Geographical Journal, 94 (February–March 1977), 56–63.

FULLER, W. A., "Canada's Largest National Park," Canadian Geographical Journal, 91 (December 1975), 14–21.

GIBBENS, R. G., "How Hydro Power Brought Aluminum to Canada," Canadian Geographical Journal, 93 (August–September 1976), 18–27.

GILL, DON, "Modification of Northern Alluvial Habitats by River Development," Canadian Geographer, 17 (1973), 138–53.

HARDING, LEE, "What Are We Doing to the Northern Yukon?" Canadian Geographical Journal, 92 (January–February 1976), 36–43.

HARE, F. KENNETH, AND J. C. RITCHIE, "The Boreal Bioclimates," Geographical Review, 62 (1972), 333–65.

HARMAN, J. R., AND J. G. HENRY, "Lake Breezes and Summer Rainfall," Annals, Association of American Geographers, 62 (1972), 375–87.

HARRINGTON, LYN, "Thompson, Manitoba: Suburbia in the Bush," Canadian Geographical Journal, 81 (November 1970), 154–63.

———, "Thunder Bay: The Lakehead City," Canadian Geographical Journal, 80 (January 1970), 2–9.

———, "The Yukon River in Canada," Canadian Geographical Journal, 85 (1972), 200–209.

HAYTER, ROGER, "Corporate Strategies and Industrial Change in the Canadian Forest Product Industries," Geographical Review, 66 (1976), 209–28.

INGLIS, GEORGE ERSKINE, "Yellowknife: Capital of the Northwest Territories," Canadian Geographical Journal, 80 (February 1970), 38–45.

LANGMAN, R. C., "Northeastern Ontario Under the Microscope," Canadian Geographical Journal, 93 (August–September 1976), 70–72.

NAYSMITH, JOHN, "Changing Land Use Patterns in the North," Canadian Geographical Journal, 90 (January 1975), 11–18.

PUGH, DONALD E., "Ontario's Great Clay Belt Hoax," Canadian Geographical Journal, 90 (January 1976), 19–24.

PROVINCE OF BRITISH COLUMBIA LANDS SERVICE, The Peace River Bulletin Area. Victoria: Queen's Printer, 1968.

"Richard Harrington's Yukon," Alaska Geographic, 2, no. 2 (1974), entire issue.

RITCHIE, W., AND H. J. WALKER, "River in the Frozen North," Geographical Magazine, 46 (1974), 634–40.

ROBERGE, ROGER A., "Resource Towns: The Pulp and Paper Communities," Canadian Geographical Journal, 94 (February–March 1977), 28–35.

ROBINSON, J. LEWIS, Resources of the Canadian Shield. Toronto: Methuen Publications, 1969.

SHORTRIDGE, JAMES R., "The Collapse of Frontier Farming in Alaska," Annals, Association of American Geographers, 66 (1976), 583–604.

SPRAGINS, F. K., "Syncrude: Full Steam Ahead," Canadian Geographical Journal, 90 (February 1975), 46–49.

SYMINGTON, FRASER, Tuktu: A Question of Survival. Ottawa: Canadian Wildlife Service, 1965.

WALLACE, A. I., AND P. J. WILLIAMS, "Problems of Building Roads in the North," Canadian Geographical Journal, 89 (July–August 1974), 40–47.

WIGHT, J. B., "Water Distribution and Regional Planning: Northwest Territories," Albertan Geographer, 9 (1973), 40–49.

WIGHT, PAMELA, "Peaceful Progress in the Peace River Country," *Canadian Geographical Journal*, 92 (March–April 1976), 36–43.

"Wilderness Proposals: Which Way for Alaska's Lands?" *Alaska Geographic*, 4, no. 4 (1977), entire issue.

WONDERS, WILLIAM C., ed., *Canada's Changing North*. Toronto: McClelland and Stewart Limited, 1971.

———, "The Canadian Northwest: Some Geographical Perspectives," *Canadian Geographical Journal*, 80 (May 1970), 146–65.

———, "Japan's Role in Land Resource Development in the Canadian Northwest," *Journal of Geography*, 75 (1976), 200–208.

———, ed., *The North*. Toronto: University of Toronto Press, 1972.

YLI-JOKIPII, PENTTI, "Recent Trends in Mining Activity in the Upper Peninsula of Michigan and Their Effect on Regional Development," *Acta Geographica*, 25 (1971), 1–21.

20

THE
TUNDRA

The Tundra, one of the largest regions in Anglo-America, is the most sparsely populated, the least productive economically, and certainly the least promising as far as humanity's future occupance is concerned.[1] In few parts of the earth is nature more niggardly and more unyielding, and nowhere else are people's ways of living more closely attuned to the physical environment. The Tundra Region is primarily the land of the Eskimos; yet they have established themselves permanently only in small numbers.

Parts of this region have long been known to white men. Five centuries before Columbus reached the New World, Norsemen had visited the coast of Labrador. Explorers, whalers, sealers, and fishermen came with surprising frequency to what is now Canada's eastern Arctic coasts and the Bering Sea fringes of Alaska; however, only rarely did they establish anything more than very temporary settlements. Along with the hot deserts, the rainy tropics, and the lofty mountains, the tundra is one of the least desirable places for settlement. The few white inhabitants have gone to the Tundra Region to get furs, exploit minerals, convert the natives to Christianity, represent their respective governments, or man defense or weather stations.

[1] *Tundra* is a Finnish word meaning "barren land."

Cities and towns like those in the mid-latitudes are virtually nonexistent. In the more remote areas, a settlement nucleus may include only three or four families. Nevertheless, wherever they are and whatever their size, the settlements of the region are always dominated by the immensity of the environment. The inhabited places are also separated by great distances of trackless and treeless land or by equally barren water or ice. Within a settlement, the buildings and artifacts of people take on a peculiarly aggressive significance. There are no trees or shrubs to cover mistakes, provide transitions, or ease the exposed rawness. The sparse, slow-growing, unobtrusive vegetation finds it difficult to survive, and where it has been ripped away by human endeavor, the nakedness persists for a long time. Settlements are inevitably scars on the fragile landscape.

This, then, is a region in which nature thoroughly dominates mankind. Matters such as ice thickness, windchill factor, permafrost depth, caribou migration route, hours of daylight, blizzard frequency, abundance of harp seal, and formation of fast ice are critical to human existence.

Conversely, what people do in this region has remarkably long-lasting effects on the environment. Although the surface of the land is rock-hard through the long winter months, during the brief summer period it is extremely susceptible to the impress of human activities. The structural fragility of the ground-hugging tundra plants and the spongy soil beneath them is such that any kind of compression leaves a mark that is not soon erased. The scrape of a bulldozer blade will leave a scar for generations, the track of a wheeled vehicle will be visible for years, and even a single footprint may be obvious for months.

The Tundra Region includes the part of Anglo-America that extends from the Bering Sea on the west to the Atlantic Ocean on the east and from the Boreal Forest on the south to the Arctic Sea on the north; it also includes the vast Arctic archipelago north of the Canadian mainland (fig. 20–1).

There is considerable ignorance of the Tundra Region. More firsthand information has been gained about it in the past three decades than in the preceding three centuries. Probably the most important concept is that this is not a totally uniform area; there are many areas, and few if any statements apply to all of them.

Particularly notable in this respect is the fact that the eastern and western extremities of the region—coastal Labrador in the east and the Bering seacoast–Aleutian Island area in the west—have a pronounced orientation toward commercial fishing that is quite unlike the situation over most of the tundra. This is a function of the availability of exploitable resources—cod in the east and salmon and fur seals in the west—which is governed largely by climatic differences.

fig. 20–1 The Tundra Region (base map copyright A. K. Lobeck; reprinted by permission of Hammond, Inc.).

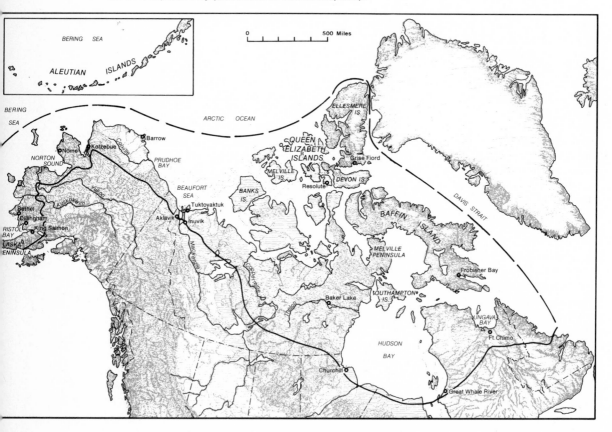

the physical setting

CLIMATE

The tundra is not, as novelists would have it, a land of perpetual ice and snow. Winter temperatures are low, but they are higher than in the taiga to the south. Point Barrow has yet to record winter temperatures as low as those characterizing certain stations in North Dakota and Montana. Extremes become greater south of Point Barrow, since the country increases in altitude and is more remote from the ameliorating effects of the ocean. Thus the temperature range at Allakaket, 350 miles to the south, is much greater; whereas the lowest and highest temperatures at Point Barrow are −56°F. and 78°F. respectively, those at Allakaket are −79°F. and 90°F. But everywhere in the Tundra Region winters are long and summers short. Although the temperature range at Point Barrow is the more limited, the growing season is only 17 days; at Allakaket, however, it is 54. There can be two to four months without snow. The growing season along much of the Arctic coast is less than 40 days.

Air at low temperatures cannot absorb or retain much water vapor, so the precipitation is light and varies over most of the region from 5 to 15 inches. In the far east and far west there are higher totals, but part of the High Arctic is the most arid area of Anglo-America; most of Ellesmere Island, for example, is a frigid desert that receives less than 2 inches of moisture annually. The precipitation that does fall in the region is mostly fine dry snow, or sleet.

Winds, especially in winter, are very strong and frequently howl day after day. They greatly affect the sensible temperature; thus on a quiet day a temperature as low as −30°F. is not at all unpleasant if one is suitably clothed, but on a windy day a temperature of zero may be quite unbearable. The wind sweeps unobstructed across the frozen land and sea and packs the snow into drifts so hard that they often take no footprints, and no snowshoes are required for human locomotion. Winter windchill not only discourages people and animals from moving about but also significantly contributes to the slow growth of plants. But it is not always cold. The long daylight hours of summer combine with continual reflection off water surfaces to produce heat that can occasionally become intolerable.

The coastal areas of Labrador, the Bering Sea, and the Aleutian Islands experience widespread overcast conditions, considerable fogginess, and more storminess than other parts of the region. The relative warmth of the Aleutians contributes to much heavier precipitation there; persistent mist and rain are characteristic. On the average, the Aleutians experience only two clear days per month.

Perhaps the climatic phenomenon of greatest significance to humans is the seasonal fluctuation in length of days and nights. Continual daylight in summer and continual darkness in winter persist for lingering weeks, and even months, in the northerly latitudes.

TERRAIN

The gross topographic features of the Tundra Region are similar to those of other parts of the continent; only in relatively superficial details does the unique stamp of the arctic environment appear. Most typical are flat and featureless coastal plains, which occupy much of the Canadian central Arctic, as well as most of the northern and western coasts of Alaska. Prominent mountains occur in several localities. The massive Brooks Range separates the Yukon and Arctic watersheds in northern Alaska (fig. 20–2). The eastern fringe of Arctic Canada, from Labrador to northern Ellesmere Island, is mountain-girt with numerous peaks over 6,000 feet, rising to the 8,544-foot level of Barbeau Peak in the far north.

Of special interest is the 1,000-mile long chain of the Aleutian Islands, extending westward in a broad arc from the tip of the Alaska Peninsula. These treeless, desolate, fog-shrouded islands are essentially a series

fig. 20-2 The snowy labyrinth of the Brooks Range in winter (courtesy Alyeska Pipeline Company).

of volcanic mountain tops, comprising 14 major islands, 40 lesser ones, and countless islets and rocks.

The coastline adjacent to Baffin Bay and the Labrador Sea is notably embayed and fiorded as a result of glacial modification of the numerous short, deep, preglacial valleys that crossed the highland rim. Along the east coast of the three islands (Ellesmere, Devon, and Baffin) and Labrador are innu-

merable fiords, some of which penetrate inland for more than 50 miles. Offshore is a fringe of rounded, rocky islets called skerries.

A number of large rivers flow into the Arctic Ocean and Bering Sea from the continental mainland, but the Arctic islands have no streams of importance. Most notable of the rivers are the Mackenzie and the Yukon, both of which form extensive deltas (fig. 20-3); that of the former river contains literally thousands of miles of distributary channels and as many as 20,000 small lakes.[2] Other major rivers of the region are the Kuskokwim and Colville in Alaska and the Coppermine and Thelon in the Northwest Territories.

DISTINCTIVE TOPOGRAPHIC FEATURES OF THE ARCTIC

There are three kinds of distinctive landform features in the Tundra Region that are limited to this harsh environment.

Icecaps Icecaps and glaciers constitute less than 5 percent of the ground cover of Arctic Canada, but many of them are quite large in size.[3] Baffin Island contains two icecaps that are larger in area than the province of Prince Edward Island, and the islands north of Baffin (Bylot, Devon, Axel Heiberg, and Ellsemere) each contain icecaps that are still more extensive in size (fig. 20-4). Almost all these ice features have been diminishing in area and thinning in depth during the twentieth century, and the evidence of glacial recession is conspicuous.

Ground newly uncovered by the retreating ice front is raw, light-coloured, unvegetated, in contrast to the ground beyond the trimline which was the position reached by the glacier at its greatest recent extent. Many small glaciers have completely disappeared since the turn of the century, larger ones have become 300 to 500 feet thinner and in some instances their snouts have retreated several miles.[4]

[2] J. Ross Mackay, "The Mackenzie Delta." *Canadian Geographical Journal,* 78 (May 1969), 148.

[3] J. Brian Bird, *The Physiography of Arctic Canada* (Baltimore, Md.: Johns Hopkins Press, 1967), p. 23.

[4] J. D. Ives, "Glaciers," *Canadian Geographical Journal,* 74 (April 1967), 115.

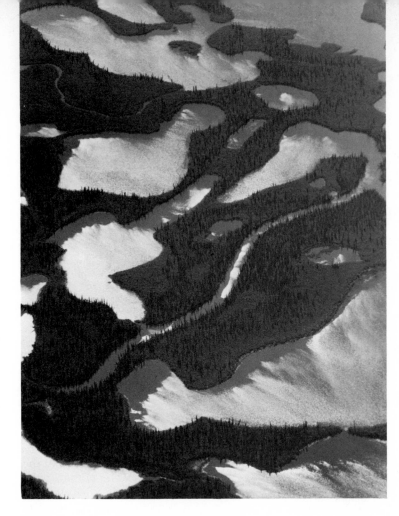

fig. 20-3 Looking south across the watery expanse of the Mackenzie River delta, frozen by an August cold snap (courtesy Information Canada Photothèque).

fig. 20-4 Ice conditions in the Tundra Region.

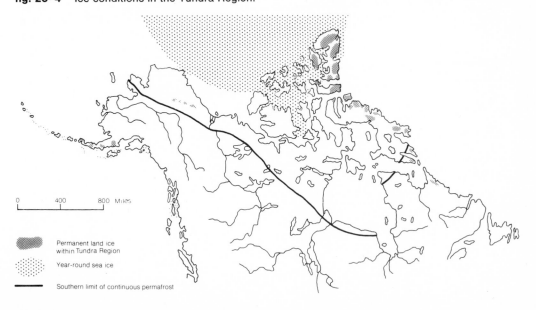

Raised Gravel Beaches Adjacent to many portions of the present coastline are relics of previous sea levels. Characteristically these appear as gravelly beaches that may extend inland for several miles and may reach heights several hundred feet above the contemporary coastline. These subaerial beaches indicate emergence of the land after the great weight of Pleistocene ice sheets was removed by melting. The postglacial recovery of the land from ice depression varies from 100 to as much as 900 vertical feet in some places.

Patterned Ground The most unique and eyecatching of tundra terrain is patterned ground, the generic name applied to various geometric patterns that repeatedly appear over large areas in the Arctic. The patterns, consisting of circles, ovals, polygons, and stripes, are of apparently varied but still unknown origin, although it is generally accepted that frost action is instrumental in their formation.

A very distinctive type of patterned ground is the tundra polygon . . . [which resemble] enormous mud cracks, such as those of a dried-up muddy pool, but with diameters of from 50 to 100 feet. The tundra polygons may be nearly as regularly shaped as the squares on a checkerboard, but most are irregular, somewhat like the markings on turtle shells. The boundary between two adjacent polygons is a ditch. Beneath the ditch there is an ice wedge of whitish bubbly ice which tapers downwards, like the blade of an axe driven into the ground. Some ice wedges are more than ten feet wide at the top and are tens of feet deep. . . . On a smaller scale, the ground observer may see stones arranged in circles or garlands a few feet across, like stone necklaces; or the ground may have stripes trending downhill. . . . Of particular interest to people in the western Arctic are the conical ice-cored hills called pingos, an Eskimo word for hill [fig. 20–5]. The pingos are most numerous near the Mackenzie Delta, where there are nearly 1,500 of them. The pingos may reach a height of 150 feet and so are prominent features in the landscape. They are found typically in shallow or drained lakes and are believed to have grown as the result of the penetration of permafrost into a thawed lake basin. Each pingo has an ice core of clear ice. If the ice core should melt, a depression with a doughnut-shaped ring enclosing a lake is left behind.[5]*

[5] J. Ross Mackay, "Arctic Landforms," in *The Unbelievable Land*, ed. I. Norman Smith (Ottawa: Department of Indian Affairs and Northern Development, n.d.), p. 62.

fig. 20–5 A pair of pingos near the northern edge of the Mackenzie delta. These ice-cored hills are conspicuous in an otherwise featureless landscape (courtesy Canadian Government Travel Bureau).

The principal significance of patterned ground is that it demonstrates the mobility of tundra terrain, emphasizing the role of soil ice in producing geomorphic processes that are largely unknown further south.[6]

PERMAFROST

Most, but not all, of the Tundra Region is underlain with permafrost. In the Aleutian Islands and part of the Alaska Peninsula, it is unknown. In most of the region, however, permafrost is both continuous and thick.

NATURAL VEGETATION

Most of the Arctic region as here considered refers to that part of Anglo-America lying north of the tree line, the great coniferous forest belt. The line on the map separating the tundra from the forest symbolizes a zone within which the trees gradually become smaller and more scattered until they disappear altogether (fig. 20–6). It coincides rather closely with the 50° isotherm for the warmest month. This zone, in most instances, lies south of the Arctic Circle, even reaching the 55th parallel on the west side of James Bay.

From area to area, however, the boundaries between taiga and tundra differ, and the extent to which the taiga penetrates the tundra seems to depend on a combination of low temperatures, wind velocity, and availability of soil moisture. The forest boundary extends farthest north in the valley of the Mackenzie River, where a forest of white spruce reaches into the southern part of the delta, at about the 68th parallel. There are also significant, although not large, forest outliers in the valleys of the Thelon and lower Coppermine rivers.

The characteristic vegetation association of this region is tundra. The tundra consists of a great variety of low-growing and inconspicuous plants that belong to five principal groups:

[6] J. Brian Bird, *The Natural Landscapes of Canada: A Study in Regional Earth Science* (Toronto: Wiley Publishers of Canada, Ltd., 1972), p. 160.

fig. 20–6　The treeline north of Great Whale River in Quebec. In the distance a scattering of trees marks the northern margin of the boreal forest. In the foreground is the characteristic tundra association of grasses, forbs, and lichen-covered rocks (courtesy Canadian Government Travel Bureau).

1　lichens, which grow either on rocks or in mats on the ground where they form the principal food supply of the migrating caribou herds

2　mosses

3　grasses and grass-like herbs

4　cushion plants

5　low shrubs

This is one of the world's harshest floristic environments, and the growing season is so short that there is simply not time during the brief summer for the life processes of annual plants to be completed. Instead the plant cover consists of hardy perennials, which can remain dormant for as long as ten months and then spring to life for an accelerated annual cycle during the abbreviated summer period. This means that arctic plants have a very slow weight increase. Studies of arctic willow (*Salix arctica*) on Cornwallis Island, for example, show an an-

553

nual increment of only one-third of total plant weight; in the midlatitudes such an increase can take place in a week.[7] Nevertheless, this limited vegetation has great value because directly or indirectly it is the food of all the land animals. It is assimilated directly by the herbivores, and these are the prey of the carnivores.

NATIVE ANIMAL LIFE

The regional ecosystems are characterized by simplicity and sensitivity. Only a few animal species inhabit the lands and waters of the region. Although they must be hardy to survive the rigorous environment, at the same time they are vulnerable, largely because of a limited food supply, a slow growth rate that delays maturing and restricts reproductive potential, and wide oscillations in population abundance that frequently results in local extinction of species.

In no other region is the fauna so important to people. There has long been an intimate association between the abundance or scarcity of animal life and the welfare of the natives of the region. This close relationship is diminishing but is still pronounced.

Aquatic mammals have long been the mainstay of Eskimo livelihood. Several varieties of *seals* range throughout the region, and they are the most common quarry of Eskimo hunters. The ringed seal is the most successful and widespread of the marine mammals because it can use breathing holes to live under fast ice (solid surface ice) all winter.

The *walrus* is a ponderous, slow-breeding (the female does not reproduce until the sixth year, and then has only one pup every other year) creature that is verging on extermination over much of its range. It must live in an area of strong currents that keep the sea ice moving all winter, for it does not gnaw a breathing hole through the ice as

does the seal. The Atlantic walrus inhabits most of the eastern Arctic Ocean, with particular concentration around the Melville Peninsula and Southampton Island. The Pacific walrus inhabits the Bering Sea; there is a 1,000-mile gap between the ranges of the two.

Whales of various species are much sought by the Eskimos, but by far the most common is the white whale, or *beluga*. They occur in considerable numbers throughout the Arctic, mostly in salt water but often going up the larger rivers (they have been seen as far up the St. Lawrence as Quebec City). They gather in remarkable abundance upon occasion; for example, up to 5,000 individuals cluster off the Mackenzie delta in summer. The *narwhal* is much less common but is highly prized because of the ivory-like horn of the male. Varieties of the larger whales, such as the *bowhead*, are taken whenever possible for their meat.

The *polar bear* ranges widely in the Arctic, living mostly on sea ice except for land denning to give birth. They are sometimes found several tens of miles from the nearest land. There is an unusual denning concentration along the Hudson Bay lowland between James Bay and Churchill, where the Ontario government has established a large provincial park for their protection. Unlike other bears, which are omnivorous, polar bears are almost wholly carnivorous. There is considerable concern for their survival, partly because of natives' overuse but especially because of hunting by airborne "sportsmen" in such places as the international waters north of Point Barrow.

The outstanding land animal is the *barren-ground caribou* (fig. 20–7). During its migrations between tundra and taiga, it is a vital factor in the economy of thousands of Indians, Eskimos, and whites in the Arctic. The Keewatin herd (occupying the so-called Barren Grounds, the tundra area west of Hudson Bay) is the principal herd, but its numbers have decreased from several million in the 1940s to a low point of about 200,000 in 1960; there has been a moderate

[7] Patrick O. Baird, *The Polar World* (New York: John Wiley & Sons, Inc., 1964), p. 112.

fig. 20–7 Caribou grazing on Alaska's North Slope with an oil drilling rig operating in the background (courtesy Alyeska Pipeline Company).

upward trend since then. A more recent crisis has befallen the so-called Western Arctic herd in northern Alaska, where there was a decrease from 250,000 in 1970 to about 50,000 in 1976. Stringent hunting regulations have been enacted and wolf control instituted in an effort to alleviate the decline.[8] There are three other principal herds of caribou: one in Alaska, another that ranges between northeastern Alaska and the northern Yukon, and a small herd on Baffin Island.

The only other native ungulate of the tundra is the *musk ox*. There are some 2,000 on Ellesmere Island, with the greatest concentration around Lake Hazen in the north, in the shelter of a high mountain range that provides a protected area of much milder climate and better forage. Another 500 or so occupy the Thelon Valley in the Keewatin

district, where there is another mild area. Smaller numbers are scattered in other parts of the Northwest Territories. Musk oxen were exterminated in Alaska long ago but were reintroduced in the 1930s to Nunivak Island in the Bering Sea, where they have flourished enough to provide seed stock for reintroduction to the Alaskan mainland.

Furbearers of note include the *arctic fox,* a prolific breeder whose population seems to run in cycles; the *lemming,* a queer nocturnal burrowing rodent noted for its seemingly pointless migrations; the *arctic wolf,* principal large predator of the region; and the *arctic hare,* whose population pattern follows wildly fluctuating cycles.

Fish life is abundant, if not particularly varied.

Of the birds, the snow owl, ptarmigan, gyrfalcon, raven, and snow bunting are year-round inhabitants. Others, summer residents, arrive by the thousands to breed in the seclusion and security of the tundra. They are also attracted by the prolific insect life.

Because of the abundance of poorly drained land, insects find this region a paradise during the short summer season. "On a

[8] It is widely recognized that most of the caribou kill from this herd has been for subsistence purposes by native people (some 30,000 annually in comparison with perhaps 12,000 killed by wolves and 1,000 by trophy hunters); however, wolf control will be carried on as a temporary emergency measure, in addition to limiting subsistence hunting take to about 3,000 per year.

warm cloudy, windless day, the insect life on the Barrens defies description."[9] Happily such days are rare; most days are windy and cause the insect hordes to lie low.

the people

In this vast region there are less than 75,000 inhabitants. About 67 percent consist of Eskimos or mixed-bloods in which the Eskimo strain is dominant, about 25 percent is white, perhaps 6 percent is Aleut, and about 2 percent is Indian. These people mostly reside in widely scattered small settlements, of which there is a total of about 130. No single settlement has a population of more than about 3,000.

THE ESKIMO

The Eskimos are one of those rare races that is readily identifiable by all three basic anthropological criteria: physical characteristics, culture, and language.[10] They have well-marked physical homogeneity, a distinctive culture, and a language spoken by themselves and nobody else.

These short, Mongoloid people are dispersed throughout arctic America from northern Greenland to the islands of the Bering Sea and the Siberian mainland, making them the only native people to be found in both Eastern and Western hemispheres. Although various dialects are recognized, there is remarkable linguistic homogeneity among the widespread Eskimo groups. A single language, Inupik, is spoken from Greenland to Norton Sound in Alaska. In southwestern Alaska (south of Norton Sound) and Siberia is a different Eskimo tongue, Yupik, said to be related to Inupik more or less as English is related to German.

In their native state the Eskimos have shown remarkable ingenuity in adapting themselves to an almost impossible environment. They live in one of the coldest and darkest parts of the world, and in one that is among the poorest in available fuel; yet they have not only survived but have also enjoyed life in self-sufficient family groups. Originally their entire livelihood was dependent on fishing and hunting, whereas practically all Eurasian tundra people were herders.

Eskimo culture history revolves around successive waves of people and cultural innovations spreading eastward from the Bering Sea area. The earliest Eskimos, or "proto-Eskimos" of North America, presumably derived their culture in Siberia and originally migrated from there. This culture stage—called the Arctic Small Tool Tradition, or simply Pre-Dorset—had an idefinite tenure in Alaska but lasted in Canada until about 800 B.C. when it was replaced by the eastward-spreading Dorset Culture. After about twenty centuries the Dorset Culture was in turn replaced by the Thule Culture, which also spread eastward from Alaska.

Thule Culture had two principal attributes lacking in the Dorset era: domesticated dogs to aid in hunting and in pulling sleds, and a full range of gear for hunting the great baleen whales, a major food source not available to Dorset people.[11] Thule Culture evolved into the contemporary Eskimo culture in about the eighteenth century, in a transition stage marked by the decline of

[9] Eric W. Morse, "Summer Travel in the Canadian Barren Lands," *Canadian Geographical Journal,* 74 (1967), 162.

[10] Canadian Eskimos are often called Inuit, which is the self-preferred indigenous name in the central and eastern Arctic of Canada. In the western Canadian Arctic, however, the people generally refer to themselves as Inuvialuit, and in Arctic Alaska their preferred name is Inupiat. The natives of western Alaska are mostly Yupik people. The term *Eskimo* is still apparently the most satisfactory collective name for these groups, although Inuit is increasingly used in its stead. (The authors are grateful to Canadian geographer and Arctic specialist Peter J. Usher for this summation of appropriate nomenclature [personal communication of 17 July 1977].)

[11] William E. Taylor, Jr., "The Fragments of Eskimo Prehistory," *The Beaver,* Outfit 295 (Spring 1965), 14.

whale hunting and the almost complete depopulation of the northern Canadian islands.

The coming of the white man to Eskimo country marked the beginning of the end for their way of life. European diseases, midlatitude foods, liquor, rifles, motorboats, and a new set of mores were introduced, and the overall result was more often bad than good.

The Eskimo today has drifted toward "civilization." Relatively few exist by subsistence hunting and fishing. More and more take temporary jobs on construction projects, in salmon canneries, and at other white outposts in the Arctic. The trading post, the DEW line station, the tuberculosis sanitarium, and the relief check are now well established in their way of life.

THE ALEUTS

The origin of the Aleuts is unclear, although generally they are considered to derive from Eskimos, or proto-Eskimos, who settled in a maritime environment in southwestern Alaska and developed a livelihood based almost entirely on fishing and sealing. Aleuts occupied the Aleutian Islands, the Alaska Peninsula, and the Kenai Peninsula in considerable numbers (perhaps 25,000) at the time of Russian contact in the eighteenth century. They were killed and enslaved by the Russian fur seekers, and in relatively few years their number was reduced by 90 percent.

Today there are some 6,000 Aleuts in southwestern Alaska, most of them of mixed blood. They are mostly commercial fishermen, sealers, or workers in salmon fishing and canning in the Bristol Bay area. In addition, they provide most of the labor for the international fur sealing industry of the Pribilof Islands.

THE INDIANS

There are only about 1,000 Indians in the entire Tundra Region, and practically all are in Canada. Generally speaking, the tree line has served as the northern boundary of Indian occupance, just as it has served as the southern border of Inuit settlement. Indians and Eskimos live adjacently in any numbers in only five localities: Aklavik and Inuvik in the Mackenzie delta, Churchill, Great Whale River on the eastern shore of Hudson Bay, and Fort Chimo at the southern end of Ungava Bay. The Indian livelihood in this region is based on hunting, trapping, fishing, and temporary construction work.

THE WHITES

Whites living in the region now number more than 20,000, a total that is growing. Well over half are in Alaska, where, except for military bases in the Aleutians, Nome is the largest white settlement by far (approximately half of the town's population of 2,500 is white). Most of the whites who live in the region today man the defense and weather installations, or are government officials, oil company employees, prospectors, fur traders, fishermen, or missionaries.

the diminishing subsistence economy of the region

Throughout history most of the population of the Tundra Region has been involved in essentially subsistence activities: fishing, hunting, and trapping. Since World War II, there has been a decline in these pursuits and their replacement by a money economy. More recently this trend has been markedly accelerated all across the region, from the Aleutian Islands to the High Arctic. Despite the downturn in subsistence activities, however, they still contribute significantly to the well-being of the people in providing "country food" (the name given to subsistence food obtained from the land or water), material for clothing and implements, blubber for fuel, and furs for sale or trade.

Hunting for sea and land animals is widespread (fig. 20–8). In some areas where winter conditions persist almost year-round, such as in the Queen Elizabeth Islands, ice hunting for sea mammals is a specialty. In other areas, such as the Colville River country of Alaska, there are inland groups that specialize in caribou hunting. But most native settlements are on the coast, and there are well-marked seasonal changes in hunting patterns. A typical "quarry rotation" might be seals in early fall, walrus in late fall, bear and fox in winter, seals in spring, fish and beluga in early summer, and caribou in late summer. In the hunting areas, late winter and spring are the most important seasons for resource utilization. Midwinter is too dark and cold; ice and fog handicap long trips by small boat in summer; and autumn is stormy and newly forming ice is hazardous.

Some animals, such as caribou, birds, and hares, are hunted on land. Others, such

fig. 20–8 A just-killed seal is about to be skinned (courtesy Information Canada Phototèque).

modern arctic anachronisms: harpoon, kayak, and sled dog

In association with the continuing decline of subsistence activities has been the introduction of outside inventions that have significantly changed the life of the tundra people. Of particular note has been the replacement of harpoon by rifle, of kayak by motorboat, and of sled dog by motorized toboggan.

The rifle was introduced to the region in the nineteenth century, but its impact was not really felt until the twentieth. As a substitute for harpoons and arrows, the rifle proved to be much deadlier. In much of the region it resulted in overkill of animal life, particularly such larger species as the caribou, musk ox, and walrus. The rifle is now common in the region, although harpoons have two advantages that keep them from being entirely abandoned: when used more than once, they are much less expensive than guns and bullets; and a rope attached to the butt of the harpoon allows the harpooned

animal to be retrieved, whereas a shot animal frequently sinks and is lost.

Kayaks and umiaks, the famous skin boats of the Eskimos, are rapidly becoming a thing of the past, with small motorboats and motor-driven whale boats replacing them. Kayaks are now virtually nonexistent in the entire Canadian Arctic. They are still built and used to some extent in Alaska, particularly by residents of the various islands in the Bering Sea and by walrus hunters.

The demise of the sled dog is a more recent phenomenon, essentially transpiring since 1960. "Husky," a corruption of the word "Eskimo," has been the general name applied to all sled dogs, including Samoyeds, malamutes, and Siberians. At the height of use, in the 1920s and 1930s, it is estimated that there were from 40,000 to 50,000 working huskies in the North American Arctic. But recently almost

as walrus and narwhal, are taken from boats.[12] In many cases the most important hunting is done on the sea ice, largely for seals and polar bear.

A notable crisis has developed with respect to caribou hunting, especially for the Western Arctic and Keewatin herds. The rapid decline in numbers of these herds has already been mentioned. Causes of the decrease are many, including diseases, parasites, wolf predation, windchill, drowning, and inclement weather at calving time; but the leading mortality factor by far has been improvident overuse by natives (both Es-

kimos and Indians). The ready availability of modern guns and ammunition has led to orgies of overhunting of the migrating herds. Education of natives to the problem and to other sources of food has begun to make an impression, but the crisis is far from past.

The Inland Eskimos of the Barren Grounds are now but a footnote to history. Apart from coastal settlements the vast expanse of tundra in the Keewatin district is now totally unpopulated, with the exception of a small settlement at Baker Lake, largely because of the caribou decline.

FISHING

Subsistence fishing is carried on wherever possible. Stone fish traps are constructed along some streams, but most fishing is done in the ocean. Summer fishing is easier, but ice fishing also takes place throughout the winter. Subsistence fishing is less important now than in the past because sled dogs, which are major consumers of fish, are much more scarce (see vignette below).

---

[12] In spite of their intimate association with the ocean, few Eskimos can swim. Ability to maintain balance when jumping from ice floe to ice floe is an important capability, however. Thus one of the most popular Eskimo outdoor sports, *Nalukatok,* or blanket tossing, has a practical origin and application. In Nalukatok, each participant is tossed high from a blanket or walrus hide, and strives to land on his feet and continue bouncing. The winner is the one who can be bounced the most times before losing his balance.

---

any Eskimo who could afford to do so has replaced his dogteam with a motor-toboggan, usually called snowmobile or ski-doo (fig. 20-a). For example, at the settlement of Resolute on Cornwallis Island in 1962 there were 14 dogteams and no ski-doos; by 1966 there were 3 dogteams and 14 ski-doos.[a] By 1970 it was estimated that there were only 2,000 sled dogs remaining in the Canadian Arctic.[b]

The advantage of a ski-doo over a dogteam is that it extends the radius of travel; a man can hold a regular five- or six-day job and still be able to get away to hunt or trap on the week-

---

[a] Don Bissett, *Resolute: An Area Economic Survey* (Ottawa: Industrial Division, Department of Indian Affairs and Northern Development, 1968), p. 107.

[b] Fred Bruemmer, "Sled Dogs and Dog Sleds," *Canadian Geographical Journal,* 80 (April 1970), 125.

fig. 20-a Modern Eskimos, using their ski-doos for recreation, near Barrow, Alaska (courtesy Alaska Travel Division).

(Continued)

As well as supplying meat and clothing, trapping has long been the major source of money income for natives of the Tundra Region. Various animals are trapped, but by far the most important is the white arctic fox. Fluctuations in the international fur market have caused much uncertainty in the industry in the past and will undoubtedly cause more in the future.

Trappers are licensed and carefully regulated in both countries. Only natives are allowed to trap in the Canadian Arctic, and only a very few white trappers are permitted in Alaska.

The outstanding trapping area is the Mackenzie River delta (which is largely in the Boreal Forest Region), where muskrat are numerous and prolific. Fox trapping in the delta, however, is rapidly dying out. The Arctic's richest fox-trapping area is on Banks Island, the southwesternmost of the Arctic Archipelago, where the bulk of the community income of Sachs Harbour is derived from trapping. Other important trapping areas include northern Labrador, the Grise Fiord area of southern Ellesmere Island, and the deltas of the Yukon and Kuskokwim rivers.

The precipitous decline in trapping is amply demonstrated by the decrease in fur trading establishments. In the entire Canadian Arctic there were only a dozen fur trading locations in the mid-1970s, in contrast to more than 100 in the late 1920s. A strong international fur market in the decade of the 1970s, however, stimulated an increase in both the amount of trapping and trappers' income.

the rise of a money economy and agglomerated settlements

The most important trend in the contemporary geography of the Tundra Region is the increasing concentration of the population into fewer and larger settlement centers, where life is based on a money economy. This pattern is being followed throughout the region. Wage labor is now the preferred means of livelihood, and more and more families are abandoning their seminomadic hunting camps and settling down to a sedentary existence in a settlement node, where the younger generation grows up relatively ignorant of the techniques requisite to a subsistence economy.

---

end. Also the perpetual burden of providing feed for the sled dogs is eliminated. A sled dog annually requires about 400 pounds of meat, which means that many Eskimos have to spend an inordinate amount of time hunting meat just to feed their dogs. On the other hand, ski-doos are expensive to buy and costly to fuel; their replacement parts are often difficult to obtain; and there is always the potential hazard of a mechanical breakdown under dangerous conditions.

Initially game is more easily obtained with the use of ski-doos, although in the long run local extermination may result. Eskimos use ski-doos to hunt polar bear around Cornwallis Island, where ice conditions are usually smooth. A bear can simply be run until it is exhausted and then shot. As a result, Cornwallis Island natives kill about twice as many polar bears as do people from any other Canadian settlement, and a quota system has had to be instituted.[c] A compensating advantage in the use of ski-doos is that hunting pressure has been relieved on such species as walrus and beluga, which were major sources of bulk meat for dog feed.

Thus the impressive silence of the Arctic is now punctured with the staccato sputter of motors. With the rapid proliferation of outboard motors, ski-doos, and other cross-terrain vehicles, it is now reported that the most common artifact in the Tundra Region is the Johnson 40 hp motor.

[c] Bissett, *Resolute: An Area Economic Survey*, p. 141.

As a result, large areas of the tundra, such as the Keewatin Barrens, the Colville delta, and much of the northern Labrador coast, are now virtually unpopulated. Dozens, and sometimes hundreds, of Eskimos have moved into settlements that previously had very small populations. The possibility of a steady job, and the lure of stores, medical facilities, and perhaps housing are proving irresistible.

Unfortunately the rate of natural increase in the population is very high—generally the highest on the continent—and the supply of jobs is inadequate. Construction work has been the principal provider of wage labor in the past. During and after World War II, there was a great deal of construction of defense and meteorological installations: radar stations, communications bases, and airfields. Such construction activity has inevitably decelerated, but it has given the people of the region a taste of sedentary regularity that they cannot forget.

Population clusters have clearly been a mixed blessing. When people abandoned a dispersed, seminomadic life for settled living, illness statistics began to rise. Many of the settlements are hygienically as well as socially grim. The provision of water and removal of waste are problems everywhere, and litter is a common eyesore (fig. 20–9). Alcoholism is an almost overwhelming menace, even in such settlements as Barrow that have voted themselves dry.[13] Yet there have also been many positive results such as the growth of local cooperatives, rudimentary

[13] It is reported that 90 percent of Royal Canadian Mounted Police work in the Arctic involves liquor problems. See Carroll Holland, "Central Arctic Settlements," *Canadian Geographical Journal,* 86 (June 1973), 209.

fig. 20–9 The traditionally frugal Eskimos utilized almost everything provided by their niggardly environment. Western technology, however, supplies them with more than they can use or recycle. Thus the environs of settlements—in this case, Barrow, Alaska—are sometimes engulfed with debris, which is mercifully hidden under the snow most of the time but is glaringly obvious during the brief summer (photo by James H. Davis; reproduced by permission of *Landscape*).

community government, a well-developed school system, generally improved housing, access to medical facilities, introduction of "outside" amenities (ranging from A&W root beer stands to color television brought by satellite transmission to communities that had never known newspapers or magazines), and an awakening cultural awareness.

The agglomeration continues. Where jobs are not available, there have been varied attempts to promote native handicraft output or cooperative commercial endeavors in such fields as fishing or mining. Government assistance in relocation has also been attempted. Inland Eskimos of Keewatin were resettled on the shore of Hudson Bay, and High Arctic resettlement has brought Eskimos back to Ellesmere and Cornwallis islands after an absence of many generations.

This pattern is now clearly established and will undoubtedly continue. In many settlements, however, the maintenance of a viable economy will be increasingly difficult.

nodes of settlement

Since the people of the Tundra Region increasingly tend to cluster, a nodal pattern of population distribution is beginning to become apparent. Most of the settlements lack

many of the attributes of towns in other parts of the continent: their form is often sprawling, amorphous, and unregimented to a street pattern; their urban functions are extremely limited; their buildings are often raised above ground level to keep the permafrost from thawing and buckling the foundations; and provision of utilities is generally primitive or totally absent (sometimes the piped conduits for water, sewerage, and gas are in "utilidor" or "servidor" systems raised above the ground in heavily insulated tunnels).

Despite the agglomerating tendencies, there are only a few settlements of any size (table 20–1). There are only seven communities in the region with a population in excess of 1,000, and none of these exceeds 3,100 in size. In only one locality, Nome, does the nonnative population exceed 1,000. The following are the larger settlements:

1 *Bethel, Nome* (fig. 20–10), and *Kotzebue* are Bering Sea towns of primarily Eskimo population but some diversity of function. Commercial fishing is significant at Bethel. Nome has been a limited commercial center since its gold-rush days at the turn of the century. Both Nome and Kotzebue are visited by considerable numbers of tourists in the summer.

2 *Barrow* is an administrative and military center for the Arctic coast and has the largest Eskimo population of any settlement in the region (fig. 20–11).

3 *Inuvik* is a planned town and a major administrative center in the western Canadian Arctic. Its site is actually on the edge of the boreal forest, but it has a strong functional relationship with the Tundra Region.

4 *Frobisher Bay* on Baffin Island is the administrative center for Canada's Eastern Arctic and is distinguished by an impressive town center, a large federal building, a high-rise apartment block, a relatively busy commercial airfield, and a weekly newspaper. It contains the largest Eskimo community in Canada.

5 *Churchill* is a busy grain-shipping port during its three-month navigation season.

table 20–1 Largest Urban Places of the Tundra Region

name	population of principal city	population of metropolitan area
Barrow, Alaska	2,418	
Bethel, Alaska	2,931	
Churchill, Man.	1,009	
Frobisher Bay, N.W.T.	2,291	
Inuvik, N.W.T.	3,039	
Kotzebue, Alaska	1,813	
Nome, Alaska	2,512	

fig. 20–10 The historic town of Nome, on the Bering Sea (courtesy Alaska Travel Division).

Smaller settlements in the region are mostly either isolated technical stations (radar, meteorological) or outpost service settlements in which a dominant native population is serviced by a handful of government and commercial agents, and increasingly by local people.

economic specialization

The commercial economy of the Tundra Region involves only a few specialized activities on a generally limited scale.

COMMERCIAL FISHING

There are two areas where commercial fishing is of considerable significance. In both places it is primarily a seasonal activity, and many of the participants are outsiders who come into the region for only a few weeks during the fishing season. The Bristol Bay area of southwestern Alaska is one of the state's principal salmon fisheries. Canneries operate at a feverish pitch during late summer and fall at King Salmon, Dillingham, and other localities. Along the north coast of Labrador there has long been an important commercial fishing venture, primarily for cod but also supplying char and salmon for sale. Many Newfoundlanders come to this area as "stationers" or "floaters" in the summer to join the Eskimos and "liveyeres" (white settlers of Labrador) who fish these coastal waters.

Small and sporadic commercial fisheries are also in operation at other places in the region, mostly for Arctic char, which is frozen and flown to luxury markets in the south. Char can be taken only during a short period of the year, however, and the yield is limited; hence expansion opportunities are small.

fig. 20–11 The blessings of shopping centers have come to the Arctic, too. The bulging side of this Eskimo-owned shopping center in Barrow encloses a heated indoor playground (photo by James H. Davis; reproduced by permission of *Landscape*).

COMMERCIAL SEALING

Seals of various species are widely hunted and trapped in the Arctic. Many of the pelts are sold, bringing an important cash income to the native hunters. The only large-scale commercial sealing enterprise in the region, however, is on the Pribilof Islands of the Bering Sea, which are the breeding grounds of the Alaska fur seal. From the discovery of the Pribilofs until the present, nearly 9 million fur seal pelts have been taken. The history of sealing there has been one of alternating periods of ruthless exploitation and of careful conservation. At present, under conditions controlled by international convention, between 50,000 and 100,000 fur seals are "harvested" each year (fig. 20–12). A single company, employing mostly Aleuts, makes the entire kill, about one-third of which is allotted to Canada and Japan under the international agreement.

COMMERCIAL REINDEER HERDING

Reindeer were introduced into Alaska from Siberia in the 1890s, with the idea of establishing a viable pastoral enterprise among the Eskimos. The Canadian government subsequently brought some Alaskan rein-

fig. 20–12 Fur seals on a hauling-out beach, the Pribilof Islands (courtesy Alaska Travel Division).

deer to the Mackenzie delta in the late 1920s to serve as a nucleus for eventual dispersal.

In neither case, however, has the reindeer experiment been very successful. Although the Alaskan herds increased to a total of more than 600,000 reindeer in the 1930s, problems developed and the numbers diminished rapidly. There are now about 30,000 reindeer in Alaska in 17 separate herds, mostly on the Seward Peninsula. Five of the herds are noncommercial, and slaughtering is for home use only. Of the other dozen only one is a successful commercial operation, and it is a government herd on Nunivak Island that is operated by the Bureau of Indian Affairs.

The Mackenzie delta herd reached a peak of about 9,000 animals in 1942, but interest waned and the herd has declined to less than 3,000 today (fig. 20–13). In 1968 the Canadian Wildlife Service took over the operation of this herd, which is maintained on a reindeer reserve where it provides scant employment and little income.

MINERAL INDUSTRIES

Considerable mineral wealth is known to exist in this region, but transportation is so expensive that mining is virtually nonexistent at present. Exploration for oil and gas has been extensive and is continuing. The only commercially feasible discovery thus far has been the tremendous reserves of Alaska's North Slope, centering on Prudhoe Bay. Upon completion of the TAPline in 1977 the Prudhoe Bay field immediately went into commercial production, with the result that for the first time in seven years the continuing downtrend in total United States crude oil output was reversed.

Considerable oil, especially in the Mackenzie delta–Beaufort Sea area, and natural gas, particularly on Melville and King Christian islands, have been discovered in the Canadian Arctic, but the indicated reserves thus far are considerably smaller than those of the North Slope. Moreover, production costs are very high (drilling expense in the Beaufort Sea is

fig. 20–13   A herd of domesticated reindeer in a temporary corral in the Mackenzie River delta country (courtesy Information Canada Photothèque).

about $30 million per hole), and the massive problem of transportation awaits future solution.

There has also been accelerated exploration during the late 1970s in "Iceberg Alley" off the coast of northern Labrador.

Prospecting and proving of metallic ore deposits have been continuing in various locations, but most appear to be economically questionable. Nevertheless, Canada's first mine north of the Arctic Circle has been developed at Strathcona Sound on the north end of Baffin Island, with initial shipments of lead and zinc ore made in 1977.

transportation

Inadequate transportation is the outstanding deterrent to economic progress in the Arctic. All-weather roads are virtually non-existent, and the only railway line is that connecting Churchill with the Prairie Provinces. In other words, conventional forms of land transportation are almost totally lacking. Tractor trains, temporary winter roads, and ski-doos provide minimal transport during the cold season, and there is some useful riverboat service during summer. By and large, however, regional transport depends on oceangoing vessels, which have a short navigation season, or on aircraft, which are expensive.

There is now a great deal of scheduled air service in the region. For example, Resolute on Cornwallis Island receives regular air traffic from both Montreal and Edmonton. A surprising number of small settlements is served at least occasionally by scheduled flights. Nonscheduled flying fills in many of the gaps. Construction of an airfield has therefore become an essential for most population nodes, and frequently the airfield is the location of the most modern and desirable facilities to be found locally. As Ralph Brown has noted, "The ubiquitous light aircraft is the bond between most rural Alaskan natives and the products and services of the civilization upon which they have become dependent."[14]

Many of the settlements, however, are still dependent for their bulk supplies on government patrol boats that often cover thousands of miles on a single summer trip bringing foodstuffs, fuel, and other materials that must last until the ship returns the following summer. This is particularly characteristic of the eastern Canadian Arctic and the northern coast of Labrador.

the outlook

The region will continue as a land of great distances and few people, where nothing more than a scanty livelihood is obtainable by trapping, hunting, fishing, or grazing. Cities in the true sense will, as now, be nonexistent. Trapping will continue to be important to the natives, but it is too dependent on the vagaries of fashion, fluctuation of prices, and biological cycles to provide a steady means of livelihood for large numbers of people.

Expansion of commercial fishing offers considerable promise in a few localities, but in most of the region its growth possibilities seem quite limited. Expansion of reindeer herding seems logical in theory, but the lesson of seven decades of history is thoroughly negative.

The overwhelming problem of the region is that the population is rapidly increasing, concentrating in settlement nodes, and acquiring a taste for alien foods and creature comforts, but it has scant opportunity to make a living. Many of the small arctic settlements have a very questionable resource base. Even some of the larger ones,

such as Frobisher Bay, are unpromising examples of artificial growth centers based on inadequate resources and government subsidy. A Canadian economist has stated the matter in unequivocal terms:

Having deemed it desirable to mould the Eskimo in our social image, an industrialized society may now be experiencing hesitancy, and uncertainty, about the outcome of the whole process of Eskimo acculturation. Unless the tenet of the desirability of formal education is abandoned, and the Eskimo is encouraged to return to a subsistence economy more heavily weighted in favour of a higher degree of seasonal mobility and an increased dependency on the harvesting of faunal resources, the process of formal education will inevitably interfere with the perceptions, ability, and desire of the Eskimo to return to, and be content with, a lower standard of living than he is able to attain if given the opportunity.[15]

It is clear that the population increase will only accelerate problems. There are not enough wage positions now, and there will be a continually increasing demand for such positions. There is a small but growing trend to take Eskimos "south" for training and then return them to the tundra with a new skill. This has been successful, on a small scale, with hard-rock miners at Rankin Inlet, with fur dressers at Aklavik, and in a few other instances, and it could be the beginning of formation of a nucleus of semi-skilled labor. Two somewhat broader native training programs were formulated in northern Canada in the 1970s: a federal program called Hire North, and the NOR-TRAN project sponsored by oil and pipeline companies. They have experienced only mixed success, however, and the lasting benefits are still questionable.

The formation of cooperatives has been a positive step in several places, but their principal function may be only as local palliatives.

Most natives of the tundra will doubtless make the transition to a "civilized" way of life, and no doubt the transition will be a difficult and painful one in many ways.

[14] Ralph C. Brown, "Changing Rural Settlement Patterns in Arctic Alaska," *Professional Geographer,* 21 (September 1969), 324.

[15] D. Villiers, *The Central Arctic: An Area Economic Survey* (Ottawa: Department of Indian Affairs and Northern Development, 1969), p. 171.

They love the North and are adjusted to northern living, and so could become the backbone of northern development if they could acquire new skills without losing their identities. But with the perishing of the "old" way of life, employment opportunities must be made available or the native is likely to sink into a slough of apathy and degradation, as the monumental problem of alcoholism clearly demonstrates. Is it possible to develop a sound economic base for the native peoples of the tundra without endangering their cultural survival?

Mineral exploitation will almost surely provide the major economic development stimulus for the region. The actualities of Prudhoe Bay and the potentialities of the Beaufort Sea area and the Mackenzie Valley corridor will be the principal foci of activity. What will this do for the local inhabitants? Will they receive "early, visible, and lasting benefits" from such developments, as is the Canadian government's stated ambition? Oil drilling and pipeline operation can be either a boon or a burden (or both) to the region.

The regional and village corporations in the Alaskan portion of the tundra now have considerable capital to work with, and it is quite likely that native claim payments will significantly augment the economy in the Canadian tundra as well (as is already the case with the James Bay Eskimos). The wise use of these windfall monies could do much to alleviate the bleakness of the long-term prospects for the native peoples.

In Anglo-America the "underdeveloped" regions frequently have their economies bolstered by tourists and sportsmen. The transportation handicaps in the tundra, however, which are greater than in any other region, are strong inhibiting factors. A few hunters fly into the region on expensive expeditions for polar bear or walrus, but this cannot—and should not—be expected to expand much. A trickle of tourists visits Kotzebue to see Eskimos or to Frobisher Bay to see the "true Arctic," and this trickle should grow—but only gradually.

Heavy pressure on a limited resource base by a burgeoning population poses an almost insoluble dilemma for the governments of both nations. Or is this the basic problem of the world in microcosm?

selected bibliography

Area Economic Surveys (Ottawa: Industrial Division, Department of Indian Affairs and Northern Development)
   1958. Ungava Bay
   1962. Southampton Island
   1962. Tuktoyaktuk–Cape Parry
   1962. Western Ungava
   1963. The Copper Eskimos
   1963. Keewatin Mainland
   1963. Yukon Territory Littoral
   1965. Banks Island
   1965. Northern Foxe Basin
   1966. East Coast–Baffin Island
   1966. Frobisher Bay
   1966. The Mackenzie Delta
   1966. Rae–Lac La Martre
   1967. Central Mackenzie
   1967. Lancaster Sound
   1967. South Coast–Baffin Island
   1967. South Shore–Great Slave Lake
   1968. Central Arctic
   1968. Keewatin Mainland Re-appraisal

BIRD, J. BRIAN, *The Physiography of Arctic Canada.* Baltimore, Md.: Johns Hopkins Press, 1967.

BOND, COURTNEY C. J., "Two Communities in the Eastern Arctic," *Canadian Geographical Journal,* 81 (1970), 184–93.

BRITTON, M. E., *Alaskan Arctic Tundra.* Washington, D.C.: Arctic Institute of North America, 1973.

"The Brooks Range: Environmental Watershed," *Alaska Geographic,* 4, no. 2 (1977), entire issue.

BROWN, RALPH C., "Changing Rural Settlement Patterns in Arctic Alaska," *Professional Geographer,* 21 (1969), 324–27.

BRUEMMER, FRED, *The Arctic.* Englewood Cliffs, N.J.: Prentice-Hall, 1974.

———, "The Eskimos of Grise Fiord," *Canadian Geographical Journal,* 77 (1968), 64–71.

———, "Northern Labrador," *Canadian Geographical Journal,* 82 (1971), 158–67.

———, "The Polar Bear," *Canadian Geographical Journal,* 78 (1969), 98–105.

———, "Sled Dogs and Dog Sleds," *Canadian Geographical Journal,* 80 (1970), 118–25.

BUCKSAR, RICHARD G., "The Squatter on the Resource Frontier," *Arctic,* 23 (1970), 201–4.

CHANCE, NORMAN A., *The Eskimo of North Alaska.* New York: Holt, Rinehart & Winston, 1967.

COWAN, IAN MCTAGGART, "Ecology and Northern Development," *Arctic,* 22 (1969), 3–12.

CROWE, KEITH J., *A History of the Original Peoples of Northern Canada.* Montreal: Arctic Institute of North America, McGill-Queen's University Press, 1974.

DANIELSON, ERIC W., JR., "Hudson Bay Ice Conditions," *Arctic,* 24 (1971), 90–107.

DAVIS, JAMES H., "Barrow, Alaska: Technology Invades an Eskimo Community," *Landscape,* 21 (1977), 21–25.

DE BELLE, GAIL, AND P. H. BEAUBIER, "Threatened Wilderness," *Geographical Magazine,* 44 (1972), 536–44.

DUNBAR, M. J., "On the Fishery Potential of the Sea Waters of the Canadian North," *Arctic,* 23 (1970), 150–74.

GRAINGE, J. W., AND J. C. ROYLE, "How Arctic Community Life Has Changed," *Canadian Geographical Journal,* 91 (December 1975), 38–45.

HARDING, L., "Mackenzie Delta: Home of Abounding Life," *Canadian Geographical Journal,* 88 (May 1974), 4–13.

HARE, F. KENNETH, "The Atmospheric Circulation and Arctic Meteorology," *Arctic,* 22 (1969), 185–94.

HARRINGTON, RICHARD, "Herschel Island," *Canadian Geographical Journal,* 85 (November 1972), 172–77.

HEMSTOCK, R. A., "Transporting Petroleum in the North," *Canadian Geographical Journal,* 90 (April 1975), 42–49.

HERRINGTON, CLYDE, *Atlas of the Canadian Arctic Islands.* Vancouver: Shultoncraft Publishing Co., 1969.

HINDLE, WALTER, "Piping Arctic Gas South via Hudson Bay," *Canadian Geographical Journal,* 20 (June 1975), 14–19.

HOLLAND, C., "Central Arctic Settlements," *Canadian Geographical Journal,* 86 (June 1973), 202–13.

HUME, JAMES D., AND MARSHALL SCHALK, "Shoreline Processes Near Barrow, Alaska: A Comparison of the Normal and the Catastrophic," *Arctic,* 20 (1967), 86–103.

KELLEY, J. J., JR., AND D. F. WEAVER, "Physical Processes at the Surface of the Arctic Tundra," *Arctic,* 22 (1969), 424–37.

KING, ROGER H., "Dynamics of Polar Desert-Like Soils on Devon Island, Canadian Arctic Archipelago," *Proceedings,* Association of American Geographers, 6 (1974), 18–21.

KORANDA, J., "The North Slope: Its Physiography, Fauna, and Its Flora," *Alaska Geographic,* 1, no. 1 (1972), 7–37.

KRESSE, D. T., ET AL., *Briston Bay: A Socioeconomic Study.* Fairbanks: University of Alaska Press, 1974.

MCCANN, S. B., P. J. HOWARTH, AND J. G. COGLEY, "Fluvial Processes in a Periglacial Environment: Queen Elizabeth Islands, N.W.T., Canada," *Transactions,* Institute of British Geographers, 55 (1972), 69–82.

MACKAY, J. ROSS, "The Mackenzie Delta," *Canadian Geographical Journal,* 78 (1969), 146–55.

———, "The World of Underground Ice," *Annals,* Association of American Geographers, 62 (1972), 1–22.

NAYSMITH, J., "Changing Land Use Patterns in the North," *Canadian Geographical Journal,* 90 (January 1975), 11–18.

PIMLOTT, D. H., "The Arctic Offshore Gamble," *The Living Wilderness,* 38 (1974), 16–25.

REEVES, RANDALL R., "Narwhals: Another Endangered Species," *Canadian Geographical Journal,* 92 (May–June 1976), 12–19.

SMITH, I. NORMAN, ed., *The Unbelievable Land.* Ottawa: Queen's Printer, 1964.

USHER, P. J., "The Growth and Decay of the Trading and Trapping Frontiers in the Western Canadian Arctic," *Canadian Geographer,* 19 (1975), 308–20.

WEBB, KENNETH, "What Made the Hudson Bay Arc?" *Canadian Geographical Journal,* 92 (May–June 1976), 20–25.

WONDERS, WILLIAM C., "Community and Regional Development in the North," *Arctic,* 23 (1970), 281–84.

INDEX

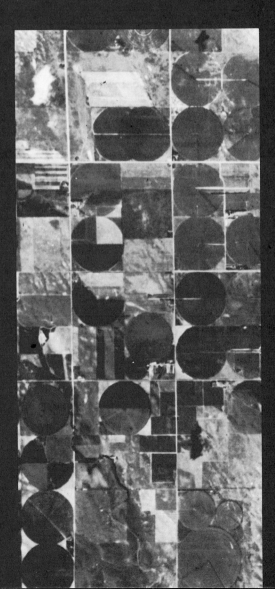